THE LIFE OF
SHIVAJI MAHARAJ

THE LIFE OF SHIVAJI MAHARAJ

FOUNDER OF THE MARATHA EMPIRE

N. S. TAKAKHAV,
K. A. KELUSAKARA,

Published by

FacsiMile Publisher
12 Pragati Market
Ashok Vihar, Ph-2
Delhi - 110052, India
Phone: 011-47034999
Email: www.facsimilepublishers.com
info@facsimilepublishers.com

Distribution Network
gyanbooks.com
India, USA, Canada, UK, Australia

ISBN: 978-93-3336-851-3 (HB)
First Published, 1921

2nd Impression 2025

Printed at: Gyan Press, Delhi.

**THE LIFE OF SHIVAJI MAHARAJ,
FOUNDER OF THE MARATHA EMPIRE**
Author: N. S. TAKAKHAV, K. A. KELUSAKARA

SHRI CHHATRAPATI SHIVAJI MAHARAJ,

FOUNDER OF THE MARATHA EMPIRE

THE LIFE OF SHIVAJI MAHARAJ

FOUNDER OF THE MARATHA EMPIRE

BY

N. S. TAKAKHAV, M. A.,

PROFESSOR, WILSON COLLEGE, BOMBAY

ADAPTED FROM THE ORIGINAL MARATHI WORK

WRITTEN BY

K. A. KELUSKAR,

TEACHER, WILSON HIGH SCHOOL, BOMBAY

BOMBAY, MANORANJAN PRESS,

1921

SHRI CHHATRAPATI SHAHU MAHARAJ,
G. C. S. I., G. C. I. E., G C. V. O., LL D., etc.,
KOLHAPUR STATE

TO

H. H. SHRI CHHATRAPATI

SHAHU MAHARAJ

KOLHAPUR STATE

THIS BIOGRAPHY OF HIS MOST ILLUSTRIOUS ANCESTOR IS MOST RESPECTFULLY AND GRATEFULLY DEDICATED

BY THE PUBLISHER

PREFACE

At a time when the whole of the Indian Continent is entering upon a new phase of political life and bold schemes of social and political re-construction are being daily pressed for acceptance, no apology would seem to be necessary for the publication of a new life of Shivaji For among the glittering multitude of mighty kings whose names adorn the pages of Indian History, the name of Shivaji stands forth in bold relief as the author of a momentous national revival that changed the destinies of India. And this is a fact allowed by all historians, even though the editors of the Rulers of India Series have chosen to ignore him and denied him a place in their Series, while including many other "Rulers" who were more or less mediocrities, when compared with the great Shivaji. If ever in the pre-British period of Indian History, there was anything that might be compared with the great national movements of Western countries, it was the political movement which laid the foundations of the Maratha Swarajya. And that movement would have been utterly destitute of all its national glory and significance, were it not for the genius and originality of one master mind who presided over the whole event, built a nation out of chaos and breathed life and purpose into the dead clay and *disjecta membra* of Maharashtra society and institutions.

Such a man was Shivaji. Of the empire which he built up, only a few fragments have escaped the ravages of time. The rest has crumbled down and gone the way that all great empires in the world have gone. But the spirit of it has remained behind. He has left no pyramids, no rock-cut temples, no architectural marvels to attest his greatness. But the name of Shivaji still lives to kindle and inspire the growing manhood of Maharashtra.

Inspired by the stirring events of the late war, when the Maratha soldiers were called upon to display their native valour on the battle-fields of the West, this work was undertaken at the special request of the author of the Marathi original, as a grateful tribute to the genius of the founder of the Maratha nation. At the time when this work was undertaken, there was no worthy biography in the English language of the life and career of the great King who during the night of Mahomedan despotism dreamt the dream of national independence and realized it. It seemed a standing reproach to the Indian community, with their newly awakened political consciousness, that there should be no biographical record, commensurate with the greatness of the national hero, in that language which has done more than anything else to unite us into a nation and stimulate our national aspirations.

This English version was taken in hand about seven years ago. As the work proceeded it was found necessary to make considerable alterations in the original Marathi text of Mr. Keluskar's Life, as published in 1907. It was found necessary to take notice of the mass of new material and discoveries which have accumulated in the course of the last fourteen years. In its final draft the present English version has practically become a new and independent work and has already served as a basis for the second Marathi edition, which in a revised and considerably enlarged form, as compared to the first edition, was published by Mr. Keluskar early in 1921. This work has been thoroughly revised and retouched from time to time during the last seven years. It is quite up-to-date, so far as our knowledge of Shivaji and the men and things of his time extends and the conflicting theories that have been proposed as regards the purpose or policy for which he strove and the men of wisdom or action who counselled or co-operated in his plans.

While the preparation of this work was in its various stages of progress, three important English works on Shivaji appeared in print, one of which has already gone into a second edition. Some explanation would seem to be necessary to justify the publication of a fourth work on the same subject. The first and obvious answer is that none of these works can be called a faithful biography of Shivaji, that is to say, a biography which is at once full and exhaustive and traces the development of his life-work from beginning to end in chronological order. The work of Mr. Kincaid reviews the work of Shivaji as a fragment of the History of the Maratha People, that of Prof. Jadunath Sarkar discourses upon "Shivaji and his Times" and often forgets the hero while discoursing upon his "*Times*", that of Prof. Rawlinson is avowedly a monograph, too meagre in its scope to comprise the life-work of a great hero like Shivaji. The thanks of the Maratha reader are due to all these scholars for the new light they have thrown on many obscure points in the life of their national hero, and to Prof. Rawlinson and Mr. Kincaid in particular for the generous way in which they have interpreted the motives and character of the great King. The earliest of this triad is the Life of Shivaji by Principal Rawlinson. It is a generous appreciation of Shivaji's work and character. But the monograph, besides being too meagre in size for the magnitude of the task, devotes a good deal of its contents to discussions upon somewhat irrelevant topics. The impression that remains after a perusal of the book is that the author's purpose is to show that the new era of Shivaji after all inaugurated a new type of bureaucracy, and the author seems to suggest that from the times of Ashoka and Chandragupta down to present times, the bureaucratic form of government has prevailed in India and must inevitably prevail for all time. The author forgets that there are bureaucracies and bureaucracies and that a bureaucracy with a Shivaji at its head ceases to be a bureaucracy, both in form and substance. Mr. C. A. Kincaid, who writes in collaboration with Rao Bahadur D. B. Parasnis, has devoted some 170 pages of the first volume of his History of the Maratha People to the story of Shivaji. The authors have taken little notice of the stirring events of the career of Shahaji and have chosen to ignore many a controversy which has caused an acute tension of feeling among scholars. This history is full of legends and folk-lore tales and apparently attaches as much importance to them as to matters of serious history. Its highest virtue is its picturesqueness. Although Mr. Kincaid has repeated the orthodox version as to the date, when Shivaji enrolled himself as a disciple of Ramdas Swami, it is some consolation to think that Mr. Kincaid has not allowed the infatuation of the Ramdas cult to blind him to such an extent as to ascribe to the preceptor the credit of Shivaji's glorious achievements. He has had sense enough to see, as some patriotic and over-zealous Maharashtra scholars have not, that such a representation of the relations between the preceptor and the disciple would reduce the national hero to a mere puppet. The supreme merit of Mr. Kincaid's work is his enthusiastic and unreserved admiration of the Maratha people.

Prof. Jadunath Sarkar's "Shivaji and His Times" is the last of this triad.[1] It is a noble work marred with strange flaws. Mr. Kincaid's History and Prof. Sarkar's *Shivaji* stand at two opposite extremes of historical method and style. The one is romantic in conception and uncritical in method, the other is hypercritical in method and sceptical in its intellectual outlook. The merits of Sarkar's work are great. He has had access to a wealth of Mahomedan and British sources and authorities, the very existence of which had not been previously suspected. The fundamental fault of the work is that it appears as an overflow of the vast amount of historical material he had collected for his monumental work upon Aurangzeb. His sympathies are with the Moguls and the commanders of the Mogul empire. His sympathies are with the British factors at Surat and Rajapur. His sympathies are anywhere except with Shivaji and his gallant companions. Shivaji has fallen into the

[1] Since his Preface went to the press, another monograph on Shivaji has been published by Mr. S. V. Raddi, B A., which appears to be based chiefly on the works of Prof. Sarkar and Mr. Kincaid.

back-ground. Sarkar's pæans of praise are poured forth in unstinted measure, now in honour of Shaista Khan, now in honour of Jay Singh. He conducts his reader into the Mogul camp, he brings him in the wake of the Mogul armies and the Mogul standards. Shivaji is at best patronised here and there with a nodding familiarity and spoken of as a familiar underling with the name of "Shiva". This is not intended, but such is the effect produced. The critical estimate of Shivaji's character and work in the last seven pages of this work is an appreciative review of the character and life-work of the great King and is, strange to say, quite at variance with the hyper-critical denunciations expressed in the fourteen pages that immediately precede it, and on the whole gives the lie direct to many of the generalizations which are found interspersed in the earlier part of the work. By far the most valuable service rendered by Prof. Sarkar is his vindication of Shivaji from the charge of murdering Afzul Khan. Again he has not fallen into the error of exaggerating the influence of Ramdas Swami upon Shivaji. Indeed he seems to have gone to an opposite extreme and failed to recognize, in anything like a proper estimate, the intense spirituality of outlook which distinguished Shivaji among the nation-builders and rulers of India. Finally, it must be said of Prof. Sarkar's work that it is arranged in too scrappy a manner to suit the purposes of a serious biography and hence arise the contradictions which are noticed above.

In the present work Shivaji is depicted as the director and entrepreneur of the greatest movement for the assertion of national liberty and independence that India has known in pre-British times. His character, his institutions and the greatness of his work are set forth at length in the 24th and in the concluding chapters. The prejudices against Shivaji on the part of the Mahomedan chroniclers are here shown to be of the same sort as those with which the student of Roman History becomes familiar when he finds Roman authors like Livy and Cicero passing uncalled for strictures upon Hannibal. There is indeed a close parallel between these two heroes. Both strove hard for the liberty and independence of their country from foreign aggression. Both were endowed with the most brilliant talents and genius. In both their powers of invention and resourcefulness baffled the understanding and vigilance of their enemies. Both have been denounced by biassed historians for their imaginary acts of treachery and cruelty. But the contrast between the environments of these two conquerors brings out the superior mettle of the Maratha hero. Hannibal had not to make an army, much less to make a nation. Shivaji had to make everything for himself in order to build the Maratha nation. And that he did build a nation and found an empire which lasted longer than the power of Carthage did after the death of Hannibal, is no little testimony to the superiority of the Maratha hero over that of Carthage. It has been the fashion in some quarters to compare Shivaji with great conquerors like Cæsar, Alexander or Bonaparte, and a tendency is seen now and then to compare him with ardent but obscure patriots like Viriathus, Vercingetorix or Caractacus, or at best with King Alfred, Robert Bruce, or William Tell. But the fact is that he combined in himself the righteous purpose and patriotic fervour of leaders like Bruce and Alfred and Vercingetorix with the superior military genius and statesmanship that characterized the world's great heroes like Cæsar, Alexander, Hannibal and Bonaparte; and in so far as these two different sets of qualities characterizing the two groups are found to unite together to a certain extent in the character of Hannibal alone, the latter seems to be the one unique military genius of the ancient world with whom we may compare Shivaji with an approximate measure of accuracy. But the truth is that the character and the life-work of the Maratha hero were both alike so unique, that it is idle to make any comparison.

The present work is an attempt to give a faithful likeness of Shivaji and an estimate of his great work, chiefly based upon the indigenous bakhar chronicles of the Marathas. Nearly all the Maratha chronicles have been laid under contribution, together with other authorities, which will be found cited in the foot-notes, Most of these foot-notes are of a critical kind, supplementing, illustrating, and giving the authorities for the statements made in the text. The works of Mr. Kincaid and Prof. Jadunath Sarkar have been of great use, and the latter is freely quoted, especially as regards his citations from the *Factory Records* in the India Office, which are not otherwise available in India. Of great use have been the writings of Mr. V. K. Rajwade and Rao Bahadur Parasnis, the reports of the Bharat Itihas Sanshodhak Mandali of Poona, the Jedhe *Shakawali* or Chronology published by the late Mr. B. G. Tilak, and the *Itihas Sangraha*.

Attention may be invited to the following features in the present work :—

(*a*) It gives a complete account of the career of Shahaji and a critical exposition of his attitude towards Shivaji.

(*b*) It gives a re-constructed version of the Chandra Rao More tragedy.

(*c*) It clears Shivaji from the charge of murdering Afzul Khan.

(*d*) It re-arranges the chronology of the events of Shaista Khan's invasion, in the light of the Jedhe Chronology and the Mahomedan chronicles.

(*e*) It examines the relations between Shivaji and Dadaji Kondadev and between Shivaji and Ramdas Swami in the light of modern authorities and discoveries.

(*f*) It throws new light upon the naval battle of Khanderi, from British Factory Records and Correspondence, hitherto not handled by any previous historian of Shivaji.

(*g*) It re-constructs the military career of one of Shivaji's great commanders, whose services have fallen into an unmerited oblivion,—Anandrao Bhonsle (Appendix II).

(*h*) It re-constructs the career of one of Shivaji's great plenipotentiaries at the Mogul Court–Ragho Ballal Korde–wrongly charged with murdering Chandrarao More (Appendix IV).

(*i*) It vindicates Shivaji from the charge of cruelty and treachery, by proving that the Mogul commanders were more guilty than Shivaji.

(*j*) It gives a new explanation of Shivaji's so-called plundering campaigns.

(*k*) It discusses the various theories of the late Justice Ranade, Rajwade, Kincaid and others about the origin of the Swarajya movement, its authorship, the relation of the Bhagwat School towards Swarajya and kindred topics.

I have to express my thanks to all the authors mentioned above for the assistance derived from their works, as also to Principal G. C. Bhate, Principal Rawlinson, Mr. G. S. Sardesai, R. & O. Strachey, Mr. S. Dev, Mr. S. Sen, Mr. Vasudev Shastri Khare, and a host of others whose works have been quoted or made use of, in different parts of this book. I have especially to thank the Rev. Dr. N. Macnicol, M. A., D. Litt. of the United Free Church of Scotland Mission, a distinguished scholar and a sympathetic critic, for kindly revising and correcting the MS. and the proofs and for the many valuable suggestions he made which have greatly advanced the usefulness of this biography. The sympathetic "Foreword" which he has so kindly contributed to this work may be taken not only as index of his genuine interest and sympathy in all Indian aspirations, but as a noble tribute to the greatness of our great national hero.

Bombay,
6th May 1921.

NILKANT S. TAKAKHAV,

THE PUBLISHER'S NOTE

The Publisher's cordial thanks are due to Prof. N. S. Takakhav, M. A., for having readily undertaken this very difficult and arduous task. He as a student of history was not content with the original Marathi text. He went to the very sources of information from which it was compiled, and brought under contribution almost all the recent researches and discoveries regarding the life story of our national hero. In his hands the work has assumed a highly critical and exhaustive form and is calculated to dispel many groundless and uncharitable notions about our hero which have hitherto, almost unchallenged, gained currency in the historical literature concerning our land.

The value of this work has been enhanced by the fact that the Revd. Dr. N. Macnicol M.A., D. Litt., a distinguished missionary scholar of the United Free Church of Scotland Mission, was gracious enough to revise the MS. of this work and go through the proofs as the work passed through the press. His kind and appreciative Foreword appended hereto is a noble tribute from a high-souled and sympathetic friend of India. For this noble and generous act the publisher owes him a deep debt of gratitude.

The MS. of this work was lying for several years with the publisher for want of funds to put it through the press. He was helped out of this difficulty by Shrimant Major Sardar Maloji Narsingrao Sitole of Gwalior, who advanced a large loan at the instance of Shrimant Sadashivrao alias Khasesaheb Powar, Home Member, Gwalior State and Rao Bahadur Khaserao Bhagwantrao Jadhav of Baroda. But this fund was soon exhausted and the publisher was again in a fix, from which he was helped out by his esteemed friend Rao Saheb Harischandra Vishram Rajwadkar, J. P., who advanced another large loan. For this financial help the publisher is very grateful to these generous gentlemen.

His thanks are also due to the Proprietor and Manager of the Manoranjan Press for the great care and interest with which he has printed this work and afforded him all reasonable facilities to bring it out in this very decent and acceptable form.

The work is now before the English reading public and it is earnestly hoped that all who love fair play and wish to see a true image of Shivaji, not distorted by racial or sectarian prejudices, will be generous enough to patronize this patriotic attempt.

FOREWORD

Mr. K. A. Keluskar has asked me to write a brief foreword to the English edition of his *Life of Shivaji Maharaj*, and I have consented to do so because of the high regard that I have for him both as a man and as a Marathi scholar and because of our long-standing friendship. I have no other claim than these give me to take it upon myself to introduce this book to the public. At the same time I feel that it is only fitting that this story should be told by one who is sprung from the same robust and manly stock to which the great Maratha soldier himself belonged, and I feel that, if that be so, there is no one so well able to tell the story with sympathy, with knowledge and with critical judgement as Mr. Keluskar. Shivaji belongs to no class or caste; he is a national possession. He may be said indeed to have come to rebirth in the hearts of his countrymen, not of Maharashtra alone but of all India, in the national awakening of the last twenty years. But at the same time it is inevitable that some aspects of his life and work can be best understood and appreciated by one whose kinship with him is not of race or nation only but of caste as well. The rivalry between various classes, seeking to prove that their ancestors had a share in the accomplishment of the task of this Maratha Liberator,—a rivalry that stirs wide and vivid interest at the present time,—is indeed a testimony to the inspiration that his memory and example bring to his fellow countrymen still. Perhaps an element of class jealousy, not yet wholly extinguished, embitters sometimes these disputes and renders an impartial judgement difficult. But the growth of a critical spirit in the young historical students of to-day, among whom the translator and editor of this book has a distinguished place, as well as the influence of a wider patriotism, will speedily exorcise this evil and enable India to view her great son as he actually was, unobscured by either depreciation or flattery.

The view of Sir William Hunter that affirms that Shivaji won his supremacy "by treachery, assassination and hard fighting" is as unhistorical and as partial as that which exalts him to the position of a super-human being. Both views do injustice to the foresight, the statesmanship, the tenacity of purpose of the king himself and to the loyalty and the courage of his subjects. One of the hateful aspects of war is, as a Greek historian has said, that it takes away your freedom and puts you in the region of necessity. That fact makes it only fair that we should judge a soldier, not only in the 17th century but even to-day, by a lowered standard. When we remember this we must agree that India has every right to set the Maratha warrior-king in a high place among those whom she remembers with gratitude and pride.

Poona,
May, 1921.

N. MACNICOL.

CONTENTS.

LIFE OF SHIVAJI MAHARAJ

CHAPTER I

ANCESTRY

SHIVAJI MAHARAJ, the illustrious founder of the Maratha Power, derived his descent from the renowned Bhonsle family. This noble Maratha house claimed an ancient Kshatriya origin. It is said that the family was transferred to the uplands of Maharashtra by a Rajput warrior, Devraj Maharana by name. The family tradition tells a long tale of chequered adventures and vicissitudes. In what is now known as the modern province of Oudh, there ruled for centuries the ancient princes of the royal Sesodia family. They claimed descent from the mythical Solar Race, which along with the Lunar Race comprises the genealogy of every Kshatriya family in the land. One of these Sesodia princes crossed the Narbada and became the founder of an independent principality on its southern banks. The fortunes of this family were, however, destined to wane before the rising glory of the famous Shalivan, who inaugurated a new Hindu era, which is still current south of the Narbada. The ruling Bhonsle prince of the time was defeated and his kingdom annexed. At this crisis the afflicted queen of the prince escaped with her young son of five or six years across the Narbada and sought shelter in the inhospitable regions of Mewar in the vicinity of the Vindhya Mountains. There she found an asylum in a poor Brahman family, her son keeping the Brahman's kine. Once while out engaged on his cow-herd duties the boy discovered a hidden treasure. This he disclosed to his patron and acquainted him with the story of his origin and fall. The Brahman listened with sympathy and encouraged and exhorted him to endeavour to recover his royal power, giving him to that end every assistance within his means. It was a mountainous region in the possession of the Bhils, with whom they had to fight. When the conquest of the country was completed, they erected a fort upon those mountain heights under the shadow of a temple of the goddess Bhawani. This fort they named Chitrakote. They restored the ancient temple of Bhavani and built another within the fort in honour of Eklingji Shiv. The descendants of this prince are said to have reigned at Chitrakote for about five hundred years. This fort of Chitrakote became afterwards famous in history as the fort of Chitore.

Then followed the establishment of Mahomedan power at Delhi, and the interminable wars between the Mahomedan emperors and the Rajput princes. Many Hindu kings had to acknowledge defeat and become vassals of the Mahomedan emperors. These rulers carried on constant wars with the Rajput state of Chitore, but with little success to boast of. The Chitore princes defended their kingdom and independence very bravely. About 1275 the Maharana Lakshman Singh succeeded to the throne of Chitore. The affairs of the administration were in the charge of his uncle, Bhim Singh. This Bhim Singh had for his consort one of the greatest beauties in the land, Rani Padmini[1]. This princess is said to have come from Ceylon. Her great reputation for beauty reached the ears of Allauddin Khilji, the emperor of Delhi, who conceived an unholy passion for her. With an immense army he advanced upon Chitore and laid siege to the fort. The Rajputs fought with the valour for which they are famous; they beat back the enemy in all their advances, but still Allauddin would not raise the siege. He had invested the fortress on all sides with very powerful forces. The garrison had now exhausted all their resources. Driven to desperation the Rajput king resolvod at the head of his whole army to make a sudden sortie upon the enemy and meet a warrior's death on the field of battle. All the

---

1 Some chronicles describe the Rani Padmini as the wife of the Maharana Lakshman Singh.

Rajputs to a man applauded the plan. But surely it was not desirable that the whole race of the Sesodias should be extirpated from the earth, and means must be found to perpetuate it. The king had twelve sons. They all vied with each other in the desire to sacrifice their lives upon the battle-field. But the second prince Ajay Singh was the special favourite of hisroyal father. The Raja explained to him, how undesirable it was that his royal race should be totally extinguished and commanded him to betake himself to an inaccessible part of the Aravalli Mountains, known as Kailwada, and save himself. This advice was by no means palatable to a prince of the courage of Ajay Singh.. But overcome by the urgent entreaties of his father he was obliged to acquiesce in this plan, and according to his father's wishes escaped to Kailwada[1]. Thereupon at Chitore, the Raja with his followers and kinsmen dashed forth upon the enemy, and nearly fourteen hundred of them were cut to pieces. The fort fell into the hands of the Mahomedans. The whole place was pillaged and plundered; not even the royal insignia were saved; the gigantic war-drum and the massive gates composed of an ingenious amalgam of five metals, celebrated throughout the land, fell into the hands of the enemy.

When, as related above, Ajay Singh made his escape, he took with him Humbir Singh, the minor son of his eldest brother. He then rallied the remnants of his people and again formed a fairly large principality. As Humbir Singh grew in years he proved himself a brave and capable leader. Ajay Singh was a man of a very pious disposition and loved his nephew with a father's love. He crowned him king of his forefathers' realm and himself took charge of the administration. They built the fortress of Rajnagar and made it their capital. For they had sworn not to

[1] Chitnis's chronicle gives a different version to the effect that at Lakshman Singh's desperate sally his queen escaped to the Bhil country with two princes, who subsequently propagated the race.

return to Chitore until they had retrieved from the enemy the royal drum and insignia. Until they had curbed the insolent pride of those hostile bands who had decimated their race and desecrated the capital of their hereditary kingdom, they were resolved not to carry their war-standards before them, and to deny to themselves the luxury of plate and couches, and not even to trim their beards. This hatred of Islam they transmitted to their posterity. They made new conquests; they built new forts and consolidated their power; and at last with Udaipur as their capital, they established their independence.

On the demise of Ajay Singh, his son Sajan Singh thought it unwise to quarrel with his cousin for a partition of territory, and considered it more glorious to win new realms for himself. With this design, this brave prince advanced southwards. The territory of Sondhwad was conquered by him, and there he made his capital. Among his descendants we read the names of Dilip Singhji Maharana, Singhji Maharana, Bhosaji Maharana, and Devrajji Maharana in succession. All these constantly fought with the Mahomedans and preserved their kingdom. But at length Devrajji, quite exhausted with the frequency of the Mahomedan invasions, gave up his kingdom, and coming down to the south maintained a precarious independence as a *polygar* in the valleys of the Krishna and the Bhima. On coming to the Deccan he changed his name for fear of the Mahomedans and assumed that of Bhosawant Bhonsle. His object was, if possible, to lay the foundations of a new sovereignty in this land. But the Mahomedans carried everything before them and his high ambition was not destined to be realized. At last he had to content himself with the Patelship of Singnapur.

His descendants afterwards obtained by purchase the Patelships of various places, such as, Khanwat, Hingnsi Begdi, Dewalgaon, Verul, Vavi, Mungi etc. In the line of direct descent from Devrajji we have Indrasen, Shubhkrishnaji, Rupsinghji, Bhumindraji, Dhapji Barhatji[1], Khalaji[2] alias Khalkarn, Karnasinghji alias Jayakarn, Sambhaji and Babaji alias Shivaji. The last named Babaji was born in 1533[3]. Babaji was a man of piety and character. He had two sons, Maloji and Vithoji. Maloji was born in 1550 and Vithoji in 1553. They were both men of ability and character. When they came to years of discretion and began to look after their estates they had many land disputes with the agriculturists of Dewalgaon. They, therefore, came and settled at Verul (Ellora), near Dowlatabad. But agriculture is at best an "arida nutrix," and gives little scope for the free play of genius. They began to look out for an employment which might better develop their virtue and talents. This they found by enlisting themselves in the service of Lukhji Jadhav of Sindhkhed in the humble ranks of the "bargir" infantry. Lukhji Jadhav, a scion of the 'Yadavs' of Devgiri, was Deshmukh of Sindhkhed. Under the Nizami Dynasty of Ahmednagar he held a *mansab* or command of 12,000 horse and he had

---

1 Chitnis gives the name as Barbatji.

2 Elsewhere given as Kheloji.

3 This genealogy chiefly follows the account in Chitnis's Bakhar or Chronicle history. It agrees in all particulars with the genealogy prepared by the Rajah Pratapsinh of Satara. The latter has been printed and published at Kolhapur under the auspices of the Maharajah of that state. Col. Tod in his History of Rajasthan refers to a genealogy of Shivaji which he had obtained from the Bhats or troubadours of Mewar. This genealogy agrees generally with the one followed in the text with a few variations. While referring to the above mentioned genealogy Col. Tod remarks that it was reserved for the house of Sajan Singh eventually to produce a hero, who would overthrow the Mahomedan powers, and that this was realized by Shivaji, the founder of the Satara dynasty. It may be remarked that many discrepancies and variations from the story followed in the text are to be found in other *Bakhars* or chronicle hristories, as for instance in the famous bakhar of Shivaji called the Shivadigvijaya or Triumph of Shivaji. This is not to be marvelled at, as many of these bakhars contain various traditional tales indifferently strung together. Mr. Keluskar in his original note gives the variant versions of other chronicles. The name "*Bhonsle*" is derived by most chroniclers from "*Bhosi*" or "*Bhosavant*", a fortress near Chitore. Khafi Khan gives some legends about the meaning of "Bhonsla" (Vide Elliot VII, 255).

a *jahgir* made over to him for the maintenance of his forces. He had great influence in the councils of the Nizami Government, and there were indeed very few generals in that state who could compare with him in bravery and power. Jadhavrao was delighted to welcome Maloji and Vithoji into his service, offered them a salary of five *hons* (pagodas) each, and ordained that they should keep him company at table.

THE CAREER OF MALOJI.

Maloji was strong and burly in figure, so that few horses could bear his weight on a prolonged excursion. He was therefore chosen to mount sentry at the outposts. With his talents and brilliant parts he soon won the favour of Jadhavrao, who introduced him to Murtezashaha Nizam and recommended him to the royal favour as a man of integrity and honour. The Sultan was pleased with him and retained him as a "shiledar" or cavalry officer in his service Henceforth Maloji served the Nizam at the head of his own foot and horse, but seems to have still remained a dependent of Jadhavrao.

Maloji was married to Dipabai, the sister of Jagpalrao Nimbalkar, the Deshmukh of Phaltan. After his admission into the Sultan's army his rise was rapid. His brother, Vithoji, had also been promoted to the position of Shiledar. Vithoji had eight sons but Maloji as yet had no children. This was a source of great affliction to his wife Dipabai. True to Hindu sentiments the pious pair made endless vows to the gods and practised many a rite of religious merit that their home might be blessed with children. At length he made a vow at a celebrated shrine at Nagar, that of the Pir Shaha Sharif. Every Thursday Maloji used to give alms and doles to *fakirs*. This he practised continually for six months. At last Dipabai had the good fortune to get her heart's desire, being delivered of a son in 1594. Deeming the birth of the child as an act of benefaction on the part of the Pir, Maloji named the child, after the Pir, Shahaji. After some time he had a second son, whom he named Sharifji.

Shahaji was a handsome boy, and with his sprightly ways, no less than with his sweet childish prattle and precocity, he made a most favourable impression upon all people. There was a peculiar charm in his manners, gait, and voice. Jadhavrao conceived a great fondness for the boy. He often took him home, decked him with clothes of various styles and embroideries, and indulged him in all his boyish whims. Now Jadhav had an only daughter two or three years of age, with whom Shahaji used to play and romp for hours. Thus the two grew up together, playmates and companions almost from their cradles. Thus Shahaji grew to five years of age; and now once it happened that Jadhav was celebrating the Hindu festival of the *Shimga*. On the day of the *Rang-Panchami*, he had invited all his friends and relations to his house. Among those who had received the invitation was Maloji. He attended the social function, which was a kind of durbar, with his son. Jadhavrao called the youngster towards him and seated him on his lap. Soon after his daughter, Jija, came running from the inner apartments of the house and sat down on the other knee of her father. Both the children were so pretty and handsome and equally matched in age, that it was nothing strange that Jadhav addressing the young girl asked her in jest whether she would have the boy for her husband and, turning to the company, exclaimed that they would be a proper pair indeed! Scarcely had he spoken when the children, snatching handfuls of the red powder which was standing near in a plate, began to throw it upon each other. The company present were much amused at this display of childish fun and spirits and laughed outright exclaiming that they were indeed a pretty match. At this, Maloji and Vithoji stood up, and, "Listen, gentlemen," they exclaimed, "from this day, Jadhavrao and ourselves have become related by betrothal. Jija is now our daughter-in-law. You have just heard what Jadhavrao has said. His resolution is made. Great men never recede from a declaration made in public." Thus calling all the company to bear witness to what had occurred, they sat down. The spectators assented. Jadhavrao was astonished at this scene. He had never imagined that any one would place such a construction upon words uttered in jest. But he made no reply.

The next day Jadhavrao invited his friends to dinner. Maloji also was invited. But he in return replied in these terms: "We are now to be related by the marriage of our children; the wedding will be the proper time for us now to feast together; kindly do not invite us till then." When Jadhavrao's wife, Mhalsabai, came to learn of these proceedings, she resented this impertinence of Maloji. That a common Shiledar like Maloji should dream of a marriage alliance into the house of a rich mansabdar of the rank of Jadhav was in her eyes the height of folly and insolence. Mhalsabai remonstrated with her husband for his unguarded words in the assembly. "It was wrong of you," she exclaimed, "to have uttered those words; more wrong still not to have replied when Maloji stood up and spoke. Maloji is a dependent of ours. It will never do to give our daughter into his house. What will the world say, if we pass over eligible youths from the houses of the Mahadiks, the Shirkes, the Nimbalkars, our equals in rank and wealth-Mansabdars and Deshmukhs—, and stoop so low as this house of Maloji? Yes! what will the world say?" Thus she fumed in spite of all the efforts of Jadhavrao to console her. "I spoke in jest," he declared, "I don't think I am any way bound in honour." Then he sent a peremptory message to Maloji: "A truce to this talk of a marriage union! Our people cannot entertain it. What I spoke before the assembly was merely in jest. It is preposterous to construe it into a solemn declaration. Do accept the invitation. The gods alone know the future." Maloji retorted upon this, "A pronouncement made in presence of so numerous a company—how could it be void? We claim an affiance with your house." Jadhavrao was very angry at this insolent reply. After the feast he summoned his clerk to him and ordered him to make up the accounts of Maloji and Vithoji, pay up the arrears due to them, and discharge them immediately from his service, with notice to quit his territory at once, bag and baggage.

Thus the two brothers now lost the high positions of command so nobly earned and were forced to return to their paternal homestead at Verul, again to become farm hinds and till the land.

This was a great insult to the haughty spirit of Maloji. He felt the degradation all the more keenly, because he saw that Jadhavrao had dared to treat him thus only because he was a dependent without wealth and rank; and he now firmly resolved to make every effort to retrieve his fortune. This now became the one desire of his life and he dedicated his nights and days to the realization of his lofty aim. To a man of his spirit and character death itself seemed better than the ignominious repudiation by Jadhav of what he considered a solemn avowal of betrothal in the presence of the assembled chiefs and nobles, the elite of Maratha society. The sense of dishonour rankled in his heart. In this agitated and disconsolate frame of mind, the two brothers went out one night to watch their crops. It was the full moon night in the month of *Magh*. They kept watch by turns. At first Vithoji went to sleep while Maloji remained watching. There was an ant-hill at the spot where he had stationed himself. After a little while, he saw a bright and lustrous hand like that of the goddess Bhavani, bejewelled with armlets of gold, coming out of the ant-hill and beckoning to him, and after waving once or twice it vanished out of sight. Maloji awakened his brother and described to him the vision he had just seen. "It is all an illusion," cried Vithoji, and he undertook to watch himself and asked Maloji to sleep. Now as soon as he was asleep he had a wondrous dream. He saw in his dream the goddess Bhavani standing before him, draped in silver white, with the red-powder mark on her brows, and decked with the richest jewels. He thought she stroked him on the back and awoke him, and addressed him in these terms: "Behold, oh mortal, I have of mine own accord become propitious and lavish my favours on thee. The snake thou wilt find haunting this ant-hill is nought but my divine self in another guise. Be it thine to salute the snake and dig up the ant-hill; and take thou the gold thou shalt find therein, but harm not the reptile, for it shall go its way. Twenty-seven of thy descendants in the direct line shall reign in the land!" Maloji awoke from his dream and described the marvellous vision to Vithoji. The two brothers now resolved to test the truth of the wonderful prophecy and began to dig the ant-hill. They found in it a great quantity of gold and precious gems. They brought it home and buried it safely, in the yard behind their house[1].

This unexpected windfall gave a new stimulus to Maloji's energies. He caused a rumour to be circulated among the people that the goddess Bhavani had been pleased to be specially propitious to him and had put him in possession of an untold amount of gold, and had given her divine promise that there would be born in their house an invincible hero, who would inaugurate a new era in the land. They then deposited their money at the house of a great banker at Shrigonde, Shesava Naik Pande by name. They had an old family connection with Shesava. With his help Maloji purchased a thousand horses and enlisted many *bargirs* and *shiledars* in his service. From the beginning he had been known for his piety, and this new accession of wealth which he attributed to divine favour only served to accentuate his natural predilection for religion. He resolved to devote a great part of his acquisitions to objects of benevolence. He made bountiful presents to deserving

[1] Grant Duff thinks that Maloji must have acquired his riches by plunder. But the imputation is quite gratuitous. It was nothing strange in those exciting and revolutionary times to discover a hidden treasure, and it was the common practice to bury precious things under ground as the only effectual way of saving them from the hands of the spoilers.

Brahmans upon the farm which had been the scene of the discovery of his treasure, and he erected a beautiful temple upon the site of the ant-hill. There is in the Satara District the famous hill of Shambhu Mahadev. On the top of this mountain there used to be held every year a great religious fair in the month of *Chaitra*. No less than 500,000 persons used to gather at the fair at this time, but they suffered from a great scarcity of water. The devout pilgrims had to provide themselves with water from a distance of over five or six miles. With a view to mitigate this grievance, Maloji built a great reservoir of water upon a suitable site. He spent freely upon this work. On the completion of the raservoir, he gave a great feast to Brahmans and liberal alms to *fakirs*; he also erected some *dharmshalas* at this place. He restored the dilapidated temple of Krishna at Verul and built a reservoir near that town. In the same way he built tanks, wells etc. at different places and spent much in charity at the various shrines.

By the performance of these and other similar acts of religious merit so congenial to the sentiments of orthodox Hinduism, Maloji earned a great reputation for wealth and munificence. He now commenced to put into practice the great scheme of his life. It has already been mentioned how he had begun to maintain a cavalry force of ten to twelve hundred retainers. He went on adding to his retinue, and when he found himself well established he renewed his demand for the daughter of Jadhav. But Jadhav would not upon any terms consent to this proposal, which he could only regard in the light of a mesalliance. Maloji now began harrying the territory under Jadhav's military control and opened communications with the Nimbalkars to the effect that they should co-operate with him with a reinforcement of two thousand horse and curb the insolence of family pride which had caused Jadhav to break his promise. These negotiations proved successful and Maloji now concerted a systematic war of invasion and depredation upon Jadhav's jahgir. But nothing that Maloji could do to molest him would make Jadhav swerve from his decision. Then Maloji had recourse to a strange stratagem. At the head of the cavalry force of the Nimbalkars, Maloji and Vithoji marched up to Shrigonde. Leaving behind them their heavy baggage and artillery at this place, they poured down the pass of Nimbdevara and crossed the Godavari past the village of Nevase. There they killed a couple of pigs and threw the carcases into the mosque at Dowlatabad, having previously tied round their necks letters enclosing a petition to the Nizam Shahi Sultan of Ahmednagar. The petition recited the grounds of these disturbances, how Jadhavrao had forsworn himself in deference to the whims of the ladies of his house and had basely discharged the Bhonsle brothers from his service, and how they had sought shelter with the Nimbalkars and taken revenge with their encouragement and support. The missives concluded with threats of further disturbance and desecration. When the news of this desecration came to the ears of Nizam Shaha his anger knew no bounds, but it was curiously directed against Jadhavrao, whom he summoned to his presence and threatened with menaces. He told him that it was most improper on his part to have made a declaration of a betrothal and then to have broken it off, and declared it was owing to his headstrong obstinacy that a sacred mosque of Islam had been desecrated so. He expostulated with him on the folly of protracting a private dispute at the expense of the public weal and ordered him peremptorily to put an end to it by conciliating Maloji and signalizing the event by giving his daughter into the Bhonsle house. Jadhavrao replied that his objection to the match was based on the inequality of social position between the two houses; otherwise they stood related by ties of race and blood, and that his people desired that his daughter should be given into a house of the same fortune and standing as his own.

On hearing this reply the Sultan reflected that the high honours enjoyed by Jadhav had made him insolent, and that the only way of making him eat humble pie was to exalt Maloji to rank and honour, by conferring a high *mansab*, or military command, upon him. Strange that the Sultan should have thought of this kind of friendly treatment towards the Bhonsles! In truth Maloji and Vithoji had been guilty of an atrocity which outraged public opinion and Islam sentiment, and which under ordinary circumstances would have instantly called forth the retribution it deserved. But the Nizam Shahi State of Ahmednagar had fallen on evil days. The Emperor Akbar was endeavouring to overthrow the kingdom and absorb it within the ever widening bounds of the Mogul Empire. The Mogul armies were every hour gaining ground inch by inch into the sultan's realm, and the only breakwater capable of keeping off the accumulating tide of invasion was the solid and united front of the Maratha nobility. If at this critical time the state were to embark on a policy of fomenting dissension among the Marathas, it would have been fatal to the best interests of the ruling dynasty. The disaffected Maratha chiefs were sure to go over to the enemy's camp, and every accession of strength to the Mogul meant a corresponding loss to the Mahomedan prince of the Deccan. Thus the sultan had to think deep before committing himself to a hasty step, and his final decision was the rather startling proposal to conciliate and heap honours upon men who had given him mortal offence. He invited Maloji and Vithoji to the royal presence and received them with courtesy, conferring upon each a *mansab* of 12,000 horse and the title of "Rajah" upon Maloji[1], together with the forts of Shivneri and Chakan and the adjoining territory for his maintenance, and the districts of Poona and Supa in jahgir.[2] This event took place in March, 1604.

---

1 Other accounts mention a mansab of 5,000 for Maloji only.

2 The Shiv -Digvijaya gives a longer list of jahgir lands which would include some parganas of Poona, Nasik, Ahmednagar and Khandesh.

Now that the sultan himself had espoused the cause of Maloji and had given him an exalted rank at his court, Jadhav could no longer withstand the demand. The sultan ordered both the parties to bring their families and relations to Dowlatabad; and the nuptials were celebrated with great pomp and eclat in the royal presence. The fact that the sultan himself attended the wedding and took a personal interest in it was sufficient cause for all the Omrahs of the court to attend it without exception. Under such auspices was celebrated the marriage of Shahaji and Jijabai. Maloji grudged no amount of expense on this great occasion, which, in truth, was the crowning glory of his life. He gave a grand banquet to the Omrahs, and distributed large sums in charity to Brahmans and fakirs. This wedding took place in April 1604. Maloji had not only won his object, but had secured a mansab and the title of Rajah into the bargain.

After the marriage, the Rajah Maloji, now a mansabdar or commander of the Nizam Shahi kingdom did very useful service to that government in those troublous times. By his bravery and talents he soon gained an overwhelming ascendency at that court. He earned the gratitude of the state for his success in the most difficult operations of war and his services both civil and military. It soon became apparent that though the high command was originally conferred upon Maloji merely on account of the sultan's displeasure at Jadhav's obstinacy, the recipient was well worthy of the honours lavished upon him. The state officials now consulted him in all questions of moment. Besides by his conciliatory and courteous manners he always kept on terms of the utmost cordiality with the high officers of the court. Shahaji used to attend the court in company with his father. His fine figure and noble bearing, his penetration and sagacity, his habitual courtesy and persuasiveness soon won for him the golden opinions of the sultan and the court. He became a "persona grata" with all the great Omrahs and courtiers. After enjoying his great *mansab* and prosperity for fifteen years with ever increasing influence in the state, Maloji died in 1619. The Nizam Shaha conferred his jahgirs and honours upon the Rajah Shahaji.

CHAPTER II

THE CAREER OF SHAHAJI

AT the time when Shahaji succeeded to the *mansab*, the renowned Malik Ambar was at the head of the Nizam Shahi State. It is indispensable at this stage to have some general notion of the state of Ahmednagar, on the eve of its extinction. The town had fallen into the hands of the Moguls about 1600, and the illustrious Chand Bibi Sultana, whose noble defence of it had excited the admiration and envy of the Mogul conquerors, had been stabbed by one of her own perfidious *sardars*. The infant prince she had placed upon the Nizamshahi throne was now a captive in Mogul hands, being immured within the prison-fort of Gwalior. The capital was gone, the prince was lost, but this did not daunt the noble heart of Malik Ambar, who rallied the Ahmednagar chiefs and again presented a united front to the invaders, having proclaimed an infant prince who stood next in succession under the name of Murteza Nizam Shaha II[1]. He transferred the new king's court to

---

[1] Most of the chroniclers call this Nizamshahi Sultan as Sultan Murteza Nizam Shah II, and the puppet prince set up by Shahaji at the extinction of the dynasty would then be recognized as Murteza Shah III. However there is much confusion. Meadows Taylor speaks of the puppet supported by Malik Ambar as Murteza Shah II and the Sultan reigning at the time of Khan Jehan Lodi's rebellion as Murteza Shah III. Prof. Jadunath Sarkar in his article on Shahaji in the Modern Review (September 1917) calls the prince supported by Malik Ambar by the name of Buran Nizam Shaha, against the authority of Ferishta who calls him Murteza II. This prince reigned over a long period, 1601 to 1632. At any rate Murteza II, the protege of Malik Ambar was a grandson of Buran Nizam Shah I, and might have been known as Buran Nizam Shaha before succeeding to the throne. Grant Duff and other historians including the Marathi chronicles have concurred in calling him Murteza II. The puppet set up by Fatteh Khan was Hoosein Nizam III, though Prof. Jadunath Sarkar speaks of him both under this name and as Bahadur Nizam Shaha. It may be here noted that the *Jedhe* chronology, (see *Bharat-Itihas-Sanshodhak Mandal, Chaturth Sammelanvritta*, page 178) states, under Shaka year 1553, that Fatteh Khan put to death the Sultan Buran Nizam Shaha.

The gist of the article of Prof. Sarkar above referred to is that Shahaji came to greatness only after 1630-32, and that entirely owing to the Bijapur

the strong fort of Dowlatabad and again unfurled the defiant standard of the house of Bheiry. This led to a concentration of all power in the hands of Malik Ambar, and the Abyssinian element in the state, which was Malik Ambar's party, now had it all their own way. The Maratha nobility resented this and factions arose. The leader of the Maratha party was Mian Raju, who had co-operated with Malik Ambar in recovering a great part of the territory conquered by the Moguls. Now Mian Raju kept in his own hand all the recovered territory north of Dowlatabad upto the limits of Guzerat and south-wards down to Ahmednagar. The country further south remained under Malik Ambar. Both outwardly professed allegiance to Nizam Shaha, but had no desire to surrender their power. Murteza Nizam Shaha was kept in the fort of Avsha, and the revenue of the territory adjoining the fort was ceded for the expenses of his court.

Some time afterwards we find Mian Raju making peace with the Moguls and waging war with Malik Ambar. In this contest victory at last smiled upon Malik Ambar, and Mian Raju himself was soon a prisoner in his hands. The Maratha nobility had now to give up their opposition and acknowledge the supremacy of Malik Ambar. After overthrowing all opposition Malik Ambar devoted all his attention to the reorganization of the state. He had in a short time restored order to the different departments of the state, but the crowning glory of his administration was his reform of the revenue system. By this reform he at once made a name throughout Maharashtra. Later in 1610 he founded a new town, Khadki, afterwards more famous under the

---

ministers Khawas Khan and Murarpant, and he states that the fall of his patron, Fatteh Khan, and the murder of his father-in-law Lukhji Jadhavrao were *crushing* blows to him. The latter of these statements is opposed to all Marathi Chronicle authorities; nor can any justification for it be seen in the rest of Prof. Sarkar's article, which would appear to contradict itself in terms by giving us the further information that between 1620–30 Jadhavrao fought under the Moguls, that is against Ahmednagar and against Fatteh Khan, the patron of Shahaji.

name Aurangabad. This he now made the capital of the Nizam Shahi Kingdom. He waged endless wars with the Moguls, many of them with conspicuous success. He recaptured the town of Ahmednagar, which had passed under the Moguls. While Malik Ambar was thus waxing in resources and chastising one Mogul army after another, Jehangir, the then Mogul emperor of Delhi, sent his son Shaha Jahan with a great army to the Deccan to reconquer the Nizam Shahi dominions (1617). A desperate engagement took place between Malik Ambar and the Mogul forces in 1620. The Maratha nobles fought with great bravery, and it was in this battle that the bravery and generalship of the Rajah Shahaji were first recognized. Malik Ambar was indeed defeated and had to retire, still the Rajah Shahaji, undaunted by any reverses, made raid after raid on the Mogul camp and tired them out. For this perseverance and valour he received great honour at the Nizamshahi court. No one had now a doubt left about his bravery or proficiency in the tactics of war. He at once rose in the high esteem of Malik Ambar.

Shaha Jahan saw that as long as the Nizamshahi was supported by the solid strength of the Maratha power, it was impossible to subvert it. He, therefore, began to sow intrigues. He corrupted Lukhji Jadhav and other nobles and drew them over to the Mogul side. These nobles were already disaffected with Malik Ambar and had no great scruples about deserting a sovereignty of which he was the mainstay. It is said that Jadhavrao received a mansab of 24,000 horse from the Moguls, and that many of his relations got mansabs in their own right[1]. This occurred in 1621.

---

[1] Some of the *Bakhar*-writers attribute the defection of Jadhavrao to his envy of the sudden rise of Shahaji in the Nizamshahi state. They likewise assign to it a date subsequent to the death of the Sultan Murteza II. According to them Shahaji being practically appointed as vizier and guardian to the reigning Nizami prince who was only an infant, Jadhavrao did not like to dance attendance upon Shahaji, and therefore went over to the Moguls. As to the total amount of the mansab obtained by Jadhavrao, see prof. Jadunath Sarkar's article in the Modern Review, (September 1917, page 249 and Elliot VII, page 11.)

The Rajah Shahaji was the only one of the great Maratha nobles, who was proof against this corruption. He still adhered to the party of his patron, Malik Ambar.

After this wholesale desertion of the Maratha nobility, Malik Ambar saw there was little prospect of success in stemming the tide of Mogul invasion, and was content to make peace by a large cession of territory. A little later events compelled Shaha Jahan to return to Delhi. Malik Ambar seized this opportunity to expel the remnant of the Mogul garrisons and reconquer the ceded territory. Shaha Jahan soon returned to the scene of these war operations. The old fields were fought again and the territory so recently recovered by Malik Ambar again came under the rule of the Mogul Empire. Malik Ambar had now exhausted all his resources. Shahaji still kept loyally supporting his chief. But all his efforts proved vain before the great military resources of the Moguls. Malik Ambar now thought it proper to make his submission and save the remnants of the territory for his Nizam Shahi master rather than to stake all upon the uncertain chances of a decidedly unequal war. He soon found a favourable opportunity for overtures of peace. This honourable peace he observed till the last day of his life. He did not live long after this. He died of a sudden malady in 1626 at the age of eighty.

Immediately on the death of Malik Ambar the Moguls renewed their hostilities with the active support of Lukhji Jadhav. Shaha Jahan had to return to Delhi about this time, on account of the death of his father, the Emperor Jehangir. He marched to Delhi, leaving but a small Mogul force to co-operate with Jadhavrao. At this time the sultan Murteza Nizam Shaha was at Mahuli, and Shahaji was in attendance upon the Sultan. Jadhavrao laid siege to Mahuli with all his forces. Shahaji defended the fort with great valour for six months, but with all his efforts he did not succeed in forcing the enemy to raise the siege. However he was resolved never to give in to the enemy. Shahaji was indeed the last of the loyal officers still left in the service of the Nizamshahi who combined in himself the will and the capacity to save the Nizamshahi kingdom. But the good fortune of the state seemed to have forsaken her for ever. For as misfortunes never come singly the state lost the services of a good and loyal servant, on account of a strange prejudice that Murteza Nizam Shaha's mother now conceived against Shahaji. This was due to an intrigue which Lukhji Jadhav had set on foot, under the pretence of reconciliation and peace, but in reality to extinguish the Nizami power. Shahaji saw the changed aspect of affairs, but he could only regret it. When the sultan had himself lost heart and was bent upon submission at the sacrifice of every idea of honour and advantage of what avail was it, he reflected, for himself to continue the opposition single handed, perhaps at the risk of his life? His loyal and devoted service to the state seemed to have been rendered in vain. Why should he now, when the state was being blindly driven to the brink of ruin, incur the gratuitous odium of hastening on its fall? Far better for him to turn his back upon the impending destruction! With these counsels, he prepared for his departure from the beleaguered town, having previously apprised the sultan and his mother of his intention. He sallied out of the fort one night with a small band of loyal veterans and broke through the besieging lines. This is just what Jadhavrao wanted. He pursued him and continued the pursuit for several days with great earnestness until the barriers of Phaltan were reached. There the vengeful Jadhavrao had to stop his relentless chase of his son in-law. For he knew of the old alliance of the Nimbalkars and knew well too that were Shahaji, re-inforced with the militia of the Nimbalkars, to turn upon him, he would have little difficulty in dispersing his pursuers.

At the time that the Rajah Shahaji burst forth from the fortress of Mahuli he was accompanied by his wife

Jijabai and his little son Sambhaji, who was then only three or four years of age. Jijabai herself was far advanced in pregnancy. Hard-pressed by their pursuers, the fugitives had to make forced marches and Jijabai had to be conveyed on horse-back. A few miles' journey sufficed to cause her intense sufferings, so that Shahaji was reluctantly forced to find an asylum for her on the way[1]. Now Junnar was the stronghold of a certain Shriniwasrao, an independent chief with whom Shahaji had a long standing alliance. Under his promise of protection the lady Jijabai was placed for shelter in the fort of Shivneri, and Shahaji detached a small body of cavalry from his slender retinue to defend her from harm. No sooner had Shahaji left the place than his pursuers arrived. With difficulty could Jadhavrao be persuaded to yield to the importunate pleading of those who argued that whatever grudge he might have against Shahaji in person, his own daughter Jijabai was an innocent party and that public opinion required it of him to take measures for her safety. Whose would be the disgrace if the Jadhavrao's daughter were to fall into Mogul hands? This last argument carried weight with the haughty warrior. He pitied the forlorn state of Jijabai and went to see her. The meeting between father and daughter was very painful. She reproached him for his lack of generosity and of a father's love and exclaimed that, now that she had fallen into his hands instead of Sahaji, he was welcome to wreak his revenge on her instead of her husband. His heart was touched and he endeavoured to comfort her saying: "What the gods had ordained has taken place; the bitterness of after-regrets is of no avail." He tried to persuade her to accompany him to Sindhkhed, the seat of the jahgir he had received from the Moguls. But she steadfastly refused, and Jadhavrao, seeing that nothing would shake her resolution, detached from

[1] Some *bakhars* represent Shahaji to have been forced by necessity to leave Jijabai on the way with a small escort and attribute her removal to the fort of Shivneri to Jadhavrao, who detached a force of 500 horse-soldiers for her protection.

his army an escort for Jijabai's protection and went forward. Thus did the high-minded Jijabai continue to dwell in the place chosen for her by her husband. That her father, of all persons in the world, should prosecute these hostilities against her husband was an offence she could never forgive. Notwithstanding all the tumults of war that were raging all round her, she persevered in staying at Shivneri, and never more in after life did she set her foot in her father's jahgir.

Meanwhile Shahaji did not slack his flight till he reached Bijapur. He had previously sent a trusty officer, Balkrishnapant Hanumante, to the Bijapur Durbar, on a political mission, as soon as he had got the first inkling of the intrigue meditated by the mother of the Nizam Shaha at Mahuli. The principal statesmen of the Bijapur state, Murar Jagdeo and Randulla Khan, knew the ability of the Rajah Shahaji. The Adil Shahi Sultan received him with honour and cordiality, promised to co-operate with him in his labours to preserve the Nizamshahi dynasty from utter extinction and re-inforced him with a small complement of Bijapur forces.

In the meantime a great revolution had taken place in the affairs at Ahmednagar. On the death of Malik Ambar, his son, Fatteh Khan, succeeded to the viziership. He possessed none of the tact and ability of his father, or the courtesy and considerateness by which he had won over the gentry and nobility towards himself. He waged arduous wars with the Moguls, but seldom with success. The Mogul general Khan Jahan Lodi was in charge of military operations in the south. A timely peace concluded with him by Fatteh Khan gave a new lease of life to the Nizam Shahi.

Not long after the Nizam Shahi sultan had reason to resent the insolent and arbitrary ways of Fatteh Khan, who possessed all the autocratic tendencies of his great father without his genius. Takrib Khan was accordingly appointed to supersede him as vizier[1]. This change of ministry induced Jadhavrao to return to his allegiance and the service of the Nizamshahi; and with this end in view he started overtures for a reconciliation. But the Nizam Murteza Shaha was a man who was led by the impulses of passion. With him desire for revenge weighed more in the balance than counsels of prudence; and against Jadhavrao he had conceived the bitterest hatred and animosity. It did not occur to him that the exigencies of the state might not permit him to nurse his grudges. A great general of the empire was coming back in sack-cloth and ashes. True statesmanship required the sultan to forgive and forget the past, to receive the repentant general with open arms, to unite him to his interests and make him a pillar of his state. But these thoughts were too noble and too generous for his pusillanimous spirit. He chose to work in darkness and intrigue and return treachery for treachery. Resolved to revenge himself on Jadhavrao for his past desertion, he invited him to a personal interview in the fort of Dowlatabad. In reply to the invitation Jadhavrao attended by his son Achloji, came to the Nizam's durbar. Soon after they had been ushered in, the sultan left the audience hall, on the pretence of a secret consultation with his ministers, and three Mahomedan nobles, in accordance with a previously concerted plan of treachery, drew their swords, fell upon the unsuspecting Jadhavrao and his son, and in an instant deprived them of their swords. Alarmed by this treachery both father and son drew their daggers and fought with bravery, but the odds were against them and they were cut to pieces.[2] The

---

1 Khafi Khan says that Hamid Khan, an Abyssinian noble, who had risen to power on account of the fascination of his wife's beauty upon the sultan, succeeded Fatteh Khan as vizier.

2 Modak's history of the Adilshahi kingdom (Marathi) gives quite a different version of this story. It represents that a feeling of unrest had sprung up in the mind of Jadhavrao and the Maratha nobles generally on account of the incarceration of Fatteh Khan. He intrigued to secede to the Moguls, and the sultan's suspicion being once roused he determined to apprehend and keep him in custody. Then follows the story of the trea-

wife of Jadhavrao was encamped with a small force at the reservoir outside the town. When the story of the treacherous murder of her husband and son reached her ears, she at once escaped with her little army to Sindhkhed. In reply to her petition, the Mogul court transferred the mansab and jahgir of her husband to his brother, Bhotajirao. This branch of the Jadhav family remained true to the Mogul sovereigns to the last day of the empire and rendered distinguished and loyal service to their Mogul masters.

The Rajah Shahaji was then at the fort of Parinda and having conquered the adjoining territory reigned there an absolute master. When he heard of the treacherous circumstances of his father-in-law's murder, he saw that it was useless any more to try to get reconciled with the Nizam Shaha or lead the Nizami standards, as he had done on many a battlefield in the past, in the impending struggle with the Moguls. He was convinced that Murteza was an irredeemably treacherous and vindictive man. Shahaji accordingly resolved to conquer whatever territory he could and make himself independent. In consequence of this plan he reduced all the country from Sangamner to Poona under his personal sway and captured all the forts in the neighbourhood. In the confusion of these conquests, certain parts of the Bijapur kingdom came in for a share of his acts of violence. It was but natural that the Bijapur authorities should resent his encroachment upon their dominions, and send a general at the head of a large army to chastise his audacity. This general conquered some of Shahaji's districts and captured Poona, consigning to flames Shahaji's mansion in that town. Shahaji did not yet feel himself strong enough to challenge the large Bijapur army. He, therefore, again

chery in the durbar. The *Basatin-i-Salatin* relates the story of Jadhavrao's murder in full, and this version agrees with the one followed in the text. Some chronicles change the name of Bhotaji into Vithoji or Nathuji, perhaps the same as Jagdevrao. Vide *Abdul Hamid* in Elliot VII, page 11.

had recourse to the friendly aid of Shrinivasrao of Junnar. When the tide of the Bijapur invasion had ebbed away, Shahaji once more emerged from the hospitable walls of Junnar, on a new career of adventure. He found the fort of Pamegad in an utterly dismantled and abandoned condition. He repaired and fortified this fort, named it Shamgad and made it his head-quarters[1]. From this fort he recovered in gradual succession nearly all his old fortresses and possessions, assembled a force of five or six thousand and subjugated all the territory from Junnar and Sangamner to Ahmednagar and Dowlatabad. He also captured the Baleghat district.

About this time the redoubted Mogul commander, Khan Jahan Lodi, had suffered an eclipse of the imperial favour. He had deserted from the service of the emperor Shaha Jahan and found shelter with the government of Ahmednagar. A mighty army was sent after him from Delhi. Khan Jahan found many warm partisans among the landed gentry and nobility of the south, the *deshmukhs* and *jahgirdars* of the Ahmednagar kingdom, who espoused his cause and made it their own. This was the beginning of a prolonged war with the Moguls. Shahaji took up his cause and rendered him such valuable assistance that for a long time the Mogul armies made little head-way in the field. When the news of these events reached the ears of Shaha Jahan, he at once perceived that the sinister conjunction of the Nizamshahi sultan and the Maratha nobility with the forces of Khan Jahan Lodi portended disaster to the Mogul crown, and nothing but an immediate annihilation of the forces of Khan Jahan and his confederate partisans would avert the danger. With this conviction he marched to the Deccan in person and issued a proclama-

[1] The names are variously given as Bhimgad for Pamegad and Shahagad for Shamgad (*Basatin-i-Salatin*, page 441). This confusion or variation of names is found in nearly all the chronicle authorities. Bhimgad or Pamegad was the fort where Shahaji ruled afterwards in the name of the puppet prince he had set up.

tion that whosoever aided or abetted or sympathised with Lodi would be considered by him his personal enemy and would be utterly extirpated by the Mogul army. He then despatched his army in three divisions, under three different commanders, against Lodi and his confederates. Lodi was too weak to withstand these tremendous forces and fled southward, imploring the assistance of Bijapur. But that state held wisely aloof. Lodi directed his flight again northwards in the direction of Dowlatabad and was re-inforced by the Nizam Shahi sultan. The result was a pitched battle between the Mogul and Nizami armies, in which the former were victorious. Thus with his hopes frustrated on all sides, Lodi with his chosen horse, determined to make his way to the north and escape to Kabul. The Mogul armies pursued him so relentlessly that at length driven to utter despair, Lodi turned upon his pursuers with a handful of his loyal supporters and fell fighting bravely.

Upon the destruction of the forces of Khan Jahan Lodi Shahaji was in extreme terror lest Shaha Jahan should carry out his threats and turn the vanguard of the Mogul army upon his possessions. He found but one expedient to save himself from such a dire contingency, and that was to tender his submission to the Mogul Court, procure an amnesty for his offences in the past and offer to take service in the Mogul army. He began his overtures for peace on these lines, through Azim Khan, a nobleman of the Mogul court. He memorialized the emperor to the effect that he was ready to join the Mogul service, and if a promise of pardon and safety were vouchsafed to him he would throw himself on the emperor's mercy. Shaha Jahan had already received personal proofs of Shahaji's valour and bravery. He also thought that the active co-operation of a powerful chief and practised general like Shahaji would be of the highest advantage in the accomplishment of the great object of his life, namely, the extinction of the Ahmednagar kingdom. He, therefore, acceded to Shahaji's request and giving him his royal promise of pardon invited him to a conference. Shahaji went to meet the emperor with his corps of two thousand horse. He was received with great honour and a mansab of five[1] thousand was conferred upon him, in addition to which he received some districts[2]. Shaha Jahan went so far as even to give mansabs to the relatives and dependents of Shahaji, among them to Kheloji, the son of his uncle Vithoji, who attended Shahaji on this occasion. This event took place in 1629. The districts of Junnar and Sangamner now came under Shahaji.

About this time there was a great famine in the Deccan, the greatest severity of which fell upon the inhabitants of the Nizam Shahi state. To the horrors of famine were added the ravages of cholera. People died literally in thousands. Whole districts were depopulated. On the top of these horrors came the furies of the Mogul war. The Moguls deposed many *jahagirdars* and *mansabdars* in the Nizam Shahi kingdom and installed their own officers in their places. Amid all these disasters, the Nizam Shaha now felt that his sceptre was falling from his grasp. Many of his greater nobles had openly gone over into the camp of the enemy, the loyalty of many others was open to question; all had been tampered with. In his despair he began to reflect upon the causes of these evils. He somehow persuaded himself that his new vizier was at the bottom of his present misfortunes. He accordingly proceeded to depose this vizier, released Fatteh Khan from his captivity and again placed him at the head of affairs. The deposed vizier

---

1 Some of the Marathi chronicles describe Shahaji's mansab as a command of twenty-two thousand horse, and Khafi Khan rates it at 6000 personal and 5000 horse. (Elliot VII. 15.)

2 These districts probably include Ahmednagar to which Shivaji at a later date laid claim. Some *Bakhars* state (and this is supported by the *Badishahinamah*) that Kheloji mentioned in this connection was later on apprehended and executed by Aurangzeb. It would seem that the Marathi chronicles have exaggerated the value of the mansabs. According to the *Badishahinamah*, Shahaji's mansab amounted to five thousand horse, but his relatives were given separate mansabs in their own right.

Takribkhan was not a man to brood over his degradation in silence; he openly joined the enemy. The Moguls appointed him a commander of 6000 and retained him in their service for the operations of the war.

No sooner had Fatteh Khan been restored to the viziership than he began to concert a plot to revenge himself upon the sultan for his heartless ingratitude towards himself. He caused a rumour to be circulated that the sultan had gone mad and had him placed in confinement under this pretence. The sultan thus placed at his mercy was secretly strangled to death. This atrocious deed was followed by the simultaneous massacre of some twenty-five of the prominent nobles, who were partisans of the king. By such infernal plans did Fatteh Khan endeavour to concentrate all authority in his own hands, and in order to secure permanently to himself the absolute power which he had thus usurped, he petitioned the Emperor Shaha Jahan, stating that in doing what he had done he only wanted to give a practical proof of his anxiety to remain and be reckoned upon as a loyal vassal of the empire, and that for the present he had placed on the Nizam Shahi throne a puppet prince of ten years, the son of the late sultan, and requested the favour of the emperor's orders in the matter. Shaha Jahan was a shrewd and astute statesman. He could at once read between the lines of this petition what the secret aims and objects of Fatteh Khan were. He reflected that most of the provinces of the Nizam Shahi kingdom were already in his grasp, and only a few hill-forts, more or less strongly fortified, remained to be taken. He thought he could get Fatteh Khan to play into his hands so as to secure all his objects. With this view he sent orders to Fatteh Khan that the imperial pleasure was that all the state jewels from the Nizam Shahi treasury and the state elephants should be sent to the imperial camp, that all the territory which still remained with Ahmednagar should remain under the rule of the young Nizam Shahi king, and that special lands would be assigned to Fatteh Khan in jahgir. Fatteh Khan was at first very indignant at the imperial demands. He could by no means make up his mind to send away the state jewels and elephants. Shaha Jahan sent a large army to overawe him into submission. Fatteh Khan had no resources to maintain a contest with the Moguls. Alarmed at this measure, he had no alternative but to bow to the imperial pleasure, to undertake to cede all the valuables demanded of him without protest, and to crown all, to pay an indemnity of eight lakhs of rupees in cash and agree to pay an annual tribute in future. When these demands were complied with, Shaha Jahan gave him permission to carry on the administration of the Nizam Shahi state in the name of the young sultan, in the restricted territories assigned to him, and also completed the grant of a personal jahgir made to Fatteh Khan. In this grant of jahgir-lands were included some districts which had been before assigned to Shahaji. At this Shahaji took umbrage and again meditated a renunciation of the authority of the emperor and set about to carve out an independent principality for himself[1].

The first step in this direction was to make his peace with the Bijapur State. He succeeded in conciliating to his interests Murarpant, the chief minister to the vizier and indeed the pillar of the Adil Shahi State, and through him conducted his negotiations. He drew the attention of the Bijapur Government to the absolute anarchy reigning in the Nizamshahi government and the public distrust in the administrative acts of Fatteh Khan, and urged how easy it was at the present juncture of affairs to conquer that kingdom and even to capture its capital, the fort of Dowlatabad itself. The garrison of the fort had lost their faith in the government; and the control of its defences was never more lax. If the Bijapur government thought it proper, now was the opportunity to send its armies against

---

[1] Abdul Hamid in Elliot VII, 36, 37.

that fort, and Shahaji undertook in person to serve the Bijapur interests and carry the fort with that bravery and strategy that never failed him in the midst of war. The Bijapur government approved of this plan. The sultan of Bijapur thought that the accession of a powerful and experienced commander like Shahaji to his fortunes would be of inestimable advantage in confronting the Mogul armies. The Adilshahi sultan placed his army under the command of Shahaji and ordered him in concert with Murarpant to advance against Dowlatabad[1].

The consternation of Fatteh Khan knew no bounds, when he learnt that Shahaji having made friends with Bijapur was in full march upon Dowlatabad at the head of the Adilshahi army. He scarcely had the strength to challenge a conflict with them. He tried negotiations with the Moguls and promised to yield to them the fort of Dowlatabad, if only the state were saved from the Bijapur invasion. Shaha Jahan ordered Mohabat Khan to march to the aid of Fatteh Khan. This Mogul general came up with the invading hosts of Bijapur and a hard fought contest followed. Shahaji put forth all his arts and bravery in withstanding the imperial forces, but was at length beaten back and forced to retreat on account of their overwhelming numbers[2].

Shahaji and the Adilshahi ministers now thought to gain by craft what they had failed to gain by arms. Negotiations were secretly opened with Fatteh Khan, and he was warned that in making over the fort of Dowlatabad to the Moguls he was digging his own grave. On the other hand the Bijapur government was ready to conclude a defensive and offensive alliance with him and to keep up the friendly relations between the two states, if he placed

---

[1] Abdul Hamid's *Badishahnamah* (Elliot VII, 23, 28) says that the chief minister at Bijapur was then Khawas Khan, originally a slave and *Kalawant* (musician) named Daulat. Murarpant was Khawas Khan's confidential friend and counsellor.

[2] Elliot VII, 37.

the fort of Dowlatabad in their hands and indemnified Shahaji for the losses he had sustained. Fatteh Khan was quite won over by these promises and had the hardihood to break with his Mogul overlord. The Mogul army was lying encamped in the plain dominated by the fort. Without any provocation he opened fire with his artillery upon the exposed army from the height of the fortress. Shahaji leading the Bijapur troops soon appeared on the scene in aid of Fatteh Khan. The battle was hotly contested. But Shahaji could effect little against the overwhelming numbers of the enemy. Victory at length declared itself in favour of the Moguls, whose general Mohabat Khan carried the fort of Dowlatabad by storm in 1633 A. D[1].

Fatteh Khan's fortunes were now at their lowest ebb. Deprived of every means of resistance, he had to surrender himself to the Moguls. He was divested of all authority and influence and compelled to retire into private life with a fixed annual pension. The puppet prince whom he had raised to the insecure throne of the Nizamshahi state was relegated to the prison-fortress of Gwalior, as was the fate of most political prisoners, and the remnants of the territory of that state were now permanently annexed to the Mogul Empire. Thus the year 1633 was the last year of the Nizamshahi dynasty of Ahmednagar. Its conquest had been the life-dream of Shaha Jahan. He experienced all the thrill of a gratified ambition. As far as the Deccan went, his cares and anxieties were now at an end. Thus thought the exultant emperor. Little did he dream that the now vanquished Shahaji would again rise from his fall and attempt to revive the extinct monarchy. Little did he dream that the same old battles would have to be fought over again.

During the last campaign the Mogul commander had tried his utmost to bring Shahaji into difficulties. While the Mogul siege-lines were lying round Dowlatabad, Shahaji

---

1 *Vide*: Abdul Hamid's Badishahnamah in Elliot, VII, 36, 37.

caused constant diversions amongst them by his nightly attacks and surprises. In order to wreak revenge upon Shahaji for these constant incursions, Mohabat Khan hit upon the unchivalrous plan of surprising Shahaji's wife Jijabai at her residence at Byzapur, and by fair or foul means bringing her a captive to the Mogul camp. Now, as fortune would have it, the governor of a Nizamshahi fort had just deserted to the Mogul camp and wanted to transfer his services to the emperor. As an earnest of his good faith and loyalty he was ordered to effect the arrest of Jijabai at Byzapur, and he was asked to trust for all the rest to the imperial favour should he be so fortunate as to pass this test. These conditions were accepted by the commander. He exhausted all his ingenuity and ultimately succeeded in capturing Jijabai and bringing her down into the Mogul Camp. But the brother of Lukhji Jadhav was in the Mogul service and was indeed present in the camp itself. He was naturally much irritated at what had just occurred. He interceded with the general, urging as was well known that the families of Jadhavrao and Shahaji were at daggers drawn with each other and that on this account Shahaji had abandoned his wife and son and had two or three years previously married Tukabai, a daughter of the Mohite family. In consequence it was urged that Jijabai and Shahaji were very much at variance with each other, that the arrest of his wife was in no way an injury to Shahaji, but on the other hand, as she was a daughter of the Jadhav family, it would be a gross affront and insult to that noble family. This argument carried weight with the Khan and he made over Jijabai to the protection of the Jadhav, who sent her back in safety to Kondana, one of the hill-forts under Shahaji. Thus was a great danger averted from the infant career of the great empire-builder who is the subject of our biography[1].

---

1. Byzapur or Bezapur is 25 miles west of Aurangabad. As may be inferred from Abdul Hamid (Elliot VII, 15, 17) it came into Shahaji's occupation after Junnar and Sangamner, perhaps as part of his jahgir from the Moguls when he left Khan Jehan Lodi and was co-operating with Azam

Repulsed in the manner described above the Bijapur troops were forced to retire, and Shahaji also had to retire with them. But he did not lose heart under this defeat and disappointment. His ardour and enthusiasm were as fresh as ever; his defeat served to enkindle them all the more. He resolved to restore the Nizamshahi dynasty that had just been extinguished by the Moguls. The task he had proposed to himself was not a light one. It meant a deadly encounter with a formidable foe like the Mogul. Instead of returning to Bijapur with the retreating army, he left it on the way and marched from Nasik to Bhimgad. This fort had all along been in his control. He mustered an army in its mountain fastnesses, and when his muster had swollen considerably in numbers, he proceeded to wrest from the Moguls all the districts from Poona and Chakan to Balaghat. In this way he went on carrying one Mogul outpost after another. The Mogul officer in charge of the garrison of Dowlatabad, Iradatkhan by name, sought to devise some way to put an end to these encroachments of Shahaji. Shahaji's uncle Vithoji had a son of the name of Maloji Bhonsle. He formed a friendship with this man, and by his mediation he opened communications with Shahaji. He offered again to bestow on Shahaji from the emperor the old mansab of twenty-two thousand. This

Khan and other imperial generals (*Vide* Prof. Sarkar's article on Shahaji in the Modern Review, September 1917). The story of Jijabai's abduction is omitted in Sarkar's Life of Shivaji, though the story of a similar abduction of Kheloji Bhonsle's wife is related by him. The abduction of Jijabai is described by most of the Marathi chronicles, and the story of the abduction of Kheloji's wife lends probability to the abduction of Jijabai. Mr. Kincaid relates the story in his History. Mr. Sardesai (*Marathi Riyasat*) while relating the story avers that Jijabai was staying with her mother's relations at Byzapur. But since Shahaji had seized possession of Nasik, Trimbak, Sangamner and other lands which he had held under the Moguls, even after defying their authority, it might well be that Byzapur was one of these places and Jijabai was living there as one of the places in her husband's possession, and not with her mother on account of estrangement with Shahaji at his second marriage.

was not acceptable to Shahaji. The time was gone when such an offer would have brought him over[1].

Shahaji maintained at this time a force of eight to ten thousand and had already won back a portion of the Nizamshahi provinces that had fallen into the hands of the Moguls. He knew well enough that he must prepare for an attack by the great Mogul armies. He knew likewise that he was not strong enough to meet them single-handed. He saw that without the active co-operation of Bijapur his high ambition could not be realized. The chief minister at the Bijapur court was a nobleman named Khawas Khan. Through the good offices of Murarpant, Shahaji opened overtures for an alliance with Bijapur, promising to revive the fallen Nizamshahi and restore the fortunes of the House of Bheiry[2]. Many statesmen of Bijapur doubted the expediency of this plan; but Shahaji answered all their objections and dispelled their doubts. They were soon assured of the wisdom and the generosity of his plans, and subscribing to these views they undertook to render him every assistance. Between both parties a covenant was entered into to the effect that Shahaji should select an eligible descendant of the Nizamshahi family, instal him on the throne and conduct the government of the Nizamshahi districts in his name. True to this covenant, Shahaji released a young prince of the name of Murteza who was on parole at Shrivardhan, and crowned him king at Bhimgad, the new capital. This event took place in 1634. This prince having been proclaimed as the king of the Nizamshahi state, Shahaji

---

1 Modak's history of the Adil Shahi Dynasty (Marathi) gives a different version representing that the proposal here referred to emanated from a noble of the Bijapur kingdom and that a treaty was struck between Shahaji and the Bijapur *Durbar* by which Shahaji was to receive a mansab of 22000 horse, and the territory of the Nizamshahi state recovered by the joint co-operation of Shahaji and the Bijapur forces was to be equally divided between the two parties.

2 Bheiry or Bahiry was the nickname of the founder of the Nizamshahi dynasty of Ahmednagar, who is said to have been originally a Brahman converted to Islam.

continued the reconquest of other forts and provinces. Admiring his pluck and daring and pleased with his zealous allegiance to the sultan's family, the hereditary supporters of the Nizamshahi, the loyal gentry and nobility, now came over to Shahaji. The disbanded soldiery of the Nizamshahi state, who had for some time been roving over the country in search of adventures flocked to Shahaji's standards. Thus from day to day did his party wax in strength and his military resources continue to augment. Shahaji now subdued all the Konkan country which had once been under the Nizamshahi, all the territory upto Ahmednagar on the east and the country from the Nira to the Chandor mountains in the south. Shahaji's next move was upon Junnar. Shrinivasrao ruled there in independence. He was, as we have seen, a great friend of Shahaji. But Shahaji saw that the Nizamshahi kingdom could not regain its fallen power and prestige until the recalcitrant nobles who had declared themselves independent were brought back under its allegiance. He, therefore, tried to conciliate Shrinivasrao into an acknowledgment of his Nizamshahi suzerain. But Shrinivasrao was entirely governed by selfish plans. He refused to unite his powers with those of the sultan. He declined to accede to Shahaji's terms. Shahaji was obliged to resort to an ungenerous stratagem. He gave out that he was desirous of entering into a marriage alliance with him, and demanded the daughter of Shrinivasrao for his son Sambhaji. Under pretence of arranging about the espousals, Shrinivasrao was invited to a feast at Shahaji's mansion, and when he came there in answer to the invitation, he was put under arrest. The towns of Junnar, Jivdhan, Sounda, Bhorag and others which were under Shrinivasrao were now captured. The young sultan was brought up from Bhimgad to Junnar. Shahaji next proceeded to bring under his power the Abyssinian chief, Saya Saif Khan, who like Shrinivasrao had become independent at Bhiwandi and was raiding the neighbourhood, and likewise the Abyssinian Ambar, who was pursuing the same tactics at Janjira.

When the emperor Shaha Jahan heard of these events in the Deccan and learnt that the Nizamshahi dynasty had been restored and its territory all but reconquered by Shahaji, a great army was launched against him. A great battle took place at Perinda between the Mogul army and the forces of Shahaji who was aided by Bijapur. The Mogul army was overthrown. Then the emperor ordered Khan Dowran and Khan Jeman to start with a large army and crush the insurrectionary attempts of Shahaji. But these commanders also were much harassed by Shahaji, who was well supported by Randulla Khan and Murarpant of the Bijapur kingdom and had besides considerable forces of his own. This enabled him to defeat all the attempts of the Moguls against himself.

Shaha Jahan was naturally quite exasperated at the failure of these two expeditions, and what stung him especially was the support lent by Bijapur to Shahaji. Shahaji had in a short time proved the Mogul triumphs over the Nizamshahi and the extinction of that dynasty to have been a mockery. Affairs stood now in exactly the same posture in which they were at the commencement of the protracted war, and the emperor was all the more incensed when he saw that he had now to deal with an adversary of more mettle and superior powers of enterprise. In the height of his fury he declared his resolution to take the field in person with a mighty host, to crush Shahaji and force him to restore all the territory and, if occasion arose, to extinguish the Mahomedan dynasties of Bijapur and Golconda. With this comprehensive programme before him, the Mogul came down upon the Deccan with his invading hosts.

His first manœuvre was to separate Mahomad Adilshaha of Bijapur from the alliance with Shahaji by threats. He sent an ambassador to Adilshaha requiring him to surrender the Nizamshahi fortresses that had been taken by him, to return the famous piece of ordnance called the

Malik-i-maidan[1] which had been transferred from the fort of Perinda to Bijapur, and not to lend any assistance to Shahaji and his partisans, with a promise that if these conditions were complied with, the emperor would make over to Bijapur all that portion of the Konkan which had once been under the Nizamshahi, with the fort of Sholapur and all the territory within its influence. At the same time the emperor threatened to extinguish the Adilshahi Kingdom if these demands were not instantly obeyed. The sultan of Bijapur paid little heed to these demands, since Randulla Khan and the rest of the influential nobility were inclined to continue the alliance with Shahaji.

Seeing that this plan was frustrated, Shaha Jahan determined upon punishing the two powers together, and dividing, for this purpose, his vast army into four columns he ordered two of them to march against Shahaji and the other two to advance against Bijapur. In command of the first column against Shahaji was Shaista Khan, whose charge was to subdue Chandor, Nasik, Sangamner, and other towns and the outlying districts and forts which were under Shahaji. The other, consisting of twenty thousand horse, was under the command of Khan Jeman. His orders were to engage with Shahaji in the plains, and put him to flight, and reducing the Konkan hill-forts leave him no rallying-ground in any part of the Nizamshahi territory.

---

[1] The name "*Malik-i-Maidan*" means "the Lord of the Field." This marvellous piece of artillery is believed to have been cast by a Constantinople mechanic at Ahmednagar by order of a Nizamshahi sultan. The weight of this cannon is estimated by an English military officer at 32,000 pounds avoirdupois. It is usually given as 60 candies. It is nine feet eight inches in length. The bore is so wide that it is said that a person may be easily seated in it and in that posture be able to fold his scarf into a turban round his head. This gun is reported to have been made use of in the fateful battle of Talikot which resulted in the death of Ram Rajah and the extinction of the Vijavanagar kingdom. Aurangzeb had an inscription engraved upon it in commemoration of his capture of Bijapur in 1685. The East India Company proposed to present it to King George IV in 1823, but expert advice having proved the impracticability of hauling and transporting it to the coast, the plan had to be given up. The superstitious people of the place worship the gun and call it by the name of the goddess, *Mahakali*.

Thus at one and the same moment Shahaji had to bear the brunt of attacks by two large Mogul armies on two different fronts. But his courage did not waver for an instant. His resolution had been made to fight without flinching or yielding an inch of ground, and he persisted in this noble resolve to the end. He put forth all the arts of a redoubted warrior and general. His consummate strategy, the rapidity of his movements, and unerring tactics drew praise even from his bitterest foes. He did his best to harass the Moguls, but their great advantage of numbers began to tell in course of time, and he had to face defeat in different directions. The Moguls took twenty-five of his forts in the districts of Nasik and Chandor. All the territory between Sholapur and Bedar slipped away from his hands. Many outposts in the Konkan were seized upon by the Moguls. Repulsed from the Konkan, Shahaji had to move to Ahmednagar and wait in ambush, Both the Mogul columns now effected a junction and marched together upon him. Driven to great straits, he made good his escape from between their battle lines, by a most dexterous movement, and fell back upon the districts between Chambhargonde and Baramati. When the enemy followed on his rear into those parts, he diverted his flight to Kolhapur and Miraj. Receiving new reinforcements from Bijapur, he now turned back against the pursuing Moguls and began raiding their army and intercepting their fodder supplies. They had no energy left to give battle or to pursue Shahaji any further.

When the news of these events reached Shaha Jahan, he sent orders to Khan Jaman to let Shahaji alone, since his pursuit was attended with such severe losses to the imperial armies, and to concentrate his forces against the Bijapur territory, as on the fall of that kingdom it would take little time to subdue Shahaji. In accordance with these orders, three Mogul generals invaded the Bijapur dominions, causing havoc in all directions. Many forts and towns fell before them, and thousands of the inhabitants were taken prisoners and sold into slavery ! A large Mogul army marched straight upon Bijapur. The Sultan Adilshaha was seized with panic. He had no power to resist, and opened negotiations. A peace was soon brought about between the two powers, on terms rather favourable to Bijapur. It was arranged by the treaty that the Adilshahi Dynasty should retain possession of the forts of Perinda and Sholapur, together with the territory between them ; that the same sultan should continue his authority over Bidar, Kalyani, and Naldurg to the east of Sholapur, and should retain the Malik-i-maidan, the famous gun for which a demand had been made before the war ; that the parts of the Konkan that had once been held by the Nizamshahi kings should be transferred to the Adilshahi sultan ; as also the country watered by the Bhima and the Nira upto the fort of Chakan. In return for all this territory the Adilshahi sultan was to pay an annual tribute of 12 lacs of *hons* (pagodas) to the Mogul emperor, and the Rajah Shahaji with his followers was to receive pardon on condition of surrendering all his forts and cannon and munitions of war. Should he not do so he was not to obtain any shelter within the limits of the Bijapur state, who were to look upon him as a public foe of their own no less than as an enemy of the Mogul Empire.

By this treaty the kingdom of Bijapur extricated itself from its difficulties[1]. Shahaji now lost his great ally and was quite isolated. Undaunted by this change of circumstances, he still held on. He was bent on fighting it out with the enemy. By the treaty with Bijapur, Shaha Jahan's armies were now free to move. They were concentrated against Shahaji. They dogged his footsteps. Shahaji availed himself of an opportunity to descend into the Konkan, and put his remaining fortresses in readiness for a long war. Soon after the Mogul armies poured down

[1] The ruthlessness of the Mogul campaign can be seen from Jadunath Sarkar's Life of Aurangzeb, Vol. I page 37. Prof. Sarkar gives the terms of the treaty at length in the same volume, pages 38 to 40.

into the Konkan and took possession of the hill-forts one after another. A contingent from Bijapur under Randulla Khan co-operated with the Moguls. Shahaji soon found himself in great extremity, from which there was no escape possible except by submission. He petitioned the emperor for pardon and offered his services to the imperial army. His request was not complied with. In his reply the emperor reminded him of the mansab or military command that had once been conferred upon him, and how notwithstanding this he had declared hostilities with the empire, and had brought upon it immense losses by his rebellion. He could no more expect employment under the Mogul empire; but he was free to enter the service of Bijapur. On receipt of this reply, Shahaji purchased his peace by surrendering to the emperor the puppet sultan whom he had raised to the Nizamshahi throne at Mahuli, and with the rest of his followers came down to Bijapur. (1637).

SHAHAJI IN SERVICE UNDER BIJAPUR.

Shahaji was received with great honour by the Adilshahi sultan and the statesmen of that court like Randulla Khan. He was retained in the service of the court with his great retinue. They indeed considered the accession of such a brave, daring, and experienced general a peculiar piece of good fortune to the Adilshahi State. By the recent treaty with the Moguls, Shahaji's jahgir lands had passed over to the Bijapur kingdom. Out of these, Poona and Supa were now continued to him in jahgir[1]. The charge of administering these jahgirs was entrusted by Shahaji to a capable and faithful Brahman minister, named Dadaji Kondadev, and a force of a thousand cavalry was kept with him for defence of the jahgir[2]. In command of this cavalry force was Hilal, an Abyssinian officer.

---

[1] The Rairi *Bakhar* represents this grant to have been made by Murarpant, on Shahaji's return from the siege of Dowlatabad.

[2] Dadaji Kondadev was Patwari of Multhan, a *Mouza* of Poona Prant. Afterwards he is mentioned in records as "Subhedar, Fort Kondana" or "Muzumdar, Junnar Subha" (Rajwade: Vol. XVIII, 19 and Chitnis, 19).

The Bijapur state had entered on the task of restoring order to the province between the Bhima and the Nira, which had been made over to it by the Moguls. That government got Shahaji to accompany their general, when he set out for this province, as Shahaji knew the district so well. Shahaji rendered him very valuable assistance, for he was as good a politician as he was a brave general. The governor[1] highly appreciated the manifold talents of his gifted assistant, and the appreciation soon ripened into a close friendship. On his return from this duty he highly extolled Shahaji's abilities and urged the sultan to make much of an officer who combined in himself the virtues of war and peace in such an eminent degree. He recommended the sultan to reward his services by every mark of the royal favour and encourage him by all means in his power to remain loyally with the master with whom he had now staked his fortunes.

Some of the *Bakhars* mention the following anecdote of the ingenuity by which Shahaji had won over the favour of the Adil Shahi minister, Murarpant. The story belongs to the period when at the suggestion of Shahaji the Bijapur army was sent against the fort of Dowlatabad under the command of Murarpant. While the army was on the march it happened that there took place an eclipse of the sun[2]. Murarpant was then encamped at Nagargaon at the confluence of the Bhima and the Indrayani; and true to Hindu superstition he made the eclipse an occasion for dispensing

[1] According to the Marathi chronicles Shahaji's first campaign under Bijapur took place as an assistant to Murarpant (1637). But Prof. Sarkar has proved in his article in the Modern Review (Sept. 1917), that Murar was executed about 1635 or 36. Prof. Sarkar bases this story on a passage in the *Basatin-i-Salatin*.

[2] This eclipse took place in *Shaka* year 1555 (1633 A. D.) on new moon day in the month of *Bhadrapad* (September). An account of this event is given in the Bharat-Itihas Sanshodhak Mandali's Year Book for 1912, page 69.

various kinds of charity[1]. Among other acts of charity, Murarpant thought of weighing his elephant against silver and distributing the treasure among Brahmans. But then arose the perplexing question, how to weigh the elephant. No one could make a practical suggestion until it came to Shahaji's turn, who hit upon the following method to weigh the unwieldy beast. Shahaji suggested that the elephant should be embarked on a boat, and a mark should be made of the extent to which it sank in the water under the weight of the beast. Then the elephant should be removed and the boat filled with large stones until it should sink in the water to the same extent as before. Lastly the stones should be taken out and severally weighed, and the total arrived at would give the weight of the elephant. This simple expedient, which, however, because of its very simplicity perhaps occurred to no one else present, won him great admiration from Murarpant, who, when the weighing ceremony was done, gave to the Brahmans lands worth the weight of the silver.

After returning from this expedition, Shahaji did not make a long sojourn at Bijapur. Immediately in the following year, the Adil Shahi sultan determined to subjugate the various Hindu polygar chiefs in the Karnatic and thus to extend his dominions. Randulla Khan was placed in command of this expedition with the title of *Sir Lashkar* (Chief Commander), and Shahaji was sent with him as his deputy. In order that Shahaji might devote himself entirely to this cause in co-operation with Randulla Khan, the sultan promised to give him a jahgir out of the conquered territory. By Shahaji's enthusiastic co-operation, the expedition was crowned with success. The war with the polygars lasted for two or three years, and many of them were utterly defeated. The *bakhars* mention one or two of these contests. They speak of a certain Raya

1 This village (viz. Nagargaon) received in commemoration of this elephant weighing incident the name of Tulapur. The story that Aurangzeb gave this name to the place is therefore a myth.

Rayal, who was probably a distant survivor of the royal family of Vijayanagar, otherwise known as Shri Ranga Rayal. He was raising his head in the Karnatic and harassed the districts there that had been conquered by Bijapur. Shahaji defeated him in two decisive engagements and conquered the districts of Akalkote, Bagalkote, Bangalore, Vaskote, Balapore and Shirta from him. By these conquests Shahaji earned the high favour of Randulla Khan, who, on the return of the expedition, frequently extolled his services in the presence of the sultan. The sultan was pleased with Shahaji's valour and gave him the conquered provinces in jahgir. Not long after, the districts of Ratanpore, Deogad, Kanakgiri, and Rajdurg were added to his jahgir, and his Maharashtra jahgir likewise received the addition of Indapur, Baramati, and Maval. In addition to all this, the *deshmukhi* of twenty-two villages in the Karhad district was conferred upon Shahaji.

Thus in the service of the Bijapur state, Shahaji had at last found a good arena for the display of his talents, and, to his credit be it said, the sultan showed high appreciation of Shahaji's virtues. The sultan was convinced that Shahaji was one of the most competent and loyal of his servants. It was no mean task to restore order and establish a good system of administration in the Karnatic and Dravid parts that had been so recently brought under the Bijapur kingdom. The sultan also saw that none but the most capable and devoted of his governors would be able to administer the newly acquired territory. The leading politicians of the state concurred in the opinion that Shahaji was the most competent officer for this high post, and Shahaji was duly appointed and sent to this new province. The province, having been but lately annexed to the Bijapur kingdom, was full of disorder and anarchy. It was the task of the new governor to extirpate the elements of disorder and misrule and establish the authority of Bijapur on a sound basis. In a short time Shahaji achieved these objects. Anarchy and misrule melted away before him. A new revenue settlement was introduced in the province, which, while it made the people happy and properous, resulted in a substantial addition to the royal treasury. In order to maintain the finances in order, Shahaji brought over from Maharashtra a battalion of Brahman finance-clerks or karkuns. The descendants of these men brought over to the Karnatic in the times of Shahaji are still to be found there bearing the various office names of Deshmukh, Deshpande, Kulkarni, Shirestadar etc. Shahaji had learnt his lessons in finance at the feet of Malik Ambar, and the true disciple of such an illustrious master was not to be dismayed by the finance problems of the Karnatic. What is truly to be commended in him is not that he did not harass or oppress his Karnatic subjects, but that in all his endeavours, he made it a particular point to cultivate their love and friendly sympathy. He was careful to send regularly to Bijapur the annual quota of revenue from the Karnatic and to retain a substantial surplus with himself.

On going down to the Karnatic, Shahaji at first resided at Bangalore. When tranquillity was restored to the country he made Balapore his headquarters. At that time a powerful prince of the name of Vijay Raghav reigned at Tanjore. He was at enmity with the Rajah of Trichinopoly. The latter made an alliance with Shahaji against Tanjore, offering to make a united war against Tanjore and conquer its territory, and promising to contribute five lakhs of rupees to Shahaji for his war expenses and all the booty. Shahaji invaded the principality of Vijay Raghav. The prince was defeated and fell on the field of battle. Tanjore fell into the hands of Shahaji, who found an immense treasure there. Shahaji saw that Tanjore was indeed a fertile and wealthy country and determined to retain possession of it. He gave the Rajah of Trichinopoly to understand that he meant to keep Tanjore and he need not make any payment for the expenses of the war. The Rajah was irritated at this reply and declared war. He was defeated, and his principality too fell into Shahaji's hands. The Bijapur government confirmed him in possession of these new territories[1].

When we survey these events of the career of Shahaji, a question that naturally and inevitably arises in our mind is how a spirit, so war-like and heroical, could choose to remain humbly contented with servile vassalage to the throne of Bijapur. How could he, who was not dazzled by the pomp and splendour of Mogul power, and who set at nought the much vaunted strength of the imperial armies, forget his own worth, set aside his own ambitions and be content to attach himself to the waning fortunes of the Adil Shahi dynasty? The explanation is to be found in Shahaji's character. He was a cautious and far-sighted statesman. He was not a man to be misled by a passing caprice, or to be betrayed into a rash or irrevocable act by passion. The true statesman must at all times act with circumspection. He must weigh time and circumstance. Situated as he was Shahaji had constantly to trim his sails according as the wind blew in order to save his fortunes from destruction. When the Nizamshahi dynasty was extinguished by the Moguls, he strove to re-kindle its dying splendour with the help of Bijapur. But the emperor separated Bijapur from this coalition by tempting offers and the vanquished Nizamshahi dominions were divided between the two powers. This conjunction of powers had proved too strong for the single-handed resistance of Shahaji. He could count upon no support. Further resistance or endeavour to re-conquer the lost territory would bring down the united Mogul and Bijapur hosts upon himself. To enter upon a conflict with

---

1 Jonathan Scott and the author of the Bundela Memoirs (Naskha-i-Dilkasha) give a different account. According to these authors the quarrel was between the Rajah of Tanjore, whose name is mentioned as Panchi Rangu, and the polygar Naik Janjappa of Mudgal, the latter of whom enlisted the assistance of Shahaji and the occupation of Tanjore by Shahaji led to a subsequent war between him and the chief of Mudgal.

such mighty powers was to invite his own destruction. Under the circumstances it seemed far more to his own interest to acquire a permanent jahgir and watch future events. It was no doubt with such motives that he had entered the service of the Bijapur Government.

When he had earned the favour and confidence of the Adilshahi sultan and obtained the governorship of the Karnatic, Shahaji began gradually to develop his higher ambition. Some historians confidently assert that it was his object to lay the foundation of an independent principality in the Karnatic[1]. His object in endeavouring to earn the popularity and grateful affection of his people was that he might confidently rely upon their zealous co-operation should he ever come into a collision with the Bijapur sultan. That his conduct was shaped by some such motives becomes evident, when we consider that the deeds of grants and other *sanads* that he issued, some of which are still extant among the people of the Karnatic, make no mention of their proceeding from the higher authority of the sultan, but record the gifts as emanating from the *durbar* or court of the Rajah Shahaji Bhonsle. There is another piece of evidence bearing on his latent ambition. When Shivaji began to raid the Bijapur territory, the noblemen of this court began openly to murmur that Shahaji must be in collusion with his audacious son, and the sultan wrote to Shahaji on the subject, requiring him to bring back his rebel son to a sense of his duty. Shahaji replied to the court that he had renounced his first wife and her son and married another, and that for some time he had no kind of communication with them. The government was at liberty to take against them such steps as they liked. It seems that the Adilshahi sultan was at this time quite satisfied with this reply and did not in any manner proceed against Shahaji. It is quite clear, however, that this reply was a mere subterfuge. For, if Shahaji had really been out of sympathy with the daring and adventurous career which

[1] Wilks's History of Mysore. (Vol. I, page 75 *et seq*)

Shivaji had just embarked upon, it was within both Shahaji's power and interest to put an end to his michievous enterprise. But in excusing himself, under the pretext that he had nothing to do with his son and in refusing responsibility for his acts, he only masked his real feelings under a cloak of disapproval. But it should be transparent to every student of history, that in reality he thought Shivaji's acts to be in agreement with his own deeper projects[1].

In course of time Shivaji's rebellious attitude became more pronounced. The Bijapur kingdom could put up with it no longer and determined that it was time to punish the father for the acts of the son. Notwithstanding the assurances of Shahaji their suspicions were re-awakened. The durbar was the more inclined to suspect collusion in view of the practical independence achieved by Shahaji himself in the Karnatic and the measures he was pursuing for the accomplishment of his object. The Bijapur authorities entrusted the task of arresting Shahaji for punishment to Baji Ghorpade, chief of Mudhol. To defeat Shahaji in the open field and take him prisoner was no easy task; for a general like the Ghorpade it was well-nigh impossible. He, who had so often eluded the Mogul armios and baffled the most renowned of Mogul generals, was not likely to fall easily into the hands of a second-rate officer of the Bijapur state. Ghorpade never dreamt of achieving such a feat. He resorted to stratagem. He invited Shahaji to an entertainment and had him arrested as an unsuspecting guest[2]. When his capture was thus made by treachery,

1 Shahaji has aptly been called a king-maker; but the fact that his greatness was eclipsed by that of his greater son has been partly the cause of his claims to greatness not receiving the proper acknowledgment. It is only now that his real greatness is beginning to be realized even among the Marathas. *Vide* Mr. Sardesai's "History of Modern India" part II, Vol. I, page 157, second edition. (Marathi).

2 The account in Modak's History differs widely from the generally accepted story given in the text. According to Modak's account Shahaji, having made himself independent of Mustapha Khan, his colleague in the Karnatic, was suddenly fallen upon and apprehended by Baji Ghorpade,

Shahaji was lying encamped at Jirawady near Chandawar (Jinji). How Shivaji at the command of his father retaliated upon the Ghorpade for this act of treachery will be described at the proper place.

When Shahaji was thus arrested and brought to Bijapur, the sultan meditated his execution. After much discussion it was finally resolved that he should be confined in a stone dungeon, which was entirely closed in except for a small aperture; and it was threatened that if within a certain time Shivaji should not make his submission the aperture would be for ever closed and he be buried alive. The details of this story will be given in their proper place in a subsequent chapter[1]. Suffice it to say here that the Adil Shahi sultan must have had some substantial grounds for entertaining such a suspicion and peremptorily threatening the execution of such a valiant and influential officer as Shahaji. Shivaji extricated himself from this dilemma by negotiations with the Moguls[2]. Although on account of this intervention of the emperor the sultan did not dare to execute Shahaji, still he decided not to send him again to the Karnatic, but to detain him as a prisoner at large at Bijapur. During this period Shivaji made no disturbance in the Bijapur territory. Shahaji won over the politicians of the

under the orders of Mustapha Khan. Shahaji's party was taken by surprise and Shahaji himself was captured in an attempt to mount and ride off from the scene of the unexpected encounter. The *Jedhe* Chronology (Bharat-Itihas-Sanshodhak Mandal, Chaturtha Sammelan Vritta, page 179) says that Shahaji was arrested near Jinji by Mustapha Khan, which would mean that Ghorpade acted as Mustapha's agent.

[1] Vide Chapter VIII.

[2] According to some *Bakhars* Shahaji's deliverance was due to the intervention of his tried friend Randulla Khan. The Rairi *bakhar* improves upon the story by a romantic account of Shahaji's impending execution already decreed by the sultan (who had prepared dispatches to that effect addressed to Baji Ghorpade) being averted by Randulla, threatening to turn fakir and leave the court service for a pilgrimage to Mecca. In this way by his adroitness he is said to have obliged the sultan to yield to his wishes and thus saved the life of his veteran comrade.

Bijapur state and, re-establishing confidence in his good faith, recovered his governorship and was again sent to the Karnatic.

Thus relieved from immediate danger, Shahaji kept up ostensibly the most loyal and cordial relations with Bijapur. But to the end of his life he never abandoned his plans of aggrandizing his power so as to declare one day his independence. Of the further events of his life no historical records are available. The accounts of the Bijapur wars in the Karnatic given by Mahomedan historians are very meagre, and here and there we meet with occasional references to the brave services of Shahaji. The jahgir he had received in the Karnatic from the Bijapur government he enjoyed for life and it was considerably augmented from time to time. We have already narrated the circumstances under which he had got possession of Tanjore and Trichinopoly. In addition to these places, he exercised sovereignty over the fort of Arni, Porto Novo, and other towns.

Away from far-off Maharashtra tales were brought from time to time of the successful endeavours of his son Shivaji to lay the foundations of an independent monarchy. Shahaji was exceedingly gratified with these early indications of a noble career and had a vehement yearning to embrace such a valiant son. But the activities of Shivaji lay on the western outskirts of the Bijapur kingdom, and Shahaji had no opportunity for a long time to gratify his desire. Fortunately a few years later, a truce was effected between Shivaji and Bijapur, and the suspension of hostilities gave Shahaji an opportunity to visit his home in Maharashtra with the permission of the sultan and to meet Shivaji[1]. Shahaji might have complied with Shivaji's urgent wishes and stayed in Maharashtra for the rest of his life. But when he received the sultan's permission to visit Maharashtra it was on the distinct understanding that he was to return to the Karnatic and on no account to unite with his son. Had he broken

[1] Vide Chapter XIV.

this covenant, the sultan would certainly have confiscated his possessions in the Karnatic. Shahaji had no desire to lose the fruits of his toils, and so returned to the Karnatic.

Shahaji did not live long after this visit to his son; he died within two years. The story of his death is as follows: Two polygars of Bednore, Bhadrappa Naik and Shivappa Naik harassed the Bijapur dominions. The sultan commissioned Shahaji and Sarja Khan with the duty of subduing these chiefs. Shahaji defeated Bhadrappa Naik and forced him to come to terms. He surrendered the territory he had conquered from the Bijapur kingdom and became a vassal of Bijapur with certain jahgir lands. The Adilshahi sultan was pleased with this last service of Shahaji, wrote him a congratulatory letter upon his victory and presented him with a robe of honour, horses, elephants and other ornaments and marks of the royal favour. The politicians of the state, each in his turn, sent congratulatory epistles. While engaged upon these operations, Shahaji one day went out on a hunting expedition to a village named Bandekir[1]. He was hunting a hare, and while riding impetuously after the game, his horse's hoof was caught in a fissure, and both horse and rider came to the ground. Shahaji was kicked by his horse and immediately killed. His followers came searching for him and seeing him dead, brought up his son Venkoji, who performed his funeral obsequies. Shahaji was seventy years of age at his death, which took place in January 1664. The sultan sent to Venkoji a letter of condolence and robes of honour confirming his succession to his father's position. A tomb was erected on the place where Shahaji died and under a *sanad* or charter of the Bijapur state the revenues of the village were set apart for its maintenance.

Shahaji had three sons, of whom the eldest, Sambhaji, was born at Dowlatabad in 1623 to his first wife Jijabai, during their residence at that fort. Shahaji loved him very affectionately and always had him in his company. In 1653

---

[1] On the Tungabhadra; elsewhere called Basavapattan.

Sambhaji was killed in an assault upon the fort of Kanakgiri. The chief of Kanakgiri had long been guilty of aggression upon the district of Balapore, one of Shahaji's possessions. Sambhaji was deputed by his father to proceed with a force to punish this refractory prince. Sambhaji laid siege to the fort of Kanakgiri and opened a cannonade upon its walls, but himself fell a victim to a cannon shot.[1] His death was a great shock to Shahaji. His desire for vengeance was stirred to its depths. He himself headed a force against Kanakgiri, utterly defeated the chief and took the fort by assault. On this occasion the chief of Kanakgiri had been secretly aided by Afzul Khan, a distinguished officer in the Bijapur service. Shahaji had a great desire to avenge himself upon Afzul Khan, but, dreading the displeasure of the sultan, abstained from this step. Little did he dream at that moment that Afzul Khan was destined to expiate this deed with his life and that the death of Sambhaji was shortly to be avenged by his younger but greater brother[2].

The circumstances under which Jijabai was left behind at the fort of Shivneri, at the critical period when Lukhji Jadhav was in hot pursuit of his son-in-law have already been described at the beginning of this chapter. Shivaji, the subject of this history, was born here in 1627. This was the second son Shahaji had by Jijabai. In 1630 Shahaji married Tukabai of the Mohite family. By her he had a son, Venkoji, who was born in 1631. On the

1 According to another account Sambhaji held a jahgir in his own right from the Bijapur state and was done to death by poison administered by the queen of Mahomed Adil Shaha, familiarly known as the Bari Saheba. The "Shivdigvijaya" *bakhar* slightly differs from the account followed in the text, in that it says that Kanakgiri was part of Shahaji's jahgir, but the fort was usurped by the chief Appa Khan.

2 The date 1653 assigned in the text as the year of the death of Sambhaji is based on the authority of Grant Duff and the Marathi chronicles. But on the authority of certain stone inscriptions discovered in the Karnatic the question is raised whether he did not live up to the year 1663. Vide Parasnis's "History of the Tanjore Dynasty" in his "*Itihas Sangraha*" 1912, footnote at page 23.

conquest of the district of Chandawar, Shahaji kept Tukabai and Venkoji there. On the death of Shahaji, Venkoji succeeded to the entire jahgir in the Karnatic. Some years afterwards Shivaji marched upon the Karnatic for a share of the paternal jahgir, but the history of this expedition will be chronicled at the proper place.[1] It is said that on his return from Shivaji's realm, the aged Shahaji called his younger son and addressed to him words of advice as follows: "Thy elder brother," exclaimed Shahaji, "has by his heroic enterprise secured a kingdom for himself. Thou art to succeed to my possessions in these parts, and as such thou shalt look after the family of my uncle, Vithoji, and my brother Sharifji. Thou shalt govern thy possessions with justice and mercy. It is the grand plan of thy elder brother to be a world-conqueror and if by God's grace his noble ambition is realized, he will be the protector of all our family. But if by mischance he should meet with any vicissitudes of fortune, remember, my son, that I have acquired for you both this jahgir, with the full consent and sanction of the sultan. Remember that I leave it in trust for you both, though thou shalt have its immediate usufruct. Remember thou art my favourite son and the brother of the valorous Shivaji. Hearken to the advice of my chosen and trusty servants and thy path shall be thornless in this world."

CHAPTER III

THE CHILDHOOD OF SHIVAJI

WE have already described in the last chapter how Jijabai far advanced in pregnancy was left behind at the fort of Shivneri, while Shahaji was being pursued by Lukhji Jadhav past the confines of the Nizamshahi kingdom. To look after his wife, Shahaji had detached from his secretarial staff three officers noted for their personal devotion towards himself. These were Balkrishnapant Hanumante, Shamrao Nilkant and Raghunath Ballal Korde.[1] The Jadhav had also on meeting his daughter at Shivneri deputed some men from his staff for her protection. She also seems to have found a watchful protector in Shrinivasrao of Junnar. Though we find her thus living in comparative safety amidst the troublous storms that were beating about her on all sides, a secret sorrow and anxiety seem to have preyed upon her mind as to the fate of her husband and her first-born, a child of three or four years, whom she had been compelled to part with at a time when they were fugitives before the vindictive rage of her father. Amidst these tormenting cares and anxieties, she made a solemn vow to Shiwai, the guardian divinity of the fortress, that if by her favour the gloomy clouds should be dispelled from Shahaji's fortunes and she delivered of a male child she would christen him after the goddess's name, as the fruit of her divine favour. The founder of the Maratha Empire was born on the 10th of April 1627 (Monday, the 5th of the first half of *Vaishakh* of the *Shaka* year 1549).[2]

---

1 In Malhar Ramrao's bakhar Hanumante's name is given as Krishnaji Hanumante. Instead of Shamrao Nilkant some chronicles give the name Shankraji Nilkant. Malhar Ramrao mentions a fourth officer Sonopant Dabir. Sabhasad in his well known bakhar says that these officers were sent with Jijabai from Bengalore.

2 There are discrepancies about the date in the various bakhars. Malhar Ramrao and Shivadigvijaya give the second of the first half of *Vaishakh* as the date and Thursday as the day of the week. But the date and day do not seem to agree. The Rairi's *bakhar* giving the same date and day as in the text gives the year as *Shaka* 1548. Here again the date and

The birth of this child, reserved by the call of heaven for such momentous events in the history of the Indian Empire, took place at a time of great political upheavals in the Deccan. He was born, however, in the comparatively secluded and at that time neglected neighbourhood of Poona. Shivneri is within fifty miles of that town. This was an event of great rejoicing in the little colony of exiles and refugees at Shivneri, and was celebrated with such pride and pomp as their present means and the humble circumstances of the place afforded. Women from the neighbouring villages coming to the fort with provisions were entertained with hospitality in honour of the joyful event aud presented with gifts at their departure. Shahaji who was then at Bijapur had the news sent to him by special messengers, who received handsome rewards from the delighted father for the joyful tidings they had brought to him. The child was christened Shivaji after the goddess Shivai, in consequence of the vow made to that effect by Jijabai.

Jijabai spent three years at this fortress in company with her son. She was probably transferred to Byzapur from this place, for it will be remembered that in 1633, as described in the last chapter, she was captured by the Mogul army at Bijapur. On her release from the Mogul camp she was removed to the fort of Kondana by Jagdeorao Jadhav, and she seems again to have passed a part of her life at Shivneri and the fort of Mahuli. It does not transpire where she found safety during the tumultuous period of the interminable contests between the Moguls and Shahaji which then set in. So much at any rate is clear that she

day cannot agree. In Wilks's History of Mysore and the Chronicle called the bakhar of the Maratha Swarajya the same date is followed as in the text. Calculations of an astronomical character upon certain data furnished by Mr. Kashinath Krishna Lele to the Kavyetihas Sangraha are in accord with the time followed in the text here. Vide Rajwade's "Marathyanchya Itihasachi Sadhane" (Materials for the History of the Marathas, Section IV.) The Shedgaokar bakhar gives Saturday the 3rd of the first half of *Vaishakh, Shaka* year 1549 as the birth-day, while the Jedhe chronology dates the event in *shaka* year 1551, *Falgun*, which would be February 1630 A. D.

never sought shelter under the roof of her relatives on her father's side, in order to save herself or her child from the wrath of the Moguls. There is not a shred of evidence to show that she ever sought refuge with the Jadhav family. It must also be considered that the Jadhavs were vassals of the Mogal emperor with whom Shahaji was at open war and it would have been extremely hazardous for the wife of Shahaji to throw herself upon the protection of a family which had entirely passed under the Mogul domination, nor would Shahaji have ever approved of such a step. It follows, therefore, that Jijabai and her son led an isolated life in the midst of great political hazards and turmoils, moving from fortress to fortress within the sphere of Shahaji's influence. Shahaji did what he could from his head-quarters to ensure the safety of his wife and son. Had Jijabai indeed desired the protection of the Jadhav family–she, who had spurned the offers of her vindictive father in the delicate situation in which she was when she first came to Shivneri–that occasion had surely presented itself, when she was taken a prisoner to the Mogul camp. That she did not choose to accept the hospitality of Jadhav at that time of necessity and distress is a sufficient proof to show that she had no desire for any protection at the hands of her paternal relations. One might well imagine to himself the dreadful cares and perils to which her life was exposed in these days. Flying from fort to fort, in imminent danger of being surprised by the enemy, she had to look helplessly on at the dreadful political drama that was being played out, the most conspicuous figure in which was her own gallant husband, whom the numerous Mogul hosts were closing in upon from all sides. It reflects the highest credit upon the spirited Maratha lady that during all this time of stress and strife her confidence in her hnsband's courage and bravery and her own refined sense of dignity as a mother did not falter even for an instant. The annalists make no mention of the manner in which Jijabai conducted the education of her son Shivaji. It is, however, clear that during this time he seems to have made considerable progress in riding and horse management, archery and marksmanship, the use and exercise of the *patta*, the national Maratha javelin, and other warlike exercises, as also in reading and writing.

When Shahaji became a vassal of the Adilshahi sultan he took his wife and son to Bijapur. Shortly afterwards he was confirmed in the possession of his old jahgir by the Bijapur state, and was deputed to the province of the Karnatic as second in command to Randulla Khan. Upon this occasion he entrusted an experienced and faithful Brahman secretary, Dadaji Kondadev, with the administration of the family jahgir, and placed Jijabai and Shivaji under his guardianship. The education of Shivaji was entrusted to his care. Dadaji Kondadev brought mother and son with all their retinue to Poona and had a spacious mansion raised for their residence. In the following year Dadaji had to travel to Bangalore to submit to Shahaji the accounts of the jahgir. Dadaji was accompanied on this occasion by Shivaji and Jijabai, who again returned to Poona in his company.

On Shahaji's return to Bijapur from his successful campaign in the Karnatic, he wrote to Dadaji Kondadev expressing his desire to bring Shivaji to Bijapur and celebrate his marriage there. Shivaji replied that as Bijapur lay purely in a Mahomedan atmosphere, he preferred to have his marriage celebrated at Poona, where the ceremonies of the Hindu religion could be performed unobstructed with due pomp and solemnity. Such being the wishes of Shivaji, Dadaji Kondadev obtained Shahaji's consent to have the marriage solemnised at Poona. In consequence of this arrangement the marriage of Shivaji took place at Poona in 1640, with great pomp and eclat. The bride chosen was Sayibai, a daughter of the distinguished Nimbalkar family.

In 1641, Shahaji invited Shivaji and Jijabai to Bijapur, and seems to have kept them with him for two or three years. As the boy watched the persecution and sectarian bigotry of this Mahomedan capital, the purpose began to form itself in his mind of overthrowing the supremacy of Islam.[1] The rudiments of that political wisdom and sagacity, which afterwards evoked the ungrudging admiration of the whole of the Indian continent, were also instilled into his mind during this period.

He was only fourteen, but already at that early age he was fairly advanced in all the arts of war. Handsome and endowed with great muscular strength he was most agile in his movements. With this he combined unique powers of observation. From infancy he was fond of examining the qualities of horses and elephants and visiting military depots and magazines. He behaved with remarkable courtesy towards persons eminent for their wisdom, learning or experience, and endeavoured to acquire knowledge and to win their favour by the tactful and respectful manner in which he inquired into the various subjects or studies they had mastered. He hated vice and luxury. He treated age and experience with the honour they deserved. These qualities soon won him the high regard of the nobles and gentry in the neighbourhood.

The nobles were so fascinated by the young Shivaji's manners that on one occasion they spoke of him with great enthusiasm in presence of the sultan, who at once expressed a desire to see a youth of such promise. It was, therefore, decided to introduce Shivaji to the court. But Shivaji was by no means pleased with the prospect of a meeting with the sultan. He pleaded with great modesty and submission that he was not inclined to flatter or to prostrate himself before the Mahomedans or their king, since they were so mean and insolent in their ways. He could not, he pleaded, tolerate the scant respect with which his religion and the Brahman expounders of that religion were generally treated in Mahomedan courts.

---

[1] The Basatin-i-Salatin gives details of the repressive policy of the Adilshahi sultans towards the Hindus, even in the halcyon-days of Sultan Mahomed Adul Shaha.

When he passed to and fro in the streets, he constantly came across the hideous spectacle of cow-slaughter, and his blood boiled in his veins, and he could scarcely restrain the impulse to destroy the slayer of the kine. But out of regard for the feelings of his elders he had restrained his impulses. However he submitted that he could not contemplate calmly the prospect of visiting or paying court to Mahomedan nobles or princes or in any way coming in contact with them. When such a meeting took place, he could not breathe freely till at least he had changed his clothes!

Strange fancies these in the case of a youth of fourteen! It was pointed out to him by the officers in the service of Shahaji that his ancestors had risen to greatness by doing service to Mahomedan princes, that under the circumstances it was not becoming in Shivaji to hate the Mahomedans, and that in doing so he did not show proper reverence towards his elders. This sort of persuasion was also practised upon him through the mediation of his equals in age. Jijabai herself strove to persuade him to change his stubborn attitude, but without success. At last Shahaji called him to his presence and addressed him in this strain: "The Mahomedans" said he "are rulers of the land. What is the harm in serving them, while keeping the observances of one's own faith? It is a divine ordinance that in these unhappy times we should eke out our daily bread by serving the Mahomedans. If God had not decreed this, why should the Hindus have waned in power and the might of Islam waxed? I have risen to my present position and power by steering my bark according to the times, and to keep and continue what I have attained, it is but fair that you should seek to win the favour of the sultan." To all these remonstrances Shivaji, with all due deference and submission, returned but one answer: "I bow down," he exclaimed, "to the word of command, but I protest, I cannot look on a passive spectator of the cruelty towards kine and the desecration and degradation of our shrines and priesthood!"

It is plain that no one could have more regretted than Shahaji the anti-Mahomedan sentiments which had by this time taken root in the mind of Shivaji and already threatened to overshadow other considerations. But he did not deem it prudent to chastise with severity or crush under the weight of anthority the impulses of such a promising youth. Not that he was himself a blind admirer of Mahomedan excesses, but it had always been a part of his policy to conciliate the followers of Islam, and thus to accomplish his objects in life. He does not seem to have much resented the obstinacy of Shivaji. But by constantly speaking upon the subject and by skilful appeals to Shivaji's filial obligations he succeeded in inducing his stubborn son to consent to accompany him to the durbar. Shahaji had instructed his son about the court etiquette of saluting the sultan by bowing down to the ground, as soon as he came into his presence. But Shivaji only made a slight *salaam*, and seated himself by his father. The Sultan, observing that Shahaji was accompanied by a boy, inquired whether it was Shahaji's son, and was told that it was so, and that it was the first occasion for young Shivaji to come to the durbar. This answer was given lest the sultan should be provoked at the scant salaam made by Shivaji, unaccompanied as it was by the courtly prostration. The sultan presented jewels and robes of honour to the young jahgirdar as a mark of his favour. But as soon as Shivaji returned home, he discarded the courtly dress and, as though it had been a contamination, had an expiatory bath.

After this Shivaji often accompanied his father to the durbar, but on every occasion he made only a slight salaam and took his seat in the hall. This conduct naturally excited a suspicion in the mind of the sultan, and doubting whether this was done on purpose to affront him, the sultan once called Shivaji aside and questioned him point-blank about it. But Shivaji replied with great presence of mind that though constantly reminded to make his salute according to the etiquette of prostration, at the critical moment he forgot it and made the usual salaam. He could only make an apology for this and beg that the salaam might be taken to stand for a prostration. Besides he made no difference between the sultan and his father, and until he learnt there was a difference he would continue to make the salaam. The sultan burst into a fit of laughter at this witty reply.

On the way to the court, there were butchers' shops, in which were set out for sale beef and heads of slaughtered cattle. In the same manner hawkers sat in their booths with cooked flesh for sale opposite the palace gates. Shivaji was much offended at the loathsome spectacle and could scarcely restrain his indignation. But he had to restrain his angry feelings for a long while. Once it happened that while Shivaji was on the way to the palace, he came across a butcher in the act of slaughtering a cow. Shivaji instantly fell upon the offending butcher, belaboured him with blows and delivered the cow from the axe. This event was much talked of in the bazaars and even reached the sultan's ears but on account of the weight of Shahaji's influence, no inquiry was made into the matter. Shivaji was now quite disgusted with the constant scenes of cow-slaughter. He could bear it no longer, and thought to leave the Adilshahi capital for ever and never more visit the state durbar. With this resolution formed, he entreated his father not to press him any more to accompany him to the durbar, as he could not bear to look upon the cow-flesh booths on the way, that if as a servant of the state Shahaji was obliged to connive at these things, there was no such obligation upon him and that until this cruel slaughter and traffic in cow-flesh was put a stop to he could not think of attending the court. Shahaji was in great perplexity. For the sultan was sure to remark the absence of his son, and what answer was he to give ? In this perplexity Shahaji consulted Mir Jumla, an old and tried friend at the court. After some deliberation, it was decided that Shivaji might stay at home for the day and that they should broach the subject with the sultan if they found him in good humour.

Accordingly the two nobles, one a Hindu and the other a Mahomedan, attended the durbar and, seeing that the sultan was in very good humour, submitted their views in the audience-hall. Mir Jumla reminded the sultan that he was the father of his people, both Hindus and Mahomedans. The royal favour was bestowed equally upon all his subjects. There were both Hindu and Mahomedan officers in the service of the state, and it did the state great honour that it allowed its servants to follow each his own religion. According to the ideas of the Hindu religion, it was a gross sin to kill kine and to traffic in cow-flesh. But cow-slaughter openly took place in the thoroughfare round about the royal palace, and flesh-booths lined the palace road. This was a mortal affront to the Hindu servants of the state, and to none more than to Shahaji, one of the sultan's most tried and honoured servants. But he did not dare, submitted Mir Jumla, to lay the complaint before the sultan. His son had not attended the court that day, as he could no longer put up with the abomination of cow-slaughter, and had quarrelled with his father upon the subject. It was for the sultan to restrain this license. The sultan listened calmly to this petition of Mir Jumla's and thought a good case was made out requiring his immediate intervention. He forthwith issued an injunction against cow-slaughter in the vicinity of the palace and forbade the sale of cow-flesh within the city-limits. No one doing this in defiance of these orders would receive any redress for any retaliation or chastisement he might have at the hands of the Hindus. A proclamation was made to this effect and the slaughter-houses were removed out of the city, to an isolated place to the south. The butchers were ordered to migrate in a body to this place. When these orders were carried out, Shivaji began again to attend the durbar in company with his father. The sultan was struck with his lofty spirit and address, and occasionally signalised his favour with presents of robes and other marks of honour.

As ill-luck would have it, one day a butcher with a basketful of cow-flesh was squatting at the city gate to sell his wares, just as Shivaji with a band of his chosen friends was coming out on horse-back. To glance at the butcher, to draw his sword and to cut him down was the work of a moment. The butcher's wife filled the air with lamentations and went to lodge a complaint at the court, and called the gate-keepers to swear to the truth of her complaint. The sultan, however, defended the deed as a condign punishment for breach of his edict on the subject. He paid her a small sum for the expences of her husband's funeral and fixed a small payment for her maintenance.

This event was naturally much talked of. Murmurs arose on all sides that in a Mahomedan capital the Mahomedans had no hononr. Had the Mahomedan rule already become a dead letter? Strange that an infatuated king should allow such things to be done in the light of day! And by whom? By one who refused to make obeisance by prostrating himself as a vassal before his lord. And to humour this insolent subject, this same figure-head of a monarch deported the honest butchers from the town-limits, to the great inconvenience of loyal Mahomedans. What depths of madness! This son of Shahaji's had lost all restraint and balance. He was running amuck among innocent Mahomedans. There was something rotten in this state of Bijapur.

Such mutterings could be heard in all the thoroughfares, by no means disguised or measured in language; and no doubt there was truth in this incoherent strain of impotent rage and abuse. These murmurs soon came to Shahaji's ears and filled him with dismay. Adroit man of action that he was, he could not help contrasting the lofty virtues and talents of his son with these erratic and wayward acts of violence. Was the noble life, of which such earnest was given by Shivaji's youthful brilliance, to be after all destroyed by the violence of his bigotry and race-hatred? Had he made so much of his shining virtues and placed him on the high road to fortune and preferment, only that he might by such a puerile indiscretion not only wreck his own career, but drag his father and the achievements of a life-time into ruin? These thoughts flashed across Shahaji's mind and filled him with dismay. His wide experience of men suggested to him how he should deal with this case. He saw that mere rebukes or punishment would have the most undesirable effects upon a mind so proud and impetuous as that of Shivaji. The advice must be seasoned with an appreciation of his noble qualities and a lively appeal to his dutiful instincts. Armed with this resolution he is said to have addressed himself to Shivaji in Jijabai's presence to the following effect: "You are still in your teens, young man, and have no experience of life. It does little credit to your understanding to fly into a passion and commit excesses without provocation. Not to bow down before the Mahomedans to put your hand to your sword at the slaughter of a cow,— is this the sort of conduct by which you can achieve success in life? If we are to serve the Mahomedans, we must be prepared to submit humbly to them in these matters. Had I followed such a course of action, where in the world should I have been? It was by serving the Mahomedans, young man, that your ancestors rose to greatness from the humble rank of a peon in the infantry to the highest eminence! Need I describe the hardships and perils through which I have passed, in attaining to my present greatness? Reflect upon the trials and tribulations of your father in the uncertain times of the Nizamshahi dynasty, and count the steps by which, when I had emerged from those clouds, I have risen to the full height of my position in the service of this Adilshahi state. It is natural that I should desire you to tread in my foot-steps, please and conciliate the powers that be and extend your fortunes. Nothing can exceed your happiness and glory, if following your father's example, you behave with prudence and circumspection. Continue in these wild pranks and fancies, and the heavens themselves will not be able to save us. We shall be sent away in exile and disgrace, despoiled of our fortunes and possessions. That such a catastrophe has thus far been averted is due to the intervention of our influential friends at the court. But if we have friends, we have enemies, and the moment they get an opportunity of injuring us, it is but the question of an hour to bring down upon us the royal displeasure and drive us away into exile. I appeal then to your own sense of duty and prudence and self-interest, and trust you will at once amend your ways." Shivaji listened in silence and replied not a word.

Shahaji did not rest here, but got Jijabai to advise the young man in the privacy of her apartments with her own tender and persuasive eloquence. She dwelt on the respect for elders, the virtue of obedience and the gratefu co-operation with the ambitious labours of a father like Shahaji. She appealed to the high traditions of his ancestors and conjured him not to stain the noble escutcheon, coming down from a long line of illustrious ancestors. Shivaji listened to these words of love and replied that the least wishes of his parents were sacred commands to him and he was always ready to act according to their wishes. "But in this matter," he protested, "I cannot alter my nature. I cannot reconcile myself to bend my knees before Mahomedans or to tolerate cow-slaughter and other insults to my religious instincts. Forgive me, but when my eyes fall upon such atrocities, my passions rebel in my breast and I am no longer myself; I am helpless. Whatever may be the inscrutable dispensation of Providence, it is clear I cannot continue to eat the bread of a Mahomedan prince. Something tells me it is pollution, a falling off from heaven, an obstacle to my religious ideals To save me from such deeds in future let me be sent away, I pray, far off from this place, yes, far beyond the barriers of any Mahomedan state. If I say this, in all sincerity and frankness, it is not in a spirit of rebellion and disobedience, but from a perfect knowledge of the feelings and passions in my breast, I entreat and implore you to grant my prayer."

Jijabai communicated these wishes to Shahaji and pointed out the undesirability of punishing the boy for this sort of eccentricity, though otherwise so humble and docile and obedient. His mysterious hatred of Mahomedans, she thought, agreeably to the feelings of a Hindu woman, must be a legacy inherited by him from a former birth. It was clear he could not be happy doing service to Mahomedans, and there was no use to seek to change his nature. She suggested that the best plan under the circumstances was to place him at a distance from the Mahomedan capital. If from love to his son he should keep him any longer, there was risk of his fortune and reputation being ruined. Shahaji sighed to hear this opinion of Jijabai and upon consultation with a few nobles who were in his confidence came to the same conclusion. About the same time, Dadaji Kondadev happened to come to Bijapur to submit the jahgir accounts, and he was ordered to escort Jijabai and Shivaji back to Poona.

Before leaving for Poona, Shivaji married a second wife at Bijapur. It is said that this second marriage took place at the express desire of the sultan. Once, when according to his custom Shahaji attended the durbar with his son, the sultan asked Shahaji whether his son was married. Shahaji replied that Shivaji's marriage was celebrated at Poona. The sultan ridiculed the marriage as celebrated in the absence of the father and far from the court and insisted that he should be married again in presence of the court, with all the pomp and circumstance befitting his rank. In deference to the sultan's wishes Shivaji was wedded to his second bride chosen from the select Maratha nobility. All the omrahs of the court and the sultan himself attended the wedding, at which great festivities and exchanges of bridal presents took place. This second wife of Shivaji was named Soyarabai.

As described above Shahaji had to bid farewell to his wife and son, who came back to Poona, in the company of Dadaji Kondadev. This parting was final: they never lived again under the same roof either at Poona or Bijapur. The fact is that Shahaji soon afterwards marched to the Karnatic and had no occasion any more to reside at Poona or Bijapur. Upon this slender foundation, some historians have raised a fictitious story of a quarrel between Shahaji and Jijabai, and the old quarrel between Shahaji and Lukhji Jadhav has been brought under contribution to lend a plausible colouring to this theory. But a close observation of the events as they have been thus far chronicled in these pages will show the absurdity of such a theory. For the first ten years after the birth of Shivaji, Shahaji was involved in such political complications that he had no leisure whatever to give to family life. Nor can the second marriage of Shahaji lend countenance to this view. For the custom of polygamy was much in vogue among the Maratha families in those times and still prevails among them. Hence a second marriage does not necessarily mean estrangement from the first wife. When Shivaji began his attacks upon the borders of the Bijapur territory it was natural that Shahaji tried to relieve himself of all responsibility by giving out that he had no connection with Shivaji and Jijabai. But this at best was a transparent pretext. Had there been a real cleavage between husband and wife, Shahaji would certainly not have taken his wife and son to Bijapur, as he did, as soon as his fortunes were well establishsd in the service of the Bijapur state.[1] If in 1643 again Jijabai and Shivaji were permanently stationed at Poona under the care of Dadaji Kondadev, we must credit Shahaji with having done so, on account of the insuperable difficulty of keeping Shivaji at

[1] Grant Duff (Ch. III) sets forth the theory of a disagreement between Shivaji's parents. Ranade (Ch. IV) assumes it as true. Mr. Sardesai assumes the theory of her disagroement with her husband but praises her for not seeking for shelter with her father's people (Marathi Riyasat, I, page 159.)

Bijapur. It is clear Shahaji was convinced that Bijapur was no congenial residence for a young man obsessed by a virulent hatred of Islam. Judging by these circumstances, we find no reason to accept the theory of a family feud to account for the divergence of the fortunes of father and son and of husband and wife, which commences from this stage. Jijabai's elder son, Sambhaji, always remained with Shahaji, a sharer in his toils and supporter of his ambitions. From this it does not follow, however, that Shahaji's love and affection for Shivaji were in any way less.

CHAPTER IV

THE EDUCATION OF SHIVAJI

A GREAT career is determined by favourable circumstances for the growth of genius. It is also shaped in a great measure by a good education. Both these influences played a great part in moulding the mind and character of Shivaji. The first ten years of his life were spent in his mother's company, an influence of most vital character on the life of a man. It is the age when the mind is most tender and plastic, and the impressions then formed are the very foundation of life. The months and years as they roll on in their course only serve to render these early impressions more deep and vivid, their full development only requiring a train of favourable circumstances and events. Whether these early influences are to be productive of good or evil depends mainly on the character of the father and the mother, more especially on the latter. The virtues and disposition of the mother are strained and filtered into the character of her child, and the goodness or evil of the one depends on that of the other. We can see the foundation of Shivaji's greatness in the circumstances in which he was born. When the future hero was yet in the womb, Jijabai lived through a time of great stress and revolution in the state, and in that revolution her husband and herself played a conspicuous part. Living in the midst of constant alarms, with her husband, once the mainstay of the Nizamshahi state, in flight and exile, and the ungrateful Nizamshahi sultan blindly in league with her husband's and his own enemies, her own scorn and disdain of the puny Mahomedan powers, her contempt of their pusillanimity and grovelling incapacity and her indignation at their impotent cruelty and barbarities were at that most delicate period of psychical excitement reflected and transfused into the mind of the future hero. Here then is some explanation of that mysterious and all absorbing anti-Mahomedan passion which possessed Shivaji from his earliest years. Nor was this all. The first ten years of Shivaji's life were passed in the midst of constant alarm and fear of treachery, and naturally enkindled a relentless hatred against those–the Mahomedan powers–who were the authors of these atrocities. Add to this Jijabai's proud and independent spirit, her personal ambition and self-reliance, her strong intellect and penetration. With these intense predisposing causes and influences constantly at play, is it a wonder that the smouldering discontent in Shivaji's breast burst into a flame in the form of an uncompromising anti-Mahomedan passion ?

It follows then that Jijabai was the most powerful influence on the youthful genius of Shivaji. Jijabai was born of a family that had once wielded the sceptre at Devgiri, the same that acquired the name of Dowlatabad on the fall of its Jadhav (Yadav) sovereigns. The once mighty family had fallen upon evil times. It had to serve its Mahomedan lords in those very scenes which had witnessed its power and grandeur. The children of the Jadhav family were not the sort of men to forget its noble past and the grandeur of its traditions, least of all Jijabai, a woman of a haughty and indomitable spirit. The treacherous murder of her father and brother by the vindictive Nizamshahi sultan served to add fuel to the flame of her hatred of Mahomedan rule. Nor was she likely to forget that it was the Mahomedans that had quenched the light of the Sesodia Bhonsle family. Later on for a time by his brilliant genius and valour, her husband Shahaji endeavoured to revive a Hindu sovereignty from the wreck of the Mahomedan state of Ahmednagar, but with all his valour and resources, he was forced to yield to overwhelming odds and remain content as an honoured vassal and feudatory of the Bijapur state. And how nearly had he succeeded! With the puppet of a Nizamshahi prince in his grasp, Shahaji had destroyed one Mogul host after another and stirred up the living remembrances of a not quite forgotten past in the depths of his loyal wife's heart. But inexorable fortune had stood in the way of his ultimate success, and the chagrin and disappointment occasioned by the failure was the crown of all her sorrows.

And then the family tradition to which Maloji had given currency,-that the House of Bhonsle would produce a world-compelling hero—ever flashed across her mind,—a prophecy which Shahaji's temporary success had all but verified. Despite her crushing disappointment and suffering, this tradition kept all her passions and aspirations awake. She believed in it with the faith of a woman, with a religious heart, and she looked forward wistfully to its accomplishment.

What though Shahaji had at last failed and seceded to the Mahomedan dynasty of Bijapur? Had not his temporary success proved that the defeat of the Mahomedans was no mirage, no idle phantom flitting before a fevered mind, but a tangible thing within the range of practical accomplishment? This was the subject to which she constantly recurred in her conversation with her son. She poured forth into his eager ears the story of the fall from royal power of both the Jadhav and Bhonsle Houses and pictured to him their former greatness, with the inevitable contrast of the inglorious present that could not but obtrude itself upon his sensitive mind. Again by repeated recitals of the story of Shahaji's heroic achievements, she sought to enkindle in his heart the same noble ambition and love of heroic enterprise. In her daily discourses she ever laid stress on the inherent degradation, however great the worldly splendours, of service to an alien Mahomedan power, the steps of whose rise had been marked by the overthrow of many a Hindu sovereignty and whose progress was attended with the slaughter of kine, the pollution of temples and shrines and the violation of the Brahmans,—cruelty and treachery in all forms and guises. To these were added readings from the *puranas* and the sacred texts, the main theme of which is the struggle of virtue and the ultimate triumph of good over evil. Shivaji from his earliest infancy developed a strong taste for these readings, listening with rapt attention to the recitals. It was these readings which infused in him an overpowering sense of piety, religious zeal, and enthusiasm. His eyes kindled and his breast throbbed with religious fervour as he listened to the tales of chivalry and self-sacrifice from the Ramayan and the Mahabharat and he followed every tone and undulation of his mother's voice, as she related the inspiring legends. It was as if she had said in so many words: "Go thou and do likewise". The seed was not cast upon rocky soil, for, from the time he began to understand things, these repeated counsels and exhortations began to take root, and by imperceptible degrees, a strong passion was kindled in his breast to emulate not only his father's exploits, but the epic chivalry of the puranas.

By nature Shivaji was a man of great intellectual strength and alertness. His powers both of understanding and memory were of a high order. Jijabai was a woman of great earnestness and courage, and the instinct for honour and esteem was the great motive force in all her actions. By daily contact and conversation with his mother, Shivaji had assimilated these noble virtues in all their perfection. She watched over him with all her maternal solicitude and was careful to see that he followed the best example, moved in good company and kept away from the snares and blandishments of vice in all its forms. From early boyhood, she made provision for his military education. Thus the highest impulses of life and human character were evolved in Shivaji's heart by his close contact with this noble matron,--bravery, enterprise, courage, love of truth and religious fervour. But more important than all the rest, there was one impulse that came to him from his mother,— an impulse upon which all his greatness was founded, and which will for ever obtain for him a niche in the temple of fame and an honoured place in the world's great roll of patriots -his unquenchable thirst for liberty. He never faltered in his opinion of the intrinsic unworthiness of the highest glory and honour that a servile allegiance to a Mahomedan prince could bring to a man, that indifference and ingratitude were the invariable return for the most loyal and devoted service to the sultan, and that an alien despotism like that of the Mahomedan states stood for all that was mean, vindictive and tyrannical. Of this the days of his own childhood had given him sufficient proof. Personal experience combined with maternal exhortation to inflame him with a passion for freedom. In boyhood already he had made up his mind to defy foreign domination even if it should cost him his life. It is well known how Dadaji Kondadev endeavoured to turn him aside from his determined course, but we find no account in any of the the extant chronicles of any attempt to dissuade him on the part of Jijabai. This very circumstance strengthens the view that it was Jijabai herself who was primarily instrumental in inspiring Shivaji with the enthusiasm and enterprise of revolting from the domination of Islam and unfurling the standard of Maratha liberty. That Jijabai endeavoured at Bijapur to persuade Shivaji to suppress his anti-Mahomedan sentiments does not in any manner militate against this conclusion, nor need her conduct upon that occasion be taken to stand as an indication of her real opinion upon this subject. As a Hindu wife, to whom devotion and obedience to the husband is the highest dower, she had to carry out the instructions of her husband and become his mouth-piece, whatever her feelings on the subject might be. In short, it was due to the rare combination of a mother, who with her noble convictions and ideals could inspire and dominate her son's future, and of a son, who while allowing himself to be stirred to the noblest moods and passions could lead and impress the world with the resources of his master-mind, that the record of a career was made possible, by which the Hindu population of peninsular India was liberated from the yoke of Islam.

In 1637 Dadaji Kondadev was entrusted with the administration of the jahgir lands by Shahaji, and the charge of young Shivaji's education was also made over to him. From this time forth, therefore, the burden of Shivaji's education fell upon Dadaji, and his mother's influence became secondary. This does not of course mean that Jijabai ceased altogether to look after the upbringing of her son. He was all in all to her, the prop of all her hopes and ambitions. The mysterious instincts of the maternal heart had enabled her to foresee his future greatness. In her impassioned moods, she often thought with ecstacy that Shivaji might be just the man to whom the restoration of the Jadhav and Bhonsle sovereignties had been reserved by fate, the hero whom the divine prophecy current in the family had ever been beckoning on to the task of national emancipation. She, therefore, continued to watch over him in spirit, with all the zeal of maternal solicitude. It was left, however, to Dadaji to initiate Shivaji in those arts and sciences and that practical knowledge which was essential to a person in his position.

It will not be out of place to give a brief account of the great man to whom the education of Shivaji was thus confided. It is not known at what period Dadaji Kondadev entered into Shahaji's service. Shahaji was early satisfied with his tact, abilities and uprightness and appointed him to the management of his jahgir estates at Poona, Supa, Baramati, Indapur and the Maval tracts in Maharashtra. These districts he administered with great efficiency. The long wars of the Moguls and the Deccan Mahomedans had reduced these parts to mere wildernesses. To this were added the horrors of a most terrible famine in the year 1630.[1] Dadaji re-populated these districts and reclaimed them for cultivation by holding forth the inducement of immunity from the land-tax for a succession of years. There was at once an influx of cultivators from the adjoining districts, and the lands in a short time had changed their forlorn aspect. The people were contented and happy. Bumper crops swelled the granaries. Dadaji then instituted a survey and classification of the land and introduced the revenue system of Malik Ambar, the essence of which was

[1] This terrible famine is referred to in Jedhe's Chronology (page 178) and in the Padishahnamah of Abdul Hamid.

that the revenue dues were to be based on the ascertained crops of the year. This gave a great stimulus to agriculture. The settlements made with the agriculturists gave them permanent proprietary rights subject to the payment of revenue, and a large residue of the income after the deduction of revenue still remained for the enjoyment of the prosperous peasantry.

The district of Maval was inhabited by a poverty-stricken people called the Mavalis. Even by toiling day and night these semi-civilized people found it difficult to earn enough to provide food and clothing. Dadaji saw the fidelity and industrious habits of these people and assiduously set to work to ameliorate their condition. He encouraged them to till their rocky and barren soil by granting remissions of revenue taxes. Many of them he enlisted in his service as peons or soldiers and engaged them in the collection of revenue. They were satisfied with the most meagre pay, one or two rupees a month, and a bushel or two of the coarsest millet, such as *nachni* or *vari*. It was a mountainous country infested by wild animals. To put an end to the mischief they caused from year to year, Dadaji maintained a corps of Mavali javelin-men and gave them a reward for each tiger or wolf that was slain. Many wild beasts were exterminated in this way, and the country became more settled.

The country was also infested with brigands. Dadaji endeavoured to minimise the evil by establishing watches and a sort of rude police.[1] He encouraged the plantation of fruit-trees and orchards. Groves of mango and other trees grew on all sides. He kept the fortresses under Shahaji in an excellent state of repair, installed suitable garrisons in each of them, and recruited a small army of Maval is for general defence. In this way Dadaji administered the jahgir and considerably augmented its income. All the balance, that accrued to Shahaji's credit after payment of the different charges, such as salaries of peons and

[1] Vide Chitnis, page 29 and the Tarikh-i-Shivaji (page 9 (a)).

soldiers, clerks and executive officers and other incidental expenses, was faithfully remitted to Shahaji's head-quarters. An anecdote illustrating Dadaji's extraordinary sense of duty and uprightness has been recorded by the Maratha chroniclers. It is said that while Dadaji was going one day in the company of Shivaji through one of Shahaji's orchards he happened quite casually to pluck off a mango from its stem. Instantly it occurred to his mind that what he had done was a misdemeanour, and he commanded his attendants to mutilate the hand with which he had committed the offence. Shivaji replied that his reasoning was not correct, that he had cultivated the park and was its master. On hearing this reply he shortened one of the sleeves of his robe and to the time of his death he wore a shortened sleeve[1].

Dadaji was then a man of extraordinary integrity; and devotion to his master was the ruling passion of his life. He was already advanced in age and experience when Shahaji nominated him to the jahgir. He was very pure in his morals and pious in the observances of his religion. It was an article of faith with him that his personal interests and prosperity were identical with those of his master. It was natural that Shahaji felt not the slightest misgivings in his heart in giving over his son to the tutelage of such a man, who united with a most exalted sense of righteousness a complete devotion to his master's person and interests. Needless to say that Dadaji acquitted himself of the trust beyond the most sanguine expectations of his master.

He spared no pains to see that Shivaji and Jijabai should labour under no privation. He thought that a warrior's son should have the best military education obtainable, and

1 The Rairi bakhar gives a slightly different version of the story, by making the mango the property of a peasant cultivator. Shahaji is reported to have heard of the incident and marked his sense of appreciation of Dadaji's integrity by a present of 700 pagodas and urged him to wear his sleeves as usual. The version followed in the text is that of Chitnis. (P. 29.)

provided every facility towards this object. He made him go through a regular system of drill and physical discipline. Jijabai had laid the foundation of this discipline. Dadaji carried it forward with great zeal. Besides physical culture Dadaji arranged for a course of intellectual discipline[1]. This too had been anticipated by Jijabai and was promoted with greater zeal by Dadaji, on the mother and son coming to reside at Poona. Shivaji made considerable progress in Urdu and Persian and had made a beginning in the elements of the Sanskrit language[2]. It is said that certain devotional odes composed by Shivaji contain a number of Urdu words. Dadaji's religious temperament served to foster Shivaji's own instincts for piety. He got many opportunities to listen to religious lectures and rhapsodies from the puranas. His natural enthusiasm for religion was stimulated by Dadaji's example.

The seed of all this had already been sown by Jijabai. But there was another departmant in which Dadaji was a past master, and that was finance. He knew the art of keeping the peasantry happy while doubling and trebling the revenue. He had the tact and courtesy to extract the best work from his servants without wounding their feelings. He excelled as a judge, and his decisions were conclusive and impartial. He took a paternal interest in the welfare

---

[1] Vide Chitnis's bakhar (page 28). While it may be admitted that the account in the Shivdigvijaya is too extravagant for credence, it is not too much to assume that if the warrior class of the time of the puranas could successfully unite an all round intellectual culture with the military craft, a boy brought up with such an absorbing admiration of the puranic lore might have received a fairly good literary education.

[2] Vide Mr. Rajwade's work in Marathi, entitled "Materials for the history of the Maratha", Vol. IV, page 74. The same author in a learned article on the subject of Shivaji's literary education contributed to the Marathi Magazine, "Saraswati Mandir" (Vol. 5, No. 5), has completely exploded Grant Duff's hypothesis of Shivaji's illiteracy. Most of the Maratha nobility contemporaneous with Shivaji, as also those who preceded or followed him in point of time, knew the simple arts of reading and writing. This is the contention of Mr. Rajwade, and the present author has no hesitation in endorsing that opinion.

of the people. Shivaji studied with close and minute observation those arts of administration under Dadaji. Shivaji's faculty of observation was very early developed. His questions were at times very trying even to the experts in the various subjects. He paid to Dadaji the honour due to his position and experience and made it a point to acquire from him his varied knowledge of affairs. Now there were some affairs which Dadaji used to transact without Shivaji's knowledge. Shivaji took this to heart and one day expressed himself rather frankly upon this subject. "What though I am young ?" said he, "Your duty it is to acquaint me with all affairs, that I may acquire experience under your guidance. For are you not to me in the position of a father ? How could I otherwise learn wisdom ?" Dadaji admired this boyish curiosity and consulted him thereafter upon all affairs. Young Shivaji discussed the pros and cons of every question with the gravity of an elder. Dadaji trained him to give decisions in disputes, where the most complicated issues were involved. With his wonderful grasp and penetration the most complex problem could never elude his judgment, and he could use these precedents in dealing with similar questions that recurred from time to time. It was thus under the kind guidance of Dadaji that Shivaji mastered the various subjects of finance, agriculture, the discipline of his infantry and cavalry, and supervision over ths various grades of servants in his service. This early knowledge and experience, it is needless to say, was of immense service to him in the near future.

But there was one subject upon which there was the greatest divergence of opinion between Dadaji and Shivaji, and that was the attitude of Shivaji towards the Mahomedan rulers. The hatred of Islam which he had almost literally sucked in with his mother's milk, and his ambitious plans of the restoration of a Hindu sovereignty were never approved of by Dadaji. Dadaji was not a man who could even dream of the great ambitions of his ward. He never possessed that wide outlook of vision. His was a philosophy of simple contentment. He thought, and from the ordinary stand-point of human prudence rightly thought, that his duty was in the first place to behave with submission and humility towards that power, owing to whose favour and benevolence, his master enjoyed his jahgir, and in the second place to protect and administer the jahgir to the highest advantage of his master. To incur the wrath of the Mahomedan rulers–were it only by seeking to expand the jahgir–was too audacious an enterprise for the placid mind of Dadaji to think of. Soon after the return of Shivaji and Jijabai from Bijapur in the company of Dadaji Kondadev, Shivaji communicated his ambitious plans to the trusty confidante of his father. "I do not consider it proper," said Shivaji, "to live as an underling of the Mahomedans on the wealth my father has earned in their service. I am resolved to carve out my fortune with my own right hand. What good is it to have been born in the Bhonsle family, if I add no new honours to the family escutcheon? The worth of a manly life, what is it to be found in, if not in a life of toil? Not surely in fortune's smiles? Do you not see how the Mahomedan domination has crushed the life out of Hindu society and religion? Kine and Brahmans, gods and shrines have been polluted and desecrated in all the land, and no champion has sprung forth from the groaning soil. I have pondered deep over this subject and have resolved to devote my life to this object of reviving our independence and our religion. I cannot recall the past; but the future is in my hands." Dadaji was astonished at the proposal and tried to divert his mind from the project. "How impossible", he exclaimed, "is the task you speak of and how dreadful! The whole land lies panting under the oppression of Islam. All forts and positions of strategic value are commanded by them. Their armies man the garrisons. Enough for you to have and keep what your father has wrested from the general wreck. Try to think of aggrandising your fortunes and that moment you will be declared a public enemy, and you will involve your father in your ruin.

Just think of your father and his fiery valour! Even he had to bend before the Mahomedans."

Later on when Shivaji began to realize his plans of forming an independent Hindu state and in pursuance of the same to make expeditions against the Bijapur territory, Dadaji was filled with consternation. He called Shivaji and began to expostulate with him in the most vehement terms. "You have embarked," he said to Shivaji, "on a most hazardous enterprise, which will one day bring you and your jahgir to ruin. On the four sides of the continent, the great Mahomedan sovereignties are holding undisputed sway, each in the plenitude of its power and glory. What are you and your puny resources before their power? Don't you see that you are only jeopardising your father's position? He is there in the midst of the enemy, in the power of the sultan. For your rash acts the sultan is sure to retaliate on your father. You will be evicted from your jahgir and will be a bye-word in the land. It is to your own interest to maintain loyal relations with the Adilshahi dynasty, if indeed you value your estates." This chilling advice was repeated from time to time. Shivaji, as was his wont, always listened in calm silence, but to the eternal good fortune of all Maharashtrians, he did not allow himself in the least to be swerved from his glorious enterprise.

It is said that when Dadaji saw how ineffective all his counsels to Shivaji upon this one subject were, the upright man was filled with dismay, not knowing what to do. Shivaji's conduct preyed upon his heart, and the good man could only think of the counsequences with a shudder. The boy had been confided to his care, to be brought up as a youth of character and noble promise. But he had conceived this wayward passion and lent countenance to lawless acts. The excesses of the son were bound to recoil upon the innocent head of the father. And had not Shahaji the right to ask of him how he, of whom he had expected so much, had allowed his son to run wild, governed by a frenzied passion for liberty? Yes, the blame would rightly fall on him, and not all his past services would avail to atone for it. With such remorseful thoughts the good man sickened and slowly pined away.[1]

Dadaji indeed did the only thing he could do under the circumstances, to shield himself from blame, and that was to inform Shahaji of the strange passion for liberty now awakened in Shivaji's breast, warning him to take the proper steps to suppress it in time. Shahaji did not take particular notice of the warning and ordered no change whatever in Shivaji's discipline or mode of living. The truth is that Shahaji knew the true state of affairs at Bijapur better than any man of his time, and he was himself secretly preparing for the inauguration of an independent sovereignty, of which more will be said at its appropriate place. The conclusion, therefore, which thrusts itself inevitably upon our minds is that the glorious thoughts of founding a new Hindu dynasty were not implanted in Shivaji's mind by Dadaji Kondadev, who on the other hand laboured hard to counteract them; and indeed had Dadaji to deal with a common man without insight, the current of those thoughts would have been stopped for ever. The real impulse then came from Jijabai. How true is it that one sweet and loving word from the lips of a mother makes a deeper impression on the heart than ten thousand speeches!

Filled with the ambition to do great deeds, Shivaji did not hearken to Dadaji's advice. But this disobedience only affected his master passion. In other regards nobody could be more docile. Shivaji honoured him like a father, did whatever he commanded him and always remembered in his actions that Dadaji was the trusted friend of Shahaji. Dadaji sought to wean Shivaji from his violent enterprise by occupying his mind with other subjects. He took him round the different jahgir villages, explaining the revenue

---

1 In the bakhar, called the Bakhar of the Marathi Swarajya (Chronicle of the Maratha Empire) Dadaji is represented to have resorted to poison and committed suicide, being unable to withstand this consuming anxiety. The *Tarikh-i-Shivaji* tells the same story.

systems and the forms of administration. He entrusted many of his duties to Shivaji who executed them with great skill and enthusiasm. But this did not divert his mind from his cherished schemes. It only brought him into immediate contact with the revenue officers, administrators and other persons of rank within the limits of the jahgir and created in him a greater sense of confidence for administrative work.

Dadaji's spirit groaned in him to see that nothing could stop or stem Shivaji's violent ambition. He was agitated with a devouring anxiety, which shortly affected his health. Jijabai and Shivaji attended him with assiduity. Shivaji was always by his bed-side. They tried all remedies that were suggested to them But medicine and attendance notwithstanding Dadaji kept steadily sinking. When the moment of death was at hand, Dadaji confided the keys of the treasury to Shivaji and described the management of the hill-forts, the districts and the army, exhorting him to deal kindly with the officers, and expatiating on the merits of every individual. He also had the clerks and officers brought into his presence and with his dying voice exhorted them to serve Shahaji with loyalty and devotion, and making them clasp young Shivaji's hand he adjured them to look upon him as their master. Having settled these public duties, he is said to have exhorted Shivaji to look after his family and dependents and to have expressed a cordial wish for his happiness and glory and the fulfilment of his noble vow to inaugurate a new state, for the protection of cows and Brahmans and the higher glory of his religion. With these words on his lips, the loyal Dadaji Kondadev expired. He was seventy years old at his death.

We have so far described two sources of Shivaji's education, the one being Jijabai and the other Dadaji Kondadev. But there was a third source, and that was Shahaji himself. True, the period of the operation of this educative force was brief, but, brief as it was, it was of the highest value in its effect upon Shivaji's career. In his short sojourn at Bijapur Shivaji had endless opportunities to watch the working of the various departments of the Bijapur government, the methods of administration, the etiquette of the court and the manners and fashions of the nobility. Shahaji commanded great influence at the Bijapur court and was on terms of cordiality with many of the leading Mahomedan and Maratha nobles, and Shivaji, instead of idling his time like the sons of the other nobles, turned these opportunities to good account. He frequently visited and made constant observation of the cantonments, the war-horses, the artillery parks and the batteries, and, constantly making inquiries of expert officers, he resolved his doubts and registered all vital information upon the tablets of his memory. Shahaji himself was gratified at his son's desire to learn and indulged him in these pursuits. Shahaji had often his son beside him when arguing subtle questions of war or diplomacy. He had him in his company when attending the durbar, where his remarkable faculties of comprehension and observation found active exercise. All this produced two general effects: first, by being always in the company of his father, he got much useful information of vital influence upon his subsequent career; and secondly, his disgust of Mahomedan rule was accentuated and embittered by all he had witnessed, and became the master passion of his life.

Such was the discipline by which a great career was moulded and made possible. It was more or less a moral and an administrative discipline. As to whether, in addition to this, he made a systematic study of any great authors or not, we have no information in the authentic chronicles. The account in the chronicle called the Shiv-digvijaya is very much exaggerated and is not supported by any other sources of information. From the praises of Shivaji by such saintly poets as Vaman, Tukaram and Ramdas, among his contemporaries, it might be inferred that he had a fair acquaintance with books. But it is plain that the biographers of Shivaji, being more or less men of action, set little store by bookish knowedge and scarcely, if ever, refer to it. And the life of this great man has to convey, among others, this lesson that practical wisdom is often times a more efficient factor of success than literary knowledge.

CHAPTER V

THE PREPARATION FOR SWARAJYA

THE Marathi chroniclers are silent upon the early preparations of Shivaji in furtherance of his ambitious plans. That ambition in its essence comprehended the deliverance of his country from a very unbearable Mahomedan tyranny, the raising of the fabric of an independent national government, and the expulsion of Mahomedan bigotry from the land. The scanty material available on the subject has been laid under contribution but with extreme caution and reserve in the account that follows.

On his return to Poona, as described in the last chapter, Shivaji went out on various reconnoitring expeditions over the surrounding mountain tracts under pretence of a personal inspection of his jahgir. Attended by persons who from birth were familiar with the geographical conditions of the upland parts of the Western ghats, and forming acquaintance with the chiefs and men of position in every town and village, he surveyed all those inaccessible regions with a close scrutiny into the mountain fortresses and places of military advantage. He examined the routes of communication, the by-paths and mountain defiles, the glens and the valleys. His companions admired the ardent zeal he manifested in informing himself about the topographical conditions of these mountains. It was natural for them to be astonished that this young heir of a rising jahgirdar should expose himself to sun and shower, surmounting ascents and precipices, defying the attacks of wild beasts and a hundred other dangers, apparently with no other motive than an insatiable thirst for geographical information. Young Shivaji spent whole days and nights, wandering from forest to forest and mountain to mountain, with the swiftness of foot and gliding movement peculiar to the aboriginal tribes of these mountains. It was not easy for his companions to conceive how necessary these tours of inspection were to the career to which the young chief felt himself to be called as it were by the voice of duty. While making these explorations he was silently achieving another object of equally great importance, that of winning over a loyal body of followers and supporters.

There was a kind of personal magnetism by which young Shivaji attracted every heart towards himself. A few moments' conversation sufficed to draw with a magic fascination the highest and the lowest persons in the land to follow his least inclinations. In conversation with young Shivaji every man instantly forgot all the restraints of reserve and laid bare before him his most secret thoughts and the innermost impulses of life. Shivaji put all men at their ease with such magic tact and courtesy that all thought they were pouring out their hearts to one who was their equal. He listened to their tales of sorrow and anguish and won them over to his heart with the closest bonds of affection, friendship and gratitude. His purse was always at the call of these companions of his early boyhood.

This lavish generosity entailed a large expenditure which considerably exceeded his slender allowance. Dadaji remonstrated with him for this drain on the jahgir revenues "You are, of course, the master," said Dadaji, "and I am bound to make any payment to anybody you want on your account. But when you exceed your allowance, it must be at the expense of the annual remittance to be sent to Shahaji, and I shall have to account for the shortage. You must therefore get your allowance increased, and I shall have no objection to your extravagance." Shivaji retorted it was not for Dadaji to be anxious about his prodigality, and he would procure his father's sanction for the expenses beyond his fixed allowance. Dadaji was quite mystified at this reply. He did not see that there was rhyme or reason in Shivaji's mad extravagance. He had no wide range of thought or outlook upon affairs. His practical wisdom and philosophy was directed to the one absorbing task of procuring the largest possible revenue for Shahaji from year to year.

Thus did Shivaji go on forming a large circle of clients and dependents, every one of whom was imbued with a thorough faith in his master's nobility of heart. Their enthusiasm kindled into a loyal devotion and self-sacrificing passion towards the person of Shivaji. It was a strange attraction they felt towards him. In this circle of dependents, a large number of those who had won the entire favour and confidence of Shivaji were the Mavalis. These were rude and semi-civilized people, with an aspect anything but prepossessing. But under their rude exteriors, burnt hearts the most faithful and upright amoung Shivaji's followers. They had a strong faith in the unerring wisdom of their master and executed his most difficult orders with a display of sagacity and agility for which no one could have given them credit. They were brought up in the creed of passive obedience and unquestioning service. To them once a master always a master. Inured to poverty and frugal in their living, the employer who provided them with the means of coarse subsistence and clothing earned from them such a gratitude that they would court the greatest dangers and sacrifice their lives in his service. Dadaji Kondadev was the first to detect the sterling virtues in the heart of these rude mountaineers, and he maintained a corps of them in his service. Shivaji did not take long to ascertain their qualities. By his affection and generosity towards these humble people he made them his own. These mountaineers lived in the highlands of Shivaji's jahgir. They obtained a precarious living from the roots and shrubs in the mountain forests. They were quite at home in the zig-zag paths and mountain defiles over these woodlands. When Shivaji went on his tours of inspection he took these men as his guides. He soon became their idol. Only in him had they found in their experience of centuries one who was not repelled by their rude rusticity and sylvan manners, but who on the contrary treated them with courtesy and affection. This conviction bred in them a great pride and enthusiasm for their master, for whose prosperity they would renounce their fortunes, the ties of personal affection and life itself. Their spirit of self-surrender was many a time put to the proof, and no adversity, however great, could turn them away from the feet of the master. The leaders of these Mavalis, occupying the rank of *deshmukhs* among their tribes, were the earliest and closest of Shivaji's friends. The names of three of them have become famous in Maratha history. These three were Yesaji Kunk, Tanaji Malusare[1] and Baji Fasalkar. These three men commanded great influence among the Mavalis. They had a share from the beginning in all the young ambitions of Shivaji, and as the exigencies of his statecraft developed themselves in course of time, they performed the most glorious feats and exploits, sacrificing even their lives on the altar of personal friendship and devotion.

Although Shivaji's ambitious designs received scant encouragement from Dadaji Kondadev, he succeeded in winning over all the assistant staff of that loyal financier. When the deshmukhs or procurators of revenue, from the various towns came on business to Poona, Shivaji was for hours closeted with them, setting forth his projects, asking their opinions and pleading for their adherence; and such was the fascination exercised upon their minds by his speech and courtesy, that the conversation invariably terminated in a league of enduring friendship. When Shivaji himself went in person on his tours of inspection over his paternal estates, he allowed no opportunity to elude him of interviewing the various deshmukhs and drawing them into his alliance. Such of the Maratha nobility and gentry in the neighbourhood as had occasion to visit him at Poona were entertained in such a lavish and magnificent style, that they invariably departed his fast friends and sympathisers. Much as they might criticise his comparative youthfulness

---

[1] Tanaji Malusare however was not strictly a Mavali deshmukh. He was a deshmukh of Umrathe in the Konkan lowlands beneath the Mavals.

and inexperience,they could not help testifying to his courage and enthusiasm, or acknowledging the practicability of the schemes he submitted to their approval. Their assent was promptly given, and their cordial sympathy and co-operation was secured to the cause. There was indeed a singular persuasiveness in the youthful hero, which, along with the cordiality of his offers, his religious enthusiasm and the unmistakable ring of sincerity in his hatred of Mahomedan rule, made even the most self-centred of them partake of his enthusiasm, reciprocate his feelings and embrace his proposals. They had besides the object-lesson of Shahaji's great triumphs; and the conviction was easily bred in them that the son of such a father would certainly lead them forth to victory and deliverance from the thraldom of Islam. Thus they became willing partisans in the cause; and the few who hesitated or refused soon had occasion to repent of their error.

It is time to review very briefly the influences which seemed to favour a id for the restoration of the national independence of Maharashtra.

The first asset in the cause of the national regeneration that Shivaji possessed was the example of his father. He had the great example before him of the defender of the Nizamshahi dynasty against the Moguls, and the reviver of that sovereignty after its extinction. It was plain that the ultimate discomfiture of Shahaji could only be ascribed to the overwhelming armaments of the Mogul invaders. The curtain had fallen upon these early activities of Shahaji, only to disclose a new scene of almost regal pomp and splendour in the Karnatic. The experiences of Shahaji, both in his victories and failures, had established the fact that with a proper band of disciplined followers it was not only possible but easily practicable to overthrow the Mahomedan power in Maharashtra and to establish an independent Hindu sovereignty in its place. Fired with a desire to outshine his father's greatness, Shivaji had the sagacity to perceive and to remedy the defects in his system.

He often openly expressed his regret that Shahaji should have thought it necessary, after his distinguished career against the Moguls, to take service under Bijapur and shine by the reflected light of the Adilshahi dynasty.

Another circumstance which confirmed Shivaji in his ambitious resolves, was the discontent of many of the local chiefs and procurators of revenue or deshmukhs, with the Mahomedan government.[1] Emboldened by the prevailing disturbance and misrule, the inevitable precursors of revolution and change, these men carried on an uncertain war and brigandage among themselves. It was indeed a time of "*bellum omnium contra omnes*," and the Bijapur government exercised little of the rights of a sovereign state over these parts. It was almost an impossible feat to unite together these warring chiefs under a common standard or to give their bellicose spirit a higher purpose, Shivaji succeeded in the seemingly impossible task, healed the scars of private feuds and concentrated their powers to be brought into action for the higher ideal of a national enterprise.

The third circumstance, which it is necessary to advert to, is the fact that the districts of Poona, Supa, Maval and other tracts had for a long time been under the Nizamshahi state of Ahmednagar, and the troublous times of the Mogul invasions and the rapid vicissitudes through which the Ahmednagar state had passed had produced a general laxity of administration, with next to no supervision on the part of the central government. It is true indeed that these districts had at the time of the final partition and territorial adjustment passed under the Bijapur flag, but this change was so recent and the transfer had created such complications, that the Bijapur government had scarcely felt its way to bring under its direct authority these frontier parts of its dominions. There was a marked insufficiency of the military garrisons and equipments in the hill-forts, and the

---

1 A good deal of light has been thrown upon the social, political and economic condition of the Maval deshmukhs by Mr. Rajwade in the later volumes of his work (Vol. 15 to 18).

growing dissensions in the Bijapur council were not calculated to improve the situation. But the government of Bijapur had lulled itself into a belief in its security by continuing these districts in jahgir to Shahaji, who had held them from time to time since the times of Maloji. Dadaji Kondadev had administered the jahgir with great skill and wisdom. The people were happy and prosperous under a practically Hindu regime and had no desire to pass under the direct authority of the sultan. What wonder then that when they saw a noble spirit like Shivaji, himself the son of an approved leader like Shahaji, embarking upon the ambitious plan of a revived Hindu sovereignty and marked his never-failing genius and enthusiasm in all his operations, they came forth to acclaim the hero and devote themselves unreservedly to his cause and service?

That Shivaji had the ability to conduct the affairs of a new monarchy from its very foundation has been amply shown by the original administrative reforms he introduced as a ruler, the rudiments of which he had learnt at home, in listening to the conversation of Dadaji Kondadev, Jijabai and the jahgir officers. To this was joined the experience he had gained during his short residence at Bijapur. On account of the pre-eminent position of Shahaji at that court, Shivaji was able to watch the despatch of public business on some of the most momentous questions then engaging the attention of that state. Shivaji's followers therefore had no misgivings on this ground. Nor on the other hand was there much fear to be entertained on the ground of the arduous nature of the task and the inadequacy of the means for its fulfilment. The peculiar facilities for the undertaking of such an enterprise, which were offered by the political situation of the time, Shivaji had seized upon with an intuitive judgment that well qualified him for the duties of a ruler. More than this could not be expected and surely was not needed for a general of such natural talents and abilities, stimulated as his ambition ever was by the impulsive zeal of his mother and the glory shed on the Bhonsle name by his father.

CHAPTER VI

THE BEGINNINGS OF SWARAJYA

IN THE last chapter a brief sketch was attempted of the early preparations of Shivaji for the realization of his ambition: the exploration of mountain fastnesses and hill-forts, mountain paths and defiles, and the mustering together of a band of devoted friends and supporters. In this chapter we propose to trace his earliest activities as parts of a premeditated aggressive programme.

At the outset we meet with a heresy to which certain historians, the principal of whom is Mr. Rajwade (Vol. IV, page 73 of his "Materials for the History of the Marathas"), have given currency. These historians maintain that the beginnings of independence were made not by Shivaji but by Dadaji Kondadev and his officers at the instance of Shahaji himself, and that at a time when Shivaji was barely eleven or twelve years of age. In support of this contention, Mr. Rajwade quotes the chronicler, Sabhasad, to the following effect: "Immediately on the return from Bangalore to Poona, Dadaji captured the twelve Mavali glens and slew the Mavali deshmukhs who were raiding the country."

It does not however follow from this statement that the idea of an independent Hindu state had been already conceived and its execution entrusted to Dadaji Kondadev by Shahaji. The context of Sabhasad's statement makes it clear that the districts of the twelve Mavals, with Baramati and Indapur, were added to Shahaji's jahgir for his eminent services in the Karnatic, and that in 1638 on his return from Bangalore, Dadaji Kondadev in pursuance of the orders he had received from Shahaji proceeded to take possession of the recently ceded districts by a war of conquest and the defeat of the local deshmukhs. Shahaji was just feeling his way to a permanent position at the Bijapur court, and he was not likely to contemplate any act of rebellion against Bijapur at the imminent risk of wrecking his new-built fortune. As a motive for this imaginary plan of forming an independent monarchy in the Maval districts, in concert with Dadaji Kondadev Mr. Rajwade points to the private enemies of Shahaji in the Karnatic, such as Afzul Khan, Maloji Ghorpade and other nobles of Bijapur who looked askance upon his rising power in the Karnatic. Such private enmities had probably no existence in point of fact so early as 1638. The animosities between Shahaji and Afzul Khan and other nobles of Bijapur began eight or ten years later. The history of Bijapur at this earlier period of Shahaji's career in the Karnatic makes scarcely any allusion to Afzul Khan and the other enemies of Shahaji of a later time. And if Dadaji had ever concerted with Shahaji a plan for establishing an independent power in the Maval districts, it is difficult to conceive why seven or eight years later the same individual should have entered such emphatic protests against Shivaji's designs. Such a position would have been quite ridiculous for a prudent man of affairs like Dadaji to take up in dealing with the enterprising programme conceived by Shivaji and is entirely at variance with the received tradition that the pertinacity of Shivaji brought Dadaji to an early grave, or, as is sometimes asserted, made him commit suicide by resorting to poison. Nor was an experienced statesman like Shahaji likely to entrust such a serious charge to Dadaji's insignificant force of a thousand men or thereabout when he had whole regiments at his command in the Karnatic. Nor is there any shred of evidence that a large army was ever sent under Dadaji from Bangalore to Maharashtra. Lastly there is this consideration: why should Shahaji have ever confided an enterprise of such gravity and consequence to another, when he was himself the greatest military leader of his time in all the Deccan? In short, the best that can be said for this theory is that it is an inconsiderate attempt to cast a shadow upon Shivaji's greatness by transferring the originality of his design to a lesser personage. Our line of argument is quite consistent with the view that Shahaji himself had his own designs of independence, a subject which we have sufficiently adverted to in a foregoing chapter. The crux of the question is whether upon Shahaji's advice a plan for a campaign of independence in Maharashtra had ever been conceived. If such an attempt had really been made, what circumstances conspired to put an end to it? And why should Dadaji have shown seven years later such a total change of front on the subject?

As against our line of argument an objection may be raised somewhat to this effect. If Shahaji harboured no designs for independence in Maharashtra, it may be argued, why should he not have taken steps to punish Shivaji,—nay even expel him from his jahgir,—when complaints were made by Dadaji Kondadev, and when the Bijapur government itself took him to task for it? It is easy to reply to this objection. By the time Shivaji began his aggressions against Bijapur, Shahaji's authority was well rooted in the Karnatic, his jahgir possessions had been expanded on all sides, and his will was supreme law in the south. The Bijapur government was rent by party factions, and he had profited by the confusion to place his authority on a sort of autocratic basis. It was at such a time that the complaints against Shivaji came to him, a time which Shahaji felt was eminently favourable for such an attempt. With a secret approval of his son's designs and a belief in their practicability, and yet wishing to have no interruption in his chosen paths to independence, he disavowed responsibility for Shivaji's actions and professed a sort of time-serving neutrality upon this subject. His conduct clearly shows that the thoughts of liberty were in his heart, nor was he so debased or perverted as to prefer a gilded servitude to true independence. But there is nothing in his conduct to lend countenance to the view that he had begun to defy the Bijapur government so early as 1638. It is true that in the latter part of his career he was practically independent in the Karnatic. But never did Shahaji like his son openly defy the Bijapur government.

Shivaji saw the Mogul and Mahomedan power spread over the western ghats, but he was shrewd enough to see, as others were not, that the foundations of the Mahomedan power over the ghats were not rooted deep enough to defy either the assault of a foreign power without or of rebellion within. It was apparent that the Mahomedan powers had always made little of these mountain fastnesses and had never troubled themselves about strengthening their outposts on the frontiers or garrisoning the hill-forts with sufficient forces for defence [1] He therefore resolved

---

[1] From papers published by Mr. Rajwade (Vol. XV of his "Materials for a History of the Marathas") some evidence of Shivaji's pioneer attempts for independence, dating already as early as 1645, is now forth-coming. From a letter of Shivaji in reply to the Prabhu Deshpande, kulkarni of the vale of Rohida, in which the name of Dadaji Kondadev is mentioned as being privy to certain intrigues between this deshpande and Shivaji himself, an attempt is made to represent Dadaji Kondadev as not merely the promoter but the inspirer of Shivaji's plans. Dadaji's work in the conquest of the Mavals was however a part of his administrative duty as the procurator of Shahaji's jahgir, and was probably made in pursuance of his general orders for the settlement of the district. Whatever the original compact with this Prabhu family might have heen, it is clear from Rajwade (Vol. XV pp. 272-73) that they undertook to devote themselves to the prosecution of Shivaji's designs for the achievement of Swarajya and espoused his cause, though the enemies of their family carried tales to the local Bijapur authorities at Shirval. The Jedhes, who were the deshmukhs of Rohida, very early espoused Shivaji's cause. They had originally been in the Bijapur service, but about the time when Randulla Khan and Shahaji marched against the Moguls (1635 A. D.), they joined Shahaji (Jedhe Chronology, p. 178) probably with a view to enlist his support against the Khopde family who disputed the deshmukh rights over that particular district. The result of this intervention was that at a later date we find the Khopdes on the side of Afzul Khan, while the Jedhes and most other Maval deshmukhs or at least their followers remained on the side of Shivaji, whom they also assisted in the war with the Mores of Javli (Jedhe Chronology, pp. 180 and 181). Another enemy of the Jedhe family was Bandal of Hirdas Maval who had usurped their lands. Dadaji Kondadev marched agaist Bandal, but was defeated (Rajwade's Vol.XV,316, 393) and had to retreat to his head-quarters at Shivapur. In the end with the help of Kanhoji Jedhe, Dadaji Kondadev made his peace with Bandal and brought about a good understanding with the leaders of the twelve Mavals, excepting the Khopdes, and after the death of Dadaji we find them co-operating with Shivaji in all his operations. In 1648 we find Jedhe Naik was with Shahaji in the South and was arrested along with him by

to direct his first operations against the ghat country, subjugate the hill-forts and carry the adjoining tracts of mountain land along with them. He knew that, do what the Mahomedan powers could, they would never get permanent control over his highlands, unless and until the Hindu population itself chose to put themselves entirely in their hands. The first part of Shivaji's programme therefore was to make his own what the Mahomedans had so long failed to dominate, and use the hill-forts both for purposes of defence and offence, as strategical positions commanding the entire ghat country and compelling the adherence and allegiance of the deshmukhs in the neighbourhood. On nearly all the hill-forts there were nominal garrisons maintained by the Bijapur government, who were practically like mounted sentinels keeping watch. It was not to Shivaji's interest, nor was it then in his power, to declare open enmity with them. He resolved to carry his point by stratagem. About twenty miles, to the south-west of Poona, lay the fort of Torna. Shivaji despatched Yessaji Kunk, Tanaji Malusare and Baji Fasalkar to open negotiations with the governor of the fort, asking him to make over the fortress for the present to Shivaji, who, it was represented to them, was in communication with the sultan for the purpose. By these insinuations, reinforced by persuasive gold, the fort of Torna fell into Shivaji's hands in 1646[1].

Mustapha Khan. After his liberation Shahaji thanked him and exhorted him thenceforth to anchor his fortunes with those of Shivaji at Poona and support him with all his power. Thus it was that the Jedhes, the Silimkars and even the Bandals co-operated with Shivaji enthusiastically in the wars with Chandrarao More and Afzul Khan (Vide Jedhe Chronology pp. 179,-180). This is clear proof that Shahaji not only secretly sympathised with the plans of Shivaji but did his best to promote them by furnishing his son with the services of a most loyal body of auxiliaries. It will be seen that in his petty wars Dadaji Kondadev only follod out the policy of Shahaji, the eventual complications of which that able administrator did not probably foresee.

1 Khafi Khan says that the first fort captured by Shivaji was Chandanwandan.

This was the first overt act of spoliation against Bijapur, and to lend it an ostensible colouring and retain possession of his prize, Shivaji promptly despatched his deputies to Bijapur, representing to that government that the taking over by Shivaji of the fort of Torna was entirely in the interest of the government, that a loyal servant like him had better be in charge of a sequestered fortress like Torna, in preference to adventurous officers, and that in virtue of his new position as governor of the fort, he would be able to compel the deshmukhs to render true accounts of revenue to the state, thus saving immense sums of money annually to the government. As a practical proof of his good intentions, he undertook to pay over to the government a far larger revenue than the average of the last ten years. The government took a long time to draft a reply to these representations, which was just what Shivaji wanted, for in the meanwhile his agents were lavish with presents and bribes among the officers of the court and secured a favourable reply to the petition. Meanwhile the fortifications of Torna were being radically overhauled and renovated, and when completely restored the name of Prachandgad was given to it. In course of these operations Shivaji had the good luck to unearth a quantity of buried treasure among the debris of the fort. Shivaji ascribed the find to the favour of the goddess Bhawani and caused a rumour to be spread that this was a proof of her favourable interest in his enterprise This made his cause a popular cause, and the enthusiasm of the multitude knew no bounds. Shivaji devoted the treasure to the purchase of arms and ammunition and the erection of a new fort of his own.

To the south-east of Torna fort, at a distance of about three miles there was a barren mountain called Murbad,[1] of considerable strategical value. This Shivaji resolved to transform into a fortress-town with impregnable defences. The mountain spurs projected on three sides. They were also

[1] Variously called Mudrodev and Durgadevi Mount by other chroniclers. The Shedgavkar bakhar calls it Musaldev (p. 19.)

strongly fortified with ramparts. The central fort was christened Rajgad and it was adorned with a spacious palace. The projecting redoubts were named Suvela, Sanjivani, and Padmavati respectively. The Shivadigvijay states that only the projecting forts were the creation of Shivaji. The central fort existed before and was won by a stroke of diplomacy. Dadaji Kondadev had reclaimed the dense jungle around the village of Khedber between Poona and Shirval and by the careful culture of mango groves in this wilderness converted it into a thriving centre, under the name of Shivapur, after the name of his master Shivaji. This new town was peopled by inhabitants from the Maval and Konkan regions, who gladly acknowledged the authority of Shivaji. At Shivapur he gave laws and heard cases, civil and criminal.

While the entrenchments of fort Rajgad were in progress, a report of these doings of Shivaji reached the Bijapur government. The sultan immediately issued orders to Shivaji to put a stop to the fortifications and demanded explanation of these acts from Shahaji in the Karnatic. That warrior replied that neither had Shivaji consulted him in these things, nor was he doing anything upon his father's advice; but he and his family were loyal vassals of the Adilshahi state, and that being so, whatever Shivaji was doing in the way of fortification must be for the improvement or safety of his jahgir. The Bijapur state possessed no reliable fortress in the neighbourhood of his jahgir, and Shivaji might have thought of curing this defect. In this Shivaji could not be said to be doing any disservice to the Bijapur state. Such was the purport of Shahaji's reply. At the same time he wrote to Dadaji and Shivaji protesting against these acts of his son and exhorting him to reform his ways. Dadaji had already notified Shahaji of the latest doings of his son and exhausted his eloquence in vain to bring back Shivaji to the paths of worldly wisdom and easy security,—with what effect, has already been described.

Soon after followed the death of Dadaji Kondadev, and Shivaji took up personal charge of the jahgir, administering it in the name of his father. Shortly after, Shahaji's agents came to demand the arrears of the jahgir revenue. Shivaji dismissed them with the curt reply that the produces of the sterile fields scarcely sufficed for the cost of administration, and as the Karnatic estates of his father were both extensive and fertile, he had better maintain himself on that source of revenue. Shahaji does not seem to have resented this answer. It would seem that he was gratified with the early promise of a great career in the resourceful conduct of his son. Some time later he voluntarily made over to Shivaji the entire charge and usufruct of the Maharashtra jahgir, with an expression of delight at the skill and statesmanship of which his son had already given unmistakable evidence. And wisely indeed was this step taken by Shahaji. There were civil dissensions at Bijapur and anarchy reigned in all departments of government. The wiser plan for Shahaji was to watch events calmly, with a firm grasp upon his Karnatic possessions. Shivaji's progress in Maharashtra was also fraught with grave danger to his personal security. By keeping a distance between himself and Shivaji and putting him in full authority over his Maharashtra interests, Shahaji might be free at any moment to renounce any responsibility for his daring acts. With this prudent counsel, Shahaji now settled for good in the Karnatic.

Now it happened that among these jahgir estates was the district of Supa, which hitherto had been administered by Baji Mohite, the brother-in-law of Shahaji, being in fact the brother of his second wife. He was also in charge of a squadron of 300 horse. On the death of Dadaji, Shivaji wrote to him to bring the squadron and the jahgir accounts personally to Poona. Mohite did not obey this order and, instead of replying to the message, expressed his astonishment to the bearer of the despatch that Shivaji should play the landlord in the life-time of his father, whose great position alone had hitherto screened him from condign punishment for his acts of lawlessness and rapacity within the Bijapur territory. He wound up this solemn denunciation with an expression of alarm for the safety of Shahaji, should his son persist in his hare-brained enterprise, not forgetting to give the gratuitous counsel: *ne sutor ultra crepidam*. The messengers made a faithful report of these utterances to Shivaji, and one can well understand how his blood must have boiled in his veins at this representation of his acts. His revenge was swift and sudden. The Shimga festival coming on, Shivaji called on this refractory step-uncle with a small guard of Mavalis, under pretence of asking and receiving the customary Shimga presents. The trick succeeded. Mohite was taken prisoner, his territory and horse captured and the jewels and treasury seized.[1] Mohite was treated as became his rank and relation with Shahaji. Shivaji tried his best to persuade him to side with him. But persuasion had no force with Mohite, who with his followers was at last sent to Shahaji in the Karnatic, with a proper escort.

A small event this, but it had great influence upon the minds both of supporters and strangers. They saw the sort of man they had to deal with. A man who had acted so sternly towards the brother-in-law of his father, and withal a faithful and zealous officer of Shahaji, was certainly not a person to be trifled with. The circumstance aroused a sense of responsibility and fear among his followers.

The fort of Chakan lies to the east of Poona. It commanded the line of communication between Poona and the Deccan plateau. The possession of this fortress went a great way towards securing the sovereignty of the country. The fortress had recently been the scene of important events

1 Other bakhars speak of a midnight raid upon Supa resulting in the capture and imprisonment of Mohite and his followers. The Jedhe chronology gives a very late date to this event, viz. 1656. Sabhasad calls him Sambhaji Mohite.

in the career of Shahaji. That redoubted warrior had first obtained it in jahgir from the Nizamshahi sultan. When Shahaji had to fly the country from the vindictive pursuit of Jadhav, the possession of this important fortress passed into the hands of two turbulent polygar chiefs, Martand Dev and Honappa Deshpande. These chiefs were reduced and taken prisoners by Shahaji's friend, Murar Rao Jagdev of Bijapur, who made over the fortress again to its legitimate owner, Shahaji. Dadaji Kondadev, in his administrative capacity as Shahaji's minister of affairs, had appointed Firangoji Narsala as havaldar, or garrison commander of this fort. On the death of Dadaji, Firangoji made himself independent at Chakan. Shivaji opened negotiations in a conciliatory spirit and induced him to surrender the fort. Firangoji submitted quietly and was rewarded with a continuation of the garrison command of the fort in Shivaji's service. The old officers under Shahaji threw in their lot with Shivaji, excepting an old cavalry officer, Bilal Pagya, who was permitted to revert to his old allegiance at Shahaji's head-quarters.

In course of time, Firangoji Narsala captured the fort of Shivneri and planted Shivaji's flag upon his birth-place. Firangoji was entrusted with the command of this fort, in addition to his former command, and it was left to him to introduce Dadaji Kondadev's improved revenue system in the neighbouring villages.

Shivaji now turned his attention to the fort of Kondana, in the immediate vicinity of Poona. With his innate military instincts, he at once saw how indispensable the possession of this fort was for the permanent security of Poona. The seizure of this fort would strengthen Shivaji's jahgir possessions around Poona. But it was no light task to capture this fort. The Bijapur government maintained a strong garrison upon the fort under a Mahomedan officer. Shivaji was not yet powerful enough to advance openly to an encounter with such a force, an event which would have been the prelude to a larger movement on the part of the

Bijapur government. An open war with Bijapur at this stage of his career would have been a suicidal act. Shivaji therefore made up his mind to win over the fort by bribing the commander, and in this he had immediate success. The fort was no sooner won than Shivaji proceeded to overhaul its fortifications. With its new entrenchments and munitions of war, the fort entered upon a new career of vigorous activity under the name of Sinhagad, or the Lion's Fort.

The fort of Purandar and the neighbouring territory was in the charge of a capable Brahman officer, Nilkant Haibatrao, who held the fort and lands in *inam* from the defunct Nizamshahi dynasty. When the Nizamshahi territory came in course of time to be annexed to the widening Mogul Empire, Nilkant succeeded in carving out an independent fortune for himself within the secluded fastnesses of fort Purandar. He maintained a friendly attitude towards Shivaji and Dadaji till his death, which occurred within a short time after that of Dadaji. He left behind him three sons, of whom the eldest Nilopant succeeded in swallowing up the entire patrimony, regardless of the interest and birth-right of his younger brothers, Pilaji and Sankraji, who not unnaturally maintained that they should all have equal rights to the succession and command of the fort. The family bickering had been in progress for some time, when Nilopant observing what strides Shivaji was making in the expansion of his power cultivated his friendship. Shivaji was much perplexed over this fort, the acquisition of which seemed essential for the success of his enterprise. Open hostilities were impossible on account of the ties of alliance which had descended from sire to son. Public opinion was sure to be outraged by a declaration of hostilities. But for the efficient military control of his jahgir districts of Baramati, Indapur and Supa the acquisition of Purandar became an act of imperative necessity. Shivaji saw the accession of military strength the fortress was bound to bring to his possessions, and the insecurity to his own interests that the passing of the fort into hostile hands was sure to bring in its train. This, at any rate, he was resolved to prevent.

While the fraternal dissensions were at their height, Shivaji, with a chosen band of his Mavalis, entered the Purandar territory, with the ostensible purpose of a tour in the Supa district. No sooner were the two younger brothers apprised of Shivaji's approach than they sent to invite him to fort Purandar to arbitrate upon the dispute.[1] Upon this Shivaji made a halt and quartered his men at the temple of Narayan under the fort. A sudden march upon the fort might rouse Nilopant's suspicion, and this Shivaji wanted to avoid as much as possible. On the other hand the younger brothers had no courage to descend and openly join Shivaji. In this uncertainty, the soldiers and officers of the garrison began to reflect upon the growing evils of the fraternal strife. Things were drifting they could not see how and might end in the seizure of the fort by an outsider. Far better they thought if the fort were to pass under Shivaji, their neighbour, than under an utter stranger. Shivaji owned the surrounding country and was fast becoming the lord of the hill-forts round about. Under his iron hand anarchy was impossible. What leader more valiant and chivalrous could they ever hope to serve? Such thoughts were passing through their minds. They concerted their plans and determined to invite Shivaji to the fort. They represented to the dissentient brothers the wisdom of cultivating friendly feelings between their family and that of Shivaji, and that the valiant leader being under the walls of the fort and the time being that of the Divali festival, the most festive time of the year in the Deccan, it would be but an exercise of common courtesy to welcome him to partake of the hospitality of the fort. They further advised the brothers to lay their mutual complaints befor Shivaji and abide by

[1] The author of the Rairi bakhar says that Shivaji asked for and obtained from Nilopant permission to spend the autumn at the foot of fort Purandar, and upon this Shivaji came into the country under the fort in company with Jijabai.

his decision. Thus persuaded, the three brothers descended from the fort with the object of according a warm welcome to Shivaji and invited him in the most cordial terms to accept their hospitality in the auspicious season of Divali. Shivaji protested that he was not alone and could not indeed leave his followers in the season of festivity. Upon this the welcome was extended to the whole party, and for three days they enjoyed the hospitality of the fort. During this time, it is but due to Shivaji to say that he used all persuasive arts to pour oil upon the troubled waters, but nothing that he could think of could heal the feuds in the family. The arts of reconciliation were tried in vain. The two younger brothers pleaded that they had no hopes of justice at the hands of their brother and offered to put themselves under Shivaji's protection. On the night of the third day, while the company were conversing, Nilopant feeling drowsy retired to sleep. Shivaji suggested to the younger brothers that they should seize this opportunity and imprison a brother who turned a deaf ear to all conciliatory proposals. The brothers eagerly fell in with this proposal. Shivaji called his Mavalis and enlisted the sympathy of the garrison forces for a concerted *coup de main* with the mutual help of his own soldiers and the garrison. Nilopant was surprised while asleep and put under arrest. The three brothers were marched out of the fortress, which itself was taken possession of by Shivaji's men. Their *inam* lands were equally divided among them, and they were ordered to reside on the lower heights under the fort. In course of time they were given offices in Shivaji's government and prospered in his service. Thus was the fort of Purandar captured without a drop of blood, with the result of a great accession of military strength to Shivaji's districts of Supa and Indapur.

Soon after this event, Mankoji Dahatonde captured the fort of Visapur under Shivaji's orders. An Abyssinian officer of Shahaji, Sidi Bilal the Abyssinian, was in authority at this fort, and Shivaji intended at first to continue him in command. But when the proposal was made to him, the Abyssinian replied that Shivaji was a lawless adventurer, his career one of unrestrained violence, his course ultimately bound to end in ruin: he would not take service under Shivaji's flag. Shivaji showed no resentment at this scathing criticism on the part of a veteran officer of his father. Without the least insult or indignity to his person, but rather with many marks of esteem and laden with a profusion of favours, the veteran was allowed to return to Shabaji.

In this manner did Shivaji proceed to reduce the numerous hill-forts bordering upon his jahgir and render his position as secure and impregnable as possible. Upto this period he had had no occasion to court open hostilities with Bijapur. True indeed, two or three forts, such as those of Torna and Kondana, were seized directly from the military authorities of the Bijapur government; but they had been taken without shedding a drop of blood, and there was this excuse in their case, that they lay immediately upon his jahgir estates. While their maintenance in the highest state of efficiency was naturally more possible from the fact of their being vested in Shivaji's hands, and on the retention of them to a great extent depended the permanent security and tranquillity of his jahgir, the turbulent deshmukhs, or revenue lords, of the neighbourhood would now be under greater control, and what was of far greater moment, they would no longer be able to avoid paying their contribution of the government dues. The forts of Chakan, Purandar and several others had passed under usurping chiefs who defied the government. In reducing these restive chiefs, Shivaji could make it appear that he was in reality doing a service to Bijapur. It was therefore quite natural that the Bijapur government made little of this apparently insignificant movement of Shivaji. How could they be induced to believe that young and inexperienced as he was, the son of a loyal veteran like Shahaji could ever lend himself to the prosecution of any seditious designs against the state?

His schemes must of necessity, so they thought, be in the interest of the government. Another circumstance contributing to the same result was the fact that the reigning Adilshahi sultan (Mahomed Adil Shaha 1626–56) was absorbed in the erection of monumental edifices, the architectural beauties of which still redeem the ruins of the Bijapur capital. His political programme comprehended the subjugation of the whole of the Karnatic country, in the prosecution of which enterprise Shahaji had already rendered such splendid service. The sultan must have thought that to confiscate Shahaji's jahgir and take stringent measures against young Shivaji's present career would lead to unnecessary irritation and unpleasantness in his relations with a gallant officer who had already rendered such meritorious service to the state. It is needless to expatiate at large upon Shivaji's objects and purposes at this stage of his career. Suffice it to say that he was laying deep the firm foundations of that imperial edifice under whose arch the people of Maharashtra were able to breathe freely the spirit of liberty and independence. The mountain forts were the keys that opened up before him the dominion of the surrounding territory. Under the shadow of their rocky walls, his own realm could thrive in prosperous security, in spite of all the alarms of war.

In this manner Shivaji brought under his rule the whole territory from Chakan fort to the Nira. Each fort was re-entrenched as it was captured and kept in a state of high efficiency under a garrison of his faithful Mavalis. The deshmukhs of the districts around paid in their dues of land revenue without a murmur. The revenue system of Dadaji Kondadev was introduced everywhere. Favourable settlements were made with the ryots, with the result of great regularity in the payment of revenues; and a desire to improve the land was bred in their minds by reason of the sense of security they began to feel about their estates. Shivaji actively promoted this instinct for improvement, and his efforts made him the idol of the people. The Hindu cultivators in all directions hailed him as an ideal sovereign. His officers admired his wisdom and sagacity. Admiration and gratitude ripened into a feeling of reverence. Among the Mavalis this sense of reverence was most intense. They looked upon him not only as their king, but almost as their father. They were ready to sacrifice their lives for his glory. They were resolved to carry out his behests, regardless of consequences.

Not less important than the efficient management of his territorial possessions was another part of his policy, which was the retention in his service and favour of as large a number of followers as possible, and of men of ability both military and civilian. There was an emulous zeal to join his service. Shivaji was an extemely good judge of character and ability. He was deft in assigning the right duty to the right man, and wherever possible this was done by Shivaji in person. He never let slip an opportunity of extending his patronage to a brave soldier or a capable civil officer. Men of honour and ability swarmed round him from all parts, and Shivaji left no stone unturned to infuse his own spirit of enthusiasm in them, and convert them into efficient instruments of the great cause looming before him in the future.

In a short time, he was at the head of ten thonsand Mavalis and three thousand horse, including the scattered cavalry left behind by Shahaji, which was now mustered together. There were civilian officers deputed by Shahaji and others nominated by Dadaji Kondadev, who still continued under Shivaji and rendered him every assistance. They were nerved to action and fired with enthusiasm by the exalted spirit with which they saw their master dash forward for the glorious stake of national independence. They recognized that talent for enterprise and genius for invention which swayed Shivaji's comparatively youthful form. They obeyed his least wishes. Shivaji on his part was not slow to honour and appreciate, where honour and appreciation were due. Acknowledgments of merit and promotion followed in quick succession. For the present, Shivaji was resolved that the idea of Swarajya or independence should be commensurate with the boundaries of his jahgir, and with a view to instil this idea, and as a foretaste of the future, he appointed Shamraj Nilkant Rajekar (Kanzekar)[1] to the rank and office of *Peshwa* or prime minister, Balkrishna Dikshit to that of *Muzumdar*, (acountant general), Sonopant to that of *Dabir* (foreign secretary) and Raghunath Ballal Bokil to that of *Sabnis* (paymaster). Besides these, Yessaji Kunk, Tanaji Malusare and Baji Fasalkar were appointed to the command of the Mavali troops, Shivaji himself being the commander-in-chief of his army. The honour of *Sirnobut* (marshal of the royal drum) had not yet been conferred upon any individual, though some chronicles describe the appointment as having been made as early as this period.[2] In short, though Shivaji's power had not yet extended beyond the natural boundaries of his jahgir, the foundations were laid and the machinery of self-government was already in motion, to work with an added impetus, when the outline was more fully filled in and the entire superstructure was complete in all its parts..

1 The Shivdigvijay gives 1643 as the date of the appointment, and this seems to have been accepted by Mr. Rajwade; but such an early date does not seem probable. In the bakhar of Chitragupta the name of the Peshwa is given as Sankraji. Raghunath Ballal Sabnis was probably Raghunath Ballal Korde.

2 According to Sabhasad and Chitragupta, the Maratha commander of the Supa district, Tukoji Chor, had the honour of the Sirnobut conferred on him. But the same authorities record a little later that the honour was conferred upon Mankoji Dahatonde (*alias* Dutonde, *alias* Datavda).

Foot note to page 91:—The passage from Sabhasad referred to by Mr. Rajwade occurs at page 7 of that bakhar. It literally seems to mean that "the Maval deshmukhs were bound and subdued and the lawless raiders amongst them were killed." But the passage has been differently interpreted, the word "*bound*" being interpreted as "bound to the cause," or "united." The twelve Mavals referred to in the passage are in the neighbourhood of Poona. They are little valleys generally named after the rivulet irrigating the mountain declivity in each case. They are (1) Rohidkhore, (2) Velvand, (3) Muse, (4) Muthe, (5) Jor, (6) Kanad, (7) Shivthar (8) Murrum, (9) Powd, (10) Gunjan, (11) Bhor and (12) Pavan. There were similarly other Mavals in the neighbourhood of Junnar, such as Shivner, Bhimner, Ghodner, Parner, Jamner etc. (Vide Sardesai's *Marathi Riyasat*, 1907, p.166). These Mavals have the characteristic suffix *khore* or *ner*. As to the fact of Shivaji's seal being found impressed on a document published by Mr. Rajwade in his volume XV and dated as early as the year 1639 A. D., and the inferences drawn from the date and the language of the motto of the seal ("This is the seal of Shivaji, the son of Shahaji, whose glory waxes over the world like the crescent glory of the moon") by historians like Messrs. Kincaid and Sardesai, it seems to us that the use of such a seal even at so early a date cannot be taken *per se* as an evidence of a set purpose to inaugurate an independent kingdom, since it was customary for every jahgirdar to have his own seal; and the language of the motto might be taken as a piece of conventional extravagance However it is important in the light of other circumstances as furnishing an index to the hidden motives in the mind of Shivaji, and possibly also of Shahaji, viz: the irrepressible desire for founding an independent monarchy. Beyond this there is no warrant to infer that the empire-building actually began as early as 1639.

CHAPTER VII

DEVELOPMENT OF SWARAJYA

IN the last chapter we attempted to trace a faint outline of the pioneer labours of Shivaji as the founder of a sovereign power. In this chapter we shall follow the further expansion and development of his boldly conceived plans.

The country enclosing the jahgir domain of Shivaji was, as we have already observed, in the hands of ambitious nobles, who owed more or less a sort of hereditary allegiance to Bijapur, but for the most part were engaged in adventurous warfare among themselves. On the southern bank of the Nira, as far to the east as Shirval and southwards up to the mountains that skirt the upper courses of the Krishna, a petty deshmukh of the Maval regions, Bandal by name, held despotic sway. His head-quarters were the fort of Rohida. He harboured an ancient grudge against Shivaji and envied his rise. He always maintained the defences of his fortress in a condition of high efficiency and had a strong garrison. When fort after fort fell before Shivaji in his victorious career, Bandal was resolved that his fort at any rate should form an exception. He looked moreover with greedy eyes upon the fair fields around the fort of Purandar. When Purandar was surrendered to Shivaji, Bandal was naturally all the more anxious for the safety of his fort.

The uplands of the western ghats, from the Krishna to the Warna, acknowledged the rule of Rajah Chandrarao More. Javli was the head-quarters of this chief and the fortress of Hashamgad was in his power. Shivaji's arts of conciliation were not likely to succeed with him. With his large feudal forces he defied everybody.

Wai was under a *mokassadar* of the Bijapur government, who also had Pandavgad, Kamalgad and other forts under him. Another great Mahomedan officer had charge of Kolhapur and the important fort of Panhalla in its neighbourhood.

Kalyan had once been under the Nizamshahi kings of Ahmednagar. By the treaty made with the Moguls in 1636, Bijapur had acquired possession of this strategical position. The district was divided into two parts and administered by separate officers. The northern half extending from Kalyan-Bhiwandi to Nagotna was under a Mahomedan noble of high family, 'Mullana' Ahmed by name, whose head-quarters were at Kalyan-Bhiwandi. This was an extensive tract of land and comprised many of the hill forts on the ghats and the lowlands beneath. These fortresses were as a rule rarely kept in an efficient condition. The southern half of the province was under the sway of an Abyssinian nobleman. It was, indeed, in some sort, a jahgir which his Abyssinian forefathers had enjoyed from the Nizamshahi government, in acknowledgment of the services of the naval contingent maintained by them for the defence of the commerce on the western sea and the conveyance of Mecca pilgrims to and from the Red Sea. Not that it was a hereditary jahgir in its origin. The best naval officer of the Abyssinian corps in the service of the Nizamshahi state generally enjoyed this jahgir with the style and title of *vizier*. This high admiral had a staff of officers and sailors, who were generally of Abyssinian origin. Thus it came to pass that in course of time there arose a small but powerful colony of these Abyssinians on the Konkan littoral. The head-quarters of the Abyssinian naval squadron was Danda-Rajpuri. There was a little island off this harbour, which was strongly fortified. This island became famous under the name of Janjira. At the time under review Fatteh Khan was the high admiral of the Abyssinian corps. He had many forts under him, the principal of which were those of Tala, Ghosala and Rairi. These forts were all in charge of Maratha officers.

The Bijapur government had for a long time ruled over parts of the Konkan. That government had ceded considerable districts in jahgir to the *deshmukhs* of the

Deccan and the jahgirs had been handed down from father to son. They absorbed the major part of the revenue among themselves. The chief command of the harbour towns of Dabhol (Dabul), Anjenwel, Ratnagiri and Rajapur was however still centred in the hands of government officers, who collected the revenue in the surrounding territory. Predominant over the rest of these deshmukhs was the Sawant family of Wadi. This Deshmukh was virtually master of the mountainous regions on the frontiers of Goa, which owned the rule of the Portuguese. Next in power under Sawant was Surve, the deshmukh of Shringarpur.[1] On account of the isolated state of their jahgir the Surves were comparatively independent like the Mores of Javli.

Such was the political condition of the neighbouring jahgirs and fiefs, when Shivaji launched forth upon his venturous enterprise of enlarging his dominions, and under the circumstances it was perfectly natural that he should direct his first energies against these fief-holders. As for the *ghat-matha* regions and the lowlands beneath, Shivaji was already, thanks to the co-operation of his Mavali friends, in full possession of all the requisite information and had made the deshmukhs his own. For a similar purpose in order to sound the views of the Konkan deshmukhs and governors of forts, as also to make reconnaissances in that region and announce his general intention of declaring his independence of the Mahomedan government, Shivaji despatched Brahman and Prabhu officers of acknowledged merit as diplomats. They traversed the Konkan in its various parts and conciliated the sympathy and adherence of several deshmukhs and Maratha nobles.

Shivaji had by this time a very large following and several more were ready to throw in their lot with him. The difficulty was how to maintain this steadily growing number of followers. The revenues accruing from the terri-

---

[1] Grant Duff gives Dalvi as the family name of this chief. Chietni, Sabhasad and Chitragupta style him Surve. We think Surve was the cognomen and Dalvi an agnomen of this family.

tory already in his possession fell far short of his growing requirements. Prompt payment is the secret of military obedience. A large increase of cavalry and infantry was a *sine qua non* to the enterprise he had entered upon. The forts recently captured entailed a vast expenditure for their defence, while their safety from future assault on the part of the enemy depended on a large supply of food and provisions being constantly maintained for the emergencies of war. All this meant money, and it was essential that the scarcity of specie should no longer come in the way of his aspirations. Shivaji therefore set about to procure money. He commenced to borrow on a large scale from wealthy capitalists, and against those, who would not willingly part with their gold, compulsion was resorted to. There is no denying the fact that there was a grave injustice in this. But Shivaji believed that the great cause he had embarked upon was to the advantage of all and rendered imperative a large accumulation of capital.

While in this anxiety he received news that Mullana Ahmed, the *subhedar* of Kalyan, was forwarding a large sum of money to the Bijapur government by way of Wai, through the Konkan. Resolved to intercept this precious treasure and divert it to his own ambitious purposes, Shivaji set off with 300 horse and the flower of his Mavali infantry and falling upon the convoying party dispersed them in no time, transferring the precious treasure immediately to the fort of Rajgad.[1] The convoying force deputed by the subhedar was by no means contemptible, for the subhedar had every reason to fear the emergency of the treasure being cut off by Shivaji or the marauding chiefs of the neighbourhood. In the contest that ensued, Shivaji lost about ten of his followers and had something like 25 men wounded. On Mullana's side about 25 were killed and a hundred wounded. With his wonted liberality, Shivaji rewarded the gallant soldiers who had rendered him this

[1] According to the Shivdigvijay the convoy was looted by Yessaji Kunk and Tanaji Malusare under Shivaji's orders.

useful service and devised means for the maintenance of the families of those who were killed or wounded. This fresh proof of his liberality still further enhanced his popularity.

This event was followed by the outbreak of open hostilities with Mullana. Abaji Sondev who was despatched against him captured Kalyan by a surprise attack, seizing all its forts, and taking Mullana prisoner. No sooner did Shivaji hear the joyful news than he proceeded in person to Kalyan, and liberating Mullana sent him with all honour to Bijapur. Now in the assault on the fort, Abaji had seized upon the daughter-in-law of Mullana.[1] Abaji informed Shivaji that he had made prisoner a woman of distinguished beauty and prayed that Shivaji might accept her as a fit person for his zenana. Shivaji bade him introduce her in open durbar; and when the beautiful lady was introduced, apparelled in the loveliest raiment, Shivaji smiled and exclaimed, "Would that my mother had equalled her in beauty, for then he who was born of her might have been as beautiful!" These words caused great amazement in the assembly. To those gathered there such self-restraint appeared truly marvellous. Shivaji continued his speech: "It is written that he who hankers after victory, should beware of love's meshes and other people's women. It was this which brought low the proudest towers of strength like Ravana of Lanka. What then of poor mortals like ourselves? Let the king look upon all persons as his children." These words of wisdom created a great impression upon the assembly. No circumstance could have stamped more vividly upon their minds an idea of the magnanimity and high worth of their master. The truth dawned upon their minds that they had to deal with a man whose rectitude would never swerve an inch, and in whose service no act of iniquity on the part of his followers would ever find countenance. Shivaji treated the lady with great

[1] The version of the Shivdigvijay is that she was a daughter of Mullana and had been openly made over to Abaji by her father for a sum of money. The text follows Chitnis, page 34, which is corroborated by the Tarikh-i-Shivaji, page 14 (a)

consideration, presented her with ornaments and robes of honour befitting her dignity, and sent her with a proper escort to her father-in-law at Bijapur.

Abaji Sondev having earned the grateful acknowledgment of his generous master for the conquest of Kalyan was rewarded with the governorship of that important province. The reformed system of revenue was speedily introduced here, and the ryots oppressed under Mahomedan misrule now breathed a new atmosphere of hope and confidence. The old village organizations and institutions that had disappeared during years of confusion and anarchy were revived. The annual grants once conceded to temples and Brahmans were restored, and those which had remained despite the adverse circumstances were confirmed. The poor Hindu subjects were gratified at this beneficent and auspicious commencement of Shivaji's regime, and his fame as a merciful and benignant ruler spread far and wide.

This was the beginning of Shivaji's great triumphs. A spirit of noble exaltation and emulation now entirely possessed the hearts of his followers. Mullana having been so cheaply got out of the way, Shivaji's further career was signalized by the capture of fort after fort. The officers of the different forts were won over where possible; if they proved obstinate in their opposition, a surprise attack followed, leading inevitably to the capture of the fort. The Mavalis and warrior chiefs under Shivaji were as a rule armed with full information concerning the intricacies and vulnerable points of the different fortresses, and where this information was lacking, it could be procured from local experts. The sentinel guards of the hill-forts could be corrupted where other means failed, or the local contractors of supply outside the fort, who undertook to provide the thatching and roof-material against the expected monsoon for the buildings within, could be won over to the side of the assailants against the garrison who employed them. In this manner Shivaji's warriors could enter a fort, carrying on their heads bundles of hay, under which their swords were concealed, and with the assistance of the sentinels who were already in the secret, they could make an onslaught on the rest and conquer the fort. By this plan of operations, the forts of Kangari, Tung, Tikoni, Lohgad, Rajmachi, Kuwari, Bhorup, Ghangad, Kelna, Mahuli and others were captured. The deshmukhs in this territory who were a perennial source of oppression to the ryots were reduced to allegiance, either by conciliation or by force, and the Maval region was delivered finally from their tyranny. The Hindu population of these districts hailed with delight the advent of a capable Hindu ruler, who put an end to the rule of Islam and the reign of terror and license that had accompanied it. They had a foretaste of freedom under Shivaji's banner and rejoiced in the unrestrained exercise of their religious rites.

The Hindu inhabitants of the southern half of the province of Kalyan which was under their Abyssinian ruler now envied the happier lot of their brethren in the northern half of the province. There were at the time two Maratha officers of the rank of Jamedar, Sodawlekar and Kodawlekar, in the Abyssinian service. They sent word to Shivaji that they were quite tired of their dependence on their Abyssinian oppressors and undertook to give over the fortresses of Tala and Ghosala to Shivaji, should he be pleased to make an expedition into the Konkan. They held out the prospect of a large accession of territory with the conquest of these forts and the secession of a large number of Maratha combatants from the service of the Abyssinians. Under these favourable auspices, Shivaji turned his attention in that direction, with the result that the fortresses above mentioned fell before him. With them was conquered the neighbouring fort of Surgad and the low-lands commanded by its guns. It was however difficult to maintain his firm hold over this conquest, for the Sidi or Abyssinian ruler was a powerful chief. On this account, Shivaji erected new fortifications, the chief of which was at Birwadi, upon a spot prospected for the purpose. The fortifications of Rairi were also strengthened, and the fort of Lingana was built thereupon. This fort was afterwards further entrenched and became famous under the name of Raigad. In all these forts Shivaji maintained his own garrisons.

It was in this campaign that Shivaji obtained his famous sword Bhavani. As Shivaji was returning from a visit to the temple of Harihareshwar, he was told that there was a famous long sword worth 300 *hons* (pagodas) with a chief, Gowalkar Sawant by name. It was suggested to Shivaji that he should wrest this sword by force. Shivaji's reply was characteristic. He said, "A brave man should never covet what belongs to another. You will remember the puranic legend about that precious stone called the Syamantmani. The feuds that arose from the theft of that diamond required all the energies of the Lord Shri Krishna to settle. We poor mortals had better not raise such storms for trifles.' Impressed by his austere attitude his people kept silence. Now while these conversations were going on in Shivaji's camp, the Sawant received independent advice from his ministers to seize the opportunity for conciliating Shivaji and seal the compact of amity by making him present of the precious sword. The Sawant saw the wisdom of this proposal and seeking an interview with Shivaji presented him with the sword. Shivaji was highly gratified with the gift and in return presented to the Sawant, as an earnest of his good will, a purse of 300 hons and a robe of honour, and also received him into his service. Shivaji, it may be said without exaggeration, simply adored this sword. He never started on an expedition without it. He gave it the name of his tutelary deity Bhavani. From the time of the acquisition of this sword, he never knew defeat in any campaign. This he attributed to the sword, and he loved and adored it as something divine. During the nine days preceding the Dasara, dedicated to the worship of the goddess Bhawani, he placed the sword on the consecrated altar next to the image of the goddess and worshipped it as a visible favour from Heaven. On the tenth day, the auspicious festal day of the Dasara, he used to take it up devoutly from the altar and with this Bhavani blade in his hand set out upon his campaign.

In the course of the Konkan campaign, Shivaji attacked Rajapur. This was a town under the Abyssinians. Shivaji established a strict blockade and prepared to pillage the town. On the other hand the *kamavisdar* or civil commissioner in charge of the town made some show of resistance, but being thoroughly worsted had finally to yield. Shivaji levied contributions from the rich merchants and wealthy citizens of the town. But no material wealth Shivaji found in this town could compare with that sterling specimen of humanity, the loyal Balaji Avji, whose accession to Shivaji's side dates from this expedition against Rajapur. The father of Balaji Avji was Abaji Hari Chitre, once a *dewan* or minister under the Abyssinian chief. In a fit of passion occasioned by a trifling offence the Abyssinian put Abaji Hari and his brother to death and ordered the women and children in their family to be transported to Muscat and sold into slavery. This dire sentence was on the point of being executed. However, Abaji's wife, the mother of Balaji, was a woman of remarkable prudence and sagacity. She won over the sailors of the ship which was destined for Muscat and induced them to take them to Rajapur and in the mart of that town sell them as slaves. At Rajapur was her brother, Visaji Shankar, a merchant of great local influence. Visaji bought them without letting the sailors know that they were his relations. The eldest son of this lady was Balaji and the other two were Chimnaji and Shamji. Visaji gave a good education to these three children. Balaji was a *karkun* or clerk under a revenue officer in charge of a *kasba*. On hearing the news of Shivaji's arrival in the Konkan, he wrote to him detailing the tragic misfortunes of his family. Shivaji was filled with admiration at Balaji's hand-writing as exhibited in that letter and wrote in reply that he would with pleasure entertain Balaji as a *karkun* in his service

Upon this Bàlaji replied that he laboured under considerable obligations to his uncle and until that debt was cleared he could not think of joining Shivaji. On Shivaji's arrival at Rajapur he inquired after Balaji Avji and ordered him to be brought into his presence. Balaji was accordingly brought before Shivaji. Balaji's mother, unable to conjecture the cause, was filled with terror and came with maternal solicitude before the conqueror, prostrating herself before him and narrating the tragedy of her life. Shivaji was overwhelmed with deep emotion at the recital of this narrative, so full of pathos, called up her two younger sons, and gave her an assurance as to their safety, entreating her to look upon himself as a fourth son, and to send them all to try their fortunes in his service. The good opinion that Shivaji had formed about Balaji from his hand-writing was greatly heightened by the personal interview. Pleased with his brilliant talents and the honourable precedents of his family he appointed Balaji to the post of *Chitnis* or Private Secretary. Chimnaji being versed in accounts was appointed to the Audit Department, and the youngest of the three, Shamji, was placed in charge of the stores at fort Raigad.

Balaji Avji was in the highest favour with Shivaji. He was the first person in his confidence and the repository of the most secret of his plans. This confidence was the well-merited reward of his unimpeachable loyalty and uprightness. Despatches of the greatest consequence and significance passed through his hands. Possessed of great activity of mind and considerable literary ability, he could at once grasp the vaguest thoughts floating in the mind of his royal master and express them with a lucidity, appositeness and precision that was simply astonishing. An anecdote told about him, whether true or false, is very characteristic of the man. In the course of a busy campaign he had received orders from Shivaji to write despatches on some affair of moment. Balaji's time was somehow occupied with other urgent affairs, and until night-fall he found no leisure to carry out the mandate. At night Shivaji summoned him to his presence and inquired whether the despatches were ready. Balaji was in great perplexity. He was quite aware that if he were to confess his fault, Shivaji would make an example of him for inadvertence and negligence as regards his express orders. He thought he must somehow tide over the present difficulty, and without any sign of dismay replied in the affirmative. Shivaji's next order was that he should read it aloud. Balaji opened his desk and, taking out a blank piece of paper, pretended to read out the despatch from the blank paper, and he did this without halting or stammering for a word. Shivaji was pleased with the supposed despatch and praised him for the deftness and skill with which he supposed him to have executed it. But this was too much for the torch-bearer who was holding up the light on the paper. He burst into a fit of laughter, and on Shivaji's inquiring the cause, he let the cat out of the bag. Balaji had to confess his fault and explain how he had no leisure to write out the despatches. Gratified with the marvellous proof of Balaji's powers of memory, Shivaji for once excused this dereliction on the part of his trusty secretary.

FOOT NOTE to page 116:—The Bhawani was a "*firang*" i. e. a sword of European (Portuguese or Spanish) make. It was a long straight-bladed sword, probably from the famous armoury of Toledo in Spain.

CHAPTER VIII
SHAHAJI ENTRAPPED

THE disturbances caused by Shivaji in the Bijapur territory had been overlooked for two or three years; but the Kalyan affair was the last straw, and even that apathetic and indulgent government had now to bestir itself. For the plunder of the royal treasure on the way to the capital, the conquest of Kalyan and the out-lying forts, and the rumours that were now bruited abroad about Shivaji's future projects had caused great consternation and raised an out-cry against the lethargy of the government. The sultan, Mahomed Adil Shaha, hastened to the wrong conclusion that the master mind of Shahaji must be at the bottom of this affair. Nor was this suspicion quite unreasonable. On the retirement of Randulla Khan from the Karnatic, Shahaji had succeeded to the government of that province, and having in a short time won popularity and affection from the grateful population both by his conciliatory spirit and consummate statesmanship, as described in the second chapter, he was now half way towards the establishment of an independent sovereignty, under nominal allegiance to the Adil Shahi dynasty. Added to this was the fact that the country which was the scene of Shivaji's incipient activities was one which in quite recent times had owned the practically absolute authority of Shahaji. It was natural under these circumstances that Mahomed Adil Shaha should have jumped to the conclusion that Shahaji was the real author and inspirer of his son's rebellion.

But for a time the Adil Shahi sultan could do nothing more than nurse his suspicion in secret. To declare open hostilities against Shahaji was really not in his power; but to despatch a sufficient force against Shivaji was under the circumstances quite as inexpedient. Such an overt act of hostility against his son might possibly precipitate the growing ambition of Shahaji into active defiance, and Shahaji's defiance might, between the Mogul on the north and the rebellious chieftains in the south, jeopardize the very foundations of the Adil Shahi empire. The sultan therefore decided that the only way open to him was to make peaceful overtures to his powerful vassal and pointed out to Shahaji how regrettable it was that the son of a loyal vassal like him should turn traitor, fall upon the sultan's forts all round his jahgir in Poona, and end with the atrocious seizure of Kalyan. He enjoined him in his own interest to see to it that Shivaji was adequately chastised for such rebellious conduct and compelled to give up his marauding career and make submission as became a loyal citizen and vassal of the Adil Shahi state. This injunction culminated in threats of reprisals against Shahaji in person and his son, and a hint that if Shahaji was not able to manage his son, he should hand him over to the Bijapur government.

Shahaji replied that Shivaji was no longer in his power. He was not responsible for his evil ways. He was himself a loyal servant of the state and had no art or part in Shivaji's doings. Should any direct charge be made against him, he would come to the sultan's presence to answer in person. It was open to His Majesty to move his forces against Shivaji, put him under arrest or wreak his royal will in any manner upon him. He would not oppose it. It was for His Majesty to reduce Shivaji to allegiance, and he had nothing more to say on the subject. Such was the tenor of Shahaji's reply, but it brought no conviction to the sultan's distrustful mind. He sent secret despatches to Baji Ghorpade of Mudhol to procure the arrest of Shahaji by stratagem. Only thus he thought he could bend Shivaji to his will.

Such is the traditional account of the cause of Shahaji's incarceration as handed down to posterity by Chitnis and other Marathi chronicles, and as accepted by all leading historians from Grant Duff to Kincaid. But the Jedhe chronology (page 179) says with characteristic brevity that Shahaji was arrested near Jinji, along with the

Mavali deshmukh Kanoji Naik Jedhe of Rohida by Mustapha Khan. The Basatin-i-Salatin states that Shahaji was arrested by Baji Ghorpade and Yeshwant Rao Asad-Khani by treachery under orders from Mustapha Khan for disobedience. It would seem from these authorities that the neighbourhood of Jinji was the scene of the arrest and that Mustapha was in authority, and got Baji Ghorpade to arrest Shahaji for non-compliance with his orders. Prof. Jadunath Sarkar quotes a Bijapur chronicle, the *Muhammadnamah* (pp. 371–372) to show that Mustapha was the Adil Shahi commander-in-chief in the south and that Shahaji was in charge of siege-operations around Jinji. Shahaji wanted to retire to his own country leaving the siege-works incomplete and said he would do so without writing for permission, when Mustapha got him arrested and had him sent to Bijapur. As will be seen from a foot-note at page 47 in the second chapter, this version is also followed by Modak in his History of the Adil Shahi Dynasty (Marathi). Modak constantly copies the Basatin-i-Salatin and the Adil Shahi chronicles like the Muhammadnamah. But the Jedhe chronology is an altogether independent piece of evidence. However if Baji Ghorpade acted treacherously upon the orders of Mustapha Khan, it is just possible that the latter acted upon the orders of the sultan.

Whatever the original reason for the arrest of Shahaji might have been, the sultan treated the captive as a hostage for the submission of his son. Naturally, therefore, have the Marathi chronicles represented the whole event in this light. Incidentally it may be remarked that here is presented to us an array of facts that establishes beyond doubt the attitude of Shahaji as regards the movement his great son had entered upon. There is first the presence of Mavali chiefs in Shahaji's camp. There is the fact that at this particular time of his career Shahaji wanted to retire to his country in defiance of orders from his superiors. There is lastly the fact that immediately after his liberation he bound the Jedhe family (Vide Jedhe chronology, pp. 179-180) by solemn oaths to serve Shivaji in all his wars, even against the Mogul and the Adil Shahi armies.

How Ghorpade effected his treacherous object has already been described in the second chapter. Shahaji was brought to Bijapur and enjoined to put a stop to Shivaji's rebellious acts. Other nobles of the court were asked to exhort Shahaji to the same purpose. But to all of them Shahaji returned a reply in the same strain as before. At length the sultan compelled Shahaji to compose in his royal presence an urgent letter to Shivaji, calling upon him to come straightway to Bijapur and make a complete restitution of all forts and territories seized from the government, and apprising him of the forlorn condition to which he had been reduced by Shivaji's disobedience.

The receipt of this letter and paternal mandate presented a great dilemma before Shivaji's mind. On the one hand it was unfilial to disobey his father and desert him in the perilous situation in which he found himself. On the other hand obedience to his father's command meant disgrace, forfeiture and surrender. To surrender the hard-won forts and territories, to declare submission and vassalage to the Mahomedan despots of the Deccan, to leave his great designs half-executed were proposals from which his nobler instincts recoiled. And what could he gain in exchange? That, the hatred of which had been the main spring of all his actions, a state of sordid and servile dependence upon the powers of Islam! In this disconsolate frame of mind he was observed by his wife, Sayibai, who inquiring into the cause and learning the reason, replied to Shivaji's request for advice that it was not for a woman to advise in affairs of such moment, that Shivaji indeed had captains and ministers more qualified to give an opinion, but so far as her home-spun wit as a simple woman went, she thought it nobler to pursue the great design of liberty and independence and freedom of worship. She asked him to act with unshaken faith in Providence; that private affections must give place to political forces; and that Shahaji himself would have applauded such a plan, were he not an exile on foreign soil. This was some re-assurance to Shivaji's perplexed mind. His mother, ministers and officers concurred in this line of reasoning. Strengthened by these re-assurances Shivaji replied to Shahaji's letter that his coming in person to Bijapur would serve no useful purpose and he was not prepared to surrender the conquests he had made. They must follow–the father and the son –the divergent lines of fortune ordained for them by inevitable destiny.

This letter was submitted by Shahaji to the Adil Shahi sultan, with fresh importunities that he might be now set at liberty, and that the sultan might take such action against Shivaji as he deemed proper. But the sultan was not satisfied with these representations of Shahaji and persisted in the belief that Shahaji was the secret instigator of his son's rebellion. He thought that the direst punishment in his power must be inflicted to curb his obstinacy. The sultan ordered a wall to be built with a stone niche just large enough to accommodate a person seated. Shahaji was confined in this niche, which was all but built in, except for a single opening, and he was threatened that even this opening would be permanently closed in with masonry, if Shivaji did not make his submission within a given time. Twice during the day he was released for a few minutes from the niche and again confined in that living tomb.

The news of this horrible punishment inflicted upon his father by the enraged sultan came to Shivaji's ears and filled him with sorrow. The thought that the impending death of his father should be due to his acts was most maddening! His high ambition and enterprise had thus far not provoked any censure from his father, and this he had so long interpreted as a mark of his acquiescence and even of his approval. Inspired by this silent sympathy and approbation, he had zealously carried forward his designs, never dreaming they would lead him to such a tragic issue. For he was sure of the great prestige of his father in the Karnatic and never imagined that he would ever be at the sultan's mercy. The treachery of Ghorpade had led to this unexpected denouement.

It is critical occasions like these that test the mettle of a truly heroic spirit. The crisis brought forth the most eminent qualities of Shivaji's character. His unswerving filial devotion was in the first instance put to a glorious proof. Had he been merely selfish and greedy of power, he might have recked little of the safety of his father. For in the very age in which Shivaji lived, Aurangzeb was soon to exchange a father's love for a throne. Had Shivaji been governed by a similar strain of ambition, why think of voluntarily surrendering a power and sovereignty built up with such patient toil from the debris of an alien empire, merely to rescue his father from his impending fate? But Shivaji was not a man of such sordid ambition. Another great virtue of Shivaji that was tried on this occasion was his iron determination not to leave half done what he had so well begun, for all the dangers and obstacles in his way. His filial duty and affections and his ambitious labours for the political emancipation of his countrymen now seemed to be at cross purposes. One seemed to demand the sacrifice of the other. It was left to Shivaji's statesmanship and resourcefulness to steer straight between Scylla and Charybdis, without the least detriment to his ambition or the pious affection due to his father.

Up to this time Shivaji had maintained the most friendly relations with the Moguls. One obvious reason for this was the fact that it was highly inexpedient to be at war simultaneously with two Mahomedan powers. Besides the provinces on the Mogul frontier were well-secured and fortified. The Mogul emperor himself must have thought fit in the interest of expediency to have friendly relations with Shahaji, of whose valour he had a foretaste, and with his son Shivaji. Lastly Shivaji must have looked upon this power as an asylum in reserve for any extreme emergency.

Apprised of the intentions of the Moguls with regard to the Deccan powers, Shivaji saw that the temper of the Mogul emperor was such that any aid he might solicit against Bijapur would be granted without demur. With this knowledge of the currents of political thought, Shivaji decided to assume a supplicatory attitude towards the padi shah, invoking his patronage and instant aid against the danger Shahaji ran of being immured in the fortress wall, and offering, both for himself and Shahaji, to enter into the Mogul service. Shivaji petitioned that the part Shahaji had formerly played in arresting the onward march of the Mogul standards in the Deccan might be generously forgiven and urged that in saving the life of such a distinguished general the emperor would strengthen the foundations of the Mogul power in the Deccan and could count upon the grateful assistance of Shahaji and himself. Shahajahan had personal proofs of Shahaji's dash and daring and from time to time had heard favourable reports of Shivaji's valorous enterprise. Such towers of strength he thought he could not afford to despise in his future plans against Bijapur and Golconda. With these views, he graciously complied with Shivaji's request.[1]

The Emperor Shahajahan accordingly sent peremptory orders to the Bijapur durbar that the Rajah Shahaji Bhonsle be immediately set at liberty.[2] Shivaji was informed that

---

[1] Shivaji did not negotiate directly with the emperor at Agra, but with his son Prince Murad, governor of the Deccan. This is amply borne out by the *Parasnis MS.* and Appendix A at page 149 of Mr Kincaid's history, where by a strange mistake a letter under the seal of Murad is described as Shahajahan's letter to Shahaji. From one of the letters of the Mogul authorities it is clear that Shivaji sent Ragho Pandit (probably Raghunath Ballal Korde) to treat about the restoration of the deshmukh rights over Junnar and Sangamner which had been formerly granted to Shahaji (Vide note on page 27, Chapter II).

[2] Prof. Sarkar thinks that notwithstanding these Mogul promises the Mogul government did not probably in the end actually intercede for Shahaji.

the imperial court had forgiven Shahaji's past offences and were prepared to admit him again to military service under the empire, and as to Shivaji himself they were prepared to grant him a mansab or command of 5000 horse. The Adil Shahi sultan dared not despise the peremptory mandate of the Mogul. The tenure of his power was precarious and depended on a recent treaty between himself and the Moguls. In displeasing the latter power, he was sure to incur the gravest risks to his independence. Shahaji was, therefore, released on his giving sureties for his loyalty in the future, but he was ordered to remain at Bijapur as it were on parole.[1] This event took place in 1649. For four years thereafter Shahaji remained in enforced inaction at Bijapur. He tried every expedient to get permission to march to the Karnatic, and his friends tried to intercede for him, but the sultan was inexorable. At length after four years when it became obvious that the slackening of government control in the absence of the powerful grip of Shahaji had encouraged all the elements of anarchy and unrest in the province of the Karnatic to come to a head, and it was felt that none but a brave and experienced commander like him could be safely trusted to deal with the rebellious naiks and deshmukhs of the south, he again received orders to march to the scene of his power and greatness. But before proceeding southwards he was compelled to pledge his word that he would in no way molest the treacherous Ghorpade of Mudhol or his jahgir. The sultan did not content himself with this promise; but further to reconcile them to each other and induce them

[1] Some of the bakhars attribute the credit of Shahaji's eliverance to the intercessory aid of his friends Randulla Khan and Murarpant. It is said that these veteran ministers represented to the sultan that the cruel execution of such a tried and experienced commander would redound to the discredit of the state and cause disaffection among the sultan's vassals. There is no ground to believe such a story, for both these ministers seem to have been dead by this time. The tradition of the strange device by which Randulla Khan attempted to intercede for his friend is referred to in a foot-note in the second chapter. Prof. Jadunath Sarkar is inclined to think that Malhar Ramrao Chitnis is right when he ascribes the release of Shahaji to the mediation of Randulla Khan.

to let bygones be bygones, he got them to make an exchange of their inam and jahgir lands. In accordance with the terms of this exchange, the Ghorpade gave to Shahaji all his jahgir in the Karnatic and received from him all his rights and titles in the district of Karhad.

But Shahaji did not bury the past in oblivion. No sooner did he reach the Karnatic than he sent word to Shivaji that as a true son of Shahaji it was left to him to wreak vengeance on Baji Ghorpade. In fact this was an unnecessary spur to a willing horse. Shivaji hated the Ghorpade with more than a mortal hate and was only waiting for an opportunity to avenge on him his dastardly conduct towards his father. But he had to wait for nearly eight or nine years for this consummation of his wishes. About 1661, the chiefs of Sawantwadi, Khem Sawant Desai and Lakham Sawant Desai, called for the help of Bijapur against Shivaji, and upon that occasion the services of Baji Ghorpade were lent to them by the Bijapur government. Ghorpade marched from Bijapur into the Konkan at the head of his forces, but before descending to the sea-board he paid a visit to his jahgir town of Mudhol. No sooner did Shivaji hear tidings of these movements of Baji Ghorpade than he swooped down from Vishalgad and by forced marches suddenly presented himself before Mudhol. A desperate encounter took place between Shivaji's and Ghorpade's forces and in the mêlee Ghorpade was slain. Mudhol was laid waste with fire and sword. All the kith and kin of Ghorpade perished or were seized and executed. The massacre is said to have reached three thousand.[1] Never before or since did such cruelty stain Shivaji's wars. Savage as the punishment meted to the

---

1 A son of Baji Ghorpade, named Maloji, managed to make his escape during this crisis. This Maloji afterwards rose to great eminence and succeeded to the paternal jahgir. At a subsequent date Shivaji attempted to conciliate him and in a letter addressed from Bhaganagar (Hyderabad) made overtures to him to unite with the Bhonsle power and jointly turn the scale against the Mahomedans. But Maloji remained obdurate and to the end served his Adilshahi sultan.

Ghorpade family was, it illustrates the price Shivaji considered must be paid for the treachery which had all but extinguished before its time the glorious career of Shahaji. It illustrates above all his keen sense of filial duty.[1]

During the period of five years, 1649 to 1653, when Shahaji was at Bijapur on parole, Shivaji abstained strictly from any act of hostility against Bijapur. Nor was it possible for him to take the offensive against the Moguls, whose friendship had so recently stood him in such good stead, and an estrangement with whom was again likely to endanger the life of Shahaji. He had indeed to congratulate himself that the Bijapur Government was so far cowed by the threat of Mogul intervention that they did not insist on his surrendering the conquered forts and provinces as they might have done by fresh threats to Shahaji, who, while he lived on parole at Bijapur, had constantly this sword of Damocles hanging over his head. Shivaji turned this period of enforced quietude to good account, overhauling the conquered fortresses and completing the revenue settlements in his new provinces. The Bijapur government seems at this period to have been under the impression that any further protests against Shivaji would directly have the effect of making him throw in his lot with the Moguls and with their active support or connivance renew his depredations upon their territory on a still more extended scale.

---

[1] From a letter of Shivaji to his father (Vide Kincaid vol I, page 175,) it would seem that the latter gave a clear mandate for vengeance against Baji Ghorpade. It was Shahaji himself who informed Shivaji about the proposed movement of Baji Ghorpade to carry succour to Lakham Sawant and Khem Sawant of Wadi.

CHAPTER IX

RELATIONS WITH THE MOGULS. 1650-57

THE alliance between Shivaji and the Moguls was destined to be a deceptive move in Shivaji's game of politics. By this diplomatic stroke he had cut a gordian knot which might have proved too serious for the resourcefulness of any statesman of the time. His readiness to enter the Mogul service was a feint that had deceived both the Bijapur and the Mogul governments. In reality he desired nothing of the kind. When the deliverance of his father was once achieved, his ardour for the Mogul service at once cooled. While tempting the Padishaha with this offer, he was resolved to remain true to the vow of his earliest youth: never to do service to a Mahomedan ruler whatever the gains or emoluments.

But Shahajahan, through his viceroy, Prince Murad, continued his demands that Shivaji should according to the terms of his promise enter the Mogul service and receive a mansab or command in the military forces of the empire. Shivaji met these proposals with great tact. He sent an envoy to the imperial governor, Prince Murad, alleging that his family possessed the hereditary rights of sirdeshmukh over the provinces of Junnar and Ahmednagar, but for some time these dues had been withheld from them. He should, therefore, be restored to the enjoyment of his family rights over these provinces.[1] Shahajahan did not acknowledge these demands at the time, but replied that when Shivaji came to the imperial court his rights would be duly considered. In this manner Shivaji put off to a future date the question of entering into the service of the empire.

In 1657 Shahajahan deputed his son Aurangzeb and the experienced general Mir Jumla to lead an army against

---

1 Vide Parasnis's MS, and Kincaid, Appendix B. page 149, where Murad acknowledges the demands of Shivaji made through his envoy Ragho Pandit (Raghunath Ballal Korde (?) and replies that the same would be considered when he reached the royal camp in person.

Bijapur for the express purpose of conquering and annexing that kingdom. They carried in rapid succession the barrier forts on the frontiers of that kingdom, such as Kalyani, Bedar and others. Shivaji, ever watchful for the preservation of his interests, wrote to Aurangzeb that he owed service to the head of the empire and was prepared to render all possible assistance to the Mogul generals in their present campaign, on condition that the secure possession of the Bijapur forts and territories already under his power was assured to him. He on his part would be quite willing to co-operate with the Mogul forces in the conquest of Dabhol and other positions on the Konkan sea-board. It was quite in the nature of things that the imperial commander knowing Shivaji's worth should close with this proposal. Aurangzeb assured Shivaji that he did not meditate any interference with the Bijapur territories already under his sway and informed him that he should by all means turn his victorious arms to the Bijapur possessions in the Konkan low-lands. 1657 A.D.[1]

Such was the purport of Auragzeb's letter to Shivaji. Aurangzeb seems to have been anxious to have a personal conference with Shivaji and urge upon him the expediency of his making common cause with the Moguls against Bijapur and the numerous benefits that might accrue to him from such an alliance. Aurangzeb at a later date wrote to Shivaji upon this subject. His desire was to yoke Shivaji to active service under the empire. But Shivaji was too astute a statesman to swallow the alluring bait. He kept up his repeated assurances of loyalty and service to the padishaha, but always managed to avoid the abject dependence of an imperial courtier. Thus playing adroitly upon Aurangzeb's wishes and fears he secured the peace and tranquillity of his possessions from the grand Mogul's invading hordes. With the Mogul and Bijapur forces engaged in a deadly conflict, he set about concerting measures for the expansion of the Maratha power.

---

1 Grant Duff, I, 161-62, and Prof. Sarkar's *Aurangzeb*, II, 261-69.

It will be remembered that Shivaji had often asserted certain hereditary claims upon Junnar and Ahmednagar. The former was reputed a wealthy town in those days. The emperor had so far turned a deaf ear to Shivaji's claims. Shivaji determined to retaliate by surprising these towns. With this plan he suddenly fell upon Junnar by a night attack and sacked the town. He carried away the richest spoils to Poona, about 300,000 pagodas, 200 horses and other valuables. The booty was safely transferred to Rajgad by officers deputed for the purpose. Shivaji made a similar attempt upon Ahmednagar, but did not succeed here so well as at Junnar.[1] For while he was plundering the suburban parts and the business quarters of the town immediately after the first onslaught, the city forces poured down in sufficient strength from the citadel and stopped the spoliation. However the first shock had already yielded a considerable booty, including 700 horses and four elephants. Shivaji carried them off in triumph through the ranks of the garrison forces, though not without many casualties in his gallant little army.

With these additions to his treasury, Shivaji resolved upon enlarging his cavalry forces. The sack of Junnar and Ahmednagar had as above described resulted in the capture of many horses. These he supplemented with his own purchases, and besides maintaining his own *bargirs*[2] he began to entertain in his service many a willing *shiledar*. The general in command of the cavalry force which

---

1 On the authority of Kambu's Amal-i-Salih, Prof. Sarkar says the attack on Ahmednagar was made by Minaji (Manaji) Bhonsle and Kashi. Was this the same Minaji Bhonsle who as a Mogul mansabdar is said to have treacherously surrendered the fort of Mahuli to Shahaji (Vide *Abdul Hamid's Badshanamah* in Elliot, VII, page 57). The same authority states that at the time when Shahajahan gave a mansab to Shahaji, the emperor also gave a mansab to his son Samaji (Sambhaji) and his brother Minaji, while the Marathi chronicles generally state that an imperial mansab was conferred upon Kheloji, the son of Vithoji Bhonsle.

2 These represent two classes of cavalry soldiers, the shiledar maintaining his own horse and being a sort of cavalier, the bargir using a horse lent by the state.

up to this time had served under Shivaji was Mankoji Dahatonde, who had received the title of sirnobut or lord of the royal drum. Mankoji was an old veteran who had seen service in the stirring times of Shahaji's fights with the Moguls. He had maintained Shivaji's cavalry in the highest state of efficiency. On his death, the brave Netaji Palkar was appointed to succeed him. Palkar commanded great influence among the Maratha gentry, many of whom now eagerly sought to obtain commissions as shiledars in Shivaji's cavalry.

Meanwhile the Moguls were inflicting defeat after defeat upon Bijapur, and this augured very unfavourably for Shivaji's future career. For it was plain that the extinction of the Bijapur kingdom would turn the Mogul conqueror upon Shivaji himself. Anticipating this exigency, Shivaji sought to conciliate Aurangzeb, submitting himself and his fortunes to the Mogul protection and offering an humble apology for the spoliation of Junnar and Ahmednagar. With a petition couched in these terms he sent his envoy Raghunathpant Korde, a trusty officer well versed in the diplomacy and finesse of Indian courts, to the imperial camp, that he might add verbal assurances to the entreaties for pardon made in the petition.

Fortunately for the future of Shivaji's enterprise, Aurangzeb received a confidential report of Shahajahan's illness from the princess Roshanara, who watched over his ambitious interests at the capital, and the imperial general concluded a hasty peace with Bijapur and with as large a force as he could collect in the southern subha, he immediately set out for Delhi. Emboldened by the sudden diversion of the imperial forces to the north, Shivaji forthwith sent another embassy representing his regret for the necessity that had led to the spoliation of Mogul territory by his forces, offering to place a large force of cavalry at the service of Aurangzeb, and undertaking the defence of the imperial territory in the south during Aurangzeb's enforced absence. In return, Shivaji prayed, he might be reinstated in the hereditary rights and privileges he claimed over certain territories that had passed under the Moguls, as also the jahgir lands of his family which had now come under the imperial power and the commission of deshmukh or zamindary rights over the districts of Junnar and Ahmednagar. The restoration of these rights and dues would be an ample return for his proffered service to the imperial crown. In conclusion he pointed out that the government of the Konkan districts had long been neglected by the Adil Shahi power and represented that the transfer of this province to himself would be of very great advantage to the empire.

These were serious demands couched in the adulatory language of court etiquette, but the great excitement in the Mogul camp did not leave to Aurangzeb sufficient leisure to indulge in resentful feelings. He rather chose for the present to leave Shivaji in a state of expectancy with regard to his demands and encourage him to continue his disturbances in the Bijapur territory, for in this the wily prince discerned the only means of preservation for the Mogul conquests in the Deccan during the strenuous civil wars which were now impending and were certain to jeopardize the security and integrity of the empire. Resolved to pursue this line of conduct Aurangzeb made answer in the most guarded manner possible. In the first place, while censuring Shivaji's conduct, he was pleased to extend to him that royal mercy which he craved. Secondly, he granted permission to Shivaji to turn his attention to the conquest of the Konkan. Lastly Shivaji was desired to depute Abaji Sondev to a conference where Shivaji's hereditary rights and perquisites would be duly considered, and pending a final adjustment of these claims Shivaji was required to send 500 horse to the assistance of the Moguls and keep his forces in a state of readiness and efficiency for the maintenance of peace and security in the Mogul province.[1]

These negotiations led to no tangible results in the

[1] Parasnis M S

end. It was only a make-believe sort of alliance on either side. In fact there was no time to seal a conpact of permanent friendship. Aurangzeb was too much occupied by the stress of the civil wars that followed. It was his unnatural task to fight, slay, or execute his unfortunate brothers and to imprison his father in his helpless dotage, literally wading through slaughter to an inauspicious throne. That was just what Shivaji wanted. Right well did Shivaji know that the demands which he had made were too ambitious for the haughty prince to grant. On his part it was only a ruse to gain more time to pursue his ambitious plans in a leisurely manner.

Tradition has it that on reaching Delhi, when Aurangzeb finally resolved to usurp the throne and imprison his helpless father in his palace, he wrote to the Deccan nobles to come to his assistance, and that among others Shivaji too received such an invitation. Whereupon it is said that Shivaji shuddered at the contents of the letter and openly expressed his horror of the unnatural crime formulated by Aurangzeb in such a cold-blooded fashion. Nay, the story goes that he spurned the poor courier who was the bearer of the proposal and drove him from his presence and had the traitorous missive bound to the tail of a mongrel cur to be dragged over the mire and filth of Poona. On hearing of the contemptuous manner in which this proposal was received by Shivaji, Aurangazeb is said to have burst forth into a passion and vowed to avenge the indignity. But this plan of revenge he never had the opportunity to carry out, and it would even seem that his resentment must have been of short duration. For shortly afterwards when the news of the death of Afzul Khan at the hands of Shivaji reached Aurangzeb's ears, he congratulated the Maratha warrior by letter and presented him with two or three hill-forts on the borders of Bijapur. Not content with this he advised Shivaji to continue this plan of aggression against Bijapur and promised to confer on him tax-free all the lands he might succeed in wresting from the Bijapur government. It is obvious that in all this Aurangzeb was inspired by thoughts of his future dealings with the Adil Shahi dynasty, reflecting no doubt that Shivaji's pioneer work in the dismemberment of that kingdom would render his programme all the easier of accomplishment. As to the ultimate defeat of Shivaji he took it as a matter of course. Little did he then dream, with all his political sagacity, that the most stubborn problem of all his life, reserved as the crowning wreck and disgrace of his declining years, would be just this—the war with the newly founded Maratha power.

CHAPTER X

THE CAPTURE OF JAVLI AND OTHER EVENTS

1654-58

AFTER the complete liberation of Shahaji from the Sultan's watch at Bijapur and his return to the Karnatic, Shivaji revived the aggressive policy he had slackened in the interim. His object was now to win over from the sultan the entire region of the Konkan and the uplands of the ghats, and to round off these possessions with the conquest of new hill-forts. The news of these freshly awakened activities threw the Bijapur durbar once more into consternation. For they were in the dilemma that if they were to move their forces openly against Shivaji, he might in all probability enlist the sympathy of the Moguls and demand their protection, and thus they would only accelerate their downfall. Thoughts of public hostilities could not therefore be entertained, but a force of a thousand horse was entrusted to a nobleman, Baji Shamraj by name, who undertook the arduous task of surprising Shivaji and making him prisoner. Shivaji was then encamped at Mahad. Baji Shamraj with the active support of Chandrarao More of Javli formed an ambuscade in the defile of the Parghat, lying in wait to fall upon Shivaji unawares and apprehend him. But Shivaji was apprised of this plot of Baji by his faithful scouts, and the result was that far from Shivaji falling into the trap, Baji Shamraj's party itself was suddenly attacked and dispersed in all directions. Shamraj returned to Bijapur defeated and crest-fallen.

The active support lent to his enemies by the More family naturally rankled in Shivaji's mind, and he now set about to teach them a lesson they would ever remember.[1] Chandrarao More held sway in the districts which formed the watershed of the Krishna and the Warna. He entertained more than a thousand Mavalis in his

[1] Chandrarao More was the hereditary title of the fief-holders of Javli. The feudal lord of Javli at the time was Krishnaji Baji. (Parasnis: *Itihas Sangraha, Sphuta Lekh* I, 26.)

service and was one of the principal feudal lords under the Bijapur durbar. The payment of the annual tribute left him an ample surplus upon which the family had thriven and prospered for centuries. He was the lord of many a hill-fort and mountain defile, his principal position being Hashamgad. Several times before this Shivaji had tried to win over this mighty chief and bind him to his interests, and had represented that he might either stop the tribute paid to Bijapur and divert it to Shivaji or might enjoy all the revenue to himself, on no other condition than that of helping him with a force of 5000 in time of need. To these proposals the loyal More had systematically turned a deaf ear.

Now it was quite apparent that this little world of hill and dale under the rule of the More family stood in the way of Shivaji's complete domination over the zone of the highlands of the Western Ghats. It comprehended many a mountain fastness, the keys to the mastery of fields and pastures in the valleys. Shivaji's ultimate plans to strike at the Mahomedan power required that he should be first safely ensconced among these rocky wilds as the undisputed master of the Western Ghats. This must inevitably bring him into collision with the More family. But the More's was an ancient name, and he had thonsands of brave Mavali retainers in his service, and many a gallant warrior and chief strove night and day for its prestige. Among them Suryarao, the brother of Chandrarao More, and Hanmantrao, his private secretary, were men of acknowledged military genius. To put his forces against those of the More family in an open encounter was in Shivaji's opinion likely to prove a bloody experiment without much probability of ultimate success. Shivaji, therefore, according to the traditional bakhar account, had to act with circumspection and avoid any act of overt hostility. With this object in view, he got two of his officers, Raghunath Ballal Korde and Sambhaji Kavji, with a small escort to proceed to the principality of Javli to reconnoitre the place and report on its hill-forts and positions of strategic value.[1] To facilitate this plan, Shivaji's officers feigned as an excuse for their intrusion that they had come on an embassy to negotiate a match between Shivaji and Chandrarao More's daughter. Relying upon this assurance More gave orders to arrange for the comfort of his guests. Now More was much addicted to drink. He had not the least suspicion of the ulterior intentions of these alleged ambassadors. These men on the other hand were scrutinizing everything they saw or heard. Raghunath Ballal did not take long to discover the reckless security in which the drunken More lived and the dissensions that existed in his garrison. Conceiving the plan of surprising and assassinating the unguarded chief within the walls of his own fort, he consulted his comrade Sambhaji Kavji and with his concurrence wrote to Shivaji that they had it in their power to settle the last account with More, provided Shivaji advanced with his army in the vicinity of Javli and at a given signal appeared on the scene. Shivaji descended from Rajgad with a small army and came by forced marches to Mahabaleshwar by way of Purandar. He arranged his troops in the forest and remained on the alert for further developments, having notified Raghunathrao of his arrival. Having set the trap ready, Raghunathrao proposed a confidential conference with Chandrarao and his brother Suryarao. In the course of the conversation he found an occasion to draw his dagger and killed the brothers on the spot, and set forth straightway to descend the castle with the band of his followers, who were drawn up all ready for the start[2] But they were interrupted by the

1 According to Chitnis, Sabhasad, and Shedgaokar Raghunath Ballal Sabnis was sent upon this mission, with a few soldiers. According to Shedgaokar Bakhar, Sambhaji Kavji was later on sent to Hamantrao and murdered him.

2 According to the version in the Shivdigvijay, Ragho Ballal came to an interview with More's secretary, Hanmantrao, on pretence of a marriage alliance, and finding him off his guard killed him by treachery. Upon this Shivaji marched upon Chandrarao More, defeated and slew him in the field and captured Javli. The Rairi bakhar gives nearly the

sentry mounted at the gate who had meanwhile received word of the murders committed within. Shivaji's men forced their way at the sword's point through their ranks and made good their escape into the forest. The retainers of More made little serious attempt to pursue the treacherous guests. For the lord of the castle having himself fallen, who was there to rally the pursuers and keep up their spirits? Shivaji now descended from Mahabaleshwar by the Nissan ghat, or *Pass of the Stairs*, to Javli and blockading Hashamgad on all sides gave battle to the More hosts. Chandrarao's sons Bajirao and Krishnarao and the minister Hanmantrao fought with the energy of despair. But at length Hanmantrao fell dead on the field and More's brave sons were wounded and made prisoners.[1] These brave warriors with the ladies and children of the More family were kept in confinement upon fort Purandar. Shivaji intended to confer a suitable jahgir on the heirs of More so as to keep up the prestige of an ancient name. But they were detected in a traitorous correspondence with Bijapur for arranging a flight to that court. This correspondence was intercepted and put in evidence against them. They were found guilty of treason and executed. The ladies of the family were then set at liberty.

Such is the traditional account of this event, as it has come down to us from the pens of the leading chroniclers. As regards statements of details they differ much from one another, as will be seen from the foot-notes. Let us put together these divergent statements, and they lead to one

same version with this addition that Hanmant was first overtaken and slain in a battle at Mahabaleshwar and next Shivaji advanced against Chandrarao More and defeating him conquered Javli and Mahabaleshwar.

[1] There are other versions:—(1) According to Sabhasad this Hanmantrao was a brother of Chandrarao More. On the conquest of Javli he retired into the Konkan and set up a small principality there. Fearing he might return and repeat his attempts for the recovery of Javli, Shivaji sent Sambhaji Kavji on a diplomatic mission to Hanmantrao. The envoy opened the discussion of a marriage alliance between Hanmant and Shivaji and despatched the unsuspecting chief with his dagger. (2) Chitnis omits these gruesome datails and only says that Sambhaji killed Hanmantrao.

conclusion, that there was an offer of a marriage alliance, that under pretence of such an offer, *either* Chandrarao More himself *or* his captain and kinsman, Hanmantrao More, was treacherously slain, *either* by Raghunath Ballal *or* by Sambhaji Kavji. For it is too much to believe that Raghunath Ballal proposed a marriage alliance to Chandrarao More and stabbed him, and *at the same time* to believe that after this murder had taken place Sambhaji Kavji made a similar proposal to Hanmantrao and murdered him. We hold that if Chandrarao More was deceived and murdered, Hanmantrao, who is described as a brave and wise man, the actual administrator of Javli and the only pillar of strength to the More family, was too shrewd a man to fall into the same trap. The probability is that if the one was murdered, the other was not. Hanmantrao would not be deceived by offers of a marriage alliance (Shedgaokar bakhar, 81), if Chandrarao More had been done to death by a similar treacherous proposal.

The Jedhe Chronology tells us plainly that the fighting with the Mores was a prolonged affair and not to be settled by the murder of one man or another. This chronology gives no account of treachery, it speaks only of fighting. The struggle lasted for above five months, from December 1655 (*Pousha* of Shaka 1577) to at least April or May 1656 (*Vaishakha* of Shaka 1578). Under the first entry (December 1655) we are told that Shivaji captured Javli with the help of the Jedhe deshmukh and the followers of Bandal and Silibkar (Silimkar) and other Mavli chiefs, and we are distinctly told that with their help Shivaji *fought* and took Javli. Before proceeding to the second entry, we will remark that this first entry confirms the statement of the bakhar account published in Parasnis's *Itihas Sangraha, Sphuta Lekh I*, 26, where we are told that after mutual recriminations and challenges, Shivaji sent an ultimatum to Chandrarao (presumably through Raghunath Ballal Korde) and descending from Mahabaleshwar by the Pass of the Stairs (Nissan ghat), laid siege to Javli for a month. This account further states that at the fall of Javli, Chandrarao More escaped to Rairi, seized it from Shivaji's men and fought the fort for *three* months, at the end of which he was forced to capitulate. Now these statements (*Itihas Sangraha Sphuta Lekh I, 26–29; II* 11, and Parasnis's *Mahabaleshwar, 19–21*) are supported by the second entry in the Jedhe Chronology (pp. 180–81), which is undoubtedly an independent authority. This entry, under the month of *Vaishakh, Shake* 1578, reads as follows:—"In *Vaishakh* the Rajah Shivaji took (recovered) Rairi. Along with him were Kanhoji Jedhe deshmukh, of Taluka Bhore, and Bandal and Shilibkar deshmukhs, and a force of Mavalis. Haibatrao and Balaji Naik Silibkar used their mediation and Chandrarao descended the fort. The *Itihas Sangraha* account further states that Chandrarao More was pardoned and re-established in some of his old possessions and honours as a fief-holder under Shivaji, until he opened an intriguing correspondence with the Ghorpades of Mudhol, when he was executed at Chakan, perhaps along with his sons, and then the glory of Javli came to an end. On the other hand the Jedhe entry concludes with a statement that Shivaji rewarded the services of Haibatrao Silibkar in bringing about a reconciliation with Chandrarao and that the territories of the latter were divided between him and his brothers. There is nothing contradictory between this and the *Itihas Sangraha* account. They mutually confirm one another. The Shedgaokar bakhar says expressly that the quarrels of the brothers wrecked the realm of Chandrarao. Reconstructing the whole story, we may proceed to state, as related in some of the bakhars, that Hanmantrao More still continued to defy Shivaji after the submission of Chandrarao, that Sambhaji Kavji was therefore sent to him (Sabhasad 10) perhaps under pretence of a marriage alliance (Sabhasad and Shedgaokar) and that under some such pretence he stabbed him to death (Chitnis, Sabhasad and Shedgaokar). When it is considered that Hanmantrao belonged to the More family and that

Chandrarao More was only the hereditary title of the fief-holders of Javli, it seems possible that the Marathi chronicles describing the events full two generations after they had occurred would make a muddle of the whole affair and some of them proceed wrongly to state that Javli was taken by tricking Chandrarao More into a proposal of marriage. There is nothing improbable in such a reconstruction of the whole event, which is the only intelligible form in which it commends itself to our acceptance in sympathy with the general tenor of the conflicting versions. Prof. Sarkar (Shivaji, 54) might well have spared his gibes against recent "discoveries" of "old chronicles", for it is not necessary to press upon the reader the acceptance of that part of the *Itihas Sangraha* narrative which asserts that Chandrarao More had attempted to seize Shivaji by treachery and had intrigued with the Ghorpades of Mudhol against him. This attempt to represent that event in a retaliatory light has unnecessarily provoked the ire of Prof. Sarkar. That intrigue was probably the last incident of the tragic tale. It led to executions and reprisals, and the practical extinction of the More family (Shivdigvijay, 131) though, as Prof. Sarkar shows, some of the members of the More family unquestionably escaped and attempted to avenge themselves by co-operating with the Rajah Jaysingh at a later date.

In this manner was effected the conquest of Javli and the fortifications comprised in that demesne. Shivaji's flag was now flying over all its hill-forts. The large treasures in gold and specie accumulated by many generations of the More family fell intact into Shivaji's hands. Under the auspices of the Mores a Brahman named Babaji Kondadev had waxed in power in the valley of Shivthar. This man now constituted himself into a sort of independent ruler, plundering the neighbourhood and defying Shivaji's authority. He was arrested and though under ordinary circumstances he would have been straightway executed for his arrogant defiance, his character as a member of the priestly class excited commiseration in Shivaji's eyes. Instead of inflicting the extreme penalty of the law, Shivaji ordered his eyes to be put out.[1]

The deshmukh of Hirdas in the Maval region, Bandal by name, was another of these turbulent chiefs whom Shivaji had long meditated to bring under his allegiance. He had hitherto evaded Shivaji's peaceful proposals. His head-quarters were the mountain-fort of Rohida. According to Chitnis, about this time, Shivaji concerted a successful night attack upon this fort and Bandal found himself overwhelmed on all sides. Bandal knew well that he had little hope of safety, being so completely hemmed in by Shivaji's forces. But he was resolved never to yield and launched a violent attack on Shivaji. Both parties put forth their utmost efforts. Bandal himself rushed over the field, sword in hand. He was at length defeated and fell mortally wounded. The few surviving followers of Bandal made their submission, the chief among them being Bandal's minister, Baji Prabhu Deshpande. Shivaji, pleased with Deshpande's bravery, treated him with great generosity, confirming him in his privileges and estates. When Shivaji had received further proofs of his loyalty, he got him to enlist in his service. He was placed in charge of a battalion of infantry. What signal services he rendered to Shivaji, and in bow heroical and self-sacrificing a manner, will be seen in the sequel.[2]

---

[1] Sabhasad gives a different name, viz. Baji Kodanerao, and the Shedgaokar bakhar names him Dadaji Mahadev (pp. 20, 21.)

[2] Chitnis's version is followed in the text as regards the conquest of Hirdas Maval. On the other hand the Jedhe Chronology, as menticned before, says that Bandal deshmukh, or at any rate his followers, co-operated with Shivaji, in capturing Javli. Prof. Sarkar remarks that the twelve Mavals were completely conquered by Dadaji Kondadev, and rejects this version of Chitnis. But Prof. Sarkar seems to contradict himself when he states that the fort of Rohida (Rahira) was gained some time after wards (Prof. Sarkar: *Shivaji* 39, Foot-note and 41). Moreover the name of Baji Deshpande is not mentioned before this event. It would seem that Bandal made war and peace according to his convenience, and hence these discrepancies among our authorities. (Vide Foot-note (1) in Chapter VI).

After the extirpation of Bandal and his party, Shivaji's rule over the Maval region knew no check or interruption. The elements of discord being exterminated, the peasantry became secure and fearless and in consequence happy The introduction of a regular system in the collection of the land revenue contributed greatly to their prosperity. The settlements were neither arbitrary nor oppressive. The people's interests and wishes were everywhere studied and consulted. Those who were willing to serve in the field had ready access to Shivaji's army, as new recruits were being constantly picked up wherever they could be discovered. Shivaji admitted a large number of More's brave retainers to serve in his field force.

In order to consolidate his conquest of Javli and the adjacent parts, Shivaji resolved to erect a central fort among the mountains at the sources of the river Krishna and entrusted the building operations to Moro Trimal Pingle. Pingle was a gallant officer who had accompanied the Rajah Shahaji upon his first expedition into the Karnatic. He had received his training in finance and war under the expert guidance of his own father and the Rajah Shahaji, in the disturbed times which had marked the early vicissitudes of Shahaji's life. From the Karnatic he returned to Maharashtra about 1653 and took service under Shivaji. He won the confidence of Shivaji by the loyalty, zeal, and ability he displayed in the execution of every duty entrusted to him. He carried out the building of the fortifications quite up to Shivaji's standard. The fortress was christened Pratapgad. The old temple at Mahabaleshwar was re-modelled and repaired. A new temple, with a massive court and walls, was erected next to the fountain head of the Krishna. An image of the tutelary goddess Bhavani was here set up in imitation of the ancient Bhavani of Tuljapur. Shivaji adorned the temple with rich ornaments and made frequent pilgrimages to this shrine.

A little later Aurangzeb marched southwards and

defeated Bijapur and concluding a new treaty retired to North India. We have already seen the precautions Shivaji had taken to ensure his possessions from the ravages of the Moguls. By professions of humility Shivaji had succeeded in deceiving a past master of state-craft like Aurangzeb and obtained permission to have his own way in the Bijapur territory. On Aurangzeb's retirement to the North, Shivaji turned his attention to the conquest of the Konkan. In quick succession the sea-board towns of Ratnagiri, Vijaydurg, Suvarnadurg, Salsi and Kharepatan fell before Shivaji.

About this time a troop of 700 Pathans came to Shivaji to seek employment in his army. They had been disbanded by the Bijapur Government after the last treaty with the Moguls. They came straggling to Poona and applied to Shivaji for employment submitting that they had been attracted to him by the fame of his name and the martial renown of Shahaji Bhosle. Shivaji was much at a loss whether to entertain or not a corps of Mahomedan soldiers in his service. Some of his intimate followers distrusted them and represented to Shivaji that they might be in a secret league with Bijapur or the Mogul camp and sent on purpose to sow sedition in his army, and might turn traitors at any moment. But among the trusty officers of Shivaji was a havaldar, Gomaji Naik Pansambal, who had seen service under the redoubted Lukhji Jadhav and had come over to Shahaji in Jijabai's escort at the time of her marriage. He had shared in all the vicissitudes of Jijabai's career and served in Shivaji's earliest enterprises with undeviating loyalty and courage. Shivaji had raised him to the rank of havaldar, having appreciated his zealous loyalty towards himself and his services in the development of his ambitious plans of independence. This veteran counselled Shivaji to secure the services of these strangers who had been drawn to him by the glory of his military exploits and argued that for the final triumph of his cause, the establishment of an independent power, it was essential that his realm should be an asylum to all men of worth and talent, irrespective of the religion they professed. "The true ruler," exclaimed this honest soldier, "shall be equally impartial to all castes and creeds. He shall give freedom of religion to all his subjects and vassals, and shall recruit his servants from all races and classes of men, worth and valour being the sole tests of selection." In this way the gallant havaldar prevailed over Shivaji's wavering mind, with the result that the latter summoned the strangers into his presence, and having by a close scrutiny and cross-examination satisfied himself as to the sincerity of their profession and the genuineness of their desire to enter into his service ordered them to be enrolled. [1]Ragho Ballal Atre was placed in command of this Pathan Division. After this incident Shivaji began to enlist Mahomedans both officers and sepoys,on a large scale, some of whom are known to have risen to great eminence by their zeal, loyalty and bravery.

The Abyssinians at Janjira were now the only considerable power that impeded Shivaji's progress towards the reduction of the entire Konkan coast under his hegemony. The Chief of Janjira[2], strong in his naval resources, time and again harassed Shivaji's possessions in the Konkan. Perceiving that his conquests there could not have even the shadow of security till this foreign ruler was subjugated, Shivaji determined to concentrate his forces upon the reduction of this enemy. Resolved to carry out this part of his programme without delay, Shivaji ordered Shamrajpant, the Peshwa, to move his forces against Janjira. Fatteh Khan was the Abyssinian chief then bearing sway over Janjira. This chief knew that Shivaji's intentions towards Janjira were by no means friendly and had prepared himself for an encounter. Between Fatteh Khan and Sham-

1 This officer's name must not be confounded with that of Ragho Ballal Korde who figures in the tragic story of the capture of Javli.

2 The word "Janjira" means an island-fort or sea-fort, and the island of Zanzibar off the coast of British East Africa is said to have been so called from its being an island-fort under its Moorish masters.

rajpant several skirmishes took place near Danda-Rajpuri, and the Peshwa got the worst of these engagements. Shivaji's forces had to retire before the skilfully concerted military movements of Fatteh Khan, and numbers of the Peshwa's expeditionary force perished. Shamraj had to return home disgraced and dispirited. This was the first considerable reverse sustained by Shivaji's arms, and he took it ill to such an extent that he discharged Shamrajpant from his office of Peshwa and entrusted Raghunathpant with the campaign with a considerably re-inforced army. The office of Peshwa was conferred upon Moro Trimal Pingle, who exercised the duties of this position of trust for the rest of his life. Among other transfers of office Nilo Sondev was given charge of the duties of Muzumdar, (accountant-general), Gango Mangaji those of Waknis (record-keeper) and Yessaji Kunk was appointed to be the commander-in-chief of the infantry force, with the title of sirnobut.

In the course of this war with the Abyssinians, the chief of Sawantwadi came to learn of the great armaments embarked by Shivaji upon the conquest of the Konkan coast. The Sawantwadi chief had little of internal resources to stem the tide of the expected invasion. The chief owned the hegemony of Bijapur and had hitherto paid little heed to the rise of Shivaji. But the annihilation of the power and prestige of the great More family, the discomfiture of neighbouring feudal chiefs and the surrender of numerous hill-forts and positions of vantage without any successful resistance on the part of Bijapur, added to the utter paralysis of inaction and dissension which had overtaken that state after the last Mogul invasion, opened the eyes of the Sawantwadi chief to the utter futility of any expectation of aid in the hour of peril and the advisability of entering into an understanding with one whose star was unmistakably in the ascendant. A treaty followed, by which it was agreed that the Sawant should cede half his revenues to Shivaji, who was empowered to collect his moiety by his own agency. The Sawant was to enjoy the rest of the revenue with all the rights and prerogatives of *deshmukhi* or *zamindari* lordship over Sawantwadi without let or hindrance. In pursuance of this plan the Sawant chief was to discontinue payment of the time-honoured tribute to Bijapur, to maintain his garrisons all over the forts, and keep an efficient infantry force of 3000 to be placed at Shivaji's service on demand. In effect, the chief disowned the hegemony of Bijapur and acknowledged that of Shivaji.

The treaty thus entered into was plainly not the outcome of the Sawant's free will, and in a short time he repented of the step to which he had rashly committed himself. It was too galling to his spirit to submit to Shivaji's domination which he soon made shift to change for that of Bijapur. How Shivaji visited this fickleness on the Sawant's head will be described in a later chapter.

Meanwhile the forces sent against the Abyssinians had met with foemen worthy of their steel and the monsoon setting in made the protraction of the struggle impossible. In the following campaign the command was entrusted to the Peshwa Moropant assisted by Netaji Palkar. The campaign was interrupted by the monsoons, which began rather earlier than usual. Meanwhile a new crisis threatened to overtake Shivaji's fortune which made a pause necessary in the Maratha enterprise and required the exercise of all their concentrated resources. This was the invasion of Afzul Khan.

CHAPTER XI

THE TRAGEDY OF AFZUL KHAN, 1659

THE Bijapur government had been waiting with patience. Fort after fort, district after district had passed from their inert grasp into the grip of the Maratha warrior. Their feudal vassals were being seduced to defection, the zealous Mores of Javli had paid for their loyalty with death and ruin, the Sawants of Wadi had been seduced from their allegiance to their traditional suzerains, the province of Kalyan dissevered for ever from the Bijapur monarchy, and their Abyssinian admirals beset on all sides and all but forced to withdraw from the Konkan. These events were too serious each of them to be lightly passed over, but taken together they would have roused to action the most lethargic government that ever bore sway in any part of India. It is said that no less than forty of the Bijapur fortresses were by this time in Shivaji's hands.[1] The government had seen all, heard all, but had not moved. One remedy indeed they had tried. They had incarcerated Shahaji. They had hoped to tame the son by threatening the life of the father. They had hoped in vain. They had not fully counted upon Shivaji's resourcefulness. They had yet to fathom the depths of his diplomacy. They were bitterly undeceived. Their attempt had recoiled on themselves. It had drawn Shivaji into a league with their Mogul spoilers and given the support of the imperial authority to his excesses. They had served him as a shield against the wrath of Bijapur. He had become the Mogul poniard in the bosom of the Adil Shahi State. Once more after the liberation of Shahaji, they had tried to entrap the quarry they dared not bring to bay, but they had been signally disappointed in Baji Shamraj. Then the Mogul cavalry had suddenly invaded their land and drenched it with blood The peace at last made with the Moguls and the absorption of Aurangzeb in the fratricidal war in the north allowed them now to breathe freely for a while.

[1] Modak's History of Bijapur.

This interval of peace with the Mogul emperor they hoped to turn against Shivaji.

Ali Adil Shaha II then held the sceptre at Bijapur. He was a mere youth, without experience, about twenty-one years of age. His mother, famous among native historians under the popular name of the *Badi* (*Bari*) *Saheba* or the queen dowager, carried on the affairs of state in person with the assistance of the able minister, Khawas Khan. One day calling all her ministers and generals to an audience, she ordered them to put the state armies in motion and capture the rebellious Shivaji alive and at the conclusion of her harangue inquired who would take the glorious task upon himself. No one offered to risk the undertaking. They had heard enough of Shivaji's valour to feel that it was better to keep well out of his way. They all dreaded a rencontre with him.[1] But there was one amongst them in whom vanity outweighed his discretion. This was Afzul Khan.[2] He was elated with pride. What a noble chance to play the hero! He would not flinch or waver. Let the queen but give the word, he would make Shivaji dance to the tune of his sword. This language of bravado filled the queen dowager with elation. She knew he was a general of high eminence in the state. She presented him with robes of honour and bade him start on his campaign with 12,000 horse and a goodly number of infantry with a suitable complement of artillery, rockets, and war material in charge of a camel corps.[3] It is said that the

[1] Sabhasad, 3; Shedgaonkar, 24.

[2] He is said to have originally belonged to the caste or profession of a cook-shop keeper, *bhatari*, and to have risen to greatness and the rank of a commander by his talents. His name is said to have originally been Abdulkhan. He is referred to by this name in some of the bakhars and powadas i. e. the ballads of Maratha minstrelsy.

[3] The figures are variously given. Grant Duff mentions 5000 horse and seven hundred foot. Chitnis puts down the whole invading army at 30,000, while Chitragupta exaggerates the number to 70,000. The powadas limit the number to 12,000 horse. The English *Factory Records*, Rajapur, give the strength of his army as 10,000 horse and foot, and it is said that because this number was so small, the queen told Afzul Khan to pretend friendship with Shivaji, and seize or slay him by treachery.

provisions and war-material were plentiful enough to have lasted for three campaigns. Besides these forces Afzul Khan was provided with a corps of two or three thousand Mavalis. These he had entertained knowing well how indispensable they were for a campaign in the Maval regions, especially as Shivaji's fighting force was chiefly recruited from these people. But what a world of difference there lay between Shivaji's Mavali militia inspired by the highest feelings of loyalty and patriotism and the Mavali soldiers of Afzul Khan hired for a soulless enterprise! But it was not for Afzul Khan to discern this difference.

At the very outset let us take notice of the spirit of bravado in which Afzul Khan had undertaken this enterprise. In open durbar he had boasted that he would bring back Shivaji alive, a captive in chains. The dowager queen had besides instructed him to effect the *capture* or *murder* of Shivaji by "pretending friendship" and rousing hopes of the sultan's pardon.[1] He hoped to succeed in this heavy task by tampering with the loyalty of Shivaji's Mavali deshmukhs[2] and by a policy of striking terror among the Marathas.

Afzul Khan crossed the Krishna with his troops, and forcing his marches with great rapidity arrived at the ancient temple of Bhawani at Tuljapur, where he temporarily encamped his army. Learning that this temple was sacred in the eyes of the Marathas, the Bhavani of Tuljapur being indeed the guardian patroness of certain leading families of the Maratha nobility, and in particular of the Bhonsle family, he desecrated the temple. The original stone image of the goddess, which was considered the more sacred, was concealed by the priest under water. But the larger image of the deity was seized and ground to powder between mill-stones![3] Breaking up his camp, Afzul

1 Factory Records, Rajapur, 10th October 1659, quoted by Prof. Sarkar, *Shivaji* p. 69.

2 Jedhe Chronology, pp. 182–83.

3 A powada describes how the idol was broken, the temple converted into a mosque, and further polluted by cow-slaughter.

Khan made for Pandharpur, polluting the temple of Mankeshwar on the way. This was a circuitous way that Afzul Khan had taken, urged to the step, it is said, by the fact that the straight road over the mountain ghats was rendered impassble to an army by the heavy rains. Having encamped on the Bhima, he resolved to destroy the historic temple of Vithoba at Pandharpur. But the hereditary priests of the temple concealed the image and the affrighted citizens deserting house and home fled for safety to the neighbouring forests [1] Afzul wreaked such vengeance as he could on the shrine and turned his march to Poona, reducing such of Shivaji's forts and possessions as lay right on his line of march.

Shivaji was at Rajgad when his scouts brought word of the impending descent of Afzul Khan, with the avowed purpose of seizing him alive and carrying him as a prisoner in chains to celebrate his triumph through the streets of Bijapur. Upon this Shivaji held a conference with his chiefs and nobles, whose opinion was that the Khan should be hemmed in within some narrow defile and Shivaji should keep his forces ready under the protection of the fortifications of Pratapgad pending the invasion of the Khan. There was also another opinion expressed by a minority of the chiefs in council, who held that there was little prospect of success in a conflict with the Khan's armies and advocated peaceful overtures with the Bijapur commander. Shivaji did not disguise his contempt of this proposal, expressing his want of confidence in the good faith of the Adil Shahi government or of its general and declaring that they could not afford to trust any offer of friendship from men who were incapable of forming a true conception of peace and good-will. He hoped to meet them on the field of battle. He would beat them on their own ground. He would make them abate their insolence!

Now tradition has it that while his mind was racked

---

[1] However the powada, already referred to, speaks of the breaking of the image of Vithoba and the drowning of that of Pundalik.

with these cares and depressed with the weight of the responsibility hanging on his actions, he had a vision of the goddess Bhavani of Tuljapur whose temple had just then been desecrated. The goddess bade him be of good cheer, for his was to be the hand that would compel Afzul Khan to expiate these atrocities. His campaign would be crowned with glorious success. Such was the dream. Shivaji roused himself from his slumbers, performed his morning ablutions and had his mother awakened in order to communicate to her the dream he had just experienced. At dawn when the civil and military officers gathered to his levee he expounded to them his dream, exclaiming that when the great goddess herself was to stand by his side, what did he reck the force of a mere mortal like Afzul Khan? By the divine blessing he had found a way to put Afzul Khan's army to utter rout and confusion. The courtiers present declared it was too serious an enterprise and its miscarriage was bound to have a tremendous recoil on the people of Maharashtra. Observing the embarrassed looks of his adherents, Shivaji declared with animation that talk of conciliation was vain and would lead inevitably to ruin. An open fight and fair field was the only salvation for them. Death or victory, either was welcome. He would welcome a death which stood for glory; but to surrender, to whine and to die—this was alike inglorious and unprofitable. He for one was resolved to fight to the death. If the war ended in victory, he would say, all's well that ends well. But should it prove otherwise, he looked to his followers to guard his little realm and maintain the renown of the Bhonsle name, under the instructions of his mother.

With his heart thus steeled to do or die, Shivaji gave immediate order to move his camp to Pratapgad, and entered the ladies' apartments to communicate his final plans to his mother. Prostrating himself reverently, as was his wont, at the feet of his mother, he described to her the resolution he had formed. Mother and son were overwhelmed with the tenderest emotions at this crisis. Both knew the gravity of the situation and the small probability of success. But the brave matron faced the situation without faltering and putting aside all the softer emotions roused in her breast, she nerved herself to cheer on her son, after a great mental struggle. Laying her hand proudly upon his head she poured out her blessings and expressed her conviction that by his valour and heroism, she might earn the satisfaction of having given birth to a hero. Having received his mother's blessing Shivaji set out for Pratapgad.

Apprised of Shivaji's movements Afzul Khan diverted his march from Poona to Wai, desecrating the temple of Shambhu Mahadev at Shingnapur on his line of march. At Wai the Khan found himself in the midst of his fief-lands. He encamped his army with great caution. From this base he wrote to the Mavali chiefs and the Adil Shahi zemindars to flock to his standards.[1] Chief among these were the Khopdes, the rivals of the Jedhes for the deshmukh rights over Rohidkhore. Kedarji Khopde seems to have joined Afzul Khan already before; and on receipt of this order Khandoji Khopde of Taluka Utroli hastened to join him at Wai. Similar orders were received by Kanhoji Naik Jedhe along with the other deshmukhs, already when Shivaji was at Rajgad. The Jedhe chief and others went to Shivaji at Rajgad on receipt of these orders. Shivaji told these men to join Afzul Khan, if they cared for their estates and their lives, after receiving some guarantee of protection. But they swore obedience to Shivaji and at his advice removed their families for better protection to Talegaon (Dhamdhere). Among those who refused to obey Afzul Khan's call were the Jedhes, the followers of Bandal, Haibat Rao Silibkar, Fasalkar, Marne and Dhamale, and the deshmukhs of Maral.[2]

Afzul Khan was quite taken aback by Shivaji's posting himself on the inaccessible cliff of Pratapgad, for he

1 Rajwade XV, 393; XVII, 31.

2 Jedhe Chronology.

well knew of the difficulties of a march in that direction, and knew at the same time the risks of a battle with Shivaji, in a place which was very disadvantageous for the manœuvring of his forces. His idea was to contrive some plan to lure the Maratha prince from his vantage-ground. By various pretences and overtures of friendship he hoped to throw him off his guard, arrest him in person and take him in triumph to Bijapur.

When Afzul Khan reached Wai, Shivaji appointed Vishwas Rao Nana Prabhu of Muse Khore in the Maval country to the important duty of reconnoitring his camp and observing the number and quality of his forces. Vishwas Rao used to wander night after night in all parts of the hostile camp in the disguise of a fakir, and send information to Shivaji. The result of this scouting sufficed to prove to Shivaji the magnificent preparations of Afzul Khan and the costliness of a victory, supposing that victory itself was assured. He concluded, therefore, that he must tread his path with circumspection and make up by stratagem for the inadequacy of his forces. Could he not hit upon some plan so as to conserve his resources in money and in men and withal cause Afzul Khan's fury to recoil upon himself? Shivaji's courtiers encouraged him in this preference of policy above rashness. Having at last made up his mind, he assumed an attitude of humiliation and sent word to Afzul Khan that he would be the last man to think of challenging comparisons with such a distinguished general as he was, and that he had now no other desire than to sue for peace and pardon from the authorities of the Bijapur government. He had affronted that government in the grossest manner possible and doubted how far he could secure pardon even though he presented himself before them in sackcloth and ashes. He, therefore, craved this favour that Afzul Khan might with his well-known magnanimity condescend to intercede for him with the Bijapur durbar. Should he consent to do so and procure his pardon he would consider himself to have been especially favoured by fortune. He was ready to put himself entirely at his mercy, relying on the generosity and greatness of his soul. He now repented of his folly and would restore to the Bijapur state all the conquests he had made. He only wanted to be assured of the royal pardon.

Afzul Khan took all this in serious earnest. It seemed to him natural that Shivaji should bate his pride and proclaim his readiness to surrender. He thought nothing else could be expected of him when confronted with such a general as himself. That surrender he thought now depended entirely on his movements. But Shivaji must first be dislodged from the impregnable position he occupied. By promises of pardon he might attain this object. With this view he deputed Krishnaji Bhaskar[1], a Brahman well-versed in the arts of diplomacy, to proceed on an embassy to Shivaji's camp, having tutored him at a private interview how he was to conduct himself with Shivaji and lure him to his ruin. The ambassador received instructions to represent to Shivaji that he should repose in Afzul Khan the same confidence he did in his father, remembering that the Khan was a comrade in arms to Shahaji; that the Khan had great affection for Shivaji, and he expected him to reciprocate his feelings, that in view of the bravery and services of Shahaji, Shivaji's past career would be forgiven and forgotten; and the Khan would undertake to procure for Shivaji a modest principality in the Konkan, with permission to retain the fortresses he had captured and a military grant or *saranjam* for the maintenance of an army corps. Lastly Afzul Khan would undertake to reconcile Shivaji with the sultan and procure for him all the

---

[1] According to the version of some of the bakhars Afzul Khan was the first to send an envoy, without any message from Shivaji, and this seems to be the view taken by Prof. Sarkar. Grant Duff gives the name of the Khan's envoy as Pantaji Gopinath; Chitragupta gives it as Dattaji Gopinath and the Shivdigvijay mentions a second envoy, Govindpant, from the Khan. In the Mahad copy of Sabhasad's bakhar the name of this celebrated envoy is given as Pantajipant. The Shedgaokar bakhar calls the Khan's envoy Dattaji Bhaskar.

honours and privileges of a trusted nobleman of the Adil Shahi court. With these honeyed messages Afzul Khan urged upon his ambassador to use all his arts to induce Shivaji to come to a personal conference dispelling all fears and jealousy from his mind, and if after all this persuasion he declined to accede to this proposal, to prepare him to receive a private visit from Afzul Khan himself.

Learning that the Khan's envoy was coming to him with proposals of such import, Shivaji descended from his fort to meet the honoured guest half-ways and receiving him with cordial welcome brought him with all due pomp and ceremony to his citadel. A durbar was soon held for the purpose of giving a public audience to the Khan's envoy, who delivered the message he was charged with. Shivaji in reply expressed his gratitude for the Khan's kindly intentions and declared that the restoration to him in jahgir form of however small a territory could not but give him great satisfaction. After all he was but a vassal of the sultán, and as such had cleared the country of refractory chiefs and nobles, established peace and good government, repaired old fortresses and erected new ones, raised a militia force of no mean ability, and added in a variety of ways to the fortunes of the state. All this would now come unto the sultan as an unearned increment and make him acknowledge Shivaji's services to the state. As to Afzul Khan Shivaji looked upon him as his father. He would come to pay his respects to him with the greatest affection and good will in the world. These things passed in the public durbar, and after its dissolution the envoy and his party went to take their rest in their appointed quarters.

Shivaji had so arranged it that the camp appointed for the residence of the envoy-in-chief, Krishnaji Bhaskar, should be a little apart from the quarters of the rest of the members of the diplomatic mission. This was done with the premeditated object of conducting secret conversations with the head of the mission. Shivaji no doubt expected to be able to interview the ambassador in the privacy of his apartment and induce him to come over to his side. On the night after the durbar, when all had gone to rest and all around was still and silent, Shivaji came secretly to the tent of the envoy and rousing him from his sleep addressed himself to him in a persuasive strain, submitting that his ambitions were not selfish. He adjured Krishnaji to remember that he belonged to the sacred Brahman caste, the repositories of the Hindu learning and religion. To the glory of that learning and religion and the preservation of every Hindu interest his life's labours were dedicated. He had a clear call from above. He was but the passive executor of a divine mandate, for the spirit of Bhavani inspired his acts and bade him go forth to protect Brahmans and kine, chastise the violators of temples and shrines, and slay the bigots of Islamic intolerance. Humble as he was he had taken upon himself this sacred task and had thus far carried it forward. But the holy cause would never succeed without the sympathy and support of noble and learned Brahmans like Krishnaji. A Brahman of his lofty spirit could not but be greatly distressed at the wreck of Hindu religion and society. The gods and the preceptors of their holy cult were alike the objects of a relentless and inexpiable persecution. Scarcely a vestige of the purest forms of Hinduism remained in all the land of Hindustan. Heresy and persecution prevailed throughout the land. His heart must bleed over these acts of religious violation and vandalism. Shivaji's was a humble but conscientious beginning to the task of restoring happiness to this land of blasted honour and blighted glory. This work of revival was a noble work. It could only succeed with the help of noble spirits like Krishnaji. Would he not join him in retrieving the fortune of Hinduism? This honeyed speech quite changed the man. His religious pride was touched. The flattering attentions and inspiring words of the warrior won him over from his allegiance. He reflected that here was a man who had staked all his worldly fortunes upon the deliverance of his country's religion from bondage. Moreover he was possessed of all those qualities that were essential to the attainment of his noble object–courage, valour, enterprise. All his exploits had been invariably crowned with success. His name was already a household word in thousands of admiring Maharashtra families. Was it not desirable and certainly more meritorious from the point of view of his religion that he should participate in this prince's glorious triumphs? Such thoughts crowded upon his mind and he finally announced to Shivaji his determination to espouse his cause and swear allegiance to him. After this exchange of promises and pledges he took Shivaji into his confidence and revealed to him the real object of his diplomatic mission. It was no less than a trick to delude Shivaji into a surrender on promises of pardon and protection, lure him to an interview so that he might be seized, and then taken in irons to Bijapur and paraded in the bazaars of the capital as a prisoner of war to grace Afzul Khan's treacherous triumph. This revelation made, it was proposed to let the Khan proceed with his projects and cherish his hopes of the impending capture of Shivaji, Krishnaji Bhaskar was to continue playing the role of a zealous envoy and induce the Mahomedan chief to approach Pratapgad for his treacherously planned interview, and when he had come within his power Shivaji was to fall suddenly upon him and surprise his panic-stricken forces. Having thus checkmated Afzul Khan's plots, Shivaji returned warily home.

In public conversations with Krishnaji during the days that followed Shivaji continued his professions of submission, and it was definitely agreed that Afzul Khan should advance to Javli for a conference where the terms of the alliance between the two parties should be finally settled. On Shivaji's side, his envoy, Pantaji Gopinath, was to accompany Krishnaji to confirm this proposal and represent Shivaji's views before Afzul Khan. This minister was one of Shivaji's intimate circle. Before despatch ing him upon this mission, Shivaji explained fully to him in private conference how Krishnaji Bhaskar, while continuing to play the part of Afzul Khan's envoy, had really been won over to his views and had vowed to advance his interests.[1] Gopinath was instructed to represent to Afzul Khan that while Shivaji fully admitted that it was his duty to come to Afzul Khan and pay his respects to him, his natural timidity and fear of the Mahomedan camp prevented him from complying with these essentials of diplomatic etiquette. He had no courage to come to Wai to meet Afzul Khan. But as he looked upon him with the affection of a father, it would be extremely kind of him to comply with his request to approach nearer to Javli where he undertook to come and meet the Khan at an interview. As to his encouraging him in his difficulty and promising to intercede in his behalf with the sultan and arrange to admit him again to the Adil Shahi court, this was only an index of the greatness of his soul. Afzul Khan's approaching Javli without hesitation would be considered by Shivaji a proof of his good intentions towards him. In this fashion Gopinath was to acquit himself of this mission, taking heed to be prodigal of compliments and watchful not to excite suspicion. Without betraying any anxiety as to the Khan's intentions he was to probe minutely into his thoughts and report on the discipline and equipment of his forces. Shivaji bade farewell to Afzul Khan's ambassador with many marks of honour, presenting him with embroidered robes, a set of pearl earrings, bracelets and lockets, a fine Arab horse, and a gift of 5000 pagodas. Gopinathpant was also suitably honoured and sent with a fair retinue befitting his rank.

On his return to Afzul Khan, Krishnaji Bhaskar informed him that Shivaji was ready to meet him to tender his submission but hesitated to come to Wai, where he feared treachery. Shivaji's envoy had accompanied him

1 Sabhasad omits the account of the secret meeting between Shivaji and Krishnaji Bhaskar given by Chitnis.

in order to communicate his reply, if the Khan would graciously grant him an audience. The audience was granted and Gopinathpant had an opportunity to represent Shivaji's proposal. Krishnaji Bhaskar commenting on this proposal urged upon his master to agree to these terms, and pointed out that the Khan was sure to succeed in his aim. By marching up to Javli and advancing so far at Shivaji's request, he would disarm his suspicions, lure him to a meeting and get him easily into his clutches. The Khan objected that Javli was a difficult region for the deploying of his army and what guarantee was there that Shivaji meant no harm? Upon this Krishnaji assured the Khan that for his part he was convinced that there was nothing sinister in Shivaji's proposal and asked him not to entertain any doubts on that head. He urged on the Khan not to lose the opportunity that had in so unforeseen a manner presented itself and contended that Afzul Khan might advance with all his army to Javli, where there was ample room to canton his troops and no difficulty in the supply of water and forage. Afzul Khan's fears of an advance into the defiles of Javli were gradually dispelled and he was confirmed in the plan of marching into the enemy's stronghold ostensibly to bring about an interview with the Maratha leader and seizing upon him by force under that pretence. Satisfied with the assurances of his envoy, Afzul Khan ordered the camp to be moved for a march to Javli and in the hope of somehow or other securing the arrest of his opponent, he agreed to waive his former demands and humour Shivaji by granting all the concessions asked for. Having formed this resolution he wrote to Shivaji that he was coming down to Javli and Shivaji himself in his turn should descend from the fort of Pratapgad for the conference.

On the receipt of this final reply from the Khan, Shivaji summoned a council of his nobles and veterans and asked their opinion. They all concurred in expressing their loyalty and readiness to carry out any task their master might choose to entrust to them. They were prepared to lay down their lives for their chief. Shivaji then conferred with Jijabai,[1] who advised him to act in concert with his friends, reposing his confidence in Providence. For herself she had no fear but that now as formerly his auspicious enterprise would be crowned with the success it deserved. Armed with these reassurances Shivaji proceeded to make his plans.

To ensure the implicit confidence of Afzul Khan in his professions of humility, Shivaji took every precaution to render the Khan's march as easy and unobstructed as possible. The ascent up the ghats was made less toilsome by cutting down the brushwood and thickets and cutting new paths. An open space was made ready for cantoning the Khan's troops by clearing away the trees and shrubs. Outposts of soldiers were stationed at intervals on the Khan's line of march under direction of competent civil officers whose instructions were to supply every want of the Khan's forces, and make ample arrangements for the supply of their meals. The path cleared for the Khan's march was, however, prepared so cleverly that a dense growth of trees and brushwood obstructed the view on either side of the route beyond a certain distance. All by-paths and cross-ways were closed up by huge trees cut down across the glades.

Shivaji unfolded his secret counsels to Netaji Palkar, Moropant the Peshwa and Tanaji Malusare. Netaji Palkar was ordered to bring up his battalions from the Konkan immediately to the ridge of the ghats and maintain a close ambush under cover of thick foliage, a little to the east of the fort of Pratapgad. This was a precaution against a possible movement of part of the Khan's army in that direction. Moropant, a veteran general, received orders to loiter about the precincts of that prepared clearing where Afzul Khan's grand army was to encamp, and

[1] According to Sabhasad, Jijabai was at Rajgad, but Chitnis and the author of the Shivdigvijay say that she was at Pratapgad.

remain under cover of the shady trees to watch events. Raghunath Ballal was to be Netaji's lieutenant, and Trimbak Bhaskar, lieutenant to Moropant. A bugle was to give the signal for Netaji to advance and burst upon the hostile bands emerging on the heights, while on the discharge of five cannon shots from the fort Moropant was to make an onslaught on the army encamped in the vale of Javli. They were to be on the alert and booty was to be no consideration with them. While making these preparations without the fort, Shivaji had the fort itself placed in siege order, with a sufficient garrison and adequate equipment of guns and ammunition, food-stores and provisions all under his personal supervision. All accesses to the fort were closed. Every tower in front of the fort was manned with a defence force of a hundred men and half as many men formed the defence complement to each battlement in the rear. Besides a large number of warriors was drawn up in the passages leading to the main entrance, group by group, and these were ordered, on the signal of a trumpet blast after Shivaji's descent from the fort, to come forward gradually in little groups of one or two thousand and station themselves at fixed distances from each other, so that the outermost group would be within an arrow-shot from the place of the meeting and the last group would be at the portals of the fortress. A picked band of veterans was to escort Shivaji up to almost the very place of the conference.

At the foot of the fort where there was an open space near a battlemented tower was fixed the place for the conference between the two leaders. A spacious and magnificent pavilion was erected here for the purpose, with a grand couch of state in the centre and two or three smaller seats on the dais. A silken cloth lined the ceiling, with borders formed of strings of pearls and the divan was spread with cushions and carpets of various shapes and designs.

When all was ready word was sent to the Khan to start for Javli. He set out with his troops by the ghat of Radtondi (the "tearful" pass, so called from the steep ascent) where a path had been prepared on purpose. He came without his guns and heavy encumbrances, though this is contradicted by some chronicles. Descending the Radtondi ghat, Afzul Khan halted near the village of Par on the Koyana. The ascent that followed greatly harassed the Khan's followers, and the Pathan mercenaries in his army were heard to say that Shivaji was a rogue and no one could probe the depths of his cunning and subtlety. It was not a good sign as to how things would fare with them after all this ascent. The echoes of these complaints often reached Afzul Khan's ears. But he was strangely infatuated. So sure was he of out-witting Shivaji and making him a prisoner that he paid no attention to the hazards he was running. Shivaji did all in his power to make the Khan persevere in the fatuous course he was pursuing. At every halt tents, pavilions, camp equipments and all manner of provisions were officiously kept in readiness. These zealous attentions served to keep the Khan continually in good humour. Yes! Shivaji was off his guard, so thought the doting invader. The Maratha chief was absolutely without suspicion of his evil intentions. He would walk straight into his trap and be exhibited as a captured fool to the people of Bijapur! Such were the Khan's thoughts.

On his arrival at Javli, the Khan despatched Krishnaji Bhaskar up the fort to announce his arrival and summon Shivaji to the conference without loss of time. With this message the envoy went up the fort and delivered his instructions to Shivaji in presence of the assembled durbar. The formal business done, Shivaji had a private audience with the envoy, when Krishnaji declared that true to his compact he had brought the Khan to Javli. Now it was only left to him to bring the leaders together to a conference. The further development of the plan rested entirely in Shivaji's hands. He must now make use of all his resources. It was then decided that the conference should come off on the third day from that date. Krishnaji was to work upon the mind of the Khan and induce him to present himself at the pavilion with only two companions, and Shivaji was to give an undertaking to the same effect. The rest of the soldiers on either side should stand off at a distance. Krishnaji promised to obtain Afzul Khan's assent to these conditions and left the fort. On his return, Krishnaji communicated the conditions of the conference and further represented that Shivaji's timidity was without example, and he did not yet quite trust the Khan's assurances. Krishnaji then suggested that Afzul Khan should agree even to this condition as his main object was now on the point of fulfilment. Afzul Khan was eager to trap Shivaji. He shirked no conditions and gave his immediate consent to all these proposals. He sent his trusty officers to inspect the place of the meeting. They reported that the pavilion lay in an open plain, and there were no forces in covert.

At last the fateful hour arrived. The Khan set forward with 1,500 of the pick of his army. The crafty Krishnaji intervened representing that if Afzul Khan were to proceed with all that cavalcade, Shivaji's fear and distrust might be re-awakened, and he might not even be induced to descend from his fortress. Then he applied the soothing balm of flattery. "You, a pillar of strength to the Adil Shahi state, are a cavalier of renown! Shivaji is but as a rush in comparison with your prowess. Why, oh, Khan! so much ado to snare such a simpleton?" He then asked him to attend the pavilion with one or two attendants like Shivaji.[1] The Khan approved this plan and detailed his soldiers to wait in detachments along the way, and having stationed a fair number of soldiers within an arrow-shot of

---

1 The powada above referred to states that Moropant and Shamrajpant, Shivaji's ministers, who had been sent to conduct the Khan to the place of meeting protested when Afzul Khan set out in a palanquin with 4000 horse, and requested him to station his men at a distance as also to put down the palanquin away from the place. According to Sabhasad, Pantaji Pant (i. e. Gopinathpant) protested against Afzul Khan's taking such a large retinue, not the Khan's envoy, Krishnaji.

the pavilion proceeded in a state palanquin to the conference. He was accompanied by two attendants, along with a redoubted veteran soldier named Said Banda and the envoy, Krishnaji Bhaskar. All he now wanted was that Shivaji should, in terms of the agreement, present himself at the conference. He felt sure he would straight make a prisoner of him, without the least resistance. What was the puny Shivaji before Afzul Khan? So sanguine was he of success and confidence in his strength that he was merely attired in such a vest and cloak as it was the custom to wear when attending a public office. Clad in a flowing robe of thin muslin, he carried no other weapon than a sword. The Khan reached the pavilion, seated himself in the audience hall long before Shivaji's arrival and sent his envoy to the fort to bring down Shivaji. From him Shivaji learnt that Afzul Khan was accompanied by an expert veteran, and sent word to him that he did not dare to come down to the conference unless he appeared in the hall with no other companion than a single attendant. Upon this Afzul Khan bade Said Banda stand at a distance.

Meanwhile Shivaji having made all arrangements to meet the worst that might occur, had his bath and went through the usual ceremonial rites. He then addressed his prayers to the goddess Bhavani, the guardian deity of his family, and it is said that such was the fervour of his devotion on this occasion, that he had an afflatus of the divine spirit and became possessed by religious frenzy. It appeared to the observers that he became the medium of an oracular assurance on the part of the deity, bidding Shivaji "be of good cheer; that he would triumph, thanks to her powerful protection; that blinded by a mental gloom of her raising, the Khan had walked on unsuspecting to his doom. Let him fall a victim to her divine wrath and let the avenging victor immolate a buffalo with its brows stained with the blood of Afzul Khan!" These words—ascribed to the deity but uttered by Shivaji in a sort of trance induced by the extraordinary fervour of religious enthusiasm into which, agreeably to the devotional constitution of his mind, he was probably thrown by the tremendous pressure put upon his nervous system—were noted down by the officers present and communicated to him when he came back to his senses. He was still more elated by this prophetic assurance. Then Shivaji addressing his nobles announced to them that in going out to meet Afzul Khan he knew he was carrying his life in his hands. If the event ended in success there was nothing to fear; if the result were inauspicious they must not give way to despondency. They were to fall upon the enemy in the manner previously devised, put him to rout and defend their state. He trusted entirely to their bravery and valour. That he cared not a straw for the Mahomedan powers was due entirely to the co-operation and loyal support of the men standing before him. It was for them to exert themselves to the best of their power in order to save the glorious achievements of the past. This moment was to try their mettle. They would stand the test like heroes and win immortal renown. This was a stirring appeal and aroused in them the liveliest battle spirit. They bowed assent declaring not one of them would swerve an inch from his orders. They would lay down their lives. Their lives were not their own, having been once dedicated to his service. Their greatest honour would be a loyal death.

Having thus exhorted his companions, stimulated their national pride, and discussed further plans, Shivaji prepared to dress, for the hour of the ordeal was fast approaching. He wore the usual flowing robe in white over a mail-coat of links and a similar mail-cap under his turban. He girt himself with the waist-band and loin-cloth which Indian wrestlers and fighters habitually wear. He had a little poniard hidden under the sleeves of his right hand, and wore the sharp steel instrument called the "Tiger's Claws" on the fingers of his left hand. Thus accoutred he again visited with reverence the temple of his guardian deity and prostrating himself at his mother's feet entreated her parting blessing. Jijabai's heart was full to overflowing with affection for her son, but restraining her emotion, she gave him her blessing bidding him repose his trust in the protection of his tutelary deity. She compared herself to Kunti, the mother of the heroic Pandavas of Mahabharat fame, and said that he would shed lustre on the name of Bhonsle. She asked him to avenge himself on Afzul Khan, for the death of his elder brother Sambhaji, to which Afzul Khan had lent his countenance.[1]

Shivaji slowly descended down the fort, under the escort of Tanaji Malusare, Yessaji Kunk, Hiroji Farzand, Gopinathpant and about fifty other men. On arriving at the pavilion hall, Shivaji entered in company with Jiva Mahalya and Sambhaji Kavji.[2] Shivaji saw the Khan and made as if he was affrighted and faltered in his movements. Krishnaji Bhaskar who was with the Khan pointed out how Shivaji was seized with terror at beholding Afzul Khan and trembled in all his limbs. He proposed that Afzul Khan might even dismiss his attendant and encourage Shivaji to approach him, as he might feel more confident to encounter the Khan when he found him alone. Shivaji advanced nearer. His attendant bore a sword in either hand, a circumstance to which the Khan made no objection. On Shivaji drawing near, the Khan raised himself from

1 The Rairi bakhar gives the curious information that doubtful of success and fearing for his safety, Shivaji sent Brahmans laden with treasure to Kashi (Banares) and Gaya to perform his funeral rites in those holy places in case of his death, and that at the same time he made lavish largesses to the Bramans and shaved his beard, at which tears came into Jijabai's eyes, who had in consequence to be removed from his presence. As to the allusion to the death of Sambhaji, Shivaji's elder brother, *vide a* foot-note in Chapter II. It was a general belief that Afzul Khan had instigated the rebellion which led to the death of Sambhaji.

2 According to Sabhasad, Chitragupta and Shedgaokar bakhars, Shivaji was accompanied by Jiva Mahalya and Shambhaji Kavji, and this is followed by Mr. Kincaid and Prof. Sarkar. According to the powada Shivaji gave his sword into the hand of Jivaji Mahaldar and had him to attend on him. Granf Duff says Shivaji was attended by Tanaji Malusare. Jiva Mahalya was a barber by caste, (*Bharat Itihas Sanshodhak Mandal Sammelan Vritta*, Vol. V, p. 16).

his seat and advanced two or three steps forward to meet him. He was very eager to encounter the Maratha. He felt sure that Shivaji was unarmed and would easily fall into his clutches. The reason was plain,as the Khan was a man of giant built, though Shivaji while shorter of stature was far more wiry. Krishnaji Bhaskar formally introduced them to one another. They advanced to the embrace. The Khan contrived to get Shivaji's neck under his left arm, squeezed his head under the arm-pit, and drawing bis dagger attempted to drive it between his ribs. But it merely grazed the mail under his robe and caused no harm.[1] Recovering from his surprise and the agony of strangulation, Shivaji fastened the "Tiger's Claws" upon the Khan's abdomen. At the same time he drew out the poniard from under his sleeve, delivered thrust after thrust, and dexterously extricated his head from under Afzul Khan's arm. The "Tiger's Claws" pierced the Khan's bowels, drawing out the entrails and blood after them. Afzul Khan held down the wounded part with one hand and lunged with his sword upon Shivaji with the other. Shivaji warded off the stroke, by jumping off with great agility, but the blow glanced across his head-gear and dashing it to the ground caused a slight wound. In an instant Shivaji delivered

[1] Grant Duff's version is that Shivaji was the first aggressor, driving deep his "Tiger's claws" at the first embrace. The general tenor of the bakhars is quite different and is followed in the text here. Modak's History of the Adil Shahi Kingdom gives a radically different version of the event, briefly to this effect:—Convinced that it was impossible for him to prevail over Afzul Khan, Shivaji made a pretence of friendship, put on a show of humility, appeared before Afzul Khan at his tent and induced him to come to a banquet at Pratapgad. When the unsuspecting guest came with a dozen or so of his followers, Shivaji's armed bands suddenly fell upon him and cut him to pieces. Modak derived his account probably from the Basatin-i-Salatin, which gives nearly the same story. Chitragupta's bakhar and the powada introduce other details, viz., angry speeches between Shivaji and Afzul Khan followed by a duel. The Khan was apparently angry that Shivaji should make such a show of his magnificence in the upholstering of the pavilion. This led to mutual abuse. The Shedgaokar version is that the Khan complained about it to Shivaji's envoy, who propitiated him by replying that these costly things would eventually be surrendered to Bijapur.

another powerful blow and tried to wrest the sword from Afzul Khan's hand. The Khan raised an outcry of "Murder! treason! help!" which drew the soldiers on either side nearer to the scene of the tragedy. Said Banda first came up to the rescue and attacked Shivaji with his double-edged sword. Shivaji took a similar sword from Jiva Mahalya in his right hand and with his own poniard in the left began to ward off Said Banda's blows. In the meantime Jiva Mahalya rushed upon Said Banda and lopped off from the shoulder the arm with which he brandished his long sword, so that the loyal defender of the Khan collapsed on the ground.[1] Then there followed a general melee, in which the followers of Afzul Khan contrived to place him in a palanquin and bear him off.[2] Yessaji Kunk and Tanaji Malusare extricated Shivaji from the melee around him and pursued the Khan's palanquin. They came up with the litter and wounding the bearers in the legs compelled them to throw down their burden. The Khan's head was severed from the trunk and borne off wrapped in a scarf.[3] Afzul Khan had a Brahman civilian of the name of Krishnaji with him. He, compassionating the fate of the ill-starred Afzul rushed upon Shivaji, sword in hand, flaming with indignation. Shivaji parried one or two thrusts and then declared that he acted upon his father's command not to slay a Brahman. He had better make the best of his way home. With this order he was let go.[4]

1 According to Chitnis Yesaji Kunk slew Said Banda.

2 According to Sabhasad and Chitragupta Afzul Khan himself leapt down from the dais and began to run away with shouts of "Murder! treason!" at which his men rushed to the rescue, put him into the palanquin and began to take him away.

3 According to Grant Duff it was Khando Maley and other followers who cut off the head of the unfortunate Khan. Chitragupta and Sabhasad say it was brought down by Sambhaji Kavji at Shivaji's order. The powada represents Sambhaji Kavji to have maimed the bearers and Shivaji himself to have cut off the head.

4 Prof. Jadunath Sarkar on the authority of the Marathi bakhars, the Tarikh-i-Shivaji, the English Factory Records of Rajapur &c. concludes that Afzul Khan fell a vicitim to his own treachery.

Delivered from all these dangers Shivaji reached the main gate of Pratapgad in safety. It was still an hour or two before sunset. True to the concerted plans signal guns were fired and bugles sounded. The Khan's army encamped in the low-lying plain heard the cannonade and took it for a salvo in honour of the meeting. Thus they remained unguarded and unconscious of the great event. Meanwhile following the concerted programme Netaji Palkar fell upon the 1,500 warriors who had come up in Afzul Khan's cavalcade. By this time the news of the tragic end of the Khan had spread to this chosen body-guard. The guard was seized with surprise. The confusion became worse confounded when Netaji Palkar directed his onslaught upon them. But brave and expert veterans as they were they got the better of their panic and stood at bay. They struggled long and valorously with their Mavali assailants. At last the scales of fortune were turned against them. They had exhausted every art of defensive warfare. Then there was a head-long rush and they fled for their lives. The Mavalis pressed on in pursuit of them and cut down every Pathan they could overtake in the chase.

On another side Moropant Pingle followed up the appointed signal with a sudden onslaught on the main body of Afzul Khan's army peacefully quartered in their camp in the plain of Javli. They had not the least expectation of such a sudden charge by the hostile bands against them. Their panic was in proportion to their unpreparedness.

He thinks that Shivaji would have been considered but a fool, had he not provided against such a contingency at the hands of Afzul Khan. The late Mr. R. P. Karkaria more than twenty years ago made a defence of the version disclosed to us by the Maratha chronicles. The late Mr. Ranade in his "Rise of the Maratha Power" attempted a halting defence. A circumstance that must never be lost sight of is the fact that the Khan had made a solemn vow that he would take Shivaji alive or dead, and Shivaji had to elude his object. Besides the Khan's intrigues with the Khopdes (Rajwade XV, 302) clearly show his intention was to seize Shivaji, somehow or other. Scott Waring, in his *History of the Marathas*, 1810, defends the Marathi bakhar version of the tragedy.

Even thus they turned round to confront the enemy. But their defeat was a foregone conclusion, and the little resistance they made was prompted by the energy of despair. After repeated attacks they were at last driven into a precipitate rout. Shivaji's standing orders to his generals were not to put to death those who would give up their arms and surrender. Many who were wounded thus surrendered. Many took flight into the neighbouring jungles. Hiding and flying from forest to forest for some time they evaded capture. But this did not last long. They lost their way in the tangled woods and were at length detected and seized, worn out and starving, by Shivaji's search parties.

The captives thus taken were treated by Shivaji with his wonted courtesy and generosity. They were accorded treatment befitting their rank and released with grants of money for their travelling expenses. Persons of noble rank received due honour, horses and gifts of apparel being provided for their return to Bijapur. Many a Maratha soldier in the Bijapur service observing the magnanimous bearing of the victor transferred his allegiance to Shivaji. They were retained with cordial welcome. Among the great nobles captured on this occasion was a Maratha sardar named Zunzarrao Ghatge. Between Ghatge's father and the Rajah Shahaji there had once subsisted, as Shivaji was aware, a most cordial friendship. It was, therefore, natural that Shivaji should have tried with all the persuasiveness at his command to induce Ghatge to serve under his flag. But he declined to give up his Adil Shahi master even for the cause of freedom. Shivaji with great reluctance parted company with this scion of a family with which he had a hereditary alliance. He arranged for his return to Bijapur with presents of robes of honour and of jewellery as a mark of his esteem.

In the general affray, Fazal Khan, the eldest son of Afzul Khan, was wounded and took to flight. Applying bandages to his wounds he tried to escape by a concealed flight between the thickets and brushwood. But the unfortunate man with the members of his household fell into the hands of Khandoji Khopde.[1] They offered him a bribe and he volunteered to lead them in safety to Karhad along the bank of the Koyana, instead of surrendering them to Shivaji. When this was known Shivaji ordered Khopde to be executed.

Shivaji gained much booty in this defeat of Afzul Khan. It comprised about a hundred elephants, seven to eight thousand horses, a thousand camels, the entire artillery park and field-guns, about ten to twelve lakhs of rupees in specie, gold, pearls, and precious stones of the value of more than two lakhs, two thousand packages of cloth, tents, camp equipages and other material of use on a march. More important than these material gains was the accession of strength to Shivaji's army, for Marathas even from the Khan's hosts were astonished at Shivaji's bravery and generosity and willingly came over to him, company after company.

The severed head of Afzul Khan was presented to the goddess Bhavani, whose desecrated temple at Tuljapur was thus avenged. After visiting the temple of his guardian deity, Shivaji presented himself before his mother. Jijabai was overjoyed to welcome him to her arms again. Clasping him to her bosom, she congratulated him on the victory and exclaimed that the death of his brother, Sambhaji, was now avenged by his heroism. The day of his safe return from victory was indeed a red-letter day in her life. Uttering these words with maternal solicitude she went through the usual form by which Hindu matrons ward off

---

1 Chitnis and the author of the Shivadigvijay maintain that Khandoji Khopde, the commander of Afzul Khan's Mavali corps, led Fazal Khan and the unfortunate Afzul Khan's family in safety to Karhad with a force of two hundred men, and that some time later Khopde having fallen into the hands of Shivaji was executed. Instead of Khopde the name Kankde is also found. Sabhasad says that among other sardars two of Afzul Khan's sons were apprehended and brought before Shivaji.

the 'evil eye' from their children. Then turning to his companions she acclaimed them one and all for the triumph, saying the credit was due to them both for the victory and the preservation of their master's life. She loaded them with gifts in the shape of personal decorations or articles of attire in recognition of their valour.

Shivaji again descended from the fort to inspect the condition of his combatants. He arranged for the care and nursing of the wounded and encouraged them by visiting and conversing with them one and all. A comprehensive list was made of all who had fallen in the fight, and condolences were sent to their families and promises of pension, *vatans* or grants of land made to the veteran officers in their life-time were continued in their families as a hereditary right. The wounded received compensation in proportion to the seriousness of the wounds they had received, the amounts ranging from 75 to 200 pagodas each. Other favours and marks of honour were lavished in profusion upon men who indeed had nobly deserved them. The senior officers and nobles were presented with horses, rings, pearl pendants or crests, necklets and armlets, robes and head-gear embroidered with gold. There were grants of *inam* lands and revenue rights. These were graduated according to the quality of the service rendered. Many an infantry sepoy received promotion in the cavalry. Some received higher command in the army, others received special recognition in the shape of a palanquin grant, in itself no light honour. The sons of the deceased, if of mature age for the army, were at once enrolled in place of their father. These gifts and promotions were all made in presence of the whole army, with public acknowledgment of each meritorious action or warlike exploit. This had the effect of stimulating their enthusiasm and rousing the spirit of emulation among men and officers. The generous rewards made by Shivaji carried conviction to the breast of each soldier that their merit would receive due acknowledgment. Nor was Gopinathpant forgotten. He was given the village of Hivre as inam in perpetuity.[1]

At Pratapgad and other places there were great rejoicings in honour of the victory. Music was to be heard everywhere. Each private house was decorated with flags of victory, hoisted upon the verandahs. Sugar aud sweets were distributed from huge panniers carried by state elephants from house to house, a time-hououred feature of a triumphal celebration with Indian rajahs. The Brahmans received noble presents in the form of *dakshina*, and the poorest had alms. There were dinners and banquetings at which the Brahmans as usual figured conspicuously. Saints and *gosavis* of ancient shrines were honoured with gifts and offerings. The news of Afzul Khan's defeat and death was sent round to all friends and allies. A special messenger was sent to the Rajah Shahaji in the Karnatic to convey the tidings of victory. The event was celebrated as a national triumph. The death of the desecrator of the national shrines of Tuljapur, of Pandharpur, of Shingnapur was universally hailed as the death of a demon, and the finger of Providence was seen in his fall. A strong wave of patriotism overswept the whole country, such as it had not experienced for centuries. These feelings found vent in the stirring ballad or powada that celebrates the event. It is said that this powada was composed by the court minstrel at the express order of Jijabai. Afzul Khan's head was buried at the scene of the tragedy, and a castellated tower built on the site, to which the name was given of the Afzul *Buruz* or Afzul Tower. The sword wrested from Afzul Khan was preserved as a memento of the victory. Ascribing the victory to the propitious favour of the Bhavani of Tuljapur, it is said that Shivaji vowed to install and con-

[1] The Rairi bakhar says that the inam of Hivre (plus one lakh of pagodas) was conferred upon Shivaji's envoy Dattaji Gopinath, which is perhaps a mistake for Gopinathpant. The Shivadigvijay says that the inam of Hivre was conferred upon Shivaji's envoy, Pantajipant. As regards the variations of the name of Shivaji's envoy, notice has already been taken in a previous foot-note.

secrate an image of that goddess within the battlements of Fort Pratapgad. A Brahman expert was despatched to the banks of the Gandaki, famed for their veins of stone fit for artistic carving. The stone block thus carefully selected was sent to Tuljapur and a model of the original image made at the hands of an artist. The image was installed in a court on the topmost fortification at the summit of Fort Pratapgad and a beautiful temple raised over it. Provision was made for the maintenance of the daily rites and offerings and the periodical banquets to Brahmans on auspicious days in honour of the goddess. The same festivals and periodical fairs were ordered to be held here as at Tuljapur. According to other authorities the temple was erected after the fall of the Mores of Javli.

The Adil Shahi sultan and the dowager sultana at Bijapur were shocked to hear of the tragedy of Afzul Khan and the dissipation of his grand army. It is said that when the messengers brought word of the catastrophe the sultan sprang from his throne in grief and alarm and betook himself to his bed-chamber. The dowager queen gave herself to wailing and lamentation. That such a mighty nobleman as Afzul Khan should be so utterly defeated, his head dissevered from his body and carried in triumph, his forces annihilated and his camp despoiled showed a culmination of Maratha power which threw the omrahs of the Adil Shahi court into the deepest gloom. The fortunes of the Adil Shahi state seemed to totter At any hour Shivaji might knock at their gates, at the head of his victorious legions. The capital was full of these rumours. For three days, it is said, the royal drums remained silent and the sultan and his guardian mother lost all appetite for their meals.[1]

[1] Many curious legends have gathered round the tragic fate of Afzul Khan. The most striking is the story which is told in Marshall's Bijapur, and which is related by the local guides to travellers visiting Bijapur about Afzul Khan having a premonition of his death before starting against Shivaji and having killed his 63 wives that they might not share another man's bed and buried them in the tombs which are still shown to the traveller in the ruined and deserted suburb of Afzulpura, where the Khan had his mansion (vide Shedgaokar's Bakhar.)

CHAPTER XII

ADIL SHAHI NOBLES DISCOMFITED

THE terror of Shivaji's name was now felt in all parts of the Bijapur kingdom. The defeat of Afzul Khan was followed by the rapid conquest of several forts and rural tracts in the neighbourhood. On the announcement of Afzul Khan's invasion, the Abyssinian chief of Janjira had lost no time in laying siege to the Konkan forts of Tala and Ghosala. The report of Afzul Khan's tragic end coming quickly on the heels of the first report had induced him to raise the siege of both these places. Shivaji put his army in motion to punish the Abyssinians. But an opportunity for the conquest of Panhala having unexpectedly supervened Shivaji's forces were drawn in that direction.

For the officer in charge of this important fortress had of his own initiative opened communications with Shivaji and signified his intention to place the fort at Shivaji's disposal. This was a matter of surprise. That the commander of such an impregnable fort should without any suggestion on his part offer to make such a proposal naturally excited suspicion. Was he sincere? Was he acting thus at the dictation of the Bijapur authorities? It was necessary to ascertain that there was no plot or stratagem at the bottom of this offer. But the capture of this fort was bound to be of incalculable advantage, and it was worth attempting. A Mavali battalion was at once got ready under a trusty general. He was ordered to start for the fort in answer to the invitation. The choice had fallen upon Annaji Datto. Shivaji in person started with a larger force of infantry and cavalry to station himself in the vicinity of the scene of Annaji's operations to await the issue and support him in case of treachery. But there was no occasion for fighting. The governor of the fort kept his word. The fort was delivered unconditionally to Shivaji's general in October, 1659.[1] The fort of Pavangad fell under

[1] Another version of the capture of Panhala is as follows :—Shivaji

similar circumstances. Vasantgad was captured by a sudden assault. The acquisition of these forts established Shivaji's power on the upper courses of the Krishna. The revenues of these districts came into Shivaji's hands. Revenue stations were appointed all over these newly conquered possessions. These stations extended in a line up to the miniature fortress of Battisshirala.

On the fall of Panhala Shivaji marched up to that fort and detailed his forces for the conquest of a number of little hill-forts lying in all directions on the crest of the Sahyadri or the Western Ghats. Most of these fell without his generals being forced to strike a blow. But the forts of Rangna and Khelna had to be taken by storm. The conquest of Khelna indeed required tremendous sacrifices, in commemoration of which circumstance, Shivaji changed its name and it emerged on a new career of historical renown under the name of Vishalgad or Fort Tremendous. It has come down to our times under this name. All these acquisitions were made in little more than the space of two or three months after the Afzul Khan tragedy. Thus the fertile country of Kolhapur and its numerous fortresses came under Shivaji's domination.

During these times the Bijapur government maintained an important military station at Miraj, the governor of which was a general named Rustom Jeman. His military control extended from Kolhapur to Ratnagiri and included a part of the Kanara district. This general, strange to say, presented no opposition to the onward expansion of Shivaji's power within the sphere of his authority. Whether it be

had long meditated the capture of this fort, but had been deterred by the difficulties of the task. To effect its capture, Shivaji made use of a stratagem. He made a pretence of discharging from his service some seven or eight hundred of his followers, who representing that they were discharged by Shivaji offered their services to the governor of Panhala and were enrolled for garrison duty at that fort. Subsequently Shivaji laid siege to Panhala, when some members of the besieging party were secretly admitted under cover of night by the ex-soldiers of Shivaji and by their united arms the defenders of the fort were defeated and the fort captured.

that he stood in such fear of Shivaji's onslaught that he felt it more prudent to remain passive, or, as was alleged by the British merchants of the period at Rajapur, his silence and inactivity were purchased by a bribe, it is difficult to decide. But soon afterwards he received express orders from the sultan to take the field against Shivaji in defence of the district of Kolhapur. He had then under his command a force of three thousand horse with a small complement of infantry. He put himself at the head of these forces and marched upon Panhala. As soon as he drew near enough to the fort, Shivaji sallied out and charged with all his cavalry. So complete was Rustom's defeat that he was driven beyond the Krishna and chased for many miles. The chase lasted almost to the gates of Bijapur. The larger towns on the way were plundered and destroyed, and the shops and markets laid under contribution. Having inflicted such immense damage on the Bijapur government Shivaji wheeled round with such amazing rapidity, that the enemy had no time to pursue his galloping columns. His celerity of movement did not permit even a thought of pursuit.

On his return to Vishalgad, Shivaji put himself at the head of an infantry force, which had been kept ready in marching order by Annaji Datto under Shivaji's advice. His present objective was Rajapur and the seaport towns in the Konkan.

The town of Rajapur was at first spared because, as the English merchants in the Rajapur factory wrote, this port belonged to Rustom Jeman with whom Shivaji had a secret understanding. Shivaji fell upon Dabhol and carried all the little stations dependent on its maritime fortifications. When he had refreshed and recruited his forces by a brief stay at Raigad he was ready to fall upon Cheul, a wealthy harbour town, which was plundered for three days in succession. The military governor of Cheul, Khojoji by name, was taken prisoner, the town occupied, and the booty transferred safely to Rajgad. Meanwhile the

Adil Shahi refugees from the Konkan seaport had found shelter at Rajapur. The defeat of Rustom Jeman at Panhala had filled these refugees with great alarm. They had just heard rumours of Shivaji's depredations in the neighbourhood of Bijapur, when they were astonished to learn that a flying column of Maratha horse was actually storming the gates of their own town. The local governor attempted to escape in one of Rustom Jeman's cargo-ships. The Marathas tried to stop him. The governor pretended it was a cargo-ship of the East India Company. Henry Revington, the English Company's agent, became a party to this collusion. He pretended that the ship was attached for unpaid debts owing by the governor to the Company. In reality there was only a private transaction between the governor and one of Revington's brokers. He refused to restore the ship to the Maratha general. Upon this two of the Company's brokers and an English factor, Philip Gyffard, were arrested and sent for detention to Kharepatan. Meanwhile Shivaji heard of these events at Rajapur, and condemned the attack upon the port. He ordered all the plunder taken from the citizens to be restored and the prisoners set at liberty, though it seems that Gyffard had been already rescued by a party of Revington's mercenary soldiers, while being removed from Kharepatan to another fort. (February 1660).[1]

The discomfiture of two great generals of the Bijapur state, Afzul Khan and Rustom Jeman, of whom one had lost his life and the other had fled precipitately before Shivaji's squadrons, filled the people of Bijapur with terror. Nor was this mitigated by the sweeping march of the Maratha leader to the gates of the capital carrying fire and sword. The name of Shivaji had now become a terror to every Mahomedan sardar and killedar in the Adilshahi kingdom. Their consternation was so great that it emboldened many an adventurous marauder to profess himself a follower of Shivaji, enter the Bijapur territory unresisted and unchal-

[1] Factory Records, Rajapur, quoted by Prof. Sarkar.

lenged, and levy tribute and plunder with impunity. The tottering government was in utter despair. The omrahs of the court in their anxiety at the common peril forgot their civil dissensions for the present. No prominent general was forth-coming to take the field against Shivaji. It is said that Afzul Khan's son Fazal was burning with desire to avenge his father's death and continually clamoured for a campaign of vengeance against Shivaji. But even he did not dare to take the field alone. There was a party that suggested that the next campaign should be conducted directly under the auspices of the sultan himself, and that no single general, however great, could be entrusted with a task of such gravity. Others, on the contrary, declared that it would be derogatory to the crown that the sultan should take the field in person against a rebel, that Shivaji's rashness and craft might lead him to any extremities, and the sultan's life and with it their honour would be in jeopardy.

Thus they remained in uncertainty looking for a champion who would deliver them. At last such a champion was discovered. He was a brave Sidi or Abyssinian of the name of Johar. The fields of the Karnatic bore testimony to his prowess. A quarrel with the sultan had led him to declare himself independent in the province of Kurnool. The sultan bore him a grudge on that score. Later on he endeavoured to become reconciled with the sultan and tendered an apology for his behaviour in the past. The sultan now wrote to him in reply that he could purchase his pardon only by leading the Adil Shahi standards against Shivaji and returning in triumph after the complete overthrow of the Maratha leader. Greater honours, greater rewards would await his successful return. The Abyssinian joyfully accepted these conditions, and embarked on the new expedition. Fazal Khan accompanied him seeking revenge for his father's death.[1]

---

[1] According to Chitnis and the Shivadigvijay there was a third general named Sarja Khan.

The forces sent down with Sidi Johar were considerably larger than any previously launched against Shivaji. Some say they were twice as many as Afzul Khan's army. On the eve of his departure the sultan honoured the Abyssinian with a new title, Salabat Khan, the object being to enkindle his loyal devotion and enthusiasm upon which the success of the expedition so vitally depended. As to Fazal Khan, his desire for vengeance wss a spur more potent than any title. While Shivaji was attacked on one side by these two generals, the Abyssinians of Janjira with the co-operation of the chief of Sawantwadi were to make a diversion in the Konkan possessions of Shivaji. Such was the plan of the invasion. Sidi Johar and Fazal resolved to strike the first blow on Panhala. With this object they marched to that fort (May 1660). The arrangement was that Sidi Johar should complete the siege of Panhala and Fazal should descend the ghats into the Konkan to ravage Shivaji's territory on the coast. About the same time the Moguls began their campaign under the lead of Shaista Khan.

Shivaji's scouts promptly brought tidings of what was happening. Apprised of these hostile movements in good time, Shivaji issued orders for defensive preparations to be made in each fort and the armies to be on the alert. The tide of invasion was to be held back on all sides. Raghunathpant Korde was ordered to fight Sidi Fatteh Khan of Janjira in the Konkan; the defence of the Kalyan and Bhiwandi districts was imposed upon Abaji Sondev, the conflict with the Sawants of Wadi was entrusted to Baji Fasalkar. On the uplands of the ghats, there was Moropant Pingle in defence of Purandhar, Sinhagad, Pratapgad and other fortresses and the territory commanded by them; Shivaji in person was to conduct the defensive operations at Fort Panhala, and Netaji Palkar with the light cavalry was instructed to harass Sidi Johar from a distance and cut off his communications and supplies. Shivaji had undertaken the defence of Panhala in person owing to the news he had received from his scouts of the intention of the Bijapur leaders to concentrate their attack upon that fort. Concluding, therefore, that the major operations on the defensive must be centred in this spot, Shivaji had taken up this post. But the events proved that it would have been better if he had done otherwise.

Sidi Johar approached Panhala without opposition. Shivaji's object was to bide his time and punish him only when he had advanced so far that retreat became impossible. When the Bijapur forces had at last encamped close before Panhala Netaji Palkar took the aggressive. He made midnight raids upon the Adil Shahi camp. He cut off their supplies and harassed them by falling upon their foraging parties. Netaji's light cavalry used to emerge suddenly from a valley, burst upon those quarters of the hostile camp which seemed to be closely guarded, inflict immense slaughter and with lightning speed make good their escape before the enemy had time to think of pursuit, after discharging their mortar-bombs to add to the enemy's confusion. Johar saw the first necessity of the campaign was to get rid of these skirmishing parties of Netaji. He therefore took the offensive against Netaji's light horse killing all the skirmishers he could capture. But he soon found it an extremely arduous and interminable task to pursue and capture the Mavalis in that mountainous country. Having thus decided to let Netaji alone he concentrated the detachments which had been located in far-off stations and pressed forward the siege with greater rigour. Though the weather was unfavourable for a siege, his cannonading never slackened for a moment. Strict orders were issued under no circumstances to permit any one from the garrison to emerge from the besieged fort nor any outsider to enter in. Nor was this all. It was proclaimed to all ranks of the besieging army that no Maratha combatant they might come across should be allowed to escape alive. Distinct units of watch-parties were constituted of privates and officers to mount guard in rotation both day and night, the object being that there should be no relaxation whatever in the maintenance of a strict blockade. He himself set an example of untiring vigilance in supervising the operations of the siege.

Thus Shivaji was closed in for four months. There seemed to be no chance of the siege being raised by the enemy. The besieging army was large enough to keep up a strict blockade and its discipline was of a most efficient order. Do what Netaji Palkar might in the way of raids and surprises, the besiegers' efforts were not likely to grow weaker on that account. The cannonading from the brow of the fort, however steadily maintained, had little effect on the enemy. The worst of the situation was that the enemy had got news of Shivaji's presence in the fort, and he was not likely to leave this quarry, however long it might stand at bay, in search of more ignoble game. Sidi Johar no doubt thought that sooner or later the fort must fall before him and with it Shivaji must come into his hands. He would thus easily achieve what had foiled so many generals before him. His prestige at the Bijapur durbar would be established beyond dispute. These ambitious thoughts kindled his vigour and enthusiasm. On the other hand, Shivaji's foresight had made such ample preparations on the fort as might have sufficed for even a siege of over two years. There was no likelihood of any shortage of provisions or ammunition for that period even if his communications with the outside world were entirely cut off. What Shivaji chiefly regretted was that, being thus cooped up at Panhala, he was cut off from all sources of information as to how things were shaping themselves abroad and from issuing commands to his officers elsewhere. He therefore became very anxious to escape. Heavy siege lines encompassed him on all sides. There could be seen no weak point in the siege-works. To sally out and give battle was impossible, for the enemy far out-numbered the garrison. He had therefore to contrive his escape by daring and stratagem. With this view he opened communications with the Sidi stating that he was prepared to deliver the fort upon certain conditions, to state which he would himself come down to the lower slope, if the Sidi undertook to guarantee his safe return. The Sidi was overjoyed at the turn events had taken and willingly gave the guarantee. Shivaji attended by a small body-guard came down to the Sidi's camp in the evening. At the conference Shivaji played a part which quite imposed upon the Sidi. First he consented to surrender the fort. The discussion then turned on the conditions of the surrender, and the principal articles of the treaty were settled after some discussion. By this time it was very dark, and adjourning the conference for the night to be resumed the following morning for the settlement of minor details, Shivaji returned to his fort.[1] The Sidi was relieved of his cares and felt quite jubilant at Shivaji's submission and was ready to consent to any terms proposed by him. He concluded the war was now at an end and the fort as good as gained. He stopped the cannonading. The sentinels relaxed their watch and for the first time after a long period of tension gave themselves to mirth and frolic.

This was just what Shivaji wanted and for this it was

[1] In Modak's History of the Adil Shahi Kingdom we have quite a different version of this interview. There it is mentioned that Shivaji begged leave for a friendly interview with Johar in company with two or three of his followers, stating he wanted to sue for pardon and communicate further proposals at the interview. The Sidi was considerably elated with this and made answer that Shivaji might safely entrust himself in his hands, for that though he served the sultan and made the campaign under his orders, he wished him well and would willingly promote the terms of any accommodation proposed by Shivaji. Upon this assurance, Shivaji came down at midnight for a conference with two or three of his chiefs and was courteously entertained by Sidi. Preliminaries were settled and Shivaji returned to the fort. When the sultan heard of these events at Bijapur he was greatly incensed and moved the army to take the command into his own hand and conduct the war against Shivaji. (Page 202, Modak's History of the Adil Shahi Kingdom). Prof. Sarkar apparently follows a similar account, which is based upon the Basatin-i-Salatin.

that he had planned the meeting. With the flower of his bravest Mavalis, Shivaji slipped down the fort walls and marched right through the enemy's sentinel outposts.[1] Amid their boisterous carousals this movement at first escaped their notice. But they soon observed that Shivaji had given them the slip and began to prepare themselves for pursuit. Meanwhile Shivaji had used his advantage to good purpose and made such speed that he was now abreast of Fort Vishalgad.[2] But now there followed a pursuit in deadly earnest. Fazal Khan, the son of Afzul and Sidi Aziz, the son of Johar[3] led the cavalry with the infantry following at a distance. It was not till sun-rise however that they could come in sight of Shivaji's fugitive squadron. When they first observed it, the squadron was dashing up a ghat about six miles from Vishalgad. Now that the pursuers had gained so much ground upon him, Shivaji thought it necessary to leave a detachment in the gorge below to hold the enemy in play. A corps of Mavalis was detached and told to occupy the gorge in the glen of *Pandhare Pani* or the White Water, through which the enemy had of necessity to pass if he wished to continue the pursuit. Shivaji himself continued his flight. A leader of heroic mettle, Baji Deshpande of Hirdas Maval, was left in command of these daring Mavalis. Five cannon-shots pealing from the brows

---

1 The Rairi bakhar says that at the head of 20,000 Mavalis Shivaji sallied upon the besieging army and making his way with the sword, effected his escape to Vishalgad with Fazal in his pursuit. The pretence of a treaty to put the besiegers off their guard is not mentioned in this bakhar.

2 Grant Duff and Ranade following Chitnis say that Shivaji fled to Rangna. It is now generally agreed that the fort to which Shivaji escaped was not Rangna, but Vishalgad. *Pandhare Pani* is six miles from Vishalgad. The Jedhe Chronology also states that Shivaji escaped to Khelna, which is the same as Vishalgad. Rangna is about 75 miles from Panhala while Vishalgad is nearer. Ranade compared the heroic defence of the mountain pass by Baji Deshpande with the self-sacrifice of Leonidas and his three hundred Spartans at the pass of Thermopylæ. The death of Baji in the moment of victory may be compared with the triumphant deaths of the heroes of Quebec, of Corunna and of Trafalgar.

3 The Tarikh-i-Shivaji calls him Sidi Halal.

of Vishalgad were to be a signal that the Maratha prince was safe in its towers. Till then the gallant Baji was to keep the enemy at bay. No better choice could have been made for such a perilous enterprise. Never was confidence in a general more brilliantly vindicated. There stood the gallant hero, with his 5000 Mavalis in a defile which became literally a valley of death, without shelter to right or left, under no cover but hedges of bramble and brushwood. The vanguard of pursuing cavalry were scattered by bullets and chain-shot. They kept at a respectful distance below the defile. But the infantry soon came up and desperately charged the Mavalis. The Mavalis met the charge with equal impetuosity. The charge was broken and the attacking columns were rolled back. They formed again this time with increased numbers, and delivered a second assault. But even this was beaten off by Baji Deshpande. The battle then became a hand-to-hand struggle and was fiercely disputed on both sides. The fighting had now lasted for three hours and the dauntless guardians of the pass had not yielded an inch of ground. The enemy was still at the foot of the defile, storming and raving with impotence. This annoyed Fazal Khan. He rallied his Karnatic infantry to a third charge more furious and obstinate, supported by artillery. By this time the Mavalis had been reduced to half their numbers and the enemy had lost nearly five thousand. Baji Deshpande, nothing daunted, advanced to meet the charge, but while rallying his men to the attack was struck down by a cannon-shot. Bravely had he stood his ground and before his death he had the satisfaction of knowing that he had done his duty. For Shivaji had reached the fort and the loyal Baji had the joy ere he closed his eyes in death of hearing the five signal shots from the guns of Vishalgad. His was the happy death of a patriot who died for his king and country. His work was done and that of the gallant brigade of his Mavalis. After the glorious death of their leader and the arrival of Shivaji at his destination their mission was ended. They made for the fort, following diverse paths, taking care to bear on their shoulders the mortal remains of their gallant general. At the cost of many lives they saved his body from the hands of a vindictive and sacrilegious foe. The Mahomedans did not dare to pursue them through the mazy tangle of those forests. (July, 1660).

The enemy occupied the gorge, filed through the pass, and presented himself at the foot of Vishalgad. It was the hottest part of the year. The streams had all dried up. The valleys under the fort were scarcely commodious enough to plant batteries for purposes of a regular siege. Fazal Khan began thus to weigh anxiously the risks and chances of a blockade. The risks were that Shivaji with his wonderful capacity for achieving the impossible might invent some plan for his destruction were he to establish his lines before his stronghold. Moreover Johar had no desire to raise the siege of Panhala only to transfer the batteries to a new scene at Vishalgad and go through the preliminaries of a siege all over again. Upon these grounds, Fazal Khan gave up the idea of commencing a siege and returned to Panhala. But at Panhala, Shivaji having escaped, there was no strong motive to persevere doggedly in the siege. Shivaji was now free to counteract the designs of the besiegers. The monsoons were approaching, and their violence was more to be dreaded in these mountainous regions, especially by an army entrenched behind siege-works. Besides Raghunath Ballal who was entrusted with the command of the fort, when Shivaji effected his escape, was putting up a gallant defence. Shivaji had sent re-inforcements to co-operate with the garrison from without. When the besiegers advanced to plant batteries and storm the fort, these bands hovered round the rear of the enemy's army from below and wrought much havoc, slaying and plundering all that came within their reach. Again when the van of the storming party ran down to meet the alarm on their rear, the garrison seized the occasion to wreck the batteries. Between this double fire Johar and Fazal Khan gave up all hope of carrying the fort by storm. They had one recourse left open to them, corruption. This they now resolved to try. They sent word to Raghunath Ballal that it would be to his advantage to surrender the fort and come over to the besiegers' side. They would recommend him to the special favour of the Bijapur government. They promised him titles and jahgirs. But Raghunathpant was a man of sterling worth. He replied fearlessly that he thirsted not for gold and would never break faith with his master. So in this also the besiegers were foiled. All their resources had been tried to no purpose. Johar's resolution began to waver. His mind vacillated between opposite extremes. At one moment he thought to postpone the siege till after the rains, spend the interval at Bijapur, and after the enforced inactivity recommence the siege on a greater scale. Then again he thought he had led such vast forces to disgrace and ruin, without performing any feat of arms worthy of the sacrifice. His return to Bijapur would have no other construction than an inglorious defeat, and draw down the sultan's wrath upon his devoted head. Better then to spend the autumn in this inclement place with the chance of renewing the siege after the monsoon storms had exhausted themselves. He resolved to encamp at Gajapur between Panhala and Vishalgad. This proposal became known to the army. The despondent soldiery were seized with consternation and clamoured for furlough. Nothing could assuage their fears. Their obstinacy increased from day to day. It was plain Johar could not persevere to remain around Panhala with a discontented army. With great reluctance he broke up his camp and ordered a retreat to be sounded for the walls of Bijapur.

Ali Adil Shaha took it much to heart that all his great army should have returned home without achieving any success worth the name. Sidi Johar had only achieved this that the army he led back to Bijapur was considerably reduced in numbers compared to the army he had led forth upon the enterprise. The sultan was a rash and choleric man by disposition, and Johar's failure was not calculated to put him in good humour. Envious courtiers added fuel to the fire. They circulated a rumour that Sidi had been corrupted by Shivaji, that his escape from Panhala was due to a collusion. Had Sidi Johar been in earnest he would surely have surrounded Vishalgad. Far from doing so, the traitor had continued his make-belief siege of Panhala, and had now impudently arrived at Bijapur to practise further impostures upon his royal master. The credulous monarch readily believed these stories and accused Sidi Johar of premeditated treachery. Sidi was so offended with these imputations of treason that he became quite frantic with rage. He raved and fumed, violently affirming his innocence. But this defiant manner only served to confirm the sultan in his belief of Johar's treason.

At Shivaji's court there was joy and revelry. The state had tided over a great storm. The ruler had escaped from grave personal danger by the skin of his teeth. Baji Deshpande's self-sacrificing heroism was the cause of all this jubilation. Shivaji invited Baji's son, Balaji Baji, to his presence and having expressed his admiration of the great services of the hero, invested the young man with the father's honours. Balaji Baji was given the government of those hill-forts which had lately been under his father. He was given the honorary title of *bakshi* or paymaster of the forces, and a jahgir for his mintenance. Baji's seven brothers were similarly presented to Shivaji, honoured with stipendiary grants and state palanquins for the maintenance of their dignities, and appointed to the offices of paymasters of forces (sabnis) over the Mavali corps.

Raghunath Ballal, the defender of Panhala, came in also for a share of the royal favour. His services were handsomely acknowledged by his appointment to the governorship of Panhala and the country in its sphere of influence. He acquitted himself in his new civil duties just as creditably as he had discharged his military duties in the late war. He rallied the poor peasantry who had deserted their homes and farms in the troublous times of the siege. He made new revenue settlements to suit their convenience. He established in them a confidence of security and undisturbed enjoyment of their gains and increased the total output of revenue by putting new lands under cultivation.

While the siege of Panhala was in progress, the Sidi of Janjira pursuing the compact with Sidi Johar had launched his naval forces against the Konkan regions that had been acquired by Shivaji. It will be remembered that at the outset of his defensive campaign Shivaji had entrusted the conduct of the Konkan war to Raghunathpant Korde. The Abyssinians gained several advantages in the beginning. Their two chiefs Khairat Khan and Yakub Khan had even advanced to lay siege to the fort of Tala, when the tidings came to them that Shivaji had sallied out of the besieging lines round Panhala, beaten off his pursuers, and was coming thence on his way to Raigad. The news filled them with dismay and they hastened to raise the siege. Raghunathpant had now a fresh lease of activity. He retrieved his losses, drove off the enemy, and reduced the Abyssinian harbour of Danda-rajpuri. The Abyssinians now made overtures for peace. The campaign was thus brought to a triumphant conclusion. The Sidi gave to Raghunathpant as a mark of his esteem and appreciation presents of costly apparel and a horse with trappings.[1]

And now the Sawants of Wadi remained. It will be remembered that the plan of the Bijapur government was

[1] Orme says that on his escape from Panhala Shivaji came straight upon Dandarajpuri with a big army and presented despatches purporting to be from the hand of Sidi Johar requiring the Abyssinians to make over the fort of Dandarajpuri in exchange for Panhala. Having no reason to suspect any fraud, since Shivaji's coming away from Panhala seemed impossible without Johar's permission, the beguiled Abyssinian chief made over Dandarajpuri to Shivaji. Later his suspicions were roused and he refused to part with Janjira.

that simultaneously with the invasion of Sidi Johar the chiefs of Janjira and Wadi were to overrun the Konkan in concert. Acting upon this plan the Sawants had assumed the aggressive in the last campaign. Baji Fasalkar,[1] a comrade in arms to Shivaji from his earliest youth, was entrusted with the task of chastising the Sawants. Many skirmishes took place, in several of which Baji Fasalkar came off victorious. At length Kai Sawant with an army of five thousand, re-inforced by the Abyssinians of Janjira, advanced upon Baji Fasalkar. A decisive battle took place at Rajapur. Fasalkar himself, sword in hand, fought the enemy in every part of the field. Fasalkar and Kai Sawant were at last brought face to face. The battle now resolved itself into a duel between these opposing leaders. The combat was fiercely disputed, though each leader had received several wounds at the hand of the other. Both received mortal wounds and the same moment sank lifeless on the field. Fasalkar's men, though their chief had fallen, did not get dispirited, but fought their way to victory. Shivaji mourned the death of Baji Fasalkar as of a dear companion in arms and resolved to avenge it on the Sawant and the Sidi in whose quarrel his life had been sacrificed.

1 Fasalkar was one of the earliest companions of Shivaji's childhood and second to none in valour and uprightness among his leaders. Versed in all the arts of war, he was distinguished for a powerful physique. He was originally a resident of Muse Khore (the valley of the Musa) and was deshmukh of eight villages. He lived at the village of Kurdu near Chhatri-Nizampura, at the foot of Raigad and defended the entrance to its defile. According to the powadas he possessed three incomparable jewels in his far-famed shield, and sword, and mare,-the last named Yeshwanta (i. e. Victrix) being coveted by the Bijapur sarkar and the innocent cause of a combat between Fasalkar and Sonoo Dalvi, who had come to carry her by force to Bijapur.

CHAPTER XIII

THE BIJAPUR GOVERNMENT ON ITS KNEES, 1661-62

THE Bijapur Government was in a sullen mood. The disgraceful return of Sidi Johar and Fazal Khan had filled the sultan with indignation. In the first impulse of his wrath he announced his intention of taking the field in person against the Maratha leader. With a large army under his command, the sultan moved to Karhad. This movement had the immediate effect of stirring up those of his feudatories on the border who had consented to pay tribute to Shivaji These chiefs now hastened to the royal camp with humiliation and consternation and began to proffer their allegiance and service to the sultan. Sidi Johar at the same time supplicated for pardon. But he did not volunteer to attend the sultan in his campaign, knowing as he did by experience the petty envy and personal spite that reigned supreme with such disastrous results in the sultan's court. He retired to his jahgir.

The sultan began well. He besieged and captured Panhala. (August, 1660). Pavangad followed. The minor hill-forts in the neighbourhood fell one after another, but the forts of Rangna and Vishalgad held out. The rains having set in as he did not desire to expose his army to the heavy rains on the crest of the Sahyadri, he returned to Chimalge on the banks of the Krishna to canton his army during the season of storms.

Shivaji's plan was to encourage the sultan to fritter away his forces. He was no match for the overwhelming forces of the Bijipur durbar. Shivaji's army had already been considerably impaired by the stress of the campaign with Sidi Johar. The new storm had burst so soon after the last that he had scarcely any time to make up his losses. The sultan might meanwhile waste his strength on the capture of minor forts, and when his forces were affected as they were bound to be by the tear and wear of the desultory campaign, Shivaji resolved to put forth all his strength and beat back the invader. On the repulse of the sultan it would be so easy to recover the lost ground. Such were Shivaji's plans.

Nor was he quite idle. He turned the vanguard of his army once more upon the town of Rajapur. The Maratha horse entered the port a second time. The British East India Company, as has already been mentioned, held an important factory or entrepot at this flourishing town. The company incurred heavy losses during this invasion. Four British merchants including the agent, Henry Revington, were taken prisoners and confined for three years at the fort of Waisati and afterwards at Raigad. The reason of this harsh treatment was that the British factors at Rajapur had supplied ammunition to Sidi Johar during the last invasion, and some members of the Rajapur factory had been actually bribed by the Bijapur authorities to join their camp and help in the bombardment of Panhala fort.[1] Three years afterwards the British prisoners were allowed to be liberated on ransom.

On the fall of Rajapur Shivaji turned his forces against Shringarpur, where a Maratha noble of the name of Surve had set up an independent principality.[2] He had got together an army of about 10,000 and confident of his strength, he had been carrying on a marauding warfare with the landed gentry in the neighbourhood. His chief officers were two Maratha nobles, Pilaji and Tanaji, of the Shirke family. Pilaji attended Shivaji's camp in the capacity of Surve's vakil or agent. By way of retaliation on Surve for his insolence Shivaji threw Pilaji into chains a nd marching upon his master, took Shringarpur by a sudden assault. Though deprivedof his head-quarters, Surve did not acknowledge defeat. He rallied his men and continued the war. At length Shivaji advanced against

[1] Rajapur, *Factory Records*, quoted by Prof. Sarkar, p. 299.

[2] Grant Duff names him Dalvi and says Surve was his minister. He does not mention Shirke. The account followed in the text is that found in the Marathi bakhars. As explained before Dalvi was an additional name of the Surves.

the post where Surve had concentrated his forces. A desperate battle ensued, in which Surve was defeated and slain. But Tanaji Shirke made good his escape from the field of battle. On the destruction of Surve some of his feudatories took shelter with the Abyssinians of Janjira. Shivaji foresaw what this would lead to. The adherents of Surve, such as Tanaji and others were going to concentrate on Janjira soil and with the active co-operation of the Abyssinians deliver a combined attack upon Shivaji. In order to forestall such a combination, Shivaji conciliated Tanaji Shirke, giving him Shringarpur and other districts in inam. Shirke acknowledged the feudal suzerainty of Shivaji. Encouraged by this act of generosity on the part of the victor, the fugitive retainers of Surve returned from Janjira and were permitted to enter again upon their old *vatan* or hereditary rights of property. Such of them as were willing and fit for active service were enrolled in Shivaji's army. A little later, Shirke's daughter was married to Shivaji's eldest son.

The rains had now begun in earnest. But Shivaji could not afford to remain inactive. Simultaneously with the invasion which the sultan had undertaken in person, the Abyssinans, throwing to the winds the treaty recently made with Raghunathrao Korde, renewed their incursions into Shivaji's territory. Shivaji resented the treachery and wanted to accelerate his operations, so as to exterminate the foe before either the sultan or the confederate chief of Wadi could come to his help. The command was given to Venkoji. After a protracted struggle, Venkoji conquered Dandarajpuri with the territory surrounding that town. The conquered country was occupied by a strong expeditionary force of five or six thousand, and fortifications were raised at suitable points to overawe the district. Only their stronghold of Janjira remained with the Abyssinians. Shivaji opened a cannonade upon this fortress, but had soon to give up this attempt, for want both of sufficient artillery and of expert artillery-men. On the close of the monsoons, Shivaji had to relax this campaign and concentrate his attention upon the movements of the sultan.

That prince, as we have seen, had postponed active operations for the autumn and encamped his army at Chimalge. While encamped at Chimalge he received despatches from the Karnatic announcing an extensive revolt against the Adil Shahi power. The sultan decided to send Sidi Johar to the Karnatic to quell the rebellion and with this object invited him with all honour due to his position to lead an expeditionary force to the Karnatic. But Johar who distrusted the sultan and was at bitter enmity with Ibrahim Khan, the prime minister, declined the responsibility and straightway returned to his jahgir. The sultan construed this action as a proof of his being in secret league with the rebels in the Karnatic, as also with Shivaji.

The sultan was in great perplexity at being thus caught between two fires. He had embarked upon this campaign with Shivaji with the firm resolve of never turning his back upon the operations, before the name of Shivaji was wiped out of the country. Some of his adherents were even now of the same opinion. But there was also a weighty expression of opinion on the part of those who maintained that the situation in the Karnatic, both for its gravity and the magnitude of the issues involved, required the immediate attention of the durbar. The pursuit of the elusive Maratha warrior over valley and mountain, forest and plain, and the sacrifice of vast armies to secure this paltry end would be at best, they fancied, an illustration of the mountain in labour and the proverbial mouse. While the sultan was distracted between these conflicting opinions, the proposal of the deshmukhs or chiefs of Wadi came as a great encouragement to him. For the Sawants of Wadi, Lakham Sawant and Khem Sawant, applied for liberal reinforcements to enable them to prosecute hostilities against Shivaji and undertook to destroy utterly all his authority over the entire Konkan coast. This proposition was most welcome to the sultan as it immediately relieved him from an anxious dilemma. The prayers of the Sawant chiefs were readily acceded to. It was decided that Behlol (*Bahlol*) Khan and Baji Ghorpade, the chief of Mudhol, should muster all available forces and march to the succour of the chiefs of Wadi. The three leaders were required to concert together a plan of operations against Shivaji and the sultan in person was to take the field against the rebels in the Karnatic.

Preparations were being rapidly made on an extensive scale for a campaign on which mighty issues seemed to rest. While the forces were mustering, Baji Ghorpade had occasion to pay a flying visit to his jahgir of Mudhol, a movement of which instant intelligence was conveyed to Shivaji by his spies. This was the man who bore the stigma of having been the instrument of that treacherous capture of Shahaji which had almost culminated in a frightful tragedy. When Shivaji with wonderful tact and resources saved his father from the sultan's vengeance on that occasion, he had, as it will be remembered, sworn a deadly feud with the chief of Mudhol. The hour he had long waited for to vindicate the family honour had now at last arrived. For the gates of Mudhol fly suddenly open before Shivaji's columns and with streams of blood and heaps of slaughtered dead the treacherous chief and his clansmen atone for their villainy.

Khawas Khan took the place of command made vacant by the death of Baji Ghorpade. But the Mahomedan generals had not advanced more than a few days' march before they were ordered to divert their forces from the Konkan and required to present themselves without loss of time at the scene of war in the Karnatic. The flames of rebellion in the southern provinces of the kingdom had assumed very grave proportions and required a larger effort to quench them than had been anticipated by the sultan.

Shivaji could have prayed for nothing better. While the deadlock in the Karnatic engrossed the armies of the

Adil Shahi state, Shivaji swept rapidly from fort to fort recovering lost ground and adding many a new province he had never conquered before. The Sawants of Wadi who had paraded their loyalty to the sultan and applied to him for help in a concerted attack upon Shivaji had certainly not even endeavoured to veil their malignant animosity against the rise of the new power. Nemesis was not slow to overtake the chiefs of Wadi. Shivaji swiftly overran their dominions. The Sawants were in despair. They could scarcely put forth any resistance, without the active aid of the sultan, and this aid the sultan's present embarrassments had prevented him from sending. Shivaji made immediate conquest of Kudal, Bande, and other territorial possessions of the Sawant Wadi chief. The latter found an asylum in the hospitable country of Goa, the capital of Portuguese India. Shivaji sent a peremptory reprimand to the Portuguese authorities, whose eyes were now opened to the risks they were incurring in harbouring the refugees, and the latter were again cast adrift to encounter the forces of Shivaji. At length, deserted by every prince or feudatory chieftain, they made humble appeals to Shivaji, through their vakil or agent, Pitamber Shenvi. They averred that the Sawants were related to the Bhonsles by many ties of relationship. They deprecated the fact that the two families should act as enemies. They protested their readiness to transfer their allegiance to Shivaji, praying him to forgive and forget the past and admit them again to a feudal dependence upon him. Shivaji was gratified to see them acknowledge the error of their ways and profess their loyalty. He gave them pardon and invited them to an interview, at which it was decided that they should continue to enjoy in perpetuity the revenues of their fief as deshmukhs of Wadi, subject to an annual tribute.[1] Their infantry force was transferred to Shivaji's service and sent on campaigns far away from their homes, while their own

---

[1] Sabhasad says that they were to receive a fixed revenue of six thousand pagodas, reside at Kudal, and abstain from any building or entrenching operations or mustering an army.

possessions were placed under a defence force composed of Shivaji's veterans.

Now there were two valiant commanders in the service of the Wadi chief, viz., Nan Sawant[1] and Rama Dalvi. Pleased with their address and chivalry Shivaji received them with open arms in his service. Rama Dalvi was indeed a name to conjure with in the Konkan. This valiant leader was entrusted with a large army for the reduction of the outlying parts of the Konkan. The Sawants thus lost for ever two of the main pillars of their strength.

During this campaign Shivaji first came into collision with the Portuguese. By rapid conquests he got under his occupation the Portuguese districts of Panch Mahal, Mardangad and Bardesh, and threatened the land communications of Goa itself. To deliver Goa from a possible blockade and escape further hostilites at his hand, the Portuguese made overtures for a peace through the medium of Anant Shenvi, who was the sabnis or paymaster of the forces under the Desai or Chief of Kudal. But Anant Shenvi professed a friendly attitude towards Shivaji only to cloak his treacherous intentions. He represented to the Portuguese authorities that the sending of a peaceful embassy would throw Shivaji off his guard and the occasion should be seized to entrap him by a midnight raid upon his camp. But Kanhoji Tandel, the skipper of a local barque, divulged the sinister plot to Shivaji. Profiting by the information, Shivaji remained in readiness awaiting the development of the treachery. True to the information received, Anant Shenvi noiselessly led an ambushed force of 10,000 Portuguese to surprise Shivaji's camp. But what was his anguish to discover that Shivaji had fallen back about a mile and placed his men in battle order in evident expectation of his midnight assailants! Come what may, the Portuguese had now to open fire, which they did as soon as they came up to the encampment. Shivaji

[1] Sabhasad names him Tanaji Sawant.

held in his men till day-break, when his cavalry dashed down upon their opponents and cut them to pieces. The Portuguese were utterly routed. Scarcely a thousand of their men escaped with their lives. Some fell dead upon the field of battle; others were drowned in the creeks, and a large number were wounded. The Portuguese government was now in great fear. Shivaji harried the entire Bardesh with fire and sword. Portuguese captives without exception were put to the sword. The Portuguese merchants were arrested and subjected to heavy war-fines. The military cantonments of the Maratha cavalry stationed in the various parts of Kudal, Bande, Sakli, (Sankhal or Sankhali), Maneri and other places were extended to Bardesh. The landward portions of Goa were, in one word, brought under permanent occupation, and events had come to such a crisis that it seemed that the whole of that little peninsula would slip for ever from the hands of the Portuguese. The Portuguese government now repented of their folly in listening to the treacherous counsels of Anant Shenvi. They sent ambassadors for peace and made an ample apology. The ambassadors came laden with presents to Shivaji's camp, the presents consisting chiefly of a sum of 20,000 crowns and magnificent suits of apparel. The treaty now made with the Portuguese provided that they should annually furnish a certain number of new cannon to Shivaji as also jewellery and should obtain from him warrants for the passage of their mercantile vessels.

The Bijapur government now mourned the downfall of the Sawants. The chief of Wadi was the last of their great barons in the Konkan. His fall left little scope for the recovery of that region in the future. The Abyssinian chief of Janjira, once the high admiral of the Adil Shahi crown, was equally maimed and crippled by the repeated onslaughts of Shivaji. The Abyssinians saw that henceforth they could not depend on the fostering care of their Bijapur sovereign. The fate of the Sawants made them indifferent towards their masters. The Bijapur durbar was in great perplexity as to the next move they should make in the game with Shivaji. No general at their court would undertake a new campaign against him. Wearied with the constant internecine struggle, the grand vizier of the court at length opened secret communications with Shivaji. There were reasons for this secrecy. The grand vizier plainly saw that the courtiers, whose craven spirit shirked the perils of fighting, would be the first to throw themselves into attitudes of injured honour on hearing of a treaty with this enemy. They would stand with folded hands, spectators of the rapine and bloodshed, and try to redeem their indifference by an insincere outcry against a peace. The vizier knew the temper of these gilded popinjays too well not to perceive that they might even attempt to taunt him with accusations of breaking faith with his sovereign, if not in formal terms at least by innuendo. They were even capable of using back-stairs influence with their sovereign to procure the banishment or death of the advocate of a conciliatory policy. The chief conditions of these informal negotiations, which shortly afterwards resulted in a treaty, were that the conquests hitherto made by Shivaji should be allowed to remain in his hands and the Adil Shahi durbar should make no further attempt at their recovery. The durbar was to recognize Shivaji as an independent sovereign, cede him certain defined districts and stipulate to pay him an annual tribute of seven lakhs of hons amounting to about Rs. 35,00,000 at the ruling rate of exchange. There was to be a defensive alliance between the two powers, and Shivaji's ambassador, Shamji Naik Pande, was permitted to reside at Bijapur and represent him at the Adil Shahi durbar.

If the durbar acquiesced in such terms, they did so manifestly because of the utter exhaustion of their military resources. Never was defeat more complete or acknowledgment more ample on the part of a sovereign towards a former vassal. Shortly afterwards the Rajah Shahaji obtained permission, as is told in the following chapter, to revisit

Maharashtra. On this occasion the Bijapur durbar exhorted Shahaji to use his influence with his son to continue these friendly relations with their court. The result of Shahaji's advice was that Shivaji ceased to attack Bijapur.

Shivaji may now be said to have attained the crown of his earliest ambition. Every crisis had tried the high spirit and sterling virtues of which he had given promise from his early years. The plans and visions which Dadaji Kondadev and others had considered so chimerical had been proved to be not only practicable but to have been actually realized. He who had been so recently no more than a petty jahgirdar was now famous and feared throughout the whole of south India. The lesser glory of envious deshmukhs and haughty sardars of the Maratha gentry had paled before his. The spectacle of a sovereign state paying tribute to its tributary vassal filled his rivals with wonder and dismay.

This will be the proper place to review Shivaji's possessions at this period of his career (1662). His territory comprised in the first place the whole of the Konkan coast from Kalyan to Goa, a strip of 300 miles in length. From the Bhima to the Warna, the uplands that rise above the Konkan were also in Shivaji's hands. This territory was on an average about 160 miles in length and about 100 miles in breadth. His military resources comprised 50,000 foot and 7,000 horse. This army was much too large considering the dimensions of his kingdom. But living as he did in the midst of constant alarms and compelled to keep himself on a war-footing so as to meet at any time the forces of two empires, this army cannot be said to have been too numerous. Of these the first had been worsted; with the second he had just come into collision. The result of that collision was not a long way off.

CHAPTER XIV

RE-UNION OF FATHER AND SON

It goes without saying that no person could have been in greater ecstasy at Shivaji's successive triumphs and the crowning glory of the peace that made Bijapur a tributary to a vassal's son than his father Shahaji. He was naturally most anxious to meet again a son whose valour and good fortune had well-nigh proved invincible. Frequent correspondence passed between father and son, the one reporting in brief the events as they developed one after another, the other exhorting and felicitating him on his victories. But the correspondence was most guarded. Shahaji had no desire to have it disclosed that he had any part in Shivaji's affairs. Such a disclosure in his opinion would have been prejudicial, nay fatal, to his far reaching designs in the Karnatic. He had already had experience of the mistrustfulness of the Bijapur durbar. It was only when peace was made between Shivaji and Bijapur that he applied for leave to pay a short visit to Maharashtra, ostensibly to visit the old shrines and temples and perform the traditional rites and ceremonies. He exerted private influence on the durbar to have this request granted. In sanctioning his application for furlough the durbar wrote to him in reply that now that he was returning home, he ought to persuade his unmanageable son to be obedient to the central power and bring him to pay his respects to the sultan. He should become a noble or omrah of the court. If he presented himself at the durbar, they would be but too eager to give him the grand viziership of the kingdom. At any sacrifice Shahaji ought to use his diplomacy to make Shivaji a willing feudal lord under Bijapur. To this Shahaji replied that the durbar already knew well enough how little Shivaji cared for the parental authority, but he would do his best to advance his chief's fortunes. After his vows to his guardian deities had been discharged, he would call upon Shivaji and give him good counsel. Shahaji received a reply exhorting him to try his best to persuade Shivaji.

Should he, however, persist in keeping aloof from the Bijapur influence, Shahaji was exhorted that he at any rate should not make common cause with him. He was asked to return to his sovereign's service, unaffected by the ties of a parent's love.

Under such circumstances Shahaji left the Karnatic to visit once more his native land after a long term of absence from home. He was accompanied by his second wife and the son she had borne him, Venkoji. Shivaji was apprised of his father's coming home again with the permission of his sovereign.

On reaching the shrine of Tuljapur Shahaji attended the temple of Bhavani to discharge his vows. Large sums of money were distributed in charity. It is said that Shahaji had made a vow to the deity of Tuljapur that if his son's noble enterprise for the establishment of religious and civil liberty among his countrymen were by the deity's blessing to be crowned with success he would adorn the temple with votive images and offerings to the value of a lakh of rupees. The events of Shivaji's career had turned out so auspiciously that Shahaji had now come with the greatest eagerness to make good his vows. He had statuettes in gold cast by the artists of the Karnatic which he now dedicated to the goddess. Shahaji visited several other holy places, among others the temple of Mahadev at Shingnapur and the Vithoba of Pandharpur. At every holy place, Shahaji performed acts of charity including the banqueting of learned Brahmans and alms to the poor.

On the arrival of his father within the limits of his kingdom, Shivaji appointed officers to provide for his comfort at every halt. If Shahaji was so eager to clasp in his arms his glorious son, Shivaji was no less eager to welcome his beloved father. To Jijabai indeed it was a great occasion. The reunion between wife and husband, father and son, which after such a prolonged absence was now under the auspices of the gods to take place, was arranged by consultation with the Brahmans to take place in a temple. The celebrated temple of Jejuri was selected for the function. The cavalcades of father and son were to approach this place at an appointed hour. On the arrival of the Rajah Shahaji in the neighbourhood of Jejuri, Shivaji sent forward his commander-in-chief accompanied by foot soldiers, cavalry and elephants to greet and receive him in the name of Shivaji, while the Maharajah himself waited at Jejuri. Amid strains of music and jubilation on the part of the multitude Shahaji advanced escorted by the procession that had gone forth to receive and lead him to the temple. The sacred rites performed, Shahaji went through a quaint Hindu solemnity of renewing old love with relations meeting together after a prolonged separation. A large basin of bronze was brought filled with clarified butter, and the long lost relations had their first sight of each other silently and simultaneously in the reflection of their faces mirrored on the surface of the liquefied *ghee.* The persons to whom Shahaji was thus introduced in the quaint forms of the family reunion ceremony prescribed by Hindu tradition, were his wife Jijabai, his son Shivaji and Shivaji's two wives. After this solemnity, Shivaji saluted his father prostrating himself at Shahaji's feet, who raised him up with great emotion and clasped him in a loving embrace. The tears started to their eyes with joy and gratitude. Shahaji was then taken in a palanquin to Shivaji's camp, Shivaji walking bare-footed by his side and holding his father's slippers in his hands. On arrival Shahaji was seated on the divan, while Shivaji stood before him with his father's slippers still in his hands in a reverent attitude and addressed him somewhat in the following strain: "I have transgressed your precepts and made war upon Bijapur. This has brought your life time and again in jeopardy. It was most gross and improper that a son's misdeeds should recoil upon his father. The son now pleads guilty to the charge and now that he has repented of his misbehaviour he offers himself for any punishment at the bands of his injured father." These words stirred tumultuous feelings in Shahaji's breast and drew tears from his eyes. He embraced his heroic son and seated him next to him, not without much resistance and made reply in the following terms: "Your deeds, indeed, are no misdeeds, but such as may be expected of a scion of the Sesodia line of warriors. I am proud and gratified to behold the record of valorous deeds by which you have vindicated and established the civil and religious liberty of our countrymen. You have fulfilled the family tradition that there should be born in our house a ruler who was destined to inaugurate a new era and restore the Hindu liberties and religion. Your valour and wisdom have revived the glories of our historic house. What greater happiness in heaven or on earth than to have been the father of such a glorious son?" At these words of praise and encouragement Shivaji acknowledged his thanks by again bowing down reverently at his father's feet, exclaiming that his was the glory and the praise if any meritorious deeds had emanated from so humble an instrument as himself. Shahaji's good wishes and paternal blessings had wafted him onward to victory and the little success he had achieved was entirely to be credited to his account.

When the interchange of loving greetings and confidences had lasted some time, Shivaji introduced to his father the officers and dignitaries of his kingdom. Then he saluted his step-mother Tukabai with affection and reverence and embraced his step-brother, Venkoji. Shivaji was then introduced to his father's officers. Every one was gratified at the filial piety of their chief towards his father. Unstinted eulogies of father and son were heard on all sides. In honour of the joyful event, Shivaji made liberal largesses to the poor and banqueted the Brahmans. Joy beamed in every countenance.

The camp was then moved to Poona, where Shahaji

stayed for two months.[1] Shivaji treated his father's attendants and followers with royal hospitality. He personally superintended the arrangements for Shahaji's comfort. Shivaji made a full recital to his father of the civil and military arrangements he had made in his principality, and while his father was under his roof he transacted no state business without consulting him. Nay, all was done in Shahaji's name while he remained in his son's territory. Shahaji's gratification knew no bounds at these marks of honour and affection. Who could have expected such humility and filial obedience in one who had practically been the architect of his own fortune? Shivaji showed him all his treasures. Shahaji was astonished at the vast accumulation of treasure and precious stones which he had got together in so short a time—treasure, indeed, which might have done honour to the ruler of a world empire.

Shahaji had brought with him from the Karnatic some swords of exquisite workmanship, which he presented to Shivaji, and as a special mark of his esteem and satisfaction he gave to Shivaji a be-jewelled sword which he himself usually carried. Shivaji received it with reverence and gratitude, and as having been hitherto wielded by his

---

[1] We have followed the traditional account of Shahaji's visit to his son at Poona in 1662. However according to the Jedhe Chronology, Shaista Khan had already captured Chakan and taken possession of Poona by October (or November) 1660. Prof. Sarkar, basing his conclusion on the Persian chronicles, states that Chakan was captured by the Moguls in August 1660, and soon afterwards Shaista Khan returned to Poona. As the city of Poona was occupied by the Moguls at least till April 1663 (Jedhe Chronology pp. 186), we have to conclude *either* that Shahaji's visit to Shivaji was paid at some other place than Poona, or that it took place, as it seems more probable, after the retreat of Shaista Khan, in the middle of 1663. The trend of thought in the chronicles is to the effect that Shahaji paid his visit before Shaista Khan's occupation and this is accepted by nearly all historians. But the statements in the Jedhe Chronology and the Alamgir Namah, which Prof. Sarkar relies upon, are in favour of the view that Shaista Khan began his offensive almost about the same time that Shivaji was besieged at Panhala by Sidi Johar. Khafi Khan gives no date as to the occupation of Poona by Shaista Khan, but states that he marched from Aurangabad towards Poona and Chakan about the end of January 1660 (Vide Elliot, VII, p. 261).

victorious father he gave it the name of the 'Tulja' sword and kept it with great reverence side by side with his sword 'Bhawani.' In normal times these swords were the objects of certain acts of worship at the hands of Shivaji, a superstitious belief which was much in fashion with Indian soldiers of all ranks.

During these days Shivaji spent all his time in the performance of filial offices. No great events or campaigns requiring him to turn aside from these filial duties were entered upon during this period. Shivaji attended not only upon his father but also upon his step-mother, Tukabai, towards whom he made no difference in his affection or behaviour from what he observed towards Jijabai. The same evidence of zeal and service he showed in his relations with his brother, Vyankoji.

After some days Shivaji requested his father to inspect his principal fortresses and give him the benefit of his opinion upon their equipment. Shahaji made the tour of inspection in Shivaji's company, the latter describing the circumstances under which each fort was captured and noting the suggestions made by Shahaji, with his wide experience of the art of fortification. Shahaji was taken to Pratapgad and shown over the fort, the temple of Bhawani, and the tower or buruz commemorating the death of Afzul Khan. Shahaji now learnt in detail the stratagems pursued at that crisis culminating in the great tragedy. The officers in charge of the different forts, and the leading nobility of every district that was visited were introduced to Shahaji throughout the tour.

When at last they came to the fort of Panhala, Shahaji signified his intention to return to the Karnatic. Shivaji requested him to reconsider his decision and spend the close of his life in his mother-land, superintending the affairs of his kingdom there. Shahaji pointed out in reply that were he to yield to the dictates of his family affections he would have to give up the fortune he had acquired in the Karnatic. Another weighty argument in favour of his departure, said Shahaji, was that his occupation of the Karnatic might be of service to Shivaji in carrying forward his higher ambitions, the ultimate goal of which was to expand his power over the entire Indian continent and expel the heresy of Islam. Shivaji listened to these reasons and abandoned his importunity and began to prepare for his father's impending departure. There was another round of banquets and entertainments at Panhala in honour of the departing guests. Magnificent presents were exchanged with Shahaji's followers. His chief officer, Trimbak Narayan Hanmante, was presented with an embroidered suit, gifts of jewellery and a sword and shield. Shahaji himself and his second wife and son received costly offerings befitting their rank. A large force of cavalry and elephants was got ready to attend them on the way.

The final farewell was most sad and pathetic. Shivaji was sincerely affected at the prospect of his father's old age being spent in the service of an ungrateful court, and quite convinced as he was of the essential degradation and unhappiness of such a position, he desired nothing better than that his father should spend the ripe years of his old age in the tranquil calm of his native country and amid his kindred. But Shahaji's firm decision and the grounds he had mentioned for it had disarmed him of every argument. The final moment, however, overwhelmed him with grief and he exhorted Shahaji's officers, again and again, to take care of the aged veteran assuring them that he would reward them for their painstaking zeal, as he soon expected to return Shahaji's visit.

Tradition affirms that Shivaji entered into an undertaking with his old father not to enter on any further warlike operations against Bijapur during the rest of Shahaji's life. Shahaji first reported himself at Bijapur and at a private conference with the sultan made over to him the jewellery, horses, and elephants which in reality Shivaji had presented to his father, but which Shahaji averred were sent by his son as a nazar or state present to the Adil Shahi durbar. He also announced that he had effected his mission with Shivaji and with these assurances betook himself to the Karnatic.

Shahaji did not live long after his return to the Karnatic, and this was the last meeting between father and son. The tragic circumstances of his death have already been described in the second chapter. The news of the tragic event filled Shivaji's heart with sorrow. His one protector was gone, he exclaimed, by whose silent support and approbation he had been nerved to defy his Mahomedan foes. The pride and satisfaction of a loving parent at the exploits of his son, which are such inestimable spurs to noble action and enterprise, were lost to him for ever. And thus he grieved. Jijabai was more disconsolate still. Her grief it was impossible to calm or restrain. She prepared to perform the rite of *sati*, with the devotion of a faithful *Kshatriya* wife. This resolution of his mother aggravated Shivaji's sorrow. He begged her, besought her, held fast to her feet, but she would not yield. The ministers of state, Moropant, Niraji, Dattaji and others at length intervened representing to Jijabai that Shivaji would so much take to heart her self-immolation by the act of *sati* as scarcely to outlive her death and the empire he had built up by long years of labour was sure to collapse with his death. The name of Shivaji and together with it that of Shahaji would both alike be extinguished with her death. It was, therefore, imperative in the interests of the state that she should bear her grief in silence and patience instead of yielding to the impulsive thought of sacrificing herself on her husband's funeral pyre. This weighty argument shook her resolution. In order that she might witness the glory of her son she consented to live a widowed life.

Shivaji performed his father's funeral rites in the orthodox Hindu fashion, spending lakhs of rupees that the hero's shade might rest in peace. Shivaji erected a monumental tomb in honour of his father at the town of

Bandckir where he died.[1] For the upkeep of the monument and the celebration of periodic festivals in honour of the event Shivaji appointed officers, ceding the revenues of certain villages, which he purchased for the purpose from the Bijapur durbar, to meet the recurring expenses.

---

1 Different variations of this name are found in the different authorities, viz. Bedikare, Bedgiri and Bandgiri. Vide foot-note at the end of the second chapter. It was also called Basavpattam, a town captured by the Adil Shahi state, perhaps with the help of Shahaji, in 1639, (Vide: Jedhe Chronology., p.178.)

CHAPTER XV

SEA POWER

A LONG strip of the Konkan sea-coast was by this time under Shivaji. To secure the tranquillity of this great province, Shivaji had either destroyed or received the submission of the turbulent local nobility. Among these there was one who had still baffled Shivaji's attempts at conquest. This was the Abyssinian state of Janjira. Shivaji had indeed fought many successful campaigns with the Abyssinians and stripped them of some of their richest districts. He had even raised many a defensive fortification in the conquered territory. But his armies had never made any head-way in the reduction of the key of the Abyssinian power, the stronghold of Janjira. The naval resources of the Janjira chiefs had made an effective blockade impossible. His naval armament hovered over the neighbouring shore and making sudden descent upon Shivaji's possessions harried the country far and wide. Janjira was the base of this hostile navy; but to capture Janjira it was necessary to create a naval power that could successfully cope with the Abyssinian. Without a naval contingent a siege of Janjira was impossible. Another circumstance which helped to lead Shivaji to this conclusion was the fact that by his naval strength the Janjira chief was enabled to levy contributions upon the mercantile vessels plying in the Konkan and it was necessary to deprive him of this source of plunder.

With this determination, Shivaji collected from all ports artisans and masters skilled in the art of ship-building with the zealous co-operation of his ship-wrights. With their help he was soon able to launch a navy consisting of from four to five hundred vessels of all forms and sizes. These vessels were variously classified according to their size. Upon the construction of this nucleus Shivaji spent about ten lakhs of rupees. Naval batteries were installed and crews of marines and sailors recruited. His crews consisted of men who belonged to sea-faring tribes, such as fishers, pirates, and lascars. The chief command of this contingent was vested in two admirals, Mainaik Bhandari and another whose title was Daryasarang.[1] The ships set sail and at once encountered the vessels of foreign nationalities, such as the Moors, Portuguese, Dutch, French and English. Shivaji obtained a vast booty as the result of these naval encounters enough indeed to defray the expenses of the naval contingent. The Abyssinian chief was now in terror. His lordship of the Konkan sea was at stake. The two navies constantly came into collision with one another. The Portuguese and the English companies had to pay annual tribute to Shivaji, in order to ensure the safety of their vessels. As Shivaji's naval power rose on the western coast, that of the Abyssinians had a corresponding decline.

Shivaji had next to arrange for sheltered anchorages for his naval contingent. With this view he repaired and re-equipped many a maritime fort on the Konkan coast. He got possession of the fort of Kolaba, restored its fortifications, and made it the central basis of his naval power. Here it was that the cargo of all foreign and native crafts was searched and examined. Among other dismantled forts which were remodelled and brought into fighting order were the famous fortified sea-ports of Suvarnadurg and Vijaydurg, the latter of which became more famous in the writings of Mahomedan and European historians under the name of Gheria. Under the batteries of these forts Shivaji's fleets rode safe at anchor. The officers at each principal naval station were to report on and account for the plunder obtained by falling upon pilgrims' vessels bound for Mecca or the more richly laden fleets plying on the coast in the interest of commerce. These reports were to be submitted to the naval headquarters at Kolaba.

The Portuguese were among the first nations to take an alarm at this development of Shivaji's maritime activity.

[1] Vide: foot-note at the end of this chapter.

They sent their envoy to Shivaji's court to obtain exemption and privileges for the commerce of their nation. Articles were signed between the two powers, by which the Portuguese agreed to furnish every year to Shivaji a certain amount of guns and ammunition and other war material, in consideration for which their mercantile fleets were to pass unmolested by Shivaji's fleet. The agreement was renewed from year to year. There are some authorities who assert that between Shivaji and the British East India Company also there was a similar agreement.

Shivaji never assumed the chief command of his navy, nor did he make naval compaigns in person. Only once, on the occasion of the sack of Barcelore (Basnur) did Shivaji travel by sea. But the voyage was a very painful experience. In the first place, both Shivaji and a great number of his men suffered from sea-sickness, and secondly, Shivaji learnt by experience the helpless position of a fleet at the mercy of storms and tides and winds, and the uncertainty in a general's movement who confided himself to these elements. If a commander of the position of Shivaji were unexpectedly be-calmed in the midst of important manoeuvres or prevented by adverse winds from proceeding to his destination, he would for days be cut off from all communication with his followers. With this experience before him, he never attempted a sea-voyage again.

From a classified list of Shivaji's naval armament given by one of the Maratha chronicle writers named Chitragupta, it would appear that he had about 640 vessels of war. Of these about 30 were of the largest size known on the western coast of India,[1] about 300 of an intermediate size, and the rest smaller craft of various classes. The English merchants made lists of Shivaji's fleets on different occasions. From one record it appears

---

1 These were called *Gurabas*. The records of the British East India Company mention them under this name as also the anglicised abbreviated form, '*grabs*,'; other names mentioned are *shebars*, *pals*, *machawas* *mahagiris*, *jugs*, etc. Vide Bombay Gazetteer XIII, 345-49.

that on one occasion when Shivaji's fleets sailed to Karwar, there were 85 one-masted vessels, of from 30 to 150 tons, and three others of a larger size. On another occasion when the East India Company was allied with the Janjira chief it is recorded that Shivaji's admiral suddenly swooped down upon Bombay and appeared in the Back Bay waters on the west side of the town with a squadron of 160 war-ships.

Although this naval squadron had been brought into existence for the express purpose of challenging and defeating the maritime power of the Abyssinian chiefs of Janjira, no detailed account of these operations has come down to us. The principal object–the conquest of Janjira–was almost achieved. But the Janjira chief renounced his allegiance to Bijapur and by placing himself under the protection of the Moguls was able to save his stronghold from falling into the hands of Shivaji. Convinced that the Abyssinian Janjira was beyond his reach, Shivaji decided to build a rival *janjira* or maritime fortress of his own. For this purpose a survey was ordered to be made, with the result that the shores of Malwan were reported to possess all the conveniences and requirements of naval strategy. Besides the necessity of a maritime fortress to remain a standing menace to Janjira, it was also thought desirable to have a southerly naval base to overawe the Portuguese and the chief of Sawantwadi, who maintained a small coasting fleet of his own and was a terror to smaller mercantile craft.

The work was immediately taken in hand. Soundings were made in the waters of Malwan, the duty being entrusted to hereditary boatmen, fishers who knew the condition of the harbour and its topographical features very intimately by reason of life-long experience in those waters. These experts having submitted their report received handsome rewards from Shivaji. Many of them were appointed captains of Shivaji's war-vessels and a village was bestowed upon them in hereditary vatan or proprietary right. The ground being thus broken, building operations were taken in hand, with the customary auspicious ceremonies, including an elaborate ceremony to propitiate the god of the sea. An army of about 3000 masons, smiths and other artisans were soon at work upon the erection of the new sea-fort. It is said that 200 candies worth of iron alone were required for the tools and instruments of the masons and other mechanics. The foundations were made of hewn blocks of stones soldered with lead. The naval squadron hovered round while the building operations were proceeding, ready for battle in case of armed opposition, while on the shore a force of 5000 Mavalis was mounted on guard against a surprise attack on the landward side. Fortunately for Shivaji, the work proceeded without let or hindrance. The Portuguese were already bound by an alliance and dared not break it. The Sawants had been reduced to allegiance under Shivaji and were not likely to embark upon a new war. The sole source of anxiety was the confederate naval forces of the Moguls and the Janjira chiefs. But happily for the present hostilities with these were suspended.

In the beginning of these building operations, Shivaji superintended the work in person, and it is even said that he laboured with his own hands in the erection of the fort. He had at any rate formed the entire plan and devised his own methods for laying deep the foundations under the sea-water. When the foundations were completed and only the super-structure remained to be constructed, Shivaji returned to Raigad, having entrusted the duty of supervision to Govind Vishwanath Prabhu Subhedar. The entire fortification took three years for its completion. When all was ready Shivaji came down from the fort of Panhala to Malwan travelling by the ghat of Bavada, with great pomp and ceremony, for the express purpose of inspecting the newly constructed fortifications. Shivaji made his state entry into the fort under religious auspices, the ceremony being accompanied among other things by a salvo of guns from every ship in the harbour, the customary feasting of Brahmans and the distribution of sweets. In accordance with Hindu custom the master masons and architects were presented with robes of honour and armlets of gold. A corps of skilled artisans kindly lent by the Portuguese government at Goa were thanked for their zeal and the captain of the band honoured with suitable rewards for his services. Govind Vishwanath Prabhu's services were acknowledged with similar presents, with a crest of pearls and an embroidered head-dress, and also a sword, as a mark of special distinction.

The new fort was christened Sindhudurg, or the Fortress of the Sea. It is traditionally estimated that its erection and equipment cost a crore of pagodas. A garrison of three thousand Mavalis under the command of a Mamlatdar was stationed in it the bravest of the Mavalis being given dignities of naik (commander,) sirnaik (chief commander) or *tatsirnobat* (chief commander of the ramparts). A parapet called the *Darya Buruz* (Sea Tower) was raised to keep the waves from dashing on the battlements.[1] It is said that similar sea-forts were erected by Shivaji in other places, such as Anjenweli, Ratnagiri, Padmadurg, Sarjakote, Gahandurg, Khakeri and Rajkote.

Unfortunately the object for which this fort had been erected at such a cost was scarcely realized. The Abyssinians continued to make depredations upon Shivaji's possessions in the immediate vicinity of the island of Bombay, and it seemed they were abetted in these invasions by the authorities of the British East India Company upon that island. Upon this Shivaji planned the conquest of the rocky islets of Khanderi and Underi[2]

---

[1] Certain foot-prints discovered in the fort of Sindhudurg were devoutly believed to be those of Shivaji and a dome was raised thereupon by the pious residents of the place. An image of Shivaji was installed and became the object of certain acts of daily worship. The Kolhapur durbar has granted a fixed allowance for this '*puja*'.

[2] Kennerey and Hennerey in Grant Duff.

opposite Bombay and indeed only twelve miles from that town. These events will be described in their proper place. in Chapter XXVIII.

Shivaji's untimely death prevented him from maturing his far-seeing plans for the establishment of a naval ascendency strong enough to strike terror into the hearts of all the sea-faring nations whose ships were chiefly to be seen in the crowded ports on the coast of Western India. Chief among these were the Abyssinians, the Portuguese, the English, the Moguls and the Moors. His desire now evidently was to capture the commerce of these nations, or to bring it entirely under his control. His far-reaching aims were not understood after his death by any of his successors, and the empire of the sea and the naval instrument for wielding it were both given up, uncontested and unchallenged.

Foot-Note to page 214:—The term *Darya Sagar* of the bakhars is a corrupt form of *Daryasarang*, meaning Captain of the Sea, from the Persian *Darya* meaning the sea, a word also current in the Indian vernaculars. Similarly the name *Mainaik*, which is fairly common among *Bhandaris* and fisher folk of the Bombay coast, is a hybrid term from the Arabic *Maa*, water and the Sanskrit *nayak*, leader and means *water-lord* or leader. Sabhasad speaks of the *Daryasarang* as a Mahomedan and of Mainaik as a Hindu of the Bhandari caste. Prof. Sarkar quotes a Bombay letter of 21st November 1670 to show that the *praenomen* of the Darya Sarang was "*Ventgee*," and seems to infer that he was a Hindu. But as a matter of fact Mahomedans of the Bombay and Guzrat coasts often have their names with the honorific suffix "ji" or "gee," which can scarcely be distinguished from Hindu names.

CHAPTER XVI

THE CAMPAIGN OF SHAISTA KHAN, 1660-63.

WHILE Aurangzeb continued as Viceroy of the Deccan, Shivaji had maintained a friendly and submissive attitude. For his raids upon Junnar and Aurangabad he had made his excuses and had received an assurance of pardon. Upon Aurangzeb's departure for Delhi, Shivaji had sued for the restoration of territories which had once been part of Shahaji's jahgir and had even asked for a free hand to make conquests in the Adil Shahi Konkan. These concessions had been granted in vague and indefinite terms. Abaji Sondev was asked to attend the prince's court.[1] Then followed the blood-feud in the imperial family. Aurangzeb was no longer a prince, but an emperor. He had waded through slaughter to the throne. He had thrown his father into captivity. He had warred with his brothers and executed them, or was preparing to execute them after mock-trials. His time was taken up with plotting and counter-plotting. He had little leisure to follow events in the south. But he had played the cautious game of intrigue, of treaties and embassies. Thus, while Shivaji was asked to send his envoy, Aurangzeb had been writing to the Adil Shaha to take steps against Shivaji. While he warned the Adil Shaha against Shivaji, he congratulated the latter on the overthrow of Afzul Khan and the Bijapur forces.

When Aurangzeb was about to celebrate the first anniversary of his accession to the throne, with festivities extending over two months (5th June to 19 August 1659), it would seem that Shivaji sent an envoy to congratulate him on the occasion and make certain demands. In reply to these demands the emperor replied that he had now conquered all his enemies and by the grace of God had won everything he had wanted, and that he had just appointed the *Amir-ul-umara* Shaista Khan to the *subha* of the Deccan to whom Shivaji was referred for orders.

---

[1] Vide Parasnis MSS. 5.

The emperor sent to Shivaji the usual robes of honour.[1] This was in July 1659.

In July 1659, therefore, Shaista Khan was posted to the subha of the Deccan. He was the amir-ul-umara, or the premier noble of the Mogul court. He was, besides, a near kinsman to the emperor being his maternal-uncle. Already before he had governed the subhas of Malwa and the Deccan, and shortly afterwards he was appointed to the viceroyalty of Bengal. The principal task imposed upon him was to subjugate Shivaji, and particularly to wrest from him those territories which he had conquered from Bijapur. There was actually no war between Shivaji and the Moguls at the time. This then was the result of the treaties and the embassies.

The time was ripe for action. Seldom was a general more favoured by fortune than Shaista Khan was on this occasion. Shivaji was caught between two fires. He was already involved in the war with Bijapur. Shortly afterwards the Bijapur durbar elevated Sidi Johar to the title of Salabat Khan and sent him forth against Shivaji, with a threatened combination of the Sawants and the Abyssinians.

Towards the end of January 1660 Shaista Khan commenced his march from Aurangabad. He came down with an army of 100,000 strong. He announced his determination to subdue Shivaji and reconquer all the forts and territory that had passed into his hand. It is said his vast army comprised five to seven hundred elephants, about 4000 camels, 3000 artillery waggons drawn by bullocks and 2,000 drawn by horses, and specie aggregating thirty-two crores of rupees. With these vast encumbrances Shaista Khan's camp presented the appearance of a large movable town.

Shaista Khan reached Ahmednagar in February. Shivaji was just emerging from the Kolhapur and the Konkan terriories after his conquest of Panhala. Shaista

[1] Rajwade VIII, 7.

Khan's banners swept southwards from Ahmednagar along the eastern barriers of the Poona district. Shivaji's light horse retreated before the Khan. The Khan pressed forward to Supa. Shivaji left the place just before his arrival.[1]

The amir-ul-umara took Supa without a blow and left Jadu Rai (Jadhavrao of Sindhkhed) in charge of it. Supa was to be the base of supply to the advancing army. From this point the passage of the advancing army into the Maratha country became difficult. The Maratha light horse who had hitherto retired before the Mogul van now began a series of rear and flank attacks, and constantly cut off the Mogul commissariat. Shaista Khan detached a cavalry contingent of 4,000 horse to protect his baggage. But every day and in every march, as Khafi Khan has to admit, Shivaji's light horse swarmed round the Khan's baggage and falling suddenly upon it like Cossacks, they carried off horses, camels, men and whatever they could secure.[2]

Shaista Khan overran the entire district of Supa and capturing Poona in person, he occupied that town. He sent detachments of his army to storm the ghat of Katraj and the town of Shivapur, and scouting parties to reconnoitre the defences of the neighbouring forts, with a view to attack and conquer them seriatim, should they be reported upon as assailable.

The fort of Chakan stood in the way of Shaista Khan's communication with Junnar. He determined to reduce

---

1 Vide Khafi Khan, (Elliot VII, 261). Most historians following Grand Duff and the bakhar chronicles place the campaign of Shaista Khan in the year 1662-63. But Khafi Khan says the campaign was begun in 1660, the fort of Chakan being captured by him about the middle of the year. Khafi Khan bases his narrative on the *Alamgir Namah*, which is the standard authority for the first ten years of the reign of Aurangzeb.The Jedhe Chronology, which is altogether independent of this authority, gives nearly the same dates and supports these Persian chronicles. The text follows the dates in this chronology.

2 Vide Khafi Khan, Elliot VII, 261.

the fortress and advanced to conduct the siege in person. Shaista Khan in attacking that little fort with his vast armies had never bargained for the spirited stand made by its brave garrison under the command of its governor, Firangoji Narsala. The latter protracted the defence for nearly two months against overwhelming odds, until on the fifty-sixth day of the siege, the beleaguering army by successful mining operations exploded the outer tower at the north-eastern angle of the fort. The soldiers defending the bastion were killed to a man. A gaping aperture presented itself in the rampart, through which the besiegers pressed on to the assault. The valiant governor with the remnants of his defence force threw himself upon the invaders and successfully barred their way for the whole night. At day-break Firangoji saw it was impossible to prolong the defence.[1] The fort and its noble governor fell into the enemy's hands. Shaista Khan received him with great hononr, complimenting him upon his valour and perseverance, and requesting him to come over into the Mogul service, undertaking that he would watch in person over his prospects and promotion in the imperial army. An alluring bait, which the magnanimous Firangoji spurned with contempt. The Khan took his obstinate refusal in good part, perhaps with admiration. He released him to depart to his master, in the most courteous manner, with many marks of his favour and esteem in acknowledgment of his gallantry. Shivaji received him with much honour, congratulating him upon his loyal and valorous resistance and appointed him to the governorship of the fort of Bhupalgad.[2]

[1] According to Khafi Khan, in the final assault, 300 men of the imperial army were slain, besides sappers and miners. Six or seven hundred were wounded by stones and bullets, arrows and swords. Firangoji made his surrender through an imperialist Rajput commander. The Jedhe Chronology gives the month *Ashwin* of the *shaka* 1582 (October 1660) as the date of the capture of Chakan by Shaista Khan.

[2] The Shivdigvijay says that Firangoji was first dimissed by Shivaji for capitulating to a Mohamedan enemy, and having joined Shaista Khan in disgust was brought back by force through Netaji Palkar

While Shaista Khan was besieging Chakan by throwing up trenches and mines, Shivaji himself was besieged at Panhala by the Bijapur forces under Sidi Johar. This will serve to explain the final cause of Firangoji's surrender. Shivaji being himself immured for a period of nearly four months at Panhala was unable to direct a sufficient relief force to come to the succour of the heroic garrison. However,[1] on dark nights, the garrison frequently sallied forth into the Mogul trenches and fought with surprising boldness, and on some occasions the forces of Shivaji outside the fort combined with those inside to make simultaneous attacks in broad day-light, and placed the Mogul trenches in great danger.

An interesting anecdote is told concerning this part of Shivaji's defence preparations. There were two deshmukhs at Poona, Babajiram and Honappa Deshpande by name[3]. These men having some cause of offence against Shivaji went over to Shaista Khan's camp. Shivaji was very angry when he heard of this defection. Now it happened that a relation of these revolted deshmukhs, Sambhaji Kavji by name, stood in high favour with Shivaji. To him Shivaji spoke about the treason of his kinsmen in feeling terms, declaring that he could scarcely continue to trust a man, two of whose faithful dependents and kinsmen had thus sullied their fair name with treason. The pointed sarcasm of this speech was resented by Sambhaji, who felt highly insulted. He in his turn now went over to Shaista Khan and was received with open arms. At his first interview with Shaista Khan he attracted the attention of

from Malkur, where Shaista Khan had put him in command with a mansab of 5000. But this story seems to be a confused version of a similar story about Sambhaji Kavji.

1 Khafi Khan, Elliot VII, 261-63.

3 Chitnis (p. 97) gives the names of these traitors as Sambhaji Kavji and Babajiram Hanappa. Sambhaji Kavji was the officer, who according to the bakhar accounts murdered Hanmant Rao More of Javli, under pretence of a marriage alliance. The Shivdigvijay makes a mess of the latter part of this story, substituting the name of Firangoji Narsala in place of Sambhaji Kavji.

the Mogul general by a display of physical strength almost superhuman. Among other feats of physical strength he seized a horse by the hoofs and raised him aloft from the ground. The Khan pleased with his great strength admitted him to his service and gave him a command of five hundred horse. Sometime later when this Sambhaji was encamped at Malkur in the Mogul service, Shivaji sent against him a small force under Netaji, a general who was a fellow-townsman of the revolted chief himself. Sambhaji was defeated and slain and Malkur where he had encamped was reduced to dust and ashes.

The conquest of Chakan fort had cost Shaista Khan so many lives that he was compelled to give up the attempt to extend his conquests up to Junnar and return to Poona. The stubborn resistance offered by the little band of heroes in Chakan fort made him reconsider his programme. He had first lulled himself into the belief that Shivaji's forts would fall before him by the very magic of his name, that no resistance was possible, that the new Maratha power would collapse at the first shock of his arrival like a house of cards. But a small hill-fort, like that of Chakan, was now found capable of occupying his vast army for two months, and though it had fallen at last, its fall had only been effected by the sacrifice of hundreds of soldiers from the besieging army. This single experience made him view the situation with a clearer and less clouded vision. He now discerned the magnitude of the task he had embarked upon of wresting the mountain fortresses from the grasp of Shivaji. Aurangzeb himself laboured under the same delusion. That august monarch was all along of the opinion that it was a very light matter to conquer these mountain forts and subdue such a foe as the newly grown Maratha power. The repeated victories of Shivaji and the tales of chivalrous valour on the part of his commanders made him revise his judgment and send re-inforcements under Jaswant Singh, the Maharajah of Jodhpur, to co-operate with Shaista Khan. These new battalions remained encamped near Poona.

In 1661 the Moguls conquered the district of Kalyan-Bhiwandy. Moropant was ordered to recover this entire district and subdue the forts in the neighbourhood. Moropant carried these forts by storm together with other Mogul strongholds north of Junnar. Netaji Palkar carried his flying columns deep into the heart of the Mogul dominions, plundering town and village and levying war-fines upon market and emporium. Passing swiftly from town to town upto the banks of the Godavari he despoiled Baleghat, Parande (Parinda), Haveli, Kalburga (Gulburga), Avse, and Udgir on his victorious march.[1] He raided the country upto the very gates of Aurangabad and subdued the districts all round.

Mahakub Singh, the Mogul commander in charge of Aurangabad, incensed at these depredations, advanced upon Netaji with 10,000 men. A battle took place near Ahmednagar, in which the Moguls were completely worsted by Netaji. The Mogul horses, elephants, and war-stores were cut off by the Marathas. Laden with booty and successful beyond measure in this diversion against the Mogul strongholds in the Deccan, Netaji returned home.[2]

---

[1] According to Chitnis, Netaji Palkar had at this time been divested of the dignity of sir-nobut and Prataprao Guzar upon whom it was conferred was entrusted with this victorious campaign. Other versions about this change of title are that the title was transferred to Prataprao Guzar, about the time of Jay Singh's invasion, on account of Netaji Palkar's failure to obey certain orders of Shivaji. Parinda which is here described as one of the places plundered by Netaji Palkar had, according to Khafi Khan, been won by the Moguls without fighting from a Bijapur commander only in 1660. (*Vide* Jedhe Chronology, p. 185).

[2] According to the Rairi bakhar Mahakub Singh was watching these movements in silence, but roused to action by stringent orders of Aurangzeb took the field against Shivaji and was defeated and killed by Prataprao Guzar in a battle near Ahmednagar. The Mogul commander of Aurangabad, according to Khafi Khan, was Mumtaz Khan, left there during his own absence by Shaista Khan.

One of these Mogul strongholds was the fortress of Prabalgad, the commander of which was Keshar Singh, a Rajput officer. This Rajput chief refused to surrender the fort and Shivaji had to lead an attack against it in person. Keshar Singh defended the fort with bravery for a long time, but saw that he was helpless before the invader. The loyal warrior would not, however, outlive the defeat. Ordering the ladies of his *zenana* to perform the tragic *johar*—the self-immolation of Rajput ladies in a burning pile to escape the disgrace of captivity, the heroic warrior rallied his men and fell upon Shivaji courting a soldier's death. Not till the whole heroic band had fallen on the field of battle did Shivaji capture the fort of Prabalgad. Shivaji ordered the bodies of the heroic Rajputs to be burned with all honour according to the rites of the Hindu religion. The mother and daughter of Keshar Singh were discovered in one of the fortress towers, the sole survivors of the misfortune that had befallen their family. Shivaji received them with the honour and consideration befitting their rank and later on when they expressed a desire to return to their home in the north, he sent them away with a suitable retinue and handsome gifts of raiment and jewellery, as a mark of his esteem.

It is said that when Shivaji set out in a palanquin to examine the fort, his scarf got entangled in a cherry tree and fell to the ground. Shivaji ordered a halt, exclaiming that the omen which caused him to delay there probably showed that there was some treasure under ground. He ordered the soil to be dug out where his scarf had fallen, and marvellous as it turned out, a buried treasure was indeed discovered there. The find was a jar filled with four lakhs of gold mohurs.

Netaji Palkar with his clouds of cavalry hovered about the confines of Ahmednagar and Aurungabad, carrying fire and sword into the Mogul territory, intercepting forage and provisions, and harassing the fce by systematic surprise attacks upon his outposts. The celerity of his movements baffled all pursuit. The enemy had to endure his rapid onslaughts without the power to reply to them. When the Mogul hosts on the defensive at their southern headquarters were found too feeble to withstand Netaji's incursions, Shaista Khan was compelled to send a detachment of his cavalry to put a stop to his attacks. A critical encounter followed between the opposed squadrons, in which Netaji, by reason of his inferiority in numbers, was defeated. But he fought bravely to avert the defeat, was repeatedly wounded and, exhausted as he was, he bravely escaped from the enemy's hands. It is believed that it was due to Rustom Jeman, the Adil Shahi commander, that he escaped being taken prisoner on this occasion.

At Poona Shaista Khan took up his residence in the mansion expressly built for Shivaji by the guardian of his younger days, Dadaji Kondadev. This mansion was known as Lal Mahal or the Red Palace. The Khan knew well enough that Shivaji was near at hand at Fort Sinhagad, and might be expected to swoop down at any moment and by some unexpected *coup de main* raid the Mogul cantonment. Shaista Khan's proper tactics should have been to surround Sinhagad or carry it by storm with the chance of taking Shivaji prisoner. But the experience of Fort Chakan, which he had purchased at no small price, had sobered his ardour. The very fact that Shivaji had chosen to take shelter in this fort spoke volumes for its impregnability and the strength of its garrison in men and munitions of war. All that Shaista Khan could do and did, with the menace of a sudden onslaught by Shivaji hanging over him, was to observe the strictest precautions for the defence of Poona. The Mogul officers had orders not to admit any armed Maratha into the town without a pass-port, no Maratha shiledar was to enter his cantonment, exception being made only in the case of the small retinues of the Maratha nobility who claimed the Mogul allegiance. He denied personal interview or audience to any Maratha officer outside this circle. Sentinels and outposts were stationed at fixed intervals. Thus Shaista Khan lingered at Poona armed against all surprises, and concerting the plans of his future campaigns.

On the other hand, Shivaji watched his movements, perched on the summit of Fort Sinhagad. When Shaista Khan came down with his army to the south, resolved to exterminate the Maratha power, Shivaji had held a council of war, to devise measures of defence in consultation with his great captains and ministers of state. The latter had urged the magnitude of the war operations with the over-whelming hosts of the Moguls and counselled a policy of peace and submission. But peace seemed to be out of the range of practical politics, as on the side of Shaista Khan there appeared to be no Rajput noble of position and prestige, who would up-hold the cause of the Hindu chief or Hindu religion and intercede for a peace in the councils of the Khan. As an uncle of the reigning sovereign, Shaista Khan was not a man to be won over by gold. To expect a promise of pardon and a personal conference was not to be thought of with an invader whose object was the utter defeat and chastisement of Shivaji. The Maratha leader had, therefore, to decide upon the policy which he had so far pursued, viz. on the one hand, not to commit his fortunes to a regular pitched battle to which he plainly saw he was not equal, considering the vast hosts he was confronted with; and on the other hand, to harass the enemy by all the means in his power, cutting off supplies and forage, surrounding and intercepting the conquering hosts in difficult defiles, and raiding them when they blockaded the Maratha hill-forts.

While in this suspense, Shivaji had another paroxysm of a psychical character, when he felt the afflatus of his guardian deity, and under this spiritual obsession he uttered words which were immediately taken down by the by-standers. The words were to this effect: "Let not my child be anxious on the score of Shaista Khan. Like Afzul Khan he too is doomed. Shivaji's is the hand that shall work the dire result. Away with anxious cares!" After his paroxysm had abated, Shivaji read the words and thought they augured well despite all hazards. His hopes began to mount in his breast. His valour would yet triumph.

Shaista Khan's arrogance whetted this desire. While residing at the Lal Mahal, Shaista Khan got a Brahman who knew Sanskrit to write a taunting epistle to Shivaji, the purport of which was as follows: "You are a wild ape of the mountains; your mischievous activities break out from the sheltered coverts of your mountain lairs, and at every challenge to a fair and equal fight you fly to your mountain solitudes. But I am come to draw you out of your lairs and shall never leave the pursuit till I have hunted you out. How long shall you, with your elusive tactics of cunning and cowardice, put off your inexorable fate?" Shivaji answered defiance with defiance. "Monkey, if thou wouldst call me, oh Khan!" thus ran Shivaji's reply, "learn that I am like unto that valiant one whose glories resound in the deathless verses of the Ramayan. If he destroyed Ravana, the Lord of Lanka, I shall rout your insolent hosts and rid the world of such an abomination."[1]

Shaista Khan's camp was safely guarded against a sudden assault and the large number of his soldiers made a fight impossible. Shivaji was, however, determined to make the Khan expiate his insolence with his blood. Without its leader the Mogul army was bound to melt away of itself. Shivaji succeeded in sending two of his agents to the Mogul camp at Poona with instructions to win over a Maratha cavalry officer there. This officer was instructed to give out that he was about to celebrate

---

[1] Rairi bakhar. The Jedhe Chronology (Page 185) in one of its entries notes that Sonaji Pandit brought a message from Shaista Khan to Shivaji at Raigad.

a marriage in his family and apply to the Khan for special permission to lead a nuptial procession. The permission being granted, he improvised a fictitious marriage in concert with his intimate friends and sent back Shivaji's agents with assurances of help. Upon this Shivaji descended from Fort Sinhagad, with a picked body of fifteen hundred veteran Mavalis. On the way he fixed numerous torches to the trees growing on the ghat of Katraj as also to the horns of cattle. Bodies of trumpeters and horn-blowers were stationed upon inaccessible cliffs. The object was that at a given signal after a successful attack on Shaista Khan's camp, the torches were to be set ablaze, and the trumpets to blare and the torch-bearing cattle and trumpeters to set off in headlong flight, so as to lure the Khan's pursuing horsemen to a fruitless chase and to leave the way clear for Shivaji's retreat to Sinhagad. Shivaji placed his men in small companies along the way to Poona, advising them to gather on hearing a signal given by a flourish of trumpets. A troop of about five hundred soldiers was stationed under cover of the mango-groves outside the town and about two hundred just outside the Mogul camp.[1] True to the previously contrived plan, the wedding guests came in procession to the ramparts, when Shivaji with a handful of about twenty-five warriors, among whom were included his tried and trusty campanions, Tanaji Malusare, Yessaji Kunk, Dadaji and Chimnaji Bapuji Deshpande, smuggled themselves into the procession.[2] In those days Maratha soldiers carried their arms even at such a peaceful function as a wedding celebration. The presence of Shivaji's armed men in the procession did not, therefore, excite any suspicion.

Shivaji was arrayed in a coat of mail concealed under the ample folds of a long white robe, and under his turban he wore a helmet of mail. In his hand he grasped his

1 According to Sabhasad, Netaji Palkar and Moropant were stationed with the army a little distance from the Mogul camp.

2 According to Khafi Khan a party of two hundred Marathas entered the town with the pretended bridegroom.

sword, while he was also armed with the famous tiger-claws and dagger. Shortly after Shivaji and his party had entered into Shaista Khan's camp, in the garb and under the pretence of wedding guests, night came down and silence reigned over the scene. The soldiers mounting guard inside the camp were themselves half asleep and well they might, as the vigilant watches maintained outside the camp and at the entrance-gates were so efficient as to give the inner watch a complete sense of security. As the palace chosen by the Khan was one that had long been the residence of Shivaji himself who knew it thoroughly, it could present no difficulty to Shivaji's people. Shivaji led his men straight to this mansion and effected an entrance through a kitchen window, which he knew to exist in the rear of the mansion though the Khan had taken the precaution to build it up. To dig a way through this window and leap cautiously in with two or three companions was for Shivaji the work of a moment. But the sound of treading feet awakened the ladies of the Khan's harem, who in their turn awakened their Lord. The different chronicles give different versions of the events that followed,[1] as

[1] Chitnis gives the following version:—The Khan lived in a tent adjacent to the palace garden and was suddenly surprised by Shivaji with two of his comrades, while he was asleep. Shivaji sat on his breast and was about to kill him with his sword, when the Khan's wife interceded for his life. Upon this Shivaji got up still in an attitude to strike and compelled the Khan and his wife to follow him in silence. He cut off two of his fingers and let him escape, bidding him take a lesson by his experience and retire from Maharashtra.

Sabhasad and Chitragupta give the same version with a few variations :—When Shivaji entered the tent some ladies who were awake raised an outcry. The Khan was then awakened and hid himself among the ladies. While searching for him Shivaji discovered the Khan in the act of striking at him with a sword. But Shivaji anticipated his blow and struck at him. In avoiding the blow he had three of his fingers cut off. The Khan's men entering the tent in confusion, Shivaji managed to escape.

The Rairi bakhar tells the story of an intrigue with a *mali*, or gardener, next to Shaista Khan's residence. The mali undertook to

is but natural, considering the excitement under which they took place. Most of the chronicles agree in giving an account of what happened as follows: The affrighted Khan being awakened by his ladies thought only of effecting his escape. He rushed to the window and almost escaped unscathed. Shivaji, however, noticed his stealthy flight and made for him at the window. He struck at him with his long sword as he was gliding out of the window and cut off one of his fingers. Meanwhile Shaista Khan's son with his special bodyguard rushed upon Shivaji. The latter received the attack with such

---

introduce Shivaji at night to the Khan's bed-chamber. Shivaji came from Rajgad in haste to Poona and was accordingly admitted with a few followers. Twenty-five sentinels at the door and a eunuch still awake were cut down; but by mistake the mali led Shivaji into the chamber of the Khan's son. Shivaji killed him on the spot and compelled a servant-maid to lead him to Shaista Khan's chamber. Meanwhile the Khan had been awakened by the noise and was escaping by the window, when Shivaji struck at him and cut off one of his thumbs. Torches were now lighted and a crowd gathered. Shivaji returned by the way he had entered but found the garden surrounded. He charged one party and escaped, cutting down all that opposed him, and mounting his horse returned safe to Rajgad.

The Shivadigvijay gives a version which is a compound of the versions given by Chitnis and the Rairi bakhar. Acccording to the Shivdigvijay Shivaji entered the chamber of the Khan's son and killed him. The wife of the deceased noble was awakened by the sound, and being asked as to the identity of the slain person, told Shivaji it was the son of the Khan. She had then to lead Shivaji to the Khan's chamber. Shivaji raised his sword to strike the Khan, but the light of the lamp flashing on it, awakened the Khan's wife. She interceded for the life of her husband, and both she and the Khan complied with Shivaji's order to follow him and a finger was cut off as in the version given by Chitnis.

Khafi Khan (Elliot VII p. 270) says that the Marathas entered the cook-house, where, it being the month of Ramzan, some cooks were at work, but were killed. The noise awoke a servant in the next room, but Shaista Khan did not mind his report. A maid-servant then awoke and took the report, when the Khan got up and armed himself. Just then a Maratha got up to him and cut off his thumb. The maid-servants in the end got the Khan to hide himself. Some Marathas worked their way to the *nagar-khana* or band-room and ordered the drums to be beaten in the Khan's name. Others killed the drowsy sentinels, saying, 'This is how they keep watch'. Next day when Jaswant Singh came to express his condolence, Shaista Khan replied, "I thought the Maharajah was in His Majesty's service when such an evil befell me."

promptitude that in a few seconds the corpses of most of his assailants were strewn on the floor. Shivaji now burst victorious from the palace (5th April 1663). Cries of murder and treason rent the air and the whole camp had now become a confused pandemonium. While a confused search was being instituted for the raiders of the camp, Shivaji and his party joined in the outcry and escaped safe out of the town. Collecting the soldiers whom he had stationed in detached outposts on the way, Shivaji made for Sinhagad. The trumpets gave the signal to kindle the torches in the Katraj ghat. The Khan's pursuing parties, as had been foreseen by Shivaji, were lured on in this direction, leaving the way open for Shivaji's escape to Sinhagad. The Mogul pursuers discovered late in the morning how they had been led on a fool's errand, when they saw the torches attached to the trees and the horns of cattle.[1] Dispirited with the unsuccessful result of their pursuit, they turned back and feeling sure that by this ruse Shivaji must have ensconced himself again behind the shelter of the battlements of Sinhagad, they gathered in full force at the foot of that fortress. Shivaji permitted them to come within range of the fortress guns unchallenged. They came flourishing their swords and sounding their trumpets quite under the fortress walls, resolved to storm the fort and apprehend or slay Shivaji. But at length the Sinhagad cannon replied with a loud salvo, and with the first discharge carried dismay and panic into their disorderly ranks. Hundreds fell mortally wounded; others fled in a sudden panic; the elephant carrying the imperial standard was killed by a cannon-ball; none cared to stand by

---

[1] As regards the stratagem of the torches bound to the horns of cattle and set ablaze, the reader will recollect that the same stratagem was used by Hannibal to outwit Fabius Maximus in the pass of Tarracina (*Vide* Livy, Bk. XXII Ch. XII.) This does not of course detract from the originality of Shivaji's plan, since he could not be accused of an acquaintance with the classics. It is, however, a striking parallel and shows how a kindred genius was shared in common by the Maratha and Carthaginian leaders.

the standard; and a headlong flight ensued. While the siege was thus raised, the besiegers were themselves surprised by a detachment of horse sent against them by Netaji Palkar and Kartoji Guzar. Several hundreds of the Mogul combatants were cut down by Guzar.

Shaista Khan was beside himself with shame at this defeat and disgrace,—a defeat in which he had lost his son and the lives of so many of his zealous veterans. He had no hope left of a successful campaign. He dreaded to think what the next moment might bring forth, dealing as he was with so artful a raiding host as that of Shivaji. His good fortune had already saved him once from imminent death, and he felt it would be tempting his fortunes too much to court such perils any more. The rains made a siege of Sinhagad impossible. His soldiers had already become faint-hearted. They would scarcely entertain a proposal of further fight with Shivaji with any thing like spontaneous zeal and eagerness. To force them to fight at the point of the musket or by appealing to their sense of the gravity of the imperial mandate would be only like leading them to sure defeat and death, to the irremediable detriment of the imperial forces. To surround himself with further lines of entrenchments and remain in camp in expectation of a more favourable season to strike a final blow at the enemy was also vain. Shivaji had made his ingress into the Mogul camp through the lines of night guards and sentinels. Entrenchments and ramparts had not availed to bar his way. All this bred suspicion of treason in his own camp. Under the shadow of this fear he dared not abide longer to protract a campaign with the support of men about whose loyalty he had cause of suspicion. This would be to court the fate of Afzul Khan. He, therefore, resolved to evacuate Poona and march to a new encampment at Pedgaum.

His suspicions were directed against the Rajah Jaswant Singh. He wrote to the emperor that there was treason in his camp and that Shivaji had evidently corrupted Rajah

Jaswant Singh, and that this was the cause of his unexpected reverses. Aurangzeb was in great dismay at the news of this defeat and the enterprising spirit of Shivaji, which enabled him to triumph over all the obstructions in his way and defeat the most eminent strategists of the empire. His great campaign had only served to diminish the prestige of the Mogul name and jeopardized the safety of his southern-most subha. The emperor was convinced that there was no longer any possibility of friendly co-operation between Shaista Khan and Jaswant Singh. He recalled Shaista Khan and appointed Prince Muazzim in his place. The galled spirit of Shaista Khan was appeased with the governorship of the princely province of Bengal. The services of Jaswant Singh were retained as deputy to the prince, for fear lest the slur of a recall might throw him into the open arms of the Marathas.[1] In truth, so acute was the tension of feeling in the southern subha that Aurangzeb might have been expected to take the field in person against Shivaji, but the sinister aspect of politics in Kashmir required his personal presence near the north-western frontier.

On the departure of Shaista Khan, the Rajah Jaswant Singh endeavoured to prove his loyalty and valour by a renewed siege of Sinhagad. But it proved to be labour lost. Shivaji's raiding bands terrorized the besiegers.[2] The siege had to be raised, and Jaswant Singh with great losses made good his retreat to Aurangabad.

---

1 According to Bernier this Rajput prince, when at last recalled to Delhi, instead of going to the Mogul capital returned to his own state in Rajputana.

2 The siege of Sinhagad from December 1663 to about June 1664. (Jedhe Chronology.)

CHAPTER XVII

THE SACK OF SURAT AND BARSELOR, 1664-1665

On the retirement of the Rajah Jaswant Singh to Aurungabad, Shivaji mustered his forces in two concentration camps one at Kalyan and the other at Danda-Rajapuri, with the ostensible object of a campaign against the Portuguese at Cheul and Bassein and a final struggle with the Abyssinians of Janjira. The real motive for this concentration of his forces, however, was a sudden march upon Surat and the sack of that emporium of trade on the western coast. Among the populous and opulent towns of the orient, the port of Surat claimed a very high place. It was the seat of international trade. All sorts of foreign merchants traded in Indian wares in the marts of that town. Many of its citizens were counted among the most affluent merchant princes in India. Shivaji had sent to Surat his scout, Bahirji Naik by name, who scrutinized the fortunes of the leading citizens and furnished very valuable information to Shivaji so as to facilitate an attack. His report induced Shivaji to launch upon this enterprise. The town was shown to be an easy prey and wealth untold awaited the fortunate captor.[1]

Shivaji had decided to conduct the expedition in person, having learnt by experience of previous campaigns that much of the best results is lost when the command was entrusted to his lieutenants. The expeditionary force consisted of 10,000 Mavalis, including such leaders of distinction as Moropant Pingle, Prataprao Guzar, and several subordinate officers. With this great host he left the Konkan in a straight line of march upon Surat.[2] But

[1] According to some accounts Shivaji himself in a disguise had made his way to Surat and in a stay of three days had seen things with his own eyes and in particular the residences of the merchant princes.

[2] According to Orme to disguise his plans Shivaji encamped his forces before Cheul and Bassein and made believe that he was preparing to capture these places by storm, and that Shivaji secretly started from the Bassein camp with four thousand horse, leaving strict

in order to divert the attention of the Moguls from his real object he gave out that the march was for the sacred pilgrim place of Nasik, whence he proposed to go on a tour of inspection of the fortresses recently captured by Moropant. Having thus blinded the enemy as to his real intention, he advanced in a northerly course and by incredibly forced marches suddenly presented himself within a few miles of the city.[1]

On the morning of the 5th January 1664 the alarming news came to Surat that Shivaji's banners were seen at Gandevi, only 28 miles south of the town. The citizens were utterly taken by surprise. They had no suspicion of the coming storm. In their panic they began to flee away across the river, to the villages on the northern bank, with their wives and children. The governor sent a messenger to make a parley with the invader. The messenger was put under arrest as also the messengers of the Dutch and the English East India Companies, who had been sent to watch Shivaji's movements.[2] Next morning Shivaji's columns were already hurling themselves upon the old mud walls of the city. The governor of the city, Inayet Khan, mustered his scanty forces and advanced, not to give battle to the foe, but to flee for shelter to the inner castle. Shivaji planted his batteries against the citadel. The inhabitants were left to their own resources.[3]

orders to maintain the same vigilance as before with the usual flourish of trumpets and other war-like music.

[1] The Factory Records of the English Company at Surat give graphic accounts of the sack of Surat. The Log of the *Loyal Merchant*, an English ship then at the mouth of the Tapti, preserved among the Orme MSS., Vol 263, is of special value. Next in importance are the Dutch Records and the accounts given by Valentyn, Bernier, Manucci, and Dr. Fryer.

[2] *Vide* the Dutch version of the event in Valentyn's "*Lives of the Moguls.*"

[3] According to Bernier and Valentyn, the governor of Surat came to oppose Shivaji, but was made to retire on the understanding that Shivaji did not mean to force his entrance into the town but march outwards. Orme says that the governor of the town and the commander of the garrison in their fright betook themselves to the citadel admitting only a few who could be accommodated within, and fired upon Shivaji when he entered the town, but he made nothing of it.

On the previous night Shivaji had despatched a message to the governor, requiring him and Haji Sayad Beg, Baharji (Virji) Borah, and Haji Cassim, three of the richest merchants in the city, to attend his camp, a little outside the city-gate, and settle the ransom, in default of which he threatened to plunder the town.[1] As no answer came to this summons, the Maratha hosts poured in. The invaders very soon made their presence felt all over the town. The mansions of the leading citizens were occupied and the city was subjected to a systematic pillage for the space of three days. The rich were forced under fear of death to disclose their buried treasures. In the confusion an opulent Jewish merchant fell into the hands of Shivaji. He was a native of Constantinople and had come to Surat to negotiate the sale of certain precious jewellery to the emperor Aurangzeb. He was produced before Shivaji and commanded to surrender his treasures. He refused and notwithstanding all manner of threats against his life persisted in his refusal. Thrice was he thrown down on the ground and the sword placed at his throat. But he did not yield for a moment. His gold was dearer to him than life.[2]

The house of Baharji Borah was plundered for three days and an incredible amount of money and precious stones was carried away with twenty-eight seers of large pearls. This house stood next to the Dutch factory, that of Haji Sayad Beg being close to the English. The Marathas plundered Haji Sayad's house for two days until the English company put an English guard upon it and took its protection in their hands. This brought about an exchange of threats of defiance between Shivaji and the president of the English factory, Sir George Oxenden. In this way burning and plundering went on for three days.

But Shivaji did not act in this extortionate manner towards all in the moment of his triumph. Certain anecdotes of his conduct on this occasion illustrate the

[1] Factory Records, Surat, Letter in Forrest's Selections Vol I, p. 24.
[2] Bernier, 190.

innate generosity of his character. There lived at this time at Surat a Roman Catholic capuchin of the name of Father Ambrose. Though the dwelling-place of this priest was pointed out for plunder, Shivaji did not violate it. He is reported to have said that the *padres* were men of piety and it was improper to injure them in any way. Another story is that there was at Surat a certain citizen of the name of Mohandas Parekh who was an accredited broker to the Dutch East India Company. He was a person of high character and well spoken of for his philanthropy. He had died a few years before Shivaji's invasion of Surat, leaving behind him a large family and an ample fortune. Though reports of the vast wealth of this family were brought to Shivaji, he saved it from every species of violation, out of deference for the high renown of the deceased philanthropist.[1]

The English and the Dutch East India Companies had thriving factories at Surat at the date of Shivaji's invasion. These European merchants, and in particular the representatives of the English Company with great bravery defended their factories, chiefly with the powerful aid of the sailors on board their mercantile fleets at Swally, at the mouth of the river. Many native merchants found a safe asylum in the factories of the European merchants. An Englishman of the name of Anthony Smith was taken prisoner and brought before Shivaji. He was afterwards released.[2] He has left a brief account of Shivaji's sack of Surat. He tells how Shivaji was seated in a tent and persons suspected of hiding their wealth were taken before him. When these men persevered in their refusal to disclose the places where

---

1 Bernier, 188-189.

2 The Log of the *Loyal Merchant* (quoted by Prof. Sarkar) says that he was ransomed for Rs 350. The English chaplain, Escaliot has given a similar account of the plunder in his letter to Sir T. Browne, the author of *Religio Medici*, which Prof. Sarkar quotes from Ind. Antiq. VIII, 256, to describe the state of Surat at the time and the manner in which the loot was carried out. An equally vivid description is given by Dr. Fryer. All these authorities are naturally prejudiced against Shivaji.

their fortunes were hidden, he ordered them either to be executed or deprived of their hands. It is said that were it not for the gallant stand made by the British factors, Shivaji would have carried off a much greater amount of treasure. Their gallantry evoked the admiration of Aurangzeb. He congratulated Sir George Oxenden, the president of the factory at Surat, and presented him with a jewelled crest as a special distinction. The British merchants were granted a remission of 2½% in the customs duty; and the proprietors of the British East India Company were honoured with the presentation of a special gold medal as a mark of imperial favour.[1]

On his arrival at Surat, Shivaji had publicly announced that he had not come to do any personal harm to any of the native or foreign merchants in the city, but only to revenge himself on Aurangzeb for having invaded his own country and killed some of his relatives. Consistently with this declaration he had invited the governor of the city with three of the foremost citizens to attend his camp outside the city gates and settle the ransom there. In this demand he was quite justified. He was at war with the Mogul government. His appearance before the city-gates was a masterly move on the part of the Maratha strategist. Again, as he rightly said, the Mogul emperor had forced him to keep a large army, and he would force the emperor to become its pay-master.

It was the duty of the governor to pay the ransom or defend the city. He does neither. He leaves the city to the mercy of the invader. The invader has to enter the city-gates and exact payments from the individual citizens. The governor having failed in his primary duty does not hesitate to employ an assassin to murder Shivaji in his camp. The assassin attacks Shivaji with his dagger. Both the murderer and the intended victim roll on the ground together. The blood is seen on Shivaji's dress. The Maratha soldiers for a time actually believe

[1] *Vide* Dr. Fryer, Vol. I, letter II, Chapter V.

that Shivaji has been murdered. A cry runs through the camp to slay the prisoners. Even with this provocation there was no massacre. Shivaji's voice was the first to forbid it.[1]

As a retaliatory measure only four prisoners were executed and twenty-four had their hands cut off. Those who condemn Shivaji for the cruelty of his exactions are, therefore, less wise in their censure than the citizens of Surat were when they threw dirt upon their governor, when the coward at last emerged from behind the shadow of the castle-walls upon Shivaji's retirement. In any case the sack of Surat was Shivaji's decisive reply to the Mogul emperor for the seizure and occupation of Poona and the surrounding districts by the Mogul hosts under Shaista Khan. That occupation had lasted for three years. If Shaista Khan had not plundered Poona, it was because he found little to plunder there. In 1657 Aurangzeb had given orders to the Mogul hosts invading Shivaji's territories, after the attack upon Junnar, to lay waste the villages, "slaying the people without pity, and plundering them to the extreme".[2] That was Aurangzeb's way of making reprisals for the attack on Junnar,—the robbing, the slaying, and the enslaving of the poorest type of countrymen. This was Shivaji's way of making reprisals for Shaista Khan's seizure of Poona—the spoliation of the wealthiest citizens of the wealthiest sea-port in the empire on the refusal of its governor to comply with the demand for ransom.[3] How the Mogul armies themselves could pillage and plunder a great city was amply shown only seven years before the sack of Surat, when on the treacherous orders of Aurangzeb, in defiance of treaties and existing peace, the Mogul hosts under the command of his son entered the Golconda territory under a vile pre-

1 Prof. Sarkar's "Shivaji", 115.

2 Prof. Sarkar's "Shivaji", 62.

3 It must be remarked that the sack of Surat took place, while the Rajah Jaswant Singh was besieging Kondana (Sinhagad). *Vide* the dates in Jedhe's Chronology, pp. 186-87.

text, and plundered the hapless city of Hyderabad, then the richest city in South India, for days together.[1] It is needless, therefore, to be too censorious about the cruelty or injustice involved in the sack of Surat.

When the sacking of the town was brought to a conclusion, a huge cavalcade of heavily laden pack-horses started for Raigad, which they reached safely, without any attempt to obstruct them on the part of the Moguls. The wealth obtained in this enterprise is said to have been computed to amount to a sum of eight and a half crores of pagodas. A large number of horses was captured, brought down from Surat and formed into a new cavalry corps. On his return from Surat, Shivaji wrote to Aurangzeb in the following strain: "I have chastised your uncle, Shaista Khan; I have defiled the beauty of your fair city of Surat. Hindustan is for the Hindus. You have no business here. You have no business, too, to be in the Deccan. The Deccan belongs of right to the Nizam Shahi dynasty, and I am the *vizier* of that dynasty." Aurangzeb made no reply to this letter.

Upon his return from Surat, Shivaji learnt the sad tidings of the death of Shahaji. The mourning and funeral rites were performed at Fort Sinhagad. After the full period of these funeral solemnities Shivaji returned to Raigad, where some time was spent in the re-organization of the various departments of government. It was at this period upon the death of the Raja Shahaji that Shivaji solemnly assumed the title of Raja and struck coins in his own name.[2]

While Shivaji was for a time resting and enjoying a lull in his war-like activities, his followers were by no means idle. They harried the Mogul provinces in the south. Netaji Palkar systematically took the field with his irregular cavalry during the favourable season from year

[1] Elphinstone, 575; Prof. Sarkar's "Aurangzeb" Vol. I. Chapter X.

[2] Khafi Khan, (Elliot Vol. VII, p. 271.)

to year, and at the beginning of the stormy season he used to return with his spoils. The naval contingent was equally active, laying an embargo upon the merchant vessels wherever they could and pillaging them according as occasion served. They levied contributions upon the pilgrim vessels plying between the western coast and Mecca. Wealthy pilgrims were subjected to heavy exactions. Shortly afterwards Shivaji took the field in person and led his victorious legions to the sack of Ahmednagar and the devastation of the Mogul province of the Deccan up to the gates of its capital, Aurangabad.

Observing how Shivaji was engaged in hostilities against the Moguls, two nobles under the hegemony of the Adil Shahi ruler at Panhala[1] broke the former peace and made an energetic movement for the reconquest of the Konkan. They recaptured some of the principal stations in the Konkan. When Shivaji learned of the new crisis on the Konkan shores, he with marvellous rapidity presented himself at this new scene of war. A battle ensued, in which thousands of the Adil Shahi army were put to flight or killed. The agents of the British Company at Karwar and Rajapur have estimated the number of the slain on both sides as nearly six thousand.[2] Hubli was plundered. The people of Vengurla rose against Shivaji's commander in that town. Shivaji retaliated by reducing the town to ruins. Concluding this business with extraordinary speed, Shivaji was again back at Sinhagad. For news had arrived that the Mogul army at Junnar had been re-inforced and meditated an invasion of the territory under Shivaji's influence. Shivaji's quick return to Sinhagad nipped this hostile demonstration in the bud. When this danger had been averted Shivaji ordered his light cavalry south of the Krishna to raid the Bijapur dominions. While the people of Bijapur were thus attacked in their southern valleys, Shivaji prepared to deliver simultaneously another

1 Mohamed Ikhlas Khan and Fazal Khan.

2 Factory Reports, Surat, Vol. 86. The Bijapur general, Khawas Khan, was hemmed round by Shivaji but escaped by a gallant charge.

blow on the seaward side of that empire. This took the form of a sudden march upon Barselor and the spoliation of that wealthy entrepot of trade on the Konkan coast. The attack was to be made by sea. Shivaji's naval contingent received orders to concentrate at the sea-fort of Sindhudurg on the Malwan coast. These preparations were made with extreme caution and secrecy, and it was given out to the diplomatic world that Shivaji was mustering a strong force for a decisive attack on the Mogul camp at Junnar. Having thus thrown dust in the eyes of the enemy, Shivaji suddenly appeared at Malwan and the naval force made straight for Barselor.[1]

The invader descended upon the town quite unexpectedly before the morning twilight. It was sacked and pillaged for the whole day unhindered. The plunder which is supposed to have been almost as great as that of Surat amounted to between two and three crores.

Following on the sack of this town Shivaji extended his conquest to other sea-board towns, such as Kadwal, Shiveshwar, Miraj, Ankola, Kodre (Kadra), Humaud and others. The sacred shrine of Gokarn-Mahableshwar was taken possession of and large sums spent in religious charities at this frequented place of pilgrimage. At Bednore, further south, a jahagirdar named Shivappa Naik had made himself independent of Bijapur. This Naik had recently died and an infant prince had been put on the throne, under the regency of his mother. Before proceeding to those southern parts Shivaji had made a demand on this chief to agree to the payment of an annual tribute and the maintenance of an accredited agent at Shivaji's court; whereupon the insolent minister of the Naik challenged Shivaji to come and extort tribute from him, if he dared. Upon receipt of this haughty reply Shivaji

[1] In some bakhars, the name of the town occurs as Basnur. The Shivdigvijaya calls it Harhasnur. The Rairi bakhar calls it Hasnur. It is elsewhere called *Basrur*. It was the principal port of the Bednore Rajas.

came up by forced marches, conquering town and village and compelled the Naik to sue for peace. He sent his vakils, with abject entreaties for pardon and with royal presents, including a *nazar* of a lakh of rupees. The young Naik with his guardian came down in person to meet Shivaji at a friendly conference, where promises were interchanged and the chief finally consented to pay an annual tribute of three lakhs of rupees. The Naik sent his vakil, Umaji, to reside at Shivaji's court.[1]

On his arrival at Gokarn, the greater part of Shivaji's naval force was ordered to retire to head-quarters, and the land force continued its depredations in the interior of the country. Karwar fell but suffered no harm, the inhabitants having offered to pay the victor a fair sum of money. (1665.) It is said that the local factors of the British Company bought their safety by a prudent arrangement to pay down the modest contribution of £ 112. With these trophies the invader began his retreat, the army marching by land routes, Shivaji himself sailing with a small naval squadron, with the object of inspecting with his own eyes the aggressive preparations of the Janjira chief by a cruise along the Konkan coast. But adverse winds delayed this voyage. The voyagers were suddenly becalmed and had to spend many days and nights, in a helpless and profitless manner, on the sea. Shivaji found himself for the time being cut off from all communication with his army and all knowledge of the movements of the enemy. He never trusted himself again to the mercy of the treacherous element. A ship he now found by experience to be no better than a prison, in this that a man seemed thereby to be cut off from all communication with the towns and nations of the earth.

---

[1] Ali Adil Shaha of Bijapur had for years been fighting with this chief and his father. The father was Shivappa Naik and the son Somshekar, and in 1665, a puppet prince was reigning at Bednore under his mother's regency. Shahaji had fought against Shivappa in Ali Adil Shaha's camp.

CHAPTER XVIII

THE INVASION OF RAJA JAY SINGH

NEWS of a more portentous crisis in his fortunes than any he had tided over in his hitherto triumphant career was destined to greet Shivaji's ears immediately on his arrival at Raigad from the scene of his recent conquests in the Southern Konkan and Kanara. This was the bodeful invasion of the Mogul army under the command of two of the most illustrious generals of the empire, Mirza Raja Jay Singh and Diler Khan, who had marched down upon the south with the fullest and the most efficient of warlike equipments then known in India. They were eager to wreak on Shivaji a full revenge for the disgrace of Shaista Khan and the defeat of Jaswant Singh. At first sight it may appear strange that an emperor of the haughty and bigoted temper of Aurangzeb should have allowed any length of time to elapse before paying off old scores, and making the raider of the Mogul provinces feel the power of the empire. Yet so it was and it could not be otherwise. With all his sense of power, the usurper, whose conscience was burdened with the guilt of having deposed his dotard father and the judicial murder of his more guileless brothers, lived in an insecurity of his own. His mental torments were a veritable hell. His father's fate was the sword of Damocles that hung above his head. He distrusted Prince Muazzim even while sending him to take over the command from Shaista Khan. Thus Muazzim had come down with resources ill-proportioned to his task, but with all the gilded splendours of the mighty Mogul name. The calculating emperor was watching an opportunity when the political ferment in the north should have subsided in order to lead the Mogul legions under his personal command and destroy by one crushing blow at once the Maratha and the Adil Shahi powers. Of the military calibre of the new Maratha power he had indeed a poor notion. The surprise and discomfiture of Shaista Khan was in his opinion no proof of a genius for war; the humiliation of the

Adil Shahi power was due after all to its growing incompetence. Before the arrayed forces of the Mogul power, Shivaji seemed to him like a flying phantom, easy to overtake and crush in a moment. Not for nothing did he call him a mountain rat. He cherished these delusions for too long a time to be able to retrieve his error.

But his wrath was still further roused by the news of the recent acts of the despised Shivaji,—the spoliation of Mogul territory, the sack of Surat, his assumption of the title of Raja and his presumption in instituting a coinage of his own. This wrath was inflamed into a bigoted hatred and religious frenzy by the naval preparations of the Maratha Raja, and the systematic pillage and confiscation of pilgrim vessels bound for Mecca. He vowed to wreak a bloody vengeance upon the infidel author of these atrocities and in consequence of this determination he had now launched, as described above, a new invading host upon the impious Maratha.

The emperor's object in deputing two commanders obviously was to balance an attempted treason on the part of one by the envious vigilance of the other. The emperor lived in an atmosphere of suspicion and was convinced that Shivaji was a past master in the art of sowing treason in the enemies' camp. Aurangzeb seems to have specially enjoined upon Diler Khan to take particular care lest the infidel Jay Singh might artfully turn the tables in favour of the infidel Shivaji, that he should be prepared for every emergency and scent treason from a distance. The emperor had indeed little confidence in either of these leaders. He sent them, however, upon the great task awaiting them, under a belief that they had at least enough of that capacity which might serve to distract and weaken an enemy.

In connection with this there is a tradition of an attempted coalition between the Mogul and Bijapur powers against Shivaji. The fame of Shivaji's exploits had filled the emperor with dismay; the annihilation of Shaista

Khan's invading host had come as a staggering blow; and the emperor in his anxiety conceived the plan of a concerted campaign supported by Bijapur. With a view to securing the accession of Bijapur to this projected enterprise, Aurangzeb is said to have despatched an envoy extraordinary bearing the terms of a proposed alliance with the Deccan kingdom, wherein the emperor is believed to have expatiated at length upon the magnitude of the menace to the Islam church and dynasties, as also upon the necessity of joint action in extirpating one whose state, according to Mahomedan opinion, was a hot-bed of rank sedition and lawlessness. In short the united arms of Bijapur and the Mogul power were to be turned upon the common foe before his power and position really became impregnable.[1] Accordingly the Deccan state was invited to form an alliance with the emperor and unite with him in an attack upon the common aggressor. The Adil Shahi state felt flattered by this invitation and ordered their general Khawas Khan to proceed against Shivaji with a great army. The Maratha leader overtook the enemy and forced him to give battle on unfavourable ground. Khawas Khan was defeated and driven back in confusion to Bijapur. This was the result of the attempted coalition between the two great Mahomedan states of the north and the south, though it is pertinent to observe that Mahomedan historians and Maratha chroniclers persist in assigning the credit of the victory to their own co-religionists.

Upon the appointment of Jay Singh and Diler Khan to the Deccan province, Prince Muazzim and Jaswant Singh were naturally recalled. Their united armies had effected little worth the name, and the emperor, true to his distrustful nature, had grave suspicion of a possible collusion between these imperial commanders and Shivaji. The new commaders had a double task before them, first to exterminate the Maratha power, and secondly to exact the prompt payment of tribute from Bijapur, and to terrorise the

[1] Modak's History of the Adil Shahi Dynasty (in Marathi) p. 212.

insecure sultan, in punishment for the fickleness with which he had shaken off the last alliance and set himself in opposition to the Mogul arms.

It was in February 1665 that the great Mogul host under Jay Singh and Diler Khan crossed the Narbada. Shivaji was engaged upon the naval war described in the last chapter. It was owing to this that he remained without prompt information of the new danger from the north. The Mogul generals did not allow the grass to grow beneath their feet. They came to Aurangabad, the head-quarters of the subha or province, put its affairs on a footing of efficiency, and straightway advanced upon Fort Purandar. Diler Khan undertook the blockade of Purandar, while Jay Singh advanced to besiege Sinhagad, despatching a few detachments to operate against Rajgad and Lohagad.

Meanwhile Shivaji returned to Raigad and held a council of war to which the principal military officers were summoned. At this crisis one of the old Maratha leaders, Netaji Palkar had come under the royal disfavour inasmuch as instead of dogging the enemy's movements on his first entrance into the Maratha territory as were his distinct orders, he had diverted his light cavalry on distant forays. This conduct of his lends some plausibility to the view of certain authors who accuse him of a corrupt understanding with Jay Singh. Shivaji sent orders for his instant return. On his non-compliance he degraded him from the title of sir-nobut, or commander of the royal forces which he had so long enjoyed. This title was now conferred upon Kartoji Guzar, who is later on known as Prataprao Guzar.[1] Guzar had earned the highest praise for the able strategy he had displayed in intercepting the forage and supplies of the

[1] According to Sabhasad's chronicle, when Sidi Johar besieged Panhala, that fort having but lately passed into Shivaji's power had not been well fortified and equipped; and Netaji Palkar's failure to bring succour to it on that occasion led to his forfeiture of the title of sir-nobut. However, in any case, it is clear that he still continued in Shivaji's service. The assertion about bribery is made by Catrou.

Moguls and the vigilance with which he had guarded against all Mogul tactics to out-wit or elude him.

Jay Singh's forces amounted to 80,000, in which were represented some of the most warlike and spirited races of Hindustan. Jay Singh was himself a brave and clever tactician who was not likely to blunder easily.

He had brought with him a number of Rajput warriors. From the moment he crossed the Narbada he had tried to form coalitions with Shivaji's enemies. He enlisted the support of the Abyssinians of Janjira, the zemindars of the Karnatic and in particular the raja of Bednore who had been recently humiliated by Shivaji, and the rajas of Jawhar and Ramnagar. Lastly he had won over to the imperial cause the families of those who had sworn, so to say, a blood-feud with Shivaji. Thus there came to the imperial camp Fazal, the son of Afzul Khan still thirsting for vengeance against Shivaji. There came likewise to the Mogul side two members of the vanquished More family of Javli, on the special invitation of Jay Singh.[1] Jay Singh had realized the gravity of his task, and made his preparations accordingly. He had signalized his arrival in the Maratha country by a sudden siege of two of the most impregnable forts of the Marathas. Shivaji was shrewd enough to foresee the difficulty of subduing such an enemy.[2] The arts which had succeeded so brilliantly with Afzul Khan and Shaista Khan were not likely to stand any chance with the present commander. He was not a man to take any thing on trust. An appeal to his sense of patriotism or to his religious fervour was out

[1] Letters of Jay Singh in the *Hajt Anjuman* (Paris MS.) cited by Prof. Sarkar, and Manuccis: "*Storia*." Manucci himself instigated the Koli Rajas of Jawhar etc. on behalf of Jay Singh (Storia II, 132).

[2] Scott Waring says that Shivaji had sent Prataprao Guzar to assassinate Jay Singh. According to his story Guzar went to Jay Singh and got himself admitted to his service. He was in close attendance about Jay Singh's person, and one day seeing that there were very few people present attempted to kill him. But he was at once arrested and disarmed. He was, however, let go by Jay Singh with impunity.

of the question as the presence of Diler Khan made it necessary that he should always be on his guard.

Shivaji is said to have had one of those ecstatic fits to which he was so prone on occasions of high nervous excitement. It was believed that he again became the medium of the communication of the fiat of his guardian deity. His utterances in the trance were taken down by his secretaries. They were to this effect : "Great is the peril that is threatening thee now. Jay Singh is not fated to taste defeat at thy hands. Thou shalt have to make terms of peace and amity and go to Delhi into the sunshine of the imperial presence. Dark clouds gather round thee at Delhi. But I shall shield thee from all harm and restore thee safe and victorious again to thy realm." This oracular assurance calmed Shivaji's mind.

Jay Singh was encamped at Saswad between the siege lines around Sinhagad and Purandar. He was well informed about Shivaji's antecedents. He was prepossessed in his favour by what he had heard about his daily sacrifices in the promotion of the cause of religious and political independence. He looked upon it as in some measure a holy enterprise and his conscience did not whisper to him any assurances of success or encouragement.

He saw the heroic stuff of which Shivaji's followers were made and how they had poured their hearts and souls into his enterprise. These meditations combined to influence him also to think of peaceful methods and an honourable conclusion of the task he had undertaken. Then the fates of Afzul Khan and Shaista Khan constantly hovered before his eyes, and no concessions to Shivaji appeared in his mind too great so long as they were consistent with self-respect. From the moment he had set his foot in the Maratha country some instinct whispered to him that his life was not worth a moment's purchase and his chief desire now was to escape with honour from the hostile land.[1] He,

[1] Some of the Marathi chronicles say that he got his priests to offer

therefore, tried persuasion expatiating on the advantages of peace with the great Mogul. He referred to the family tradition of Shivaji's Rajput descent from the Sesodia stock of Udaipur, expressed his personal gratification at his religious pride, and concluded with an expression of his willingness to maintain the power and possessions of the Maratha Raja.

The hints thus conveyed relieved Shivaji from all immediate anxiety. His officers and chiefs advised a continuation of these peaceful overtures. Raghunathpant, the chief justice, was sent as an envoy to the camp of Jay Singh with the customary presents of jewellery and embroidered silks, of horses and elephants. The envoy presented a missive embellished with the most courtly compliments and couched in the most mellifluous strain of which Shivaji's secretary was capable. Shivaji professed himself to be inspired almost with a feeling of filial affection at the paternal tone of Jay Singh's epistle; he compared himself to Jay Singh's son and offered to abide by his counsel. He ascribed his operations of war to his love of the Hindu religion and his desire to set free Hindu worship, usage and law. He painted a lurid picture of the Hindu church bleeding under the talons of Islam, of Hindu temples converted into mosques. While thus striving to stir up the Rajput's Hindu pride and sentiment he professed himself ready to accept him as a mediator before the imperial throne, admitting the grounds of the imperial wrath, but pointing out that his domains and castles were acquired from other states, hoping to retain them under the imperial favour and offering to aid the imperial expansion in the South. Such in brief was the character of the epistle, the contents whereof were embellished and supplemented by Raghunathpant's oratory.

Jay Singh was gratified with the tone and contents of Shivaji's letter. He represented to Shivaji's envoy that

special prayers and perform ceremonial rites for the success of his campaign.

it was to his own advantage that the Maratha prince should come to terms with the mighty Mogul power and undertook on his word of honour as a Rajput to bring about a reconciliation and invite him as an honoured guest to the Mogul durbar. The envoy at a private audience with Jay Singh addressed himself to the Maharaja's religious susceptibilities and appealed to him to lend his active support to Shivaji's propaganda in favour of a Hindu revival, pointing out the degradation of service under a foreign anti-Hindu domination and the desecration of Hindu shrines and gods. This was done to secure the Rajput's personal intervention as against any insidious designs on the part of his sovereign. Jay Sing renewed his assurances and showed no trace of resentment at the frank language of the envoy.

Jay Singh brought about an interview between Raghunathpant and Diler Khan, where it was agreed that Shivaji should communicate his demands and stipulations, in formal terms to be submitted to Aurangzeb, being assured that these would be carefully attended to at the imperial court. The envoy then returned to Raigad and Shivaji's council after full deliberation drafted the conditions of a treaty. They were to this effect: That Shivaji should retain in his possession the forts and territories already in his power, with the rights of *chaut* (one quarter of land revenue) and *sirdeshmukhi* (one tenth of the revenue) over the rest of the Deccan, and that with these rights and concessions an alliance should be formed between the Maratha and the imperial power.

These terms and stipulations were submitted to Jay Singh by Shivaji's envoy. The Rajput leader was convinced of the *bona fides* of Shivaji and got the envoy to confirm the declaration on oath. The Raja urged Shivaji to put full confidence in himself and act according to his wishes. The ratification of the terms was postponed to be effected at a personal conference between Jay Singh and Shivaji.

When Diler Khan came to learn that the preliminaries of a treaty were all but completed between Jay Singh and Shivaji and the ratification depended merely on a personal conference between the two leaders, his jealousy was roused and he suspected that the Hindu leaders on either side were going to act in collusion to the detriment of the interests of the empire. He, therefore, held out against this proposal, urging that the final consent to Shivaji's stipulations should be withheld till receipt of the imperial orders on the subject, that their future relations with the Maratha power should be based upon the rescript from the throne, and that pending this decision they should prosecute with vigour the siege of Purandar and Sinhagad already begun under such good auspices. Upon this Jay Singh enlarged upon the wisdom of an immediate alliance between the Maratha and the Mogul and the acceptance by Shivaji of the suzerainty of the emperor. The purpose of the present campaign, said Jay Singh, would be amply served and the war fully vindicated, if Shivaji were compelled through the instrumentality of the treaty to surrender such of his fortresses and territories as belonged of right to the old Nizam Shahi kingdom and, therefore, formed part of the imperial subha of the Deccan. Apart from such an arrangement the re-conquest of the hill-forts was a difficult task. Each fort would cost thousands of precious lives, and for all these sacrifices the chances of conquest would still remain precarious. Jay Singh, therefore, deprecated any further attacks upon these forts, urging that they should calmly wait and watch, having intercepted all communications of the Maratha garrisons with the outer world beyond their mountain walls. Diler Khan would not yield. He declared that his colleague might rust and dally in sloth before the walls of Sinhagad, but for his part he was resolved to push forward the siege of Purandar and would brook no obstruction to thwart his purpose. He departed with an injunction to Jay Singh on no account to make peace without direct orders from the emperor.

And now the siege of Purandar went forward with great vigour on the part of the assailants. A steady blockade was maintained on all sides. The governor of the fortress, Murar Baji Prabhu, was no mean soldier. As the Mogul siege lines were being pushed nearer and nearer he surprised their straggling parties, exploded their ammunition bags and captured war material on an extensive scale. He sent out his light horse to cut off the enemy's supplies and starve the besieging host. These manœuvres often met with eminent success until the Moguls were able to overtake the flying squadrons or pursue them back to the rocky walls of Purandar. But the inevitable end approached steadily nearer. The siege lines drew closer round the fort and no avenue was left open by which any one could enter or leave it.

But Murar Baji was never daunted in spirit. He could muster a small but sturdy garrison of 2000 brave men—Mavalis and Hetkaris. Thanks to the liberal provisioning on the part of his government, there was an abundance of supplies and munitions of war. The undaunted garrison defended the fort for days together against overwhelming odds. They warded off the Mogul attacks and drove them off from every point of approach. Shivaji availed himself of every opportunity to send re-inforcements and fresh fodder and corn supplies from Rajgad. Thus baffled in these attempts, Diler Khan having driven in some of the outposts, commenced mining a rock under one of the bastions of the lower fort. The garrison made frequent sallies and repeatedly drove off the miners with considerable losses. But their great numbers and tenacity at length enabled them to complete these operations. After repeated failures, they succeeded in shattering the rock. The tower was levelled to the ground, and the lower fort—for the fortifications of Purandar consisted of an upper and a lower fort—was exposed to an assault. No sooner did the invading bands effect the entrance into the lower fort than they dispersed themselves to plunder, and in their heedless precipitation exposed themselves to a withering fire which the Hetkari marksmen from the upper fort opened upon them with unerring precision. So sudden was the destruction that they wrought that the assailants were driven in all directions and rushed head-long to get under cover of the rock. A new party of assailants was in the act of coming up to take their place. At this moment Murar Baji, with the flower of his Mavali infantry, sallied out and engaged in a hand to hand fight with the Mogul forces pouring within. The Mavalis fought stubbornly. Two thousand of the enemy, Pathan and Mogul, felt the edge of the Mavali blade. Hundreds of the ardent Mavalis laid down their loyal lives, but for the moment they had achieved their object, for the foe was melting away, fleeing down the hill, in view of Diler Khan himself, who mounted on his elephant near a temple beneath the fort, was watching the progress of the assault. Seeing the flight of his men he bent his bow, called to a guard of Pathans around him to advance, and rallying the flying host, charged the Mavalis in person. But Murar Baji put forth his utmost strength and disputed every step of Diler Khan's advance. The hardy Afghans recoiled from the swords of the infuriated Mavalis, whom their recent success had raised to the highest pitch of enthusiasm. The example of the leader was a stirring inspiration to every Mavali heart; for Murar Baji recked not of blood or life but put his soul into every stroke. And what should he reck of life when in spite of his brave efforts the fort entrusted to him by his sovereign lord had thus been mined and breached and the stream of Mogul foemen was steadily pouring in? It was not for him to survive its capture but to prevent it to the best of his ability. Thus, indifferent to all but the call of duty, he fought on, now here, now there, exhorting and inspiring his gallant Mavalis by word and deed. In the midst of all the dust and din of war he observed where the Khan was stationed, mounted upon his elephant, and in a moment he rushed upon him like a lion upon his prey. He had lost his shield and was now parrying the sword-thrusts of the enemy with his arm which was covered only with a scarf. When Murar Baji drew quite near, the Khan addressed him in a loud voice, declaring his unreserved admiration of the valorous deeds he had done in the field that day and inviting him to surrender relying upon his assurances, and promising that he would raise him to high titles and dignities. Upon this, it is said, the noble Murar Baji retorted: "Ye are Turks and Tartars and what care I for you and your offerings? I am a true servant to Shivaji and will not hear of terms of surrender. Sooner will I die than yield." With these words he prepared to aim a sword thrust at Diler Khan, when the latter, bow in hand, deftly shot an arrow and killed him on the spot. The garrison soldiers accompanying their noble leader fell back at once and betook themselves fighting all the while into the upper fort, closing its massive gate in the face of the enemy.[1] A timely succour from Shivaji revived their spirit and encouraged them to renew the struggle. The blare of trumpets and the booming of war-drums began to resound once more and the cannonading was again resumed from the upper ridges. The Moguls were forced to relinquish all the ground they had won.

But Diler Khan doffed his turban and vowed never to wear it again till the fortress was captured. He again carried the lower slopes, and considering the northern face of Purandar impregnable determined to carry by escalade a small detached fort lying towards the northwest, called the fort of Rudramal, or as Grant Duff calls it, the fort of Vajragad, with a view to bring up his guns upon that fort and direct them upon the main fortifications of Purandar. The havaldars in command of this fort were two brothers, Babaji Bowaji and Yeshwantrao Bowaji. Confident that Murar Baji, of whose death they had not heard, would send aid to their rescue, the havaldar brothers put up a strenu-

1 There arose a superstitious tradition that when the head of Murar Baji was severed from the trunk the latter continued to mow down the Mahomedans!

ous fight. In the end they were slain and the fort surrendered. The fort of Vajragad was a key to unlock the fort of Purandar. Diler Khan now opened a vigorous fire from the top of this fort against the upper fort of Purandar. But the rains set in shortly after and retarded the operations. The garrison, who had hitherto never lost heart notwithstanding the death of their captain and were emulous to lay down their own lives after his example, were, however, somewhat dispirited when they saw that they were now caught between two fires. The Mogul artillery was however extremely bad, and though continued for weeks was found to have done very poor execution while the rain considerably hampered the Mogul enterprise. Shivaji sent such relief as was possible and earnest instructions to hold on, until he should send them word to surrender.

While Diler Khan sat with iron tenacity before the rocky walls of Purandar, Jay Singh had not been idle. He had organized many a raiding attack in the territory surrounding these forts. The flying columns of the Moguls ravaged the villages, leaving not a vestige of cultivation or habitation, but an utter desolation, wherever they went[1] This was the usual kind of warfare with the agricultural classes favoured by the imperial commanders in the south. It was vindictive in its aims and methods. Its object was to terrorize Shivaji, to bring home to him the vastness of the military resources of the empire, and to induce him at length to make a complete surrender, reposing his faith absolutely in the good faith of Jay Singh. On the other hand the Maratha captains did not take these things quite so meekly. From April to May, Netaji Palkar pursued with frequent success his old tactics of sudden forays upon the Mogul camp. Jay Singh of course in his despatches to the emperor drew a rosy picture of his triumphs, but even he had often to admit that he had not always succeeded in frustrating the plans of the

[1] Jay Singh's letters, (Paris MS.) quoted by Prof. Sarkar.

Marathas. The brilliant successes of Shivaji's captains, their assaults on dark nights, their blockade of roads and difficult passes have called forth the admiration of Khafi Khan.[1]

While these operations were in progress against Purandar, Sinhagad was also the scene of an active siege under the direction of a deputy of Jay Singh. The Mogul commander had advanced to the wall and was planting batteries, when Shivaji's horse made a sudden raid upon the besiegers' camp just before it was day-break and looted his stores. The officer returned discomfited much to the astonishment of Jay Singh. This made a considerable impression upon Jay Singh as also did the fact that Shivaji's skirmishers had constantly carried on raids, cut off fodder, led surprise attacks, driven off sumpter beasts, and set the surrounding woods on fire. It made Jay Singh impatient to have done with his onerous duty. He remonstrated with Diler Khan for his head-strong pride and folly. A single fort had already cost so many Mogul lives, and yet the chances of conquest stood as far off as ever. Shivaji's men were of heroic mettle. One hero took the place of another and there was no end to the tale of valour. What did Diler Khan expect to do with the more inaccessible forts of the Konkan and the Sahyadri ranges? Of his own accord the Maratha prince was coming down to make peace and friendship. Diler Khan had spurned the golden opportunity only to dispel faith and confidence and play a losing game. These reproaches now seemed to make some impression upon Diler Khan, for he had learnt by bitter experience the arduous nature of the plan he had embarked upon. He replied to Jay Singh that he was not averse to a peace, provided some means could be found to draw Shivaji to a conference and the acceptance of a treaty; but he pointed out that he had sworn not to don his turban till Purandar were taken, so that the floating of the Mogul flag on the citadel of Puran-

1 *Vide* Khafi Khan (Elliot VII, 272-273.)

dar, was a *sine qua non* to any treaty proposals, though it might be open to Shivaji thereafter to have it restored to him by the terms of the treaty itself.

Upon this Jay Singh renewed the negotiations which had been suspended by reason of the obstinacy of Diler Khan. He communicated to Shivaji that his terms were generally agreeable to him, a condition precedent being the hoisting of the Mogul flag upon Purandar. The stipulations were to be settled at a private conference subject to confirmation by the emperor. Shivaji was gratified at the renewal of the overtures, though for the time he feigned anger at the abrupt breaking off of the original negotiations and the losses he had sustained in consequence. Far from his having to surrender Purandar, he declared, it was for the Moguls to surrender Rudramal and raise the siege-lines round Purandar itself. In reply Jay Singh repeated his assurance and undertook to make every concession.

Shivaji then arranged to meet Jay Singh at a personal conference. He started with a large retinue of officers and attendants with every mark of royal pomp and magnificence. His personal attendants were arrayed in rich embroideries and ornaments.[1] His courtiers and officers wore jewelled brocades. The body-guard of Mavalis and Hetkaris was also brilliantly attired. Shivaji's own attire was distinguished for its simplicity. He rode an elephant, with bow and arrows. Raghunathpant led the

[1] Grant Duff and the author of the Bundela Memoirs say that Shivaji was frightened by the large massing of the Mogul forces around Purandar and came to Jay Singh's camp with his retinue. Jay Singh sent forward his son Kirat Singh to receive him at the camp gate and himself came up to the entrance of his pavilion to welcome Shivaji. Khafi Khan says Shivaji's wife and maternal relations were in the fort of Sinhagad and the fort being besieged closely he could not rescue them. Therefore he sent men to ask for pardon and himself proposed to visit Jay Singh in his camp. The latter sent his *Munshi* to tell him that if Shivaji submitted frankly and gave up his forts his petition would be granted; otherwise he had better return and renew the war. Shivaji assured him that he was in earnest, and then the Rajah sent a person of high rank to receive Shivaji.

way to the tent of Jay Singh. The Rajput came out to receive his guest. The Maratha dismounted at the sight of the veteran Rajput. The Rajput dismounted in his turn, and the chieftains embraced. A flourish of trumpets was sounded by both body-guards. The Mogul officers came crowding out to have a look at the distinguished Maratha warrior. Shivaji's bearing and manners made a favourable impression upon the haughty aristocracy of the Mogul camp.

The warrior chief returned to the tent of Jay Singh amid great eclat. The nobles on either side were introduced. Jay Singh complimented Shivaji on his bravery which had brought the Mahomedan chiefs of North and South into so much trouble. He professed himself to be anxious to forward Shivaji's interests consistently with the interests of the empire. He would treat him as he would his eldest son, Ram Singh. He might rely on his word. Shivaji made the utmost professions of humility and respect, offering to place his kingdom at his feet, as a dutiful son to his solicitous parent. He had full faith in his honour and professions and complied with his wishes to come to a conference.[1] He was prepared unreservedly to place all his hill-forts at Jay Singh's disposal. Jay Singh was greatly delighted at Shivaji's loyal proposals, but pointed out that Diler Khan's good will must first be conciliated. He was a haughty patrician of Afghan descent and enjoyed the imperial favour as no other omrah at the court did. It was essential that he must be flattered into reconciliation. He would send Shivaji to Diler Khan's tent with an escort of Rajput officers under a brave noble of the Mogul court. Shivaji agreed to the

[1] According to Manucci (who was an artillery officer in Jay Singh's camp) Jay Singh had endeavoured to create in Shivaji's mind a good opinion about himself and assured him prior to the meeting that if he put his entire trust in him he would attain all his objects at the hands of the emperor. Shivaji had several conversations with Manucci, who testifies to the inquisitiveness with which Shivaji informed himself about things European.

proposal. Diler Khan lay encamped before the gates of Purandar. He was exceedingly mortified at Jay Singh's receiving Shivaji without reference to him, and thought that Shivaji was now visiting him after carrying things half-way with the Rajput.[1] He was smarting under the sense of his humiliation at not having yet fulfilled the vow of the conquest of Purandar. He felt that in the end the whole credit of the campaign was going to Jay Singh's account. He suspected that Hindu was acting in collusion with Hindu and was frustrating the objects of his compaign. Thus he nursed his irritation and anger, and received Shivaji in a cold and formal manner. The Khan had no faith in Shivaji and kept his arms ready beside him, even when they were seated next to each other on the *divan*. Subhan Singh, the maternal uncle of Jay Singh, began to explain the proposal for a treaty. The Khan, however, with simulated wrath threatened to persevere in reducing Purandar and putting every man to the sword. "Until this is achieved," he exclaimed, "I won't hear of a peace." This was a mere threat and Shivaji's courtly and adroit reply soothed his anger. "The fort is yours", said Shivaji. "Why put yourself to so much ado on that account? I am come here in person to place the keys of its portals in your gracious hands. With Purandar I am prepared to make over all my other forts and lands. My only entreaty is for pardon and forgiveness. Well do I know that it is not for a poor chief like me to defy an imperial general of your calibre and distinction. Your Lordship's propitious favour and mediation will be the ladder of my good fortune." The Khan was highly gratified with Shivaji's courtly flattery

[1] It appears from Jay Singh's letters that in order to impress Shivaji and induce him to make a surrender of his forts, Jay Singh had arranged with Diler Khan and his son Kirat Singh to deliver a final assault upon Purandar at the very time when Shivaji was coming for his interview to the Mogul camp, so that while the conference between Jay Singh and Shivaji was going on, the latter could see from the Raja's tent, which commanded a full view of the siege operations, the assault being delivered.

and replied that Jay Singh was his senior and in personal favour with the emperor. He was a mere satellite. The final disposition of things was in Jay Singh's hands, whose word was law to him. With this the conference broke up and with it the siege of Purandar. The operations of war were succeeded by an interchange of friendly amenities. Shivaji entertained Jay Singh, Diler Khan and the leading omrahs and officers of the Mogul camp to a sumptuous banquet. The Mogul commanders returned the compliment to Shivaji and his courtiers.

On the conclusion of the armistice Shivaji returned to Raigad. After several conferences the following terms of agreement were entered upon, subject to the imperial sanction, but granted under the personal guarantee of Jay Singh. The first condition was that Shivaji should cede whatever forts or territory he had taken from the Moguls. Of the 32 forts taken or built by him in the territory which had at one time or other been under the Nizam Shahi kingdom, Shivaji was to relinquish 20 to Jay Singh and retain the remaining 12, with the territory adjoining to these forts,[1] yielding an annual revenue of ten lakhs of rupees, and these forts and revenue together with all the rest of his acquisitions from the Bijapur kingdom were to continue under him as a jahgir depending on the emperor. Shivaji's son Sambhaji, then a stripling of only eight years, was to receive an imperial mansab of 5000 horse. In lieu of the hereditary claims on the Nizamshahi territory which Shivaji hereby undertook to cede, he was to be granted the assignments of chauth and sirdeshmukhi on certain territories above the ghats under the

[1] According to some authorities 25, and again according to others 27 forts, were to be relinquished. Khafi Khan says the forts ceded were 23 and the ceded territory yielded a revenue of forty lakhs. Prof. Sarkar says the forts ceded were 23, with an annual revenue of 4 lakhs of pagodas (i. e. twenty lakhs of rupees) and those remaining with Shivaji were 12, with a revenue of one lakh of pagodas. But Rajwade (VIII, 14) quotes an imperial rescript to Shivaji, in which the forts ceded are stated to be twenty. Prof. Sarkar gives a list of the 23 forts (Shivaji, pp. 156, 157).

Bijapur kingdom as also the cession of the sea-fort of Janjira. Should the last two conditions be ratified by the emperor, Shivaji was to pay the sum of 40 lakhs of pagodas as a premium or *peshkush* by annual instalments of three lakhs of pagodas, the charge of collecting which he took upon himself; and lastly he also agreed to maintain a special cavalry force in the Mogul service.

These conditions were submitted in petition form to the emperor Aurangzeb, with the special recommendation of Jay Singh that the terms be ratified. Jay Singh drew the emperor's attention to the service Shivaji was capable of rendering to the empire, calling him the Key of the Deccan and declaring his belief that without his accession to the imperial side, the conquest of the Deccan would never be realized. At Jay Singh's suggestion, Shivaji intimated his desire of visiting the emperor.

In a long letter to Shivaji Aurangzeb distinctly confirmed most of the terms proposed by him. As to the grant of chauth and sirdeshmukhi over Bijapur territories, Aurangzeb agreed to a cession of certain Bijapur territories on the distinct understanding that he should co-operate with Jay Singh, together with all his forces in the campaign against Bijapur and exert himself in the conquest of that kingdom and pay forthwith the first instalment of the peshkush he had agreed to pay for these assignments. The cession of Janjira was not granted.[1]

Pursuant to this agreement, Shivaji, with a body of 2000 horse and 8,000 infantry participated in Jay Singh's campaign against Bijapur. Their first operations were directed against Bajaji Naik Nimbalkar of Phaltan who

[1] *Vide* Parasnis MSS. No. 8; Rajwade VIII, 14 The chauth and sirdeshmukhi are not mentioned in Aurangzeb's letter to Shivaji. Aurangzeb apparently assigned to Shivaji the prospective conquests of the Adil Shahi Baleghat districts, with an annual revenue of four lakhs of pagodas, provided that Shivaji recovered them before Bijapur fell into the hands of the ogals and provided he actively co-operated with Jay Singh in the invasion upon Bijapur territory.

was completely overthrown, and the town of Phaltan fell into the hands of the invaders. The chief of Phaltan, though a relation of Shivaji, had never been on friendly terms with him and took greater pride in his unswerving allegiance to the Adil-Shahi house. The fort of Tattora (Tathavda), another of Nimbalkar's strongholds was escaladed by Shivaji's Mavalis.[1] All other fortified places on the line of march fell before the invading army.

Ali Adil Shaha II had prepared his troops, but at the same time endeavoured to avert the storm by promises to concede the Mogul demands. In this he had no success. Jay Singh and Diler Khan continued to advance and carry fort after fort. At length the rival powers confronted one another on the field of Mangalwedhe and a desperate battle ensued. The Bijapur army was composed to a large extent of the Maratha light cavalry and many distinguished Maratha nobles could be counted in their ranks. Distinguished among the rest was Shivaji's half-brother the Raja Vyankoji, whose gallantry in the field attracted general attention. On the Mogul side the Maratha arms were represented by Shivaji's contingent, ably led by Shivaji himself and Netaji Palkar. The valour and strategy evinced by the Maratha commanders evoked the ungrudging admiration of Jay Singh and the Mogul officers. Every detail of military duty entrusted to them was discharged with conspicuous success. The Bijapur forces, as was to be expected, were defeated.

---

[1] Shivaji's wife Sayibai is said to have been a sister of Bajaji Nimbalkar and his daughter Sakhubai was married to his son Mahadaji. After the capture of Sambhaji by the Moguls Mahadaji Nimbalkar and Sakhubai were, according to Khafi Khan, taken prisoners and confined in Gwalior Fort. Mr. Sardesai, (Marathi Riyasat, P. 490) following the Phaltan *daftar* and an article in the *Itihas Sangraha*, tells the traditional story that on account of family feuds Bajaji was taken a prisoner to the Adil Shahi court and forced to become a Mahomedan to save his life, and that in about 1657, with the active encouragement of Jijabai, Shivaji's mother, he was purified at the temple of Shingnapur and reconverted to Hinduism, and to set all doubts at rest Shivaji's daughter was given in marriage to the son of Bajaji.

Jay Singh spared no compliments in acknowledging the services of Shivaji in this battle. Courage, bravery, skill seemed to be splendidly united in his actions. He made special mention of these services in his despatches to Aurangzeb about the event, upon which the emperor addressed a second letter to Shivaji extolling his prowess and services and sent him a robe of honour and a jewelled dagger as a mark of his appreciation.[1]

In this manner the allied forces of Jay Singh and Shivaji advanced to within ten miles of the fort of Bijapur. Here their further advance was stopped. The Maratha and Mahomedan nobles of the Adil Shahi state hastened to the rescue of their capital. They laid waste the country all around and forced the invading hosts to retire for want of fodder and water. The Moguls fell back upon Perinda. Shivaji asked permission to make a diversion against Panhala, a fort of which he knew all the ins and outs. But here his usual good luck forsook him, chiefly on account of the unexpected defection of Netaji Palkar, who was won over by the Adil Shahi officers to their side by the offer of a heavy bribe.[2] Jay Singh, however, was not the man to lose the services of such an excellent cavalry officer to the imperial cause. He made still more tempting promises, offered him a mansab of 5000 horse, and a substantial jahgir. So Netaji Palkar followed the Mogul flag again and soon came back to his old allegiance.[3]

---

1 *Vide* Parasnis MSS. No. 9 and Rajwade, VIII, 15.

2 Khafi Khan (Elliot VII, 278.)

3 When Shivaji went to Agra, Netaji Palkar continued to serve under Jay Singh but was evidently considered a member of Shivaji's contingent. Khafi Khan tells us that upon the escape of Shivaji from Agra, Jay Singh acting under the emperor's order arrested Netaji Palkar and his son and sent them to court (i. e. Agra). Here in order to save himself Palkar became a Mahomedan and was given a small mansab. But afterwards in 1676 he escaped to Shivaji in the south and re-canted (Elliot VII, 280). He underwent a purification ceremony and was readmitted to Hinduism (Jedhe Chronology). We have already seen how Jijabai had interested herself in the re-admission to Hindu caste of Bajaji Nimbalkar.

The growing difficulties of the siege of Bijapur again roused the suspicion of Diler Khan that these difficulties were of Shivaji's making. Jay Singh saw the injustice of this suspicion on the part of Diler Khan. It is said that Diler Khan constantly asked him to put Shivaji to death and undertook to murder him without any impairment to the Mirza Raja's reputation. But Jay Singh had given the most solemn assurances of safety to Shivaji when he made his submission and refused to be a party to such a dishonest proposal. It may be it was partly due to this motive that he had sanctioned the diversion upon Panhala. Shivaji now retired to Khelna (Vishalgad) and in spite of the failure of the attack on Panhala was courteously treated by Jay Singh.[1] From Khelna he sent an army under a Mahomedan officer to attack Phonda.[2] This town underwent a long siege, on account of the collusion of Rustom Jeman, the Adil Shahi governor in those parts. Rustom Jeman in the end being taunted by his sultan for his remissness sent one of his lieutenants to relieve the town. Rustom Jeman endeavoured to reinstate himself in his king's favour by capturing Kudal, Bande, Sankhali, Dicholi, and other minor stations, forming the barrier territory between Sawantwadi and the Portuguese domains of Goa.[3]

Soon afterwards, Aurangzeb, at the suggestion of Jay Singh, again wrote to Shivaji and invited him to the imperial court, promising to confer on him a great rank and honour with permission to return to the Deccan. At the same time Aurangzeb sent immediate orders to

[1] *Vide* Khafi Khan, (Elliot VII, 278). As to Diler Khan's suspicion and proposal to put Shivaji to death see Manucci, *Storia*, II, 137. The Jedhe Chronology p. 187, says Shivaji took leave of Jay Singh and went to Raigad.

[2] First siege of Phonda 1666. Shivaji's Mahomedan officer was defeated by stratagem by the Adil Shahi officer, *Vide* Factory Records, Surat 104, referred to by Prof. Sarkar in his Shivaji, p. 313, foot-note.

[3] Prof. Sarkar makes wild guesses in trying to trace Sankhali and Dicholi on the atlas. These village towns form part of the Bardesh district of Goa.

Jay Singh in his capacity as the subhedar of Aurangabad to pay a lakh of rupees from the imperial treasury to Shivaji for his travelling expenses and send him to Delhi without loss of time. Upon receipt of these orders, Jay Singh advised Shivaji to proceed to Agra without any anxiety, promising that his son Ram Singh would look after his comfort and safety. Upon these assurances Shivaji resolved to visit Agra.[1]

---

1 Shivaji visited the emperor actually at Agra, not at Delhi.

CHAPTER XIX

SHIVAJI AT THE MOGUL COURT, 1666–67

When the decision to visit the imperial capital was finally made, Shivaji left the Mogul camp and proceeded to Raigad, where he had summoned his principal officers to communicate to them his intention. Not a few of them expressed their disapproval, pointing out that Aurangzeb was a sort of impious Titan, who never forgot his intrigues nor his enmities. To trust him was to take a leap in the dark. Besides Delhi was two months' journey off, and who would say what difficulties would have to be encountered? To these criticisms Shivaji replied that to go to Delhi was now a necessity, and he depended on the utterance of his tutelary goddess in this connection. For the prophecy had then been made that Shivaji would have to go to Delhi and his tutelary deity would bring him safe from harm. A journey to the north had besides its educative value. It would enable him to observe the state of the country and the Mogul durbar, to view those countries which at one time had been under the sway of his ancestors, and to visit the great shrines and holy rivers of Aryavarta. Jay Singh's guarantee had dispelled all fears and the emperor's friendly disposition had been proved by the Treaty of Purandar. Notwithstanding all the assurances, should any unforeseen calamity overtake him, he hoped he would make shift to emerge from it in triumph. In this manner Shivaji overruled the objections of his counsellors and adhered to his resolution to visit Delhi in company with his eldest son Sambhaji.

Shivaji invested three of his principal officers, Moropant Trimal, the Peshwa, Annaji Datto, the Surnis (the record keeper), and Nilo Sondev, the Muzumdar (the auditor general) with full authority during his absence, bade them conduct all the administration from Raigad under the regency of Jijabai, and enjoined upon all public officers to respect and obey their orders. To Prataprao and others of his intimate nobles he entrusted the care of his mother and second son. He made a tour of inspection throughout his kingdom. He urged all to conduct the administration with the same efficiency as heretofore, to defend the realm and add to it, and to be on the watch for any news about him from Delhi. Whatever evil might betide, he was sure to return, and the word of men like Jay Singh could not be pledged in vain. But should the unexpected happen and trouble come upon his party, it was left to his officers and ministers to cheer up his old mother and guard the kingdom and govern it in the name of Rajaram. In their zeal, their loyalty, and their ability he had complete confidence. For his escort Shivaji chose men of approved loyalty, who would never forsake him in any crisis. Among the principal officers there were Niraji Ravji, Trimbak Sondev Dabir, Dattaji Trimbak, Manako Hari Sabnis,[1] and among his aides-de-camp were Hiroji Farzand, Ragho Mittra, Dawalji Gadge, and Jiva Mahalya.[2] With these Shivaji had a corps of expert swordsmen and a Mavali brigade of three to four thousand warriors.[3] As the hour of parting came near, Shivaji had a last interview with the leading ministers, after which he paid his reverence to the image of his tutelary deity in the palace chapel and came down to the apartments of his mother for her parting benediction. This parting was the most painful of all, but as she clasped him in a close embrace and laid her hand upon his head, her hopes and blessings struggled forth into incoherent words through her tears and emotion. Shivaji listened to her blessings and the old, old precepts which he had listened

1 Chitnis substitutes for this name Jivanram Manko. He also adds to this list the names of Balaji Avji Chitnis and Narhar Balla Sabnis.

2 Sabhasad omits the names of Gadge and Mahalya. The Shivdigvijaya gives the names of Raghunathrao Korde, Yesaji Kunk, Tanaji Malusare and Balaji Avji. It is clear from Jedhe Chronology (p. 188) that Trimbakpant Dabir and Raghunathpant Korde accompanied Shivaji and were arrested after his escape from Agra.

3 Some bakhars state that Prataprao Guzar accompanied Shivaji.

to from the days of his childhood and always with increasing enthusiasm.

Before proceeding directly to Delhi, Shivaji had another conference with Jay Singh, who gave an entertainment in his honour. He also gave advice to Shivaji from his wider experience as to the ways of Delhi life and the society at court. He gave him a special letter to be handed to his son, Ram Singh[1] who was at the Mogul darbar. In this epistle, Jay Singh enjoined upon his son to pay proper attention to Shivaji and his party and supply their needs with the greatest zeal and diligence at his command. Finally, Jay Singh undertook to remain in the Deccan as long as Shivaji was at Delhi, so as to safeguard Shivaji's forts and possessions from any molestation at the hands of the Moguls, and he promised that in case of danger, Ram Singh would leave no stone unturned to effect Shivaji's rescue, even at the cost of an open rupture with Aurangzeb, nor would he himself fail in his turn by his actions to do all he could to humble the haughty emperor.

With these assurances and re-assurances Shivaji started on the fateful march to Delhi, having already sent his envoy in advance. Orders had been issued to all the *mahalkaris* (taluka-officers) and *mokassdars* (revenue farmers) to require the local *fouzdars* (garrison commanders) on Shivaji's route to provide for all the wants of his force and treat him as a prince of the empire. At every halt the local dignitaries came to pay their respects to one of whose fame and valour they had heard so much. The district and taluka officers took particular care not to cause the least annoyance or disrespect to Shivaji, who was known to be very sensitive on this subject. In connection with this subject a story is told of what had recently occurred at Aurangabad, when Shivaji called there on his way to Agra. The governor Safshikan Khan, did not come to the city

[1] Some bakhars state that Ram Singh was in the Deccan with his father and was sent thence to Agra to accompany Shivaji.

gates to receive Shivaji, but sent his nephew instead. Shivaji in anger instead of calling on the governor proceeded immediately to the residence provided for him, whereupon the governor's kinsman submitted that the governor was waiting in the audience hall to receive Shivaji. Shivaji retorted that if the governor meant to make so much of him he might have come to receive him at the gate.[1] Later when the governor and his officers came on formal visits to Shivaji's quarters they made a proper apology and banqueted the guests. Their example was followed by the other nobles in the camp.

A story that is told in connection with the preparations for the journey to the north illustrates the strictness of military discipline, characteristic of Shivaji's fort administration. With a view to test the observance of his rules of discipline, Shivaji presented himself suddenly at night at the gates of a fort and, calling out to the commander of the garrison, sent word that Shivaji in person was come, flying before the enemy and ordered the gate to be thrown open for him. The captain of the fort manned the ramparts and replied that Shivaji's strict orders were not to open the fort gates under any circumstances, that if the foe did approach he might be kept at bay from the out-posts at the outer barrier of the fort, and he would see to this being done. But as for the fugitive party they must keep without under the ramparts. Upon this Shivaji protested that he was the author both of the disciplinary regulations and of the command to open the gates. If he still persisted in his refusal, he would come in for a severe censure. A loyal soldier's duty was to obey immediate commands, no matter however inconsistent with general regulations. But the governor made little of these threats and pointing out that the night was almost turning into day assured him that the pursuing foe would be baffled in the chase.

[1] This anecdote is given on the authority of Scott Waring and the Bundela Memoirs (*Nushka-i-Dilkasha*).

Nevertheless he detained Shivaji's party outside the fort walls for the rest of the night. When morning dawned the governor and the principal offenders appeared at the gate with their hands bound, and unbolting the gate gave admission to Shivaji and prostrated themselves before him, acknowledging their guilt and demanding instant punishment. Shivaji was quite overjoyed with this proof of their adherence to discipline and regulations and far from imposing any kind of censure gave them higher positions in the army. With this moral certainty that the administration at the various fort centres would be conducted in a spirit of harmony and discipline, Shivaji left for the north.

When it was announced that Shivaji's cavalcade was about to approach Agra,[1] Aurangzeb sent Ram Singh and Makhlis Khan, a nobleman of somewhat inferior rank, to receive him. This marked slight, though it did not pass unobserved, Shivaji forbore to notice. He took up his residence at the mansion appointed for him and urged upon Ram Singh to hasten the day of the audience. He also represented to the Rajput prince that the meeting should be arranged on a footing of equality as between ruler and ruler. But Ram Singh pointed out that this was impossible, and that the haughty sovereign of the empire would never treat the ruler of a small principality on terms of equality, and declared that it would be highly imprudent to communicate to him such a proposal.

Aurangzeb indeed was disposed to play the host on a scale of imperial splendour. Nothing was wanting to the comfort of Shivaji and his party. But to kindle his old

---

1 According to Grant Duff and the bakhars, Shivaji's meeting with Aurangzeb at the imperial durbar took place at Delhi. Shivaji might have left Raigad with a view to visit Aurangzeb at Delhi. But soon after the death of Shaha Jahan in January 1666, Aurangzeb removed his court to Agra which was practically his capital for the rest of his reign. Khafi Khan is, therefore, right when he says that Shivaji visited the emperor at Agra. The Jedhe Chronology also mentions Agra as the Mogul capital visited by Shivaji. *Vide* Rajwade VIII, 23.

enmity and add fuel to his passion certain zenana influences were being exercised.[1] The wife of Shaista Khan was then at Agra. She naturally harboured an unforgiving grudge for one who had slain her son and discomfited her husband. She spread the infection of her revengeful hatred among the ladies of the imperial seraglio, urging upon them to plead with the emperor that now that Shivaji was in his power, he should, instead of treating him as an honoured guest of the empire, lead him to the execution block. This made Aurangzeb's mind waver. The gossip of these intrigues in the imperial household came to the ears of the leading omrahs of the court. They deprecated such a proposal, affirming that the imperial honour should not be stained in so foul a manner and that their own lives and fortunes rested entirely on the emperor's reputation for good faith. A treachery so glaring and unforgiveable was bound to throw Jay Singh and the rest of the Rajput supporters of the throne into open rebellion. These protestations had their effect and Aurangzeb revised his judgment.

When Ram Singh arranged the day for the audience which happened to be the fiftieth birth-day of the emperor, special precautions were taken and the most loyal nobles and the pathans of the praetorian guard stood in their appointed places, round the throne, with naked swords in their hands. The emperor had his own fears; he had heard that Shivaji was no ordinary man. Gossip said that he was a very devil at requiting an injury, and that his stride sometimes measured twenty-five cubits in length! In addition to the precautions that have been mentioned, the emperor had in readiness close to his seat five different weapons of war and was clad in mail, over which was worn a robe of muslin. Owing to a natural curiosity to see so distinguished a warrior of the south the audience hall was crowded with leading nobles and merchant princes of the capital. The zenana ladies burned

[1] The authority for this is Bernier.

with the same curiosity, and arrangements were made for them behind the tapestry. As the durbar hour drew near, Shivaji with Ram Singh and a few chosen attendants came to the hall. He made the usual salutation,[1] placed the *nazar* (loyal present) before the throne and was introduced according to the usual etiquette of the court to the emperor. Aurangzeb made the usual enquiries after his health and Shivaji gave the proper answers. This being done, Aurangzeb motioned him with his hand to take his place among the second-rate *amirs*. Ram Singh led the way to that part of the hall and Shivaji had no alternative but to follow. He could now no longer suppress his indignation and seating himself instead of standing with the rest of the nobles, he inquired what was the rank of the *amirs* among whom he was placed. Ram Singh's answer that they were *mansabdars* holding command of five thousand men only aggravated his anger and he ejaculated that the emperor had grossly insulted him in ranking him with such inferior officers, and that he could not with self-respect accept such a position. Saying this, he demanded a dagger from Ram Singh.[2] The emperor

1 According to the chronicle of Chitnis, Shivaji did not make the salutation required by the durbar etiquette and Ram Singh scraped through it somehow. Sabhasad says that Shivaji made a triple *Salaam*, reconciling himself to the act by mentally devoting the first bow to the god Shambhu Mahadev, the second to the goddess Jagadamba, and the third to his father Shahaji.

2 It may be inferred from this that Shivaji had to enter the durbar hall without his arms. It is difficult to conjecture why he now demanded a dagger. According to the Bundela Memoirs Shivaji fainted with grief at the insult and had to be removed to the bath-room where by sprinkling rose-water etc. he was brought back to his senses. The author of these memoirs believes that Shivaji was frightened at the sight of the splendour of the Mogul court and lost his senses with astonishment! He also adds that on recovering his senses he got himself to be conveyed to his residence, where he became delirious, exclaiming in his fit that he was a fool to be caught in the talons of an eagle and asking why he did not kill him outright. The bakhars and the Bundela Memoirs further state that Shivaji asked of Ram Singh the name of the Rajput commander who was standing in front of him, and hearing that it was the Raja Rai Singh exclaimed, "Rai Singh! What? Am I

inquired what was a-foot, and the *amirs* repeated Shivaji's words.[1] Thereupon the emperor, fearing that Shivaji's excitement might lead him to some excess, ordered Ram Singh to present to him the betel-nut leaf in token of parting,[2] and to conduct him to his residence, adding that the audience might be completed on the morrow.

But no more audience was granted. The emperor had no desire to see Shivaji again. The latter was now struck with dismay, being convinced that the emperor meditated evil. To know the worst and be prepared for it, he sent Ram Singh to enquire into Aurangzeb's intentions. Aurangzeb replied that it was his imperial pleasure to retain Shivaji at the Mogul court and entrust him with military duties of the highest importance. Besides the jahgir in the Deccan which had already been conceded to him agreeably to his own stipulations, the emperor professed to confer on him an additional jahgir in the north with a revenue of lacs of rupees. Shivaji might put the southern jahgir in charge of his son: and in virtue of the northern jahgir he might serve in the imperial armies at the head of his own force of 50 to 100 thousand. For a man of Shivaji's bravery, generalship and statesmanship, the Mogul durbar was the only arena for the proper exercise of his high gifts.

These prospects of high office under the Mogul were quite distasteful to Shivaji's ideas, apart from the fact

considered only equal to him?" Sabhasad and Chitnis substitute the name of Jaswant Singh for Rai Singh. But Jaswant Singh was a *haft-hazari* and a friend of Shivaji, who was not likely to make an ungenerous comparison with him. Rai Singh was a subordinate officer.

[1] Orme says that Shivaji rebuked the emperor about his motives and said that the Shaista Khan affair and the sack of Surat must have taught him who he was. With that he drew his dagger intending to plunge it into his own breast, but was prevented by the by-standers, and the emperor reassured him that he had nothing to fear and exhorted him to live in his service and take part in the Mogul campaign against Kandahar.

[2] Khafi Khan states that the jewelled-crest, ornaments and an elephant which had been kept ready for presentation to Shivaji remained unpresented on account of the sensational termination of the audience.

that the sincerity of these proposals was very doubtful. It was obvious to Shivaji that these were the blandishments devised by a naturally crafty and astute mind to entangle him in the north while undermining his power in the south. He, therefore, petitioned the emperor through Raghunathpant, pointing out that he had been invited to the durbar by hopes of promotion,[1] that his services to the Mogul flag were already too well known to require repetition, and that he was quite prepared to fulfil to the letter the terms of the treaty made with Jay Singh. He submitted that he was willing to co-operate heart and soul in the imperial project of the conquest of the Bijapur and Golconda kingdoms. He was capable of rendering much more vital service to the empire by operating in the south which was his own country and where he commanded such a large following and influence rather than in the north, where he was an exile and a stranger to the soil, without any friends or influence to boast of. Thus neither was it to the advantage of the empire that Shivaji should transfer the scene of his imperial service to the north, nor was it of any earthly use or convenience to him. Besides the northern climate did not agree with his health nor with that of his young son, or of the little contingent that accompanied him. He therefore craved the emperor's gracious permission to return to the Deccan.

---

1 According to Manucci the agreement was that Shivaji was to be given the first place when he appeared in the durbar, and the agreement was broken by the emperor, though made in writing and on the oaths of Jay Singh and Aurangzeb himself. Prof. Sarkar believes that there is a great probability in the assertion of the Maratha chronicles that Jay Singh had promised that on his return from the Mogul court, Shivaji would be given the viceroyalty of the Mogul Deccan. Khafi Khan asserts that Shivaji had a claim to nothing less than a haft–hazari (command of 7000), as his son Sambhaji and his general Netaji Palkar were already holding a mansab of 5000 each in the Mogul army. He asserts Jay Singh had made promises to Shivaji but had artfully refrained from making them known to the emperor. Sabhasad says that Shivaji had made the offer of conquering Bijapur and Golconda for the emperor if he were appointed the Mogul commander-in-chief in the Deccan, and Jay Singh had agreed to the proposal.

To this petition the emperor vouchsafed no answer, so much was he obsessed with the view that by detaining Shivaji in the north, he would further his ambitious designs in the south. By the restraint he sought to practise upon Shivaji, the emperor thought he would curb his haughty temper and reduce him to a state of helpless dependence. Shivaji was indeed entirely at his mercy and the only marvel is that he did not take more violent measures. But the stipulations made with Shivaji by the mediation of Jay Singh always came before his eyes and made him coward when the thought of violence occurred to his mind. Some Mahomedan chroniclers add that among the ladies of the imperial zenana who had seen the introduction of Shivaji in the audience hall, was a daughter of the emperor named zeb-un-nisa Begum. This princess had already before heard the fame of Shivaji's deeds and what she saw with her own eyes of his handsome person and behaviour worthy of a brave man and a soldier answered exactly to what she had expected in such a hero of romance. This princess, say some of these historians, pleaded with her father and successfully won him over from extreme measures. Besides it is easy to believe that Aurangzeb was quite sincere in professing a desire to make use of Shivaji's gifts and genius in war and might have attempted through the mediation of Ram Singh to induce him to remain permanently at the Mogul court, had not Shivaji persisted in his refusal.

Among the omrahs in the confidence of the emperor was one Jaffar Khan a brother-in-law of Shaista Khan and prime minister to Aurangzeb. This noble is credited with having made a suggestion to Aurangzeb that in case Shivaji should not willingly agree to the proposal that he should reside at the imperial court as a grandee of the empire, he should be threatened and hampered in his movements and on no account allowed to return. This proposal seems to have been approved of by the emperor. On its coming to the knowledge of Shivaji he honoured Jaffar Khan with a visit and interviewed him on the subject, addressing himself to his sense of fairness and justice and exhorting him to use his powerful influence with the emperor to make him relent and fulfil his promise to permit his departure for the Deccan, with an escort befitting his rank. Jaffar Khan made a pretence of assenting to this request. But as a matter of fact even while the conversation was at its height the Khan's wife who happened to be a sister of Shaista Khan sent a secret message from the harem advising the Khan not to prolong his colloquies with Shivaji, as there was no knowing what he might do and when. At this warning on the part of his consort the uxorious Khan cut short the interview and presented the betel-nut leaves, a sign according to Indian usage that the visit was at an end.

Aurangzeb pursued the policy of threatening Shivaji into submission and compliance with his wishes. The city *kotwal* (commissary of police) was given strict orders to place a guard of five thousand men upon Shivaji's residence, not to allow anybody to enter or depart without permission, and, in case of Shivaji's quitting the house, to provide a sufficient force that would be responsible for his custody. Shivaji remonstrated through Ram Singh, submitting that inasmuch as the emperor seemed to distrust him even when he was undertaking to subdue and make over to Aurangzeb the entire Deccan as a dutiful vassal of the empire, and inasmuch as he persisted in refusing to grant him permission, though bound under the treaty, to return to the south, he felt the only alternative before him was to reconcile himself to the emperor's wishes and to continue to remain at Agra as a nobleman of the court. Aurangzeb answered Ram Singh that the Raja Shivaji did not seem to act with sincerity. He had turned a deaf ear to all his solicitations to take service among his feudal nobility in Hindustan. His pertinacity had driven the emperor to the necessity of restraining his movements, and until his mind was clear of doubt and misgiving he would remain in this unhappy predicament. On the other hand the emperor persisted in maintaining that he could have no covert object in ill-treating Shivaji, as he was bound in honour under the terms of the compact effected by Jay Singh and Diler Khan. He concluded by earnestly appealing to Ram Singh that he should use all his influence with Shivaji to convert him into a loyal champion and dignitary of the empire, as he himself was. When that was done, things would resume their natural course.

When Ram Singh intimated to Shivaji the purport of this communication he saw that there was no prospect of success by any methods of persuasion. The police guard around his residence continued to increase in number. To elude them would tax the ingenuity of the ablest intriguer, but this was the question that now lay immediately before him. The first condition for the success of any plan he might form was to betray no sign of fear to friend or foe. The second problem was to reduce the number of those placed innocently in the same predicament as himself. It was clear that if a way could be found to extricate from Agra those loyal followers and dependents who had accompanied him from the Deccan, the problem of his own escape would present less difficulty. Shivaji, therefore, petitioned the emperor again, urging the hardship of detaining in the north his followers from the Deccan, as the northern climate did not agree with them and sickness was rife in their ranks. He, therefore, prayed that he might have permission to send most of them home, retaining only those whose services were needful. This would also mean a great saving to his exchequer. Aurangzeb was but too pleased to grant passports for the return of Shivaji's followers to the Deccan and his Maratha retinue with the exception of a few officers was ordered to return home. His loyal attendants were extremely reluctant to return, being aware of the serious predicament in which they were leaving their master, and Shivaji had great difficulty in explaining to his faithful adherents that the scheme he had formed for his own escape made it imperative that they should first leave their master. He assured them that he would return in safety and they should be under no anxiety on this ground. The imperative orders thus received compelled them to turn their backs upon their master, who was now left to face calmly what was probably the greatest crisis in his career.

Shivaji now obtained permission to exchange visits and cultivate friendly relations with the leading omrahs at the Mogul court. On these occasions, Ram Singh attended him and introduced to him the leading grandees of the court. Shivaji's suavity of manners and urbanity of social intercourse won golden opinions wherever he went. In his most intimate conversation he now began to harp on the change in his opinions and his determination to aspire to the highest honours and dignities in the empire by rendering the most loyal and devoted service in field and council. These repeated professions gradually won the confidence of the courtiers and drew them into free and unrestrained social intercourse with Shivaji, nor did it take long for the rumour of his changed behaviour to reach the emperor's ears.

Shivaji now commenced to celebrate special festivities every Thursday in the week under the pretence of a religious vow, and as a part of this function to send presents of sweets and confectionery to the great omrahs whose friendship he had taken such pains to cultivate. For the conveyance of these sweets to and from Shivaji's residence ten large baskets were ordered to be prepared. When filled with sweets, these monster baskets became so heavy as to require two persons to carry them. They were usually hung by ropes from a bamboo that rested on their shoulders. The sentinels used to order the carriers to lay down their burden and only allowed them to carry it on, after they had duly satisfied themselves about its contents. This went on from Thursday to Thursday and the sentinels got tired of the needless search, and instead of examining all the baskets one after another they began to examine just one or two to clear their conscience. The sentinels were on the best of terms with the august prisoner they guarded, having been won over by his repeated largesses and by the punctilious courtesy that the great Maratha never failed to extend to his keepers. Shivaji mingled in their blunt conversation and unreserved ways of life and they used to speak freely to him of their hopes and fears as though he were one of themselves. With equal tact Shivaji behaved towards the officers of the guard, losing no opportunity to expatiate on his allegiance to the emperor, with the natural result that they unconsciously relaxed the rigour of their surveillance.

Now that there were growing signs of the fulfilment of his design, Shivaji gradually sent away to the Deccan many of the officers who yet kept company with him. Some left on the pretence of sickness and for a change of climate, others as being wearied with his service and desiring a change of master. Thus on one pretext or another the number of his followers dwindled from day to day. They had no difficulty about their passports and were instructed by Shivaji to await his arrival at certain appointed places. Thus most of his Deccani menials and attendants were got out of the way and their places filled by Hindustani servants. At length there were left with Shivaji of his original retinue only his son Sambhaji, Hiroji Farzand and one or two attendants. Shivaji now feigned illness, sent for diverse physicians and got them to prescribe for him. Affecting to grow worse and worse, he avoided company and instructed any one coming on business to transact it from a distance. After a time he gave it out that he was on the way to recovery and out of gratitude sent large hampers of sweets to his physicians as also complimentary presents to the amirs and omrahs of the court. Alms were liberally distributed among Brahmans and the poor, and the fakirs in the mosques had sweets and confections in abundance, the monster baskets being borne to and from Shivaji's door. This occurrence had now become so usual that it no longer excited any curiosity. One evening, Shivaji ordered some four or five baskets to be made ready with sweets, in one of which Shivaji concealed himself, while his son, the Prince Sambhaji hid himself in another. After their usual practice the sentinels examined one or two baskets and let the others pass unchallenged. As it is related in one of the chronicles, the pretence made use of on this occasion was that the sweets in question were being despatched for distribution among *fakirs* and the Brahman priests of the holy shrine of Mathura (*Muttra*). The ruse succeeded perfectly. Shivaji eluded his guards and joined his party outside of the city gates.[1]

It was arranged that the trusty Hiroji should for the time put on Shivaji's robe and occupy his master's place on the sick-bed and seize the earliest occasion to make good his escape. The trusty officer willingly undertook the perilous honour, assuring his master that he might leave the scene without any anxiety on his servant's account, since by the good fortune which had always attended

[1] The Bundela Memoirs say that on account of Shivaji's practice to give sweets in charity to mendicants of all sorts every Thursday, there was a crowd of beggars at his door. A quantity of sweets had to be brought in monster hampers, which when exhausted had to be retaken empty to the confectioners' shops to be reloaded. Shivaji and Sambhaji escaped in two of these empty hampers.

Khafi Khan tells the story that Shivaji had purchased three excellent horses ostensibly to give in charity to Brahmans, for which purpose they were taken out of the city and kept ready with all their trappings and equipments at a village about 14 kos (i. e. 35 miles) from the capital. Another authority, the *Alamgir Namah* (i. e. the life of Alamgir or Aurangzeb) states that when Jay Singh heard of the captivity of Shivaji, he remonstrated with the emperor describing the impropriety of the action, upon which the kotwal's watchmen were removed from Shivaji's residence.

his loyal service he hoped to make good his own deliverance. He lay all night covered by the bed clothes, except for one of his hands on a finger of which appeared conspicuously Shivaji's ring. Thus with serene confidence he maintained the deception, a young page contributing to it by gently rubbing the supposed patient's feet. It was now morning, and as Shivaji did not appear to have left his bed though it was broad day-light, some of the sentinels approaching the door inquired the cause of the Maharaja's keeping so long to his bed. The page replied, as he had been instructed, that the Maharaja had a severe headache, whereupon the sentinels withdrew. Upon this Hiroji rose from the perilous place he had occupied the night before and putting on his dress left the palace with the trusty page, giving out that Shivaji had had the most acute pain all through the night, and as he had just then fallen into a doze after a whole night's torture, he enjoined them to observe the strictest silence, until he returned with medicine from the physician. On their making further inquiries about the unusually late hour that the Maharaja was sleeping he put them off by a repetition of the pretence of sickness, and left the place as in urgent haste to see the physician. He had a hasty interview with the Prince Ram Singh, whom he informed of Shivaji's safe escape, and bidding him a hasty adieu, he hastened away to complete his deliverance from captivity and exile.

Let us now follow the fortunes of our hero when he had turned his back on the capital. At a certain distance from the city, Shivaji found a horse that had been kept in readiness for him, and mounting it, with young Sambhaji seated astride before him[1], he put spurs to it, not drawing reins until he had reached the village[2]

---

[1] According to Bundela, Sambhaji sat on a horse which was led by the reins by Shivaji upto Mathura.

[2] The Rairi bakhar says that a Deccani potter lived outside the capital with whom an arrangement was made by Hiroji Farzand. On

where the officers of his private staff were waiting to receive him. With their advice the future line of route was determined, as it was extremely hazardous to return to the Deccan by a straight and direct route from the north, when search parties were scouring the ordinary roads in all directions. With a view to obviate the risk of capture, Shivaji ordered a portion of his party to disguise themselves and proceed as best they might to their southern homes. Shivaji himself and his chosen band of secretaries and menial attendants were now attired as *gosavis* and followed a leisurely and circuitous route from one pilgrim place to another until they reached the Deccan. Thus they came to Benares and from thence to Mathura where they had the good fortune to fall in with three good friends of their cause, Krishnajipant, Kashipant, and Visajipant, the brothers-in-law of the minister Moro Trimal Pingle. Shivaji unravelled to them the whole story of his escape and wanderings and inquired if they would undertake the charge of young Sambhaji till the Maharaja's safe arrival in the Deccan. They heartily entered into the plan. One of the three brothers joined Shivaji in his wanderings.[1] The whole party disguised themselves as gosavis, having shaved their top-knots, beards and mustaches.

---

arriving outside the city, Shivaji made his way to the potter's and there disguising himself lived in hiding at his cottage for a month. When the scouts sent after Shivaji by Aurangzeb returned without hope of finding any trace of the fugitives, Shivaji assumed the disguise of a *gosavi* and travelled as if proceeding on a pilgrimage. According to Orme, at the extremity of the city a boat was waiting in readiness to take over Shivaji across the river on crossing which Shivaji paid the boatman handsomely for the service rendered and bade him go to Aurangzeb and report that he had conveyed the Raja across the river. Having crossed, Shivaji rode at full speed for a considerable distance down the river and crossing again to the other side made his way over hills and dales baffling all pursuit.

[1] According to the Rairi bakhar, Prince Sambhaji was kept at the house of a certain Nanaji Vishwasrao at Benares. The reason for keeping Sambhaji behind was that he could not stand the fatigue of the hasty march and his health gave way. Vishwasrao was, however, the

At Mathura Shivaji's party used to perform their morning ablutions in the Jumna. On one occasion their identity was all but betrayed. Shivaji commenting on the untidy state of the river-ghat expressed his surprise that in such a place of pilgrimage renowned all through India, the river-ghats should be kept in such an unsightly condition and suggested what appeared to him the proper arrangement of such river embankments. Upon this one of the priests of the pilgrim town exclaimed that he could be no gosavi. He had such knowledge of architecture that he must indeed be some other person in disguise. At this Krishnajipant silenced him with a heavy bribe, made him join the pilgrim party on its peregrinations, and on his return to the home country, Shivaji granted him a state pension.

It is now necessary to take notice of what transpired at Agra after Shivaji's deliverance. The sentinels observed soon afterwards that there was no movement at Shivaji's residence and that the attendant who had left the place so hurriedly on the plea of calling the physician had not yet returned. To investigate the cause of this strange silence, the officers of the guard came to the door of the illustrious patient's bed-chamber and to their unspeakable consternation found out that there was no Shivaji on the couch nor any of the usual attendants there. The bird had flown! A great alarm was now raised, and search-parties were sent after the fugitives in all directions. But there was no trace of Shivaji nor of his confidential servants. The local servants in Shivaji's temporary service were quite in the dark about the mode of their master's flight. On cross-examination they declared that Shivaji was as usual sleeping in the morning and his young page attended upon him. They did not know when he had left his chamber or how he had gone. The sentinels made their report to Polad (Fulad)

title which Shivaji gave to these Brahmans after his and Sambhaji's safe return home.

Khan, the kotwal, who ran in great trepidation to the emperor with the incredible news that Shivaji had disappeared. He protested that the sentinels he had appointed to watch over the illustrious prisoner were as trustworthy and alert as they could be, but for all their vigilance Shivaji's arts had triumphed. He attributed it to the black art, of which, he claimed, Shivaji must be a master, for how else could he become invisible, when the sentinel parties were stationed all round, and watched the gates with unremitting zeal, day and night. The news came to Aurangzeb like a bolt from the blue. There was no questioning the loyalty or sincerity of Polad Khan's protestations. None knew better than Aurangzeb himself that Polad Khan had enlisted the pick of his police force for the great charge laid upon him. Yet could he not spare the helpless kotwal the fulminations of his fury. The most stringent search was ordered. Clouds of cavalry hung about every great road leading from the capital. Cavalry parties scoured the plains and the hills and the valleys. Each subhedar or talukdar was immediately informed that the Maratha eagle had flown from his cage and ordered to arrest the fugitives if found within their jurisdiction. Jay Singh received orders to put under arrest Netaji Palkar whom Shivaji had deputed to co-operate with the Mogul army, to keep an eye upon the fugitive's flight, and prevent him from making good his position at the head of the Maratha armies in the Maratha hill-forts.

Ram Singh did not quite escape a certain measure of suspicion.[1] Immediately on the escape of Shivaji,

[1] Chitnis asserts that Ram Singh connived at Shivaji's escape. Some Maratha Brahmans who were caught admitted under torture that Shivaji had escaped with the connivance of Ram Singh. But when Jay Singh heard of this charge, he protested his son was innocent of such faithlessness to the emperor. The Jedhe Chronology (p. 188) corroborates the story of the arrest of the Brahmans. In a subsequent letter to the prime minister Jay Singh proposed to give a proof of his loyalty to the emperor by trying to entrap and murder Shivaji by

when Hiroji Farzand communicated the great secret to him, the Rajput prince immediately asked for and was granted an interview with the emperor. At this interview, the prince protested that Shivaji had come to the imperial durbar relying on the assurances both of himself and of his noble father and that the emperor instead of fulfilling the conditions made with the Maratha warrior had kept him under a strict surveillance. Henceforth neither himself nor his father was to be held responsible for anything relating to Shivaji. Upon this Aurangzeb replied that Shivaji was his dependent and he might deal with him in any way he thought proper. Should Shivaji relent and submit to the imperial terms, he would be glad to raise him in dignity and position, and neither Ram Singh nor his father need have any anxiety on this subject. This was just before the intelligence of Shivaji's flight was received, the Rajput prince thinking it right to free himself from all responsibility for the event. When the news of the flight came shortly after, a certain amount of suspicion was awakened in the emperor's mind. Ram Singh came under a cloud. He no longer obtained admission to the durbar.

As to the omrahs of the court the news of Shivaji's adroitness in eluding the vigilant guard set on his movements and the daring escape from the hands of his imperial captor evoked feelings of undisguised admiration. The opinion was freely expressed that it was scarcely in accord with the traditions of imperial greatness and statesmanship that one, whose loyal co-operation with the empire had been secured by such a pillar of the Mogul monarchy as the trusty and valorous Jay Singh, should have been entrapped into an unworthy and treacherous servitude instead of having been welcomed and treated with hospitality. The emperor thus lost for ever the active participation of a brave and

pretending to enter a matrimonial alliance and enticing Shivaji to give his daughter in marriage to his son. Nothing came of this fine proposal. (Jay Singh's letter in the *Haft Anjuman* quoted by Prof Sarkar.)

resolute leader in the military councils of the empire, whose services in the Deccan conquests were bound to be invaluable. A willing ally had been turned into a relentless antagonist. Fortune had all along seemed to smile upon all his enterprises With such a foe in the Deccan, what would the fortunes of the empire avail against the southern principalities? And Shivaji's ability was as notable as his good fortune. Such a talented leader had once espoused the Mogul cause, but who could now expect him to do the like again? Such and other criticisms rumour brought to the ears of the disconsolate emperor. The forlorn reports of talukdars and subhedars deepened his chagrin. A vague fear succeeded this despair, lest Shivaji might be skulking somewhere in some obscure corner of the capital itself, maturing some plan of revenge or treachery. The emperor had to look warily to himself, lest Shivaji might spring upon him from some unexpected quarter. He became a stranger to sleep and rest. Nemesis seemed to threaten him on every side.

From Mathura Shivaji continued his journey in the garb and the company of gosavis. At every halt at a pilgrim town Shivaji performed the proper religious rites, doling out alms and giving religious offerings on a modest scale. He travelled to Allahabad, Benares, and Gaya, the celebrated shrines in the north, and thus he traversed the country from shrine to shrine up to the regions of the Deccan. In these extended tours of piligrimage he had to put up with many vexations and inconveniences. The autumnal monsoons had already burst when he left Agra. The streams were so deeply flooded as to make it impossible to ford them. At many points the travellers had to swim from one bank to the other. Forests and mountains had to be crossed and it was most trying to have to surmount these obstructions on foot. But obstacle or no obstacle—steady *zeal* and patience overcame them all. At a certain village the local fouzdar or police officer, on some cause of suspicion, put him under arrest, when nothing but a prompt confession of his identity could save him from the predicament in which he found himself. The fouzdar was quite taken aback at the revelation of the arrested person's identity and made his apology for the discourtesy of which he had unwittingly been guilty towards so illustrious a person. Shivaji made him a sufficient recompense in money and requested him not to disclose to any Mogul officer the fact of his having travelled by that way. In another place when Shivaji, intending to perform his ablutions with due ceremonial, had entered the river and ordered the attending priest to recite the sacred chants, another priest conversing with the first happened to remark quite casually that Shivaji, the Raja of the south, who was for some time under arrest at Agra, had escaped and was wandering over the country. These words fell like molten lead upon his ears. He somehow completed his ablutions and hurriedly left the place[1]. At Cuttack Shivaji was quite prostrated with the fatigue of his wanderings and decided to purchase a horse so as to prosecute the rest of his journey on horse-back. A horse was selected for the purpose and Shivaji had to pay down the purchase price. Not finding any silver coins about him, he inadvertently opened his purse in presence of the horse-dealer, who was astonished to see that it was crammed full of pagodas. Upon this the horse-dealer exclaimed : "When you offer gold for this common sort of horse, you must be none else than the Raja Shivaji." At this, says the chronicler of the Bundela Memoirs, Shivaji flung the money at him and beat a hasty retreat.

On his arrival in the Deccan, Shivaji did not proceed directly to his own principality, but diverted his route to Puri, Gondwan, Bhaganagar (Deccan Hyderabad), Bijapur and so on to Panhala and thence to Raigad. He continued to wear the garb of a gosavi, having previously sent word of his arrival *incognito* in his own dominions. When Shivaji first presented himself at the Raigad gate in the coarse habiliments of a gosavi and demanded an interview with

[1] Khafi Khan is the authority for these two anecdotes.

Jijabai, the sentinel conveyed the intelligence within the fort that a stranger gosavi desired to see her. When introduced within the fort, Nirajipant played the part of a gosavi in earnest, invoking blessings on her in true gosavi style. But Shivaji could not longer sustain his part in the comedy, and advancing prostrated himself at her feet. She did not recognize him: to such an extent had the constant anxieties and privations of his long journey altered his features. She was astonished at the amazing conduct, as she took it, of the gosavi in falling at her feet. Shivaji doffed the pilgrim's garb and laid his head on her knees. Then indeed did she recognize him by the old marks upon his person dating from the earliest days of his childhood. Mother and son embraced each other joyfully. Tears streamed from her eyes. It was not merely that her son had returned,—he was re-born to her!

The happy interview with his mother over, Shivaji gave audience to the leading chiefs, ministers and distinguished gentry in his kingdom. Shivaji's return was celebrated on a lavish scale by all classes from the greatest to the humblest. Men vied with one another in their eagerness to have a glimpse again of his well-beloved and familiar features. Shivaji celebrated the occasion with proper observances. He was open-handed in his hospitality and largesses to the Brahmans. He scattered alms, food and raiment among the helpless and the poor. Special thanks-giving ceremonials were celebrated in honour of the tutelary Bhavani and pearls were plentifully showered upon her image. Sugar was distributed in oriental fashion to the joyful multitude from panniered elephants. Each nobleman and garrison officer received his honorary present of sweets. Sweets and alms were distributed to men of learning and piety, to hermits and sages. Each fort fired its *feu de joie.* The whole land celebrated the restoration in a spirit of jubilation such as they had never experienced before. Their hopes were aroused to the highest. Here was a chief that knew no defeat. His was a cause that was bound to triumph. The air was filled with admiration for Shivaji's exploits, his tameless spirit and the inexhaustible resources of his inventive mind.

Nor did Shivaji forget to reward the gallant services of that devoted band of followers who had shared with him the perils of captivity in the Mogul capital. The rewards took various shapes according to the merit of each zealous vassal. In the case of some personal honours and dignities were granted, in other cases annual allowances or assignments of revenue over villages and mahals. Presents of horses, elephants, trappings and personal ornaments were bestowed upon the most devoted of his personal attendants. None merited these more eminently than the self-effacing chief Hiroji Farzand. He was made a commander of a corps of cavalry and the honour of a palanquin was conferred upon him.

An interesting anecdote is related of Shivaji's adventurous flight. Shivaji was compelled one night to seek a lodging at the house of a peasant and to procure provisions from him for his immediate use, and when he demanded them the peasant's aged mother is reported to have said that they would gladly have offered provisions to gosavis, (as Shivaji and his party appeared to be) but that Shivaji's army had quite recently sacked the place, and among the booty much of their moveable property had been carried away. 'Shivaji,' continued the old woman in her garrulity,—'has, we hear, gone to Delhi, and we don't know why the emperor Aurangzeb does not chastise him, for, to say the truth, he was a great nuisance to us peasant folks.' From this Shivaji knew that in his absence his followers had not been idle, but had carried forward the old programme of making forays into the enemy's country. He gave his assurance to the old woman that things would after all turn out happily for her family, took down the peasant's name and other particulars, and on his safe arrival in Maharashtra, sent an escort to bring down the peasant's family and, having made them full compensation for their losses, admitted the head of the family to his service[1].

---

[1] *Vide* Chitnis, 118.; Shivdigvijay, 254.

According to previous arrangements the guardian of young Sambhaji at Mathura was invited to the Maharashtra court with all his family. On receipt of this invitation, Kashipant left Mathura escorting Sambhaji to his father's kingdom. On the way this party fell in with a Mogul commander, whose suspicions were roused at the princely bearing and handsome features of young Sambhaji, with the result that the latter was on the point of being arrested.[1] Kashipant and his brother submitted that they were Brahmans of Mathura and that he was a son of the family. The commander desiring to put this to the test bade him dine out of the same plate with Sambhaji, which a Brahman would under no circumstances do with a non-Brahman. Kashipant had to obey the command.[2] A dish of curds and pounded rice (*poha*) was hastily improvised and was served out on a plantain leaf to Kashipant and Sambhaji, and the Brahman and the Maratha prince partook of the common meal. Upon this the commander let them off[3]. The company reached Raigad without any further adventures. Sambhaji's arrival was greeted with great jubilation. Kashipant's enthusiastic services to the cause were duly acknowledged and the title of *Vishwasrao* or lord of good faith was conferred upon him. His two brothers received similar marks of recognition and appreciation of their noble services.[4]

---

1 The author of the Bundela Memoirs says that the young Sambhaji having long hair was disguised as a girl and Kashipant made the journey in company with his wife and the prince thus disguised.

2 Chitnis, 1 0; Shivdigvijay, 255, 256.

3 Other bakhars give the version that Aurangzeb came to be informed that Prince Sambhaji was in hiding at the house of Kashipant and had his house watched, upon which the Brahman dispelled the Mogul officer's suspicion by dining in the manner described.

4 Shivdigvijay says that the title *Vishwasrao* was conferred upon all the three brothers. The sanad conferred upon them is published in Rajwade VIII, 3. This sanad refers to Shivaji's flight from Agra, not Delhi, showing that Shivaji attended the Mogul durbar at the former town.

A more romantic incident is interwoven by certain writers in their version of the Agra episode. It is related that on the occasion when Shivaji was invited to the durbar the ladies of the imperial harem, out of a natural curiosity to see with their own eyes one of whose romantic escapades they had heard so much, were seated behind a curtain. Among these ladies was an unmarried daughter of Aurangzeb, known as Zeb-un-nisa Begum. The princess was twenty-seven years of age. It is said that the Begum fell in love with Shivaji, though it was not perhaps merely a case of love at first sight.[1] Already had she heard, so runs this romantic account, of his valour and efforts for the advancement of his country's liberties. Already had the fame of his romantic and soul-stirring adventures ravished her heart. His generosity towards the fallen foe, his filial devotion, his exemplary piety towards the gods of his country had touched in her breast a chord of sympathy. And now had he come after achieving so many labours in the furtherance of his country's cause, after so many shocks of battle with her father's invincible forces,—now had he come as a conciliated friend and ally, to honour the hospitality of the Mogul court. These feelings had prepared her heart for the first advances of a passion, which Shivaji's conduct in the durbar only served to make even deeper than before. It is said she vowed a firm resolve that she would either wed Shivaji or remain a virgin for life.

It is even said that Shivaji came to know of the sentiments of the princess towards himself and that the matter was duly represented to him on her behalf that should he be prepared to embrace the faith of Islam, the

---

[1] *Vide* Douglas: Bombay and Western India, I, 349–51. The so-called love-intrigues of the princess Zeb-un-nisa are discussed by Prof. Sarkar in his "Studies in Mughal India" pp. 79–90. He has proved these stories of love-intrigues to be entirely baseless. None of the Marathi bakhars contains the least hint as regards the supposed passion of the princess for Shivaji, nor does any of the Persian authorities or European contemporaries like Bernier, Manucci or Dr. Fryer mention it.

princess would be glad to be united with him in wedlock. Shivaji was naturally opposed to any thing like this proposal. To him the social and religious traditions which were his birth-right were dearer than any connexion with the imperial family. Had he been merely a creature of ambition, had he been swayed by no higher feelings than self-aggrandizement, he might eagerly have grasped at this offer of love and obtained a *de facto* sovereignty of the south, as the son in-law of the reigning emperor. However, the whole story appears too much like romance to have been true, and appears to have arisen from a traditional belief, current at any rate in some of the chronicles, that a daughter of Aurangzeb remained a life-long virgin on account of her love, not indeed for Shivaji, but for his son Sambhaji.[1]

The princess Zeb-un-nisa at any rate vowed to remain unmarried till her death, which took place in 1702. She was involved in Prince Akbar's rebellion and her last days were spent in the prison-fort of Salimgarh near Delhi. This princess is said to have been a lady of considerable intellectual attainments.[2] The Marathi chronicles have apparently not distinguished between this princess and the second daughter of Aurangzeb named *Zinat-un-nisa*, as they speak of the latter only as *Nisa Begum*, a term that could be applied to all the daughters of Aurangzeb. It was Zinat-un-nisa who accompanied Aurangzeb in camp during his interminable wars in the Deccan and who after the barbarous execution of Sambhaji and the fall of the fort of Raigad interested herself in the guardianship of the stripling son of that ill-starred Maratha sovereign. The young prince, the last hope of the Maratha race, was brought up by this princess with a tender care as if he

---

[1] *Vide* Sarkar's Studies in Mughal India, pp. 89–90,

[2] It is said that like her father Aurangzeb she knew the Koran by heart and that she wrote poetry under the pseudonym of *Makhfi* or the Concealed One. *Vide* Masir-i-Alamgiri, (Elliot, Vol. VII, p. 196) and Prof. Sarkar's Aurangzeb, Vol. I. Ch. IV, and Vol. III, p. 61 and Studies in Mughal India, pp. 79–90.)

were her own son. The Marathi chronicles, like the Shedgavkar's bakhar, represent this princess to have remained unmarried on account of her regard for Sambhaji, who, it is known, had made an insolent demand for her hand after his capture.[1] The Begum's ward became afterwards distinguished in history as the Maharaja Shahu.

CHAPTER XX

RE-CONQUESTS, 1667-69

No sooner did the news of Shivaji's captivity after the sensational scene at the durbar reach the Deccan than the great officers, whom Shivaji had appointed as the high stewards of his kingdom during his absence, began to make retaliatory invasions of Mogul territory in the southern subhas. The announcement of Shivaji's escape and presently his safe return put new life into the Maratha campaigns. The English factors at Karwar made a correct forecast in one of their letters of the time: " If it be true that Shivaji hath escaped, Aurangzeb will quickly hear of him to his sorrow." How correct this forecast was, was soon proved by the events that followed.

Before Shivaji's return to the scene of his Deccan triumphs, the Bijapur and the Mogul arms had been pitted against one another in a decisive campaign very much to the disadvantage of the latter. Jay Singh laid siege to Bijapur. The Deccan light horse under the Adil Shahi government had resumed those century-old tactics that had saved the capital from many a blustering conqueror. The Adil Shahi troops hovered round the Mogul camp and cut off all its supply of corn and fodder. A season of drought added the miseries of thirst to those of famine. To crown these difficulties an auxiliary force from the sultan of Golconda came opportunely to the aid of his oppressed neighbour of Bijapur, while Jay Singh's petitions for re-enforcements to his imperial sovereign might as well have been addressed to the wind. It is clear that the suspicious mind of the emperor exaggerated the danger of the good understanding subsisting between Shivaji and Jay Singh; and he seems to have been the victim of a fancy that Jay Singh was going to make himself more powerful than was consistent with loyalty, and that with Shivaji's aid he would presently defy the armies of the empire. While the emperor continued in this attitude of studied indifference, Jay Singh himself began to conclude that it was a thankless task to sacrifice the lives of his gallant Rajput veterans only to court an inglorious defeat by the Bijapur forces, which indeed was inevitable in view of the attitude of indifference adopted by the emperor. He began, therefore, of set purpose to withdraw his armies from the invaded country. The forces gradually retreated in the direction of Aurangabad. The enemy gave chase. But the gallant Rajput succeeded in making good his retreat to the Mogul head-quarters in the Deccan.

Jay Singh indeed found his resources both of men and money so exhausted that he had scarcely enough forces at his command to garrison the fortresses ceded to him by Shivaji as also those which he had succeeded in capturing with Shivaji's aid and assistance. Nor had he sufficient balances in his military chest for the maintenance of these mountain garrisons. He had to eke out his resources with the utmost caution and prudence, maintaining large garrisons upon only the principal hill-forts such as Lohagad, Sinhagad and Purandar in the ghat country and Mahuli and Karnala in the Konkan. In these five forts large forces were maintained, with a sufficient supply of war-material. In other places, where there was a possibility of obtaining local supplies of food and fodder, moderate garrisons were stationed. But as regards the greater number of other fortresses, as he could afford neither men nor money for their maintenance, he withdrew his garrisons demolishing the gates and defences of the fortresses and leaving no necessity for any garrison at all. Having thus made the best of his scanty resources and secured his conquests as best he might, he calmly awaited orders at Aurangabad. He was at last recalled by his ungracious sovereign, and Jaswant Singh and Prince Muazzim (Mauzam) were jointly appointed governors of the Deccan. It is sad to chronicle the death of this noble and magnanimous prince. On his march to North India after his recall the gallant Rajput was taken ill and died.

Meanwhile Moropant Pingle, the minister of Shivaji,

occupied fortress after fortress as it was evacuated by the Mogul armies and, arranging for such improvised defence works as were practicable at the moment, re-established the Maratha rule round about. When just a small force of Mogul troops still remained in garrison, Moropant defeated and expelled the occupants and re-garrisoned the fortresses with Maratha troops. This he did with fort after fort with the gratifying result that already before Shivaji's arrival in the south, many of the ceded forts were already flying the Maratha flag. On Shivaji's arrival he lost no time in recovering the entire district of the Konkan.

The final failure of the great armies sent down with Jay Singh and Diler Khan, the capture and subsequent escape of Shivaji, the junction of the military resources of Golconda with those of Bijapur, and the accession of strength they were likely to gain from the possibility of Shivaji's throwing in the weight of his immense resources on their side showed how seriously imperilled was the Mogul cause in the south, and the magnitude of the interests at stake was sufficient to have induced the emperor himself to gird on his armour and take upon himself the supreme command of the new army of invasion. But there were disturbances on the northern frontier which obliged the emperor to remain at the capital. He had his own misgivings at having mismanaged things so as to force Shivaji into a bitter hostility with the empire, and he was now placed in an unfortunate dilemma with regard to the course he should pursue. Were he to entrust the command of a very considerable army to his son or to the Raja Jaswant Singh, and with all these armaments at their command should they be beaten, the prestige of the empire which was now at stake would be lost for ever. If on the other hand the prince triumphed over his enemies and found himself at the head of a large army, he might perhaps be so much flushed with his victory as to forget the allegiance due to his father and raise the flag of revolt. In view of these misgivings the emperor deemed it prudent not to commit himself to a special campaign against Shivaji, who on his part was the last person to fail to turn to his utmost advantage the opportunities presented to him by the procrastination and mistrustful character of the emperor.

In many respects the appointment of Prince Muazzim and the Raja Jaswant Singh to the satrapy of the Deccan was favourable to Shivaji's wishes. He had cultivated the friendship of Jaswant Singh during his enforced sojourn at Agra. The Raja was a Rajput prince of a haughty character and had much of that religious pride which is rarely absent in a noble-spirited Rajput. When Aurangzeb entered on a rebellious war against his father to secure his succession to the throne, Jaswant Singh at first opposed his wicked ambition. It was only when it seemed clear that victory would at last smile on the rebel prince, that he turned round to his side. He was naturally never in the closest confidence of the emperor. His greatest weakness was avarice, and Shivaji turned it to very good account. Well did Shivaji call him a calf with a fondness for the oil-cake of a bribe. And Shivaji managed him so well by taking advantage of this weakness, that he always played the tune which was agreeable to the Maratha leader. The Mogul prince was a magnanimous and high-spirited general. He had nothing of his father's distrustfulness in his disposition. An open hand and a love of luxury were the distinguishing traits of his character. He was a fickle-minded young man, and the slightest persuasion turned him from his purposes. Upon such a plastic mind Jaswant Singh exercised a considerable influence. He scarcely, if ever, deliberately crossed his wishes. On his departure for the south Aurangzeb had given him much wholesome advice. He had warned him not to try conclusions with Shivaji. He would be no match for the Maratha in diplomacy or intrigue. He had been the ruin of many a general. A fresh discomfiture at his hands would recoil on the Mogul state with the most grievous results. He thus advised him to aim at conciliation in his dealings with the Marathas, to please them and so to save the Mogul fortunes from their interference. This advice was addressed to ears that were naturally willing and sympathetic. The prince had never approved of Aurangzeb's futile attempt to entrap Shivaji. It was his conviction that the highest interests of the empire required that Shivaji should be treated as a valiant and enterprising feudatory of the empire.

There is a tradition that when the intelligence came that the prince was marching to the south, Shivaji, disguised as a poor peasant, overtook him at a village near Brahmapuri and presented to him a pot of curds, which was accepted by the prince on account of its exquisite flavour and ordered to be served to him at table. A little pellet of wax, says the story, was found in the midst of the curds, and it was found that a little note was rolled up in the wax. The note purported to say that Shivaji had resorted to this expedient that he might be able to see with his own eyes what manner of man was the noble prince who was entrusted with the war against himself. If there is any truth in this story, we can well judge what reflections must have been roused in the prince's mind about the enterprise and daring of the author of this curiously presented epistle. He must have been convinced of the great hazard of war with a general of such inventiveness and enterprise. On his arrival at Aurangabad negotiations for a peace were opened through Jaswant Singh. The latter had already been bribed. Shivaji was thus able to shape a treaty according to his wishes. The time was not yet ripe for a complete break with the Moguls, and a conciliatory attitude towards a magnanimous prince like Muazzim might be productive of future results. Upon the conciliatory proposal of Muazzim, therefore, Shivaji sent his private secretary, Balaji Avji Chitnis, as an envoy extraordinary to wait upon Muazzim at the Mogul camp, with special instructions to find out the prince's real intentions. According to court etiquette, presents of jewels, brocades, and elephants accompanied the envoy. On Jaswant Singh introducing Chitnis to the prince, he began with the preamble of the treaty between Jay Singh and Shivaji, as a consequence of which Shivaji had gone up to Agra for the favour of a personal audience with the emperor. After the personal interview, proceeded the envoy, it was Shivaji's intention to get imperial ratification of certain clauses of the treaty and take service under the emperor, but that in spite of the mediation of sardars like Jay Singh, Ram Singh and others the emperor had distrusted the whole thing and put him under arrest. This, submitted the envoy, could not be said to have been done with a good grace. The prince protested that the emperor neither had then, nor now, any evil intention against Shivaji. The emperor's sole motive had always been that there should be thorough cordiality between himself and Shivaji and that the latter should seal this friendship by immediately enlisting in the service of the empire. As Shivaji had not approved of the emperor's arrangement, the latter had proceeded to obtain his consent by force and therefore kept him under restraint. Shivaji had not appreciated the kind intentions of the emperor and had effected his escape and come down to the Deccan. The prince then explained that on his setting out for the Deccan he had received special injunctions from his father not to enter upon any hostilities with Shivaji, of whose extraordinary ability he was perfectly assured. The emperor had told Muazzim that his own attempts to pacify Shivaji had unfortunately taken an untoward course. Shivaji had shown he had no desire to live at Agra, but would live only in his Deccan home. So far, so good. What the emperor now wanted was to ratify the former treaty and to enlist Shivaji's services in the Mogul campaigns in the south. Had the emperor indeed, continued Prince Muazzim, any hostile purposes against Shivaji, he would certainly have prosecuted his designs when the Maratha leader was at Agra. Such being the case, Muazzim wanted to know Shivaji's real opinion upon this proposal.

Upon the report of this conversation being duly submitted by Chitnis to Shivaji, the latter signified his wishes for a treaty, when the following conditions were mutually approved of between the two parties: (1) that there should in future be mutual peace and friendship; (2) that the former treaty be ratified; (3) that unless and until all mutual distrust was clearly swept away, Shivaji should send no forces to co-operate with the Moguls, and till then there should be no friendly intercourse; (4) that on cession of territory being duly made for the maintenance of his auxiliaries, Shivaji should furnish a contingent of 5000 to co-operate with the Moguls; (5) that the talukas of Avdhe and Balapur in the Berars be ceded in jahgir to Sambhaji for the maintenance of his mansab of 5000 horse in the Mogul service as provided for in the last treaty; (6) that Shivaji should have full power to levy the chauth and sirdeshmukhi contributions as asked for in the last treaty; and (7) the fortresses and territories of the Nizamshahi and Adil Shahi states now in the possession of Shivaji should continue to be in his possession.[1] Upon the draft setting forth these conditions the Mogul prince affixed his signature and told Shivaji to prepare as a matter of conventional form the draft treaty in the form of a petition to the emperor, upon which he would forward it to him with a personal recommendation for its acceptance. This was done and the prince added to it his warm recommendation that the present offer of such a valiant warrior as Shivaji should be accepted by the government and the bonds of friendship drawn closely together. (March, 1668). It was convenient to Aurangzeb to accede to this request and the treaty was duly ratified. The title of Raja was conferred upon Shivaji, the mansab conferred upon Sambhaji was confirmed, and the jahgir described in the treaty sanctioned, the proper sanads for the same being sent down by the emperor.[2]

---

1 According to Chitnis's chronicle the twenty-seven forts ceded under the first treaty had to be ceded over again to the Moguls.

2 Rajwade, VIII, 17.

The management of the revenue of this jahgir was entrusted to a Brahman revenue clerk, named Ravji Somnath who was promoted to the rank of mokasdar and sent up with proper equipments. Sambhaji presented himself at Aurangabad as a mansabdar in the imperial army, with his 5000 horse, attended by the experienced commander, Prataprao Guzar.[1] The Mogul prince received him with due honour for his rank and assigned to him an independent place for his residence, which became quite a new ward of the town. As Sambhaji was quite a stripling he was soon permitted to return, and Prataprao remained in the Mogul camp in command of Sambhaji's contingent. Shivaji himself managed to avoid the servile position of a mansabdar in the imperial army.

By this friendly peace, Shivaji again recovered possession of the districts of Poona and Supa and most of the other territory lost under the first treaty. However the important forts of Purandar and Sinhagad still remained with the Moguls. In offering such conciliatory terms, the emperor's plan was gradually to entice Shivaji to the position of a dependent and so to lure him on inevitably to his final destruction. But Prince Muazzim had no such sinister designs. His liberality and purity of motives were incapable of any baseness or double dealing.

It is even affirmed that some years later Muazzim, weary of the emperor's perpetual distrust and duplicity, was prepared to rebel from his father and invited the assistance of Shivaji. Suspecting some stratagem, the Maratha chief warily replied that in case of a serious conflict between the prince and the emperor he would be glad to join him with an army at the out-break of hostilities. With a view to assure Shivaji of his seriousness and to dispel his suspicions, the prince suddenly marched with his army to the north and sent urgent messages to Shivaji for instant help, employing an officer of high rank upon this embassy so as to impress him all

[1] This occurred in October, 1667. (Jedhe Chronology, p. 188.)

the more with the earnestness of his request. Shivaji sent word in reply that while the prince was fighting in the north, he would watch and defend his interest in the south, that this would be the best plan under the circumstances, as Muazzim had an army large enongh to encounter the emperor; and should fortune frown upon his attempt he invited the prince to come and partake of the hospitality of his dominions. Muazzim tried once more to tempt him by offering to place his army under Shivaji's command. But the latter was too prudent a man to yield to such an allurement. Despairing of Shivaji's support, the prince gave up his chimerical project and having by his abject repentance obtained the emperor's pardon, he returned to the Mogul head-quarters at Aurangabad. But true to his magnanimous nature, he harboured no grudge whatever against Shivaji for his prudent refusal to join him in his rebellious folly. The event served only to draw closer the bonds of their mutual friendship and good opinion.[1]

In his despatches to the prince, Aurangzeb advised him to encourage Shivaji to continue his invasions of the Bijapur and Golconda territories, so that the Deccan monarchies with their foundations undermined by these repeated onslaughts might fall easy victims before the Mogul invaders. Part of the territory thus captured by Shivaji was to be ceded to him for the maintenance of his armies. Following these orders Shivaji made repeated descents upon the Deccan kingdoms. When the Bijapur government saw how they were caught between two fires

---

1 Catrou (Manucci) tells the story of a mock rebellion of Prince Muazzim got up under Aurangzeb's special order, for the triple purpose of deceiving Shivaji, testing the good faith of the Mogul commanders, and discrediting Muazzim in case he should at a later date seriously think of rebelling against his father. Prof. Sarkar (*Shivaji* p. 212-219) shows that this event, which at one of its phases threatened to wear the aspect of a civil war between Muazzim and the emperor, was due to a quarrel between the prince and Diler Khan who had been despatched in 1670 to co-operate with the former in the prosecution of the war with Shivaji. On this occasion Muazzim and Jaswant Singh pursued Diler Khan into Khandesh against the wishes of the local governor, and invited Shivaji (with whom they carried on a pretended war) to help them in the pursuit.

and how the invasions of Shivaji were parts of a general policy prosecuted with the co-operation of the imperial armies, they determined to make their peace with the Moguls, which they did at the price of the cession of the fort of Sholapur and the territory adjoining to it, yielding an annual revenue of eighteen thousand pagodas. Upon receiving intelligence of this treaty Shivaji had a private conference with Muazzim and Jaswant Singh at which he got them to consent to connive at any expedition he might conduct on his own account in the territories of Bijapur and Golconda. With this permission Shivaji embarked on a vigorous campaign to levy the chauth and sirdeshmukhi contributions throughout the Adil Shahi dominions, until helpless before these depredations and with a view to purchase peace and security at any price, the tired ministers of the Adil Shahi state agreed for a second time in the history of their dealings with Shivaji to pay him an annual tribute of three lakhs of rupees, a sum which some chroniclers raise to seven lakhs. This second treaty with Shivaji like the first was a private understanding. It would have served no useful purpose to give out the fact that a Mahomedan state was actually reduced to the condition of paying tribute to a Hindu chief and of living as it were on his sufferance. The haughty nobility at the Mahomedan capital would have reckoned it an unspeakable disgrace to their manhood, and by an unseasonable and impotent outcry would have added to the embarrassments of the government. The secret treaty was however approved of by the sultan, who now retained Shivaji's ambassador to reside at his court. The ambassador thus nominated to this charge was Shamji Naik Pande.[1]

[1] Prof. Sarkar makes no mention of this treaty. He, however, quotes from the Factory Records, Surat, to show that there were no acts of hostility between Shivaji and Bijapur. (Prof. Sarkar's Shivaji pp. 204 and 315.) The Jedhe Chronology p. 188 affirms that peace was made with Bijapur in May 1667. It states the name of the Maratha ambassador at Bijapur as Bawaji Naik Pande. Shamji Naik Pande also acted as Shivaji's ambassador after the secret treaty with Abdul Mahomed, the chief minister of Bijapur, (*Vide* concluding portion of Ch. XIII). Pande died at Satara in December 1675 (Jedhe p. 192).

Shivaji then turned his attention to the Golconda kingdom, making the same predatory incursions into every province of that state. The sultan of the state scarcely possessed the resources to resist successfully these repeated invasions, and the knowledge that Shivaji was acting on a secret understanding with the Moguls made him realize that any such resistance would be useless. The sultan was thus reduced to the arts of conciliation. His two ministers, Madanna and Akanna, advocated a peaceful policy. With their mediation a treaty was made with Shivaji, the Kutub Shahi chief agreeing to pay an annual tribute of five lakhs of rupees. Both parties were pledged to mutual friendship and alliance and the admission of embassies at their respective courts The ambassador deputed by Shivaji under the operation of this treaty to reside at the court of Golconda was Nirajirao.[1]

Having reduced the two principal Deccan monarchies to the condition of tributaries, Shivaji turned his attention to the Konkan. Here the Abyssinians and the Portuguese still wielded considerable influence, which it was part of Shivaji's policy to wipe away and so to bring the Konkan littoral under his undisputed power. With this view he fell suddenly upon Goa, resolved to expel the Portuguese

---

1 Khafi Khan (Elliot, VII 286-87) says that on his return from Agra, Shivaji saw the Sultan Abdulla Kutub Shaha and formed an alliance with him, in virtue of which he undertook to conquer for Golconda from Bijapur some forts which the latter had wrested from the former power. Some of these forts Shivaji gave up to Golconda and others he kept for himself. But some of the forts mentioned were obviously conquered later and Khafi Khan himself mentions a report that Shivaji first went to Hyderabad in the first or second year of the reign of Sultan Abdul Hassan, who came to the throne in 1672. Grant Duff bases his account of the treaties with Bijapur and Golconda on the Marathi chronicles and Scott's Deccan. The Jedhe Chronology under date *Jeshta*, Shaka year 1594 (June 1672), states that Niraji Ravji made a treaty with Golconda which was to pay a tribute of one lakh of pagodas, of which he brought 66,000 to Shivaji (Jedhe, p. 190). It would seem to have been a fresh demand on the accession to the throne of a new sultan and is no argument against an earlier stipulation for tribute. At any rate about 1669 Niraji Ravji was at the Mogul head-quarters at Aurangabad, along with Prataprao Guzar, and could not then have been Shivaji's ambassador at the Golconda capital. (Jedhe, p. 188).

from this province. He does not seem to have met with the success he had reckoned upon. The chronicles are silent upon these operations, lending countenance to the view that no great encounters took place. Shivaji then made a renewed effort for the conquest of Janjira, but with no greater success than on the former occasion. The Abyssinians were seriously handicapped in the operations against Shivaji and had to apply to the East India Company's representatives at Bombay for help. Shivaji had to return without realizing his ambitious projects.

On the formation of the alliances with the Mogul, the Adil Shahi and the Kutub Shahi powers, as has already been described in the beginning of this chapter, peace reigned all over Shivaji's dominions and he had leisure to devote himself to the organization of his kingdom. But the subject of the re-construction of the country on Shivaji's own lines may be held over for a later chapter. (Ch. XXIV)

The alliances formed for the present with the Mahomedan powers naturally created an impression that Shivaji's ambition was quenched and that he was now going to rest upon his oars, devoting his energies to the establishment of a regular administrative system in his dominions. For had he possessed the grit and the resources to try conclusions with the Mogul power, why should he court their present friendship at the cost of an implicit acknowledgment of their supremacy? Why observe such patience with the Mogul pro-consuls? Why keep them propitiated with a periodic interchange of presents and social amenities? Thus it is that Shivaji's attitude must have struck the superficial observer. But the events that were yet in the womb of time and had scarcely cast their shadow before them ought to help us to understand that this was a delusion, and that the great Deccan warrior was but resting awhile with eyes wide awake, giving to his exhausted countrymen a necessary period of recuperation after all their triumphs and vicissitudes. There was a risk at all times, and never more so than after what had happened in the matter of the defeat of Jay Singh, that Bijapur and Golconda might make common cause and turn a united front against a Hindu power that was still in its birth-throes. To have the imperial assurance and an asylum in the back-ground of all his political plans was, therefore, an indispensable weapon in his defensive armoury. Shivaji could not count on that imperial assurance to shield him in the prosecution of any extreme measures with the Deccan monarchies. The fanaticism of the emperor would scarcely permit him to look with stoical indifference upon an infidel pressing hard upon the kingdoms of the faithful, and the moment it was discovered that it was no longer to the advantage of the empire to connive at his ally's forward movements, the emperor's wrath was sure to burst forth suddenly upon his nascent enterprise. There was moreover a point beyond which the Maratha leader could not proceed without coming into direct collision with the wishes of the emperor, who for so many years had looked upon the domains of the Bijapur and Golconda kingdoms as his own royal spoils and would scarcely permit a partner in the chase to appropriate the trophies to himself. The time was not yet for such an open defiance.

But the Maratha-Mogul *entente* was not destined to endure. The distrustful emperor soon began to suspect that Shivaji's present humility was merely a cloak to cover his ambitious designs. He guessed that Shivaji had managed by bribes and other arts to lead the imperial commanders to fall in with his wishes. He, therefore, sent fresh orders, warning Prince Muazzim against the perils of Shivaji's political blandishments and his professions of love and amity. He pointed out that Shivaji's ambition soared far higher. He was about to pounce upon the prostrate sultanates of the south, and presently when he had disposed of them, he would launch an attack upon the central power. It would then be too late to repel his invasions. He was presumptuous enough, even as matters stood now, to turn to his own uses the revenues of forts, towns and territories which he had won from the southern sultanates with the active connivance of the Mogul generals, and never felt himself to be under any obligation to account for these revenues. This was not as it ought to be. The good relations established with him by treaty must now be broken off, the forts and territories made over to him recovered, and the auxiliary contingent sent by him discharged, and if such a splendid chance did indeed present itself, that contingent should be surprised and Prataprao Guzar, Shivaji himself and the other great commanders, who owned him allegiance, must be apprehended, if possible. A reluctance to obey these orders, so the emperor plainly hinted, would bring down his displeasure upon his head.[1] Before these despatches were actually received, the prince got intelligence about their contents from his confidential spies and was able to inform Prataprao Guzar about it and advised him to ensure his safety by flight. That very night Prataprao left the Mogul camp at Aurangabad along with the cavalry contingent in his charge and accompanied by Niraji, Shivaji's envoy at Aurangabad, reached Poona in safety. (December 1669.) On receipt of the imperial despatches, Prince Muazzim, to avert suspicion of any collusion, attempted a feigned pursuit of the retreating Marathas. The pursuers returned, as was anticipated, to their general, without achieving any success. The prince wrote in reply to his father's despatches that the ungrateful traitors, the Marathas, had already left before receipt of the imperial *firman*, and in consequence could not be put under arrest, as he had been directed to do.

---

1 The Bundela Memoirs give the version that the jahgir conferred upon Prince Sambhaji was revoked on the pretext of reimbursing the amount of one lakh of rupees which had been paid to Shivaji when he started from the Deccan for Delhi. When the news of the resumption of this jahgir reached Shivaji, he at once recalled Prataprao Guzar with his contingent; and his representatives in the jahgir districts likewise returned to the south, carrying off such booty as they could lay their hands upon. The text follows Sabhasad, 61–62 and Shedgavkar, p. 62.

Shivaji was gratified at Prataprao's safe return with all his party and the unmistakable proofs which he brought with him of the imperial prince's esteem in the form of presents sent with every precaution for secrecy and concealment. Little did he regret the interruption of his peaceful relations with the great Mogul. He had spent two years in almost profound peace in looking after the internal organization of his kingdom. For two years without any overt warfare he had the satisfaction of supporting a not inconsiderable part of his forces at the cost of the Moguls. But now it was time again to be up and doing.

CHAPTER XXI

RENEWED CAMPAIGN AGAINST THE MOGULS, 1670-72

THE campaigns that Shivaji now undertook were conducted on a scale to which we have no parallel in all his previous career. The first plan was the recovery of the important forts of Sinhagadh and Purandar, the possession of which by the Moguls enabled them to obstruct Shivaji's free communication with Poona, Chakan and adjoining parts. Jay Singh had furnished the bravest of his Rajput soldiery to man these forts. The garrison armies were as vigilant as they were brave and loyal. Shivaji aimed his first operations against Sinhagad. The governor of the garrison was a brave Rajput veteran named Uday Bhanu. His loyalty was not to be tampered with by any means. The picked men under him were tried veterans, whose chivalrous valour had been proved on many a well-fought field. The conquest of this fort, therefore, was one of the most perplexing tasks that ever presented itself before Shivaji, who was all the more keen about its conquest, because, as the national ballads (powadas) of the Maratha minstrels would lead us to infer, he had entered upon the undertaking at the urgent desire of his mother Jijabai.[1] In this perplexity, Tanaji Malusare, the veteran general and the companion of Shivaji's youthful adventures, presented himself before Shivaji and undertook with his younger brother Suryaji and a corps of one thousand Mavalis of his own choosing to capture the fort. According to the ballad celebrating the event, Tanaji was attended by a force of 12,000.

---

[1] The powada says that Jijabai challenged Shivaji to a game of dice and having defeated him demanded the fort of Sinhagad as the forfeit. The fort was then under the Moguls, and thus Jijabai got him effectually to conquer it. Tanaji Malusare was engaged in the festivities in connection with the marriage of his son Rayaba, when the orders of Shivaji reached him to come with his Mavalis straightway to Raigad. And so the hero came, putting off the festivities.

About Tanaji himself almost incredible accounts are given in the native chronicles as to his valour and personal appearance. He is described as a man of gigantic proportions, of an aspect most terrible, with chest-nut hair and blood-shot eyes, and a marvellously long, bushy moustache. He had such muscular strength that, we are told, he could control the movements of an elephant, by drawing him about by the tusks at his pleasure. On the field of war, no one would stand before him face to face. Shivaji had not his equal. He was as versed in the theory and practice of arms, as he was distinguished for his personal valour and physique.

Sinhagad lies on the eastern side of the great Sahyadri range. The hills projecting from Fort Purandar extend right up to it, with which indeed by steep and narrow ridges lengthening from west to east Fort Sinhagad communicates. On the northern and southern sides the fort rears itself up into a huge precipice, with an ascent of half a mile, rising abruptly from the depths below. Arrived at this height, the traveller finds the mountain overtopped by a craggy summit, consisting of a huge mass of black rocks upwards of forty feet in height. Surmounting the rocky mass, arise the stone fortification and its towers. The fort is of a triangular shape, the area enclosed being about two miles in circumference. Except at the gates, it seems to present no entrance. The summit of the fort commands a prospect of the beautiful but narrow valley of the Nira on the east. On the northern side a great plain unfolds itself before the eyes, ths city of Poona being its chief attraction, while masses of undulating mountains rise on the west and south. In this quarter rises Fort Raigad, from which Tanaji Malusare proposed to lead his faithful Mavalis.

This force of a thousand Mavalis set forth by devious paths known only to themselves. Over hill and glen the veterans followed separate tracks until they united together at the trysting-place near the fort in the darkness of the night. It was the night of the eighth day of the dark half of the moon, in the month of *Magh* (February). Tanaji divided his forces: one-half posted themselves at a little distance, with orders to advance at a pre-arranged signal, and the other half took up their position unobserved at the foot of the rock.[1] A part of the fortress most difficult of access and on that account less likely to be guarded by the sentinel parties was chosen for attempting an escalade. Here it was that a Mavali warrior, most daring and resourceful among his fellows, scrambled up the crag with the aid of a *ghorpad* or iguana and making fast a ladder of ropes to a rock enabled his comrades to ascend the rampart one after another. As each Mavali scaled the ladder in silence he laid himself down to prevent discovery. But scarcely had 300 of them entered the fort[2], when the sentinels began to suspect that some unusual event was brewing around them, and their attention being attracted to the quarter in which the Mavali escalade had in part been effected, one of them ran up to ascertain what was the matter. An arrow shot with deadly aim was the silent answer to his inquiry. An alarm was now raised and presently the garrison camp became a babel of confusion with mounting and arming in haste. The scene of panic determined Tanaji to a bold charge with the handful of Mavalis who had made good the ascent. Soon a shower of the Mavalis' arrows was directed towards the spot whence the out-cry proceeded. By this time the sentinels had kindled their torches, and a blaze of light discovered the plight of the garrison and the cool intrepidity of their assailants. A desperate conflict then ensued, reducing itself to a series of hand-to-hand encounters. Though surprised in the middle of their plan and out-numbered by the Rajputs, the Mavalis fought with such terrible earnestness that the enemy had to retire on all sides. Meanwhile the leaders of the opposite

---

1 According to the powada, Tanaji did the scouting himself as a village Patil (headman).

2 The powada says that the rope gave way after fifty Mavalis had climbed up the rampart.

sides, Tanaji and Uday Bhanu[1], were engaged in deadly conflict. They were both known to fame for their perfect mastery of the science of self-defence. They had at last discovered in each other foemen worthy of their steel. The combat was long and arduous, a succession of thrusts and parries, and much blood was shed on both sides. At length both heroes fell mortally wounded. When the Mavalis saw that their leader was slain and that the tide was turning against them, then for the first time they lost heart and began to retire. The retreat had almost turned to a rout, each making for the place where the escalade had been made, when Suryaji, the brother of Tanaji, appeared on the rampart, bringing up the remainder of the escalading party. On learning what had happened Suryaji rallied the fugitives, pouring scorn upon them for flinching from the post of duty at such a crisis. He declared escape was impossible, for he had cut down the scaling ladder, and he asked who among them was so base, such a faint-hearted craven as to leave his father's remains to be unceremoniously dealt with by a common *mahar* (sweeper)? For Tanaji was as good as a father to them. "Now is the time," he exclaimed with growing animation, "to prove your loyalty to Shivaji, to try your mettle as heroes. Come then and attack the enemy!" With a deafening cry of "Har! Har! Mahadev!", the Hindu war-cry invoking their principal deities, the whole party as one man again turned round upon their pursuers: Suryaji's words had infused new vigour, new ambition, new life into them. They steeled themselves to the task of avenging the death of Tanaji, the idol and the hero of every loyal Mavali, and of paying their last honours to his mortal remains. The tide turned. One victorious charge and the fort fell before them. Three hundred hardy Mavalis laid down their lives. Nearly five hundred valiant Rajput soldiers lay dead upon the field of battle. A few—very few—kept

---

[1] The powada describes Uday Bhanu as the husband of eighteen wives and father of twelve sons. A fearful account is given of the quantity of meat he consumed at his meals.

in hiding and surrendered. Many precipitated themselves over the rampart and were dashed to pieces.

According to the pre-arranged signal the glad tidings of victory were conveyed to Shivaji by setting on fire a thatched house in the fort. Shivaji hailed the news with joy, but when he heard that the victory was purchased by the death of the gallant Tanaji, his joy was turned to sorrow. "The fort is taken," he exclaimed, "but the lion is slain!" in allusion to the name of Sinhagad or the Lion's Den which he had given to the fort, though according to some historians the fort had up to that time been known as Kondana, and received the name Sinhagad after this event. The gallantry of the faithful Mavalis received handsome acknowledgments. Every member of the expedition received a silver armlet in token of the victory. The officers were amply rewarded. Suryaji's services were duly acknowledged by his being promoted to the command of the garrison of the captured fort.[1]

On the capture of Sinhagad, it took little time to reduce Purandar, About a month after the victory of Sinhagad, Suryaji led his gallant Mavalis to Fort Purandar, which was escaladed by a night attack, the garrison cut to pieces, and Shivaji's standard planted on the flag-staff. The Rajput garrison of Purandar knowing but too well how ineffectual had been the resistance of their comrades at Sinhagad lost heart and with all their preponderating numbers offered little resistance. The Mavalis carried the fort without much loss on their side.

The next move was against Fort Mahuli the conquest of which was assigned to the minister, Moropant. This

1 One of the most interesting historical novels in the Marathi language is on the subject of the conquest of Sinhagad. The author was the late Mr. Hari Narayan Apte popularly known as the Sir Walter Scott of Marathi Literature. In the four pages of his description of the capture of Sinhagad (pages 227-31) Mr. Kincaid has crowded together the romantic and fantastic incidents celebrated in the powada but in a foot-note at page 231 he refers to the "less romantic but more probable story" to be found in Sabhasad's bakhar, which in the main is followed here.

warrior surrounded the fort and led a sudden assault. A bloody battle followed, in which Moropant lost a thousand lives and was obliged to fall back. Nothing daunted by this reverse, Moropant Peshwa continued the siege while the garrison within the walls redoubled their effort to hold out. After some rest, Moropant Peshwa again advanced to the assault, but again a second time was he obliged to retire. The Peshwa's siege force still continued the blockade without the least sign of irresolution, while the defenders relying on the expectation of a relief force from the Mogul camp at Junnar maintained the defensive with a dogged determination. This went on for two months, neither party giving way. At length the defenders lost faith in the ability of the Mogul commanders to effect their rescue and surrendered the fort to the Peshwa.[1] Soon after the capture of Mahuli the fort of Karnala was captured by assault and the whole of the district of Kalyan was recovered before the commencement of the monsoons. Other stray forts, here and there, under the Moguls, such as Lohagad, Rohida, Shivneri, fell before Shivaji's storming parties without much resistance.

Shivaji in person had advanced against Janjira, which was subjected to all the rigour of a land siege with ceaseless cannonading. Even with the advent of the monsoons the siege was not relaxed, Shivaji having resolved to carry the fort before the cessation of the rains. While Shivaji spared no exertion to press home the blockade, he tried at the same time with gold to win over the commander of the garrison.

---

[1] According to the Bundela Memoirs Shivaji conducted the siege of Mahuli in person. The Commander of the fort was a Rajput named Manordas. When the provision in the fort came to an end Manordas sent a message to Shivaji that he and his garrison soldiers were Rajputs and would not surrender the fort till every man had fallen on the field of war. Shivaji knew the secret passages leading to the fort and tried to escalade it by one of these paths. But the enemy within was on the watch and attacked the raiders in full force, Shivaji losing many men in the contest. He had to return, raising the siege for the time being. But eventually he made another raid and captured the fort. The Jedhe Chronology gives the date August 1670 for the capture of Mahuli.

Fatteh Khan, the lord of the sea-fort, at first resented these offers, but as the blockade became more and more stringent he was glad to entertain these conditions of surrender and accept a feudatory dependence under Shivaji. But his three principal officers scorned any such proposals. Theirs was an inveterate enmity with Shivaji. Their bigoted hatred was far too pronounced to admit of any *pourparlers* with the enemy, and if they hated the Hindus in general, they had a special racial antipathy against the Marathas. They made up their mind to frustrate Fatteh Khan's design, enlisted the sympathy of the Abyssinian leaders, and with their assistance apprehended Fatteh Khan. Having thus excluded the possibility of the proposals for surrender, they opened negotiations with the Mogul governor at Surat soliciting his intervention and promising to transfer the fort from the suzerainty of the Bijapur sultan to that of the Mogul emperor and to make over to the empire the services of their magnificent navy and hold their lands as in jahgir from the emperor.[1] These proposals were duly submitted to the emperor with the favourable comments of the governor of Surat and were sanctioned by Aurangzeb. One of the Abyssinian petitioners was declared the lord of the fort and placed in command over it, with the imperial title of Yakut Khan.

The result of the Mogul intervention was decisive. Shivaji had to break up his camp and move his forces in pursuit of objects more easy of realization. The fulfilment of his intention to chastise the Abyssinians had to be indefinitely postponed. With a view to inflict an immediate and summary vengeance on the imperial subhedar of Surat whose intervention had such disastrous effects upon his

1 Khafi Khan gives the names of the confederate Abyssinians as Sidi Sambal, Sidi Yakut and Sidi Khairiyat. But his account is rather confused, for Yakut Khan seems to have been in general the title of the Sidi admirals under the Mogul and not of a particular Sidi chief. (Khafi Khan in Elliot VII, 289-290).

plans against Janjira, Shivaji suddenly turned round upon that wealthy town when the rains had scarcely subsided and fell upon it unawares with a squadron of 15,000 horse. Unhappily for Shivaji sudden sickness and death had removed the subhedar from the reach of the Maratha vengeance. But the hapless town fell an easy prey to the victorious invaders, the more easy inasmuch as a goodly proportion of the city guards had recently been diverted by the local governor, whether under orders of Muazzim and Jaswant Singh out of collusion with Shivaji's plan, or merely by the blind operation of chance, there is no means to determine. And so it came that though the governor of Guzerat had prepared a large squadron of horse to face the anticipated invasion of Shivaji, the third of October on which Shivaji reached Surat, saw the governor of the city in command of a defence force of barely three hundred men. For some days before the invasion news had leaked out that Shivaji had gathered a large body of light horse at Kalyan, and the British factors at Surat had rightly conjectured that their own town was the objective of this light armed force. They had taken steps to remove their goods to Swally, where the new president[1] Gerald Aungier and most of the councillors of the English company had betaken themselves. The English factory and ware-houses in the city were left in charge of Streynsham Master, who was then on the Surat council, and afterwards governor of the Madras factory.

Shivaji plundered the city at leisure to his heart's content. The citadel was stormed, but an attempt to demolish it by mining was according to the English traveller Dr. Fryer beaten off by the Moguls. The Marathas spread themselves over the whole town except the European factories. For three days the sack of Surat continued. (3rd to 5th October 1670).[2]

---

[1] Aungier succeeded to the governorship of the Surat factory in 1669 Sir George Oxenden, the hero of the first sack of Surat, having died in that year.

[2] According to Dr. Fryer the old mud walls of Surat had by this time been replaced by a solid rampart of masonry. According to the

Once again the English merchants fought on the defensive and saved their possessions from wholesale plunder. They resisted two of the invader's attacks, but in the end consented to make a small present to Shivaji. This the company's agents took to the invader's tent outside the town. Shivaji told them that he wished to be on friendly terms with the English and assured them that he would do them no harm.[1] The Dutch factory lay rather isolated from the busy part of the town. Shivaji sent a letter assuring them that no harm would be done to them, if they remained quiet.[2] The French by prudent management and the payment of a fine saved their factory. They remained neutral permitting Shivaji's troops to pass through their factory to attack a Tartar prince, once King of Kashgar, who having been deposed by his son had just returned from a pilgrimage to Mecca and was then living at Surat under the protection of the emperor. Shivaji obtained a quantity of gold, silver, jewels and many other valuable articles in the pillage of this unfortunate prince's residence.

On the third day Shivaji received intelligence from Barhanpur, that a great Mogul army was coming with all speed for the defence of Surat. Shivaji immediately broke up his camp and evacuated the plundered town, having left a letter to the townsmen, demanding a tribute of twelve lakhs of rupees per annum, as the price of their exemption from future pillage.

On receipt of the news of Shivaji's invasion of Surat, the subhedar of Aurangabad had forthwith despatched a force of eight to ten thousand under two commanders, Mohabat Khan and Daud Khan, to the aid of the town.

Marathi chronicles the Mogul governor made a show of fight; but the Factory Reports state that he fled to the castle.

[1] *Vide* letter of the Surat Council to the Company, of 20th November 1670, quoted in Hedge's Diary.

[2] Dutch Reports, Translations, Vol. 29, quoted by Prof. Sarkar (Shivaji, p. 222).

When Shivaji swiftly pursuing his return march along the great road of Salheri had passed Kanchan-Manchan near Chandor (Chandwad) he was overtaken by the Mogul officers near Vani-Dindori.[1] This he did not mind, his object being to descend upon the Kolwan by the great pass near Nasik. But when he perceived that a large Mogul force was likewise holding this pass, he saw the situation had become an embarrassing one and became anxious for the safety of his booty. He, therefore, divided his forces into four or five parties. One of these began to skirmish with the enemy posted in the front, while two others were ordered to manœuvre on his flanks. Another party was entrusted with the safe convoy of the precious spoil obtained at Surat. They had orders to elude the enemy held in play by the other divisions, to sweep across the hostile positions beyond the mountains and to make the best of their way home into the Konkan. As Shivaji himself accompanied this division, there was a hot pursuit by the Moguls under Daud Khan. Shivaji wheeled round on the enemy with a column of this division and kept the Moguls engaged, while the rest of the party successfully cleared the defile. The skilful manœuvring of the Marathas and the simultaneous attacks delivered on different sides of the Mogul divisions led to a concentration of the Mogul forces and a pitched battle with Shivaji. Leaving Prataprao Sirnobut to defend the Maratha rear, Shivaji charged the united Mogul armies, fighting and exhorting his men in every part of the field, conspicuous with his burnished arms and helmet, his spirited war-horse, and the mighty sweep of the double-edged sword he wielded in either hand. Fired with the example of their chief the Marathas met the Mogul charge, broke it and turned it into a rout. Such was the battle of Vani-Dindori. It lasted above three hours. Three thousand Moguls lay dead on the field. The remnant were driven into headlong flight. Instead of pressing the pursuit, Shivaji turned his attention to the Mogul encampment, which yielded an

1 *Vide* Scott's Deccan, Vol. II, p. 25 & Sabhasad, 64-65.

abundance of spoil,—horses, elephants and war-material. When Shivaji's men heavy laden with this booty turned towards the defile, they found themselves intercepted by a brave Maratha lady, Rai Bagin, her son Jagjivan and their corps of feudal retainers. This lady was the wife of a brave officer in the Mogul service, Udaram, the deshmukh of Mahur. In a former battle the deshmukh having fallen fighting with great bravery, his place was taken by his wife, who exhorted her men and led them to victory. Admiring this marvellous presence of mind and valour in the woman, Aurangzeb had conferred upon her the title of Rai Bagin, in appreciation of her noble service. On this occasion, the brave lady had again with her wonted fidelity taken up arms in behalf of her imperial master. But she had taken up arms in vain. She was encompassed on all sides by Shivaji's followers. Baffled in all attempts to escape, she had to surrender and sue for pardon. The chivalrous victor received her with every mark of respect and had her escorted home, laden with presents of jewelled ornaments and dresses.[1]

On his return from Surat, Shivaji made preparations by land and sea. Prataprao Guzar at the head of ten thousand horse and Moropant Peshwa in command of 20,000 foot were ordered to march northward into Mogul territory. The people of these parts were on the whole in fairly affluent circumstances, and the military control being lax, great hopes were entertained of a rich and easy booty. These hopes were abundantly fulfilled. Prataprao invaded Khandesh and Berar, a region teeming with wealth and, considering the conditions of the time, also with population. The larger towns were pillaged and annual tributes imposed upon them. Written agreements were made with the leading citizens, by which the latter bound themselves to pay a quarter of the annual tribute due to the imperial authorities into the hands of Shivaji or his accredited agents. The due payment of the annual

[1] Shedgavkar p. 64 and other bakhars.

tribute was to exempt the particular towns and villages from any molestation at the hands of Shivaji's hosts. Shivaji on his side was to ensure their protection from incursions by any other power. This was the first imposition of the famous chauth on a province immediately subject to the Mogul rule. The principal incident of this expedition was the capture and pillage of Karanjia. Prataprao made a halt of three days at this town and plundered it at leisure.[1] The citizens were found to have buried their valuables in their houses, and Prataprao made a strict search of the houses of the wealthy, dug up their treasures, and carried them away as prisoners of war. A few escaped in women's clothes, Shivaji's orders on the subject being strict, that under no circumstances and on no account should a female be molested or interfered with. In another part of the Mogul dominions, West Khandesh and Baglan, Moropant's victorious infantry carried town after town and fort after fort. Daud Khan, the governor, was campaigning near Ahmednagar. He came up too late to save these places. The leading conquests were those of Aundha, Patta, Salheri, Mulheri, Trimbak and Ramnagar. Salheri was in the end carried by Shivaji in person. He invested the fort with a force of 20,000 horse and foot and captured it by escalade, after the Mogul governor of the fort had fallen in battle. Many new fortresses were erected in these newly conquered parts.

The fleet set in motion comprised one hundred and sixty war-ships. The object of the fitting up of this flotilla was

---

[1] The Jedhe Chronology, page 189, says that after the battle of Vani-Dindori, Shivaji retired to Kunjargad and in the following month proceeded to Karanjia, capturing on the way the forts of Ahiwant, Ravla-Javla and Markanda.

According to Sabhasad's chronicle the sack of Karanjia was made by Shivaji in person. Grant Duff adds in a foot-note that the East India Company's factors at Surat were under the impression that Shivaji made the incursion upon Karanjia in person, and that of the leading people of the place few escaped except such as ran away in women's clothes. From this Grant Duff concludes that the Moguls must have known Shivaji's regulations regarding protection to females.

that the naval forces should co-operate on the coast, when the port of Broach should be attacked, as was projected, on the landward side. But shortly after the fleet had weighed anchor from the vicinity of Bombay, it was recalled. On the return voyage they captured off Damaun a large Portuguese war-ship, which was safely brought to Dabhol creek. It is said about the same time the Portuguese brought to the port of Bassein about a dozen of Shivaji's war-ships intercepted by them. These events point to the probability of a sea-fight between the Portuguese and Shivaji's navies between Bombay and Damaun.

It would appear very strange that while Shivaji was winning these new triumphs, the Mogul authorities should not have moved a finger. But this inactivity of the Mogul commanders is chiefly to be ascribed to the absence of an adequate supply of troops in the southern subha. It had become an article of faith with the mistrustful emperor that to send additional forces to the distant satrapy of the south was fraught with singular danger to the empire. Whilst the Peshwa Moropant was storming Mahuli, a considerable force was stationed at Junnar and 5000 additional troops lay at Surat for the defence of the country around. There was likewise the usual quota of troops at the Aurungabad head-quarters. But these numbers were insignificant when compared with the numbers at Shivaji's command. At any given moment, if the Mogul armies in the south were to combine together for any initiative, it was within Shivaji's power to put up forty thousand men to try conclusions with them. And this without any weakening of the garrison forces maintained at each fort and station. While the deficiency of forces crippled the Mogul offensive, the rumours and divisions in the camp made the stagnation complete. All action was paralysed by the common report of a secret league between Shivaji and Prince Muazzim. The friendly relations between Shivaji and Jaswant Singh were well known. The repeated applications of the prince for reinforcement were rejected by the suspicious emperor. It is not too much to believe that the main object of Prince Muazzim was to make friendships in the south so as to pave his way to the throne on the emperor's demise. For between a Mogul prince and the grave, the only alternative stages were the peacock throne at Agra or the prison-walls of Gwalior fort. The growing depredations of Shivaji were to him a new excuse for obtaining re-enforcement from the emperor. Lack of troops was his stereotyped answer to the emperor's complaints about the Marathas. It was to his personal advantage to maintain good relations with a valiant chief like Shivaji, and though he could not altogether abstain from action, he managed to send against the Maratha generals such insufficient forces that defeat was a foregone conclusion.

But Aurangzeb was not an emperor to be thus baffled. He recalled Jaswant Singh and appointed Mohabat Khan in his place with powers almost independent of Prince Muazzim. The latter had barely a thousand men left under his command at Aurangabad. The rest of the Mogul force took the offensive under Mohabat Khan. Diler Khan was sent to co-operate with him. The subhedar of Surat was charged with neglect in the performance of his high duties. The censure was too great for the haughty subhedar to bear and he put an end to a life that had ceased to give pleasure to himself or to his master by poison. The new subhedar received orders to build a number of war-ships at Surat and Bombay, the object being to co-operate actively with the Abyssinians of Janjira, with a view to extinguish the new sea-power of Shivaji.

Immediately on his arrival in the Deccan, Mohabat Khan began the offensive. He had recovered Aundha and Patta, when the monsoons compelled him to suspend his operations. On the opening of the fair season, he formed his army into two divisions. The one under Diler Khan advanced against Chakan, which was immediately taken and all persons within the fort above nine years of age were put to the sword.[1] Upon this success, he received orders to start

1 Prof. Sarkar (Shivaji, p. 242, Foot-note) is inclined to think

against Rawla-Javla, and Ahiwant. His assaults on these two forts were gallantly repulsed by the Maratha garrisons, and on the approach of a relief force of twelve thousand sent up by Moropant, he had to break up his camp from before these forts. He next advanced to Kanergad[1] and captured it. A gallant attempt to recover this fort was made by Ramaji Pangare[2], the naik or commander of the personal retinue of the governor of the fort. With two thousand Mavalis[3] he made a mid-night attack. Observing the small force of the assailants, Diler Khan sallied out with a larger body. Nothing daunted, the resolute Pangare rallied the bravest of his Mavalis to the charge, asking only those to follow who were prepared to lay down their lives. Seven hundred Mavalis responded to the call. A furious charge ensued. The seven hundred fell along with their brave leader, with wounds all over their bodies, but in their fall they carried down two thousand Pathans to bear them company. Diler Khan was filled with admiration at this noble exhibition of valour. The rest of the Mavalis, seized with a passionate desire to emulate the prowess of their comrades, continued the unequal contest, but at last broke and fled.

While Diler Khan was thus occupied, Bahadur Khan, the governor of Guzerat, was directed to take charge of Mohabat Khan's division. He advanced and laid siege to Salheri. This position was considered to be of high strategic value and Shivaji determined to exhaust every mode of resistance in defending the fort. A shortage of food supplies was reported by the garrison and Shivaji had to exercise all his ingenuity in making good the deficiency.

---

that the description in the English Factory Records that "*Poona Chackne*" was captured by Diler Khan really stands for the conquest of Poona and not that of Chakan, judging by the language used.

[1] Chitnis calls the fort by the name of Konargad.

[2] Chitnis gives the officer's name as Ramaji Nalage.

[3] According to some chronicles the gallant officer led one thousand men only. Prof. Sarkar (Shivaji, page 243, foot-note) would place this event after the battle of Salheri.

For the siege lines lay all round Salheri and it was no easy task to convey the necessary provisions to their proper destination. Fully resolved, however, that the garrison should not be starved into surrender, Shivaji mustered a large army and drew nearer to Salheri as if for battle. Diler Khan, then under the orders of Bahadur Khan, was not slow to accept the invitation. Diverting the greater part of his army from the siege, he came readily to give battle. But Shivaji had merely practised upon the simplicity of the Mogul general, for no sooner were the siege lines relaxed in consequence of the lure of battle, than the baggage and ammunition trains dashed into the fort of Salheri from the north. Two thousand of Shivaji's horse sent to raid Diler Khan's camp were, however, charged by the Mogul commander and cut to pieces. The situation had become grave. Moropant was ordered from the Konkan with his personal corps to march against Diler Khan and Prataprao had to speed with his flying columns to relieve Salheri. Thus a force of nearly 20,000 horse was flung against the Moguls. The Mogul commander anticipating this movement deputed Ikhlas Khan with a great part of his forces to oppose their approach. Prataprao saw the advancing standards of Ikhlas Khan, ordered a halt and prepared for battle. The Moguls charged. Prataprao remained steadily on the defensive. The battle having lasted some time, the Maratha general sounded a retreat. The Marathas dispersing like the wind, the Moguls broke order and joined eagerly in the pursuit. Upon this Prataprao suddenly turned round in flight, drew up his men in order and charged straight at the disarrayed ranks of the pursuing Moguls. Meanwhile Moropant had arrived on the scene with the troops in his command, and uniting his arms with those of Prátaprao added to the confusion of the enemy. Ikhlas Khan re-formed his forces with the addition of a few fresh troops and renewed the battle. But again the Moguls had to sustain a Maratha charge more fiery and spirited than before. They wavered, broke and fled. The flight became a reckless rout. Five thousand of their bravest were killed, among them twenty-two high-placed officers. Several of the leading commanders were wounded and fell into the hands of the Marathas. Among these were Ikhlas Khan himself and Mukaham Singh, the son of Rao Amar Singh of Chandawat. They were released after some time and returned to Ahmednagar. On Shivaji's side, the loss amounted to between ten and fifteen hundred slain. Among others they mourned the loss of Surrao Kankde,[1] a hero of many battles, who was killed by a chain-shot. Kankde was one of Shivaji's earliest followers and was commander of a corps of thousand Mavalis. He first earned his laurels at the capture of a Javli and afterwards distinguished himself in the escalade of Rohida fort. Shivaji received the news of his death with great sorrow, exclaiming that in his death he had lost an old, valiant and devoted officer. The total defeat of Ikhlas Khan and the loss of such a numerous army took the edge from Mohabat Khan's offensive. He had no heart to persevere in the campaign with the remnant of his army. Bahadur Khan raised the siege of Salheri and retreated straight to Aurangabad. The Marathas hung on his rear almost to the gates of that town.

This was the battle of Salheri, 1672. The Maratha victory was as complete as it could be. The spoils of victory were great and various. The booty comprised 125 elephants, 700 camels, 6000 horses, innumerable draught animals, and an enormous quantity of treasure, jewellery and war material. Dresses and presents of jewellery were conferred upon Anandrao Bhonsle, Venkoji Datto, Rupaji Bhonsle, Khandoji Jagtap, Mansing More, Visaji Ballal, Moro Rangnath, Mukund Ballal and other distinguished officers, for the great daring and courage they had displayed in this battle. The Mogul officers and commanders wounded and taken prisoners were sent to Raigad with the respect due to their position, and when their wounds were healed they

---

[1] Sabhasad gives a variation of the name as Suryarao. The Shedgavkar bakhar calls him Surerao.

were courteously given leave to depart with the customary presents. Such of the prisoners as chose to throw in their lot with Shivaji were gladly entertained in the Maratha service.[1]

This was the most considerable victory hitherto gained by Shivaji over the Moguls. It exceeded every other success that had previously crowned Shivaji's arms. It enhanced his prestige at every court. It made a revelation of Maratha chivalry and generalship such as had never been witnessed in the past. The Mogul armies were eloquent in their testimony to the fighting spirit of their opponents. The dread of Shivaji's name pervaded every camp in South India. Maratha *sepoys* deserted in shoals the Mogul and Adil Shahi governments and came flocking to Shivaji's standards. Shivaji captured the opposite fort of Mulheri and dominated the entire Baglan region. This was a permanent menace to Surat.

Fresh from the scene of this victory Moropant was ordered to march towards Surat with ten thousand horse. As already related Aurangzeb having enrolled the Abyssinians under the protection of the empire had given orders for the construction of a fleet at Surat with a view to making descents upon the Konkan regions under Shivaji and destroying his sea-power. The imperial fleet at Surat was now believed to have well approached towards completion and Moropant's instructions were to destroy the incipient naval force before it could effect a junction with the chief of Janjira. But in this design Moropant was

---

1 In view of the fact that the charge of cruelty is often thoughtlessly made against Shivaji by his traducers, it is but fair to his memory to state that these observations about his good treatment of prisoners of war are made by no less a historian than Grant Duff himself. Indeed the ethics of war practised by Shivaji in the treatment of the fallen foe and prisoners, of women and children and persons of the priestly class, whatever their religion, and of mosques and other places of worship would put to blush the many examples of military and political outrage and acts of ruthless vandalism which have been recently perpetrated upon the war fields in the west.

completely foiled, for the fleet had already set sail for Janjira before Moropant's arrival. He now threatened the approaches of Surat, cut off all supplies and trade communications and demanded a heavy tribute. The governor of the city pretended to agree to this condition and extorted huge sums of money from the leading citizens, a part of which he paid over to Moropant as tribute and put all the rest into his own private coffers.[1]

Shivaji now resolved upon reducing the territory surrounding Surat so as to bring it under his own dominion that he might be in a position to command the approaches to that town and place it entirely under his control. With this view he invaded the territories of two petty princes reigning at Jawhar and Ramnagar in the northern Konkan. On the last two occasions when Shivaji invaded Surat he had marched through their territories having purposely taken this circuitous mountain route to evade the attention of the Mogul commanders and divert them from his real objective, which was the wealthy town of Surat. The services of these Rajas in their dominions were handsomely acknowledged on the return of the victorious armies. The state of Jawhar had, during the late struggle, sometimes been on the side of the Moguls, sometimes of Shivaji. Moropant entered Jawhar at the head of a large force and captured it. He then advanced to Ramnagar. When welcomed to the fort of Ramnagar by the local prince, Shivaji declared that the fort must now remain permanently with himself, for this stronghold was the key to unlock the banking house of Surat and it was fair to keep the keys of his safe with himself.[2]

The Raja had no alternative but to acquiesce in this demand. The territory of this prince comprised a few

[1] According to Prof. Sarkar, the governor pocketed all the money subscribed by the citizens for a defence force and attempted to extort further sums for a ransom, which the citizens refused to pay.

[2] The Jedhe Chronology (p. 190) states that the Raja of Ramnagar fled to Damaun. The Raja Vikram Singh of Jawhar fled to join the Moguls at Nasik, which place was attacked by Moropant Peshwa six years later.

mountain forts, the outlying territory on the sea-coast, forming the district of Damaun,being under the Portuguese. The latter were accustomed to pay an annual tribute to the Raja, to secure their immunity from his incursions. Shivaji having occupied these mountain forts turned upon the Portuguese power at Damaun. The Portuguese were seized with panic. The fortress ramparts had just been completed, but the cannon had yet to be mounted. With difficulty the garrison erected a few guns on the bastions and sent an officer to inquire what errand Shivaji's men had come upon. They made answer, as they had been previously tutored, that they had come to enforce and confirm the annual tribute to the lord of Ramnagar. The Portuguese willingly consented, glad that the storm had passed without further damage.

At Aurangabad there was a fresh transfer of command. Incensed with the defeat of Mohabat Khan and the impairment of the Mogul forces, the emperor recalled both Mohabat Khan and Prince Muazzim and appointed Khan Jehan Bahadur (Bahadur Khan) subhedar of Guzerat to take charge of the Deccan subha with an army of 70,000 strong and to operate against Shivaji. When this governor came upon the scene of his activities he realized that the force at his disposal was inadequate for a direct offensive against the Marathas and determined to have recourse to Fabian tactics, warding off the Maratha incursions and protecting the peaceful inhabitants of the Mogul dominions from these repeated attacks. This resolution made, he planted batteries upon the mountain defiles and secured the ghat passages through which the Maratha armies used to pour down on the fruitful plains below. The policy was not approved of by Diler Khan, elated as he was with his cheap victory at Chakan and being on that account in the good graces of the emperor. He was eager for an aggressive campaign. He advised Khan Jehan that there was no advantage in station-

1678, when Vikram Shaha was defeated and killed. (Jedhe Chronology pp. 190–194).

ing his men at the ghats, but that the squadrons must be hurled against Shivaji's force, one after another. But this argument had no effect upon the new viceroy and he persisted in his own method of warfare. The result was that the extensive invasions upon Khandesh and other northern parts were indeed stopped, but the Maratha armies divided into small parties kept hovering about the territories of Ahmednagar and Aurangabad being prepared to strike a blow as occasion served. The governor went after them in various directions but with little success and at last encamped for the rainy season at Pedgaum on the Bhima, where he erected a mud-fort for the defence of his camp and gave it the name of Bahadur-gad.[1]

While the Khan was thus passing the time in a state of inaction, Shivaji undertook a campaign further a-field. His envoy at the court of Golconda informed him of a plan adopted by that durbar to embark on war operations on a considerable scale against the French who had recently created trouble within the Kutub Shahi frontiers.[2] True to his usual plans in such operations, Shivaji observed great secrecy as to his objective, when starting upon this new campaign from Raigad with ten thousand horse. For aught that his followers knew, Shivaji might have meant to swoop down upon Aurangabad, or Ahmednagar or Bijapur. With extraordinary celerity and advancing by forced marches, Shivaji made a sudden diversion into the Golconda territory and presented himself all at once before the gates of Hyderabad (Bhaganagar). The city was seized with panic. Shivaji threatened to use fire and sword unless

[1] *Vide* Prof. Sarkar (Shivaji pp. 248–54) for a detailed account of these minor operations. A Maratha light horse column 750 strong charged an imperial force of 10,000 at Bakapur on the barriers of Berar and was repelled by the gallant Bundela general Subhakarn. Dr. Fryer (I, 330-340) describes an unsuccessful attempt on the side of Shivaji to capture Shivneri. Apparently this fort (Jedhe p. 189) was besieged, perhaps captured, by Shivaji in 1670, and subsequently lost.

[2] M. De La Haye, the French governor, seized St. Thome and drove out the Golconda garrison. Upon this the Kutub Shahi sultan prepared his army and sent it forth to recover St. Thome.

the officers and leading citizens paid a tribute of twenty lakhs of pagodas. They submitted to these terms, levied what sums they could upon the citizens and delivered their town from the horrors of an invasion. Content with what he received, Shivaji withdrew from the town, without further molestation to any of the Kutub Shahi possessions, and with the same rapidity as before brought home his victorious squadrons to Raigad.[1]

While Shivaji was intent upon this expedition, the united navies of the Moguls and the Abyssinians had made a descent upon the Konkan coast, with much destruction to the towns and villages. The Maratha batteries at Danda-Rajpuri were stormed and destroyed, and the officer in charge, Ragho Ballal Atre, though he resisted bravely, was defeated and slain.[2]

The Abyssinian attack was made during the Holi carnival and the garrison soldiers were caught napping. Sidi Khairiyat made a demonstration on the landward side and while the Maratha soldiers rushed in full force in that direction the sea-ramparts of the stronghold were carried by Yakut Khan, with a fleet of forty war-ships. There was great slaughter. The powder magazine caught fire and blew up with a number of men, including a dozen or so of the Abyssinians. It is said that when the magazine blew up, Shivaji, who was forty miles away, started from sleep, and said some misfortune must have occurred to Danda-Rajpuri. He sent his men forthwith to ascertain what had happened. In the neighbourhood of this sea-port were six or seven forts belonging to Shivaji. Yakut attacked them and six of them surrendered after two or three days' resistance. But the *quilledar* of one fort held out for a week in the hope of relief from Shivaji. He was at last obliged to surrender. Sidi Yakut granted quarter to the garrison and seven hundred of them came out. With true Abyssi-

1 The entry at page 190 in Jedhe's Chronology has reference to this event.

2 *Vide* Khafi Khan, (Elliot. VII, 290-92)

nian treachery, he violated his promise, made the children and handsome women slaves and forcibly converted them to Islam. The old and ugly women he set free, but the men he put to the sword. In this way he fulfilled his promise to the garrison to let them go without injury. He boasted the of exploit and wrote about it in a grandiloquent vein to the Mogul commanders. The latter made themselves parties to his perfidy and atrocities by increasing his mansab and sending him presents of robes of honour. On Shivaji's return from Golconda he was able to take ample vengeance.[1]

The Mogul and Abyssinian admirals about this time arranged to get into Bombay harbour and make a descent upon Coorla, then under Shivaji, and applied to the British governor of Bombay, Mr. Aungier, for permission to disembark their troops at Bombay. This permission was not granted. Nevertheless they made their entry into Bombay harbour by force after devastating some of Shivaji's villages and made overtures to the Bombay government for joint action against the Maratha king. Shivaji's representative at Bombay having got wind of these proceedings threatened the British authorities with an invasion of the island town by the Marathas the moment they threw in their lot with the Abyssinians. In the face of these threats Aungier considered it a wise policy to maintain strict neutrality and sent the Abyssinians about their business.

There was war at this time between England and Holland (1672). A Dutch fleet of twenty-two war-ships under Commodore Reickloff Van Goen had just arrived, sailing up the Malabar coast, with a view to attack and capture Bombay. The Commodore applied to Shivaji for aid against the Bombay government with a land force of three thousand, promising in return to co-operate with him with his sea-

---

1 *Vide* Khafi Khan (Elliot VII p. 292). The narrative of the events is taken from Khafi Khan. Surely after this admission of a Mogul mansabdar's perfidy and inhuman atrocities by a Mogul historian, the charges of perfidy and cruelty against Shivaji cannot be easily sustained.

forces against Janjira. The Dutch admiral waited for a reply, but Shivaji was engaged in a wider project of his own and had no leisure to attend to these proposals. The Dutch fleet is said to have returned, not finding it easy to commence their operations without that active co-operation which they had so confidently counted upon.

CHAPTER XXII

BIJAPUR WARS RENEWED, 1673-74

As related in a former chapter the wars with Bijapur had been concluded by a secret treaty between Shivaji and the chief minister of the Adil Shahi state, by which the latter had bound themselves to pay to Shivaji an annual tribute of three lakhs of rupees. From the conclusion of that treaty up to the date of the operations described in the last chapter the Bijapur government had faithfully paid the tribute as it became due from year to year. But Alli Adil Shaha II in whose reign this treaty was concluded having died in 1673, the sceptre had come into the weak grasp of a minor prince, five years of age, and the actual powers of government were exercised by the regent Khawas Khan. The latter was indifferent to the treaty obligations incurred by his predecessor, Abdul Mahomed. Khawas Khan gave himself the most arrogant airs. The other nobles of the court were gradually estranged from him and the durbar was split into factions. Each leading chief had his Brahman secretaries, and through them Shivaji was kept informed about the latest changes occurring in the state. It did not escape his watchful eye that the dissensions and distractions now reigning at Bijapur gave an excellent opportunity for beginning a new campaign. A great army was assembled at Vishalgad. The Adil Shahi commander, Abdul Karim Bahlol Khan, on the other hand, enlisted the support of the Moguls and prepared for war.

Of the entire Maratha force, fifteen thousand were told off for the re-capture of Panhala. The siege had just commenced, when Abdul Karim came down with a large army upon the besiegers. The battle was hotly disputed but in the end victory rested with the Khan, who proceeded to refresh his exhausted army by cantoning it for a short time at Tikota. But Shivaji was immediately on the scene with his relief forces. The Marathas once more charged the enemy and turned the Khan's victory into a complete rout.[1]

Fresh from this triumph, Shivaji pressed forward to attack Hubli. This town was a flourishing centre of commerce and its marts were a meeting-ground for merchants of diverse nations. Shivaji was able to pillage it at leisure, without let or hindrance, and is said to have obtained a larger booty here than in any other town. Among others the English factory at Hubli came in for a share of his attention. According to their records they lost seven to eight thousand pagodas. Mr. Aungier, the governor of Bombay, who, as we have seen, maintained friendly relations with Shivaji and avoided to the best of his power giving any offence to the Maratha ruler, made at the next favourable opportunity a demand for indemnification as regards these losses.[2] In reply Shivaji made answer that the English merchants at Hubli had not been molested by his people, nor had they suffered such losses as were complained of. In support of his contention Shivaji called for the inventories of the booty obtained as compiled by his commanders, and he proved by reference to these that only two hundred pagodas' worth had been taken from the English factory. He undertook to reimburse the company to this extent as also for the losses they had suffered at the sack of Rajapur. While giving these undertakings Shivaji also urged upon the company to re-establish their factory at Rajapur. This request was subsequently complied with, but when Shivaji demanded naval guns for the purposes of his fleet, Aungier declined to comply with Shivaji's wishes, having no desire to provoke the enmity of the Moguls and the Abyssinians. In maintaining these friendly relations with the English and promising them compensation for their losses, Shivaji

[1] In Modak's chronicle of the Adilshahi state, it is stated that Shivaji executed those of his men who had fled from the field of battle. The Jedhe Chronology (page 190) says that Panhala was won by Annaji Datto by tampering with the loyalty of the garrison in March 1673.

[2] Prof. Sarkar quotes Factory Reports, Surat, Vol. 87, and refers to Original Correspondence, 3779 and 3800.

was guided by a deeper purpose: he was eager to enlist the naval help of the Company in his conflict with the Mogul and Abyssinian fleets. Shivaji did not make any mystery about his motives but frankly proposed to Aungier a concerted attack upon Janjira. If this were undertaken he offered to make up immediately all the losses that had been sustained by them in his expeditions. But Aungier was too wary to swallow the bait. The Moguls and the Abyssinians were allies. Surat was under the Moguls, and Surat was the largest entrepot of the East India Company's trade in India. It was certainly not to the interest of the company to court open enmity with the Mogul power and an offensive alliance between the English and Shivaji would be a sufficient ground for the expulsion of the British merchants from Surat. Aungier had likewise similar invitations from the Abyssinians against Shivaji himself and had to decline them also on similar grounds. For Bombay was almost entirely surrounded by Shivaji's dominions and it would have been perilous in the extreme to court hostilities with such a neighbour. It was for this reason that Aungier adhered to his policy of strict neutrality. With both parties he behaved with equal friendship and equal indifference. Again and again did the Abyssinians apply to the Bombay government to permit their fleets to enter Bombay and make it the base of their operations. But he sternly set his face against such proposals, allowing neither party the advantage of making use of Bombay harbour for naval purposes. He had however permitted four Mogul warships to sail into the harbour, but on the condition that they must not on any account attempt to disembark. For this impartial neutrality Aungier was in the long run highly respected by both parties.[1]

Shivaji's high ambition was to bring the western coast under his undisputed authority, and it was in furtherance

[1] Factory Records, Surat 87, Original Correspondence, Nos. 3952 and 3570 (Quoted by Prof. Sarkar in his *Shivaji*, pages 347, 445 & 447).

of this object that his fleets scoured the seas and made new descents upon Karwar, Ankola and other towns. The deshmukhs in the interior were instigated to rebel against the Bijapur commanders, who in many parts were obliged to desert their stations and save themselves by an immediate flight.

To concentrate his efforts on the Bijapur conquests and carry them through to a decisive issue, it was imperative that he should be on peaceful terms with the Great Mogul. With this view Shivaji made conciliatory overtures to Khan Jehan, on the old plan of beseeching the emperor's favour and forgiveness and requesting that the rights of deshmukh all over the south should be conferred upon him and the imperial patronage extended to his enterprise. Shivaji also claimed the mansab promised to his son Sambhaji, and undertook, on the fulfilment of these conditions, to serve the imperial interests truly and loyally at all times. These petitions were forwarded by the Khan to the emperor with a request for favourable consideration. The true inwardness of these negotiations was that Khan Jehan having failed in his design had perforce come to a private understanding with Shivaji. He had learned by experience the arduousness of the struggle and the impossibility of forcing the Maratha chief to surrender his conquests. The Mogul armies had greatly suffered in strength and numbers and there was no prospect of fresh contingents being sent by the emperor. In these circumstances the only alternative open to him was to humour Shivaji and ward off his furious onslaughts from his province. Later when Shivaji had launched upon this new war with Bijapur, he maintained a mysterious silence; and it would seem he himself made a suggestion for Shivaji's present approaches to the emperor to obviate personal risks. For the present, therefore, the war had turned its course entirely against Bijapur. Perfect peace reigned all over the south as between the Moguls and the Marathas.

About this time, Mian Saheb, the fouzdar (military governor) of Karwar, declared an open rebellion against

Bijapur. Those of his Mahomedan subordinates who refused to be accessories to his plot were forthwith apprehended. The deshmukhs who still held out for their Bijapur sovereign found themselves hard pressed on all sides. The rebel chief became a source of general annoyance to the Portuguese subjects of Goa and to their possessions. He made demands for a supply of guns and ammunition from the English factory at Karwar. On their refusal to grant his request he pillaged the English factory. When the news of these events reached Bijapur, an army of eight thousand was sent down to chastise the recalcitrant fouzdar. Apprised of these proceedings Shivaji resolved to deal a blow while the Adil Shahi state was agitated by these internal convulsions.

The fort of Parali[1], which was then under the government of Bijapur, was suddenly surprised and captured by the Mavalis. The fate of Parali put the garrison of the neighbouring fort of Satara on the alert and the attempt to surprise it failed. Shivaji was obliged to have recourse to a regular siege. Well provisioned with food and ammunition supplies as it was, the fort held out strenuously for four or five months. But at length it had to surrender and a good deal of booty fell into Shivaji's hands, which was duly transferred to Raigad. Then fell in quick succession into Shivaji's hands the forts of Chandan-Wandan, Pandavagad, Nandgiri, Tattora and others. The towns of Wai, Karhad, Shirol and Kolhapur were his next captures, bringing Shivaji's possessions upto Hookeri Raibag. About October, Shivaji was reported to be engaged in raising an army of twenty thousand. The Moguls, in doubt as to its destination, feared Shivaji might contemplate a fresh invasion of Surat and arranged to strengthen its defences. The Bijapur government, on the other hand, feared that Shivaji intended to make common cause with their rebel fouzdar at Karwar. The fears of both the parties proved false. A large Maratha army of twenty-five thousand descended the

[1] Jedhe Chronology, p. 190.

ghats by various defiles, and having plundered Bankapur, presented themselves suddenly before the walls of Phonda which they proceeded to invest. The Bijapur army sent down against the rebels at Karwar was seized with sudden dismay when Shivaji's host presented itself in such close proximity to them. The soldiers lost heart, left Karwar to its fate and retreated up the mountains.

When the affairs of Bijapur were reduced to this state of hopeless confusion and the Maratha hosts were spreading devastation far and wide, the regent Khawas Khan was at last moved to send a large army under Abdul Karim[1] against Shivaji. Abdul Karim marched with a large force straight upon Panhala and laid siege to that fort. Prataprao Guzar received orders to advance against him. This general proposed to raise the siege of Panhala by a strategic movement without appearing directly with a force of deliverance before the beleaguered fort or engaging the besiegers under its walls. With this plan in view he moved his force straight upon Bijapur and advanced, pillaging and destroying, to the gates of Bijapur itself. With Guzar at the city-walls Khawas Khan was thrown into great consternation. There was no army in the city to meet the invader. It was necessary to recall Abdul Karim from Panhala and raise the siege of that fort. Abdul Karim returned but was intercepted by Prataprao at Umrani on the way between Miraj and Bijapur. The Mahomedan forces were threatened on all sides and subjected to all the rigours of a blockade, foraging and provisioning parties being cut off. No one could leave or straggle away from the Mahomedan camp, without instant fear of being captured and put to the sword. There was at the same time a constant skirmishing in front. The Khan was now in great extremity and, acknowledging his defeat, applied for an armistice. Prataprao permitted him to make his way unmolested to Bijapur. The terms of this truce are

[1] The Marathi chronicles call this officer sometimes by the name Bahlol Khan or Ballal Khan, which is properly the name of his father, an Afghan follower of Khan Jahan Lodi. He subsequently arrested Khawas Khan and made himself prime minister at Bijapur.

not known. Shivaji at any rate was greatly displeased at this act of Prataprao and wrote to him severely censuring his conduct, at which he felt so mortified that out of sheer discontent he led his victorious troops to a most remote and isolated scene of operations, an unnecessary excursion to the Pain Ghat in the Berars. This unprofitable expedition was doubly disadvantageous at that particular time. For Shivaji having put forth all his strength in the siege of Phonda, it was essential to have a reserve force in hand nearer home as a check upon Bijapur, and he had expected Prataprao to fulfil this necessary function. He had, therefore, grave reasons to regret these errant and maladroit ways of Prataprao.

While Prataprao was thus giving vent to his feelings of discontent and leading his squadrons miles away from the actual scene of the Deccan war, Abdul Karim put together his scattered forces and again advanced towards Panhala. Shivaji was duly informed of the revived offensive of the Bijapur authorities but was hampered by the absence of a suitable general or army to take the field. As to himself he had staked all his resources upon the conquest of Phonda, an enemy town between his dominions old and new, the fall of which would make his Swarajya realms one connected, inter-linked chain, north and south. Abdul Karim was already operating against Panhala, backed by a numerous army, when Prataprao getting intelligence of this new move hastened into the Deccan plains and was drawing up his cavalry for a charge, when a despatch from Shivaji was placed in his hands, couched in severest terms of censure. Shivaji complained of his disobedience to orders. "The very person," wrote Shivaji, "whom you have allowed to escape scot-free from the most hopeless of predicaments has turned round upon us and is now devastating our lands. On what ground could you put faith in such a man? Had he been crushed on the spot, there could have been no storm of his raising." The letter held Prataprao answerable for all this, and concluded with these peremptory words: "Never come into my presence until you have extinguished the army of Bijapur!" The high-souled commander was stung to the quick and determined at once to attack the enemy. With the most fearful odds against him he charged the serried ranks of the enemy, paying no heed to the risk he incurred. He discarded his usual methods of attack,—to skirmish and tempt, advance and retire, draw the enemy into a pursuit and turn round and overthrow the pursuers. These tactices which had usually stood him in such good stead he now despised in his sullen rage and thought to redeem his laurels by an impetuous onset upon the enemy. Heavy was the price he paid for this impulsive act! The Marathas broke and were cut to pieces. Prataprao himself was slain in the general mêlée. The death of their leader paralysed the Marathas, and the flight became a rout. Abdul Karim pressed the pursuit with great slaughter, until the remnant of the fugitive army found shelter behind the ramparts of Panhala, the garrison of which opened an effective fire and kept back the pursuers. But the unforeseen was yet to happen. Hansaji Mohite, a commander of five thousand had somehow been left behind with his division. On his coming up and learning the fate of those whom Prataprao had led to the charge, he pushed forward and finding the enemy dispersed carelessly in all the excitement of a reckless pursuit about the approaches of Panhala, he fell unexpectedly upon them at Jessary and changed the whole aspect of the battle. For defeat was turned into victory and the erewhile fugitives became themselves the pursuers. Thousands of Mahomedans were overtaken and slain.[1] Such was the battle of Jessary (1674). With a heavy heart Abdul Karim turned his

---

1 *Vide* Sabhasad 78, 79. The Basatin-i-Salatin is silent about Jessary, but gives a long account of the battle of Umrani. Jedhe chronology (p. 191) says Guzar fell at Nivte. We have followed Sabhasad's version of the event. Prof. Sarkar following the account of Narayan Shenvi, British interpreter at Raigad at Shivaji's coronation shortly afterwards, states that Prataprao Guzar with only six Maratha horsemen rushed

foot-steps towards Bijapur, which he reached not without many impediments to his retreat.

Shivaji was highly gratified with the marvellous bravery of the man who in the hour of darkest disaster had so triumphantly turned the scales against the enemy. He extolled the conduct of Hansaji Mohite, appointed him to the cheif command or sir-nobut, and gave him the title of Hambirrao, by which he is generally known. Two illustrious warriors, whose names were destined to become immortal in the history of Maharashtra, won their spurs in this battle under Hansaji's command. Right valiantly had they fought and done deeds of which tales might be told. The heroes whose sterling worth was first seen and admired in this battle were Santaji Ghorpade and Dhanaji Jadhav. They were introduced to Shivaji, who complimented them on their noble prowess and promoted them to higher command. No one mourned the death of Prataprao more than Shivaji himself, as he saw that his stinging words had so much to do with that mental anguish and excitement which had moved him to head a reckless charge and court a hero's death in battle. Shivaji felt he had lost in him one of his bravest and most devoted generals, and had now the melancholy consolation of testifying to his gallant services by making handsome provision for his relations and dependents and marrying his daughter to his second son, Rajaram.

Meanwhile the town of Phonda was undergoing a siege. The town had already been invested for a long time and had so far baffled all attacks. Shivaji was now convinced

---

upon Bahlol Khan in a narrow passage between two hills and the gallant seven were cut down by the swarming hosts of Bijapur, and that the general who rallied the Marathas and led them to a second attack was not Hansaji Mohite but Anandrao, upon whom, according to this version the title of Hambirrao was conferred. This view is apparently supported by two entries in the Jedhe Chronology, dated February and March 1674, page 191. Narayan Shenvi's letter is dated 4th April 1674 (Factory Records, Surat, Vol. 88). But in a subsequent entry immediately afterwards, the Jedhe Chronology speaks of Hambirrao Mohite as the sir-nobut, appointed as such about April 1674.

that there was little wisdom in keeping engaged such a large army for the capture of such an insignificant town and decided to raise the siege, but while doing so, he made a treaty with the subhedar of the fort to the effect that he should not interfere with a force Shivaji intended to station in its neighbourhood to arrest the free movement of the Bijapur army into the ghats below. As long as they would abide by this condition Shivaji undertook not to molest the fort or the territory within its range. It is said that for the purpose of this siege Shivaji had purchased from the French at Surat a supply of ammunition and eighty cannons and that this war material was brought to Rajapur.[1] During this campaign Shivaji conquered and brought under his absolute sway the entire sea-coast from Rajapur to Bardesh, and, having arranged for the military occupation of these new conquests, he returned to Raigad. The whole of Shivaji's cavalry cantoned this season at Chiplun owing to a shortage of water and fodder above the ghats occasioned by a scanty rain-fall.

While Shivaji's armies were occupied with the protracted siege of Phonda, the united Abyssinian and Mogul fleets made fresh descents upon Shivaji's Konkaṇ dominions. Many naval encounters took place between Shivaji's fleet and the Abyssinian sea-forces but with little success on Shivaji's side. Many of his war-ships were captured and borne off by the invaders. There were repeated irruptions of the Mahomedan fleets upon the territory of Coorla, and in spite of the protests made by the governor Aungier, these fleets constantly sailed into Bombay harbour and made it the base of their operations against Salsette. They abstained from no species of violence against the inhabitants, plundering, massacring and kidnapping men, women and children to be sold into slavery. Aungier continued vainly to represent to them, that by these rapacious acts, they would bring down upon him and the island of Bombay

1 The ammunition was purchased from the French East India Company founded by Colbert.

the vengeful bands of Shivaji. At length an army of three thousand came down from Raigad and, engaging the Abyssinans in a decisive contest, put them to rout. When they were thus beaten and a good many of them put to the sword, they finally weighed anchor and quitted the harbour of Bombay, fearing lest the victorious Marathas might enter the harbour and make a holocaust of their fleets.

CHAPTER XXIII

THE CROWNING OF SHIVAJI, 1674

THE victory of Hambirrao over Abdul Karim had cost many lives to the Bijapur army which remained appreciably crippled for some time. Neither was it possible to muster a new army against Shivaji, nor did a capable general offer himself for a renewal of the contest. For a long time to come, Khawas Khan thought it was imperative to let Shivaji alone. Nor was there any likelihood of trouble brewing from Aurangabad. The subhedar there had, as we have seen, an amicable understanding with Shivaji and was not over-anxious to risk his troops beyond his frontiers. He considered it a great matter for congratulation that the periodic incursions of the Marathas were stopped and was anxious to keep good relations with Shivaji. Aurangzeb was involved in complications in the north. He no longer considered Shivaji the insignificant enemy he once had been inclined to believe him to be. A personal defeat at the hands of one whom he had affected to despise would be not merely a disgrace but a danger to the empire. He remembered too the treachery he had often practised upon Shivaji and feared the Maratha chief might seek to avenge himself upon him. He had also heard of the valour and bravery of the generals under Shivaji and could not help contrasting with them the knights of the sorrowful countenance whom he was able to send upon the Deccan campaigns. Could he count on the co-operation of Golconda and Bijapur against this incipient power? He who had done his best to subvert them from their foundations? Verily, the Southern Mahomedan feared the Mogul more than the Maratha. Nay, the emperor was rather glad at the rise of the new power, so far as it had weakened the powers of Islam in the Deccan. For he was biding his time to sweep down upon the Deccan with the avalanche of a Mogul army and overwhelm the Deccan sultanates, and after them the Maratha Power,—so he proposed to himself. No need then to quicken the movements of his tardy generals or send them the re-inforcements they kept crying for. There was indeed Shivaji's application for a treaty as mentioned in the last chapter. The shrewd monarch was not to be over-reached in this manner and saw plainly enough that it was only a make-shift alliance that Shivaji wanted. Such being the attitude of Aurangzeb, Shivaji saw that for the present there was no fear from this quarter. The only other power to consider was the state of Golconda. The prospect of any storm blowing from this state had not yet arisen. As things went for the present there were good relations indeed. The annual tribute came with clock-work regularity, and the chief minister Madanna was most favourably disposed towards Shivaji.

Having thus no need to dread the Islamic powers, Shivaji thought it a favourable opportunity to assume the insignia of royalty and be duly crowned king of his people. From the death of Shahaji, Shivaji had already borne the title of Raja and had struck his own coins. But it was felt desirable to consecrate his authority by the solemn sanction of the Hindu religion, by going through the elaborate ritual prescribed by Hindu usage for a consecrated monarchy. Unless he was invested with the visible symbols of regal pomp and power, the throne, the canopy and the umbrella of state, there would always be an appreciable deficiency or inferiority in the homage of his people and the respect of his enemies, in the opinion of princes and states, and the few agents and factors of foreign powers then established in India. Without such a religious confirmation of his power, both Indian princes and foreigners might continue to reckon him as an exalted polygar and confound his systematic war programme with the random depredations of a free-booting chief. These thoughts were now passing through his mind. It was necessary to rally the Maratha nobles still serving the Mahomedan monarchies in the south or carrying on independent wars and marauding excursions on their own account. It was necessary to teach them that the new power that had sprung up in their midst was based on broader and deeper foundations and was not an isolated effort for dynastic aggrandisement. It was necessary to unfurl the standard of Maratha unity, freedom and self-government, rally their wavering spirits, and unite their wayward forces under the ægis of a Maharashtra monarchy. To this end he had laboured for thirty years. The standard, to which all Marathas were to rally as an undoubted national cause, was by the nature of things required to be the standard of an independent sovereignty.

It is rather a matter for astonishment that this step should have been postponed to so late a period of his triumphant career. But in the first place as long as Shahaji lived—and he died only in 1664—Shivaji would not have cared to have his name emblazoned with royal pomp, while his father was content to shine by the reflected glory of Bijapur. Had Shahaji elected to remain in Maharashtra when he paid his last visit to the land of his fathers, it is possible that Shivaji, as was to be expected of his filial devotion and his strict adherence to religious ideals and precedents, might have invested him with the sovereign power and conducted the administration in his name. The ten years that had elapsed since the death of Shahaji had been a period of stress and excitement, chequered with Mogul and Mahomedan wars, when the best of his time and resources were taken up with the fortification and entrenchment of his strongholds, the maintenance of his fleet and armies and the consolidation of his possessions. The bustle and excitement of war allowed no time for thoughts of coronation, pageantry and ceremonial. Now that peace reigned undisturbed over his varied realms, the thought of the assumption of the ensigns of sovereignty again recurred to his mind.

An incident occurred at his court which led Shivaji to hasten this event. There was a dinner at his palace to which invitations were issued to the leading Maratha nobility. Due arrangements were made in the banquet-hall where the guests were to be entertained. A cushioned seat or *chaurang* was in the centre, higher than the rest. This seat was intended for Shivaji, and to the left and right the guests were to seat themselves at dinner. Among the assembled guests were included the ancient Maratha nobility, the Mohites, the Mahadiks, the Shirkes, the Nimbalkars, the Ghatges, the Jadhavs and scions of other families. On noticing the elevated seat unoccupied, evidently reserved for Shivaji, they were chagrined in the highest degree and their vexation was so great that they began without respect for place or person to criticise the arrangement: "And is Shivaji now become such a great personage in the land, and have we become mere cyphers? We the representatives of illustrious ancient families, entitled to the princely honour of the *morchel*?[1] The honours and dignities we have enjoyed Shivaji's father never earned for himself. It is an insult to us to be seated on a lower level than Shivaji. Far better for us to leave the hall than submit to such an indignity." Muttering such complaints they were about to leave the banquet-hall, when the officers of the household tried to pacify them, entreating them not to irritate Shivaji on the auspicious occasion but to represent their grievance to him personally at a more suitable time. However the commotion in the hall reached Shivaji's ears and he was considerably embarrassed at the ill humour of his guests. The representatives of some of the second grade noble families, however, on being privately interviewed by Shivaji said they had no objection to the banquet arrangements. Shivaji then spoke privately to the great sardars like the Ghorpades, Nimbalkars and others and asked what their grounds of complaint were, upon which they made answer that they were the hereditary officers of the Mahomedan sultans for four or five centuries past, they could not brook Shivaji's taking precedence over them at such a social function, and that it was for Shivaji to consider the matter. Shivaji

1 The *morchel* was a tuft of pea-cock feathers used as a fan, and waved over the heads of princely personages as an attribute of royalty.

replied that if they made so much of their family prestige they ought not to attend his court. If need arose for their presence, they might be invited. Those who did not like the banquet arrangements had leave to depart. And with these words he presented "pan" to his obstinate guests, the usual ceremony according to Indian etiquette for bidding farewell to a departing visitor. This incident more than anything else impressed upon Shivaji the necessity of proclaiming himself a crowned king in these parts of India, since for lack of such a ceremony even the Maratha nobles showed a certain hesitation in recognizing his sovereign authority.

While these thoughts were revolving in his mind it is said that his tutelary deity appeared to him in a vision and assured him that his desire to be duly crowned and invested with the insignia of sovereignty would by her grace be fulfilled, and that one who had fought so nobly and strenuously in the cause of his country's gods and religion deserved more than any one else the divine attributes of sovereignty. Encouraged by the thought of a divine sanction to his proposal, he broached the subject to his mother and on obtaining her support submitted it to others. Shivaji sent a confidential officer to communicate his intention to Ramdas, his spiritual adviser, who cordially approved of the proposal. Other persons of sage and saintly character in his kingdom were similarly consulted and concurred in the proposal. The acute scholars and learned expounders of Hindu law, the pillars of the Brahman community, were next invited to a council, with all the honour due to their learning, palanquins and other conveyances being sent to bring them to court from their residences. To this council the great nobles, commanders and ministers of state were also summoned. The question of a solemn coronation was submitted to the meeting. They all expressed themselves in favour of the idea and it was unanimously decided that Shivaji should go through the coronation ceremony according to the Hindu Shastras and be invested with all the insignia of royalty.

The next question to investigate was what things were essential according to Shastric requirements for a complete coronation ceremonial on orthodox Hindu lines. And here an initial difficulty presented itself which rendered the traditional ceremony of a Hindu coronation well-nigh impossible. For according to the prescription of the shastras only the twice-born who had duly gone through the ceremony of the investiture of the sacred thread were capable of going through the forms of a shastric coronation. To all others this ceremony was denied. The circumstance that Shivaji had not been invested with the sacred thread placed him in the eyes of the pandits and the preceptors of the Hindu law in the category of Shudras or serfs. The pandits, therefore, declared that in his case a shastric coronation was impossible. Shivaji was then already far past the age for such an investiture, being now forty-six years of age, and had been married more than once and had children by his wives. A man of such an advanced age, a husband and a father, could by no means be capable of such investiture.

It was not easy to cut this knot, but one of Shivaji's most trusty and sagacious officers, Balaji Avji Chitnis, suggested a remedy. He advised Shivaji not to rest satisfied with the decision of the local pandits but to appeal to other shastris in India. He said that hitherto with God's grace he had triumphed over every difficulty and achieved his highest ideals and there was no reason why he should be baffled in this one object. He then spoke of a learned scholar of Benares, Gaga Bhatt by name, who was versed in all branches of Sanskrit learning--the four Vedas, the six shastras or sciences and the commentaries on the law,—and had attained an unrivalled reputation in India for his learning. His decisions on knotty questions of Hindu law were accepted by other pandits. His pronouncements carried almost a pontifical authority with them. The officer advised Shivaji to make a reference to this learned pandit on the question of his coronation, especially as he then happened to be at Paithan. He proposed that Gaga Bhatt should be invited along with the other renowned pandits of Paithan.[1] He would not refuse the invitation, as he could not but have heard of Shivaji's fame. Shivaji was gratified at this suggestion and Balaji Avji was deputed to invite Gaga Bhatt from Paithan and bring him under a safe escort. A sum of ten thousand rupees and the necessary paraphernalia of horses and palanquins were placed at Balaji Avji's disposal for this mission.[2]

On his arrival at Paithan Balaji had an interview with Gaga Bhatt and communicated to him Shivaji's proposal. At Gaga Bhatt's instance a meeting of the pandits was held at Paithan for the discussion of this question. After a long debate it was unanimously decided that there was no objection to Shivaji's going through the ceremonial

---

[1] The family of Gaga Bhatt belonged to Paithan, which was famous as a repository of Hindu learning. Many of his ancestors and descendants have written authoritative works on Hindu religious usages. The family attained a celebrity for its learning and scholarship at Benares, and the descendants of the family still enjoy their high prestige among the Hindu princes of North India.

[2] According to the chronicles of Sabhasad and Chitragupta Gaga Bhatt came uninvited, hearing the renown of Shivaji, to pay a visit to his court. He was treated with proper hospitality and pleased with what he saw of Shivaji's court spoke as follows :—

"The forms of Kshatriya duty have been utterly extinguished during the Kali Yuga. The earth is overrun with Yavanas (Mahomedans) who have usurped the thrones of kings. No spark of valour is left in the warriors of the Solar or the Lunar race. Sacrifices are stopped ; forms of duty forgotten ; the Brahman Dharma eclipsed ; the great shrines have lost their expiatory virtue. It is only you who have put forth great valour, defeated the Mahomedan sultans, quieted Aurangzeb, vanquished his pro-consuls, won a great kingdom, and maintained in your power a hundred thousand cavalry, three hundred and sixty forts, and great wealth and possessions. This being so, you are yet without a consecrated throne. It is, therefore, my wish and the wish of many other Hindus to crown you king and have you saluted as a king of the royal umbrella by other rulers. Without a formal crowning a ruling king has no honour. By getting yourself formally crowned, you will complete the humiliation of Aurangzeb and the other sultans. Do you, therefore, indulge us in this our desire?" These words of Gaga Bhatt induced Shivaji to take up the idea of a formal coronation.

of a shastric coronation after the manner of the Rajput princes of Jaipur, Udepur and other places. Gaga Bhatt was then brought by Balaji to Raigad, where he was received with all the honour and respect due to his learning, Shivaji himself going forward to welcome him to the fort. A procession was formed and the pandit conducted to the mansion selected for his residence, amid pomp and music.

Shivaji then convoked another assembly of the pandits, ministers of state, and citizens of note, at which Gaga Bhatt and the learned men of Paithan were introduced. The question of the coronation was again taken up for discussion, and the pros and cons having been fully considered by the meeting, the learned Gaga Bhatt delivered his decision as follows :- "That it appears to this meeting that Shivaji, a scion of the princely stock of the Sesodia family, is of Kshatriya descent, and that though his forefathers, having crossed the Narbada, came to be known as Marathas and gave up the investiture and other ceremonies of the Kshatriya class, the Kshatriya character of their descendants is not thereby impaired or extinguished. That, as in the case of the princely dynasties of Jaipur, Udepur and others, the investiture of the sacred thread precedes the coronation ceremonial proper, the same proceeding may be followed in the case of Shivaji, and that such proceeding would by no means be contrary to the precepts of the shastric law or to usage and precedent. That the fact that the original stock of the Sesodias at Udepur have always been distinguished by the insignia of royalty is a special circumstance to be considered in the case of Shivaji. As to the objection that the investiture ceremony was time-barred by Shivaji's age and the circumstance that he was already a husband and a father, it was to be understood that in this case the rite of investiture would be wholly exceptional, curing a defect occasioned by unavoidable adverse circumstances and to be viewed only as a preliminary part of the coronation rites, the whole constituting together one grand, integral, religious function." This learned decision was accepted by the pandits of Paithan and the Swarajya dominions and it was unanimously resolved that Shivaji should celebrate the investiture and coronation rites.

Gratified at this decision, Shivaji hastened to make all the necessary preparations for the ceremony. The waters of the sacred rivers and the several seas, horses and elephants with the auspicious marks, the skins of tigers and beasts of chase, the lion-supported chair of state or throne, vases of gold and silver and other sacred vessels-all these were provided for. The state astrologers were ordered to investigate and determine the most auspicious time for the assumption of the title. They reported that the thirteenth day of the first half of Jesht (the 6th of June 1674 A. D.) of the current year of the cyclic name of Anand was the most propitious time for the installation ceremony.

Invitations were sent to all the notable gentry and nobility of Maharashtra, to ministers and commanders, to subject princes as well as independent kings. To start with, it was determined that Raigad should be the capital town of the newly inaugurated monarchy. It seemed the best of all the places in Shivaji's possession; it satisfied approximately the shastric conditions for the capital of a great kingdom, some of which were that the site should be sacred ground in the neighbourhood of holy places and the waters of a noble stream, that there should be an abundant supply of water and facilities for the construction of tanks and reservoirs, that the territory around should be fertile, and above all it should be impregnable to the assaults of an enemy. It was resolved that the coronation celebrations should be held at Raigad.

Shivaji had already erected a spacious mansion at Raigad for his own residence, with buildings for his various departments of stores, classified under eighteen heads. Here were the offices and residences of the great ministers of state and the secretariat staff.[1] The durbar-hall

[1] The Shivdigvijay describes many other halls which were erected

where the throne was installed was spacious enough to accommodate thousands of spectators without any discomfort. From all these arrangements, it appears clear that Shivaji had from the beginning intended to make Raigad the seat of his government. When the pandits sanctioned this decision, the palace-walls were painted and decorated in the best style of the country. The throne-room was adorned with a rich canopy and with tapestries of rare designs and texture. The throne itself was adorned with a richly embroidered canopy supported upon four columns plated with gold and fringed with strings and tassels of pearls. The other public places and edifices on the fort were similarly painted and decorated in expectation of the event. Due arrangements were made for the residence and for the comfort of the distinguished guests invited to witness the ceremony, among whom were distinguished Brahmans and subject princes. Spacious pavilions were erected for the celebration of coronation banquets and other functions. Persons showing any kind of skill were liberally patronized on the occasion. Indian musicians, both vocalist and instrumental, professional dancing girls, and entertainers of all kinds were called in large numbers for the amusement of the guests. As the feasting of Brahmans is always a special feature of such auspicious ceremonies, large pavilions were erected at more than five places, each pavilion accommodating at one and the same time more than four thousand guests. At each banquet-hall, a separate staff of cooks, waiters, attendants and overseers was appointed, and these men had orders to alter their menus and principal dishes from day to day. Separate pavilions were set up for the banqueting of friends, relations, officers and ministers of state.

---

such as the *Vivek sabha* for the debates of learned pandits, the *Pragat sabha* for giving audience to the poor and hearing their disputes, the *Nyaya sabha* the audience of Justice, the *Prabodh sabha* the hall of *Kirtans* and *Puranas*, the *Ratnagar* sabha for connoisseurs of gems and jewels, the *Niti sabha* for giving audience to distinguished foreigners etc., likewise also halls to serve as seraglios, chapels, baths etc. etc.

The fort and its lower slope were thus crowded with tents and pavilions. A staff of supervising officers maintained a general control over the stores, with clerks in charge of each camp, who were under instructions to supply the needs of each guest, small or great, and for that purpose heaps of grain and other provisions were brought together. These officers were carefully trained in their duties, which they discharged under fixed regulations. The result was that the vast assemblage of guests were entertained in a style of hospitality which evoked universal admiration.

On the fourth day of the opening half of the month of Jesht the ceremony of the investiture of the sacred thread was commenced. It lasted for two days, and during this period a hundred thousand Brahmans were feasted and received a *dakshina* of a rupee each, Brahmans versed in the Vedas and the shastras receiving the honorarium befitting their position and learning. Upon the celebration of the investiture rites, the proper preliminaries of the coronation ceremony were taken in hand, commencing with the sixth day of Jesht. With propitiatory rites in honour of the God Ganpati, with which every religious rite must commence according to Hindu usage, and of the stars and the planets, the coronation sacrifice was duly begun. During these days, till the final consummation of the sacrifice, both Shivaji and the officiating priests observed a rigid fast subsisting only on milk and fruit. But throughout the week while the host observed a fast there was a continual round of feasts to the Brahmans, fifty thousand of them being daily entertained, with frequent changes in the dishes. The other guests received the same hospitality, and were entertained with musical concerts and other social amusements. Song, dance, and revelry reigned supreme in all parts of the fort.

At length came the auspicious day, the 13th of Jesht. There was a large assemblage present to witness the *Abhishek* or solemn religious bath, the principal feature of the coronation ceremony. As partners in the labours of the state, the chief ministers likewise had to undergo similar solemn ablutions. In the first place, therefore, the eight ministers of state were duly appointed or confirmed in their several high offices. Next after them the nominations of the king's two principal secretaries, or personal amanuenses, were made. The functionaries in charge of the various departments and stores, as also the commanders in charge of towns and provinces were each either appointed or confirmed. All these functionaries went through the preliminary consecrated bath along with Shivaji. More varied and elaborate ablutions prescribed by religious sanction were then performed by Shivaji; such as the bath with various kinds of earth, the bath with a compound of milk, ghee, etc. called the *panch-gavya* dissolved in water, the bath in the water of the sacred rivers like the Ganges, and on the top of them all, the bath with the *panchamrit* or the nectareous bath, in which milk, curds, ghee, honey and sugar were blended together. These solemn ablutions over, the bathers were arrayed in robes of silver white, with flowers and wreaths, gold and jewelled ornaments, and the sacred sandal-wood or *gandha* mark impressed upon their foreheads. Shivaji then took his seat upon a gold-plated little stool made of a particular kind of wood, the wood of a pulpy tree like that of the genus Ficus being specially recommended by the shastras. When Shivaji was seated upon this quaint little stool, which was just a cubit and a quarter high and the same in width, the senior queen and the heir-apparent were asked to sit by his side.[1] The principal ministers of state then stood in the prescribed order around their king. First of all the Peshwa or chief minister with a gold vase filled with ghee stood due east of Shivaji; Hambirrao Mohite, the commander-in-chief, with a silver vase filled with milk stood due south

[1] The senior queen who took part in the Abhishek bath was Soyarabai, the mother of Prince Rajaram and the heir-apparent was of course Prince Sambhaji.

Ramchandra Nilkanth,[1] the Amatya (or Muzumdar i. e. finance minister), with a copper vase full of curds stood due west and Raghunathrao, the ecclesiastical minister, with a gold vase filled with honey stood due north. Next to these were large earthen jars filled with the waters of various rivers and seas.[2] The four cardinal points thus adjusted, the remaining four ministers of state stood mid-way between them, north-east, north-west etc., one of them holding the royal umbrella, another the fan imperial and the other two waving each a *chamar* or fly-whisk, ensigns of Indian royalty.[3] Facing Shivaji stood before him two personal amanuenses, Balaji Avji and his brother Chimnaji, to the right and left respectively, displaying writing materials in their hands. Next to these ministers to right and left stood the other functionaries of state, and next the subject princes, the nobility and the gentry. The real ablution or Abhishek proper was then begun. A capacious urn of gold, with a hundred holes drilled at the bottom, was filled with scented water and the streaming urn held above Shivaji's head, and at the same time the contents of the various vases held by the ministers in their hands were poured out upon him, to the accompaniment of the sacred chants recited by the assembled priests. This was the final ceremony of the Abhiṣhek, which was followed up by a wild outburst of flutes, trumpets and drums and the singing and dancing of the singers and nautch-girls present. After this Shivaji was bathed

1 He was the son of Nilo Sondev. Sabhasad gives the name as Naro Nilkanth.

2 The great rivers, the water of which was thus used, were the Ganges, the Jumna, the Krishna, the Godaveri and the Cauveri.

3 These ministers were Annaji Datto (the Pant-sachiv), Janardan Pandit Hanmante (the Sumant), Dattaji Pandit (the Mantri), and Balaji Pandit (the Nyayadhish or lord chief justice.) But some of the names are differently given in the different versions. For instance, Chitnis gives the name of Trimbak Sondev instead of that of Janardan Hanmante and Sabhasad gives the name of Ramchandra, the son of Trimbak instead of that of Hanmante. Sabhasad gives the name of Niraji instead of Dattaji Pandit (Mantri), and Chitnis gives the name of Niraji Ravji instead of that of Balaji Pandit (Nyayadhish).

again and the auspicious *arti*—a quaint platter with lighted wicks—was waved over him by the matrons, and he was made to view himself as reflected in a bronze ewer filled with ghee and as also in mirrors before he was permitted to put on his dress—which was pure white—for the final installation ceremony.

The throne was a piece of splendid workmanship, constructed according to the precepts of the shastras. First of all, the basal platform was made of planks of banyan and fig-trees, wood considered sacred in the shastras, and especially prescribed for coronation purposes. This dais was decorated with gold plate, engraved with devices of silvan beasts on its four sides, the lion, the tiger, the hyena, the cat and the ox. On the golden dais stood eight columns each supporting a lion in gold, upon which the cushioned seat was placed. The columns bore in embossed relief devices of flowers, leaves, trees and creepers or birds and fishes, or figures representing nymphs dancing to the accompaniment of string instruments.[1] The cushion consisted first of deer-skin and tiger-skin, with a layer of gold coins between them. Upon this was piled up a soft cushion of cotton-down encased in velvet, with the back and side cushions embroidered in gold. From the basal pedestal upwards there rose an ornamental silver plate called the *prabhaval* forming the back of the cushioned throne and surmounting it with a metal canopy of gold, studded with brilliants and fringed with pearls. Above all rose a canopy of cloth of gold raised upon outer pillars and glittering with pearl tassels. At the entrance of the durbar-hall a horse and an elephant chosen for the auspicious marks upon their bodies were standing in readiness, decked with gold trappings and embroidered housings. As the auspicious hour drew near, Shivaji performed a solemn *puja* or worship of the God Vishnu, a golden image being used for the purpose, and when the puja was

[1] Some chronicle writers affirm that the gold columns and sculptures upon the throne required gold of the weight of three candies, thirty-two seers, and thirty-two masas i. e. nearly four candies weight of gold.

over he held the image in his right hand. At last when the inauguration time came, Shivaji saluted the Brahmans and received their benedictions amid Vedic hymns. He made his reverent salutation to his mother, who acknowledged it with a stream of affectionate blessings. And now holding the image of Vishnu still in his right hand Shivaji advanced to the throne. Approaching the right hand side of the throne, Shivaji made a slight genuflexion with the right knee, saluted the consecrated throne, and with his face to the east, ascended it without touching it with his feet. The eight ministers of state took their stations at the eight columns of the lion-throne, standing with their hands clasped in reverence. First in order the ecclesiastical minister Panditrao took his post on the right and the chief minister or Peshwa on the left. Next behind them, the commander-in-chief (sir-nobut) on the right and the Amatya (finance-minister) on the left. Behind them stood the other four ministers, the Sumant (or Dabir i. e. foreign secretary) and the Sachiv (or Surnis i. e. record-keeper) to the right and the left, and the Mantri (or Waknis i. e. home secretary and lord privy seal) and the Nyayadhish (chief justice) also to the right and the left respectively. The moment the installation was completed, the air was rent with the mingled din of drums and trumpets. The musicians and nautch-girls struck up their rhythmic melodies. The roar of cannon resounded from Raigad which was taken up by the guns of the surrounding hill-forts, as previously arranged, one after another. Thus every fort in Shivaji's dominions joined in the jubilant boom of guns.

After ascending the auspicious throne, Shivaji changed his white robes for scarlet, decked himself with the usual ornaments of Indian royalty, the necklace, the plume, the pearl-crest, the pearl pendants etc, and consecrating his sword and bow and arrows with solemn chants and *puja* took the weapons in his hands. Thus attired he came out to have flowers of silver and gold showered upon him and the auspicious *arti* waved around him by a group of sixteen Brahman matrons, who received rich presents of female costumes and ornaments. The concluding ceremonies after the enthronement were now taken in hand and the benedictions of the officiating priests were received. Munificent presents were made to them. Gaga Bhatt received an honorarium of one lakh, besides valuable presents of wearing apparel and jewellery. The priests presiding over the coronation sacrifice received five thousand each, the officiating chaplain rupees twenty-four thousand. Brahmans of learning and eminence received honorariums ranging from two hundred to one thousand rupees each; Brahmans of the rank and file rupees twenty-five per head. Ample largesses were also bestowed upon gosavis, hermits and mendicants of all kinds ranging from two to five rupees each. Persons of saintly character and Brahmans of pre-eminent piety received grants of inam land. Finally, after the manner of great Indian sovereigns, Shivaji was weighed against gold and the precious treasure equivalent to his weight, amounting to sixteen thousand[1] pagodas, was distributed among the Brahmans.

The ministers of state, subhedars and the various departmental officers, both public and private, received their titles and robes of office with various personal decorations. All moreover received the sanads or patents of their various offices. The presents made to the eight ministers of state included gold-embroidered state robes, pearl crests and pendants, sword and shield, horse and elephant, the chief minister receiving besides the special insignia of his high position, viz. a jari-patka (a cloth of gold banner, an honour also conferred upon the chief commander), a nobut or state drum, and a pair of gold handled chowries (ornamental hair tassels) to be waved about him on state processions. When the state ministers came forward to greet him with their salutation, presented

[1] These 16,000 pagodas amounted to about one hundred and forty pounds in weight.

their nazars (loyalty offerings) and received their patents of offices, Shivaji bestowed upon each of them a lakh of pagodas. Balaji Avji was then invested with the robes of Chitnis or personal secretary, with similar presents, and next after him Chimnaji Avji, Balaji's brother and colleague. For each of the eight ministers a *mutaliq* (deputy) was appointed. They also came forward to receive their special robes. The lesser officers on the civil and military establishments received their respective honours.

When the distribution of honours and presentation of nazars was at an end and the levee was dissolved, Shivaji went in a royal procession for a solemn thanks-giving at the temples of the gods. He mounted a horse with gold and jewelled trappings and rode into the outer court, where dismounting from the horse he got into a golden howdah borne by a magnificent elephant gaily decked with gold and rich embroidered housings, fringed with pearls. At the head of the elephant the chief commander of the forces took his seat, holding the trident in one hand and with the other waving the morchel (a brush of pea-cock feathers waved at royal processions before the king.) In the rear part of the howdah, the prime minister took his seat, waving the morchel from behind. The other ministers and their deputies joined the procession, each riding his own elephant as also the select nobility and commanders, on elephants or horse-back. In the van of the whole procession were the elephants bearing the two principal standards of the state, first the Jari-patka or the grand ensign of cloth of gold and secondly the Bhagva-zenda or the orange-ochre ensign. Behind them marched the ensigns of the Peshwa (prime-minister) and the Senapati (chief commander) also supported on elephants. Immediately after rode the commanders of the royal horse and officers of the horse guard musketeers with their steeds accoutred with gold and silver trappings, marching gallantly muskets in hand and forming the vanguard. After this cavalcade followed gun-carriages with artillery, horse-carriages and distinguished generals on elephants or horse-back. After them came on foot slingers, swordsmen, archers, lancers and miscellaneous classes of foot-soldiers and behind them the squires and body-guards of commanders and a division of musketeers. Then followed military drums, tabors, tambourines and other war-like musical instruments; next them fifty led elephants; then a corps of one hundred cavalry and sky-rockets mounted on camel transports: then again another troop of fifty led elephants, and behind them the softer and more melodious music of clarions, hautboys, drums mounted on horse-back, horns and trumpets. Behind them marched bards, minstrels, and Indian troubadours; next after them, flag-staff-bearers, ensigns, spearmen, macebearers and ushers with staves; and after them came gymnasts, athletes and champion wrestlers of the Maharashtra palaestra, mounted upon elephants. Behind them all came Shivaji in his gold howdah, a company of brave Mavalis, gaily accoutred and glittering with ornaments, serving as an immediate body-guard and surrounding his elephant at a respectable distance. Behind the king marched the elephants of the ministers and departmental chiefs and an infantry force brought up the rear.

It is needless to say that in expectation of the coronation procession, the streets were cleansed and decorated, and in many places were washed and beautifully laid out with picturesque designs in coloured powders or *rangoli*, an accomplishment of high class women in India. The houses were painted in gay colours and beautifully draped with tapestry. Flags, buntings, arches were seen everywhere. The procession went from temple to temple, making offerings to the gods and liberal largesses to the Brahmans. On the return journey, married women stepped forth from their threshold and waved the arti at different places on the road or scattered flowers and *durva* grass from the windows and balconies. At the palace gate Shivaji changed into a chariot and on arriving at the court-yard into a palanquin and so came on to the durbar-hall, where at his entrance he went through a quaint little Indian ceremony for appeasing or counter-acting the influence of the evil eye after all this triumph.[1]

Entering the inner apartments he first paid his worship at the chapel of his tutelary deity, and then proceeded to salute his mother. He then visited the ladies' apartments where he was welcomed and honoured with auspicious arti by his queens, who received from him royal tokens of his regard and affection. Returning to the hall Shivaji again mounted the throne and held durbar. The courtiers offered nazars and made their salutes with humility. The durbar was dispersed with the distribution of *pan*, flowers and attar of rose. The Brahmans were sumptuously banqueted, and Shivaji dined in company with his friends and guests. The solemn rites were now over. Every detail of that extraordinary and well-nigh obsolete ceremonial and pageant had been worked out with marvellous precision. The subject princes and other visitors took their leave, having received from Shivaji many a token of his esteem and affection. The different *artistes* and musicians who had enlivened the entertainments with their various talents received ample rewards for their labours. The spectators went home singing the praises of Shivaji and his greatness. The whole celebration is said to have cost a crore and forty-two lakhs of pagodas.

From the date of the coronation a new era was inaugurated,[2] which was to be observed in all public business and by all people throughout Shivaji's dominions. The

---

[1] A jar of water and a handful of salt, lemon, pepper etc. are waved up and down the person of him from whom the evil eye is to be taken off and poured out on the ground.

[2] The new era was known as the Coronation Shaka, not called personally after his name as Shivaji Shaka. According to Mr. Sardesai (Marathi Riyasat, 1915 edition, page 362) this era was used in public papers and proclamations in the Maratha state for about 104 years. Mr. Sardesai's statement is based upon certain papers published in the Report of the Bharat Itihas Sanshodhak Mandal of Poona for the Shaka 1835.

date of the coronation and the inauguration of the new era was the 13th day of the first half of the Hindu month of Jesht in the year 1596 of Shalivahan and corresponds to the 6th of June 1674. Shivaji now adopted the name and style of "Kshatriya Kulavatansa Shri Raja Shiv Chhatrapati," the meaning of which title is, "the Ornament of the Kshatriya Race, His Majesty the Raja Shiv, Lord of the Royal Umbrella." The noble resolve of his youthful years, the labours of a life-time, were crowned with rich fruition,—a free kingdom, a crowning, the inauguration of a new era.

It is not needful to describe with what sad thoughts the Mahomedan monarchies must have received the news of this solemn enthronement. Up to this date they had endeavoured to persuade themselves that whatever Shivaji's triumphs and laurels, he was after all a polygar chief, not an anointed sovereign like themselves and that in consequence his name could not stir the depths of national loyalty in the people's heart. When his rebellion was crushed his name would sink into oblivion and no land-marks of his memory would be left behind. From this pet theory of theirs they were rudely awakened. Not conquest, but union, was the real key-note of his success or the end of his ambition. That Shivaji should conquer the fairest provinces and the strongest fortresses in the country and sit down with folded hands without endeavouring to unite the affections of the people towards himself and sealing the enduring compact of relationship between sovereign and his subjects, for the attainment of which a solemn consecration and coronation seemed to be the only road, was quite unthinkable. When the Brahmans of Maharashtra seemed to waver in their opinion and make mountains of shastric difficulties, he attained the crowning glory of his noble ambition with the help of the learned exponents of the law at Paithan and Benares. Sooth to say, no Brahman or pandit of the time had a doubt about his Kshatriya origin, except that a few purists vainly attempted to rank him as a Shudra as being what in the language of the law amounted to a non-user of Kshatriya rites and privileges. To clear the mist from their eyes the clear logic of Gaga Bhatt and other scholars was necessary. But to the great people reposing beneath the shade of the Sahyadri, with that strong common sense and gratitude which have at all times been the back-bone of their national character, it could scarcely have been matter of doubt, despite the croaking of a few idlers, that he, who had delivered Maharashtra from the yoke of Islam and given his country-men the first taste of freedom and independence, deserved the name of Kshatriya more than those who masqueraded under it. It was an evidence of great foresight on his part that Shivaji established beyond the shadow of doubt the foundations and ensured for all purposes the stability and permanence of a puissant Hindu monarchy, by the solemn pomp and magnificence of his enthronement. He immediately acquired greater prestige in the eyes of the Rajput princes of the north and of the European settlers domiciled in the country, whether French, or British or Portuguese. Even Mahomedan powers—Bijapur, Golconda, and Delhi—had now to show greater deference towards him. Heretofore his name had been a terror, now it became a terror not unmingled with respect.

While the coronation festivities were still running their course, a tragic event took place which put an end to the revelry. This was the death of the aged Jijabai. She did not long survive the coronation. Her work was done. The seed she had sown had borne abundant fruit. The early stimulus she had applied to her son had awakened into life a whole people. Her sage advice had accomplished more constructive work than councils and cabinets. She had seen step by step the realization of her dreams; she had seen her son's career of victory; she had seen the crowning triumph of a united people enthroning her son in their affections more firmly than an earthly throne and the final inauguration of a new era. She had seen all this and now closed her eyes in peace. She succumbed to a sudden illness within ten or twelve days after Shivaji's coronation. Coming so suddenly upon the crest of the coronation triumphs, her death overwhelmed Shivaji with grief. That his mother should rejoice with his joys and triumph in his triumphs was the highest of his personal ambitions. Without her, these joys and triumphs seemed to have no savour, his kingdom seemed a wilderness, his wealth as dross. And so he mourned. How intense his love and affection was towards his mother was now seen by all his people. The solemn obsequies were performed and lakhs of rupees were spent on the funeral ceremonies. The four months of autumn that followed her death, Shivaji spent at Raigad, where she had died. These four months were spent in mourning. During this long period, Shivaji never once sat on the throne. It was on the fifth day of the first half of Ashvin (October) that he sat in durbar, mounting the throne again after an auspicious ceremony. After this, in company with the eight ministers and army he left Raigad to offer his worship at the temple of the Devi (goddess) at Pratapgad, whence he proceeded to visit his spiritual preceptor Ramdas Swami, and make pilgrimages to the temple of Mahadev at Shikhar, and to that of Khandoba at Jejuri, and again returned to Raigad.

CHAPTER XXIV

THE WHEELS OF GOVERNMENT

It is proper at this stage to review the institutions of Shivaji and the organization of his administrative machinery. The enthronement ceremony helped to deepen the foundations of his power; his constructive genius, to broaden and regulate it. In attempting this survey from such scanty material as is at our disposal, we may preface it with the observation that the administrative system hereinafter described was not introduced abruptly after the coronation but was slowly and tentatively evolved and practically received its final form at the inauguration of the coronation era. To a certain extent indeed it will be no exaggeration to say that a certain faint outline of the future plans was already conceived and partially acted upon before the gathering of armies and territorial conquests.[1]

To start with, Shivaji was fairly familiar with the contemporary administrative systems, both Hindu and Mahomedan. He had also a fair acquaintance with the ancient Hindu systems as gleaned from the Puranas. He had weighed well in his own mind the merits and demerits, of each system and from a study of their methods evolved for himself a system in harmony with the spirit of his age, the need of the country and the highest average good, as he conceived it, of the rayat. It will again be no exaggeration to say that it will be hard to find a parallel, either in ancient or in modern history, to the extraordinary far-sightedness and constructive skill with which he evolved his methods and principles of government. To the qualities of a successful general and conqueror he joined an administrative genius and statesmanship which have seldom proved so fruitful

[1] That is almost as early as 1746 if not earlier. At the earliest period, the days of Dadaji Kondadev, Shivaji had his Peshwa, Muzumdar, Dabir and Sabnis (*Vide* Sabhasad p. 7). The Sir-nobut was added in 1647 (Sabhasad p. 8). Other officers were added from time to time, the constitution was settled about 1667, and probably revised in 1674.

of active benevolence. Considering the needs of the time and the evils of pre-existing and contemporary Indian monarchies, Shivaji saw two extremes, viz: a monarch solely swayed by the counsels of a favourite minister or one self-willed and governed by his single caprice. In either case, it meant disorder, injustice, misrule,–in one word, tyranny–tyranny with the best or the wickedest of intentions. No single individual, however capable or intellectual, could keep in touch with the varying events in all departments of life over the whole country. No single ruler, however just and even-minded, could decide with impartiality and unerring precision on all administrative questions. The interests of one department must often clash with those of another. One may often trespass on the domain of another. This friction and overlapping had often led to discontent, and discontent had always been the parent cause of the overthrow of great monarchies. Shivaji saw all this and proposed to steer clear of these dangers and misfortunes. He entrusted the direction of public affairs to a cabinet of eight officers who were to assist him in the conduct of the government. This institution of a cabinet was a feature of Shivaji's government for which there was no precedent in any contemporary system. It was also unique in this sense, that after Shivaji the institution more or less fell into desuetude. On the rise of the Peshwas when the king became a titular puppet, it came under a total eclipse. An approximation to that system may however be seen in the more advanced and developed government of our own times under the ægis and direction of the British power.

Each of these eight ministers had direct charge of a department of government. A few details of this system are given below. The names of the incumbents of the various offices at the time of the Coronation have already been mentioned in the last chapter.

(1) The Prime Minister (Mukhya Pradhan) or Peshwa, was next in rank after the king and was the head of the entire administrative system, civil and military.

(2) The Senapati or Sir-nobut was the head of the military department. There were two Senapatis–one over the cavalry and the other over the infantry. Of these the former seems to have had precedence and control over the Senapati of the infantry. The latter had no place in the cabinet.

(3) The Pant Amatya or Muzumdar was the head of the finance department. He examined all civil and military accounts and the separate accounts of each fort. The local audits of all parts of the kingdom came under his scrutiny, and the strict control exercised through his office had a wholesome restraining influence upon the spending propensities of local commanders and reduced the evils of speculation and embezzlement of public money to a minimum. The sanction of any extraordinary expenditure or reduction beyond normal limits was granted by the king upon the recommendation and by the advice of this minister. In consequence the officer had a very extensive department of clerks and accountants under him and he maintained many supervisors of accounts for each separate district, fort, or regiment.

(4) The Pant Sachiv or Surnis was keeper of the government records, superintendent of the department of correspondence and examiner of all letters and despatches from local officers, commanders and governors of the fortresses. Government despatches to local officers also passed under his scrutiny. He was likewise the registrar of all grants, inams, sanads and commissions conferred upon civil and military officers in the provinces. This minister had also a large establishment. Without his seal and attestation no public document was valid. Both the Pant Amatya and the Pant Sachiv sent their representatives from province to province to examine and report on the work of their respective departments, viz: the department of accounts and that of records. These inspecting officers were empowered to make severe awards of fines and penalties to offending local subordinates. The principal departmental

ministers at times paid visits to the provincial centres to make a personal scrutiny.

(5) The Mantri or Waknis was keeper of the private records and correspondence. He was also superintendent of the household troops and establishment. In this were included the various private departments of stores and treasure, separated under the heads of the eighteen Karkhanas (warehouses, arsenal, commissariat &c.) and the twelve Mahals or Koshas (treasury, mint, stables, parks &c.).

(6) The Sumant or Dabir was minister of foreign affairs. He superintended all business in connection with foreign states, such as the receiving and sending of letters and messengers.

(7) The Nyaya Shastri or Panditrao advised on ecclesiastical matters and expounded the shastras. He superintended state ceremonies and religious charities from the public funds. It was also his duty to see that the penalties awarded in criminal trials were in keeping with the precepts of the shastras. He was also the censor of the public morals.

(8) The Nyayadhish, or the Chief Justice superintended the administration of justice both civil and criminal. Appeals to the king from the decisions of the local panchayats or *prant* officers (i. e. subhedar) were heard by this minister, who on a revision of the evidence gave his decisions.

In this manner the different departments of government were entrusted to different ministers. It was a point of honour with each minister to put the best of his energy and ability into his work. In intricate cases the minister in charge of the department concerned would discuss the matter with the king. If it appeared to be a matter of much gravity, it might be then referred to the cabinet or council and be subjected to a full discussion. Questions of policy affecting the whole kingdom were generally subjected to a full council discussion, and a final adjustment arrived at with the concurrence of all. The confidence thus reposed in the ministers and the value thus placed upon their opinion was a further incentive to their devotion and industry and bound them to the interests of the king and the state as to their own.

Of these ministers of state, barring the Panditrao and the Nyayadhish all were required to serve in the army and were leaders of great experience. Shivaji and his state lived in the midst of constant alarms. The sword was rarely sheathed. At the slightest notice any one of these officers, though mainly in charge of civil establishments, had to gird sword and buckler and march to the scene of war. To meet such emergencies, each of the state ministers had a deputy or mutalik who exercised full authority during his principal's absence in the field. They had the authority to affix their principals' seals of office, but in matters of special importance they had to submit their decision to the approval of their principals. Under the deputy or mutalik, each department had a staff of officers as follows :—(1) A Muzumdar holding charge of the departmental audit ; (2) a Phadnis who was an assistant to the Muzumdar ; (3) a Sabnis in charge of the departmental record ; (4) a Chitnis, in charge of the departmental correspondence ; (5) a Karkhannis, in charge of the departmental stores ; (6) a Jamdar, or office curator ; and (7) a Potnis or cashier. Besides these officers there was a full complement of clerks varying with the character of the department and the volume of work passing through it. On the personal staff of Shivaji, there was a Chitnis or private secretary for correspondence, a Phadnis or accountant, a Parasnis or Persian translator, and a Potnis or treasurer. The Chitnis, as has often been mentioned in the foregoing chapters was Balaji Avji, a Prabhu. Shivaji's first personal Phadnis (or Muzumdar) was Balkrishnapant Hanumante, a close relative of the Raja Shahaji's chief minister of that family. The name of the Parasnis or translator is not known. His duty was to interpret letters or documents couched in the Persian language or to translate them into that language when necessary for despatch. Shivaji's Potnis was a grandson of Seshava Naik Pande of Shrigonde, at whose house the Raja Maloji is said to have concealed the treasure he had discovered in an ant-hill and to whom according to tradition he had made promise that when he came to have that sovereign power of which there was an augury he would make him the Potnis or treasurer of his realm. The grand-son of the promisor made good the promise by conferring the post on the grand-son of the promisee.

Besides this organization of the public departments, for the proper administration of the various crown possessions different stores establishments were created. These were private or quasi-private departments of the crown and at the head of them all stood the Waknis or Mantri. These establishments came under two groups, which were further elaborately divided into twelve Mahals and eighteen Karkhanas or Shalas. Among the Mahals were comprehended the zenana, specie, grain stores, horse stables, cows' parks, the mint, palanquins, private palaces, the wardrobe, the private body-guard, and general purvey department. In the latter class, the Karkhanas, came elephant parks, gymnasium, public granaries, music, artillery and arsenals, medical stores, drinking water, camels, tents and carpets, hunting, jewellery, kitchens, armoury, betel-nut etc., carriages, stationery, singing and dancing, and miscellaneous stores. Over all these thirty departments, there were *darogas* or superintending officers, clerks, guards etc.

There was a separate establishment for Jijabai. To he household were attached capable servants, male and female. There were peons and foot-soldiers, maid-servants, pujaris or private chaplains, puraniks or readers of the puranas and other Brahmans to officiate at religious functions. A sum was set apart for Jijabai's expenses and religious charities. Her affairs were administered by a household staff consisting of a diwan or general manager, chitnis

(secretary), a phadnis (accountant), and a potnis (treasurer) with a number of subordinates. Shivaji was very anxious to provide for the comfort and happiness of his mother.

Shivaji's army was recruited chiefly from two sources, the Mavalis on the ghats and the Hetkaris in the Konkan beneath the ghats. The Mavalis were crack swordsmen and the Hetkaris marksmen of repute. Each was armed with sword, shield and musket. They were to provide themselves with their own arms, the ammunition being supplied by the state. Their dress consisted of a pair of breeches coming half-way down the thigh, a long band, about a span in breadth girt tightly about the loins, a long scarf worn over it round their waist, a turban and sometimes a frock of quilted cotton. The Mavalis and Hetkaris were born and bred among the mountains and in consequence found themselves quite at home whether they had to thread their mazy way over an intricate defile or scale the frowning heights of an inaccessible precipice; and it will be no exaggeration to say that few races in other parts of the world could equal them in agility and swiftness of movement.

In each decury of ten foot-soldiers there was a Naik, that is to say, each decury consisted of nine infantry men under a Naik or corporal. Over five such decuries a Havaldar was in command. Over two Havaldars a Jumledar[1] and over ten Jumledars a Hazari or commander of one thousand.[2] There were also Panch Hazaris or commanders of five thousand and they were immediately under the orders of the Sir-nobut or chief commander.[3] Some

[1] Chitnis says that in the Mavali infantry there was a Jumledar over five Havaldars and a Hazari over five Jumledars. This would make an infantry battalion of 1250 foot-soldiers.

[2] A corps of one thousand under a hazari constituted an infantry battalion.

[3] Mr. Ranade (page 122) says seven hazaris made a sir-nobut's charge for the Mavali infantry. Mr. Kincaid (page 275) follows Mr Ranade. Mr. Sardesai (Marathi Riyasat, 1915 edition, Pages 475-76) say five hazari battalions served under a sir-nobut.

of the foot-soldiers used bows and arrows, double-edged swords, spears, and javelins, and some merely carried the arms of their masters. The rule was that each soldier should wield the arms in the use of which he had acquired dexterity. Each soldier and naik drew a salary per month ranging from one to three pagodas. A jumledar received a hundred pagodas per annum, and a bazari five hundred.

The cavalry were of two kinds : the Bargirs and the Shiledars. A body of horse of the first class were called the Paga or state cavalry, for their horses belonged to the state and were the property of the royal household and were looked after by state officers. The shiledar furnished his own horse and looked after it himself, for which an extra allowance was granted by the government. The shiledar horse had been a feature of the Mahomedan monarchies in the Deccan. Shivaji did not place so much reliance on cavalry of this description as on the Bargir class. The shiledars did not always care to keep their horses in proper condition for war and when tired of service might gallop away from the field. Hence Shivaji's policy was to reduce the number of these private cavalry-men, but he had to enlist them as at the time many a Maratha would only serve on this condition. When a shiledar offered to sell his horse to government, the horse was added on to the paga and the soldier served in that department of cavalry. The paga horses were each branded with the state stamp on the rump. The cavalry soldier was dressed in a pair of tight breeches and a frock of quilted cotton. He wore a scarf round the waist and a turban, one fold of which was passed under the chin so as to fasten and prevent it from falling down when he was in full career.[1] The sword was girt with the scarf round

---

1 The practice of the Maratha bargir or shiledar cavalryman to pass a fold of the turban under his chin is a good commentary on Virgil's description of the dress of Aeneas, (Aeneid IV, 216, *Maeonia mentum. mitra crinemque subnexus*) viz. "His chin and hair bound with a Maeonian turban."

the waist, the shield buckled at the back. The spear was the national weapon of the Maratha cavalry-soldier, but some also carried a match-lock. They were, as a general rule, to furnish their own arms, the shiledars had to bring their own ammunition, the bargirs received their supply from the state.

Over every troop of twenty-five horse-soldiers of either description there was a havaldar. Over five havaldars there was a jumledar and over five jumledars there was a subhedar.[1] Over ten such subhedars there was a panch-hazari and over them all stood the sir-nobut.[2] The cavalry sir-nobut was distinct from the similar officer in chief command of the infantry. For every corps of twenty-five horses there was a water-carrier and a farrier. The havaldar had to look after the feeding and grooming of the horses under him and the proper care of their trappings and equipments. The bargir drew a salary according to his grade from two to five pagodas per mensem, a shiledar from six to twelve, a jumledar twenty.[3] A subhedar's salary was a thousand pagodas per annum and he had besides a palanquin allowance. A panch-hazari of horse had a salary of two thousand pagodas and a palanquin and an umbrella-bearer's allowance. A subhedar of a shiledar contingent held command immediately under the sir-nobut. Each subhedar, panch-hazari and sir-nobut had an establishment of couriers, scouts and spies.

Besides this cavalry and infantry Shivaji maintained a brigade of five thousand horse for his personal body-guard, and this was composed of the flower of his army. Shivaji's

[1] According to some authorities, a hazari held command over ten jumledars and a panch hazari over five hazaris. This arrangement is followed by Mr. Ranade and Prof. Sarkar. Under this plan a cavalry regiment would consist of 1250 horse and a panch hazari brigade of 6250 troopers.

[2] Mr. Sardesai gives the same sub-divisions of the cavalry brigade as described here in the text. We follow Chitnis.

[3] According to Sabhasad a jumledar received five hundred pagodas (annual pay) and a palanquin allowance.

hostilities with the Mahomedan powers endangered his life at all times and his body-guard had to be on the *qui vive* day and night. Shivaji had chosen his body-guard from the pick of the Mavali youth. These were divided into companies of thirty, forty, sixty or one hundred men and placed under the bravest and most loyal of his commanders. The body-guard of foot had a rich uniform provided by the state, to be worn on state occasions, consisting of a gold-embroidered turban, a woollen mantle and a scarf of checkered silk or a Paithan shawl. For ornaments they wore sometimes gold armlets, sometimes necklaces of silver, sometimes of gold. For their swords they had scabbards with gold-mounted ends and gold-fasteners to secure their muskets. There was also a body-guard of horse, consisting of the cream of the bargir cavalry. They numbered five thousand and were distinguished from the rest by their gold and silver trappings. For the personal use of Shivaji, there was a private stable comprising about a hundred noble steeds, with housings and trappings of the most superb order. When Shivaji set forth on an excursion, the body-guard, both horse and foot, attended him as an escort, marching in front and in the rear, or to his left or right, always observing the prescribed order and keeping fixed intervals between them.

At the recruiting season, Shivaji personally inspected every man who offered himself for service, whether in the cavalry or the infantry and took security from some persons already in the service for the fidelity and good conduct of those who were to be enlisted for the first time. The sureties executed bonds for the good conduct of their proteges. None was appointed or promoted to the rank of jumledar or subhedar, hazari, or panch hazari, who had not given proofs of his bravery and chivalry, and of proficiency in arms as well as of his family connections. These officers were Marathas. Every subhedar and hazari had under him either a Brahman subordinate as sabnis or muster-keeper and a Prabhu officer as karkhannis or storekeeper, or a Brahman muzumdar or accountant and a Prabhu sabnis or despatch clerk. In the same way, under a panch-hazari there was a diwan, a sabnis and a karkhannis. Under these officers there were inferior subordinates, and beyond the prescribed number, the commander could appoint clerks and other subordinates at his own charge. Commanding officers, subhedars and hazaris were under strict regulations to observe punctuality in the due payment of salaries and allowances to their subordinates.

Shivaji possessed at this time about two hundred and eighty hill-forts. These forts played a very important part in Shivaji's military system and he attached a special value to their defence and equipment. Whatever war or invasion menaced the country Shivaji had been able to defy the enemy in campaign after campaign by the help of these forts. From a skirmish or a raid upon the enemy in the camp or the plains below he could swiftly lead his hosts to the battlemented heights of his forts and laugh to scorn the impotent rage of his pursuers spending itself in vain against their rock foundations. Rarely could a hostile army dominate for long the country within range of such a fortress. A hostile occupation would in its nature be temporary being subject to the fire and descents of the garrison of the neighbouring fort. In short the fort was the most salient point of Shivaji's military system, both as regards offence and defence. No outlay was too great whether to repair or restore old fortifications or to build new ones in positions of natural advantage or strategical value. The organization and discipline of the forts were the most efficient and strict to be found anywhere under his dominions.

The governor or commander in supreme charge of a fort had the title of havaldar. He was usually a Maratha officer of distinguished bravery, loyalty and position. Under him was a sir-nobut, or commander of garrison troops and a tat-sir-nobut or commander of the ramparts. There was besides a staff of the usual officers, a subhedar, a sabnis, a phadnis, and a karkhannis. Of these latter the first three were generally Brahmans, the karkhannis or commissary of stores was commonly a Prabhu. These officers were selected with care for their talents, loyalty and devotion. The ministers of state or distinguished nobles stood security for their good conduct. The final responsibility for the safety of the fort being vested in the havaldar, the other officers had strictly to obey his orders. He held the keys of the fort. He passed orders for commissariat supplies, ammunition and food provisions. He held the seals of the fort and papers were received or sent in his name. He had finally the supreme charge of the garrison army. The subhedar administered the revenue in the outlying villages and acted in consultation with the havaldar. The sabnis kept the records and correspondence of the fort and the muster of the garrison forces. The karkhannis kept accounts of stores and commissariat. He was also the pay-master and supervisor of the public buildings in the fort. The division of work among men of different castes, as also the system of checks and counter-checks, was a successful provision against fraud and treachery. The forces maintained at each fort were in proportion to its size and importance.

The hills beneath the fort and the sloping declivities from the foot to the summit were guarded by sentinels whose duty it was to watch the movements of a possible invader and guard the hilly woods. At the foot of the fortress, there were outposts at the cross-ways and commanding positions where bodies of Ramosis, Parwaris, Mangs or Mahars were stationed on guard. They also acted as scouts and brought to the governor of the fort secret intelligence of any stir or excitement or anything unusual taking place in the neighbourhood, put the enemy's spies or scouts inquiring about the conditions within on a wrong scent and made sudden attacks on straggling parties from a hostile army loitering in their neighbourhood.

Under the strict regulations of Shivaji it was the duty

of the havaldar to see that the portals of the fort were closed at nightfall. He had to assure himself in person that they were properly locked up, and he could under no circumstances part with the keys, but have them under his pillow when he went to sleep. The commanders in the fort by turns went their appointed rounds all over the fort during the night. The sir-nobut had general control over the patrols, but the watches at important positions over the defences were under the supervision of the tat-sir-nobut, or commander of the rampart. The havaldar was expected to be on guard at head quarters, with a posse of armed men. The officers of each department were furnished with distinct regulations for their conduct, from which they were under no circumstances to deviate. Nor were they permitted to interfere with the duties of any brother-officer, being strictly limited to their own. Unnecessary tampering with the duties of another and indifferent attention to one's own was visited not merely with a stern animadversion and censure, but a punishment which was alike rigorous and exemplary.

The fort regulations provided for punctual payment of their salaries, whether in cash or kind, to the officers and men in the garrison. Provisions of food supplies and fodder, fuel, arms and ammunition, brick and mortar, were made on a liberal scale, in quantities to last for two years or more at a time. Each fort had its own scale for these supplies, based upon its particular needs and circumstances. Easy slopes and passages up the forts were rendered steep and inaccessible by cutting down the rocks, or by mining and artificial defence works. It is unfortunately not easy to ascertain the scale of salaries of the havaldar, subhedar, tat-sir-nobut and other garrison officers. The havaldar was at any rate entitled to the privilege and allowance of a palanquin and torch-bearer. The garrison troops drew their salaries on the same scale as other soldiers. Besides the regular garrison army, there were the skirmishers, sentinel guards and the irregular and nondescript soldiery stationed at the out-posts beneath the fort. These were recruited from various castes and hill-tribes, such as Ramosis, Parwaris, Mahars, Mangs and Berads. They did not receive fixed pay but had lands settled upon them in the neighbourhood of the fort, where they were to have their allotted dwellings, subsisting on the produce of the fields they tilled and held as their own. All these men came under the general appellation of gadkaris or garrison men. The object of this plan was to make the gadkaris, especially these non-descript members of the garrison, feel a personal interest in the safety of the fort committed to their care, which was alike the source of honour and of livelihood to them. In consequence of this arrangement, as the years elapsed, a breed of brave and loyal warriors was reared up at each fort. The veteran soldier looked for no higher honour or reward at the hands of Shivaji than to be placed in command over one of these forts or promoted to the higher garrison appointments. The fort was under the general administrative sphere of the taluka next adjacent to it and the talukdar or mamlatdar, as the case might be, was under orders to supply the necessary provisions with the advice of the prant-subhedar. The dismissal or restoration to office of any of the garrison officers depended on direct orders to that effect from the sovereign.

The organization of the artillery was in the hands of separate officers, about whose names or grades the authorities are silent. Cannon were stationed at suitable points in the different fortresses. The field artillery was moved from place to place by means of waggons, arms and ammunition were conveyed in carts, both being drawn by teams of oxen, of which a special breed was reared. When the army was on march, each cart or waggon had a double team of oxen, one relieving the other when necessary. A party of mechanics accompanied the army—smiths, carpenters, tanners, gunners and the like. The artillery officers were to keep their ammunition and equipments ready for any emergency. The mounting and dismounting of guns being an operation of great skill and labour, the best experts only had these duties assigned to them. Besides the fort artillery planted in stationary batteries, there were about two hundred field guns mounted on carriages. The artillery was purchased from the Portuguese, French and English merchants or obtained from them under the special articles of the treaties concluded with their representatives.

For the purpose of administration the entire territory under Swarajya, or Shivaji's direct control, was divided into a number of circles or districts called mahals and prants. A mahal comprised territory or villages yielding an annual revenue of from seventy-five to a hundred and twenty-five thousand rupees. Two or three such mahals went to form a prant or subha. The officer in charge of a mahal was the mahalkari. He was also called a turufdar or talukdar. This officer was generally a Brahman or Prabhu by caste. Over each mahal likewise there was a havaldar, Maratha by caste. The officer presiding over a subha was the subhedar. He was also called mamlatdar. The subhedar's jurisdiction often extended over one or two forts. The officer in charge of two or three villages was called a kamavisdar. He supervised the collection of revenue in his own little circle under direction of the mahalkari, or talukdar, his immediate superior, and submitted his accounts at the head-quarters of the subhedar concerned. The head-quarter's staff of the subhedar consisted of a muzumdar, a chitnis, phadnis and a daftardar or record-keeper, together with the necessary establishment of clerks and assistants. The mahalkari superintended the work of the kamavisdar, the subhedar that of the mahalkari. The subhedar heard cases. In criminal matters he gave decision himself. In civil matters he got the cases submitted to a village panchayat and enforced their decision. The frontier districts were subject to many disturbances, and the subhedars in charge of such districts were assisted by a contingent of infantry and cavalry. The revenue levied, whether in cash or in kind, was conveyed for safe custody to the strongest fort within the district limits. The subhedar's salary was four hundred pagodas per annum and he had also an allowance for a palanquin and umbrella-bearers. The muzumdar in charge of a subha or prant drew a salary of one hundred to one hundred and twenty-five pagodas, and the other officers at the district head-quarters in due proportion. As to the salaries and allowances of the sub-divisional officers, the mahalkari and the kamavisdar, there is no information available.

An elaborate survey of the entire Swarajya territory was taken in hand and the land record in the *daftar* of the mahalkari gave the names of the owner of each agricultural holding. The unit of field measurement in Shivaji's system was the pole or *kathi* which measured nearly six cubits in length.[1] A cubit was fixed at fourteen *tasus* or inches in Shivaji's system and eighty such tasus went to make a *kathi*. Twenty *kathis* made a *bigha* and one hundred and twenty *bighas* made a *chavar*. The produce of the holding was determined by a survey of the standing crop. Of the assessed produce three-fifths were left to the cultivator of the field and two-fifths formed the amount of the land tax, which was payable either in cash or in kind. Annual *kabulayats* or agreements were entered into with the rayat with reference to the payment of the government dues. In times of scarcity *tagavi* advances were made on a liberal scale which were repayable by instalments during the four or five years following after the period of agricultural distress. When allotments of uncultivated land were made to new tenants for the first time, with a view to their being brought under the plough, grants of agricultural cattle and seed were made at government expense and advances of corn and cash to the holder

[1] The strict measure of the *kathi* was five cubits and five *muthis*. A *muth* is equal to the breadth of the closed palm.

of the virgin soil, till the first harvest was gathered. The amount thus advanced was to be re-imbursed to the state in the course of a few years. Thus the lands were settled upon the rayat with full proprietary rights, and all soil that could boast of any degree of fecundity was brought under the plough. The revenue officers were under strict regulations to apportion the tax to the produce and render the burden of government dues as light as possible.

One important modification introduced by Shivaji in the revenue usages of the Mahomehan states calls for special notice. Under the Mahomedan regime each mahal and village had its revenue lord, deshmukh or deshpandya, desai or patil, kulkarni or khot, mirasdar or zamindar, as the case might be. The government officers had no direct dealings with the cultivator or rayat, but only with the revenue lords, who collected the revenue dues from the individual cultivator. The grievous result of this system was that the cultivators were always at the mercy of these rapacious chiefs, who fleeced the unresisting multitude at their sweet will. Was the government's share over the village produce two or three hundred rupees ? Off went the rack-renting mirasdar to levy two or three thousand ! *Sic vos non vobis mellificatis apes* ! The drones carried away all the honey, the industrious multitude groaned, and the officers of government looked on helpless, the state coffers being as low as ever for all the exaction. The revenue lords were surrounded by their own satellites, swordsmen and musketeers. They lived in fortified residences and secured their villages with mud-forts and ramparts. When the government took notice of their exactions and raised the assessment, they did not scruple to defy the sovereign power or even appeal to arms. The consequence was that the whole country was seething with sedition on account of these rebellious polygars.

This was entirely changed. The taxes were to be collected from the rayat under the direct supervision of the paid officials of the central power. The usurping mirasdars and zamindars were divested of the tyrannous powers under which the peasantry had groaned for centuries. They were now entitled to fixed grants based on an average estimate of their just claims in the old regime, and these were to be levied no longer from the cultivators but from the district officers representing the central government. True indeed, the revenue lords subsided into an idle rentier class, digesting their incomes and bearing no burden in the economy of the state. But the harpies of extortion had been at worst turned into harmless grasshoppers. Their pensions were subject to yearly confirmation, a procedure which guaranteed their good behaviour towards the state. The peasantry, freed from their grinding greed, breathed more freely. The thrall in practice became a free agent towards the state, the lowly serf began to hold up his head. Desai and deshmukh became simple subjects. Their forts and walls, their strongholds and donjons were everywhere rased to the ground, their feudal bands dispersed, their private wars and depredations put down with a strong hand. The district and taluka officers watched all their movements. It is easy to understand how these insolent nobles smarted with discontent under the new discipline. But that smouldering discontent was never allowed to blaze into a fire. Wherever practicable, the old nobility found congenial employment in Shivaji's army and in the civil service; and as they waxed in dignities and emoluments they got reconciled to the new regime. Though servants of the state while they drew their stipends, their hereditary rights and their annual claims over the village revenues were at the same time assured to them. The dragon of anarchy was slain, the cultivator went happily about his smiling meadows and the arts of peace and thrift no longer languished in the land.

A word may be said about Shivaji's field regulations. The continuance of Shivaji's independence and of the sovereign domains he had wrested from the reluctant Mahomedan powers depended entirely upon the army and necessitated the maintenance of large bands of warriors ready to take the field at the shortest notice. Never did any prince, whose power rested so vitally as Shivaji's did upon the upkeep of his army, practise a more rigid system of economy and discipline. Rigid however though the system was, the military organization he had to maintain in order to meet the constant alarms of war was too great to be entirely supported upon the slender resources of the Swarajya revenue. A certain portion of the army was stationed at the various forts, and maintained upon the revenues of the neighbouring villages. The remainder of the necessary armaments required, therefore, to be supported at least in part on other resources than state revenues. Added to these was the constant drain of wealth involved in the interminable struggle with the Mogul and the Adilshahi sultan. These circumstances conspired to give rise to the Maratha practice of sending out, year after year, a definite portion of the army upon a campaign of invasion on the enemy's territory.[1] This was called *Mulukhgiri* or active service on hostile soil. While the soldier was serving out his campaign he supported himself at the cost of the enemy and at the end of his campaign brought home his spoils to replenish the state treasury. Another consequence of these ceaseless campaigns, which no doubt was aimed at by Shivaji, was that the Mahomedan powers subjected to the distracting war grew more and more feeble and inert, and gradually relaxed their control of the country, surrendering one district after another. This, as we have seen, was the ruling idea of Shivaji's life.

The sir-nobut of the horse went forth on these campaigns for eight months in the year. He levied the chauth and sirdeshmukhi dues in the Bijapur and Mogul dominions and sacked the wealthy towns in the hostile territories. When setting forth on the campaign, inventories were duly made of the goods and chattels belonging to each soldier required by him on his march, and valuations

[1] Sabhasad, page 29.

of these were made and entered in the regimental books, the object being to compare on the return of the campaigners the valuables belonging to each soldier with those he had taken at the commencement of the march, to make him accountable for anything found in excess and confiscate it to the public coffers as part of the general booty or, as an alternative, deduct its value from his stipend. On the other hand, if a soldier was found to have come by losses or impairment of his property the same was made good at the charge of the state. If a trooper of the shiledar class lost or disabled his horse while on active service in the campaign, he immediately received compensation at the rate described in the original inventory. No females, servant-maids or prostitutes were permitted to accompany any soldier on a campaign.[1] Distillers or vendors of spirituous liquors were also prohibited from joining the regiment on march. An infringement of these rules was punished with death. The reason was plain. A strict disciplinarian like Shivaji knew by intuition the value of temperance and sobriety on field service.

No sacrilege or interference with Brahmans was permitted on a campaign. No kine were ever to be carried away in plunder nor oxen except as draught cattle according to requirement. Females and peasants were not to be interfered with. Wealthy Mahomedans or Hindus in a position of dependence on the Mahomedan chiefs and able to pay the war contributions might be arrested and taxed proportionately to their fortunes, but immediately on their payment of the stipulated sums they were to be set at liberty. The rest of the poor population suffered nothing by the invasion. Women and children had perfect immunity under all circumstances. Pending the payment of contributions, hostages might be taken, never a Brahman, a Mahomedan by preference.

The campaign had to be concluded before the rains, when the squadrons were to rejoin their cantonments. On

[1] *Vide* Shedgavkar bakhar, page 39.

arrival at the frontier of their own state, a search was made into the goods or chattels carried by each trooper, in comparison with the previous inventories, leading to restorations or confiscations, where it might be thought necessary. Elaborate inventories were also made of the spoils taken from the enemy. Embezzlement of the public spoils was summarily dealt with. The returned cavalry resumed their ordinary places in the cantonment, of which there were two or three centrally situated, with long lines of stables and residences for the troopers. The brigadier had to provide the fodder and veterinary aid to the beasts, examine the musters of his regiment, and make up the salary bills for the men under his command.

When the inventories were fully made up and tallied, the sir-nobut waited on the king presenting the spoils of the war for his gracious acceptance. The accounts were then audited and the balances credited to the royal treasury or warehouses. Jewels, precious apparel etc. were cleaned or polished as required and arranged in the proper cabinets with the estimated prices put upon them. It was open to officers and soldiers to make a bid for any of these articles at the assessed prices, which could be deducted from their salaries. Individual soldiers and officers recommended for special gallantry were now introduced to the king by the sir-nobut upon the advice of the respective subhedars for promotion or rewards of merit. The widows and orphans of those that had fallen received their fixed grants from government. Soldiers disabled by grievous wounds had their life pensions settled by the state. Medical grants were liberally made to those invalided in the service by wounds or disease. The condition and grievousness of the wounds received determined the amount of compensation and entitled them to promotion or other marks of honour. Officers in the army found unfit for the duties to which they were appointed were not summarily dismissed but transferred to another sphere or relegated to the civil service. Breach of discipline or disobedience on a campaign led to a court martial and punishment and a repetition of the offence, to dismissal from service. Misappropriation of the spoils or plunder obtained in a campaign was visited with condign punishment. In all these disciplinary matters, the sir-nobut was to act under the order of the sovereign, not on his own responsibility.

About the end of the monsoons, on the auspicious day of Dasara (a great Hindu holiday in the early part of October), the squadrons of horse were to start again on a new campaign. The celebration of Dasara was one of the most festive periods in Shivaji's calendar and of great significance in his military system. Hindu traditions of hoary antiquity and from the epic period downwards recognized it as the most auspicious day for the opening of a campaign. On the day of Dasara, shiledar and bargir and whoever else had a desire to join Shivaji's cavalry or infantry appeared before the sovereign and gave a display of their agility and physique and skill in arms. Shivaji supervised the tests in person, and those who were found fit for service were immediately enrolled and appointed to duties for which they showed special aptitudes. The forces to be launched out on the new campaign were personally reviewed by the sovereign. Shivaji examined every horse taken out on the expedition. The lists of accoutrements and appurtenances of each soldier were made out once again. The sir-nobut and the leading commanders came to have their farewell audience of the monarch. The final orders were given and taken and the generals led forth their eager hosts into those hostile territories which were decreed to be the scene of their activity for the year.

Under Shivaji's system the generals and superior officers drew their salaries in advance at the time of the mobilization of their squadrons. The rank and file of the regular army and the irregular camp-followers received their accumulated wages at the end of the campaign. From the salaries thus received in a lump sum they were to provide for their families for the whole year. The stipends due for the period of inactivity while the forces were cantoned during the monsoons appear under this system to have been payable in a lump sum at the time of Dasara. While on campaign the soldier had scarcely any payment to make for his subsistence. Shivaji spared no expense to keep the army happy and contented at all times. Never was there a mutiny, sedition, or conspiracy in his camp. The passion that dominated every breast, every regiment, every camp flying Shivaji's standard was to put forth the very best of their valour and daring, and to earn the applause and admiration of their master. This was the occupation of their thoughts, this the noble emulation that inspired them.

In the other departments there was great punctuality in the payment of all salaries to public officers. At the end of each year the salary bills were made up and paid and the standing instructions were to leave no balances for the next year. The punctuality thus observed kept the men in the public service in sympathy with the government, their families well supported even in the absence of their chiefs, and the entire civilian class free from fear of indebtedness. Shivaji knew from the condition of other governments of the time that irregularity in payment was the root cause of sedition among public officers, of indifference to duty, of dullness, of ineptitude. Hence the great care with which he endeavoured to extirpate the least signs of indebtedness from the public service. The spectre of debt took the edge from all ambition and enterprise, robbed life of all its savour and drove the distracted victim to every kind of vice and iniquity. All this Shivaji saw and he wisely made provision for his officers to enable them to avoid these fears. But he saw that there were occasions, like marriages and other festive functions, when not only the poor but even the most affluent were forced to borrow. Such being the case a rule was made that public officers on such occasions might apply for aid from the state funds, and such aid was granted on a scale determined by the applicant's position and services. At the same time when an officer was found improvident or extravagant and in consequence overwhelmed with debt, he was discharged from the service.

The superior officers received their salaries in cash or by orders for payment on the revenue officers. The latter paid in cash or in kind according to the order received, which they had to follow to the letter. Punctuality of payment was the out-standing feature of the system. These orders on the treasury were duly audited from year to year. When a paid servant of the state happened to be a holder of an agricultural estate, the land-revenue chargeable on his holding was deducted from his stipend and the balance made up by an order on the treasury, which was duly paid off in cash or in kind. No military or civil officers received assignments of village lands, as the whole or part of their salaries. Such assignments of the revenues of entire villages or a portion of them went under the name of *mokasa*. The grant of *mokasa* lands had become a regular feature of Mahomedan rule, and a prolific source of every form of oppression. What with the zamindar and the mokasadar, the subjects of these unhappy governments were, as it were, ground down between two mill-stones Under pretence of government service they impressed any amount of forced labour. To avoid these evil practices, therefore, Shivaji took care, that, where orders on the revenue were made in payment, they should be addressed to and made payable by the revenue officers concerned, and debited to the revenue account, and that the recipients should under no circumstances exercise any kind of proprietary rights or claims on those villages to the revenue of which their salaries were debited.

In the same manner were jahgirs suppressed. Jahgirs were fiefs conferred on great nobles of the state in recognition of services performed. The holders of the jahgirs collected the revenues of these fiefs by their own agents, and were responsible to the state for paying a small percentage of their receipts as tribute or in lieu thereof had to serve in the field with a prescribed number of followers. With a tenure that presented such a wide latitude for freedom of action and independence and placed such multitudes under their autonomous sway, these jahgir feudatories appeared more in the character of ruling princes than obedient vassals in allegiance to a common sovereign. The cultivators looked upon them as their sovereign masters. They had their own militia of jahgir forces. They lived in fortified strongholds and secured their fiefs with many a fortress, tower and parapet. The fiefs descended from father to son in right of succession. The zeal and loyalty of the founder of the family in the service of the central power could not in the nature of things be transmitted unimpaired along with the family fortunes to the generations that followed. The strain of virtue and valour that had distinguished the first fief-holder was rarely to be discovered among scions of the same blood. Contempt of the central power and insolent disobedience to its commands were the natural consequences. The spirit of defiance had become the element in which they lived and moved. The signal of a foreign invasion might be expected to gather their forces for the defence of the central power; but it more often proved a trumpet-call for mutiny and rebellion.

Shivaji was so conscious of the festering evils to which the jahgir system gave rise in the commonwealth, that he set his face sternly against the practice. Where it happened that in territories newly brought under his flag the old practice was found to exist and the jahgirdar aristocracy of the ancient regime had in some form to be recognized, the lands held in jahgir from times of yore by these families were no longer considered as held in proprietary right, and a percentage of the revenue was all that was conceded to them for the continuance and glory of their ancient pedigrees. And this, with the additional precaution that they should not interfere with the rayats, who were responsible only to the government officers of the villages concerned. Divested of all shadow of authority and power to work their will upon the suffering multitude, the more capable and talented of these nobles found a free arena for the exercise of their virtues and genius in Shivaji's army and civil establishments. Their ancient forts were levelled to the ground. No castellated residences were any longer assigned or permitted to them. Down went *buruz* and parapet. They were required to occupy ordinary unfortified residences. The stronger fortifications over all the jahgir dominions of course passed bodily under Shivaji's military officers as parts of the ordinary defences of the country.

Thus was crushed the many-headed hydra that had turned the fairest parts of the country into a morass and poisoned its substance. For whatever name it assumed—khot, deshmukh, deshpande, desai, zamindar, mokasdar, mirasdar, jahgirdar—the evil was the same, irresponsible rapine. It was an attribute of the highest statesmanship on the part of Shivaji that though he deprived them of their voracious propensities, this brood of hawks could yet be successfully tamed for the public service. The discontinuance of the jahgir practice by Shivaji has had one unfortunate result: the names of the illustrious leaders and statesmen, who so nobly seconded their sovereign's efforts for the redemption of the liberty of their country, have fallen into an unseemly and unmerited oblivion. In any age, in any country, the names of Moropant Pingle, Abaji Sondev, Tanaji Malusare, Yesaji Kank, Baji Fasalkar, Baji Prabhu, Netaji Palkar, Prataprao Guzar, Hambirrao Mohite and a host of others would have shone in the national galaxy like stars of the first magnitude. To-day they are under an unnatural eclipse. True to his principles Shivaji conferred no jahgirs upon these illustrious partners of his labours in field and in council, though nobody else in all the land could be said to have had a better claim for any mark of recognition than these tried veterans. But not even in these cases was the "no jahgir" rule to be broken. Had the gallant services of these men received any such recognition, who knows but perhaps these great names might still have survived the ravages of time, not indeed quite unscathed but still with the family honours and the family estates?

Another important rule of Shivaji's discipline was that no public office, civil or military, was to become hereditary. However capable or brilliant the career of the father had proved to be, this was no reason in itself for the succession of his son to the same office. If the great services of the father were at all to be acknowledged by a compensatory preferment of the son, it was strictly conditioned by the capacity and character the latter had revealed in his career. Without such ability, the gates of royal favour or preferment were closed, not only as regards succession to the paternal dignities, but to any official appointment. This put an end to all manner of nepotism in the public service. The public offices never became the close preserves of a small ring of families. The duties of the state were discharged with efficiency and with unfaltering regard for the right. This is the more remarkable when we consider the sterling character, the selfless devotion, the unwavering rectitude of Shivaji's gallant companions in arms and in council, the pillars of the empire, its builders, its defenders. Remarkable again because no one,—no, not even the worst caviller,—traces the rigour of the new system to a lack of appreciation or to insolence or ingratitude. Not indifference but a just appreciation governed all these actions, no phlegmatic disregard but a keen instinct to discern merit. So lively was this sense of fair dealing as between officer and officer, so strict the measure of justice, whether distributive or retributive, that Shivaji did not hesitate, where duty required it, to rebuke the greatest of his generals, to discharge or supersede them, when the least act of insubordination or dereliction of duty was brought home to them in the exercise of their trust. The fact that these great ministers and commanders held no jahgirs and were backed by no feudal militia made their removal or supersession from office comparatively easy. Such was the new regime, the discipline of the renaissance of the Maratha power. No prototype of it can be found in the contemporary Mahomedan governments of Shivaji's time or in the fossilized systems of Hindu mediævalism that had preceded it. Unhappily for the Maratha Renaissance all vestiges of the new system disappeared after the advent of the Raja Shahu and the usurping domination of his Peshwa ministers,—with what dire results is too well known to the student of history.

While the conduct of the great officers and commanders was subject to the constant scrutiny of the sovereign and his principal ministers, there was a secret intelligence corps or service of scouts which maintained a constant watch on the actions and the movements of the local officers at each fort, mahal, or subha, each cantonment and campaigning regiment. The head of this corps of scouts was Bahirji Naik, a man in the complete confidence of Shivaji. Secret officers kept an eye on the movements of commanders despatched on a campaign, watched the booty taken and the contributions levied and reported any attempts at misappropriation or under-assessment of the spoils of war. The detectives maintained their silent watch upon the manner in which the garrison officers discharged their trust, gave warnings of any attempted collusion with the enemy, reported on the revenues levied and actually submitted to the treasury, and generally took notice of cases of oppression or misrule. But the intelligence service had not only this sphere of activity. More important was the detective work they rendered the state by reporting on the movements of the enemy, the camp news in the Adilshahi, Kutubshahi or Mogul territories, the latest ministerial and other changes of office, the latest developments in policy or plans. They were ubiquitous; they went in all manner of disguises; they saw and detected everything. The secret despatches thus received from these officers were read out in the privacy of the royal palace by Shivaji's personal secretary, Balaji Avji Chitnis. A reported case of insubordination or breach of discipline on the part of an officer was subjected to a close investigation, and, if at the end of the enquiry he was found guilty, he was immediately punished with the penalties attached to the offence. This exercised a wholesome restraint upon the other officers and made them more amenable to duty.

Shivaji did not consider there was a necessity for a separate judicial service throughout his dominions. In land disputes or contractual disagreements about transfer of property, the cases were referred to panchayats by the mahal and district officers. The village panchayat system flourished in all its vigour and vitality, and, being the cheapest and most immediate, it was, at the same time, the most convenient system to the inhabitants. Shivaji, therefore, retained the system with a right of appeal to the sovereign. The advantage of the system was that the parties concerned had not to go a long way from their homes to reach the court, the trials took place where the causes of action arose, and decisions were given by persons who could make a personal investigation of the facts and indeed bring their ocular knowledge and local experience to bear upon the question at issue; and, over and above this, there was the undeniable advantage that being of the people they decided for the people without charging any fees or salaries. It was for the mahalkari and the subha officer to see that the decisions of the panchayat were duly respected though the party dissatisfied with the judgment of the panchayat court could appeal to the king. Such appeals were heard by the Nyayadhish or the chief justice, one of the ministers of the Ashta-Pradhan cabinet. Criminal jurisdiction was vested in the subha officer, against whose decision a reference could be made to the sovereign for revision, when the case was called before the court of the Panditrao or the ecclesiastical officer, who revised the case in the light of the shastric law. Cases of insubordination in the army or breach of military discipline came for investigation before the military subhedar or other higher officer, which could be appealed from to the sovereign, when decision was given by the sir-nobut or commander-in-chief.

In the territories now reduced under Shivaji's dominions, there had once prevailed much disturbance from thieves and dacoits. This pest of thieves was considerably mitigated and in parts utterly suppressed by Shivaji. Thieves and criminal tribes such as Berads and the like, were hunted down and executed when arrested. Some were given lands within gunshot of some strong fortress or other and the commander of the fort kept them under a strict surveillance Some were indeed enrolled among the irregular infantry of the fort garrisons and the temptation to crime cured by the prospect of a fixed salary. Where a village had earned a notoriety for frequent dacoities, it was placed under the sentinel watch of a person of the Berad class, who was made responsible for the safe-guarding of the village properties and was bound to trace the theft or pay damages. If he committed a theft himself he was straightway led to execution.

Charitable grants to shrines and temples coming down from long antiquity were continued in the new regime, and where the grants formerly made were found inadequate, additional grants were sanctioned. Fresh grants were made by cession of agricultural lands to many religious institutions which had thus far struggled on without any state aid. These places of religious sanctity were placed under proper procurators and managers, and an audit was to be made of the expenditure incurred from the state grants by priests and pujaris. These audits were subject to annual inspection by state officers. Persons of high reputation for sanctity or righteousness residing at the holy pilgrim-places received annuities. For the celebration of recurring solemnities and religious festivals, assignments of village lands were made to shrines and holy places.

It was not Hindu shrines only which came in for a share of the royal bounty, but the Mahomedan mosques and shrines and the tombs of the pirs and saints of Islam throughout the Swarajya dominions continued to draw the revenues assigned to them by the Mahomedan powers. Shivaji was so far from confiscating these mortmain properties of the church of Islam, that, on the contrary, he even transferred fresh lands to Mahomedan shrines and made new assignments of revenue. Shivaji's enthusiasm for the faith of his fathers does not seem to have led him into a bigoted hatred of anything and everything that belonged to the Mahomedan religion. Among the numberless campaigns he led in person or under the generalship of his great commanders, there is no instance mentioned of any act of sacrilege or violation of any Mahomedan shrines. And this is the more to be admired since the perpetuation of any such sacrilegious crime would, among the scenes of religious frenzy into which the followers of Islam were being constantly betrayed in his times, have appeared comparatively excusable. But Shivaji's was an enlightened policy of religious tolerance, which made any form of persecution impossible.[1]

The settled sway of Islam over the plains of Maharashtra had crushed out all life and vigour from the indigenous studies of the Vedas and other branches of Hindu philosophy. With a view to encourage and revive these fallen studies, Shivaji instituted a new system of patronage for the exponents of Hindu learning and philosophy. Under this system the month of Shravan, which coincided with the season of the autumnal cessation from warlike activities, was devoted to giving audiences to learned Brahmans from all parts of the country, who were invited to make a display of their learning and submit themselves to prescribed tests conducted by the ecclesiastical minister, the Pandit Rao. The candidates coming out successful from the tests received rewards in corn, from one

[1] Even Khafi Khan had to acknowledge Shivaji's tolerant policy towards the Church of Islam. *Vide* his remarks on the character of Shivaji. (Elliot, VII p. 305 et passim.)

to ten maunds, according to the quality and standard of their attainments. Great scholars and exponents of the Vedas and of the Indian school of astronomy, were accorded the welcome due to their position. Honorariums were given them on a royal scale. Scholarly Brahmans from across the frontiers of the Swarajya kingdom were honoured with presents in cash, those domiciled within the Swarajya limits received drafts for so many maunds in corn on the local treasury of the district in which they were domiciled. Along with the patronage of Sanskrit learning, state aid was granted to the performance of religious sacrifices and other celebrations when undertaken by learned Brahmans on their private initiative on a scale of magnificence requiring such support. In short, it was a principle of Shivaji's government to make much of the existing virtue, piety and learning in his kingdom and not to cast it adrift in search of an alien patronage. Free alms-houses were opened for maintenance of the deserving poor and arrangements made for the banqueting of the Brahmans at the important temples on auspicious occasions.

Herds of kine were maintained at the state expense in select pasturages in the valley of the Bhima, in Mandesh and other places, and an army of state dairymen and cattle attendants looked after their up-keep. A high class breed of commissariat oxen was reared in these cattle farms. Farm cattle were likewise supplied to agriculturists from public stalls. There were likewise parks of state buffaloes. These were in charge of shepherds and dairymen who were to reside in meadows teeming with herbage among the valleys and the mountains. The herds were surveyed from year to year and the annual contributions in butter or ghee were settled on each individual shepherd as also the quantity of milk each of them had to supply at the public feasts of the Brahmans on state occasions. A similar arrangement was made for state flocks of sheep and goats which were allotted in groups of twenty or twenty-five to the charge of individual shepherds subject to the same method of surveying and registering and the same scale of contributions on state occasions.

It may be of interest in this place to glance at the daily routine of Shivaji's life in times of peace. He rose with the dawn which was ushered in by beating the palace drum and with songs of divine praise sung by the palace minstrels to the accompaniment of instrumental music. Awakened amid these strains the pious king offered to Heaven his morning prayers. Then followed the ablutions of the face and hands, the worship of the sacred kine, the morning bath with water mingled with sacred sprinklings from the Ganges and other purificatory streams, the rosary, the prayers and other acts of worship. After this some time was devoted to readings from the sacred puranas. These acts of religious merit were generally ended by 7-30 A. M., after which the Maharajah usually put on his full dress. He gave himself for a brief interval to his daily exercise of target-practice, and came to the audience hall. The secretaries and officers were by this time ready in their places to receive orders and confirmations. Strangers admitted to the levee made their salutes. A smile to this minister, a word to that, a charge to a third drew all hearts towards the king as by a subtle magic. There was none present there but thought that he alone was basking in the sunshine of the royal favour. Men of talents obtained ready admission and left with many an acknowledgment of their sovereign's esteem and patronage. The session in the audience hall lasted till 10 A. M.; then an adjournment was made to the office chambers for confidential consultation with one or other ministers of state. At 11 A. M. the usual number of Brahman guests was entertained to dinner, and the king himself sat down to his morning meal, with a select company of guests. After the dinner and *pan-supari* the king came again to the secretariate and had the correspondence of the day read out by his private secretary and replies dictated and drafts presented for approval and confirmation.

Urgent proposals were then taken up and a provisional audit made of the previous day's receipts and disbursements, as also the estimates for the morrow. Then the king retired to his private chambers for the afternoon siesta, after which he came back again to the audience-hall, reviewed the recent doings of the various quasi-public establishments of the mahals and the kàrkhànàs, considered appeals or references from the judicial officers, and passed final orders thereon. About an hour before sunset, the king used to leave the palace, to pay a visit of inspection to this or the other private establishment, visits to the temples or the private parks, or for equestrian or other forms of exercise, after which he returned again to the audience-hall for the evening levee. About 7 p. m came the time for night devotions, prayers and readings from the puranas to be followed in due course by the evening meal, and deliberation with a minister. After all this audience was given to secret spies and scouts, and the nicer details of foreign diplomacy and private correspondence were attended to. Such was the ordinary routine of a life subject to an extraordinary stress of public events and surprises, the punctuality and regularity of which amid the manifold disturbing events that beset his career on all sides, cannot fail to excite our admiration. The punctilious precision of the king in all things could not but impress the same virtues upon the minds of his ministers. Sloth and procrastination found no place at his court.

While Shivaji thus diffused all round among his courtiers this keen regard for precision and punctuality, he also encouraged among them a love of noble enterprise and an ambition to rise in their own departments by dint of perseverance, enthusiasm and self-help. For these were the qualifications to win distinction and promotion in his service, not the arts of the flatterer or the parasite, or the encomiums of interested friends and partisans. Thus the court became the training-ground for virtue and talent; mediocrity and inefficiency had no place within its hallowed precincts.

During the hours of business at Shivaji's durbar, indulgence in any form of raillery or banter was forbidden. Professional jesters, entertainers and sycophants were denied admission at the durbar sessions. Vulgar or obscene conversation was impossible at his court, and the rake and the voluptuary avoided his presence. His serious thoughts were occupied at all hours with discussion of arms and horses, war and conquest. In leisure hours he was capable of witty and humorous discourse in the company of his chosen confidants, nor was he a stranger to the intellectual delights of poesie, but revelled in the impromptu effusions of the court poet, Bhushan Kavi, and other bards. Shivaji was always prepared to give an audience to musicians and preachers of distinction, who never failed to receive at his hands the reward due to their talents, learning and eloquence. Nor was the art of dancing altogether discouraged. There was no puritanical embargo on all forms of song and dance. But there was a studied restraint and discrimination in these forms of amusements. They never became a master passion with him to the exclusion of graver pursuits. The same measure of restraint was observed in the amusement of the chase. As an ordinary accomplishment and a recognized obligation of the Kshatriya or warrior caste, Shivaji indulged in this sport at intervals of one or two months, hunting big game as a rule and sparing bucks and deer, except when venison was occasionally needed for the anniversary oblations to the *manes* of his ancestors and other quasi-sacrificial occasions.

A noteworthy feature of Shivaji's discipline was the spirit of friendliness and social intercourse that subsisted among the ranks of his officers. There rarely was any envy or friction among the different members of the state-service. They were required to abstain from intervention in departments not falling under their immediate care and avoid sowing discontent among their brother officers out of spite or jealousy on failing to attain their wishes. When owing to any cause, the social relations between any of the great ministers of state were found to be strained, Shivaji promptly interfered and effected a restoration of the friendly accord and good feelings that previously existed between them. To make the reconciliation complete, where the parties belonged to the same caste, Shivaji got them to seal the restoration of harmony by a matrimonial alliance. Juniors in the service were required to behave deferentially with the senior officers. No royal valet or personal attendant, however high he might stand in the king's favour or confidence, dared abuse his position to whisper slander in the ruler's ear and prejudice his opinion against any minister or officer in the public service. The acts of administration were a forbidden subject to the menial staff, nor were they allowed to turn the conversation to the subject of their own or their friends' advancement in the king's service. No petitions or complaints of this nature were directly to be placed before the king, but to be submitted in due course through the heads of their departments. This injunction was strict and universal, and even the great nobles of the court and the personal relations of the king did not escape from it No claims for preferment found an avenue to the king's foot-stool except through the natural gate-way of the department concerned. When in spite of this rule some great officer or other did plead for preferment in the royal presence, he was invariably told that the reply to his petition would be sent through the minister concerned. Complaints against public officers were not encouraged and unless an investigation clearly proved a serious lapse on the part of a state officer, he incurred no blame or distrust in the mind of his sovereign. This mistrustfulness on the part of the king against his own ministers and officers was a common weakness of Indian potentates, and many a slanderer was to be found in every principality to impose upon the credulity of the prince and turn him against the truest and most steadfast of his servants. Shivaji knew well the seamy side of human nature and the knavery of officious back-biters and informers. The knowledge that their king was above that meanness which scents suspicion on every side and gathers around him a corps of officious, eaves-dropping and meddlesome informers inspired Shivaji's officers to give of their best both as regards service and advice, in the serene confidence that there was no possibility of a misapprehension as to the purity of their motives and the integrity of their work, no alienation, in short, unless there was a grave dereliction in the discharge of their duties.

The bakhars give a picturesque account of the style of Shivaji's durbar when he sat in audience for the discharge of solemn business and to decide on public affairs, as also of the pomp and circumstance of the state processions which were held from time to time. The forms observed at these public functions were nearly the same as have been described in the last chapter in connection with the coronation festivities. In the centre of the audience-hall was the royal throne and the canopy; behind, the bearers of the *morchel* and other attendants; in front standing in two rows were the blood-relations and officers of the body-guard. Next sat in due order of precedence on either side, the great ministers of state, commanders, members of the revenue and diplomatic services, representatives of foreign powers and select nobles.[1] The deputies and secretaries to the great ministers of state sat behind their chiefs. Then came the heads of various stores and treasury establishments. Two mace-bearers or sergeants guarded the entrance, saw to the proper salutes being made by those presenting themselves at the durbar, gave them their seats according to the degree of their precedence and ushered and announced strangers coming to the durbar. The sentinel posts in front of the audience-hall were in charge of these sergeants, and when anybody's presence was specially wanted at the durbar they sent one of the

1 The Peshwa, the Amatya, the Sachiv, the Mantri and the Chitnis stood to the right of the throne; the Panditrao, the Senapati, the Sumant, the Nyayadhish etc. to the left.

peons or troopers under their command to deliver the summons for attendance to the person concerned.

At the solemn processions, on the auspicious occasions in the Hindu calendar, the order was very much as described in the last chapter. Right in the vanguard of the entire procession came the elephants bearing the dual standards of the empire, the Jaripatka or the cloth-of-gold flag and the Bhagwa-zenda or orange-coloured banner. Behind these came the two cloth-of-gold pennants of the Prime Minister and the Commander-in-chief also mounted on elephants, followed by the standards of each separate regiment of cavalry and infantry, with officers of the king's guard and the shiledar corps riding immediately behind as the general custodians of their regimental flags. Then followed trains of artillery and ammunition, squadrons of horse and elephant-corps, the skirmishers in the infantry, light-armed slingers, javelin-throwers, archers and musketeers. Behind came the war-bands, drums, horns and trumpets with their shrill war music. Behind them again came the *paga* or household horse and mounted police, followed by the softer music of flutes and pipes, and minstrels and troubadours. Then followed other bands of spearsmen, mace-bearers, peons and attendants, wrestlers and gymnasts following on foot, and lastly the elephant bearing the royal *howda*, surrounded by a ring of chosen attendants and Mavalis. Immediately behind, followed the ladies of the royal family, then the ministers of state according to their usual rights of precedence, the secretariate officers and their deputies, and nobles and commanders. The royal drum escorted by the chief commander and other officers brought up the rear of the procession.

The bakhars give a very interesting story illustrating Shivaji's fame among his contemporaries as a patron and admirer of genius, and of his anxiety to retain such men to adorn his court by their presence. At Delhi, at the imperial conrt, there was a poet of the name of

Chintamani,[1] whose business it was to entertain the emperor by singing or reciting his odes. This bard had a brother, who was also a gifted poet, but who unfortunately unlike his more fortunate brother did not enjoy the imperial patronage. He depended on his brother until somebody insulted him as an idle, stay-at-home fellow, when he[2] determined to leave Delhi, and resolved never to live any more on the bounty of a Mahomedan. In the course of his wanderings he came to the court of a raja among the mountains of Kamaun and had the good fortune to obtain his patronage. Having spent a few years in that principality, he asked for permission to leave, upon which the prince as a sign of his appreciation presented him with a sum of one lakh of rupees, accompanying his farewell present with the observation that the poet would not find on earth a donor so bountiful and appreciative as himself. This expression of conceit irritated the poet who replied then and there to the Raja: "There may be thousands on earth to equal, nay surpass, you in munificence, but scarcely a beggar, I think, who would thus spurn a present, though a lakh of rupees, accompanied by such an arrogant boast."

With these words, the imperious bard put down the gold and left the country without any recompense for his poetic labours. In the course of his peregrinations the rising fame of Shivaji reached his ears and induced him to come down to the Deccan. Seeking an interview with Shivaji he declared to him his intention of living under the auspices of one who had no love for Mahomedans. Upon this, Shivaji retained him in his patronage and settled a maintenance grant upon him. His forte was to make poems on diverse subjects in the *Braja-bhasha* a dialect of the valley of the Jumna, with which he used to

---

1 Chintamani is said to have previously lived under the Bhonsle Raja Makarandshah of Nagpur for several years.

2 This poet is said to have at first lived under the patronage of the Raja Chhatrasal of Pannah for about six months and left him in 1664 to join Shivaji's court. (*Kavyetihas Sangraha.*)

entertain Shivaji. His principal poem is a sort of epic celebrating the exploits of Shivaji, the *Shiv-Raj-Bhushan Kavya* or the poem on the glories of Shivaji.[1] Shivaji was quite charmed with this poem. After a long sojourn in Shivaji's territories, he announced his intention to return home, upon which he was rewarded with ample presents and pressed to return again, which he willingly promised to do.

When the news of the bard's return to Delhi,[2] laden with wealth and tokens of Shivaji's favour, reached the envious ears of Aurangzeb, he bade Chintamani introduce his brother to the imperial court. Bhushan is said to have attempted some sort of protest declaring that the emperor was a declared enemy of his patron, and as a loyal vassal what would he have to do with such a one, since nothing could escape his lips but the praises of Shivaji, which would only irritate the emperor? However on the insistence of Chintamani, our bard undertook to attend the durbar, on a condition proposed and accepted, that should he be required to recite a poem, the theme would be the glories of Shivaji. Some time after the first introduction, Aurangzeb bade Bhushan recite some verses. The poet said, " Your Majesty had better wash your hands first, for after the erotics of my brother, which excite a voluptuous languor in your heart, I am going to raise my song to a heroic pitch, which, I am afraid, must needs raise Your Majesty's hands again and again to your august mustache. Hence wash your

[1] This poem was published in the Marathi Magazine Kavyetihas Sangraha many years ago. It is said the poem was completed the year before Shivaji's coronation. It proposes to discuss the figures of speech etc. in Indian works on rhetoric and in the illustrative verses chosen on the subject, the poet describes the glories of Shivaji's achievements. Prof. Sarkar thinks that Bhushan's *Granthavali* (Hindi, edited by Shyam Bihari Mishra and Shukdev Bihari Mishra—Nagari Pracharini Sabha, Benares, 1907) is full of "fulsome flattery of Shivaji, by a variety of similes and parallels from the Hindu scriptures and epics", but at the same time useful "as showing the atmosphere and the Hindu mind of the time."

[2] Probably Agra, but Delhi is used loosely of the Mogul durbar.

hands. I say!" "All right," said the emperor, "and if thou failest, thou shalt answer with thy head!" With this threat, he bade him commence his verses. Bhushan began to recite the glories of Shivaji's achievements. The emperor bade him sing his own greatness, celebrating his suzerainty over all princes and the enormous streams of tribute flowing to the imperial treasury from subject vassals. Upon this Bhushan began with a simile comparing the vassal princes to trees and the emperor to a butterfly rifling the sweets of every tree. In presenting this similitude, Bhushan likened Shivaji to the champak tree, and as the butterfly abstains from the champak tree alone, as it is believed, the poet expressed in recondite terms his meaning that whatever success the emperor might have achieved against other princes and whatever tribute he might levy from them, his attempts had all failed before Shivaji. Then the emperor reminded him of the preliminary condition and told him he had got him to wash his hands in vain. The poet continued five or six stanzas, in which some martial scenes were rendered in such lively strains, that at the end of the sixth stanza the emperor spontaneously raised his hand to his mustache. Upon this the poet concluded his recitation and the emperor, gratified with his exquisite skill and poetic faculty, bestowed upon him many marks of honour and patronage. Shivaji's agent at the imperial court sent full particulars of the incident to his royal master, which was indeed very gratifying to Shivaji. He wrote in reply to his agent to send the bard Bhushan again to the south, and it is said that at sight of his letter, Bhushan returned once more to live at Shivaji's court.

CHAPTER XXV

RENEWED WARS WITH BIJAPUR AND THE MOGULS, 1674-1676

We have already described in a previous chapter how Shivaji had made his reconciliation with Aurangzeb by prudent relations with Khan Jahan Bahadur, the subhedar of the Deccan, who had forwarded to the imperial presence Shivaji's memorial for a peace, drafted in the conciliatory style which characterised his relations with the Moguls, while giving up nothing that was of practical advantage to him. The Mogul arms had been rusting for some time, but it was not to be expected that the armistice would be anything but of short duration. It was no pleasant news to Aurangzeb when he heard of the solemnities of Shivaji's coronation and the realization of the great Maratha's ambition, the formal re-establishment of a Hindu sovereignty in the south He found fault with the continued neutrality of his subhedar and suspected that he was acting in collusion with the Maratha leader. Soon afterwards Diler Khan of Guzerat marched into Shivaji's territory upon a campaign of invasion The Peshwa Moropant advanced against him, but instead of confronting the forces of Diler Khan, made a diversion into the Mogul territories, conquering one station after another. Moropant recovered passession of Aundh and Patta which had fallen into the hands of the Moguls. While Moropant was thus keeping the Moguls busy in the south, Hambirrao, the commander-in-chief of Shivaji's forces, ascended the ghats near Surat and dividing his forces into different bands sent them to ravage the Mogul dominions in different directions. One of these bands crossed the Narbada, entered the district of Broach, and levied heavy war contributions upon the inhabitants. The result of these movements was that Diler Khan had to call away his forces from Shivaji's territories for the defence of his own province.

On the retirement of Diler Khan, Moropant lay encamped at Kalyan with a force of ten thousand men. He beat off a large body of Kolis and Bhils from Dharampur, who had invaded the Kalyan district at the instigation of the Moguls and opposed the Maratha march northward. From the camp at Kalyan Moropant sent his envoy to the Portuguese at Bassein to demand a quarter of the revenue of all their territories around Bassein. This demand of a quarter, or, to give it its more famous Marathi name, chauth of the revenue on the Portuguese government seems to have been made by Shivaji now for the first time. By the treaty made on a former occasion with the Portuguese, the latter had undertaken to supply Shivaji's government with guns and ammunition every year and they had hitherto fulfilled the terms of that agreement. Religious persecution was at its height in the Portuguese territories around Bassein. Many Hindu families were forcibly converted to Christianity. To those unconverted the alternative was the prospect of constant interference with their civic and religious liberties. The report of this persecution was the cause why the Hindu king levied the chauth contribution upon the Portuguese government. From the information now available it can only be inferred that the Portuguese government could not at this moment have dismissed Moropant's envoy with a summary refusal. For there is no record of hostilities on this occasion between Moropant and the Portuguese, nor were the latter in a position to challenge the encamped forces of Moropant to a decision on the field of war. Moropant, on the other hand, is not reported to have caused any damage to the Portuguese territories. It, therefore, stands to reason that the Portuguese government must have devised some sort of expedient to temporize with the Maratha.

While Moropant thus lay encamped at Kalyan, right opposite to the island of Salsette, the Abyssinians at Janjira had much reason for anxiety, nor were they very much cheered by the report that came soon afterwards that Shivaji was about to descend in person to the coast by the western ghats. The Abyssinian fleets lay at anchor near Bombay harbour. The Abyssinians were afraid that the Marathas might not hesitate to set their fleet on fire, and hastened to remove it to a safe port with great precipitation. On the other hand at Surat the news of Moropant's encampment at Kalyan awakened similar apprehensions, and the prospect of a fresh invasion of that prosperous town appeared more immediate by reason of the near presence of Hambirrao's light horse in the territory around Broach. Surat seemed to be menaced from two directions simultaneously by two Maratha armies.

While his two ministers were thus engaged in two different theatres of war, Shivaji himself had not been inactive. The Maratha hosts were streaming continually down the ghats and regiment after regiment was arriving to swell the ranks in Moropant's cantonment The objective of these gathering hosts crowding together in the camp lines at Kalyan was for a time kept secret. When the numbers under Moropant's standard had accumulated to twenty-five thousand, Shivaji left Raigad for the Konkan, with the ostensible object of personally inspecting the arrangements of Moropant's camp. None could fathom the real object of Shivaji's sudden march to the Konkan. The fact is that the Mogul hosts had mustered at Junnar to the number of forty thousand, and it was no secret that their object was to force their way into Shivaji's territory on a fresh campaign of invasion. The king was rightly informed about these movements of the enemy, and the mysterious gathering of the Maratha squadrons at Kalyan was a movement in anticipation of the Mogul attack. No sooner did Shivaji come down to Kalyan than he took the command of his forces and before the enemy could have so much as a suspicion of his plans, his dust-stained squadrons were scouring the plain of Junnar. A fierce battle followed, in which the Moguls were completely routed, suffering on the field ten times the number of Shivaji's casualties. The Moguls fled confusedly in all directions. Shivaji's troops divided themselves into columns and pressed the pursuit with vigour. A number of Mogul horses and a quantity of useful war material fell into the hands of the pursuers. The conquering hosts destroyed and plundered the Mogul territory they passed through in pursuit of the fugitives. The chase continued as far as the town of Brahmapuri. The market-towns on the way yielded a good deal of booty to the pursuing conquerors. Piquets of cavalry were stationed on the great trade route to Surat to intercept the merchandise and bring it down to the Maratha camp.

It was,however, not so easy to carry the fort of Shivneri, which overshadowed the town of Junnar and which after the cavalry engagement Shivaji had proceeded to besiege. One assault was tried after another. Still the fort continued to elude his grasp. Two of Shivaji's men planned a stratagem, which was to climb up the ramparts in secret and throw the gates open. But the garrison discovering the stealthy attempt in time killed the treacherous assailants, rolling down upon their heads huge stones from the fortress walls. This success became a revelation of strength to the garrison who determined to pursue this method, hurling stones and rocks on the siege-lines below. In this way Shivaji lost many men and the remainder lost heart and began to flee away. The Moguls were emboldened at the panic they had caused among their assailants, and with great animation set up a pursuit. But the pursuit proved more disastrous than they had bargained for. For the flight of the Maratha soldier was merely guerilla warfare. Retreat and fighting followed by turns and the fugitives rallied and turned upon their unwary pursuers again and again. These tactics made a thorough rout impossible, as the Moguls now discovered to their loss. However Shivaji had enough experience of fort-fighting to see that it was up-hill work to lead his rallied forces to a fresh assault upon Shivneri He, therefore, ordered a retreat to Raigad.

On his return to Raigad Shivaji learnt that Mahomed Khan, the subhedar of Phonda had taken advantage of his campaign at Junnar to break the former treaty and again acknowledge the hegemony of the state of Bijapur, and to show his zeal in the service of that government, he was molesting Shivaji's out-posts in the military stations on that side of the western ghats. Shivaji was now resolved to teach a severe lesson to the governor of this fort. He prepared a large army which he conducted in person and laid siege to the fort of Phonda. The garrison held out relying on the strength of their fortifications.[1] Shivaji made many assaults without success. At last Shivaji ordered mines to be laid under the fortress walls, which being simultaneously exploded, a large breach was made in the rampart and a considerable loss was inflicted upon the garrison. Shivaji carried the breach and a fierce encounter took place within the walls of the fortress. The governor of the fort fell in the general melee, and with his death the garrison lost heart and surrendered. A Mahomedan officer on Shivaji's side named Ibrahim Khan distinguished himself by the impetuosity of his attack on this occasion. Shivaji complimented him on his bravery and appointed him to the command of this fort. This was the first occasion on which a Mahomedan in Shivaji's service was appointed to the position of a havaldar or governor of a garrisoned fort, his usual practice being to confer these positions of trust on responsible Maratha officers. This promotion bears eloquent testimony to the confidence Shivaji reposed in the loyalty and devotion of this Mahomedan commander. The governorship of an important fortress, and that too on the frontiers of his dominions, could never have been conferred on an ordinary individual. (May, 1675)[2]

On the reduction of Phonda fort, Shivaji brought the neighbouring country under his complete sway, and to

[1] Siege of Phonda, from 9th April 1675 to 6th May 1675 (Prof. Sarkar: Shivaji p. 325-27).

[2] Jedhe Chronology, p. 192.

perpetuate his hold upon these parts he had two additional forts built, Bhimgad and Pargad, and strongly garrisoned them against the enemy. The Marathas then pushed into the district of Sunda, capturing several hill-forts. Ankola, Shiveshwar and Kadra (Kodra) fell in rapid succession. The governor of the fort of Karwar would not surrender the citadel. Upon this Shivaji gave orders for the town of Karwar to be committed to flames. There were a few English merchants, representatives of the East India Company, who were treated with deference. Their factories were not interfered with. The whole territory upto the boundaries of the province of Kanara was brought under Shivaji's flag. The sovereignty over parts of Kanara was then vested in the dowager Rani of Bednor and Shivaji did not think it fair to her sex to invade her dominions. But the princess sent a petition with the usual nazar offerings and solicited his help against her ministers and relations, who were usurping her authority.[1] In response to this petition Shivaji willingly detached some of his forces to bring succour to the distressed princess, who was soon delivered from her unhappy predicament.

While Shivaji was thus operating in the district of Phonda, two Maratha nobles in the service of the Bijapur government, Nimbalkar of Phaltan and Ghatge of Malwadi, subdued all the military out-posts maintained by Shivaji between the forts of Panhala and Tattora and expelled his soldiers from these parts. The territory around these forts was recovered and restored to Bijapur. Thus on his return to the ghats after the successful campaign in the south, Shivaji had once more to recover these out-posts and territories and, to prevent the possibility of similar events in future, Shivaji erected a chain of fortifications between Panhala and Tattora. The new forts thus created were Vardhangad, Bhushangad and Sadashivgad. Not

---

[1] The principal of these chiefs was Timayya who was the minister and commander of Bednore at Shivaji's first invasion, the Rani being the queen-regent and guardian of the infant prince. (*Vide* Chitnis 70.)

that these forts were exceptionally strong, but their situation near one another contributed very materially to the security of the territory around them.

Meanwhile Hambirrao, the chief commander, had carried on a vigorous offensive in Guzerat. He had gathered an immense booty in these wealthy parts of the Mogul dominions and was now preparing to retreat with his spoils. Diler Khan watched his movements. Hambirrao's great object was to elude the Mogul army and make good his retreat to the south with the spoils of his conquests. The Khan was however soon upon him and gave chase with great vigour. It was however to no purpose. Hambirrao eluded the pursuit and brought home to Raigad all his booty in safety. Diler Khan had to return disappointed. On the close of the rainy season Hambirrao again entered the Mogul territory and repeated his onslaughts. No Mogul commander came forth to challenge him. For the Mogul and Bijapur powers were again involved in mutual hostilities, and this circumstance was very favourable to Hambirrao's designs.

The affairs of Bijapur were then conducted by Khawas Khan. When he saw the Mogul arms concentrated against Bijapur, he proposed a treaty to Khan Jehan on the basis that the young Adil Shahi king should continue to reign on the footing of a feudal relation with the Mogul power, and the minor king's sister, Padshah Bibi, be given in marriage to a son of Aurangzeb. But this treaty was not approved of by the leading nobles of the court, who conspired against Khawas Khan and put him to death. The leader of the conspiracy was Abdul Karim,[1] who now seized the reins of government into his own hands and prepared for hostilities with the Moguls. Khan Jehan took the field in

[1] Khawas Khan was the leader of the Abyssinian party and Abdul Karim Bahlol Khan the leader of the Pathan or Afghan party at Bijapur. *Vide* Jedhe, page 192, where, however, by some corruption of the text the contrary statement is apparently made that Bahlol Khan was arrested by Khawas Khan. It appears to be a case of a *lapsus calami*.

person and came down upon Bijapur. Many skirmishes followed, in most of which the Adil Shahi arms were crowned with success. With these signs of Mogul failure before him Diler Khan proposed terms and the armistice soon gave place to a ratified treaty. By this time Shivaji had established his undisputed sway over the Konkan regions overlooked by the ghats. The Moguls and the Abyssinians had at times carried on desultory wars over these territories, but had never proved themselves equal to wresting them permanently from his iron grasp. The Moguls looked with envious eyes upon the fair provinces of Coorla, Kalyan and other parts bordering on the frontiers of the Portuguese territory near Bombay. When Khan Jehan came down upon the Konkan and began tentative incursions, Shivaji got him cheaply out of the way at the price of ten thousand pagodas. Pleased with this argument of corruption and gold, the venal Khan transferred his mimicry of war to his old theatre above the ghats. But the Abyssinian chief had no such hankering for gold. He put his naval squadrons in motion and began a campaign of systematic depredation on the coast towns and villages owning allegiance to Shivaji. He descended upon Vengurla, plundering or burning every thing that came in his way. The Dutch had a factory at the town, which, though attacked by the Abyssinians, is said to have been defended with great bravery by the European factors.

Shivaji's fleet, being fitted out for the war at the ports of Vijaydurg and Rajapur, weighed anchor and put out to sea in pursuit; but though they scoured the coasts north and south in quest of the elusive enemy, the wily Abyssinians showed no trace of their presence anywhere. At length the Maratha fleet blockaded Janjira by sea, when the Abyssinian warships made all sail and hastened to the relief of their capital. This brought about an engagement between the rival fleets, but with an indecisive result. The Maratha squadrons raised the siege and retired.

On the retirement of the Mogul subhedar from the

Konkan, Shivaji saw the necessity of maintaining a fortified out-post in the district of Salsette,[1] to overawe the Portuguese, his immediate neighbours in those parts, and at the same time to serve as a sort of watch-tower with such ample range that he might easily keep an eye on the movements of the Portuguese and other foes. Now the Portuguese had just such a fort named Seebon[2] not far from Bassein, and Shivaji resolved to have a corresponding fort on his side right in front of the Portuguese stronghold. The Portuguese made many attempts to interrupt the work. But they proved abortive and the fortification works were very rapidly proceeded with.

About this time Shivaji fell ill and was confined to his sick bed for seven or eight months at Satara. This circumstance sufficed to give currency to all sorts of baseless rumours that the great king had died, having succumbed to poison administered by his son, Sambhaji, during his illness. However the report was not generally believed among the people, for this was not the first time when such mendacious tales about Shivaji's death had gone round. In his active career of well-nigh thirty years, this seems to have been the first important sickness of Shivaji. There is no previous record of such a protracted illness in his eventful life. After the stress of so many labours and adventures by which he had paved his way to the realization of his hopes, even his Herculean strength might well flag and demand peace and rest. But the rest that Shivaji wanted it was impossible to obtain. The malignant influences of the hostile powers in the Deccan were at work on all sides. He had always to maintain a vigilant watch against them. The rest that was thus long denied to him, nature exacted in this protracted illness. It was in this time of enforced inactivity that the deep-laid plans for a new campaign were evolved in Shivaji's mind, destined to be prosecuted in person, as soon

[1] The district of Salsette in the neighbourhood of the island of Bombay, not the district of similar name in the neighbourhood of Panjim in Goa.

[2] The modern Sion, still called Shiv or Sheev in Marathi.

as his health permitted it. This was the invasion of the Karnatic, the story of which may be held over to be told in a separate chapter.

While Shivaji was pondering over these plans at Satara, Moropant Pingle marched to Kalyan with a force of ten thousand strong. Arrived there he detached a few men, with a gang of masons and labourers to a dismantled fort called Parnel (Parner). The fort was forthwith occupied by Moropant's men and the work of strengthening the fortifications commenced in right earnest. The policy which seems to have prompted this capture and renovation of a ruined fortress seems to have been this, that thereby he might obtain control over the Portuguese communications with Damaun and expose to attack one of the trade-routes to Surat as well as ths movements of the Mogul armies in those parts. The Portuguese government looked languidly upon this rising menace to their freedom of communication, being as incapable of resistance now, as a few months before they had been in the case of the fort in Salsette. On his restoration to health, previously to his embarking on the Karnatic campaign, Shivaji made a tour of inspection to this fortress, thus restored and equipped for such important purposes.

CHAPTER XXVI

THE KARNATIC CAMPAIGN, 1676-78

WHILE Shivaji was taking rest during his sickness at Satara, the Karbhari or administrator of the jahgir estates of Venkoji, Raghunath Narayen Hanmante by name, came to pay him a visit. This officer was the son of Shahaji's trusty minister, Naro Trimal Hanmante. Raghunath Hanmante had on his father's demise succeeded to his position in Shahaji's government. On the death of the Raja Shahaji, he was succeeded by his younger son, Raja Venkoji, and the estates were administered for him by Raghunathpant Hanmante. But some years later, the infatuated Venkoji took a fancy to hold the reins of his affairs in his own hands, to do very much as he liked in every thing, and not consult any of his father's veteran ministers and counsellors. From the time when Venkoji took over the administration into his own charge, Raghunathpant's influence became quite negligible in his jahagir. Venkoji governed as the vulgar satellites who surrounded him were pleased to advise, and Raghunathpant was constantly treated with insults and abuse. The minister saw that to live any more with Venkoji had become impossible. He was answerable to Shivaji for the maintenance of his father's prestige. Helpless as he felt himself to avert the wreck and ruin of Shahaji's jahgir, he could not expect to shake off his moral responsibility in the eyes of his illustrious master's more illustrious son. To prevent that reproach he must completely sever his connection with Venkoji and devote the rest of his life to the observances of religion, in some secluded retreat or place of pilgrimage. Thus he thought in silence and even with that silent thought, a blush of shame overspread his features. His mind faltered. Was it right that he should stand an idle spectstor of the waning fortunes of his young master and cover up his bitter disappointment under the specious pretence of retirement? Was it not due to his loyalty to continue his service with a view to the greater glory of Shahaji and the Bhonsle name? Yes, to bear with patience the slings and arrows of his present misfortune and the more outrageous shafts of his prince's ingratitude? He would serve the prince and in spite of the prince steer his course to safety, to the best of his abilities.

Thus fortified in his mind, he once more made bold to expostulate with Venkoji. "Your Highness knows," said he, "I am a hereditary servant of the family, and I know no other standard of service than my patron's welfare. Ah! woe is me, that my dutiful offices are distasteful to Your Highness! My heart bleeds to see you misled by the counsels of fickle and mean-spirited creatures. Bethink you, sir, of the glory and valour of your father, bethink you of the world-wide fame and the noble triumphs earned by your brother Shivaji! Follow in their wake, I pray, and earn the same laurels. Shivaji will look to me to lead you to the path of noble emulation trodden before by himself and by Shahaji. Rightly does Shivaji expect it of me and sorely will he blame me if he finds it otherwise. Be it yours to command and mine to obey. Men and money Your Highness has in abundance, but they are both rusting together, and your false friends help you only to squander away your treasure. It is only by adding to the ample glory of your ancestors that Your Highness can repay the obligations of high birth." But these discourses were lost upon Venkoji. He shrank from them as from poison. He was quite tired of his company and did not hesitate openly to express his contempt.

Disgusted with the growing insolence of Venkoji, Raghunathpant wrote a letter of warning to his brother. Upon this the latter wrote to Venkoji, giving him friendly advice. The purport of the letter was somewhat as follows. Shivaji wrote that it had come to his ears that Venkoji was indifferent to the duties of administration and was a tool in the hands of vile and unworthy men; that the parasite and the pander throve at his expense, while men of worth who deserved well of his family and had given their lives to its service were languishing in utter neglect This was not as it ought to be. Shivaji hoped his brother would turn over a new leaf, and hearkening to the advice of Raghunathpant and other experienced and capable counsellors, would consult his own welfare and the expansion of the family fortunes. But even this letter did not serve to open Venkoji's eyes. He continued his usual course of life, such was the strength of his infatuation and the ascendancy of evil company upon his feeble mind. He was, if anything, even more incensed with Raghunathpant as having had the temerity to complain of him to his elder brother. Raghunathpant had now drained the cup of loyal self-abasement to its very dregs and his patience was exhausted. He resolved to proceed to the court of Shivaji, and leaving his family behind, he started upon his journey.

Raghunathpant knew well Shivaji's ambition to expand his dominions and in order to further these aims of expansion he concluded alliances to that effect with the local chiefs before leaving the Karnatic, his object being to invite Shivaji to that province that he might bring Venkoji to his senses. To facilitate these plans, knowing that Shivaji might have to march through the Golconda territories, Raghunathpant took steps to bring about a harmonious alliance between the Maratha and the Kutub Shahi governments, so that no delay or distraction might hinder Shivaji's movements.

The leading ministers of the Kutub Shahi government about this time were Akanna and Madanna, who were not only both Hindus, but sons of the same Hindu family. These two men had the control of all Kutub Shahi affairs in their hands. Raghunathpant determined to visit the distinguished ministers, but instead of interviewing them abruptly in his own person and setting forth his diplomatic objects, he thought of making his first acquaintance with them in the disguise of a pandit. For the ministers had a fair repute for piety and hospitality and religious benefactions. Raghunathpant left his retinue behind him at an obscure village and entered the capital alone, presenting himself as a pandit at the residence of the ministers about the hour they usually devoted to their purificatory bath and morning worship. It was their rule when a pandit appeared at their house to welcome him with every mark of respect and bestow upon him such patronage as became his learning and position. True to their principles they received Raghunathpant with open hospitality. Other pandits were already in the house and debate had started among them on the relative superiority of Shaivism and Vaishnavism. Raghunathpant also took part in the debate. Being himself a staunch Vaishnavite, he proceeded first to argue for the superiority of Shiv, refuting every objection. Having established the strength of the Shaivite creed, he turned the tables upon his antagonists by suddenly espousing the cause of Vaishnavism and demonstrating its truth with a display of dialectical skill equally unanswerable. Madanna was impressed with this exhibition of argumentative talent and was convinced that he must be a person of extraordinary learning and attainments. Accosting him, he said he was glad to have come across a person of such learning and sanctity, and asked him where he had come from and with what object. Raghunathpant replied that he had not at all come with the expectation of gold or land, but as his hosts were persons of such wisdom and piety, he would feel himself much flattered to have a private audience with them. Upon this the two brothers took him apart for the interview he desired. Raghunathpant declared that he was no itinerant mendicant pandit, but an officer in Shivaji's service, proceeding to wait upon his royal master with certain delicate questions of Karnatic politics, questions which might bring down Shivaji's hosts into these parts. But Shivaji required, continued Raghunathpant, the sympathetic aid of the Golconda ministers, during this campaign, and now he had come at Shivaji's orders to intercede with them and their sovereign with a view to an alliance of mutual support and amity between Golconda and Shivaji. Raghunathpant then addressed himself to their religious instincts, pointing out the labours of Shivaji for the advancement of the Hindu religion, which made it a sort of obligation on their sense of piety and religion to advance Shivaji's great purposes, the more so as it involved no treason and no detriment whatever to the interests of their own sovereign.[1] The ministers were pleased with the proposal thus introduced, being already prepossessed in favour of Shivaji by the loud and repeated acclaims with which the Deccan people had greeted his incomparable triumphs. They had been, as has been already described in Chapter XX, instrumental in bringing about a happy compromise between Shivaji and their government, by which the latter had engaged to pay an annual tribute to the Maratha power. They gave their full assent to the proposal for further strengthening the friendly relations with Shivaji and introduced Raghunathpant to an interview with their sultan, when the terms of the alliance were settled and ratified. Shivaji was to proceed upon his Karnatic campaign, for so it was arranged, by way of the Kutub Shahi capital, Bhaganagar, the modern Hyderabad (Deccan), and there the two kings were to have a conference for a further discussion of their relation and the perpetuation of their existing alliance. Raghunathpant was given an enthusiastic reception, banqueted by the minister brothers, and presented with suits of honour and personal decorations at the time of his departure. He was also charged with the delivery of a personal epistle from the sultan addressed to Shivaji.

From the successful diplomatic mission to Bhaganagar, Raghunathpant came to Satara, where, as stated at the commencement of this chapter, he met Shivaji. The latter went forth to welcome the loyal veteran who had rendered such invaluable services to his father and led him

[1] Shivdigvijay, 290-93.

to the palace with a display of cordiality and ceremonial splendour that was but rarely witnessed at Shivaji's court.[1] Raghunathpant laid at Shivaji's feet the many curious specimens of Karnatic art and precious jewellery that he had brought with him, which gave immense satisfaction to Shivaji as the evidence of that profound loyalty towards his family which had become hereditary with the veteran minister. Shivaji congratulated himself upon the accession to his cause of one who had gained such distinction in Shahaji's service. He heaped upon him all the honours at his command and proposed to confer on him the office of Amatya or Muzumdar. It is said that the incumbent of that office, a certain Ramchandrapant, was made to vacate his place in favour of Raghunathpant.[2]

As observed in the last chapter Shivaji was at this time chafing against the restraints of an enforced idleness occasioned by his ill health. To this was added the season of the rains, which extended the period of rest by four months. During these months of leisure Raghunathpant related to Shivaji in full detail the story of Venkoji's

[1] The Rairi bakhar states that on his way from the Karnatic, Raghunathpant went to Bijapur, where the sultan offered to him the post of grand vizier. When Shivaji learnt about this offer, he wrote to Raghunathpant that, as long as he lived, it would not do for a trusty servant of his family to serve a Mahomedan prince. He should come to him without any fear, where he would be welcomed with all the honour due to his position and services.

[2] Chitnis says that Raghunathpant made a request that the honoured post of Muzumdar which he had held in the Bhonsle family in hereditary succession, should be conferred upon him and that upon this request Shivaji appointed him to that high office. But the Rairi bakhar states that Nilo Sondev the Muzumdar had just then died, and the place left vacant by his death was conferred upon Raghunathpant.

Nilo Sondev was Amatya or Muzumdar from 1647 to his death in 1672. He was the brother of Abaji Sondev the conqueror of Kalayan from Mullana. Like the Hanmantes, the family of Nilo Sondev had a hereditary connection with the Bhonsles.

The Jedhe Chronology states that Raghunath Narayan was made Muzumdar in Ashwin, Shaka 1599 i. e. October 1677, or after the Karnatic campaign was half completed.

mismanagement and urged upon him the duty and necessity of a campaign in the Karnatic to place his father's fortunes on a basis of security. He laid bare before Shivaji the alliances he had already formed with the local naiks of the Karnatic to promote the plan of the prospective campaign and the results he had achieved in his self-imposed mission to the court of Golconda. He told Shivaji that he could claim his right to a moiety of Shahaji's estates, under the Hindu law of inheritance and that by embarking on this campaign on the plea of vindicating his rights, he could save the wreck of Venkoji's heritage and put together Shahaji's dismembered fortunes, and in addition to this acquire new territories and provinces which the chances of war might throw in his way.

The times were favourable for such a campaign. There was no objection to his marching through the Golconda kingdom into the Karnatic. Golconda paid tribute and the two ministers were favourably disposed towards Shivaji. Their friendship had been further strengthened to a more permanent alliance by Raghunathpant. The recent friendly overtures between the Mogul and the Adil Shahi state had thrown Golconda into ill-humour with both those powers. That peace had been arranged between Diler Khan and the Adil Shahi premier Abdul Karim,[1] who happened to be drawn to each other by some family relationship. But Diler Dhan was a sworn enemy to Golconda and to Shivaji alike. Thus the alliance between these latter powers was alike inevitable and enduring.

It only remained to take the usual precautions against a surprise attack by the Moguls upon his territories. With this view, the judicial minister, Nirajipant, was deputed on

[1] At any rate both were Afgan nobles. Abdul Karim was the leader of the Pathan party at Bijapur and had to hold his own against the Abyssinian and Deccani party. He had got Khawas Khan, the leader of the Abyssinian party and former prime minister, out of the way by assassination. Khawas Khan had been on friendly terms with Khan Jehan Bahadur, the Mogul governor of the Deccan.

a special embassy to Khan Jehan, the Mogul subhedar. Having experience of his venality, the one great weakness of that otherwise great proconsul, Shivaji loaded him with presents of gold and jewellery and extracted a promise not to interfere with his territories. To make assurance doubly sure, Shivaji paid a large sum as tribute to the Mogul emperor, thus admitting a relation of feudal dependence. It is said that on this occasion he undertook to pay a tribute of four lakhs of pagodas to the emperor and to serve him in war with five thousand horse, remarking that it was but an oil-cake thrown to the milch-cow. Aurangzeb approved of the treaty. The emperor was engaged in a campaign against the rebel Afgan tribes on this side of the Indus. He sent word to his heir-apparent that it was not the time for war with Shivaji, a peace was most expedient and such a peace as would not injure Mogul prestige.[1]

Thus profiting by the venality of the Mogul subhedar Shivaji had secured his diminions from Mogul attacks. On the southern frontier he had by this time completed a chain of barrier forts, well-manned and equipped, to ward off the spasmodic forays of the Ghatges, the Nimbalkars and the other Maratha barons of the Adil Shahi kingdom. The Konkan was the weak spot in Shivaji's system, exposed as it was to the inextinguishable enmity of the sea-faring Abyssinians. To guard against this menace and nip in the bud the first signs of active hostilities on the part of these sea adventurers, Annaji Datto, Pant Sachiv, was detached with a large force to take general charge of the sea-board forts from Kalyan to Phonda and the territories surrounding them. These forts were equipped and re-inforced in such a splendid style that in case any of them became the object of an assault on the part of the enemy help poured in instantly from all quarters, and the garrison could defend themselves without the thought of a parley, secure of ultimate deliverance. With these precautions taken for

[1] Sabhasad, 85.

immunity from foreign attack, the whole kingdom was committed to the safe management of Moropant, the Peshwa, and other ministers and commanders were ordered to defer to him in everything.

It was about the end of 1676 that Shivaji with a force of 40,000 foot and 30,000 horse started upon his Karnatic campaign.[1] To lead such a numerous army over such distant parts was a very expensive operation and Shivaji's aim naturally was to draw upon the streams of supply from without his treasury. He proposed to levy fresh contributions upon Golconda, a country which already paid him tribute and which was not, therefore, to be treated with violence. The ministers Madanna and Akanna had already been sounded previously by Raghunathpant and were prepared for the sacrifice. Shivaji, therefore, wrote to his envoy at that court, Pralhad Niraji,[2] that as he was about to commence his Karnatic campaign, he expected the Sultan Tan Shaha to contribute towards the expenses and to arrange for a personal interview at his capital, when he came there on his march. This communication caused much agitation at the Golconda capital. The sultan was overcome with fear. The presence of Shivaji with his army at his capital seemed to strike him as a contingency fraught with grave peril. He consented to the contributions demanded of him in money, and in order to avert the danger that threatened his capital, he consented to the demand with excessive alacrity, professing to the Maratha envoy that his king might command anything without putting himself to any trouble and deviating from his route merely for the purpose of a formal interview. Pralhad Niraji communicated this offer to Shivaji.

1 The total force is variously given in the chronicles of Sabhasad, Chitnis, and the Shivdigvijay. The East India Company's representatives calculated it at 20,000 horse and 40,000 foot.

2 He was the son of Niraji Ravji, the sir-nyayadhish. In the reign of Rajaram, the title of Pratinidhi was conferred upon him. At the time of this campaign he was the resident ambassador at Golconda.

But Shivaji, pursuant to the arrangement made by Ragbunathpant with the Golconda ministers had already started for that town at the head of his army, having despatched Raghunathpant and Pralhad Niraji before him to inform the sultan of his near approach for the favour of a personal conference. The near presence of Shivaji and his warrior bands alarmed the sultan. The town was in a panic. But Raghunathpant and Pralhad Niraji assured the court on oath that Shivaji's arrival had nothing hostile about it and that he was only taking the opportunity, being near at hand, for a friendly interview. Madanna and Akanna felt the sincerity of these assurances and endeavoured to persuade the sultan that the proposed interview was likely to lead to possibilities of infinite advantage to his state. With difficulty did the timid monarch allow the bold persuasion of his ministers to outweigh his fear and tried to nerve himself to face the inevitable ordeal.

On entering the Golconda frontiers Shivaji passed strict orders to his soldiers to abstain from every act of hostility towards the people and not to harass them in any way. At every halt they were to procure food, fodder, and fuel by free purchase. No booty, no violence; any one committing a breach of these orders was to receive exemplary punishment. When in a few cases these orders were found to have been transgressed, the culprits had their hands or fingers cut off, and in a few cases, were actually executed. This stringency of discipline gave perfect security of life and property to the subjects of Golconda, and even the sultan was so far reassured as to revive his drooping spirits.[1] On Shivaji's arrival within easy reach of the capital, Madanna and Akanna went forth with a suitable retinue to receive him and escorted him into the royal city with great pomp and eclat. The next day was fixed for Shivaji's audience with the sultan.[2]

[1] Sabhasad, 88; Chitnis 136.

[2] The Jedhe Chronology gives the date of this interview as March 1677.

Shivaji started in a procession with a chosen retinue, arrayed in robes of state and mounted on horses and elephants, specially decorated for the occasion. The town had, under the sultan's express orders, put on its gala aspect. The streets were adorned with flags and festoons of flowers, gay *toran* decorations were to be seen at every turn, and musical instruments discoursed liquid melodies. Amid such pomp and splendour the procession slowly wended its way to the royal palace, the Hindu subjects of the sultan in particular turning out in great crowds into the streets, fired with an intense desire to catch a glimpse of the great Hindu raja. Loud acclamations greeted him on the way, the people enthusiastically showering flowers upon him from windows and balconies. The king had been bountiful of his alms among the poor and the fakirs of the town that morning. To the citizens greeting him on the way with floral decorations and the like Shivaji paid his thanks by presentations of select articles of dress or jewellery as tokens of his good will.

The royal conference took place at the Dadmahal, (the Palace of Justice) where sumptuous arrangements had been made for a grand reception. On Shivaji's arrival within the precincts of the palace, the retinue halted outside, and the king with a few chosen officers entered the gates. As the sultan prepared to descend the grand staircase to receive him, Shivaji sent him word that he might spare himself that trouble. On reaching the upper floor the two monarchs joined in a mutual embrace and took their seats on the same couch. Madanna and Akanna seated themselves next to them, while the rest of the omrahs remained standing. The officers accompanying Shivaji, the most conspicuous among whom were Baburao Dhamdhere, the sirnobut of the guard, Raghunathpant, Pralhad Niraji, Dattopant the Waknis and Balaji Avji, the private secretary, were desired to be seated.[1]

[1] Sabhasad adds to this list of officers present at the Dadmahal reception the names of Somji Naik Vasanagar and Janardanpant.

Then followed a friendly conversation between the two rulers. The great officers accompanying Shivaji were introduced to the sultan and received suitable compliments from their royal host, each according to his rank. The sultan was pleased with the smart appearance and accoutrements of Shivaji's body-guard. Distribution of pan, attar and flowers duly followed, together with the offerings of nazar, the sultan bestowing valuable presents of jewellery, horses, and elephants upon Shivaji. It is said that at this reception the sultan presented attar and pan to his distinguished guest with his own hands, a circumstance that the chronicle-writers have thought it worth while to record. Thus the reception lasted for two or three hours, at the termination of which, Shivaji bade farewell to his host and returned to his tent.

It is said that Shivaji made a halt for a month at Bhaganagar, during which many questions of foreign policy were discussed with the sultan through the medium of Madanna. There was a round of feasting and banqueting, Madanna inviting Shivaji and his courtiers to a grand dinner, when the usual offerings of nazars took place; and Shivaji returning the compliment with a sumptuous banquet in honour of the minister brothers, with gifts to them and their officers. Shivaji also entertained the sultan and his omrahs on a magnificent scale, when valuable presents of wearing apparel and jewellery were bestowed upon the guests according to their positions in the state. Shivaji also cultivated friendly intercourse with the leading citizens and mansabdars of the state.

An amusing incident in connection with this visit is related in one of the bakhar chronicles.[1] On one occasion in the course of his conversation with Raghunathpant, the sultan of Golconda remarked to him that he had heard so much in praise of the prowess of Shivaji's soldiers, that he was eager to see a proof of their prowess with his own eyes. Upon this Raghunathpant is reported to have answered that there were soldiers in Shivaji's

[1] The Shivdigvijaya.

army each one of whom was equal in strength to an elephant. "If so," exclaimed the sultan, "will they fight with an elephant?" "Why not?" quoth Raghunathpant, "what is there impossible about it? They don't fear an elephant." "How could they fight with an elephant?" asked the sultan, "Well! I should like to witness such a fight. Do you bring one of these veteran soldiers of Shivaji!" Raghunathpant informed Shivaji of the conversation he had with the sultan, and it was arranged that Yessaji Kank should select ten of his stalwarts to undergo the test in presence of the sultan. The soldiers were introduced by Raghunathpant to the sultan, who received them with the usual honours and presents and forthwith ordered an infuriated elephant to be freed and let loose upon them. The tusked monster came straight upon Yessaji who did not falter for a moment but drawing his sword smote the charging beast with such a tremendous force that he severed his trunk from the tusks downwards. The sultan was filled with admiration at this exhibition of physical strength and inviting Yessaji into his presence, he praised him for his valour and presented him with a set of a soldier's armlets and necklaces. Not only that, but he was going to confer upon him an inam estate of five thousand rupees, but Yessaji, informed of the sultan's royal pleasure, made a respectful salute and declined the proffered lands, replying, with marvellous firmness of mind, that he considered the bread he ate, of Shivaji's giving, to be no less of the Sultan's bounty. By Shivaji's order he had shown the valour of his arm to the sultan; it was not, therefore, becoming in him as a loyal servant to accept of inam lands at the sultan's hands, for did he not receive enough and to spare at the hands of Shivaji? Were he to accept of the present offer, he might become incapable of true and loyal service to his king. The sultan might signalize his favour by presenting what he wished to his patron. His duty was only to serve and obey. It is unnecessary to say what a profound impression the disinterested loyalty of this veteran officer must have made upon the sultan.

At the end of this long sojourn at Bhaganagar, in the midst of this gay pomp and hospitality, Shivaji communicated to the sultan his intention to depart and asked leave to do so. A farewell durbar was held in honour of the event and a fresh bestowal of presents followed. The two parties undertook on oath to aid one another on all occasions, defensive or offensive.[1] The sultan paid the pecuniary contributions required by Shivaji for the campaign.[2] Among the articles of the treaty that was now finally concluded was one by which Shivaji undertook to cede to Golconda a moiety of all the territory which he should conquer in the prospective campaign exclusive of the jahgir estate of Shahaji. The sultan was to send the Golconda artillery to co-operate with Shivaji. The sultan even offered to place a portion of his army at Shivaji's disposal, but this was not accepted. It is said that there was also an additional article in the treaty by which it was provided that Shivaji should have the authority to restore any Karnatic territories which he should have wrested from the Bijapur government in the forthcoming campaign, on condition that that government should discharge its present prime minister Abdul Karim and appoint Akanna of Bhaganagar in his place.[3]

With a plentiful supply of money and an efficient artillery Shivaji continued his march in the direction of the Karnatic. On the way, Shivaji came to a small principality, namely that of Karnul-Kudappa, on the banks of the Tungabhadra, the chief of which[4] promised to pay a tribute of five lakhs of pagodas to Shivaji. From Karnul at a distance of some twenty-five miles there

1 At this interview, according to the Rairi bakhar, Shivaji declared to the sultan. that if Golconda and Bijapur would co-operate with him he would conquer the whole of India for them. Kutub Shaha had to pay a subsidy at the rate of 3000 pagodas a day. Part of it was taken in advance.

2 According to Wilks, the sultan presented to Shivaji the sum of ten lakhs of pagodas in cash and some jewellery besides. The Rairi bakhar mentions five lakhs of pagodas only.

3 *Vide* the Shivdigvijaya, 302.

4 Wilks gives his name as Anandrao Deshmukh.

is the confluence of the Krishna with a tributary stream, the Bhavnashi, called the Nivritti-Sangam. Here Shivaji bathed in the sacred waters and crossed the Krishna. While the main body of his army advanced slowly by the route of Kudappa, Shivaji, with a body of cavalry, struck off to the eastward, for the purpose of performing his devotions at a celebrated pilgrim resort, the shrine of Shail Mallikarjun.[1] Leaving his troops behind at the inner town, Shivaji proceeded with a few companions to the river-bank. Here the scenery is most rich and sublime,—the mountain towering high into the air, with its perpetual dower of dark woods and forests, and the silver sheet of the Krishna rolling seawards down the eastern slopes. The lovely scene thrilled Shivaji with a feeling of spiritual calm and exaltation. It seemed to him like a *Kailas* on earth, the Olympus of the god Shiv. It stirred into a wild commotion the spiritual impulses of his heart. It kindled a frenzy of divine love, a desire to lay down and sacrifice all earthly and evanescent things at the foot-stool of the Eternal. Under the elation of that enthusiasm he drew his sword to sacrifice himself. Bu tthe enthusiasm reacting into a convulsive fit, he fell into a stupor and, as the chronicle-writers piously relate, he was possessed of the spirit of his tutelary deity, Bhavani, who made fresh prophecies to the effect that that was not the way for final salvation, as many more duties were waiting for fulfilment; his life was dedicated to the defence of the faith; it was not for him to run such hazards. On reviving from this paroxysm, his officers communicated to him the bidding of Bhavani, and Shivaji gave up the thought of committing this act of self-slaughter. However the holy calm of the place operated so powerfully upon his high-strung emotions that he resolved to spend the rest of his life as a recluse in these sacred haunts, and addressing his officers he said to them, "By the grace of Bhavani, we have well-nigh achieved the wildest of our ambitions; now do we will and resolve to leave the cares of this temporal world and devote

[1] Grant Duff and Wilks call it Parvatam (the mountain Shrine); Sabhasad calls the place Shail Parvat.

ourselves to holy and pious thoughts and the realization of eternal life. Do ye now put an end to this campaign already at this stage and, installing our son on the throne conduct the government in his name." This was very embarrassing to the king's officers. They tried their best to dissuade Shivaji and represented that true self-realization lay in following the lines laid down by Bhavani. But all their efforts failed. Shivaji put on the dress of an anchorite and smeared himself with ashes. He gave himself to meditation and solitude, spending his days like a sanyasi, oblivious of everything but meditation on the Supreme. The companions of Shivaji were filled with anxiety and kept a constant watch upon his actions. When he was free from meditation and had intervals of calm reasoning, Raghunathpant used to argue with him, quoting authorities from the Hindu scriptures, to prove that such a life was not meant for Kshatriyas, or men of the warrior class, like Shivaji. This aversion to material things and estrangement from the worldly life lasted for nine days.[1] Then Raghunathpant's persuasions began to prevail and Shivaji became convinced of the futility of this life of penance and prayer and meditation. Shivaji now scattered alms and feasted Brahmans, had a ghat or embankment erected on the river, called the Shri Gangesh Ghat, and built many cells for devout hermits to dwell in and practise their penances. Having thus spent eight or nine days more in these religious and charitable purposes, Shivaji proceeded upon his march.

Shivaji's infantry had already entered the Karnatic, descending the Pain Ghat by the Pass of Vyankatramangiri.[2] Overtaking the main body of his army, he left the infantry and the heavy baggage behind to come up by easy stages, while he pushed forward with the cavalry and a body of Mavalis. Passing by the route towards Madras,[3]

---

1 *Vide* Wilks, History of Mysore.

2 Col. Wilks calls it the Damulcherry pass.

3 The English Records at Madras mention that Shivaji passed Madras in the first week of May. (Records, Fort St. George 1677, pp. 112-15.) The Madras Council sent presents to Shivaji.

he reached Chandi[1] (Jinji) and proceeded to plant batteries for a regular siege. The fort belonged to the Bijapur government and was in charge of Rauf Khan and Nazar Khan, the sons of Amber Khan,[2] with whom Raghunathpant had made one of his secret agreements before coming to Satara.

The capture of the fort, therefore, occasioned no difficulty.[3] The fort was placed under the governorship of Ramji Nalage, one of Shivaji's loyal Mavali commanders, with Timaji Keshav as sabnis and Rudraji Salvi as karkhannis, or superintendent of stores. This distant fort was

---

1 Chandi or Chanji of the Marathi bakhars, called Jinji or Ginji by Grant Duff and other historians.

2 Some Marathi bakhars call him Khan. Khan i. e. Khan Khanan, and Prof. Sarkar thinks it was Khawas Khan, late premier of Bijapur.

3 The Rairi bakhar has the following story about the conquest of this fort :—Shivaji informed the governor Amber Khan that he had come down after making treaties with Bijapur and Golconda. He should, therefore, come to see him. The governor of the fort believed this and came out to see Shivaji with his eight sons, when they were all arrested and the fort captured. The Shivdigvijaya says that Amber Khan came with a nazar to Shivaji, who told him to surrender Jinji, if he cared for the tranquillity of his district, or as an alternative to stay in his camp and not return to Jinji, so that the Marathas might capture the fort in any manner they pleased. Upon this he promised to surrender the fort and made a deed of surrender, thinking that his safety lay in keeping good relations with Shivaji. But his eight sons who were in the fort refused to relinquish it and prepared for resistance. However Raghunathpant had intrigued with the garrison and the governor's sons found that very few people were on their side; upon which they got terrified and consented to surrender the fort. Shivaji assigned to them some villages for their maintenance and in return they were to serve Shivaji with their vassals.

Wilks says that on his march to Jinji, Shivaji did not molest the people and gave it out that he was marching southwards as a friend and ally of Bijapur. When Amberkhan sent his envoy to Shivaji, the latter told him that he had made his peace with Bijapur and declared himself to have accepted the supremacy of that state. Under this pretence he induced the old governor and his sons to visit him in his camp, put them into arrest and captured the fort. The bakhars speak of Rauf Khan as Rup Khan. Prof. Sarkar is of the opinion that Rauf Khan and Nazar Khan were the sons of Khawas Khan of Bijapur. He disbelieves the story of the fort having been taken by treachery; and quotes a Jesuit priest of Madura (La Mission du Madure), to prove that Shivaji carried the fort at the first assault.

subjected to the same regulations and discipline as the forts in Maharashtra. The adjoining territory was reduced to subjection and Vithal Pildev Goradkar[1] appointed as subhedar over all these districts, with orders to introduce the revenue system already adopted in Maharashtra. Rauf Khan and Nazar Mahomed had grants of land or revenue settled upon them.

At the commencement of the Karnatic expedition Shivaji gave it out that the campaign was conducted under the auspices of Golconda, having drawn so largely upon that government for money, and hoping to draw more in future. Shortly after he threw this pretence to the winds and administered in his own name, by the agency of his officers, the provinces he had captured. When the sultan of Golconda came to know of this conduct, he stopped all contributions. Shivaji had, therefore, to depend on the plunder of the country under occupation for the expenses of the campaign. The depredations thus begun caused great consternation, an idea of which can be formed by the fears recorded by the English merchants of Madras at the time. They have recorded that when Shivaji came into the Dravid country, the people in all parts were seized with panic. He had the reputation of being a very dreadful man, who carried fire and sword over the provinces of western India, and whom the people dreaded on that account. Every one was afraid lest he should fall into Shivaji's hands. He had a knack of discovering where wealth was hidden and whom to attack in order to obtain it. The people believed that he learnt this by some supernatural power and that this was the cause of his universal success.

After the reduction of Jinji, Shivaji moved his forces to Trinomali,[2] a district which was then in charge of Sher Khan, a commander of 5000 horse. He was a loyal veteran

---

1 The Shivdigvijaya gives Garud as the surname of Vithal Pildev,

2 Chitnis gives Trimalli as the name of this district. Sabhasad calls it Trivadi (Trivady).

Trivadi (Tiruvadi) was, however, an important fort in the Trinomali district as also was Vellore. Jedhe, as also some of the bakhars, call the

of Bijapur and marched upon Shivaji, the moment the Maratha forces entered his district. But in the battle that followed he was outnumbered and completely surrounded on all sides. The gallant commander was wounded and a good deal of booty and horses and elephants fell into the hands of Shivaji.

At this stage Shivaji was joined by the Raja Santaji, a natural son of Shahaji. He had hitherto lived under the protection of Venkoji, but disgusted with his conduct he now came to throw himself on Shivaji's protection. Shivaji gave him a cordial welcome and enrolled him in his service, where distinguishing himself ere long by his bravery, loyalty and abilities, he was appointed in course of time to the governorship of Chandi (Jinji.)

In the meantime the remaining part of Shivaji's army which had been left in the rear had invested the fortress of Vellore.[1] This fort was very strongly fortified and defended by a moat so wide as to enable large crocodiles to move about freely in the water. The width of the fortification walls was so great that a pair of waggons could pass each other on the ridge of the ramparts The siege was conducted by Narhari Ballal with considerable skill and ability. He erected his batteries on two little adjacent hillocks, which he playfully named Sajara and Gojara, the *pretty* hill and the *tender* hill, and concentrated his fire on the principal citadel. The cannonade did such an execution that in the end the garrison were compelled to surrender.[2]

fort Tripati. For the wounding and capture of Sher Khan *Vide* Jedhe p. 193. Prof. Sarkar following the Factory Records, Fort St. George, 87 gives a graphic account of the event. Sher Khan escaped on a dark night to a neighbouring town, but was pursued and surrounded by a Maratha column. The East India Company's Brahman agent, Nellore Ramana, was in Shivaji's camp.

1 This fort is also called Vellur and Yellur by other authors. It lay in the Trinomali district. The Shedgavkar bakhar, pp. 88, calls it Yesur instead of Yelur, the letter 's' having evidently crept in instead of 'l'.

2 The Basatin-i-Salatin asserts that Shivaji took the fort by paying a bribe of 50,000 pagodas to Abdulla Khan, the governor of the fort. As a matter of fact the siege lasted till the middle of August 1678, i. e. for

While the main body of his army was engaged in the siege of Vellore, Shivaji halted his cavalry at Tirumalvadi, on the banks of the Cauvery (the Coleroon), whence with a view to open overtures with the Raja Venkoji, he sent a message that, in order to bring about a peaceful accommodation, Venkoji should send down to his brother's camp three of his ministers, named in the letter, Govind Bhat Gosavi, Kakajipant and Nilo Naik.[1] These officers were accordingly sent to wait upon Shivaji. On their arrival, Shivaji made a feeling speech, the purport of which was as follows: " It is now thirteen years since the demise of our father. All the fortunes of Shahaji were handed over by Raghunathpant to the Raja Venkoji and he entered upon the heritage as the sole inheritor. But all the same it is our patrimony and we claim our moiety. This moiety, which we ought to have claimed long ago, we have suffered Venkoji to enjoy alone. The great distance at which we lived did not permit of our coming over here to claim it. We said to ourselves 'Venkoji is Shahaji's son. He has a vested right in his fortune. He may enjoy it for the present. We may make our demand at our leisure.' So we thought and waited these thirteen years. Affairs of state took us recently to Golconda, and being there we resolved to come over here into the Karnatic. What provinces have fallen to our sword since our coming hither, is already well known to you. We, therefore, ask Venkoji to inform us without loss of time whether he is prepared to yield to us the moiety of our patrimony without a protest. It will be a great shame for the world to see us at war. For after all, though our father be no more, we are children of the same flesh and blood. United should

---

fourteen months and the fort was ultimately captured by Raghunathpant and Anandrao (*Vide* Jedhe p. 194). From the Records of Fort St. George, *Diary and Consultations*, 1678-79, page 105, quoted by Sarkar, it appears that Abdulla Khan held out the fort as long as he could, but when he could no more postpone his surrender, he stipulated for a personal payment of 30,000 pagodas.

[1] The Shivdigvijaya adds the names of Rango Naik and Timaji Naik.

we stand, sharing mutually in each other's good fortune and ill fortune. Nobody ever profited by senseless discord." Addressing Venkoji's ministers in this strain, Shivaji gave them leave to depart sending some of his own ministers to accompany them to Venkoji's court. These people communicated Shivaji's wishes to Venkoji.

But the evil advisers of Venkoji misled the prince, urging that he should not yield tamely to Shivaji's demand for partition. He should show that he was a man and could put forth a manly fight. Venkoji was also instigated by the chief of Madura and the Raja of Mysore to defy Shivaji, they assuring him of their support. He, therefore, turned a deaf ear to these demands and dismissed Shivaji's men without an answer. Venkoji attempted to move his forces and put them in readiness for a battle. But the allies on whose assurance he had counted began to draw back at the last moment. Unaided he did not feel himself equal to a contest with Shivaji. Raghunathpant entangled the Naik of Madura in the meshes of his diplomacy and induced him to give up his partisanship with Venkoji.[1]

The Naik left Venkoji in the lurch at a critical point. Venkoji was at the end of his resources. He had to consent to an interview with Shivaji.[2]

Shivaji received him with great affection. Venkoji was accompanied by three natural sons of Shahaji, Raja Bhivji, Raja Pratapji and Raja Rayabhan.

[1] It appears from the Factory Correspondence and the letter of the East India Company's Brahman agent, Nellore Ramana, to the Madras Council that Shivaji opened the negotiations with the Naik of Madura, who was in the end induced by Raghunathpant to pay a tribute of six lakhs of pagodas (*Vide* Sarkar's Shivaji pp. 389).

[2] The Rairi bakhar states that Shivaji sent a message to Venkoji to the effect that they had not met for many years, and that he had come thus far for a meeting, wherefore he would be greatly delighted if he would come to see him. Upon this Venkoji came with his army for an interview. The two brothers met in a temple of Mahadev and dined out of one dish.

They were also received with fitting honour. Venkoji enjoyed the hospitality of Shivaji's camp for fifteen to twenty days, but during this time he did not care of his own accord to broach the subject of the partition of Shahaji's estates. Shivaji saw he must open the discussion, and, calling him to a private chamber, made a very feeling appeal to his obstinate brother. Shivaji reminded him of the brotherly affection that must always subsist between them and said that, for thirteen years since the death of Shahaji, Venkoji had enjoyed the whole paternal estate, knowing well the equal share he had in that patrimony. He did not demand a share of any personal acquisitions of Venkoji, much as he would like to see him make acquisitions of his own and much as he prayed to Heaven to grant him such thoughts. But to administer the estates of Shahaji,—he could not do so without his brother's consent. He was prepared to show to Venkoji any concession, if only he showed him the papers concerning the estates. He would help him in times of stress and difficulty. Venkoji might rest assured upon this head. Such was the substance of Shivaji's exhortation, but for all the persuasion he used with his brother, no impression seemed to have been produced. Venkoji merely ejaculated a monosyllabic "Yes" now and then, as Shivaji went on speaking. But he made no decisive reply to the proposition placed before him.

Shivaji made many attempts to draw him out, but at every attempt Venkoji evaded an answer. He would not give the least inkling of his decision either to Shivaji or to any one else in his camp. On one occasion, however, Venkoji is said to have observed to some of the ministers that if Shivaji cared to give him a moiety of his conquests, he would find his way to give him a moiety of the territory in his power. On Shivaji's side the answer was, and naturally there could be no other answer, that the territory in his possession was all of his own acquisition, while that held by Venkoji was all earned by Shahaji, and no addition whatever had been made thereto by Venkoji. Under the circumstances the demand for a moiety of Shahaji's estate was perfectly justified by the rules for the devolution of ancestral property according to the principles of the Hindu Law.[1]

Thus all this time was lost in vain. Nothing would move Venkoji to a peaceful settlement. At this continued obstinacy Shivaji's first impulse was to put him under arrest and take his own share of the inheritance by force. But calmer thoughts pervailed. Shivaji reflected on the impropriety of any form of violence towards one who was his younger brother. It would be a disgrace to his family and to his reputation as a king. He would exhaust first all the arts of conciliation at his command. But Venkoji took fright and fled from Shivaji's camp in the darkness of the night, with only five attendants.[2] Next morning Shivaji learnt of his brother's flight. He could hardly restrain his indignation at the pusillanimous conduct of his brother, which meant distrust in his promise of safety. His first impulse was to arrest a few of Venkoji's officers who were left behind. But he presently set them at liberty and sent them back to Tanjore[3] with presents and robes of honour usual on such occasions. Shivaji once more sent messengers to Venkoji with a fresh proposal by which Shivaji demanded that his brother should give up to him half of Tanjore and one or two of Shahaji's forts as his share, promising that he would be quite satisfied with this and desiring him to maintain a friendly attitude. But Venkoji was governed by the advice of his short-sighted friends, and among these were a few Mahomedan depen-

1 Prof. Sarkar relying on the Factory Records, Fort St. George and Nellore Ramana's letter to the Madras Council, states that Shivaji claimed three quarters of Shahaji's possessions and treasures to himself and offered to Venkoji only the remaining quarter. (Sarkar: Shivaji pp. 390-91).

2 In the text we follow Sabhasad's version. It is corroborated by the Jedhe Chronology, p. 13. Other bakhars state that Shivaji permitted Venkoji to return to Tanjore and gave him an escort. The Shedgavkar bakhar, p. 87, says that Venkoji's officers induced him to escape.

3 This place is also called Chandawar and Chanjawar by the bakhar writers.

dants of Bijapur. These advisers said: "What though Shivaji be your elder brother? Is he not a rebel to your liege lord, the sultan of Bijapur? Reflect on the distress which your brother's rebellion brought on your father; how on one occasion his life stood in the greatest jeopardy on his account. It is due to your loyalty and obedience to your father, that the sultan has permitted the jahgirs to continue, or else he would surely have annexed all the territory. What right then has this rebel to demand as a patrimony, what you merely enjoy by an exercise of grace on the part of Bijapur? Moreover these jahgirs are the guerdon of loyal service done to your feudal sovereign and it is as a vassal of Bijapur that you enjoy them. What part could this rebel, this foe of Bijapur, pretend to have in them?" Thus did these short-sighted, brainless creatures continue to mislead Venkoji, who finally sent word through Shivaji's officers, whom otherwise he treated with every mark of honour, that he was willing to hand over to Shivaji a moiety of all the *movables*,-horses, elephants, jewellery etc.—from among the possessions of Shahaji, to be assessed by Raghunathpant as falling rightfully to Shivaji's share, in accordance with certain lists and inventories, about which that minister had the best knowledge and which he might explain to him; and that, if for so many days he had not spoken frankly on the subject, it was because he did not wish to appear immodest in his answer to his elder brother.

It is even said that on this occasion Venkoji wrote to the Bijapur government informing them of Shivaji's demand of an equal share in the paternal estate which, he contended, was the reward of Shahaji's loyal services, and applying for that government's orders as to whether he should comply with this demand. The Bijapur government is reported to have made answer to this effect:—"The Raja Shahaji was a loyal officer of this government, and in appreciation of his loyal services the jahgir lands were conferred upon him, to have and to hold and to transmit in hereditary succession; it was on this sanad that Shivaji's demand was based. For his acts of rebellion, the government were responsible to call him to account, but it was not for Venkoji to deny his brother's right, cause a family feud and refer it to the arbitration of the government. Were the government to decide against Shivaji's claim, they would incur the utmost bitterness of his hostilities and expose their territory to his incursions. Hence they laid it down that in case Shivaji should make his claim to the jahgir inheritance, the tenure of military service, the same should be made over to him. Shivaji was indeed at present at war with their government, but were he to offer to enter into an alliance with them, they would be prepared to welcome it. At any rate, Shivaji was the elder son and had a right of priority to the inheritance." This *rescriptum Caesaris* carried little weight with Venkoji, whose mind had been poisoned by his designing satellites, in particular by the Mahomedan chiefs in his service, and they represented to him that "Shivaji was a rebel and a traitor, and the sultan, their suzerain, spoke under fear and constraint. But what of that? Venkoji held the territories in his hands and was master of his own will. He should not hesitate to draw the sword in defence. He must try the chances of war. While they lived, they would not permit him to cry for mercy and to surrender. What was it Venkoji feared? Had Shivaji only sucked a true mother's milk?"

The obstinate reply from Venkoji and the knowledge that he was governed entirely by the interested counsels of the factious Mahomedan nobility kindled Shivaji's wrath and he prepared to invade Venkoji's territory and carry on a vigorous campaign. On second thought, however, Shivaji saw that such a campaign between brothers of the same flesh and blood was nothing if not ridiculous and would in the long run bring little profit and less honour, especially when such a multitude of towns and territories lay all around him, owing allegiance to alien chiefs, whom it would be both a gain and a glory to conquer.

From Trivadi (Tiruvadi), where the fruitless interview had taken place with Venkoji, Shivaji broke camp and moved to Vellore, and making it the base of his operations he proceeded to reduce the different forts in the neighbourhood, among which Maharajgad, Jagdevgad and Karnatakgad are mentioned.[1] Shivaji then proceeded to ascend the ghats in those parts, and poured his armies into the distant, outlying districts of Shahaji's jahgir. Among the districts thus overrun could be counted Kolhar, Balapore, Bangalore Shirta (Sera?),[2] and Vaskot, all forming parts of the jahgir dominions of Shahaji. Many smaller forts and citadels fell before Shivaji's sword, and new defence works and fortifications were raised in places of advantage. The lawless polygar barons scattered over many a straggling castle and stronghold in the surrounding country were for the first time cowed into humble submission. A few of these irregular chiefs consented to make terms, binding themselves to pay an annual tribute. Those who refused to submit had to face a relentless war, were chased from stronghold to stronghold, and were finally extirpated. The fort of Arni had been entrusted by Shahaji to the charge of a trusty Brahman, Vedo Bhaskar, and was at this time in the charge of his two sons. These two youths now came to Shivaji's camp to present the keys of Arni. Shivaji was pleased with their loyalty and good offices and confirmed them in command of the place, with an adjoining territory yielding an annual revenue of three lakhs of pagodas. Mansingh More and Ranganath Kelkar were detached with a small force to restore order and discipline to these parts. Shivaji then advanced through Shrirangapatam and other districts, exacting tribute.

While Shivaji was winning these laurels in the south and exacting tribute from fort and town, his agent at Delhi

---

[1] The Jedhe Chronology mentions Jagdevgad and other districts.

[2] The ancient Chera. Vaskot is also called Uskotta, and by similar fanciful names in the bakhars.

Agra) wrote that a storm was gathering in the north and the news was confirmed by Shivaji's scouts. This was nothing less than a plan for launching the imperial armies upon the Deccan under the leadership of the emperor in person. Upon the receipt of this startling news, Shivaji prepared to leave the Karnatic in great trepidation. The fortress of Jinji (Chandi) and the outlying territory which had previously been placed under the viceroyalty of Santaji was reinforced by a reserve contingent under Raghunathpant and Hambirrao, the commander-in-chief, and with the rest of his forces, Shivaji gave orders for a general retreat. His resolve to bring under his victorious arms the whole of the south down to the ridge of Rameshwaram had, at a time when every moment was drawing him nearer to the goal of his wishes, to be abandoned on account of the sudden alarm that required his immediate presence in the midst of his affectionate people of Maharashtra, the starting point of his fortunes, ambitions and projects.[1]

The real facts about politics in the north were, however, materially different from what had been reported to Shivaji. Aurangzeb's suspicions about Khan Jehan Bahadur's venality had come to a head and he expressed his disapproval of the peace made with Shivaji. Diler Khan had submitted certain proposals, which seemed to recommend themselves to the emperor. Diler Khan's suggestion was that the Mogul government should join hands with the Bijapur government, dominated as it then was by the personality of its chief minister, Abdul Karim Balhol Khan, and making united war on Golconda, overthrow that monarchy before Shivaji's return from the south. This arrangement received the imperial sanction, and Khan Jehan Bahadur was recalled.

The pretext for this combination against Golconda was

[1] On retreating to Maharashtra Shivaji left word to the Maratha commanders left behind to raid and capture the Dutch and British settlements at Paliacot, Sadras and Madras, but to leave the French at Pondicherry unmolested.

naturally the treaty which that government had recently made with Shivaji. The growing amity between Shivaji and Golconda was viewed by both the Mogul and Adil Shahi powers with anxious eyes as a sinister conjunction against their future expansion. Madanna watched the signs of the times, was informed of the changed aspect of the political powers, and prepared for the worst. When the storm burst, Madanna was able to put a sufficient army into the field and after a hard-fought battle repelled the invaders.[1] The rout had destructive effects on the Bijapur army. It was quite disorganized. With their defective arrangements for supply and transport, the soldiers began to starve and die. Those that remained clamoured for arrears of pay or for want of it deserted and fled. The soldiers defied their officers, the officers, their government. To aggravate the whole situation, Abdul Karim himself fell ill and died. The court was now in a state of complete demoralization. Diler Khan took upon himself the cleansing of these Augean stables. He met and interviewed the omrahs and forced them to put a stop to the growing anarchy. He chose one of the wealthiest of the nobles, Masaood Khan, to be chief minister.[2] This Masaood Khan was a son-in-law of Sidi Johar, and his wealth was the principal factor that guided Diler Khan in selecting him for the premiership. For he undertook to carry out Diler Khan's terms, which were to restore peace and order at Bijapur, liquidate his government's liabilities to the Moguls, make up the arrears of pay in the army, and have no intercourse whatsoever with Shivaji. The minister's personal wealth appeared a sort of guarantee that he would carry out these engagements. He did carry them out to the best of his powers, excepting the one relating to the arrears in the army. The state of the finances of his government

[1] But Jedhe (p. 193) says that Masaood Khan and Golconda combined to fight with Diler Khan, who had to retire to Naldurg.

[2] Prof. Sarkar quotes a letter of the Rajapur factors to Surat (Factory Records, Surat, Vol. 107) showing that Masaood Khan seized possession of Bijapur by a *coup d'etat* at a time when a traitor minister was negotiating to hand over the capital and sultan to Shivaji's protection. Jedhe, p. 194 says that Bijapur came under Masaood Khan, who became minister.

obliged him to give their discharge to many of his cavalrymen. These shiledars or adventurous cavalrymen, suddenly thrown out of employment in large numbers, scoured the country, scaring and plundering the hapless inhabitants. Many of them, however, were taken by Moropant Pingle into Shivaji's service, to the great relief of their former government.

Now Shivàji kept himself duly informed about these changes in the politics of the Deccan kingdoms. When the combined armies of Bijapur and Diler Khan invaded the Golconda frontiers, Shivaji accelerated his march so as to be at home in time to parry a possible attack upon his own dominions. Shivaji's van reached the barriers of Gadag-Lakshmeshwar. There was some execution here, two forts falling before Shivaji's arms. The ruling chief Khan Gouda Desai took fright and fled. The province was easily added to Shivaji's spoils.[1]

While his forces were thus rapidly hastening, a party of foragers were attacked on the line of march by the garrison soldiers from the fort of Belwadi[2] which was then in charge of a woman named Malvai,[3] the widow

[1] For the itinerary of Shivaji's return journey we follow Chitnis who differs slightly from Sabhasad. The latter makes Shivaji reach Kopal before coming to Lakshmeshwar. According to the bakhar accounts (e. g. Shedgavkar p. 88), Khan Gauda seems to be the name of a man, not of a place, as imagined by Prof. Sarkar, who complains that he cannot trace it in the maps (*Shivaji*, p. 400, foot-note). The Desai fled to Sampgaum, which the Shedgavkar bakhar calls Satgaum.Sampgaum is in the Belgaum district.

[2] Other names used in the bakhars, are Balwed, Belwada. Belwadi means a grove of Bel trees, the leaves of which are sacred to the God Shiv. Grant Duff confounds it with Bellary in Madras Presidency.

[3] The name of this lady is given as Lalbi by Sabhasad. The Shivdigvijaya gives the lady's name as Savitribai. Her husband Yesprabhu had been killed in a previous encounter. Shivaji's commander on the occasion was also a Prabhu officer, viz: Dadji Raghunath Prabhu Mahadkar. Her story and Shivaji's subsequent chivalry towards her will remind the reader of the bravery of another heroine, Rai Bagin, described in chapter XXI. But Sabhasad and the Shedgavkar bakhars say that she was captured and punished, while the Tarikh-i-Shivaji says that she was captured and dishonoured by Sakhuji Gaekwad, whom Shivaji punished with imprisonment, when he heard of his misconduct towards the lady.

of the original Desai, or revenue-lord of the fort. Shivaji erected batteries and prepared for a siege. The lady of the fort maintained the defence for a period of twenty-seven days. But at last she found herself at the end of her resources and was obliged to surrender. The lady was brought a prisoner of war before Shivaji. But she experienced the same clemency and forbearance which the chivalrous instincts of Shivaji had trained him to observe towards all woman-kind. She was dismissed with the usual presentations and ceremony, and two villages from the fort domains were sequestered and conferred upon her, as a grant of inam for her maintenance. From Belwadi Shivaji proceeded home by forced marches and coming up to Kopal, a fort of considerable strength, besieged and captured it in about a fortnight. The country within range of that fort was quickly reduced, the neighbouring fort of Lakshmeshwar[1] captured, and the irregular polygars of the district compelled to acknowledge his sovereignty. To bring this part of the country under permanent control, Janardanpant Sumant, one of the ministers, was kept behind with a detachment of forces. Shivaji hastened onward clearing stage after stage, when two commanders of the Bijapur government, Hussain Khan Maina and Lodi Khan threw themselves upon him with a force of ten thousand horse.[2] These were repulsed, and forces

[1] It would seem from Chitnis that the operations around Lakshmeshwar in the Gadag district were resumed or were being still carried forward simultaneously with the operations at Belwadi and Kopal, after the first success gained over the local Desai. In short there were more than one campaign round about Gadag and presumably also Kopal, which accounts for the different versions.

[2] The Shivdigvijaya gives a long account of the battle which took place in the valley of the Tungabhadra at its junction with the Krishna. In the Shivdigvijaya the Adil Shahi commander is called Yusuf Maina. The Jedhe Chronology (p 192) says that already as early as January 1677 Hambirrao defeated Hussain Khan Maina (or Miana) near Yalgedla and captured some elephants and 2000 horses. The same chronology later on states that about May or June 1677 Shivaji conquered Gadag and returned to Raigad and finally in March 1679, the Peshwa Moropant gained possession of the fort of Kopal (about a hundred miles due south of Bijapur)

were detached under Niloji Katkar[1] against a third commander, Bavli Khan Pathan, who was attempting diversions at Kolhapur, Tarala, and certain other districts that had recently fallen before Shivaji's sword. Katkar overtook the Pathan at Turumba and routed him. The victors received the usual acknowledgments from Shivaji, special embroidered robes and the soldier's decorations of gold and pearls, along with an elephant and a pair of horses, which were bestowed upon Katkar.

Shivaji made a halt on arriving at Torgal, when despatches from Raghunathpant were placed in his hands. From these Shivaji learnt that Venkoji had created a diversion in the newly conquered territories, taking advantage of his absence. The news was alarming enough to induce Shivaji to suspend his march for the present and put up a stationary camp at Torgal. For Shivaji learned that the moment Venkoji came to know that he had withdrawn from the Karnatic, he, with his Mahomedan friends, had marched down upon Santaji Bhonsle, Raghunathpant and Hambirrao, whom Shivaji had left behind as his representatives,[2] with the object of bringing under his complete sway the conquests recently made by him. Shivaji's commanders, apprised in time of Venkoji's invasion, put their forces in battle order. Overtaking the invader at Balgodapur, Raghunathpant made fruitless attempts to persuade Venkoji to come to terms, but the latter would not recede an inch from his position, and the bravado of his Mahomedan instigators being kindled into

through the son of Hussain Maina, whereupon the latter was released from captivity and took service under Shivaji. All this would go to show that there were two or three campaigns in the Tungabhadra region and explain why some chronicles like Sabhasad and the Basatin-i-Salatin describe the conquest of the district before the invasion of the Karnatic, while Chitnis and the Shivdigvijaya date it after that event.

1 Instead of Katkar the name Kate or Kothe is also found.

2 According to the Rairi bakhar, Venkoji did not make the attack in person but sent his minister Jagannathpant and other officers to attack Raghunathpant and the sir-nobut. The scene of the battle was Balgodapur or Waligondapuram.

a blaze, by the attempts of Shivaji's people to make peaceful overtures, a battle ensued, in which Venkoji's party was completely overthrown.[1] In this battle Shahaji's natural sons, Pratapji and Bhivji, were wounded and taken prisoners. Venkoji saved himself by a headlong flight with one or two hundred fugitives. It would have been possible to press the pursuit and capture the fugitive band, but the feeling that Venkoji had once been his patron and Shivaji himself might not be overpleased with any sort of insult or harm done to his brother prevented Raghunathpant from keeping up the pursuit. Thus Venkoji, with a handful of followers, was enabled to make good his escape.

Such were the grave contents of Raghunathpant's letter in answer to which Shivaji's brief reply ran as follows: "Venkoji is our younger brother. He may act like a naughty boy, but for all that he is our brother. It is our duty to take care of him. You must not harm his principality." A longer letter was addressed to Venkoji, expressing his vexation and disappointment, the drift of which was to this effect: "We regret to learn," wrote Shivaji, "that, misled by Turkish knaves, you made war upon our people, a war in which you have lost much, in which our half brothers Pratapji and Bhivji were taken prisoners, and several of your chiefs wounded. You being our brother, your losses are our losses, your reputation is our reputation. It was not well done—by this foolish act to have thus published your ill fame to the world! What you have thus done was not done of the free motion of your mind. The men whose wicked counsels have led you to this act have already received condign punishment by the decree of Heaven. The prejudices instilled in

1 Col. Wilks states that in the first encounter Santaji Bhonsle was repulsed, at which he was so much vexed, that he gathered his men at night and led them to a second attack, resolved to conquer or perish in the attempt. The sudden raid of Santaji against Venkoji's forces, at a time when they were off their guard in the exultation of the day's victory, threw them into a complete rout.

your mind against us have led to this step. Had you relied on us, instead of giving yourself to your Mahomedan advisers, it would have been to your own advantage. Now you will have to render us our share and bear this disgrace into the bargain. Our father's fortunes were of his own earning. That you should have entertained a doubt, on what title to yield us our share, was not fair to us. On your restoring to us our share, it is for us and the Bijapur government to discuss this question. They will not care to make you a reference. That being so, you are acting like a naughty boy. Hereafter follow the precedents laid down by our father. Leave not virtue, leave vice, with reason for your guide. Make war upon the wicked, pour blessings on your subjects. Forget not that you are the son of Shahaji, forget not the debt of *noblesse oblige.* And yet the thought of discriminating between sin and righteousness does not enter your mind. But this will surely bring you to misery. Without a sharer thus far have you alone enjoyed the common estate. Now at length yield to us our share. Live in peace and prosperity, yielding us our dues. By the grace of the Bhawani of Tuljapur, victory shall always crown our arms, and remembering this you ought not to have rashly embarked on war with us, infatuated by the advice of your Mahomedan counsellors. You should not have acted, as Duryodhan of the Mahabharata acted, so as to dig the grave of your own people. By tasting defeat at the hands of a servant of your family, you have only disgraced yourself in the eyes of the world. The losses in the war we consider as our own. Hereafter at least don't allow a repetition of such scenes. Court not new acquaintance by disregarding the old. Those who have grown gray in the service of our father, you must respect as elders and family friends. The bitter fruit of spurning such old friends and conducting yourself according to your own caprice, you are now tasting and shall have to taste in future. Think not that, by Raghunathpant's coming over to us, this mischief is done. The claiming or yielding of the family partition must always have come sooner or later. There was no escape from it. There is no need that you should be taught this by some one else. Advice given to you in good part you took in evil part. This has brought upon you this misfortune. Regard old servants of the family as family elders. Keep them in service and victory will smile upon you and your fortunes will prosper. Remember this and play your part in the future. Arni, Bangalore, Kolhar, Vaskot,[1] Shirta and other districts are already ours. Chandawar[2] likewise shall you cede to our men. Of cash and jewellery inherited from our father you shall grant us half. Act honestly by us and we shall grant you, on the other side of the Tungabhadra, territory worth three lakhs of pagodas, in the Panhala district, of our own acquisition. Or in lieu thereof, we shall procure for you, from the Golconda Kingdom, territory worth the same amount. There is no profit in kindling a family feud. That would only mean misery to you and to us. Hereafter at least let us remain as friends. What we tell you, as an elder brother, if you hearken to in good part, you will bless yourself for the rest of your life. Act in opposition to us, and you will work your woe without a cause."[3]

After this letter to Venkoji, Shivaji wrote again to Raghunathpant, not to protract war with Venkoji and widen the gulf between them. Nothing was to be done that would injure Venkoji's self-respect. Being after all the son of Shahaji, it mattered not, if he monopolised the whole heritage to himself. Nothing should be left undone

---

[1] Vaskot is elsewhere called Iskot or Haskot.

[2] The same as Tanjore.

[3] We follow the Shivdigvijaya chronicle which practically quotes the greater part of Shivaji's letter. The original letter, which was in the hand-writing of Balaji Avji Chitnis was examined by Grant Duff. It was recovered from the Hanmante family, in whose possession it was, by a descendant of the Chitnis family at Satara and it was published by Rao Bahadur Parasnis in the Itihas-Sangraha (Volume I, 1912, p. 36)

for a restoration of peace and amity. Upon these despatches of Shivaji, Raghunathpant called back the army that was sent after Venkoji. Meanwhile Venkoji was plunged into sad reflections at Shivaji's epistle. He felt he had merited the fraternal rebuke. He reflected on the rout of his forces, the capture of his horses and elephants, the men slain, the orphans and widows who came down to curse him at the doors, the shiledars clamouring for new horses in exchange for beasts slain in war, the wounded and disabled starving for food. How was he to please or console them all? On the other hand there was his elder brother who would not renounce his just rights by any means. There was Raghunathpant to give the claimant Shivaji a full inventory of Shahaji's fortunes. What was he now to do? Carry on war to the end? It would bring misery, ignominy and ruin. All his pride of wealth would go and only the bitter recollection of hostility would remain behind. He had acted madly from beginning to end! Had he behaved humbly and listened to the reasonable wishes of his elder brother when called to the interview, these depths of ignominy would have been spared! Good fortune had always attended on his career. But he had given ear to evil counsellors and made war with such a brother!

Venkoji was now filled with remorse. He could not think of food or sleep. For hours together he sat moodily buried in thought. At last his wife, Dipabai, began to inquire what acute anxieties distracted him so much? Venkoji replied, "Shivaji's generals have remained in these parts; they have reduced the polygars and brought the sultan's forts under their power. They fight every day. They know no defeat! Where the sultan himself has retreated before them, what could we do with our slender forces? Where is the good of such a fight? And yet we did fight, to our infinite loss!" Upon this his wife spoke in very feeling terms. "After the death of the Maharaja," (meaning her father-in-law), said she, "Shivaji is to you in the place of a father. You have been deceived by the advice of evil-wishers. When it was time to think soberly, you failed to care about it. Shivaji is a righteous man and a hero. Behave well with him, and he will not reject your wishes. What does Shivaji care for your fortunes? He has won his own independent kingdom and made the fortunes of so many followers. What would you have lost if you had submitted to him? Is it your own possessions he claims to share? What additions have you made to the family fortunes? And what do you accuse him of? When he made no estrangement of his affections, how strange that you should have taken up arms against him and widened the breach! Raghunathpant, an old servant of the family who should be cherished as a relation and an elder, was humiliated and despised! The only man who could have kept things going and assured your joy and happiness, was driven from your presence! Knaves and impostors were invited to help to fritter away your estates. Even yet, bury your hatred, yield to Raghunathpant, and obey his advice, and he will free you from the obstacles in your way. Persevere in your false pride and you will add only to your dishonour. Or if you would not submit to Raghunathpant, and vanity stands in your way, go, throw yourself upon your brother's mercy. Learn humility, even at this hour, and he is sure to protect you. That is the best you can do. There is no help without it."

This advice made a great impression upon Venkoji and he resolved to act upon it. He invited Raghunathpant to settle the terms of a treaty between himself and Shivaji. But Raghunathpant wrote in reply that he was awaiting orders from Shivaji and would act according to those orders, without which he could not come to see him. On receipt of Shivaji's orders, he proceeded to meet Venkoji, informing him previously that as he was an officer and representative of Shivaji, and Shivaji was his elder brother, the conference must take place on something more than a basis of equality. This was agreed to by Venkoji. The place for the conference was then determined, and pavilions were erected at the chosen spot. The two proceeded on elephant-back from their respective camps to the spacious pavilion.[1] On Venkoji's dismounting from his howdah, Raghunathpant got down, and the two entered the pavilion hand in hand. Two chairs of state had been installed within, and the two chiefs approached them together on a footing of equality, when Raghunathpant folding his hands in a respectful attitude exclaimed that he was a servant of that throne, and Venkoji only was competent to be seated upon it. So saying, he helped Venkoji to his seat, made a humble salutation to the occupant of the chair, and seated himself a little apart. Raghunathpant then continued as follows: "You are to me the same as Shivaji. When I quitted your service, I declared to you I was quite as good a man to occupy your seat, and I had to do all this to demonstrate to you the truth of my words. Not being like the general run of servants, my services were welcomed by Shivaji. You are free to employ me again, if you please. I would freely give up my life rather than do any thing to injure you. But if my patron goes astray, I shall not cease to try to bring him round. You listened to the advice of narrow-minded fools and heaped insult and ignominy upon my head. I had, therefore, to appeal to Shivaji and suggest to him the occupation of the Karnatic. He is a true soul of valour and has vowed to bring about the restoration of free religion and government and the expulsion of Mahomedan tyrants from the country. He endorsed my views and brought his squadrons from such a great distance to the Karnatic, and in a short space of time he has made conquests worth three to four crores a year. And yet he has a great love for you. His love

1 The Shivdigvijaya says that the this meeting took place at Chandavar (i. e. at Jinji, or Tanjore). At the urgent request of Venkoji and Dipabai, Raghunathpant proceeded to Chandawar without waiting for Shivaji's order, when he had a private audience with them, whereat both husband and wife prostrated themselves at his feet, exclaiming that he had the knife, he had the head, he might slay or save ! When Raghunathpant saw this proof of humble repentance, he made a treaty with them.

is boundless. He shows it in his epistles to us. Hereafter do you behave sincerely with him. Think of the devotion of Lakshman towards Ramchandra, in the epic poem, and hold it up before yourself as the mirror of brotherly respect and affection. Let this be your study, your emulation. Do thus and you shall prosper. Whatever peril may menace you at any time, do but send me word and I shall come flying to your rescue and deliverance. That you may achieve at least a fraction of Shivaji's valour and glory is all the desire that now remains to me." With such exhortations, Raghunathpant proceeded to state the terms of the compromise. Venkoji was to remit to his brother half the annual revenue of Shahaji's jahgir domains, divide the family jewels and make a cash contribution towards the expenses of the campaign. On Venkoji's acceptance of these conditions, Shivaji was to allow him to retain Tanjore and restore the other jahgir districts that he had conquered.[1]

On receipt of the documents concerning the treaty, Shivaji wrote a lengthy letter to Raghunathpant, the purport of which was as follows:—

"It is well," wrote Shivaji, "that Dipabai has brought round her husband, and that with your help a treaty has been made. This was what we had been seeking from the first, but Venkoji would not listen. It is good that now at length he has seen through his false friends and the scales have fallen from his eyes. Now you have only to see that Venkoji carries out the terms of the treaty. Should you so prefer it, it is open to you to reside there and conduct the administration on behalf of Venkoji. Janardanpant, the Sumant,[2] might be given charge of Chandi (Jinji) and the adjoining districts, and you might keep your eye on important matters from time to time.

[1] The Rairi bakhar states that Venkoji ceded on this occasion the forts or districts of Kolhar, Balapore, Maharajgad, Jagdevgad and Karnatakgad to Shivaji. These places, as already stated, had been captured by Shivaji during this campaign.

[2] He was a brother of Raghunathpant Hanmante.

On the assumption that you would choose to reside with Venkoji, we specify below certain particulars of administrative details, to which we invite your special attention. These articles are as follows:—

Art. 1:- The privileges etc. of the relations of the royal family and the titled nobility (mankaris) to be preserved; their degrees of precedence etc. to be respected. No onerous duties to be assigned to them.

Art. 2:- The officers and commanders to be consulted in important matters. Loyal and competent officers only to be appointed to positions of trust. Promotions to be made according to merit, and strife among state officials to be discouraged by all possible means.

Art. 3:- The private suite of Raja Venkoji to consist of good, loyal and upright servants who shall give sureties for their good behaviour; no favourites; all to be under equal rule.

Art. 4:- Agents and envoys to be stationed at surrounding courts, whether friendly or hostile; and arrangements to be made for prompt and secret intelligence about all changes.

Art. 5:-Cavalry, both paga and shiledars, to be properly organized. Horses and men to be both in readiness. The shiledar force as much as possible to be converted into paga. Artillery and cavalry to be both in readiness to meet a sudden invasion.

Art. 6:- Professional thieves, rowdy and riotous people, drunkards, lawless tribes, assassins etc. to be expelled from the kingdom, or if allowed to stay, under proper security, both in cash and by sureties. Such people to be properly watched.

Art. 7:- Quarrels among high and low, concerning boundary rights, contracts, treaties etc. to be discouraged. The poor and the needy to be succoured in difficulty and saved from the oppression of the rich and the powerful.

Art. 8:- Religious grants from the state, benefactions etc. to temples and holy places to be continued and on no account to be violated.

Art. 9:- Suits of creditor and debtor relations, partitions and successions to inheritances to be decided by specially constituted panchayats, and the administration of civil justice to be conducted in the best interests of the people. Corruption of justice by bribery to be prevented, and justice to be free and gratuitous to all. As regards justice the state is to consider the poor as being under its special patronage.

Art. 10:- Promises of pardon and reprieves to be strictly adhered to. The contrary has never taken place in our family.

Art. 11:-The fort of Arni, with the adjoining district, having been granted by Shahaji to Vedo Bhaskar, to be confirmed in the possession of his eight sons and heirs, without any molestation, whether they take service under Venkoji or not.

Art. 12:- The jahgir and other lands held under sanad from the Bijapur government by Shahaji; as also those acquired from the Daulatabad authorities (Nizam Shahi state) when he came over to the Bijapur service; and thirdly the territory privately acquired by him by conquest of the polygars, to be investigated, classified, and separately accounted for. Secondly, under the tenure of feudal service, Shahaji was under obligation to serve the Bijapur government with a force of five thousand strong; which tradition must continue with this modification that by the treaties made by us (i. e. Shivaji) with that government, the feudal covenant of service has been commuted into an engagement to render occasional aid, and this modification having been made in the life-time of Shahaji, Venkoji would now be under no obligation to campaign for Bijapur except under special circumstances, being released from a perpetual covenant of service by our treaty, and he would be responsible to us for the fulfilment of this occasional obligation; in default of which, should we (i. e. Shivaji) have to campaign under the auspices of Bijapur, Venkoji shall be held liable to pay us the expenses of the campaign.

Art. 13::- As to the hereditary patilships and deshmukh rights over Varghati Hingni, Beradi, Devulgaum and other places, descended in the family, we would exercise them unchallenged, by right of primogeniture.

Art. 14:- Officers or members of our court proceeding on duty or for personal reasons to Venkoji's court, and *vice versa*, to be treated in a spirit of mutual hospitality and enabled to return to their respective places, on the transaction of their business.

Art. 15:- Of the territory ceded back to Venkoji, the districts of Bangalore, Vaskot and Silekot yield an annual revenue of three lakhs of pagodas, which may be improved to five. These districts are hereby assigned in perpetual grant by us to Dipabai as a pin-money allowance, indefeasible by any right or claim on the part of Venkoji or his heirs. After Dipabai the revenues to descend to her daughters as pin-money, and so on in the female line, from generation to generation. Venkoji's government only to administer the districts and revenues *in commendam*.

Art. 16:—Of the territory ceded around the fort of Chandi, districts to the value of seven lakhs of pagodas are hereby assigned in perpetual grant to Raja Venkoji as a personal appanage, to be transmitted from generation to generation. A schedule of these districts to be submitted to us for sanction and for grants of sanads.

Art. 17:—Raghunathpant, being a tried and loyal veteran and hereditary servant in our family, and himself of no mean lineage, shall have an inam ceded from the Tanjore territory to the value of one lakh of pagodas, to hold and to transmit from generation to generation.

Art. 18:—There is to be a right of extradition as between our kingdom and the court of Venkoji, for the arrest and conviction of thieves, robbers and other run-away criminals.

Art. 19 :—Venkoji to make monthly grants or assignments for the proper maintenance of music, clerks, soldiers, horses and other equipments and honours at the tomb of Shahaji.

We shall be happy to hear that the Raja Venkoji approves and promises to abide by these nineteen articles, in token whereof a due acknowledgment of the same should be submitted to us.[1]"

Raghunathpant presented this letter with the nineteen articles to Venkoji, to whom also Shivaji had written a personal epistle, giving him further assurances. It was finally settled that Raghunathpant should remain behind to administer Venkoji's jahgirs, as also to supervise the administration of the districts recently conquered by Shivaji. On the ratification of these last arrangements, Shivaji broke up his camp at Torgal and continued his march to the north, and sent orders to Hambirrao to follow with his army.

Meanwhile Ghatge and Nimbalkar had overrun the barrier province of Panhala, and laying waste the country, went plundering the people up to Karhad. When Shivaji received intelligence of these events, he was still encamped at Torgal. He despatched Niloji Katkar with a small detachment to repel the invaders. Katkar overtook the foe at Koorli and attacked him with such force that he was completely routed. Katkar was able to recover from the fugitives a great part of their plundered spoils, which, as being the property of the king's own subjects, was scrupulously restored to the ascertained owners, not a farthing of it being permitted to find its way into the royal exchequer.

---

1 The Shivdigvijaya gives a detailed account of this treaty, from which this account is taken. This treaty is an unimpeachable proof of the high statesmanship of Shivaji. The articles on extradition and feudal service to Bijapur show how delicately he attempted to deliver Venkoji from his subservience to Bijapur and bring him under the hegemony of Maharashtra.

On the conquest of Kopal, Janardanpant had been left behind in command of that fort; and news having been received that there was likelihood of a threatened attack by Bijapur in that quarter, some troops were detached to reinforce that commander; and shortly afterwards, with a small force to escort him, Shivaji himself reached Raigad in safety.

It will be remembered that on the conclusion of the treaty with Venkoji, Hambirrao, who till then had co-operated with Raghunathpant, had received orders to retire to Maharashtra. Janardanpant, apprised of his approach, projected a combined attack upon the Bijapur forces, and Hambirrao entering heartily into the plan, a concerted attack was made on the Bijapur militia in the basin of the Krishna and the Tungabhadra. The attack succeeded most admirably. The Bijapur forces were put to utter rout, five hundred horses, five elephants and the commander of the enemy falling into the hands of the victors. The whole of the country was overrun and subdued. The refractory deshmukhs in the neighbourhood of Kopal and Belvadi who had for a long time shirked payment of their feudal dues to Bijapur and made themselves undisputed lords of their holdings, were brought to book by Janardanpant and compelled to submit to the feudal suzerainty of Shivaji. The Bijapur government never attempted thereafter to recover these districts from Shivaji. The exhaustion of that state in the wars with the Moguls and with Golconda and the practical annihilation of their cavalry by war and desertion made a show of arms almost impossible, and had there been any such disposition on the part of that government, the flooded condition of the country, on account of the rains that set in soon afterwards, precluded all hopes of an effectual campaign. Janardanpant and Raghunathpant turned the enemy's delay to the best account and brought the whole country under their permanent control.

Hambirrao continued his march to the north, attacking the fort of Devur which lay on his line of march. The

Bijapur government sent a force of ten thousand under Hussain Khan to repel the attack. But Hambirrao defeated this force and captured the fort. Another force was then sent under Lodi Khan, but he too was defeated and taken prisoner.[1] The forts of Gondal and Bahadur-banda were attacked and captured with the like success. Thus capturing fort after fort, he reached home in triumph and was received by his sovereign with many acknowledgments of gratitude for his conspicuous services throughout the campaign. Among his lieutenants, who had likewise covered themselves with glory by their distinguished bravery and valour in the field, were Dhanaji Jadhav and Bayaji Ghorpade. Shivaji expressed his warm congratulations to these young officers and conferred upon them inams and military decorations in recognition of their gallant services. All other officers who had distinguished themselves in the campaign came in for a proper share of the royal bounty and acknowledgments. Thus was this great campaign finally concluded, having covered a period of eighteen months from the start to the finish.

Some days thereafter a letter was received from Raghunathpant about affairs in the Karnatic. "The Raja Venkoji," wrote that trusty administrator, "has given himself to a settled gloom and melancholy. He closes his eyes, avoids conversation, has grown indifferent to food and drink, sulks by himself in solitude, gives curt answers or none when I approach, and gives anything in alms that the Brahmans require. We have waited and watched for six months, in the fond hope that there might be some alteration. But there has been no improvement at all during all this time, and now I think it necessary to inform you about it, hoping to be excused for keeping you uninformed so long. It is for Your Majesty to decide what is to be done." Upon this Shivaji wrote to Venkoji as follows:

[1] These generals had already been defeated once by Shivaji's retreating columns. An entry in the Jedhe Chronology under date Chaitra (April-May) shaka year 1601 (1679 A. D.) would go to show that Moropant had something to do with these conquests.

" Raghunathpant has returned from a visit to you. The particulars he has given in his letter about you have filled us with sadness. We are sad to think that you should give yourself to melancholy. Reflect that you and I are brothers of the same flesh and blood, prepared to stand by one another in every misfortune. If you would be pleased to let us know the fears that have driven you to this sadness we will at least endeavour to eradicate the cause. Do not be deterred by any sense of reserve from confiding in us. Whatever your wishes, they shall be readily fulfilled. Be assured that we will spare no pains to gratify your wishes. Do inform us, by all means, of the cause of your mental malady. Do not be so disconsolate in future, or else we shall have to bring you here under our immediate protection, and in that case you will not be able to return thither again. Please bear this in mind and act fairly by us. Be governed by Raghunathpant's advice, for that means your welfare; beyond that as you please."

This letter had much effect upon Venkoji, who began again to take an interest in his affairs.

CHAPTER XXVII

THE FINAL CAMPAIGNS, 1678-1680

THE news of the great victories and conquests of Shivaji in the Karnatic campaign gave anything but pleasure to the haughty Aurangzeb. Shivaji had purchased his non-interference by an undertaking to pay tribute. He had bought over the Mogul governor Khan Jehan Bahadur and had been able to get him to play the tune he wanted. Aurangzeb did not make much of this armistice in the beginning. He was absorbed in his campaign against the Afghans of the north-west frontier, and was not in a position to send any re-inforcements to the governor of the Deccan subha. Later on though the treaty was cancelled and Khan Bahadur reprimanded for his share in it, the campaign of Diler Khan was not directed against Shivaji, but against the state of Golconda. Nor had that campaign produced any tangible result, except losses and misfortunes for the Mogul army. It only unfitted the Mogul arms, more than ever before, to carry home the rigours of a war of invasion against Shivaji. This was not what the great emperor had been calculating upon. He had flattered himself with a picture of Shivaji's arms beaten and battered by a long and arduous campaign in the distant plains of the Karnatic,—a dispirited king, a demoralized army ready to sink to the ground before the throwing of a lance. And he thought he might bide his time when to throw that lance. But this pleasing prospect had now melted away. Shivaji had returned laden with honours and victories. The terrors of his name had not a whit diminished! He had given above all a new check to Bijapur. "Now will he," thought Aurangzeb, "draw the cord tight round that prostrate state and after strangling its power lead his squadrons to the ridge of Rameshwaram; and our dreams, our deep-laid plans to overthrow the divided sultanates of the south, and unite together, under one rule, all the country down to the southern sea, have become void and fruitless." Thus groaned the emperor. To forestall the worst consequences, he had, at Diler Khan's suggestion, conceived a project to subvert Golconda, ere Shivaji returned from the south. But it did not succeed. Bahadur Khan was recalled from the Deccan, and Prince Muazzim was sent down a second time.

In consequence of the adjustment made between Diler Khan and Masaood Khan of Bijapur, Moropant Pingle had to keep himself on the alert and secure every position from a surprise attack on the part of the combined forces of the Mogul and the Adil Shahi governments. There was besides no mitigation as regards the continued descents of the Abyssinians on the Konkan coast, an account of which may be deferred till the next chapter.

Aurangzeb was displeased with the peaceful settlement that had been just concerted between Diler Khan and Masaood Khan. The emperor reprimanded the subhedar and ordered him to force the Bijapur government to pay up the arrears of pay to their troops, to win over the leading members of the Adil Shahi nobility to the Mogul interest, to bring their affairs under his direction, and in short to bring that state under the protection of the Mogul power. Diler Khan set to work to carry out these instructions and succeeded well enough in detaching the Afghan nobility of the Bijapur state to the Mogul side. But there was a party in the state to whom the great Mogul was an abomination. They could not be brought over by any means. The Mogul agents made a formal demand for the person of the sultan's sister, Padshaha Bibi, who, as it had been previously arranged by Khawas Khan,[1] was to be given in marriage to a son of the emperor. The present minister agreed to bring about the marriage alliance. But a large faction in the state was against it, and when the Mogul envoy came to demand the princess, there was a violent outcry and threats of resistance. The pro-Mogul party, on the contrary, urged strongly the fulfilment of the promise that had been made, and both parties were on the brink

[1] *Vide* Chapter XXV, p. 417

of civil war, when the princess herself appeared on the scene and offered to go to the Mogul camp.[1] This decision paralysed the opposition of the anti-Mogul faction. The princess was welcomed at the Mogul camp with all the honours befitting her rank and escorted with a suitable retinue to Agra.

But Diler Khan was not satisfied with this sacrifice. He had already begun a campaign of invasion, breathing vengeance against Masaood Khan for non-compliance with the terms of the treaty. At this critical juncture the latter had no other resource but to supplicate Shivaji's aid. This decision was taken not without a considerable mental struggle. Shivaji's attitude towards Bijapur could not be that of sincere friendship. Whether he would respond to the appeal favourably or otherwise, there was no means to conjecture. But he was himself on no friendly terms with the Moguls, and an appeal might be made to the family connection of Shivaji with the Bijapur state, under whose auspices he had risen to greatness. Struggling amidst these doubts and hopes, he finally applied to Shivaji for immediate help with the message: "The Mogul hosts are almost at the gates of Bijapur! This sultanate is yours. Come to instant relief!"

On receipt of this urgent request, Shivaji turned to march towards Bijapur, when, to his consternation, news was brought that his son, Prince Sambhaji, had escaped and taken refuge with Diler Khan.[2] Upon this Shivaji ordered Hambirrao to proceed to Bijapur with the army and himself came away to Panhala, lost in a hundred

---

[1] Scott's Deccan, II, 52.

[2] The order of events followed here is on the whole based on Jedhe's Chronology and the Basatin-i-Salatin, which confirm one another in a surprising manner. It differs slightly from the order of events as given by Chitnis and the Shivdigvijaya and as followed in our original Marathi edition. The principal difference is that in the usual bakhar accounts the flight of Sambhaji and the siege of Bhupalgad take place after the plunder of Jalna and battle with Ranmast Khan, while according to Jedhe these events took place in September-October 1679, while the flight of Sambhaji took place in November 1678 and the fall of Bhupalgad in April 1679.

doubts how to recover Sambhaji from the hands of the enemy.

It is necessary at this stage to unravel the story of Sambhaji's infatuation. Every provision had been made for the education of the young prince. The best pandits had been engaged to act as his tutors, and they had spared no pains to cultivate his mind and heart. But these labours had been spent in vain. He was, and he always continued to be, a wanton, froward, violent-tempered youth. The efforts of his father to inculcate in him the qualities of a good statesman, administrator and ruler were all wasted. In order to get him proclaimed as the heir-apparent to the throne, the prince had been made to undergo the ceremony of the investiture of the sacred thread. But his insolent and licentious ways became steadily more aggravating. There was once a festive celebration[1] at the palace, in honour of the goddess Gauri, when the ladies of the royal harem were entertaining all the matrons of the town. At such functions only ladies assemble and the hostesses honour their guests with the distinguishing marks of red and yellow powders or pastes, which are considered auspicious and conducive to a long life of matrimonial bliss. Among the ladies invited on this occasion was a young Brahman female of exceptional beauty. Sambhaji saw her, was smitten with her beauty, and, managing to have her taken to his room, violated her chastity. Shivaji was extremely wroth at the news of this atrocity. He said the prince was the heir to the throne and yet was guilty of such a heinous sin,—the violation of a Brahman lady, a female of the sanctified class,—the basest crime possible. To the king all subjects must be like sons and daughters. The prince must receive condign punishment in proportion to the grossness of his crime. His being a son of the blood royal could not pro

[1] Called "Haldi Kunku," or the consecrated red-powder and yellow turmeric, distributed amongst married women, the application of which to the forehead, under the auspices of the goddess Gauri, is supposed to have the virtue of lengthening conjugal felicity.

cure him a pardon. If he persisted in such a violent course, he must perforce disown such a son.[1] And saying so, Shivaji ordered the prince to be incarcerated in the fort of Panhala; and though released from strict imprisonment after a lapse of time, he was still detained at the fort in a sort of informal custody. This was most galling to a man of wild and violent nature like Sambhaji. Assured that his father was engaged with the Moguls at a distance, he planned an escape to the Mogul camp, having sent previous intimation to Diler Khan of his meditated flight. Diler Khan was naturally pleased to see this rebellion in Shivaji's own house and gave orders to Ikhlas Khan to start with a force of three to four thousand horse to welcome and escort Sambhaji to the Mogul camp. (November, 1678).

Shivaji at once despatched search parties in various directions in pursuit of Sambhaji; but the prince had by this time already joined Ikhlas Khan's party about four miles from Supa and thrown in his fortunes with the Moguls. The Marathas who came in pursuit of him saw the enemy's force was too strong to be attacked. They, therefore, returned in despair to Shivaji.

Diler Khan communicated to the emperor how Sambhaji had come over from Shivaji and how he had accorded to him a cordial welcome. The commander congratulated the emperor upon what he considered a piece of rare good fortune, that there was at last some chance of a division in Shivaji's camp, for some nobles of the Maratha kingdom were now sure, said Diler Khan, to come over and join Sambhaji. The cleavage thus commenced would cripple the Maratha power and the confusion of the foe would redound to the interest and glory of the empire. For by putting Sambhaji at the head of a Mogul detachment and sending him against his father, forts and provinces under the Maratha sway would fall in no time. But the emperor did not approve of this suggestion,

---

1 Some bakhars state that on hearing these angry words, Sambhaji fled away with his wife that very night.

suspecting, as he did, that Sambhaji might be playing a part in collusion with his crafty father, as a prelude to some stroke of policy. It might be that Sambhaji was come to sow sedition in the Mogul camp or tempt the Mogul armies into some deep-laid trap and lure them to their own destruction. But Diler Khan had already put his suggestions into practice before the arrival of Aurangzeb's protest, and Sambhaji had advanced, supported by a Mogul corps, against the fort of Bhupalgad. This was the easternmost outpost of Shivaji's defence system, almost projecting into the Mogul dominions, and as such was well fortified against a surprise attack on the part of the enemy and always equipped with an abundant supply of war material. The garrison prepared for an obstinate resistance. In normal circumstances they would not have minded the utmost rigours of a Mogul siege. But the presence of Prince Sambhaji, the heir-apparent to their state, not only among the enemy, but at the head of the assailing column, filled the garrison with dismay. Was it proper to open fire upon a prince of the blood royal? If not, how were they to defend the castle? But there was no time to think. Sambhaji called aloud from without and threatened the havaldar of the fort with death, unless he instantly threw open the gates. The garrison soldiers were perplexed at this conflict of duties, and in their consternation took fright and fled in all directions. The governor of the fort was Firangoji Narsala, the same who in the campaign with Shaista Khan had won his laurels by his brilliant defence of Chakan fort.[1] But on this occasion fortune seemed to frown upon the prospect of a successful resistance. It was impossible to rally his soldiers for the purpose of a protracted defence. Many of them fled, and nothing could restore his authority over their wavering minds. To open a cannonade was out of the question, as Prince Sambhaji was the most exposed of all. Did his authority over the castle entitle him to do an act which involved the sacrifice

---

[1] *Vide*: Chapter XVI, page 223.

of the life of the crown prince of his kingdom? This was the dilemma, and there was no getting out of it, except by a precipitate retreat. In the dead of the night the governor fled away, and the fort fell easily into the hands of the assailants. (April, 1679). The Moguls put under arrest the remnant of the garrison still found at their posts. The Mogul commander sentenced the inoffensive captives to horrible punishments, mutilation of hands and feet. Many were sold into slavery. Sambhaji naturally protested against this wanton cruelty, for which apparently there was no reason, except the belief that the fate of these helpless defenders would strike terror into the hearts of the defence garrisons of other forts. On Shivaji's being apprised of this event, strict orders were issued to the governors of other forts that Sambhaji had revolted and fled to the Moguls and should he advance against any fort, he should be treated, without the least fear or respect for his position, as a traitor and an enemy. No surrender should be made on any account.

Shivaji sent one of his confidential agents to persuade and win back the errant prince. The agent protested against the conduct of Sambhaji and dilated on the suicidal character of his secession. What could have provoked Sambhaji to this step by which he now helped the Moguls to reinstate themselves in their lost possessions? Whose was the loss? As for Shivaji, he had no motive now left to think of temporal things for himself. He might as well now retire to some solitude or the banks of some holy river and spend the remainder of his life in devout meditation at the feet of some godly saint like Ramdas. If Shivaji continued to care for affairs of temporal interest at his advanced age, surely it was not out of personal interest, but solely for the sake of his son and heir. What folly it was then that that son and heir should draw his sword against such a father. Such was the manner in which the interceder pleaded with this headstrong Absalom. But persuasion had no effect upon his heated mind.

Shivaji however did his best to come to the rescue of Masaood Khan. The cavalry was ordered to muster at Panhala, whence a force of seven thousand pushed on to Bijapur. The orders given to these troops were that they should immediately occupy and take charge of the fort of Bijapur and maintain a close watch, while with the rest of the cavalry Shivaji surprised the Mogul on his rear. When pursuant to these orders Shivaji's cavalry came to Bijapur,[1] they were asked by Masaood Khan to make their camp on the banks of the Atang. The Maratha commanders refused, and, coming up to the town, pitched their camp at Khanapur and Khusraupur, sending word to the Khan to put one fortress gate and tower into their charge, and they would defend it with their lives. But Masaood Khan would not comply with this demand and refused admission to the Maratha army, with the exception of the great commanders. The Maratha force then went down to Joharpur (Zuhrapura) and encamped in an open plain opposite the city-walls. After they had lain a few days outside the walls, some of them managed to enter the city under pretence of buying supplies and provisions for the army. Loading their baggage oxen with sacks, which securely concealed their swords and muskets, one cavalry man after another entered the city leading his ox and joined to form parties in out-of-the-way parts of the town. It did not take long to discover the stratagem. However Shivaji's commander represented to Masaood Khan that, on the invitation of the Bijapur government, they had come out of their way and only found themselves exposed to the enemy. It was a great hardship for them, since in case of an attack they would find no cover within the walls of the city. But Masaood Khan would not listen to this argument. He had no faith in their professions; he believed it to be a trick, as it probably was, to gain possession of the Bijapur capital. What the Maratha army could not gain by conciliation, they attempted to carry by a show of arms, making concerted attacks upon

---

[1] This happened about August 1679. Diler Khan's siege of Bijapur became rigorous about September 1679. *Vide* Jedhe P. 195.

the city, pillaging the suburban towns of Daulatpur (Daulatpura) and Khusraupur (Khusraupura), and putting the wealthy merchants of the exposed parts under arrest. A similar assault was made upon Joharpur and the repelling force put to rout. The Maratha army lost some officers in the action. The Bijapur garrison replied with a violent cannonade from the city walls, which compelled the Marathas to give some ground, but they did not relinquish their attempts for some time to carry the town by assault. When they lost all hopes of capturing the fort by storm, they won over the commander of the garrison with a bribe of fifty thousand pagodas. Masaood Khan required the governor of the fort to give up the bribe, when the latter shielded himself behind the back of a great commander of the Bijapur court, Sarje Khan (Sarza Khan).

Scarcely had the Marathas thus forced their entrance into Bijapur, when the Mogul foe arrived on the scene. Shivaji had not been idle. He had kept his eye steadily on the movements of Diler Khan. The Mogul commander encamped outside the city and prepared to deliver an assault. This event put a decisive end to the hostilities between the Maratha and the Adil Shahi troops within the walls of Bijapur. Masaood Khan had to make fresh petitions to Shivaji for help, in most pathetic terms. Shivaji approached to within eight *kos* (i. e. about twenty miles) on the rear of the Mogul camp, with a view to surprise and carry it by storm. But he soon discovered that Diler Khan's forces chiefly consisted of picked Pathan soldiers, numerous enough to make impossible the chances of a successful raid on the Mogul lines. He thought it more prudent to lead his forces to make a diversion in other parts of the Mogul territory. With this view he wheeled round and, swiftly crossing the Bhima, made a terrific onslaught upon the Mogul territory. But Diler Khan neither relaxed the siege nor sent men after him. Shivaji's squadrons ravaged the Mogul territory from the Bhima to the Godavari, plundering all the country. Forcing his way into the town of Jalna in Khandesh, he plundered it uninterruptedly for three consecutive days. Prince Muazzim lay close by at Aurangabad, but Shivaji did not allow this circumstance to disturb him in the least. He had skill to detect the exact places where the people had hidden their treasures. On this occasion it is said that Shivaji's troops did not spare even the cloisters of the fakirs, a departure from the usual practice, it being one of the principles of his military discipline not to do any violence to persons, no matter of what faith, who had devoted their lives to religion. There is no record, however, of any soldier or officer of Shivaji being sentenced to any of the usual penalties for any such breach of his rules of discipline, as is alleged to have occurred upon this occasion.[1]

When Shivaji, laden with all this booty, prepared to retire and conduct the spoils in safety to Raigad, Prince Muazzim sent a force of ten thousand horse under the lead of Ranmast Khan to harass his retreat. Ranmast Khan followed in close pursuit and came up with Shivaji at Sangamner, and a fierce encounter followed between the two forces. Santaji Ghorpade rather overacted his part and the result of his foolhardiness was a momentary confusion in his division and the loss of a distinguished commander, Sidhoji Nimbalkar. But Shivaji did not lose heart at the temporary set-back, rallied his men, and regardless of his personal safety, flung himself upon the enemy. The Maratha soldiers inspired by the example of their king, occupying the post of danger in the forefront of the field, recovered confidence. The Maratha columns hurled themselves upon the Moguls. At this onslaught, the enemy

[1] Khafi Khan says that on this occasion Shivaji molested the Mahomedan saints and fakirs, and in consequence died soon afterwards. Khafi Khan states that Shivaji's hosts entered Khandesh and plundered Dharangav, Chopra and Jalna, a prosperous commercial town in the Baleghat (Khafi Khan, Elliot VII, pp. 304-5). Shivaji's general orders as regards military discipline are described in Elliot VII, 305. The alleged excesses of the Maratha troops may be explained by (1) military tactics to raise the siege of Bijapur, (2) excitement caused by the desertion of Sambhaji, and (3) the savage treatment of the Maratha garrison of Bhupalgad.

broke and ran.[1] Shivaji again claimed the victory and attempted by a forced march to convey his booty beyond the reach of any further attempts on the part of the enemy. But to reinforce the scattered bands of Ranmast Khan, the Prince despatched another force under Kishen Singh of Jaipur.[2] With this addition to their strength the Mogul fugitives rallied once more and again overtook Shivaji at the head of a defile. Shivaji was about to file through the gorge, when he was called upon to face this new danger. He knew his men were so exhausted with the fatigue of the march and the encounter they had just had with the enemy, that they had scarcely any life left to face an enemy who came fresh and with unimpaired spirits. In this dilemma, a plucky scout from Shivaji's reconnoitring corps, Bahirji Naik, presented himself before his master and undertook to lead both army and booty down the defile without coming in contact with the Moguls. And he was as good as his word. The whole night long the Maratha army marched through the defile, at a distance from the gorge where they had been stopped by the Moguls. The Moguls knew not when the Marathas had vanished. But when they noticed that the position taken up by Shivaji was unoccupied, they hastened forward to discover where the enemy had disappeared. But they could find no trace of the Maratha army, being unable to discover the narrow gorge by which Shivaji had escaped. They again returned to the head of the defile where they had expected to entrap Shivaji, and poured down the gorge into the vale below. But Shivaji had already[3]

[1] According to some chronicles Hambirrao Mohite was wounded in this battle. The Jedhe Chronology dates these events about October or November 1679; but Prof. Sarkar dates the events in December 1679, soon after Sambhaji's return from the Mogul camp.

[2] He was a grandson of Jay Singh. Sabhasad gives his name as Keshar Singh. Chitragupta states that this Keshar Singh pitched his camp three Kos from Shivaji's and sent him a private message that since he looked upon him as a brother, he desired him to clear away by forced marches before he could overtake him.

[3] Sabhasad gives Pavangad as the name of the fort to which Shivaji retreated.

reached Patta, and in commemoration of the fact that the walls of that citadel gave him a much needed asylum from the hot pursuit of the Mogul foe, the Maratha monarch had its name now changed to Vishramgad or the Asylum Fort. The safe retreat that Shivaji found behind the hospitable walls of Patta, threw his Mogul pursuers into despair, and they returned disappointed to Aurangabad. Aware of the valuable services of Bahirji Naik on this occasion, but for whom the campaign was likely to have had a tragic conclusion, Shivaji conferred an adequate inam upon that gallant scout. During the days of rest spent at Patta, Shivaji conceived the plan of subduing the numerous forts that surrounded it, and thought that the present juncture of events, when Diler Khan was involved in a fierce struggle with Bijapur, was the fit moment to put this plan into execution. Moropant was charged with these operations, with a complement of infantry recalled from the Konkan and a body of horse to second his efforts. Moropant set about his work very briskly, carrying fort after fort, according to his master's instructions. (November and December 1679.)

While Shivaji lay at Patta Masaood Khan sent an express courier with a request for urgent intervention against the Moguls. The purport of the missive was as follows: " By your loyal behaviour with our durbar at this time of tribulation you have indeed proved yourself a worthy son of Shahaji. You have repaid the price of the salt that Shahaji ate of our durbar. Forgetting your enmity with the durbar, you have hastened to our aid. You have made every effort to relieve us. That was a grand idea of yours, to deliver us by diverting the war to the enemy's own country and surrounding him on all sides. Following this plan you have done him much harm and inflicted on him one or two stunning defeats. Likewise in our own capital your men have proved to be of considerable assistance to us. But Diler Khan is obstinately resolved not to leave the siege of Bijapur, whatever the cost of

Mogul disasters in the south. He will not raise the siege by any means. He has advanced close to our walls. We cannot think of any other deliverer at this crisis except yourself. Wherefore we pray that, leaving all other thoughts aside, you hasten to the rescue of the Adil Shahi dynasty."

Meanwhile Hambirrao Mohite and Moropant had led their arms to Bijapur and, though overtaken by Ranmast Khan with a squadron of eight to nine thousand horse, had already rendered a good account of themselves. Mohite and Anandrao made for the Mogul camp and began a series of raids cutting off their food and fodder supplies and starving the besieging armies that surrounded Bijapur. Men, horses and elephants fell off for want of food. Diler Khan was at last forced to raise the siege for the present and fall back westwards to Aurangabad, making good his arrival at that place with difficulty. He left the neighbourhood of Bijapur in the middle of November 1679. The foiled chief wreaked a bloody revenge upon the hapless subjects of the Adil Shahi state. Men, women and children were carried off as slaves. The wives of both Hindu and Mahomedan subjects committed suicide by jumping into wells. Villages and towns were sacked. At one village alone 3,000 inhabitants were sold into slavery.[1] At Athni, a prosperous centre of trade, the town was burnt down and the Khan sold the inhabitants, who were all Hindus, as slaves. (November, 1679.) Even Prince Sambhaji who accompanied the imperialists protested against the meditated cruelty but his protests were vain. These acts of ruthless rapine, however, served to open Sambhaji's eyes to the iniquity and unrighteousness of his own conduct.[2]

---

1 The Basatin-i-Salatin, 426–480; Factory Records, Surat 108, Bombay to Surat, 1 Jan. 1680, quoted by Prof. Sarkar.

With such a record of Mogul cruelty and rapine, which likewise had characterised Shaista Khan's progress in Maratha territory, it is absurd to make a pretence of virtue and speak of Shivaji's cruelty and plunder.

2. Prof. Sarkar's view is that, disgusted with these cruelties, Sambhaji fled away to Bijapur and thence came to join his father at Panhala. Sabhasad says, Diler Khan connived at his escape.

But the Marathas were close at Diler Khan's rear. The disproportionately smaller forces of Hambirrao and Anandrao prevented them from provoking the enemy to a pitched battle. They had to content themselves with guerilla warfare, but they inflicted no little loss upon the retiring Moguls.

After plundering Athni and carrying off the doomed inhabitants to be sold as slaves, Diler Khan crossed the Krishna and, invading the Karanatic, commenced a campaign of wholesale plunder.[1] Dividing his army into two parts he directed them into two different parts of the Karnatic, being himself the leader of one of them. Janardanpant[2], the governor of Shivaji's possessions in that quarter, was apprised of the unimpeded march of Diler Khan's plundering armies and mustered a force of six thousand strong to oppose him. As the result of this encounter not only was the further career of Diler Khan's division completely arrested, but be was himself beaten back with considerable slaughter. Janardanpant then turned upon the other division which likewise experienced the same misfortune as the first.

On the news of these defeats, the emperor gave vent to his indignation that Diler Khan, instead of guarding the interests of his governorship, should have plunged into a reckless war with Bijapur. He also ordered him to send Sambhaji under arrest to Agra, considering it dangerous to permit him to entertain him as a commander in the Mogul camp, lest he might instigate a spirit of discontent or disaffection among the Mogul soldiers and insidiously work mischief to the empire. These orders of the emperor were most displeasing to Diler Khan, who caused Sambhaji to be informed about his master's intentions, whereupon the Maratha prince quietly stole away from the Mogul camp and came to rejoin his father in the vicinity of Panhala, where Shivaji had personally proceeded.[3]

---

[1] Grant Duff Vol. I, Ch. IX.

[2] He was Sumant or foreign secretary and the brother of Raghunathpant Hanmante.

[3] Sabhasad, 93; Shedgavkar, p. 91. Shivaji had at this time considerably strengthened Panhala and concentrated his forces there against

After the first embraces of welcome, Shivaji reprimanded the errant youth in words that must have seared the very soul of Sambhaji. He pointed out to the repentant prodigal the great risk he had run in committing himself into the hands of Diler Khan, the inveterate foe of the Maratha state, at a time when the hostilities between the Marathas and the Moguls were rekindled. He owed it to the protecting hand of Heaven that he had escaped alive. For this at least, once in his life, Diler Khan had earned his fervent gratitude. It would never do for Sambhaji to forget that he was the heir to the fortunes of a noble house, the residuary claimant to all that Shivaji had won and earned. Recognising the responsibility of his position, how could he at all have thought it consistent with his honour and understanding to curry favour with Diler Khan, as a refugee and an exile? His destined succession to the throne required him to exercise a due sense of discipline and a paternal solicitude for the interest and welfare of the citizens of the state. He was expected to be the defender of the lives, the fortunes and the honour of his people. And if the guardian himself turned upon his wards and robbed them of all they held most dear and precious, what friend under heaven could they look up to? What tyranny more gross than the violation of female chastity? What more subversive of past merit and reputation? He must bethink himself of the fall of Ravan and other despotic rulers of epic fame! To cure him of this heinous offence he had sentenced him to a short term of imprisonment,-sentenced him with a heart bleeding and charged to overflowing with love. He had replied by an act of treacherous desertion. Now at length he must return to his senses and no more seek to gladden the hearts of the enemy by dividing his house against himself. If Sambhaji had a desire to wield the sceptre before his time, he might parcel out his dominions into two equal lots, giving to Rajaram the territory from the Tungabhadra to the Narbada, and

---

a possible attack upon it by Sambhaji and Diler Khan. The forty pieces of artillery received from the French, as described in a previous chapter, were mounted among the batteries of Panhala fort. See foot-note (2), p. 478.

that from the Tungabhadra to the Kaveri, to Sambhaji; and as to himself he might dedicate the last few days of his life to peaceful devotion by the banks of some holy river, or to meditation on the Most High at the feet of Ramdas Swami. Pending these arrangements Sambhaji had to be kept under restraint at Panhala. After celebrating Rajaram's nuptials in the fort of Raigad,[1] the rest of the arrangements might be completed. So Sambhaji again found himself safely ensconced behind the walls of Panhala fort, with a district of three lakhs of rupees assigned for his maintenance and his affairs managed on his behalf by Vithal Trimbak Deshpande, under the name and style of *khasnis* or special steward.[2]

The defence of the fort was entrusted to three officers of proved loyalty: Somaji Naik Banki, Bawaji Naik Samsher Bahadur, and Bawaji Dhamdhere. The officers, both civil and military, were instructed to soothe Sambhaji's hurt mind and by wise discourses to wean him gradually from his disaffection and discontent. But they were not in any case to permit the prince to leave the fort, the havaldar or resident commander of the fort being armed with special powers to overrule Sambhaji. The administration of the territory assigned as Sambhaji's appanage was vested in Janardan Narayan Sumant, who also exercised a general surveillance on Sambhaji's movements.

The repulse of Diler Khan by Shivaji's forces and the deliverance of the Adil Shahi durbar from the tightening siege-lines of the Mogul armies evoked from the sultan's government an appreciative acknowledgment of the priceless services of the Maratha power. While tendering their thanks the Adil Shahi court wrote to Shivaji: " It is due to your generosity and nobility of spirit, that we have been delivered from the deadly grip of our enemies, and to the

[1] Rajaram was married at Raigad, March 1679 (Jedhe p. 195), to Tarabai, daughter of Prataprao Guzar. The Shivdigvijay wrongly makes her a daughter of Hambirrao Mohite.

[2] He was a grand-son of Murar Baji Deshpande, the hero of Purandar; see p. 257.

timely succour and adequate re-inforcements we have all along received from you. You have truly acquitted yourself in our hour of peril of the debt of filial obligation towards your father, the Raja Shahaji. That in the face of the interminable feuds that have hitherto raged between yourself and our government and in the face of the unmerited persecution to which we subjected Shahaji for your misdemeanour in the past, that in spite of all this you should have forgiven old scores, repaid unkindness with kindness and hastened to our rescue and deliverance, has carried your fame to the ends of the earth." Such were the contents of the epistle presented to Shivaji by the envoy of the Adil Shahi state together with the customary *nazar* of rich raiments and jewellery, horses and elephants. Shivaji replied in terms of equal appreciation of the favour of Bijapur. "We have to thank you," wrote Shivaji, "for that magnanimity which prompted your government to continue the jahgirs and honours of Shahaji, the moment you were freed from your suspicion that Shahaji had any complicity in that programme of active operations which has yielded to us such a large slice of the Adil Shahi territory. The same acknowledgments of gratitude are due to your government for the continuation of Venkoji in our father's estates and honours. It is under your kind auspices and patronage that we have risen to greatness, and nothing has given so much satisfaction to us as the fact that the fortunes we have built up have proved to be of some service at least to you in your day of tribulation. That you have won the final triumph is due entirely to the auspicious fortunes of your sultan. We did what lay in our power to contribute to that triumph. Hereafter in the day of trouble do you call upon us for help, without entertaining any misgivings on the subject". Shivaji sent an envoy to Bijapur, conveying this reply with the complimentary presents to the reigning sovereign of that state, as also an important document, the protocol of a new treaty with that state, based on the following conditions:—

1st. That the forts of Kopal and Belvadi with the adjoining territory, in the Karnatic, be ceded to Shivaji.

2nd. That the Adil Shahi State renounce all claims and rights upon the conquests made by Shivaji in the Dravid country, i.e. the southern part of the peninsula.

3rd. That the Adil Shahi state renounce its sovereign rights over Tanjore and the other districts constituting Shahaji's jahgir and that the said rights be exercised by Shivaji.

4th. That both parties agree to render mutual assistance in time of danger.

These conditions were accepted by Masaood Khan and a treaty was ratified upon these lines. Shortly afterwards Shivaji paid a visit to Masaood Khan at Bijapur for a secret discussion on the future policy of the two states.

But Venkoji took with an ill grace the news of the compact between the two powers by which the sovereignty over the Karnatic and the south was transferred to Shivaji. He thought he was now divested of all liberty of action. He was already vexed in spirit at the supposed loss of independence by that *coup d' etat* on the part of Shivaji which had set Raghunathpant over his head and placed him over his affairs, which meant Shivaji's influence and Shivaji's policy permeating everything. And now on the heels of that had come this surrender of authority on the part of Bijapur, an event which blighted all the prospects of Venkoji's being able sooner or later to redeem himself from his brother's yoke with the help of the Adil Shahi forces. He gave himself to a settled melancholy. Affecting indifference to all routine business, he acted like a recluse. Raghunathpant communicated to Shivaji the change that had again come upon his royal brother. This communication elicited from Shivaji the following epistle to the chief of Tanjore:—

[1] "Many days have elapsed without my receiving

1 This epistle is given *in extenso* by Grant Duff (Chap. IX) whose

any letter from you; and in consequence, I am not in comfort. Raghunathpant has now written that you, having placed melancholy and gloom before yourself, do not take care of your person, or in any way attend to yourself as formerly; nor do you keep any great days or religious festivals. Your troops are inactive, and you have no mind to employ yourself on state affairs. You have become a *bairagi*, and think of nothing but to sit in some place accounted holy, and let time wear away. In this manner much has been written to me, and such an account of you has given me great concern. I am surprised when I reflect that you have our father's example before you—how did he encounter and surmount all difficulties, perform great actions, escape all dangers by his spirit and resolution, and acquire a renown which he maintained to the last? All he did is well known to you. You enjoyed his society, you had every opportunity of profiting by his wisdom and ability. Even I myself, as circumstances enabled me, have protected myself, and you also know, and have seen, how I have established a kingdom. Is it then for you, in the very midst of opportunity, to renounce all worldly affairs and turn bairagi—to give up your affairs to persons who will devour your estate—to ruin your property and injure your bodily health? What kind of wisdom is this? What will it end in? I am to you as your head and protection; from me you have nothing to dread. Give up, therefore, all this and do not become a bairagi. Throw off despondency, spend your days properly; attend to fasts, feasts and customary usages, and attend to your personal comforts. Look to the employment of your people, the discipline of your army and turn your attention to affairs of moment. Make your men do their duty; apply their services properly in your quarter, and gain fame and

translation of the same is reproduced here, with only a few alterations in spelling. Grant Duff has almost literally translated the original letter, which is in the hand-writing of Balaji Avji Chitnis. Grant Duff characterises this letter as being "full of energy and sense." The Marathi original was published by Rao Bahadur Parasnis in his "History of the Tanjore Dynasty", in the "Itihas Sangraha" (page 42).

renown. What a comfort and happiness it will be to me to hear the praise and fame of my younger brother. Raghunathpant is near you, he is no stranger to you, consult him on what is most advisable to be done, and he will consider you in the same light as myself. I have placed every confidence in him. Do you the same. Hold together for your mutual support, and you will acquire celebrity and fame. Above all things, be not slothful; do not allow opportunity to slip past without receiving some returns from your army. This is the time for performing great actions. Old age is the season for turning bairagi. Arouse! bestir yourself. Let me see what you can do. Why should I write more? you are wise."

This must have been probably the last letter addressed by Shivaji to Venkoji. For soon afterwards, Shivaji fell ill,—an illness from which he did not recover.

FOOT-NOTE to p. 475 :—The fakir plundered at Jalna was Sayyid Jan Muhammad. In the belief that holy men were systematically spared by Shivaji's troops, most of the wealthy citizens of Jalna had fled to his hermitage for shelter, *with their money and jewels*,—a misuse of the "right of sanctuary," as understood in mediaeval Europe. No wonder, if under these circumstances the right was not respected. The very fact that the Khandesh people had such faith in the expeditionary principles and practice of the Maratha Army is itself no small compliment to its creator, though Khafi Khan and the Bundela Memoirs attribute Shivaji's death to the Sayyid's curses. If Hambirrao Mohite took part in the battle with Ranmast Khan after the sack of Jalna (see Shedgavkar bakhar p. 90, where he is wrongly reported as killed in the battle), he must have accompanied Shivaji throughout the Khandesh expedition, leaving Anandrao in charge of the operations against Diler Khan in the south. For this purpose Shivaji, divided his forces into two columns in November, 1679. For Anandrao and Hambirrao, see foot-note at page 344 and Appendix II at the end.

CHAPTER XXVIII

THE ENGLISH AND THE ABYSSINIANS

SHIVAJI had sacked Rajapur in 1661, Surat for the first time in 1664, Karwar in 1665, Surat again in 1670, and Hubli in 1673. At all these places the British East India Company maintained factories, which came in for a share of the general misfortune, on account of the victor's plunder or enforced contributions. The factory at Rajapur was abolished, soon after the passing of that port under Shivaji. In 1668, the Company's representatives at Surat established a factory at Bombay island[1] and, making it their headquarters, opened trade relations on a larger scale, with the country around them.

Adjoining Bombay harbour is Salsette, which was then under the Portuguese flag. The Portuguese residents of those parts could not easily reconcile themselves to the loss of Bombay and began to hate the English merchants. They refused permission to the English to have any kind of trade relations with their subjects in that neighbourhood. The English could procure no food or other supplies from Salsette and had to depend for food provisions on other provinces. With the exception of Salsette, the boundaries of Bombay marched with those of Shivaji's dominions. It was natural under the circumstances for the company to maintain a friendly attitude towards the Maratha monarch. Nor had Shivaji any reason to look askance at the Company's power. He had a good opinion of their enterprising spirit both as regards commerce and navigation. Their commerce, Shivaji knew, was to the advantage of his countrymen. Besides, in his frequent wars with the chiefs of Janjira, he expected to benefit by

[1] The island of Bombay had been conferred by the king of Portugal upon King Charles II of England, in 1661, as a part of the dowry of his daughter Katherine at her marriage with the Stuart King. The latter bestowed it upon the East India Company subject to an annual rent of £ 10. The transfer was made in 1668 to Sir George Oxinden, the Company's president or governor at Surat, who, as we saw, had bravely defended the Surat factory at Shivaji's first invasion in 1664.

their naval assistance. Their navy was powerful and their ships were large and strong. They might provide him with war-ships of superior strength. They might send him supplies of muskets, artillery and ammunition. Such were his calculations, nor were they unfounded in fact. Then there was always a prospect of the Abyssinians in concert with the Mogul power forcing their way into the British territory and delivering their attacks upon the contiguous district of Coorla which was under the Maratha flag. Had Shivaji so resolved, it would not have been beyond his means to expel the British merchants and plant his standard in their harbour-town; and it is only reasonable to believe that he did not consider it expedient to give needless provocation to the merchant-adventurers, or to place any obstacle in the way of their thriving trade with his subjects. Shivaji's higher ambition, no doubt, included within its scope the complete subjugation of the western coast of the peninsula. But he knew that the realization of this plan depended essentially on the raising of a capable naval contingent, and he could not afford to treat with discourtesy those mercantile powers, whom he looked upon as the most competent to contribute to his naval resources. From the same motive he acted in a conciliatory spirit towards the Dutch and the French. With the Portuguese too his original attitude was friendly. But the growth of fanaticism among these representatives of European commerce and the religious persecution of their Hindu subjects which they embarked upon, alienated his sympathy, and in the end he did not even attempt to disguise his enmity towads them. For a long time, however, the Portuguese obtained a respite from his hostilities by their regularity in carrying out the treaty obligations they had incurred with Shivaji and the punctual delivery into his kingdom of the stipulated quantities of arms and ammunition from year to year. Had Shivaji lived a few years longer, he would probably have delivered his country from the oppressive yoke of the Portuguese power.

While the head-quarters of the British Company were at Surat, under the ægis of the Mogul government, there was little expectation of Shivaji's being able to derive any active assistance from the English. In consequence he had not scrupled to pillage their factories along with the rest of the enemy possessions. But when at a later period, as mentioned above, the British transferred their principal settlement on the west coast to Bombay, the relations between the two powers became somewhat more intimate. To contribute to this result, the appointment of Mr. Aungier to the governorship of the western presidency came as an auspicious omen.[1] He was a clever and far-seeing statesman and, coming at once to the conclusion that a friendly alliance with the Maratha ruler was a condition for ensuring the stability of British trade and authority in these parts, he immediately set to work to bring about this desirable end. On the other hand the Janjira chief was casting about for British alliance, with a view to turning Bombay into a base for his intended naval operations, from which to make his attacks upon Coorla and other territories under Shivaji. He acknowledged the hegemony of the great Mogul and was indeed the chief admiral of the Mogul power. Relying on the protection of that government he had made repeated attempts to force his way into Bombay,—attempts that had only failed on account of the fortitude and adroitness of Aungier. The Mogul governor of Surat made repeated requests to Aungier to admit the Abyssinians to Bombay, but the latter persisted in his refusal, pleading the fear of reprisals from Shivaji in excuse. This

---

[1] Sir George Oxenden was governor of the factory at Surat from 1663 to 1669, Gerald Aungier was governor from 1669 to 1677, at Surat and Bombay. Aungier came down from Surat to Bombay in 1671, and returned to Surat about 1675. During the intervening period he was mostly in Bombay. The Sidi invasions and the embassies to Shivaji's court belong to this period. However the factory at Bombay was generally in charge of a deputy governor, while the governor himself resided at Surat, (Dr. Fryer.). This was reversed in the regime of Sir Josia Child, when Bombay became the British head-quarters of Western India, about 1683.

unbending neutrality on the part of Aungier won the highest respect from Shivaji.[1]

When Shivaji commenced fortification works in his territories contiguous to the Portuguese territory of Bassein and prepared for a decisive struggle against the Sidi, Aungier fearing that the English in their turn might be molested by him, sent an embassy[2] under Lieutenant Ustick to arrange a treaty with Shivaji. But this envoy preferred a demand for the re-imbursement of the English losses at Rajapur, to the amount of thirty-two thousand pagodas, as one of the articles of the proposed treaty, and as Shivaji would not yield on this point, the scheme fell through on that occasion. The following year (1673) Aungier sent one Mr. Nichols[3] as his ambassador, and he opened communication through Prince Sambhaji, for repayment of losses at Rajapur and Hubli, but again with no better result. Shivaji undertook to re-imburse the Company's losses at Rajapur, but refused to admit that the Company had suffered any such loss at Hubli as they now professed. In order to assure the envoy on this point, Shivaji produced the inventories of the booty obtained at Hubli. This difference of accounts between the two powers as regards the Company's losses at Hubli came in the way of a permanent treaty.[4] There

---

1 The Sidi's raids began about 1672.

2 Shivaji made a demand for ammunition, which was refused; upon which the king closed the Konkan forts so that the Company's boats could get no fuel. Ustick was sent to put Shivaji under hopes, but not to commit the Company to an immediate agreement to supply ammunition and to negotiate for an indemnity for the Company's losses in the sack of Rajapur. Lt. Ustick was also to obtain a firman for freedom of trade in the Maratha territory, paying a uniform two per cent customs duty. The president had written from Surat that no definite agreement should be made to supply ammunition or help against the Sidi. But Shivaji should be kept in suspense with promises, which were not to be fulfilled. (Factory Records, Surat 87, quoted by Prof. Sarkar, Shivaji pp. 439, 441).

3 This envoy was Capt. Nichols (Thomas Niccolls) who was appointed the first English judge in Bombay by Aungier. In 1677 he was sent as an ambassador with a letter from King Charles II to Goa. (R. & O. Strachey : "Keigwin's Rebellion," pages 14 and 15).

4 The Company assessed its losses at Hubli at 7894 pagodas, but

was also another difficulty. Shivaji demanded a supply of cannon from the English, which, from their fear lest it might give offence to the Moguls or the Abyssinians, they refused to provide.

Sometime later the Sidi of Janjira regardless of any permission of the Bombay government appeared with his fleet in Bombay harbour and commenced a series of naval raids upon Shivaji's territory. But Aungier proved himself equal to the occasion, forbade the Sidi to turn the harbour into a base of hostile operations, and expelled his fleets from the port. Shivaji learnt about the bold step taken by the governor against the Sidi and congratulating him upon it proposed that a new embassy be sent to his court to remove the existing misunderstanding and arrange a permanent treaty. But just at this time the Mogul governor of Surat sent repeated demands to Aungier, that permission be granted to the Sidi so that his fleets might spend the coming monsoons in the safe shelter of Bombay harbour. This was very embarrassing to Aungier, as non-compliance with these orders meant the risk of the English factory being stopped at Surat. On the other hand, Shivaji getting wind of these orders informed the governor that were he to grant any such facilities to the Sidi to turn Bombay harbour into a centre for the Abyssinian raids to be directed against the Maratha possessions, he would undoubtedly fall in with the scheme of the Dutch Company who had projected an attack upon Bombay and had sent their emissaries inviting Maratha co-operation with a force of ten thousand to conquer the island.[1] The Sidi had meanwhile already brought up his fleet and anchored it

Shivaji produced his inventories and assessed their losses at less than 200 pagodas. There must have been under-assessment by Annaji Datto and over-assessment by the British factors.

[1] This was between 1672–74, when Holland and England were at war. The Dutch commodore Reickloss Van Goen opened negotiations with Shivaji requesting his co-operation against the English at Bombay and promising help to recover Danda-Rajpuri from the Sidi. Shivaji, however, had more faith in his English friends and distrusted the Dutch proposal.

in Bombay roads. Aungier required them to leave the precincts of the Company's possessions. But the Sidi defied these orders and sent up some of his vessels into the creeks to make good their landing north of Sion, expelling the inhabitants and occupying temporary cantonments for the rains. Aungier's soldiers, however, drove them away. Upon this the Sidi embarked five hundred armed men upon boats, who approaching the harbour at Mazagon attempted to land. But they were received by Aungier with such a cannonade that they had to run away in a panic. By this time news was received that the Dutch squadron which was advancing northwards upon Bombay had been scattered by adverse winds in the neighbourhood of Vengurla, a part of it being carried down towards Ceylon, a part towards Surat, and the rest adrift towards the Persian Gulf. This news filled the drooping hearts of the little garrison at Bombay with fresh courage, with the result that they were induced to make light of Shivaji's threats. Though the Sidi had failed to make good a landing in the harbour, his fleets still occupied their anchorage off Bombay. His insistence upon his unjust demands finally forced the Bombay government to come to a compromise, it being stipulated that the Sidi might be permitted to disembark a land-force of not more than three hundred to remain under British surveillance, provided they undertook not to make any incursions into Shivaji's territories on the landward side of the harbour, in which case they would be liable to summary expulsion and prohibited from entering again.

Shivaji's envoy,[1] who came down to Bombay for the express purpose of arranging a treaty with the Bombay government, communicated to his master the details of the

[1] Bhimaji Pandit, who along with the Company's interpreter, Narayan Shenvi, had been sent from Raigad to Bombay to settle the indemnity dispute, which was finally adjusted at 10,025 pagodas. This amount was agreed to by the Surat Council, but Shivaji being soon engaged in the Kolhapur and Panhala compaigns, the treaty had to be held over. (Factory Records, Surat, 106).

compromise arrived at between the Sidi and the Company. Shivaji was satisfied with the conduct of the Bombay government and wrote to them to send their ambassador to Raigad for the purpose of concluding the long-pending treaty. Upon this Aungier sent an envoy[1] with a proper escort to Raigad, but upon his arrival in sight of that fort, he was refused permission to continue his journey, as Shivaji was then away from Raigad. Shivaji was at this time absorbed in the preparations about his coronation, and had just then proceeded to Pratapgad to make his devotions at the shrine of his tutelary deity upon that fort, as a preliminary to the imposing ceremonial that was to follow.[2] The British ambassador was informed by the fort authorities that he would obtain permission to enter Raigad upon Shivaji's return to that place, and he had to encamp meanwhile at the village of Pachada[3] under the shadow of the fort. The ambassador wrote to the British interpreter, Narayanji Pandit,[4] about the object of his embassy, and on the latter coming to interview him on the subject he showed him his credentials from Aungier and the nazar with which he had provided himself for presentation to Shivaji and the ministers of his court. Narayanji was satisfied with all he saw and undertook to bring about an interview with Shivaji on his return from

---

1 Mr. Henry Oxenden, afterwards deputy governor of Bombay, 1677 to 1679. The authorities for the account of this embassy of Oxenden (or Oxinden) are "Oxinden's Narrative of the Negotiations with Shivaji, 13th May to 13th June 1674" quoted in Bruce's Annals; and Dr. John Fryer's "East India and Persia-Nine Years' Travels 1672-1681."

2 Dr. Fryer gives a detailed account of this embassy and incidentally of the coronation. He says that Shivaji took an offering weighing one and a quarter maund in gold to be presented to the goddess at Pratapgad.

3 The name of the village is given as Puncharra by Fryer. It is also spelled Pachad or Pachada and Panchad or Panchada. It was at this village that Jijabai died soon after the coronation.

4 This Pandit acted as interpreter to Mr. Oxenden, and generally as an interpreter to the English at Bombay. He is mentioned as Naran Sinai or Narran Sunay (Shenvi or Saraswat Brahman) in Bombay Records (Forrest, Home Papers 1,80,99), as an interpreter employed in other negotiations with Shivaji.

Pratapgad. The ambassador showed Narayanji the draft articles of the treaty to be submitted to Shivaji and asked him to express his opinion upon them. One of the draft articles was to the effect that Shivaji should make his peace with the Sidi. Upon this Narayanji Pandit advised the envoy to omit this article altogether, as Shivaji could never agree to it, the destruction of the Abyssinian power and the reduction of their stronghold of Janjira not being a scheme of yesterday, but the dream of Shivaji's life, pursued with good success or bad success since the year 1648. Shivaji had made a heavy sacrifice in this enterprise, but the peace and safety of the Konkan seaboard being at stake, he was determined to prosecute the war at all costs, sparing neither men nor money, till the extermination of the Abyssinian power. "Even now" said Narayanji, "Shivaji has laid siege to Janjira; supplies of arms and ammunition, men and money are flowing daily to the front; and under these circumstances, this demand of yours will scarcely be palatable to Shivaji." This demand was, therefore, waived by the envoy, who next began to argue that Shivaji must throw open the trade routes throughout his dominions, the Baleghat route which had been closed to trade should again be opened, and that facilities for transport would encourage the merchants to bring their goods to port, which in the long run would be of advantage both to Shivaji and to the Company. "Shivaji," said the envoy, "having spent his life in the alarms of war, does not perhaps comprehend these matters of peace; but it is the duty of men like you to explain these things to him." To this Narayanji replied that all this would be done in good season, now that the war with Bijapur seemed fairly to be on the way to come to an end. That government had now come to the end of its resources and had often sent envoys to sue for peace. This peace was bound to come in two or three months at most, when prosperity would again reign in the land and merchants would have all the freedom of trade and security of property. "When Shivaji is crowned king," continued Narayanji, "be sure that he will pursue the highest ideals of kingship, the protection of the subjects and the promotion of industry and trade. While his mind has been diverted into the constant wars with the Moguls and with Bijapur, he has not had the leisure and peace of mind required to attend to these things." At the end of this interview, the British envoy bestowed a diamond ring on the Pandit, with a similar present to his eldest son, and requested him to bring about a meeting with Shivaji as early as possible.

On the return of Shivaji to Raigad permission was granted to the envoy to come up the fort and a *bungalow* was assigned to him for his residence. On the strong representations of Narayanji Pandit on behalf of the British envoy, a day was fixed for an audience four days from that date. At this audience, the envoy explained the draft articles to the king, and he signified his approval of them, promising that the English merchants were perfectly at liberty to trade in any part of his dominions, and that there was no fear of any harm either to their persons or their property. The ambassador replied that this was the very reason why he had been deputed to Shivaji's court as an envoy by the president-in-council of the Company on this side of India and that the privileges requested by the Company were exactly the same they had already obtained from the political authorities in Persia and the sea-port towns of India. Shivaji again replied in a reassuring manner and had the draft articles submitted to the Peshwa Moropant for examination and report. With this the special audience came to an end.

The ambassador now learnt he could not expect final orders on the proposed treaty until after the conclusion of the coronation festivities. He consulted Narayanji Pandit as to what should be done about the nazar presentations that were to be made to the ministers of the court. The latter replied that the nazar to Moropant should be taken over to the minister's residence by the ambassador in person, as to the rest there would be no objection to send them by his orderlies. However he advised that the presents proposed to be sent were scarcely adequate for the position occupied by the ministers and that fresh ones should be ordered from Bombay to make a proper impression on the court, especially if he desired a full and speedy success in his mission. The ambassador on his part thought it also more prudent to act handsomely by Shivaji's officers, even at some cost to his government, rather than be detained for three or four months on the fort after the commencement of the monsoons.

It is said that the draft treaty contained twenty articles, of which eighteen were agreed to by Shivaji. These articles provided, among other things, that Shivaji should pay ten thousand pagodas as damages to the Company for the losses they had sustained during the sack of Rajapur; that the Company be permitted to open factories at Rajapur, Dabhol, Cheul and Kalyan; that the Company should have perfect freedom of trade throughout the dominions of Shivaji; that they should have complete freedom to fix their own rates, without any artificial maxima or minima; and that the customs duty on British imports into Shivaji's state be fixed at two and a half per cent. *ad valorem.* Among the articles objected to one was to the effect that British money should be declared legal tender in Shivaji's dominions. This was rejected, the king pointing out that any coinage was legal tender which the people accepted, that there was no legal prohibition of any kind, and that on the other hand it would be an act of tyranny to compel his people to accept any description of money-tokens against their will, when they thought it to be to their disadvantage. An assurance was given to the envoy that if the British coinage was of the same weight and fineness as the Mogul, there would be no difficulty for it to gain currency in the Maratha kingdom.[1]

[1] Shivaji may have known that the coinage in use at Bombay was debased and fluctuated in value, which was a partial cause of the two mutinies which took place on the island between 1674 and 1683,

The other article objected to by Shivaji was in connection with the restitution of British vessels wrecked by storm or otherwise and carried adrift to the Konkan coast, and the flotsam and jetsam of their cargoes. The Company claimed that these be restored to them hereafter by Shivaji's government. To this Shivaji replied that this was not the *lex loci* so far as the Konkan coast was concerned. All wreckages and derelicts of drifting cargoes belonged by immemorial usage to the ruling sovereign, and he did not see his way to relinquish this time-honoured prerogative of royalty; for were he to abate his privilege ever so little in favour of the English, their rivals, the French and others, would insist on the same indulgence being extended towards them.[1] Such being the firm resolution of Shivaji, the ambassador could say nothing in support of the claim. However Narayanji Pandit assured him that there would be little difficulty to have this privilege granted, since the Mogul and Bijapur governments had extended this favour to them, and a way could be found to represent to Shivaji that he too should follow where the other powers had led the way.

After a good deal of discussion, all the articles were in the end agreed to by Shivaji,[2] and soon after the Coronation, the treaty was sealed and signed by Shivaji and

---

[1] Shivaji declared that so far as the crews of the stranded ships were concerned, he undertook to assist and protect them.

[2] Grant Duff says that eventually all the articles were agreed to by Shivaji. This view is followed in the text. According to Orme the two disputed articles were not sanctioned. Dr. Fryer states that some days later (i. e. after the coronation) Naranji Pandit informed the ambassador that all the articles except that relating to currency had been signed by Shivaji. The treaty was signed on 12th June 1674.

Mr. Rajwade has published a paper describing the articles of the treaty, in which it is stated that the English made demands for four concessions of which two were granted. The concessions demanded were (1) Free trade in Shivaji's dominions; (2) Freedom from customs duty for English goods; (3) British coinage to pass current in Shivaji's dominions; and (4) Restitution of British wrecks and cargoes. Of these the first two were granted, and the last two were refused. (Rajwade VIII, 29.)

the eight ministers of the *Ashtapradhan* council. As to the Company's claim to be indemnified to the extent of ten thousand pagodas on account of the spoliation of their factory at Rajapur, a compromise was finally arranged that for three years in succession the Company should purchase from Shivaji goods to the extent of five thousand pagodas, paying only half the cash price. This would clear seven thousand five hundred pagodas at the end of the term of three years and for the remaining two thousand five hundred pagodas owing by Shivaji, the British imports at the port of Rajapur, after the Company had opened a factory there, should be allowed to enter duty-free, until the accumulated duty so exempted amounted to two and a half thousand pagodas, which would liquidate the whole claim. When the treaty was thus finally ratified, a copy of the document was handed over to the British envoy by Narayanji Pandit, who expressed to him Shivaji's parting words to the effect that he had ratified this friendly treaty from the firm conviction that it was to the interest and prosperity of his subjects, that the British should establish their settlements in their neighbourhood and continue their thriving trade within his kingdom, and that he strongly hoped that this mutual friendliness would endure.

During the coronation festivities this ambassador attended the durbar as the representative of the governor of Bombay and on that occasion he presented in the name of his government a diamond ring to Shivaji. He had an opportunity to approach the king as he sat on his throne of state and has given a picturesque account of it.[1] "On the two sides of the throne," writes Oxenden, "there were gold spears, the points whereof supported many an allegorical device emblematic of temporal power. Those to the right bore two large gold fishes with horrid jaws; those to the left bore representations of horses' tails; two lofty spears poised upon their sharp points in even balance

[1] Slightly paraphrased from Oxenden's Narrative.

a pair of weighing scales made out of gold, the fish betokening the mastery of the sea, the horses' tails, the sovereignty over the land, and the golden scales, unswerving scales of justice."

Mr. Oxenden, the British ambassador, spent about a month at Raigad. Dr. Fryer, the English traveller, who was then in India, has given, in his Travels, Mr. Oxenden's account of Raigad and the buildings and royal mansions there.[1] Mr. Oxenden's conduct during the embassy and his enlightened outlook upon affairs created in Shivaji's mind a very favourable impression about the English. Pursuant to this treaty, the English Company shortly afterwards re-established their factory at Rajapur,[2] but it had a short career, and it is doubtful, therefore, whether the Company were able to recover all the indemnity they had obtained on paper. Three years after the treaty Aungier died at Surat,[3] and his mantle fell upon a successor who possessed neither the talents nor the far-seeing wisdom of that able statesman.[4]

Of the Sidi's methods of war-fare against Shivaji, by which he converted Bombay into a base of operations,

---

1 Dr. Fryer records and Mr. Kincaid reproduces the story of the native butcher who came up the fort to have a sight of his English patrons, who in one month had eaten more of his meat than all the people of Raigad together consumed in a year.

2 Sir John Child (afterwards deputy governor of Bombay, 1679-81, governor of Surat, 1682-90, and finally general with control over all the Company's affairs in India,) was appointed chief of the newly revived factory of Rajapur. The factors did not fare well at the hands of Annaji Datto, the governor of the Konkan. But the king gave them many re-assurances (Rajapur Letter, 20th April, 1675, Factory Records, Surat, 88). Another embassy was sent and the Company threatened to close the factory. Offers were made to pay the indemnity in batty, fodder, or betel-nuts. A part only was thus paid, after the Khanderi-Underi war.

3 Grant Duff says he died at Bombay in 1676; R. & O. Strachey in "*Keigwin's Rebellion*" give the date of his death as 30th June 1677. He died at Surat.

4 Aungier's successors were Thomas Rolt at Surat and Pettit and Oxenden (British envoy at Shivaji's coronation) at Bombay. There were many intrigues at Bombay owing to the ambition of John Child, who succeeded Oxenden in 1679.

mention has already been made in more than one place in this Chapter. A constant feature of these frontier raids on the part of the Sidi was the violent arrest of peaceful inhabitants, the ruthless slaughter of male adults, and the kidnapping of women and children to be sold into slavery. The rapacity of these ruthless raids had reached a climax in 1673. Do what the English might to counteract the Sidi's excesses, they had in the end to look helplessly on at the perpetration of these iniquities. They feared the Moguls who had taken the Abyssinians under their wings. They dared not openly make war upon these troublesome proteges of the imperial power. The Bombay government once wrote to the directors of the Company for permission to effect the conquest of Janjira, open a factory, and transfer their head-quarters to that strong-hold. But permission was refused. The Bombay government feared the Sidi's raids might one day bring them into conflict with Shivaji. Steering their course evenly between Shivaji and Aurangzeb, they maintained for the present an uncertain neutrality.

We have already spoken of Shivaji's great preparations for a renewed war with the Sidi. Danda-Rajpuri erstwhile captured by the Sidi with the Mogul's aid was attacked by land and sea and the district around it reduced. From Janjira to Goa the Konkan sea-board was cleared of the Abyssinian power. The Sidi's fleets were pursued from the Konkan waters north-ward upto the port of Surat. Janjira itself was subjected to a rigorous investment both by land and sea in 1675. But though the assaults were renewed time after time, the stronghold defied all the efforts of the besiegers, and in the end, Shivaji had to raise the siege and come away. The Sidi had suffered considerable loss, but he again retrieved his fortunes under the protection of his Mogul master.

The departure of Shivaji upon his campaign in the Karnatic presented an opportunity to the Sidi chief, Sambal by name, for a renewal of his naval raids upon the Konkan coast, with the concurrence and co-operation of the Mogul navy. Falling suddenly upon Jayatapur, he set it on fire; but when the garrison turned upon him and presented a resolute front, he had to stop his advance up the creek. Shivaji's warships then came in pursuit. He eluded them, betook himself again into Bombay waters, and effecting a landing at Mazagon, encamped on British territory.[1] Here a treacherous Brahman from Coorla came to meet Sidi Kassim and offered, if ably supported, to betray some respectable Brahmans of that district into his power. The Sidi naturally lent himself to this plot, and, entrusting him with a few men in a boat, sent them forth upon the secret raid, taking care that the Company's government should remain ignorant of the whole proceeding. The traitor succeeded in betraying and seizing four fellow-Brahmans, who were brought down and kept close prisoners by the Sidi upon his warships. When Shivaji's subhedar at Cheul came to learn of these proceedings he addressed a peremptory letter to the Bombay government for the immediate surrender of the four Brahmans, who, he asserted, were unjustly detained in custody within the sphere of their jurisdiction, and threatened, in case of their failure to comply with this requisition, to lay an embargo upon all transport of food, fodder and fuel supplies to their port, at the same time gravely hinting that this would not be the worst. At this ultimatum the Bombay government set on foot an inquiry into the subject-matter of his grievance. The Sidi at first pretended ignorance of the whole event, but as the Bombay government became more insistent, he tried to excuse himself, but was at length obliged to liberate the prisoners he had kidnapped. Eleven members of the crew concerned in the abduction of the Brahmans were put under arrest by the British authorities, of whom

[1] There was at this stage a quarrel between the two Sidi chiefs, Sambal and Kassim. The Moguls had transferred the admiralship to the latter. The former refused to surrender his authority, but was at length compelled to do so, and then transferred his services to Shivaji. (Orme's Fragments.)

three were led to execution, and the rest deported to St. Helena.[1]

On Shivaji's return from the Karnatic, Moropant and the other commanders represented to him the misdeeds of Sidi Kassim and the liberties taken with the Brahman residents of Shivaji's dominions and called loudly for summary chastisement of the authors of this iniquity. They pointed out that the Janjira fleets lay skulking in Bombay harbour, the authorities of which, in awe of the Mogul government, permitted them to spend the autumn lying off Mazagon. The ministers suggested an expedition in full force to set the Sidi's fleets on fire. Shivaji entered heartily into the proposal and about the month of July sent his naval commanders, Darya Sarang and Daulat Khan, with a contingent of four thousand men to Panvel to cross over into Bombay harbour. But at Panvel they found no boats or facilities for transport, and the rainy season being at its height, they could procure no boats from other quarters to take them over. Under these circumstances they had to give up the original plan of suddenly appearing before Mazagon. However Daulat Khan not liking to be thus frustrated in his purpose made a forced march to Kalyan and applied to the Portuguese government for a free passage through their district of Thana. His object,it may be presumed, was to cross over from the Thana district by way of Mahim creek into Bombay island and surprise the Sidi camp and their vessels drawn up on the Mazagon shore, and, having collected the local craft,to strike boldly forward against the Abyssinian fleets anchored in the harbour and set them on fire.

The news of the arrival of this force at Panvel caused a flutter of excitement at Bombay. The small defence force

[1] This event took place in 1677, when Mr. John Pettit (who had distinguished himself at Shivaji's first invasion of Surat, 1664) was deputy governor of Bombay. In December 1677 he left Bombay for Persia, where he held the place of the Company's agent. St. Helena had been recaptured from the Dutch and made over to the East India Company in 1673. (Orme's Fragments, and R & O. Strachey: *Keigwin.*)

of the island was brought up to garrison the Mazagon shore. On the news of Daulat Khan's presence at Kalyan, the field force was removed to Mahim and a frigate was brought up to defend the creek. But happily for the Bombay government these precautions proved needless, on account of the intervention of the Portuguese government. The latter, affrighted by the near approach of Shivaji's forces, became anxious for the security of Salsette. The Portuguese governor marched up with a select force to Thana and advanced a fleet of forty armed vessels into the creek. Daulat Khan found himself checked at Thana, broke off the meditated march, and, with a view to turn to some account his baffled expedition, he diverted his men into the exposed parts of the Portuguese dominions, plundering and laying waste village after village. His troops had scoured the Portuguese coast up to Damaun and Surat, when he received peremptory orders to return to Raigad, which he could not but obey.

Shivaji was naturally roused to indignation by the protection granted to the Sidi by the Bombay government. Their conduct was at variance with the peaceful alliance recently made by Aungier. Under that able officer, the Sidi obtained little countenance at Bombay and this was clearly the policy required of them by the last treaty. But after Aungier's death, fear of the Mogul government had, in the eyes of his successors, outweighed the advantages of neutrality, and, acting in collusion, they had harboured the Sidi at Mazagon during the height of the rainy season. Shivaji knew the helpless condition of the Bombay government[1] and how reluctantly they had been compelled to admit the Sidi into their port, and he had no desire to bring matters to a crisis with a power whose commercial operations contributed so vitally to the material prosperity of his subjects. He looked forward to the time when he could enlist the Company's powerful co-operation for the

[1] Mr. Henry Oxenden had succeeded Pettit in 1678 and remained deputy governor till 1681.

improvement of his naval resources, and in order that they might do this without fear of the Sidi or the Mogul, it seemed necessary that these powers should be first deprived of their naval strongholds, such as Surat and Janjira. On the subject of avoiding giving any cause for irritation to the Company's government, Shivaji's scruples at times bordered on the extremity of tenderness. The following incident illustrates this solicitous attitude. The subhedar of Cheul had some credit accounts against the deputy governor, Mr. Pettit, for goods and stores supplied. There were also similar outstandings against one of the English agents at Surat. These officers, under one pretext or another, had, in spite of constant demands for liquidation, put off payment. The governor of Cheul, having failed in all his attempts at recovery of the debts, proposed to take violent measures, imagining that his action would be supported by his master, who had failed in his recent attempt to set on fire the Sidi fleets in Bombay harbour. Having determined on this plan of action, he seized all the British vessels which were at the time engaged in peaceful trade on the rivers and ports within his jurisdiction. Upon this the Bombay Council fitted[1] out four warships manned with sixty armed Europeans and sent them to Cheul to release the British vessels. The British force attacked the governor's crews guarding the interned vessels and succeeded in extricating most of them. When the governor complained to Shivaji upon this subject and urged that the Maratha power was insulted and required to be avenged, Shivaji wrote in reply, that he had been rightly served and that he must forthwith restore any British ships or property which might still be detained by him. And these orders had to be obeyed.

Once again at the end of 1678 Shivaji fitted out a strong naval force under Daulat Khan for the siege of Janjira and opened a terrible cannonade from the sea-ward

[1] By this time Henry Oxenden had succeeded Pettit to the deputy governorship.

side. The Abyssinian chief, Sidi Kassim, was then encamped at Bombay. His followers were discontented on account of their pay being in arrears. The Sidi was at the end of his resources. His demands on the treasury at Surat had not yet been honoured. He could not lead his discontented marines to the relief of his capital. But such was the strength of its natural defences, that Daulat Khan was not able to make any impression on the stronghold and was once again compelled to raise the siege and return disappointed.

Shivaji now thought of devising an expedient for checking by one and the same stroke of policy the Sidi and the Mogul in their overt alliance and the Bombay government in their covert collusion with these Mahomedan powers. About twelve miles from Bombay, right opposite to its harbour, are two little islets Khanderi and Underi[1] at a distance of two or three miles from one another. These islands were uninhabited and entirely covered with woods, whence the British settlers in Bombay, now and then procured fuel. Nor were they supposed to be of use for any other purpose. Shivaji saw that the possession of these islands would enable him to keep an observant eye upon every vessel entering or leaving Bombay harbour and the movements of any enemy stationed in that neighbourhood. He resolved, therefore, to carry the islands by storm and strengthen them with fortification works, and with this view ordered a body of three hundred soldiers with an equal number of masons and artificers, with the necessary instruments of their crafts, to the islet of Khanderi, and commenced the fortification works with great expedition and despatch. The British government heard of these preparations with dismay; for they knew what these operations betokened to their safety and freedom and the secrecy of their political moves in the future. They, therefore, hastened to change their attitude, at

---

[1] *Kenerey* and *Henery* in Grant Duff, also spelt "Kendry", "Hendry" by other authors.

first pleading that the islands were aleady their own, having been transferred to them by the Portuguese with the island of Bombay. The Portuguese on the other hand took their cue from the English and maintained that the islands for many years past were in their possession, that they had not transferred their rights over them to the English, and that they had even meditated forming a settlement there, but the absence of drinking water, notwithstanding their attempts to dig wells, had compelled them to give up that plan. Shivaji paid no attention to these disputes and went on with his fortification works.

But the Bombay authorities did not think it was a moment to sit down with folded hands. They launched three armed ships with forty Europeans on board, with instructions to prevent Shivaji's boats from approaching Khanderi and to order Shivaji's garrisons to evacuate the island. They were met with the reply that the work could not be stopped without Shivaji's orders. The British warships kept hovering round for ten or twelve days, till at last they were forced, on account of a storm, to return to Khanderi. They came reinforced by a frigate, the *Revenge*, carrying sixteen guns. Again they began cruising round the island. A lieutenant on board one of the Company's warships got drunk one day to such an extent that not minding the difficulties, he brought his vessel alongside the island and landed with a few of his sailors. A scuffle ensued between this party and Shivaji's men. The lieutenant with some six of his comrades was killed in the affray and the rest were taken prisoners.[1] The ship itself was hauled up and secured by cables to the shore. The other British ships could scarcely come to the rescue of their companions, as a fierce gale was blowing and the sea was running high. Later when the wind fell and the sea had ebbed, they did not feel courageous enough to venture near Khanderi.

Nor were the British warships more successful in

[1] The lieutenant was named Thorpe. (Page 38 R. & O. Strachey, *Keigwin*).

patrolling the sea and keeping off the Maratha boats from approaching Khanderi. The light boats of the Marathas continued to dart into the island, under cover of night, with cargoes of provisions and building materials for the fortification works, leaving again as quickly as they had approached it. The British warships were unable to overtake the swift Maratha barques which were so lightly constructed, both as regards their hull and rowing arrangements, that they could move swiftly independent of wind and tide, unlike the sailing craft of the Company. The latter were also handicapped by the smallness of their number and debarred from attempting a resolute[1] attack on the Marathas. The British commander applied for reinforcements. These were granted, the Company having hired some vessels for the purpose, so as to augment the English force to eight vessels,[2] including a frigate and a fighting contingent of two hundred European soldiers, besides some sailors.

The naval force under Daulat Khan was anchored at Cheul just opposite to Khanderi, whence every now and then emerged his light craft with their cargoes of victuals, darting to and fro and eluding pursuit. Once Daulat Khan did weigh anchor and advance upon Khanderi. But so swiftly did he sail past the British vessels that they had scarcely time to haul up their anchors. While slipping past, Daulat Khan seized a solitary British ship that had strayed away from the main body and carried her away in tow. The fate of this member[3] of their force threw the

---

1 The British commander was Captain Keigwin, who was in charge of the Revenge. He was captain-lieutenant of the small squadron of cavalry enrolled by Pettit. Before coming to Bombay he had been governor of Saint Helena. He rebelled against Sir John Child in 1683.

2 The reinforcements permitted to the *Revenge* frigate comprised two *grabs* (*or gurabas*) of two masts, strengthened by three *shebars* (or shibars), and two *munchuas* (or *machavas*), the last being described by Orme as a "stronger kind of trading vessel." The crews were strengthened by 200 European soldiers, that is, the entire garrison of Bombay.

3 This was the *Dover* under Sergeant Maulverer and a certain Mr.

rest of the British vessels into a panic. They put back in headlong haste, all but the Revenge. This ship found herself surrounded by the Marathas. But she pretended to surrender. The enemy came to board her. She fired upon him by treachery. The Marathas quailed before her fire, losing, it is said, five of their vessels.[1] While this duel was going on in one part of the sea, the opportunity was seized by the Maratha transports elsewhere to carry further reinforcements, both troops and fortification materials and food supplies, to the island. Thereupon Daulat Khan satisfied with the successful execution of his main purpose[2] put back

---

Gape who struck their ensign and top-sail out of cowardice when two miles away from Daulat Khan. Mr. Gape was a factor and afterwards a member of the Bombay Council.

1 A spirited account of the stand made by Capt. Keigwin and Capt. Minchin of the Revenge is given by R. & O. Strachey at pages 38, 39 of their "*Keigwin's Rebellion.*" Keigwin and Minchin, however, made use of treachery towards the Marathas. They hauled down their sails, so as to make the Marathas believe that the Revenge had struck in the same manner as Mr. Gape's vessel. Shivaji's admiral thinking that the Revenge was going to surrender advanced with twenty-four *grabs* (*gurabas*) within pistol-shot and prepared his boats to board the English vessel, when the latter unexpectedly opened fire and in a short time repulsed the Marathas. Minchin and Keigwin of course "covered themselves with glory", but the exploit of a captain striking his sails under pretence of surrendering and then firing upon the enemy as he advanced to accept the surrender would have covered him with another sort of "glory" at the hands of the British admiralty, had the battle taken place in European waters. But in their harangue to their crew the English captains had admonished them against "the disgrace of Christians being taken prisoners by Heathens," and they perhaps believed that the laws of naval war might also not be observed by Christians towards "Heathens." And the example of the Portuguese was before them. It is significant that Messrs. R. & O. Strachey have not a word of censure about the stratagem. As English historians have accused Shivaji of fraud and treachery, it is melancholy to observe that in the only recorded battle between him and the British authorities, it was the British captains who deceived Shivaji's admiral by an abuse of the elementary laws of naval warfare. What would have Grant Duff and other English historians said, if instead of the English captains using the stratagem, Shivaji's admiral had made use of it against the English? *Vide* Keigwin's own report of the battle, (reading it in the light of Mr. Gape's surrender), as given at pages 38, 39 of R. & O. Strachey: "*Keigwin's Rebellion.*" and Appendix III.

2 The Marathas captured five English ships that had run ashore. If

into Nagotna roads and stood at anchor. The Revenge followed him in pursuit and only desisted when she found herself completely out-distanced. At Nagotna, Daulat Khan played the same game as at Cheul, repeatedly sending his light boats with the needed provisions to Khanderi, without any effectual hindrance on the part of the British squadron cruising about.

The naval skirmishes around Khanderi were at their height, when Shivaji ordered a force of five thousand to march to Kalyan with instructions to make a diversion upon the landward side of Bombay. But the Portuguese authorities as before refused them permission to march upon Bombay through the Thana district. The news of the approach of Shivaji's forces towards their northern barriers again spread consternation at Bombay, where it was feared that, should the Portuguese grant the required passage or should the Marathas be able to obtain the necessary transports to cross over by water, in either case, the island-town would be doomed to undergo all the horrors of an invasion. Nor had they enough troops to spare to make a show of defence on the Mahim barriers as they had effectively done on the former occasion, occupied as all their available forces already were, both naval and military, in operations around Khanderi. Under the circumstances the Bombay government found no other course open to it but to send an envoy to Raigad with proposals for a fresh treaty.

By this time the fortification works upon Khanderi were nearing completion and the batteries newly mounted upon the island-fort had already begun to give a good account of themselves. The British vessels already

to this is added the *grab* surrendered by Mr. Gape, it would mean that Daulat Khan had captured six out of the seven larger vessels that formed the reinforcement of the Revenge, or including that vessel six out of the total English force of eight larger ships. Certainly Daulat Khan had accomplished his main purpose, and Keigwin and Minchin had "covered themselves with glory," *Vide* R. & O. Strachey: "*Keigwin's Rebellion,*" page 39.

driven to stand beyond the range of Khanderi guns found themselves suddenly strengthened by a fresh fleet from Surat, which included another frigate, the *Hunter* carrying sixteen guns and a complement of thirty-six Europeans. This unforeseen change emboldened the British squadron at Khanderi to assume the offensive and posting themselves at the entrance of Nagotna creek they attempted to bar the way of the light cargo-boats of the Maratha navy. But it was all lost labour. For the creek had another outlet on the opposite side, whence the Marathas could pass in and out with impunity. The British captains planned a forced entry into the creek and the destruction by fire of the Maratha fleets lying at anchor. But such an atrocious plan did not commend itself either to the president or council at Surat.[1] These level-headed statesmen saw the folly of wantonly embittering the feud with Shivaji, who could easily retaliate upon them for any such excesses with a thorough-going precision, celerity and effectiveness. They placed their hopes on the chance of an amicable settlement and looked eagerly forward to the success of their embassy.

The fortification works which were going on apace at Khanderi, the frustration of all British efforts to counteract them, and the sustained neutrality of the Portuguese power were a combination of circumstances that evoked the liveliest terror and consternation in the camp of the Mogul governor at Surat. Hitherto, thought the Mogul governor, Shivaji had been able to carry all before him on land; now it seemed he stood a fair chance to grasp the mastery of the sea, and the Mogul arms were threatened with a double leaguer, by sea and land. Was Surat going to abdicate her commercial pre-eminence in favour of Shivaji? Was he to capture the overseas trade and menace the security of Surat and the other ports? And the Sidi

1 The deputy governor of Bombay, John Child, was in favour of defiance, but the authorities at Surat required him to take up a conciliatory attitude.

had his own fears for the security of his stronghold of Janjira. It seemed that the sea-girt fortress must after all vail its standards before the naval triumphs of the Maratha power.

Fain would the Sidi have mustered together all the resources of the Abyssinian power to obstruct the triumphs of Shivaji's navy. He was deterred by the mutinous spirit of his mercenary hordes, discontented as they were by their pay having long remained in arrear. He made many requisitions upon the Mogul authorities for financial aid at a juncture so critical in his affairs, but the Moguls returned no decisive answer to his entreaties. It was only when the Moguls saw the advantage Shivaji had achieved by their apathetic disregard of the Sidi's remonstrances and the decisive menace his newly acquired station on the western sea presented to the naval position of the paramount power, that they were awakened to a sense of the gravity of the situation and hastened to atone for their past neglect by freeing the hands of the Sidi. An imperial subsidy was immediately sanctioned to relieve his financial distress and the imperial fleets were put in motion to act in co-operation for a concerted offensive against the Marathas. The Sidi put into Bombay harbour with his naval forces and had an audience with the Bombay council. Whatever the result of the conference, he proceeded towards Khanderi, ostensibly to support the British squadron. He cruised round the rocky sea-fort, examining it very narrowly, and assured one of the British officers present[1] that, should the British second his efforts, he would conquer the Maratha fort for them. The British officers, however, did not seem very much to encourage the idea, having reason to suspect his ulterior objects, for they thought that he might indeed with British assistance compel the Marathas to evacuate the fort, but at the end of the campaign instead of relinquishing it to his British allies, he might appropriate it to himself and prove a worse neighbour than Shivaji. With these

[1] Capt. Keigwin.

fears to deter them, they fought shy of the very thought of a concerted campaign with the Sidi.

Disappointed in his expectation of a British alliance, the Sidi, relying on his own resources, opened a vigorous cannonade on the Maratha fort, to which the Marathas made a vigorous reply from their newly planted batteries. The British vessels remained severely neutral, passive but not uninterested spectators of the phases of the war. The Maratha vessels in their turn left the British squadron alone, and poured their broadsides on the Abyssinian foe. The Sidi had come to learn by this time that a British envoy was already at Raigad, negotiating a treaty. To discredit his pacific intention and prejudice the Marathas against a British alliance, at this particular juncture, he forced his way with some of his warships into Bombay harbour, treating the port once more as a base for his naval raids into Shivaji's territory. Four villages were put to fire and sword and a goodly number of peaceful inhabitants were seized and brought as prisoners to Bombay.

Daulat Khan, who all this while was anchored at Nagotna, employed in his well-directed plans of sending victualling and ammunition boats to Khanderi, now determined to face about and with this resolution advanced to the head of Nagotna creek. No sooner did the Abyssinian and British vessels notice the Maratha squadron emerging from the creek than they made all sail to anticipate and arrest their movements. The Maratha commander finding his way barred signalled a retreat, leaving a few vessels at the entrance to prevent the enemy from entering the creek. The Sidi, fearing lest these vessels might under cover of night approach his warships and set them on fire, quietly withdrew his fleet, and the British squadron remained alone on the scene to watch the Marathas. The Sidi returned again to his onslaughts upon Khanderi and kept up a sustained cannonade, which did not seem however to make much impression on the Marathas.

At last baffled in this enterprise, the Sidi determined to make himself master of the opposite islet of Underi[1] and fortifying it with a sufficient garrison and fortress batteries, he notified to the Bombay authorities his intention to take permanent possession of that island. Upon this Daulat Khan at last emerged from his retreat at Nagotna and came down upon the Sidi. A sustained but indecisive encounter took place. The British vessels presented themselves at the scene of battle just after the end of the conflict. Daulat Khan took up his position on an elevated part of the shore and opened fire upon Underi, ably seconded by the batteries of the rival fort of Khanderi. After this had lasted for some time with indecisive results, Daulat Khan again advanced to tempt the fortune of a close encounter with the Sidi. The battle lasted four hours, with disastrous results to the Marathas, who lost four larger and as many smaller vessels, with five hundred men, besides a large number taken prisoners by the Sidi. Daulat Khan himself was severely wounded in the battle. The Sidi's losses are said to have been light. The remnant of the Maratha fleet fell back towards Rajapur, with the wounded admiral on board his flagship. At Rajapur the battered fleet was again put into fighting trim and with fresh additions to their crews again came forth to battle.

In the meantime the British ambassador at Raigad found the Maratha monarch agreeable to the peace proposals presented by the authorities at Bombay,[2] and a Maratha envoy was sent down to Bombay to confirm the articles of the treaty. In view of these pacific arrangements, the Bombay government recalled their squadron from Khanderi and disclaimed any partiality they might be suspected to have had for the Sidi in his recent triumph. The Sidi on his part attempted indeed to hinder the conclusion of the treaty for which the Maratha envoy had expressly come

---

[1] It may be remarked that on account of the similarity of names Grant Duff confounds Khanderi with Underi and *vice versa*. Orme, who uses the right names in one place, inverts them in another.

[2] *Vide*: R. & O. Strachey, page 40.

down to Bombay. With this view he sent to Bombay harbour for sale the Maratha vessels he had captured as the prizes of his recent victory, and applied at the same time for permission to enter the Bombay waters at the head of his squadron. This was naturally refused by the Bombay government, upon which he forced an entrance into Pen creek, carrying fire and sword into the villages on either side of the channel. In the course of this raid he is said to have seized and carried away more than a thousand inhabitants.

Amid these exciting events the new treaty was concluded in March 1680 between Shivaji and the Bombay government. By this treaty the conditions of the peace of 1674 were affirmed, and the British authorities bound themselves to grant no anchorage to the Sidi's vessels within the limits of the Bombay harbour during the monsoons, or if at all they did so, they were to permit it under special covenants on the part of the Sidi not to cause any annoyance to Shivaji's dominions.

But Shivaji did not long outlive these events. Whatever naval schemes he might have evolved in his own mind, for which the conquest of the sister isles was to be the starting-point, were destined to be brought to a sudden end with his death at Raigad, which took place soon afterwards.

CHAPTER XXIX

WITH SAINT AND SEER.

THE story that we have hitherto traced of this noble career is found chequered with many an incident of marvellous heroism, of romantic enterprise, of generous magnanimity, and of filial affection. It remains now to present succinctly in a brief review a few illustrations of the intense piety and spiritual experiences of the great king.

The religious enthusiasm and fervour which characterized the king in all his life had their germ in the associations of his earliest childhood. Brought up under the watchful eye of a loving and pious mother, he had imbibed from his infant years a growing passion for the recitals of the puranas, those eloquent records of the Indian ideals of chivalry, of self-surrender, of the triumphs of faith and devotion. The religious instinct which thus at an early period was impressed upon his plastic mind was cherished and developed in the critical period of adolescence under a guide and philosopher of the undeviating rectitude and conscientiousness of Dadaji Kondadev. The spiritual bias that was given to his mind at this stage of growing inquisitiveness and rationalism remained unobliterated to the end of his life. He was always haunted with an ever-present feeling of the vanity of earthly splendours and the wealth of spiritual hopes and promises. The religion of love had been fervently preached by many generations of saints among the people of Maharashtra, and the consolations of this creed had been made accessible to all castes and classes of society. Of Mukundraj,[1] of Dnyanadev,[2] of

---

1 Mukundraj lived between 1200 and 1300 A. D. He is generally reckoned as the first saint-poet to write in pure Marathi. His chief works are *Paramamrit* (the Highest Nectar) and Viveka Sindhu (the Ocean of Reason). The poems deal with the problem of spiritual salvation.

2 Dnyanadev (1271 to 1296 A. D.,) was one of a quartette of three brothers and one sister, all noted for the purity and saintliness of their lives and the extraordinary extent of their intellectual powers. They all died under thirty years of age. Dnyanadev's chief work is the *Dnyaneshwari*, which is a commentary on the *Bhagwat-Gita* and one of the

Namdev,[1] of Eknath,[2] of many other saints and bards of the olden Maharashtra, Shivaji had heard from the eloquent lips of preachers and rhapsodists,–he had heard buth the sweet persuasiveness of their rhythmic strains and the subtle rhetoric of their gentle deeds. In his own days the names of Mukteshwar,[3] of Ramdas,[4] of Waman,[5] of Tukaram,[6] of Jayaram Swami,[7] of Ranganath Swami,[8] of

greatest poetical works in the Marathi language. Dnyanadev and his brothers were born at Alandi and were subjected to much persecution at the hands of the orthodox Brahman community at Paithan, where they lived afterwards, on account of the circumstance that their father Vithalpant having bcome a *sannyasi* or hermit had renounced his sanyasa and lived with his wife again, and in that state had begotten his children, which was considered to be incompatible with orthodox law and custom.

1 Namdev (about 1275 A. D.) belonged to the *Shimpi* or Tailor caste. He wrote in the *Abhanga* metre or stanza. His *Abhangas* are popularly believed to have run to a crore ! Devotion to Vithal and contempt of all manner of fraud and hypocrisy are the distinguishing features of his poetry.

2 Eknath, (1528—1599,) published a commentary on the eleventh chapter of the *Bhagwat* in the *Ovi* metre. He was a disciple of Janardan Swami governor of the fort of Devgiri or Daulatabad, under the Nizamshah sultans.

3 Mukteshwar, (1609-53,) was a grand-son of Eknath and a master of the Ovi metre, and of pure poetical effects. He translated parts of the Mahabharat.

4 Ramdas (1608—82,) the spiritual preceptor of Shivaji, and the author of the *Das-Bodh*. a poem unique in Marathi literature as being almost the only work in which spiritual ideas are blended with political aspirations, eventually the result of (1) the contemporary triumphs of Shivaji and of (2) his intimate intercourse with him. *Vide* Prof. Bhate's Marathi work, " Sajjangad and Samarth Ramdas."

5 Waman Pandit (1636—96) is said to have been for some time a disciple of Ramdas Swami. He was a Sanskrit scholar of considerable attainments and wrote in the different varieties of *Shloka* metre.

6 Tukaram (1568—1649), was a native of Dehu, near Poona. He was a Maratha Kshatriya by caste and a Vaishya or tradesman by vocation. He continued his father's grocery trade, but lost heavily in business. He was a most pathetic figure, and the most popular poet in Maharashtra. He wrote *Abhangas* and like Dnyanadev and Namdev was a votary of the god Vithal of Pandharpur.

7 Jayaram Swami died about 1672. He was a disciple of Ramdas.

8 Ranganath Swami lived near Nasik, about 1608 and wrote commentaries on the Bhagwat Gita etc. Another Swami of the same name lived at Nazare near Pandharpur and was the uncle of the later poet Shridhar. He and Keshav Swami were followers of Ramdas.

Anand Murti, of Keshav Swami, and of a host of other saints, poets,[1] and *litterateurs* had fallen upon his ears. Nor was he quite a stranger to their poetry. There was an all-pervading religious awakening throughout Maharashtra, the visible symbols of which were the vast congregations that assembled twice a year at Pandharpur, chanting songs of praise in honour of the god Vithoba,[2] in the hallowed strains of Dnyanadev, Namdev and other poets. The religious renascence, which stirred all Maharashtra society to its depths, could not but operate with an intensity of spiritual enthusiasm on a mind already instinct with religious emotions, like that of Shivaji.

Almost within the bounds of the new principality which he planned for himself, marking the first stage of his scheme of empire, lay the hallowed towns of Alandi and Dehu, consecrated to the memory of the poet-saints, Dnyanadev and Tukaram. It was natural, therefore, that from his early boyhood Shivaji should come to hear of the stories and anecdotes told about these saints and listen to the recitations of their soul-stirring verses. As regards Tukaram, Shivaji had the additional advantage from his childhood of listening personally to his religious discourses and abhangas as uttered by his saintly lips on the inspiration of the moment. He had thus conceived at a very early age a high admiration for Tukaram, a saint who was not only the prince of the psalmists and religious orators—*kirtankárs*—of his time, but who was also endowed with a faculty of melodious and inspired verse, the product of his profound religious experience and the earnestness of his message of love. Shivaji took a keen delight in the *kirtans* or psalmodic discourses of Tukaram, who often came to Poona to deliver them. On such occasions, as also when word was brought that the saint was going to address

[1] The English reader will find more information about some of these saints in Chapters XI and XVII of Mr. Kincaid's "History of the Maratha People". Vol. I.

[2] *Vithoba.* Dr. Bhandarkar in his "Vaishnavism and Shaivism" derives this name from Vittu, a Canarese corruption of Vishnu.

an audience in one of the outlying villages around Poona, Shivaji attended his discourses. The following story is an apt illustration of the great fascination Tukaram's oratory and personality exercised upon Shivaji.

Once on a time Tukaram was invited by some of his ardent admirers to Poona and a programme of his kirtans was arranged from house to house. Shivaji was then residing at Sinhagad, but on hearing of the kirtan cycle commenced by Tukaram among the citizens of Poona, he made it a point to attend every night, returning again to Sinhagad on the conclusion of each kirtan.[1]

His Mahomedan foes came to learn about this and prepared an ambush to capture him by surprise. The Mahomedan governor of Chakan Fort received detailed information that on a particular night Shivaji was to be present at a kirtan of Tukaram which was arranged to be performed at the house of a certain Banyan. The commander detached forthwith a body of two thousand Pathans to surprise and arrest Shivaji. The Pathans came and surrounded the Banyan's house, but ignorant as to the identity of Shivaji they prepared to lay hold of every man present and take them away prisoners. Aware of the peril with which they stood menaced, the audience got frightened and excited, and on Tukaram inquiring into the cause of the disturbance, they explained the situation and requested that they might be permitted to ensure Shivaji's safety by flight. But the saint protested against that idea, maintaining that it would not do to leave the hall in the midst of prayer and on that day in particular, it being the day of the *ekadashi*,[2] an auspicious day for fast, prayer, or solemn meditation. Death on such a day while listening to the praises of God, exclaimed the saint-poet, was a thing to be desired. Such a death would assuredly lead to salvation

---

1 It is stated by another bakhar that these kirtans took place at Lohagaum. The number of the Pathans is exaggerated.

2 The eleventh day of the first or second half of the lunar month is regarded as a fast day by pious Vaishnavas.

and put a period for ever to the travails of future births. Thus he exhorted his audience to remain in their places. The poet addressed himself to a solemn invocation of the Almighty, praying for an instant intervention in the moment of trial, and the audience hall rang with the cry of "*Vithal! Vithal!*" Shivaji decided not to leave the kirtan—hall under such circumstances but to await patiently the sequel, whatever it might be, without moving from his place. One of his faithful followers, however, devised a brilliant plan to rescue his master and executed it with the utmost composure and adroitness. He donned Shivaji's ornamented crest and head-dress and swiftly mounting his horse galloped away obtruding his action deliberately on the notice of the Pathans. The latter saw him escaping in this stealthy manner and mistook him for the prince Shivaji. Away they hurried in pursuit, putting spurs to their horses. Under a moonlit night the chase lasted a long time while they could see the Maratha cavalier flying before them. But he eluded their pursuit until the moon set and under cover of the darkness he became invisible. The few Pathans who had remained at the banyan's house joined in the pursuit, and the persons assembled at the kirtan returned safely to their respective homes. Shivaji too paid his respects to the preacher and returned to Sinhagad that very night.[1]

Here is another anecdote illustrative of the powerful impression Tukaram's exhortations could make on the youthful Shivaji. Once on a time when Tukaram was conducting a series of kirtans at Lohagaum, Shivaji attended one of them with his retinue. As the kirtan began Shivaji was thrilled with Tukaram's delivery of the opening verses. The same effect was produced on the pious audience who

---

1 The credulous people of Shivaji's time believed that the Deity saved Shivaji by assuming his form and luring away the Pathans in a vain pursuit. Mahipati and Chitnis in their respective works have followed this legend. But in Shivaji's time there was no dearth of loyal servants to risk their lives for the sake of their master.

were exalted to such an impassioned frenzy of divine love, that forgetting all thoughts of self, of place and circumstance, they sprang to their feet in a state of spiritual ecstacy, uttering the cry, Vithal ! Vithal !, clapping their hands and dancing rhythmically. Such a scene, so full of the spirit of divine love, had never before been witnessed by Shivaji. The preacher proceeded to expound the text he had chosen for his thesis. His exposition turned on the glorification of the ascetic ideal and its true tests and character, and he concluded with a demonstration of the greatness of Vithal, than whom nothing is greater, and he exhorted his audience to leave all other paths and to love Him and cleave to Him, if they would have the crown of human life, life's full worth. These earnest precepts he illuminated with apt quotations from the great masters and ever and anon with the inspired out-pouring of his own melodious and impromptu verses. The impressive oratory of the preacher, exposing the evanescence of worldly pomp and vanity, the evil of sensual gratification, and the transitoriness of human life, wrought powerfully on the imagination of his audience and created a change of outlook in Shivaji. Endowed with the liveliest religious emotion as he was, he was enraptured with the thrilling eloquence of the preacher and he resolved to follow his spiritual advice and act upon his precepts to the very letter, in all his actions in life.

When, therefore, at the conclusion of the kirtan, the audience dispersed and Shivaji returned home, he betook himself to the woods and began to meditate on the words of the preacher amidst the solitude of the wilderness. His counsellors sought to dissuade him from this course of life, representing to him the impropriety of pursuing such an ascetic ideal at this time of his youthful career. But with all their reasoning and advice, they could not persuade Shivaji to change his mind. He dismissed them from his presence, saying that they might dispose of his worldly possessions as they pleased, he was no longer interested in them and that, life being short and evanescent, he was resolved to spend every minute of it in thoughts of eternity, which he would forfeit, if he allowed himself to be entangled in the labyrinths of war and politics. The ministers were in great perplexity and communicated to Jijabai the whole story as it had occurred. She forthwith came down in a palanquin to Lohagaum and, obtaining an audience of Tukaram, besought him to bring round her son to a sense of his temporal duties, relating to him how he had retired to the woods and was spending his days there, brooding on the exhortations of the saint. She urged upon the holy man that there was no one else to look after the state, the watchword of which was the restoration of freedom, civil and religious, from the oppressive Mahomedans. Tukaram listened to her humble appeal and bade her depart with a contented mind, assuring her that as Shivaji was expected to be present at that very night's kirtan, he would snatch the opportunity to address to him a few words and make him again attend to the duties of his vocation in life.

That night Jijabai attended the kirtan. Shivaji too came as usual. The preacher expounded the concept of *Karma*, or a life of action, its necessity, its true meaning. He defined duty as action according to one's vocation in life. There was no imperative necessity to retire from temporal interests and betake oneself to the solitudes of the wilderness for the true worship of God. It was a test of true manhood to live in the world and carry on one's affairs in the spirit of integrity and humanity and to labour day and night for the welfare, be it ever so humbly, of mankind at large. To see the absolute wretchedness and misery of the people every moment of one's life,and to turn away from the forlorn multitude and seek the shades and solitudes of caves and of mountains in quest of salvation—this was not the true spirit of human duty and conduct. To live in the world in order to improve it, there was nothing so effective as the family life. Those that leave the world, and child and wife, and mortify the flesh, smearing themselves with ashes, are constantly tried by temptations, and as the frailty of the flesh rarely permits them to resist for long, they only expose themselves to the ridicule of society. Such a man forfeits all honour on earth. He forfeits his hopes of salvation in heaven. This luminous exposition of the doctrines of *Karma* and *Dharma*, Action and Duty, was followed up by a dissertation upon the duties of a king. The orator set forth the lines of princely beneficence and social service that could be fitly exercised by a sovereign who was virtuous in his private relations and had the welfare of his subjects at heart. He quoted the great examples of *puranic* fame—of Ambarish, of Janak, of Dharma, each one of whom had earned the title of a royal sage (*rajarshi*) by his holiness and wisdom, and proved by these examples that even a king had no necessity to abdicate his sovereignty in order to cultivate the love of God and the pursuits of virtue. This exhortation, illuminated by many an apt illustration and enforced with religious fervour, enthralled and captivated the mind of Shivaji. He was impressed with the truth and sincerity of the precepts and determined to practise them in his conduct in life. Prostrating himself in devout affection at the feet of Tukaram and Jijabai, he returned home to his palace, and resumed his career of conquest and empire.

Having such faith in the sanctity and worth of Tukaram, it was but natural that Shivaji should feel a strong desire to live in close contact with the saintly man and enjoy the constant opportunity of listening to his inspiring discourses. With this view he addressed a letter of invitation to the saint and despatched it by a civilian officer, who took with him a horse, an umbrella, and other state paraphernalia to escort the saint to Shivaji's court with due honour and ceremony. Much as he appreciated the prince's motives, the saint declined the invitation in verses that are well known among his countrymen, and some of the stanzas may well bear translation :—

"God has created the world, full of strange wonders and devices.

"The wise philospher is the inspirer of the intellect, but only by faith does one attain and love his guide.

"Seeing the writing in your letter, I see you have some affection of that sort.

"Rightly are you named Shiva, a holy name, lord of the umbrella, the wielder of the reins of the universe!

"You have passed through the probation of vows, rites, penances, meditation, and mystic arts.

"You are now bent on meeting me: this is the import of your letter.

"Hear then the answer, Sir King; hear our most sincere request.

"Aimless let us wander the woods; in appearance, mean and repulsive.

"Sparely clad, our person is smeared with dust; sparely fed, we live on fruits.

"Our limbs are lean and crabbed and no fit display for anybody's eyes.

"Tuka makes a friendly request, talk not to him of a visit.

"What's the good of our coming to your presence? It will only tire our legs.

"For food, alms suffice; for raiment, rags.

"For sleep, a couch of stone; for covering, the sky.

"Then why need I fix my hopes on any body? It would be a mere waste of life.

"Should we, for honour, go to court, contentment dwelleth not there.

"At the king's palace, the rich are honoured: honour for others is none.

"But the sight of men gaudily decked and apparelled, is death to us.

"Hearing this though you should grow estranged, still God is never indifferent to us.

"This is the secret we would disclose unto you, no greater happiness than to live upon alms.

"Fettered by desire the great live miserably, performing vows, penances, and sacrifices.

"But, says Tuka, we are the rich in mind, the rich inheritors of divine love, the accumulated merit of our past lives."[1]

This frank refusal put an end to Shivaji's solicitation, and though his desire remained unquenched, he did not feel any resentment towards the great ascetic. Far from feeling any anger, his respect and admiration for him were all the more heightened. And as long as the saint was alive Shivaji never wasted a single opportunity of paying him a visit or listening to his discourse. It was his great desire to settle a permanent grant upon the holy man and ease the last days of a life which had been spent in the midst of worldly misfortunes. But before Shivaji could do anything in this direction, the great master had died. However as a humble acknowledgment of the words of wisdom that had flowed from the copious springs of his poesie, and the noble lessons of virtue and faith he had inculcated upon the masses all through his strenuous and self-denying life, Shivaji made a grant of three villages to his son. The revenues of these villages are still enjoyed by his descendants.[2]

Shivaji's desire to make Tukaram his *guru* or spiritual

---

[1] The epistle, as it has come to us, consists of six stanzas or Abhangas. Some of the stanzas, however, refer to the constitution of the Ashta Pradhan Cabinet and to Ramdas Swami, and the author is persuaded to believe that these are interpolated. The constitution of the Ashta Pradhan was not completed at the time, nor had the meeting between Shivaji and Ramdas taken place. It is now almost certain that Tukaram died in 1649. Mr. Kincaid quotes five of these stanzas from the pen of Messrs. Nelson Fraser and Marathe.

[2] This narrative about Tukaram is taken without any material alteration from Mr. Keluskar's biography (in Marathi) of that poet.

preceptor, and spend his days in holy communion with him was left unrealised owing to the premature death of the saint. There were many other saintly men among his contemporaries, but none equalled Tukaram or appeared capable to fill the void created by his death. It is an accepted creed of orthodox Hinduism that without the guidance of such a spiritual mentor, the attainment of salvation is impossible. This was impressed upon Shivaji, at a *kirtan*, which he happened to attend at Mahad, when the preacher described the triumph of spiritual fortitude by the classical example of the Prince Dhruva, which however, as Shivaji saw, was not realized without the mediation of his preceptor, the Sage Narad. But having experience of the unrivalled sanctity and the spiritual faith of Tukaram, his standard of preceptorial requirements was much too high to be approached by other sages. Nor was Shivaji, with all the distractions of state affairs, able to find time to cultivate anything like a deep intimacy with the saintly personages of his time or enroll himself as a disciple of any great spiritual thinker. It was just to fill up this void that he had invited Tukaram to come and reside at his court. But that great man could not be induced by the king's pomp or importunity to give up his ascetic ideal. From this Shivaji inferred that the true saint cares for nobody and seeks nobody's patronage, and that it would, therefore, be difficult for him to come across a man of sanctity who would answer his highest expectation and yet deign to reside at his court. But he never gave up the pious hope of being able to discover such a man and to live in his society. With this view, wherever persons of acknowledged sanctity were known to live, Shivaji did not fail to pay them a visit and provide for their earthly comforts.

Ramdas Swami was a saint of this order. An ascetic of the most austere habits, he wandered over woods and mountains, having nothing like a permanent dwelling-place. Hearing that he was generally to be found at a certain hermitage and temple of Rama, in the glen of Chafal, Shivaji proceeded to this place to pay his respects to the holy man. On his arrival there, the civilian officer of the place, Narsomalnath, came to receive him and said that the Swami did not habitually reside at the hermitage, but generally led a lonely life in the forest and that at that moment he was to be found at Bahiravgad, near the ravine of Kondwan. As Shivaji was making further inquiries about the sage, two of his disciples, Vithal Gosavi and Bhanji Gosavi, appeared on the scene and presented offerings of fruits and flowers to Shivaji, as a mark of propitious favour on the part of the deity of the temple. Accepting the sacred offerings, Shivaji asked the disciples who had built the temple, and expressed his surprise that though the Swami had resided so long at that place, he had not till then come into his presence or rendered him any service. Upon this the disciples of the Swami made answer that though he had indeed not yet come to the presence of their master, all the same the money spent upon the temple had come from him. At this, the king was astonished and saying that it was only their courtesy that made them say so, he asked when and how he had supplied the funds for the erection of the temple. The disciples reminded Shivaji of a forgotten incident, how on one occasion he had attended a kirtan at the house of his family priest at Poona, when a certain Giri Gosavi Nasikkar preached in such a charming style that he was pleased to make him a present of three hundred pagodas, which the preacher hermit had refused as he had nothing to do with the money, and how, on Shivaji's declaring that the money having been offered to him he might dispose of it for any charitable purpose, the preacher had recommended that the sum be forwarded to Ramdas Swami, who was erecting at Chafal a temple in honour of Rama. This sum, said the disciples, had been duly remitted by Shivaji through Narsomalnath, the mamlatdar or révenue officer. Shivaji now remembered the incident and proceeded to inspect the foundations, which, he found, were endangered by a brook flowing from the north of the temple grounds. Narsomalnath was commanded to divert the course of the current and erect a bridge over it and debit the charge to the limit of five hundred pagodas to the treasury. Having given these orders, Shivaji proceeded to the ravine of Kondwan in quest of the hermit, but here too he was disappointed. Upon this Shivaji returned dejected to Pratapgad, thence he proceeded to the holy shrine at Mahableshwar, from which he descended again to Wai, where he performed many acts of piety and charity, and came away to Mahuli. At Mahuli Shivaji was engaged in similar acts of piety, it being deemed a holy place on account of the confluence of the Krishna and the Vena, when a letter from Ramdas, expressed in the *Ovi* metre, was placed in his hands. It was to the following effect:—

"O Meru[1] of resolution, the support of many people, the institutor of a changeless order, rich master mind!

"O thou, whose benefactions form a mighty pile; no rival to thy virtues.

"O Lord of men, of horses, of elephants; O Lord of forts, of land, of water; of cities and thrones, thou bearest these burdens on thy massive shoulders.

"Thou art victorious and glorious, mighty and meritorious, holy and virtuous, a king of wisdom.

"Thou art rich in thought and action, in charity and religion, in knowledge and good behaviour towards all.

"Thou art brave and magnanimous, prompt in thy chivalry; by thy statesmanship thou hast spurned the princes.

"The holy shrines were lying desolate; the Brahman resorts, polluted; the earth, in convulsions; religion was nought.

"To save the gods, the rites, the Brahmans, Narayan enthroned himself in thy heart and inspired it.

"Countless pandits and puraniks, poets and vedic scholars, logicians that lead the assembly, thrive at thy court.

1 Meru is the fabled mountain at the centre of the earth.

"On the face of this earth, there is none to defend religion; the Maharashtra religion has lingered in some measure owing to thee.

"Other pieties cease not, under thy rule; and many seek thy patronage. Honour to thy glory that has pervaded the universe!

"Some wicked ones are slain, some are trembling with fear, others again are pardoned; blessed is the king Shiva!

"I have lived in thy country, but thou hast failed to ask for me; whether, by the mystic law of fate, thou hast forgotten me, I know not.

"But wise are thy counsellors and they are images of piety. What more need I say? Keep alive thy glory as the establisher of religion.

"The strain of state-craft has distracted thy mind. Pray excuse me for writing thus, without occasion."

Shivaji eagerly perused this epistle and courteously entertained the disciple who had brought it to him. He composed a reply to this effect: "Great sage, I plead guilty. Your heart abounds with forgiveness. Your benedictory epistle has filled me with joy. How can I describe it? You have sung my praises, but I am not at all worthy of them. For many days I have had an ardent desire to see you. Even now I propose to come forth into your presence. May you be pleased to receive me in your presence and appease my enduring thirst." This reply he presented to the disciple and inquired of him where the holy man was then residing. The disciple replied that the Swami was then at Chafal, but there was no knowing where he would be, as he changed from place to place, as it pleased his fancy. With these words, the disciple departed bearing Shivaji's reply.

Next day, Shivaji proceeded to Chafal with his suite, and paying a devotional visit to the temple of Ram, he made his inquiries as to the whereabouts of the saint.

The disciples present told him that the Swami was at the temple of Hanuman at Shinganwadi and that his letter which had reached them the previous day about sunset had been taken over to him that very morning, by his disciple Kalyan Gosavi. They suggested, moreover, that he should not hasten his journey to the place where the Swami was at the moment, but that he should partake of the dishes which were being prepared in honour of the deity of the temple, and after they had been duly offered up to the god, he should then proceed in a leisurely manner to pay his homage to the saint, whom in the meantime they would inform of the Rajah's arrival. Shivaji however replied that, as that day was Thursday, a day specially dedicated to the worship of one's preceptor, he was resolved not to taste a particle of food before seeing the Swami. Upon this the disciples present advised Shivaji to go without a big retinue, lest the noise should scare away the holy man. Upon this Shivaji proceeded with only two officers of his suite and one of the disciples of the saint, Divakar Bhat, for his guide. In this way he came to the temple of Hanuman at Shinganwadi, where he learnt that Ramdas Swami had descended to the garden below. Shivaji directed his foot-steps thither. The Swami was found seated beneath a fig-tree. He had just been reading Shivaji's letter delivered by Kalyan Gosavi and had broken into a ripple of laughter, when Shivaji presented himself Divakar Bhat leading the way. Shivaji advanced before the sage, presented the votive cocoa-nut, and having prostrated himself humbly to the ground, stood silent before him. The Swami, in great amazement, addressed himself to Shivaji, observing that he had come at the same moment with his letter, a thing that bespoke his impatience. The Swami went on to say that he had been living for a long time in Shivaji's kingdom, and the king had not seemed to care much for him during all that time. He wondered therefore, why he had called on him that day. Upon this, Shivaji made an apologetic reply to the effect that he had been seeking for a long time to come into his presence, but had not succeeded till that day, and he could only beg to be forgiven for his misfortune. He then requested him to be good enough to initiate him solemnly into the circle of his spiritual disciples, a favour he ardently longed for and which it was in the power of the Swami to bestow upon him. The Swami acceded to the request, and upon the suggestion of Kalyan Gosavi, Shivaji ordered the sacramental requisites for the initiation ceremony to be immediately procured. When these were ready, Shivaji underwent a purificatory bath and then went through all the solemn rites of a *puja* in honour of the preceptor of his choice, Divakar Bhat, the guide, officiating as priest at the ceremony. As the solemn rite was completed, Shivaji bowed his head upon the feet of the master. The latter then delivered into his ears the mystic words which were to be the *mantra* for his spiritual meditation, accompanied by an exhortation, which, it is said, has been incorporated under the name of the "Laghu Bodha" or the Brief Instruction in the *magnum opus* of this poet, viz. : the "*Das-Bodh*" or the "Counsel of Ramdas." It forms the sixth *samas* or section of the thirteenth *dashak* or chapter of this great poem.

The exhortation of the preceptor wrought an immediate change in Shivaji, and addressing himself to the Swami he exclaimed he was now tired of the labours of empire and desired to spend the rest of his life in peace, in the society of the sage, serving him in whatever capacity along with the rest of his disciples, and he prayed that he might be permitted to live, as he desired, in immediate attendance upon the sage. This provoked a strong remonstrance from the Swami. "Is it for this," said he, "that you have come hither, a suppliant? Your proper vocation is that of a Kshatriya. The Kshatriya or warrior has to defend the country and keep the people from harm. It is also a part of the Kshatriya's duty to serve the gods and the Brahmans. Many great exploits are yet expected of your hands. The alien Mahomedan has overrun the earth. It is for you to deliver the land from them. Thus does Rama will. Bethink yourself of the sage advice that Shri Krishna gave to Arjun in the song of the *Bhagvad-Gita.* It is the warrior's path that you must tread in general. The stories of the sage kings of antiquity have doubtless come to your ears. The valorous deeds of your immediate ancestors have doubtless not escaped your understanding. Remember them and mould your conduct on the true pattern of a warrior. It is scarcely to be thought that you should turn away into any other course." These counsels quieted all the uneasiness in Shivaji's mind and he returned home, having for the present given up all intention of becoming a hermit.

After this event Shivaji used to visit Ramdas from time to time, snatching every opportunity when he could do so without detriment to state affairs. He listened to the spiritual discourses of the sage with great interest, and had the highest faith in his teaching. However the worries of his active life and the capricious wanderings of the sage from place to place prevented Shivaji from meeting him as often as he liked. He had first to send his couriers to make sure about the whereabouts of the holy man, and thus only could he propose to himself the consolàtion of direct communion with him. With these difficulties in the way of a more frequent intercourse, Shivaji desired to give a nearer place of residence to the Swami and often urged him to adopt such a place for his abode. At length the Swami complied with his request and it was arranged that he should reside at a place called Parali. Shivaji brought the sage with great ceremony to this fort. There was a mansion upon the fort which Shivaji proposed should be the saint's residence, but the latter refused saying that it was old and dismantled, and asking that a new one should be erected. "Meanwhile," said the saint, "we shall stay in the chambers to the north of the castle-gates."

This fort had but recently come into Shivaji's hands and its administrative arrangements were yet in a disorganised state. These things were now first settled and an officer named Jijoji Katkar was appointed havaldar, with instructions to act in all instances under the orders of the Swami. The garrison in the fort and the civil population immediately within and without it, were under similar orders to obey the saint. The village of Vavardare was assigned to meet the maintenance charges of the little spiritual colony at Parali, the revenue accounts being looked after by a civilian officer, Kondopant by name, who was always to reside at the fort near the person of the Swami. On Ramdas taking up his residence upon it, the fort came to be known as Sajjangad, the Sage's Fort. Holy men from various parts began to frequent the fort, coming on purpose to pay their homage to Ramdas Swami and thus incidentally the circle of Shivaji's acquaintance with such saintly men began to expand. Gradually the colony of the disciples and followers of the saint became so large that the revenues assigned for their maintenance were found to be insufficient. In consequence, Shivaji augmented the annual grant, and it is stated in the bakhar of Ramdas Swami that the addition to the previous grant was made in the same year in which Shivaji embarked upon his Karnatic Campaign. It follows, therefore, that this addition was made in 1676.[1]

This bakhar or biography of Ramdas Swami gives stories of the different occasions on which the king and the sage were brought together. But as most of these narratives are full of fables and miracles of the kind that abound in the orthodox legends of Indian saints in general, it seems more appropriate, considering the nature of this work, to pass over them in silence. But from all these accounts, however credible or otherwise, this inference may

[1] Prof. Bhate publishes from the Chandorkar papers a letter from Dattaji Trimal, the Waknis or home secretary of Shivaji, giving a schedule of inam lands conferred by Shivaji upon the Swami for the benefit of the temple and hermitage. The letter bears the date 3rd September 1677, but it expressly states that the gift was made in the previous year, but that the sanad papers had not been executed, which being prepared in 1677 were by this letter communicated to the local subhedar, Venkaji Rudra. (*Vide* Bhate's Monograph on Ramdas, pp. 123-125).

be safely drawn that Shivaji was capable of an intense love towards his preceptor, of an ardent faith in religion, and of a very high order of character in private life, and that by reason of these virtues he had captivated the heart of such a blunt and out-spoken person as Ramdas Swami.

Tradition has it that Ramdas Swami prescribed three tasks to Shivaji. First, as Shivaji was a devotee of Shiva, he was asked every year in the month of Shravan (July and August), to consecrate a crore of sand images in honour of that god, and celebrate the event by banqueting the Brahmans. Secondly, as it was Shivaji's wont to do honour and extend his patronage to learned Brahmans in the realm, the month of Shravan should be fixed as the season for the concourse of the learned, to receive the doles of the royal favour. As described in Chapter XXIV, at this time of the year the assembled pandits submitted themselves to the prescribed tests of learning under the supervision of the Panditrao, and bore away the palms of merit, each according to his intellectual attainments. Thirdly, the Hindu subjects in Shivaji's state should discontinue the practice of doing *johar* in saluting their equals or superiors, and should use the words "Ram! Ram!" by way of salutation, that is to say, they should call upon the name of God Rama, instead of any earthly lord, which is the meaning of the word "johar";[1] and the new style of salutation should also be adopted in correspondence. However the practice of saluting a person with the greeting, "Ram! Ram!" is according to some authorities of a much older origin. In connection with the institutions derived from Ramdas, there is one more subject that calls for comment. This is the *Bhagwa Zenda* or orange-brown standard of Shivaji. The tradition is that Shivaji's standard assumed this particular colour from the orange-coloured robes worn by the great sage, and in connection

[1] The literal meaning of johar is given by Molesworth as "O Warrior!" It, therefore, seems to be a mode of salutation by which an inferior greeted a superior, or which at best was used between equals.

with the translation of the colour from the robe to the standard, the following incident is usually related. Once on a time, when Shivaji was at Satara, Ramdas Swami came to that town, with his disciples, and passed from door to door, begging for alms. Not aware that the king was then in the town, he came with his mendicant procession to the mansion, where the king had taken up his quarters. The king being informed of the circumstance, got his private secretary, Balaji Avji, to write a brief deed of gift to the effect that all the kingdom he had hitherto won by his labours was hereby granted and dedicated as alms-money to the sage. Having signed the document, the king came forward abruptly and making a profound salutation to the holy man put the deed in his alms-bag. On the saint inquiring what sort of letter he had dropped into his wallet instead of the usual handful of corn, the king replied, "It is as it should be, it is something worth being made over in charity." The sage asked his chief disciple, Kalyan Gosavi, to read the paper and on hearing the contents exclaimed, "You have given away your kingdom in charity, what do you now propose to do?" Shivaji replied, he would spend his days in waiting upon his preceptor, serving him like the rest of his disciples. The sage then dissuaded him from such a course reminding him of the noble kings, Rama and Janak, who were great in earthly as well as in spiritual glory, and impressed upon him the true nobility of a great king, discharging his royal responsibilities according to law and religion. He bade him return and carry on the government as before in his name. Shivaji obeyed and changed the colour of his standard to orange, that all might know that he was conducting the government on behalf of Ramdas.[1]

[1] This story does not find a place in any of the recognised bakhars, or chronicle histories about Shivaji. Even Chitnis who says so much about Ramdas in his bakhar is silent about it; and Prof. Bhate infers that he must have deliberately ignored the incident as unauthenticated. *Vide* Bhate's Monograph, pp. 93-94.

It is necessary at this stage to return to a controvercial point. On the basis of the acknowledged fact that Shivaji enrolled himself as a disciple of Ramdas Swami and had the highest faith in his teaching, it has been maintained that the Swami was his constant mentor in affairs of policy and statesmanship. Much insistence is laid on this assertion in the extant biographies of the Swami, which ante-date the spiritual allegiance of Shivaji to his preceptor as early as 1649 A. D., when they say Shivaji was formally enrolled as a disciple of Ramdas Swami and from which date they attribute his success in political affairs to his preceptor's counsel. But in the first place, the assumed date, 1649 A.D., when Shivaji is alleged to have joined the select circle of Ramdas's disciples, is absolutely incorrect. The chronology of most of the dates mentioned in these biographies[1] is for the most part unreliable. And the suspicion irresistibly forces itself upon our mind either that from the amiable motive of aggrandizing the glory of the object of their adulation, the biographers have deliberately perverted the real facts of the case, or, at best, that following blind tradition as their guide in the most uncritical spirit they have put their faith in idle and exaggerated tales and given to them a semblance of truth by incorporating them in their biographies. These old writers pursuing the biographical methods of the Marathi poet Mahipati have retailed the most mythical romances and miracles in their so-called histories. This circumstance alone may be taken as a fair index of their love of historical truth. It being the fancy of the lay mind in India that the life of a great saint must be full of miraculous incidents, the chronicler of such

[1] The leading bakhar of Ramdas is the biography of the saint by Hanuman Swami, upon which Messrs. Kincaid and Parasnis in their "History of the Maratha People, Vol. I" have relied so much. The untrustworthiness of this book for purposes of history is exposed by Prof. Bhate in his recent monograph and has been severely criticised by other scholars. Messrs. Dev and Rajwade, however, follow the chronology adopted in this bakhar. Mr. Sardesai, author of "Marathi Riyasat" is now in almost complete accord with the views of Prof. Bhate and Mr. Kelunkar.

a life is irresistibly drawn into the temptation of the most absurd exaggeration, but the tinsel products of such minds cannot stand for the sterling gold of history. However a good deal of truth may be found mingled with the fables of these histories of the saints,and a sympathetic and critical faculty has to be actively exercised to separate the one from the other. It is not, however, all modern critics who are mindful or capable of this function. The delusions of superstition thus continue to triumph over the feeble minds of the multitude.

A word must be said here as regards the orthodox date of Shivaji's first enrolment into the circle of the Swami's disciples. The first meeting of the king with the *guru* took place, as we are told in these biographies of Ramdas, in the glen of Chafal. Further we are assured that this place then belonged to Shivaji and was actually administered by one of his mamlatdars or revenue officers. It is also related that Shivaji on his way to Chafal passed through Karhad, Wai and Mahuli, and that at the last two of these places Shivaji made many religious charities and gave banquets to Brahmans. It would seem, therefore, from these chronicles of Ramdas that at the time when Shivaji first visited the saint to obtain the favour of spirtual discipleship, he possessed and ruled over the localities mentioned above. But the facts of history actually are that these districts were conquered by Shivaji not earlier than 1672-1673 A. D.[1] They were never before in his possession. Further, we are informed that one or two years after Shivaji's admission to the circle of the saint's disciples, the latter was invited to take up his residence at Parali Fort, and that the celebrated transfer by gift of Shivaji's kingdom took place at Satara. But both the forts of Parali and Satara were first captured by Shivaji in 1673. These historic dates cut down like cold steel right across the whole web of fiction spun together by the romancing admirers of the Swami.

[1] *Vide* Chapter XXII, p. 341, supra.

On the other hand the authentic chronicles of the career of Shivaji are singularly free from excrescences of myth and miracle and, on the whole, present a continuous narrative of the events of history. Their credibility, therefore, is beyond suspicion. But in none of them is there any record of Shivaji's having consulted Ramdas in state affairs. To be absolutely correct, we may except one case, viz. the coronation ceremony in which matter, it is said, Shivaji did consult Ramdas.[1] As against this, it may be objected, that two of the chronicles of Shivaji, viz. Chitnis's bakhar and the Shiv-digvijaya, have given the date 1649 as the year when Shivaji became the Swami's disciple. There is but one answer and that a decisive one to this question. That is that the date in question is borrowed by these chroniclers on the authority of the romancing biographies of Ramdas. A circumstance that lends great support to this view is the fact that the other old and authentic chronicles of Shivaji make no reference to Shivaji's becoming a disciple of the saint at all.[2] The final decision upon the disputed date has been given by the publication of certain authentic letters in the possession of the descendants[3] of Divakar Gosavi, the disciple of

[1] Chitnis also states that Shivaji visited Ramdas before starting for Delhi. (Agra). But even he omits the incident mentioned in Hanuman's bakhar of Shivaji's visiting the sage at Parali immediately after the tragedy of Afzulkhan and of giving him certain lands in inam. As will be seen from the text such a visit was impossible. However by a strange perversity Mr. Kincaid, accepting the date 1649, not only believes in the visit of Shivaji to Ramdas after the Afzul Khan incident but actually makes it the principal argument to exculpate Shivaji from the charge of murder! *Vide* Kincaid, p. 164.

[2] The oldest chronicler, Sabhasad, wrote his bakhar only 14 years after the death of Shivaji. He does not refer to Ramdas at all. Chitragupta refers to Ramdas only twice, and the only serious statement made by him is that Ramdas gave counsel to Shivaji on the "Duties of a King", after his coronation i. e. 1674. *Vide* p. 92.

[3] These letters have been published by Mr. G. K. Chandorkar in his letter published in the Marathi weekly, the Kesari, in its issue of 26th June, 1906. From these two passages may be briefly quoted here :—

(a) Reply of Keshav Gosavi to Divakar Gosavi :-"I understand what you write, viz: that the Raja Shivaji Bhonsle is coming to visit the

Ramdas who figures in the orthodox version of Shivaji's first personal interview with the Swami. These letters establish the date of this interview and of the consequent enrolment of Shivaji as a disciple of the sage at 1672, and that of the Swami's taking up residence at Parali in 1676. Against this view, it may, of course, be urged that though the year 1672 may be accepted as the date of Shivaji's first visit to Ramdas, he might have come to know about him much earlier. To this it may be answered that there is positive evidence that at any rate before 1658, he had no knowledge whatever of the great sage,[1] and even

Samartha (i. e. Ramdas.) It is his first visit..................I understand what you write about there being nobody to make arrangements. Engage the people of the Wadi (i. e. village of Shingan-wadi?) to make arrangements............" dated the 1st of the latter half of Chaitra, of the Shaka 1594 (i. e. 4th April, 1672 A. D.)

(b) Extract from Shivaji's letter to Jijaji Katkar, the havaldar karkun at the fort of Sajjangad:—"Shri Ramdas Gosavi residing at Shivthar, will come for a few days to the fort, when you shall permit him to do so, to live as long as he pleases, and leave when he pleases to leave............, dated, 8 *jamadilakhar, san saba sabain* 1077, of the *Shaka* 1598, (i. e. 1676 A. D.)

1 Letter of Bhaskar Gosavi to Divakar Gosavi:—"We went to beg for alms at the résidence of the Raja Shivaji. He asked, 'Who and whence are you?' Upon which we replied we were the disciples of the Shri Samarth Ramdas and lived at Chafal. He asked where Ramdas lived and whence he originally came from. We told him he was originally a resident of Jamb on the banks of the Ganga (i. e. Godavari) and that at present he had formed a hermitage at Chafal with a temple of God Rama, and having instituted solemn worship and celebrations there, had bidden us all go forth for alms for the performance of the solemn rites; wherefore we were thus rambling about. On our saying this, the raja wrote a letter to Dattaji Waknis to grant an annual sum of two hundred pagodas for the celebration of the temple solemnities. The money will reach in time. Be this known. Dated, the 2nd of the first half of *Falgun*, of the *Shaka* 1580" (13th February 1659 A. D.) This letter has been published at page 46 of the preface of Mr. Dev's edition of the *Das-Bodh*. It is worthy of remark that the annuity of two hundred pagodas mentioned in this letter is not referred to in the interesting conversation between Shivaji and the Swami's disciples at the former's first but unsuccessful visit to Chafal (*Vide* page 526 *supra.*) It my also be observed that the dialogue etc. given on that page are based on the authority of the orthodox bakhars of Ramdas. Mr. Chandorkar, in his letter to the Kesari referred to in the preceding

for some years thereafter, he does not seem to have kept in his memory a strong impression about him. For, as we have seen, when Shivaji first made his fruitless journey to Chafal to visit the saint, he asked in surprise, as recorded in the orthodox bakhars of the Swami, "How it was he had not yet rendered any service to the sage?" And this lapse of memory as regards whatever knowledge he ever had about the Swami is further confirmed by the language used by the latter at the end of his poetic letter to Shivaji: "Thou hast failed to ask for me; whether by the mystic law of fate, thou hast forgotten me I know not." Such is the plaintive note sounded in that epistle. Further, the praises lavished upon the king by Ramdas in that celebrated letter are scarcely such as by any stretch of imagination Shivaji could be said to have merited as early as 1649, or for the matter of that, even for fifteen years or more thereafter.[1] In short, we may conclude that till 1672, at any rate, Shivaji had no direct personal interview with Ramdas. Whether immediately after the first interview the king entered into a relation of spiritual discipleship under Ramdas is more than can be stated in definite terms. Reading the orthodox story of Shivaji's first introduction to his preceptor in the light of history, it would seem that the conquest of Wai, Karhad etc. took place in 1672, and the capture of the forts of Parali and Satara may be put down at 1673 A. D. However an independent piece of

note, observes that among the sanads granted to the Swami by Shivaji there is not one earlier than the Shaka 1594 (i. e. 1672 A. D.) From this it follows that the annuity mentioned in Bhaskar Gosavi's letter, as quoted above, was perhaps not regularly paid and at any rate not settled in perpetuity by a regular sanad or deed of grant.

(However the annuity is referred to in the letter of Keshav Gosavi to Divakar Gosavi in 1672 from which a portion is quoted in the note to p.536.)

[1] Prof. Bhate rightly points out that the expression "*Jalapati*" or "Lord of water" is used with reference to a period after he had equipped a navy and erected his sea-forts, which activities belong to the year 1663-64. The expression "Some wicked ones are slain" evidently suggests knowledge of the king's triumphs over Afzul Khan and other Mahomedan generals, and the sentence "Thou hast spurned the princes" certainly points to a much later period than 1649.

evidence, a letter from Divakar Gosavi, the disciple of Ramdas, addressed to his son Bhairav Bhat,[1] expressly states that the Rajah Shri Shivaji Bhonsle was admitted to spiritual discipleship at the hermitage at Shinganwadi, in the year with the cyclic name *Paridhavi.* The Shaka year of that name in the period with which we are concerned coincided with 1672 A. D. Assuming that it lasted till the beginning of 1673, that is to say, till about April in the latter year, this would perhaps coincide almost exactly with the date of the conquest of these districts adopted by us on chronicle authority in Chapter XXII.

It may however be sought to establish the orthodox view upon the answer sent by the poet Tukaram to Shivaji's letter inviting him to come and reside at his court. It is urged that in Tukaram's reply, out of which two stanzas have been given above in translation form, there was a reference to Ramdas Swami, and an exhortation to Shivaji that he should devote his attention solely to that saint; and from this it is argued that Shivaji must already, previous to the date of this epistle of Tukaram, have seen

[1] An extract from this letter is published by Mr. Chandorkar in his letter referred to above. The letters published by Mr. Chandorkar were obtained by him from the descendants of Divakar Gosavi, who was for some time the manager of the hermitage at Chafal in the life-time of Ramdas and even after his death. When the Chafal estates were finally made over by King Shahu to a descendant of Ramdas Swami's brother, for the maintenance of the hermitage etc. in hereditary succession, in order to put a stop to the existing quarrels between some of the Swami's disciples, the original papers relating to the hermitage at Chafal remained in the family of the Gosavi, the quondam manager, along with his personal papers. Prof. Bhate in his monograph on Ramdas declares that he has examined the papers bearing upon this question and that he is quite satisfied about their authenticity. He reproduces them in full at pages 108 to 119 of his monograph. Though the protagonists of the earlier date, (viz. the year 1649 as the date of Shivaji's becoming a disciple of Ramdas) like Mr. Dev of Dhulia and Mr. Rajwade still cling to the traditional view by trying to explain away the objections and difficulties raised, there cannot be any doubt that these letters completely establish the view taken by Mr. Keluskar. Prof. Bhate enforces it with greater wealth of argument and illustration. (*Vide* Bhate pp. 96 to 105).

Ramdas and entered into a pupillary relation with him in matters spiritual. Very little reliance, however, can be placed upon this part of Tukaram's epistle to Shivaji, as long as the foregoing historical evidences remain unanswered. Secondly, if the orthodox date 1649 indicates truly the time when Shivaji was acknowledged as a disciple of Ramdas, it will have to be admitted that this event took place in the same year as Tukaram's death. But if we admit the authority of the orthodox version in the matter of the date of the discipleship, we shall have further to take for gospel truth the legends of various meetings between Shivaji, the Swami and Tukaram after Shivaji's enrolment as a disciple, and in particular the story of a great solemnity at Parali which Tukaram is alleged to have attended. In consequence, the date of Tukaram's death will have to be deferred to an indefinitely later time, but it is now proved to a certainty that this date cannot be extended beyond 1649. Thirdly, it is natural to suppose that Tukaram's letter to Shivaji must have preceded his death by a few days, but according to the bakhar of Ramdas, a fairly long time must be taken to have elapsed from the discipleship of Shivaji down to the date of Tukaram's epistle. In Chitnis's bakhar of Shivaji, the same version is given as regards the post-dating of Tukaram's letter after the date of Shivaji's enrolment in the circle of the disciples of the Swami. More than that, here we have proof of a more elaborate process of tampering with the simple message of Tukaram, if we examine the manner in which it is presented in this bakhar. The stanzas constituting the epistle are here divided into two groups. The first group consisting of two stanzas is here quoted as Tukaram's answer to Shivaji's solicitations at a time prior to his coming in contact with Ramdas. The second groud of four stanzas is quoted as an answer to fresh importunities for a visit on the part of Shivaji after the latter had entered into bonds of discipleship under Ramdas. A proceeding that stands discredited by the very nature of things! For if at the time Shivaji had such a firm faith in Ramdas, why go running after the elusive Tukaram? If Shivaji, after acknowledging the discipleship of Ramdas desired nothing more than just to see Tukaram, where was the necessity of sending a special mission to invite and escort him to his capital? For at various times upon his tours and otherwise Shivaji had found numerous occasions to see and hear Tukaram. The account in Chitnis's bakhar must, therefore, be condemned as a transparent gloss.

It is more natural to assume that at the time when Shivaji was importuning Tukaram to satisfy the spiritual hunger of his soul, he probably had not even heard of the name of Ramdas. But then what about the fact that the name of Ramdas does occur in Tukaram's epistle? The answer to this is that some of the stanzas alleged to constitute a part of Tukaram's epistle are decidedly spurious, or to speak without equivocation were subsequently interpolated—interpolated undoubtedly after Shivaji's coronation by the blind admirers of the Swami, as is amply borne out by the epithet "*Chhatrapati*" (Lord of the royal umbrella or sovereign of a canopied throne), used of Shivaji, and by the allusion to the Ashta-Pradhan or Shivaji's cabinet of eight ministers. For as long as Tukaram lived, Shivaji had never assumed any such title and the constitution of the regular Ashta-Pradhan was not so much as dreamt of. However admirable the motives of these interpolators might have been—and it was misdirected zeal to promote the glory of their great preceptor—their glosses and perversions of the truth have led to the deplorable consequence of circulating throughout Maharashtra a hypothesis that depreciates the glory of Shivaji by transferring it to the credit of another. For the hypothesis is that whatever Shivaji did accomplish in the direction of the restoration of a national government and the national religion to Maharashtra, he accomplished by the inspiration and under the guidance of Ramdas Swami.

There is one more objection to be considered ere we

close this discussion. If it is held that Shivaji's first interview with Ramdas took place in 1672, and his enrolment as a disciple in that or the following year, it may be asked what must be the date of the composition of those chapters in the Das-Bodh that deal with politics and other cognate subjects, and which evidently seem to have been compiled for the purpose of giving him advice? For it appears from a letter of Divakar Gosavi addressed to one Bahiram Bhat[1] that from the Shaka 1576 (1654 A. D.) for ten years onwards the Swami was engaged in the composition of the Das-Bodh. The letter in question was written in the Shaka 1576 and the passage that has bearing on this subject is as follows:—" Shri Samarth (*i. e.* Ramdas Swami) has proceeded with Kalyan Gosavi, Chimanabai, Aka, (the last two being female disciples of the Swami), and Ananta Kavi, (*i e* the poet Ananta) to the ravine of Shivthar, to stay there for ten years, for the purpose of literary composition."[2] The answer to this objection is that of the twenty *dashakas*, or chapters of the Das-Bodh, as accepted by the orthodox, the first eight comprise the original Das Bodh, which consisted only of these parts, and the others were composed subsequently and superadded to the original, either by the disciples or by the Swami himself as occasion arose. Mr. S. S. Dev in the preface to his edition of the Das-Bodh, has succinctly stated the reasons and arguments that lead to this conclusion. They may be briefly restated as follows:—

(1) There is a sustained and continuous flow of argument in the first eight chapters, without any repetitions. It is after the eighth chapter that frequent repetitions occur. The object of Ramdas's counsels was to make a dissertation on spiritual welfare. The first eight chapters comprehend

[1] Bahiram Bhat is probably the same as Bhairav Bhat and was the name of the son of Divakar Gosavi. The word *chiranjiv* is used in this letter (which is quoted by Prof Bhate at p. 108 of his Monograph,) showing the relation between the parties to the correspondence.

[2] In the letter of Mr. Chandorkar referred to in the previous footnotes, this letter is quoted as authentic.

nothing within their scope except spiritual wisdom. The word "*rajkaran*" or politics obtrudes itself nowhere upto these eight chapters. The stream of thought induced by contact with Shivaji has not yet mingled itself with the flow of the argument. In the ninth chapter for the first time, the word "*rajkaran*" does occur and that in a casual manner.

(2) The 42nd verse of the tenth section of the seventh chapter reads as follows:—

"The jingle of words is come to an end: the work is come to its conclusion. Herein we have given a clear dissertation on the love of one's spiritual preceptor." And indeed the work was now ready for a conclusion, except for the chapter on spiritual knowledge, which would have been the final chapter of the entire work.

(3) The second verse of the sixth section of the ninth chapter runs as follows:—"*This has been discoursed upon in the Das-Bodh*; it has been made clear in the section on spiritual knowledge; the five primary elements have been described in their primordial condition." It is clear from the portion italicized that this verse and the chapter of which it is a part, were not composed originally as forming a part of the Das-Bodh.[1]

The same law must be applied to the chapters that follow; and inasmuch as it is said that the latter twelve chapters contained here and there counsels addressed to Shivaji, it must be inferred that these chapters were composed after 1672. From the whole disquisition, therefore, it would follow that the counsels which are made so much of by the admirers of the Swami were really addressed to Shivaji at a time when he had almost completed the establish-

[1] Prof Bhate in his monograph on Ramdas makes a similar analysis and comes to a similar conclusion viz. that the portion of the Das-Bodh from the 9th Chapter onwards must have been written separately from the first seven and also from the eighth, which last he thinks must have been written independently by itself. (*Vide* Bhate's monograph, pages 26 to 40.) He also shows that some of the political or quasi-political dissertations are apparently addressed to the life-members of the Ramdas's conventicles.

ment of national independence and the freedom of religion, and the composition of them was perhaps made possible by the enlivening effects which the triumphs of the great king produced on the poetical imagination of Ramdas Swami. The attempt to transfer to the poet-saint the whole credit of the warrior king's achievements is a part of the same campaign that has led certain modern scholars to attribute the first beginnings of his power to Dadaji Kondadev, nay, even to the ministers and advisers of the Raja Shahaji, a refutation of which has already been attempted at the beginning of the sixth chapter.[1] And we hope that the array of facts and dates, that we have been able to bring together in the present chapter, will enable the reader to arrive at an impartial decision, as to the extent of Shivaji's indebtedness to his preceptor, in the matter of the foundation and consolidation of his power.

It is pleasant to turn from this controversy to the policy of liberal tolerance which Shivaji extended towards Islam and which he sought in vain from Aurangzeb. At the time of the defection of Sambhaji, in the midst of his last campaign against the Moguls, the great king made a stirring appeal to Aurangzeb against the imposition of the *Jazia*. This letter reveals a lofty outlook on religion and is a passionate plea for tolerance. Shivaji reminds Aurangzeb that even in the Koran God is styled the "Lord of all men," and not the "Lord of Mahomedans" only. "If it be a mosque," wrote Shivaji, "the call to prayer is chanted in remembrance of Him. If it be a temple, the bell is rung in yearning for Him only. To show bigotry for any man's creed is really altering the words of the Holy Book ......"[2].

---

1 None of the recognized bakhars of Shivaji quotes specific instances of the king consulting Ramdas Swami for his advice before starting upon any particular enterprise (the consultation, with reference to the proposed coronation, which by the way comes after 1672, being alone excepted). Chitnis does mention, however, that before going to Delhi (Agra) Shivaji visited Ramdas for the favour of his benediction. But there has been enough criticism of Chitnis.

2 Sarkar's *Aurangzeb*, Vol. III, 325-329.

CHAPTER XXX

THE END, 1680

SHORTLY after the fortification of Khanderi, word was brought to Shivaji that a large amount of treasure was being sent under convoy from Delhi to Aurangabad, for the military operations of the Mogul power. Upon receipt of this intelligence, Shivaji set out with a chosen body of horse and veiling his movements in the greatest secrecy, attacked the convoy and securing the whole of the treasure from the enemy, returned by forced marches to Raigad. The violence and rapidity of these movements brought on a re-action, that prostrated Shivaji. The extreme exhaustion was attended with pain in the chest, fever and hæmorrhage from the mouth.[1] The disease became more and more malignant from day to day. The officers at the court spared no remedies to restore the health of their king. The prescriptions of the most renowned Indian physicians, vows to the gods and prayers at the temples, magic and astrology were tried in vain, without any alleviation of the malady.

Shivaji had given strict orders to his people not to give out the news of his mortal illness. Nor would it have been easily believed in abroad, as rumours of his death had often been spread before, which, according to the Mahomedan chroniclers, had often turned out to be the preludes of some important campaigns. And at this very time a part of the forces of Shivaji had invaded the Mogul territories upto the walls of Surat, which had already commenced to feel the

[1] The chronicles of Sabhasad and Chitragupta state that Shivaji suffered only from an ague. Chitnis and the Rairi Bakhar assign the cause of death to fever. Grant Duff describes the mortal disease as an inflammation of the knee-joint. The Bundela chronicler attributes it to the wrath of heaven occasioned by the curses of the *fakirs* at Jalna, who are said to have been looted at Shivaji's last attack upon that town. The curses, so it is said, brought on the illness to which he at last succumbed. The Shivdigvijaya gives a still more romantic legend, viz., that Shivaji was poisoned by his second wife, Soyerabai, that her son Rajaram might succeed to the throne, while prince Sambhaji lay imprisoned at Panhala. In the present text as given above the author follows the versions of Dr. Fryer, the traveller, and the historian, Orme.

brunt of their assaults. The inhabitants of Surat apparently imagined that Shivaji himself led these invading hosts and the dread memory of previous invasions had thrown them into a panic. The British merchants had sent their valuables to their boats down the Tapti. The Mogul governor of Surat at last paid a heavy tribute and purchased his peace. Moropant, the Peshwa, returned homewards with these spoils. Shivaji's original plan was himself to go upon the campaign. His mortal illness prevented this project. On his return to Raigad, rich with the fresh spoils and tributes, Moropant found the king's malady aggravated beyond cure.

Convinced that his end was drawing near, Shivaji summoned his ministers and intimate relatives to his bedside. Among the dignitaries who answered the call were Moropant the Peshwa, Pralhadpant the Chief Justice, Balaji Avji Chitnis, Ramchandrapant the Amatya, Ravji Somnath, Suryaji Malusare, Baji Kadam, Mahadaji Naik Pansambal and others. Addressing himself to them, Shivaji said that he had now arrived at the end of his life; the hour of his death was approaching apace. His physical endurance could hold out no more. A patrimony of forty thousand pagodas he had converted into a kingdom of a crore. A cavalry guard of eighty thousand was maintained by him in his service. He left no son competent to preserve and defend this wide kingdom with valour, with courage, with strategy. Rajaram was only a minor, and if he grew to man's estate he might protect and augment his dominions. Sambhaji the elder son was of age, but he was not governed by reason. He had thought of partitioning the kingdom between his sons, but Sambhaji had not consented to the compromise. But with all that if he divided the kingdom, the great lords and dignitaries of the state would take opposite sides, and the end would be rivalry and dissension instead of growth and advancement. There would be no order and obedience. The law of succession was that the elder should succeed to the throne, and the younger obey and serve his elder brother. But he could see little chance of his sons conforming to that law. Sambhaji would occupy the whole kingdom after his death. The brave officers in the army would go over to his side as the elder; Rajaram as a minor would command little support from the army. The civilians and the ministers would go over to Rajaram. This would create factions. Sambhaji would cause men of worth and position to be arrested and executed. The great nobles of the state would be subjected to indignities and insults. His reign would be a triumph for the base and the vulgar. The honoured leaders and nobles who had shared his toils and enterprises would be laughed at and insulted, and the noble discipline of his state thrown into disorder. Given to habits of dissipation as he was, his reason would be clouded and he would be governed by his passion in the insolence of power. The state would be at the mercy of rash and cruel people. As to himself he had always tried diligently to discern and cherish merit, and with the support of such men he had built up the fabric of his state. These men of worth and character would be degraded and down-trodden under Sambhaji and they would have to fly the kingdom. With such anarchy reigning in the land Aurangzeb would find it convenient to subvert the new power. The emperor had preserved peace owing to the awe of Shivaji's name. He would be emboldened by the disorders in the Maratha state to launch a new army of invasion. He would extinguish the tottering powers of the Adil Shahi and Kutub Shahi dynasties and then lead his triumphant hosts against the Maratha state. Sambhaji would prove unequal to the task of defending the state from the invader. Aurangzeb would bring utter destruction upon him. Habits of dissipation easily bring a man to ruin. If Rajaram survived, then only was there some hope of recovering the kingdom from the enemy. No other way of safety seemed to open itself before his mind.

These words of final despair overwhelmed the minds of his listeners and brought tears to their eyes. Seeing them in this agonized state, Shivaji bade them be of good cheer. For death was the appointed goal to human life. This was a world of mortality. He that was born was destined to die. To none on earth was given the gift of immortality. Wealth, son, wife, valour, victory, self were illusions and must be left behind. He that loved them and was at one with them gave himself to needless agitation. It fetched no profit. The way to salvation was to take the fortune of the moment and to act disinterestedly. They were all brave. It was their clear duty to put forth their highest efforts and save the state. It was for them to act unanimously. They had exhausted their efforts for curing his malady. Their human efforts had proved to be of no avail. They must now stop these efforts. He had reached the bourne of his life and was now prepared for a flight to heaven. Theirs it was now to observe every precaution and to defend the state by deeds of valour. It was his keen desire to subdue the Indian continent, capture Delhi, liberate the Ganges from the yoke of tribute, extend the empire beyond the Attock and govern it by law; but these higher aims had remained unrealized. The streams of his life had been exhausted. They must not repine with a sense of this grief, but control their mind,balancing it with reason. Having thus consoled them, he bade them retire from his presence.

Shivaji now gave himself entirely to the performance of the last rites of religion in the few hours of life that were yet left to him.

He had a purificatory bath in the holy water brought from the Ganges, and sacrificial ashes were smeared over his body He wore upon his person necklaces of the sacred *rudraksha* beads and wreaths of *Tulsi* (basil) leaves. Seated on a part of the floor strewn with *darbha* grass, associated as it always has been in India with holy meditation and spiritual thought, he invited great pandits and ascetics to his presence, and discussed with them the problems of spiritual destiny and salvation. Resigning earthly thoughts, he devoted the few moments of life that yet remained to the glorification of the Holy Name, listening to the readings from the sacred books and the exhortations of the kirtankars. The charities usual on such occasions were dispensed to the Brahmans, the dying king personally going through the solemn rites and, where he could not stand the fatigue, making solemn vows to that effect. Recitations from the Bhagwad-Gita and songs of divine praise were ordered to be chanted. In this manner, amidst the sacred chants of the Brahmans that surrounded his person, with a mind profoundly impressed with a deepening feeling of spiritual repose, expired the great king, the hallowed name of *Shriram* still hovering on his lips. It was on a Sunday, at noon-tide, on the full-moon day of the month of *Chaitra*, in the Shaka 1802, corresponding with the 5th of April 1680 A. D., that the great king closed his earthly career.[1] He died in the pride of power, in the meridian height of his earthly splendour; and yet he died without any feeling of regret or repining at quitting the scene of his terrestrial glories, thus exhibiting in his death the greatest of earthly triumphs, the triumph over the temptations and frailties of our human nature. That serenity of his last moments was begotten of faith and fortitude. It was an earnest desire of his, and it had recurred to his mind again and again, even in this life to quit the scene of his earthly splendours, following in the foot-steps of the saintly kings of yore, whose names are enshrined in the pages of Hindu legend and history. He had fondly hoped to be able like these great kings to abdicate the throne in favour of his son and devote the autumn of his life, without hindrance or interruption, to meditation and prayer and the service of God. But a great part of his ideal, the complete over-throw of the Mahomedan hegemony and the exaltation of the Hindu power still remained to be realised. His heir-apparent had betrayed

[1] Jedhe (p. 195) states he died on *Saturday*, but he gives the same month, hour, and year.

qualities in direct antagonism to the virtues of an ideal ruler. Under these circumstances, the thoughts of abdication and the assumption of the life of a wandering recluse or a cloistered saint appeared too heroic and extravagant to be of any practical value. His wakeful anxiety for the good of his subjects and his prophetic fears of an untimely wreck of his life's work, the disgrace of which would recoil on his name, rendered the entertainment of such ideas impossible and reconciled him to a continuance of a life of political endeavour, relieved by such opportunities, as it presented, for well doing and spiritual thought, chastened by the precepts of virtue and religion, and illumined by the inspiring society of great sages.

The death of the great leader was a grievous blow to the ministers and nobles of the state and the relations of the royal family. All classes of society mourned the loss. The ministers took the precaution to close the castle gate and prevent the publication of the tragic news. The funeral of the great king was celebrated with royal pomp and honours. The third wife of Shivaji, Putlabai, performed the *sati* rite upon the funeral pyre of her husband. The obsequies were performed by a member of the Bhonsle House, Sabaji Bhonsle of Shingnapur[1], assisted by Prince Rajaram, the latter being too young to perform all the rites himself. Religious charities in honour of the event were dispensed on a liberal scale.

Shivaji married seven wives. Sayibai, the mother of Sambhaji came of the Nimbalkar family; Soyerabai the mother of Rajaram was a daughter of the Shirke family. Putlabai, the third wife, who performed the *sati* rite on the death of Shivaji, had no issue. The fourth wife Sakwarbai came of the Gaikwar family.[2] She gave birth to Kamaljabai, who was married to Janoji Palkar. The

1 Grant Duff gives his name as Shahaji Bhonsle.

2 If the entry at page 181 of Jedhe's Chronology refers to this lady, Shivaji married her in 1657. It was probably this wife of Shivaji who died about March 1674, as we learn from Narayan Shenvi's letter to the deputy governor of Bombay.

fifth wife Lakshmibai died childless. The sixth Sagunabai had a daughter Rajkuwarbai who was given in marriage to Ganoji Raje Shirke Malekar. Of the seventh wife Gunwantabai, nothing is known except that she died childless.[1]

Sayibai gave birth to prince Sambhaji in 1657. The character of this prince has already been sufficiently indicated in the foregoing pages. Rajaram, the second son of Shivaji, was born in 1664.[2] He was a prince of good character which augured well of his future, and Shivaji had high hopes about him. Sayibai died in 1659. She was a wise woman and a loyal consort to Shivaji, who loved her fondly. In fact after her death, he does not seem to have quite enjoyed the blessing of a happy family-life. Soyerabai is said to have been an intriguing woman. It was her ambition that her son Rajaram should succeed to the throne, and she had been working in this direction even in Shivaji's life-time. She had won over most of the ministers to her side. Annaji Datto the Sachiv in particular was the leader of this faction. The thoughts of Shivaji with reference to Sambhaji, were, as we have seen, most despondent and pessimistic. The ministers decided to join the party of Soyerabai and exalting Rajaram on the throne, to conduct the affairs of government in his name. With a view to carry out these plans they attempted to suppress the news of Shivaji's death till Prince Sambhaji, who was only a prisoner at large within the limits of Panhala, was made secure and kept under a strong guard. Janardanpant, the Sumant, was sent with a body of troops to Panhala, the fort of Raigad was strengthened with an addition to the usual garrison, a force of ten thousand cavalry was posted at Panchwadi,[3] and Hambirrao, the Commander-in-chief, was ordered to encamp with his army, in a state of alertness at Karhad.

1 See Appendix at the end of this chapter.

2 Some bakhars give 1661 (A. D.) as the date of the birth of Rajaram.

3 Panchwadi is the same as Pachad, where the English ambassador had to halt at the foot of Raigad.

As these operations were likely to take some time to mature despatches were forthwith sent to Hiroji Farzand, the governor in charge of Sambhaji, instructing him how he was to behave in reference to his ward. Notwithstanding all the ministerial precautions, it would seem that the news of the death of Shivaji had already leaked out and found its way to Sambhaji, or at least that he had a very strong suspicion on the subject. For when the bearer of the ministerial despatches reached Panhala, Sambhaji intercepted the courier and compelled him, on pain of death, to deliver the despatches to himself. Upon this the courier seeing no other remedy to save himself, handed over the despatches to him. Apprised that the secret despatches from the ministers had fallen into Sambhaji's hands, Hiroji Farzand took fright and fled to the Konkan. Sambhaji first put himself in possession of the fort and executed two of the officers who tried to offer resistance. He put the fort in defence order and waited to hear of further developments on the part of the ministers. Janardanpant Sumant, informed of the change of situation at Panhala Fort and seeing that it was impossible to enter it tried to besiege the fort, but shortly after leaving his troops to continue the blockade, he withdrew to Kolhapur.

Meanwhile the ministers had installed Rajaram on the throne and conducted the government under his name. But there was no cordiality of feeling among the ministers. The rivalry between the Peshwa and the Sachiv which had already commenced during the life of Shivaji now developed into a mutual hatred. Hambirrao had not been admitted into the secret cabal of the ministers and felt estranged from them. That Janardanpant withdrew from the siege of Panhala and voluntarily retired to Kolhapur was perhaps due to some similar cause. Sambhaji won over to his side some of the soldiers, who had been stationed around Panhala, and upon Janardanpant arriving there, the prince with a body of Mavalis raided his camp and brought him prisoner to Panhala Fort. Hambirrao was delighted with this exploit of Sambhaji, which went to show to him that the young prince was a chip of the old block, and he determined to throw the weight of his authority on the side of one whom he took to have inherited the valour of Shivaji. On the news of the capture of Janardanpant reaching Raigad, Moropant Pingle came out with an army ostensibly to fight and liberate Janardanpant. On arrival at Panhala he forgot his warlike intentions and threw in his lot with Sambhaji, who, satisfied with his conciliatory attitude, confirmed him in his office of Peshwa. Hambirrao came to Panhala and joined the prince with all his army. With his cause thus strengthened, Sambhaji came down upon Raigad, but already before his arrival the fort guards had declared on his side and made prisoners of his opponents. The troops cantoned at Panchwadi likewise came over to Sambhaji. Under these circumstances Sambhaji did not experience the least difficulty in making himself master of Raigad. The first order he issued on entering the fort was to put the Sachiv, Annaji Datto, into irons and confiscate his property. Rajaram was imprisoned, and his mother, Soyerabai, was arrested and, when brought before Sambhaji, insulted in the grossest manner. She was accused of having poisoned Shivaji, and ordered to be put to a cruel and lingering death. The officers attached to her cause were beheaded, and one of them, who had perhaps been more zealous than the rest, was ordered to be hurled down the rock from the ramparts of Raigad. By these acts of cruelty and revenge he overawed all opposition, and seated himself on the throne in August 1680. Happily for us the recital of the manifold atrocities that disfigured a reign commenced in so inauspicious a manner, lies beyond the scope of the present narrative.

APPENDIX

SHIVAJI'S WIVES AND DAUGHTERS

GRANT DUFF mentions four wives, "a fourth wife whose name and family are unknown." (Chapter IX). Dr. Fryer says that Shivaji married a fourth wife at the time of his coronation, (Vol I, Letter II, Chapter IV). Prof. Sarkar quotes from Henry Oxenden's letter of 27th May 1674 to the effect that Shivaji was then busy with his coronation and married two other women. (Factory Records, Surat, Vol. 88). This is supported by an entry in the Jedhe Chronology, which states that on the 4th of the first half of the month of *Jeshta* (May) Shivaji was invested with the sacred thread and on the 6th of the month, just two days later, he was married with the *Vedic mantra* rites; and another entry states that the Coronation took place on the 12th Jeshta, i. e. six days later, and it is easy to believe that in the same manner in which the thread ceremony was completed by a Vedic rite of marriage, similarly also the coronation ceremony of the 6th of June 1674 (properly speaking 13th, not 12th of Jeshta) was followed by a marriage with vedic rites, to which Henry Oxenden's letter of the 8th of June 1674 refers, citing that "the Rajah was married to a fourth wife," to which reference is also made by Grant Duff. The interpretation to be put on the words "*fourth wife*" probably is that the bride married after the coronation ceremony became the fourth living wife of Shivaji, and not the "fourth wife" married in the same season. And yet Prof. Sarkar speaks of Shivaji "marrying three young women, though he had two or three other wives, and two sons living." (Sarkar's *Shivaji* p. 428). Prof. Sarkar probably assumes that Shivaji married two wives in May 1674 and *one* in June 1675, but that does not explain how the last mentioned bride could be the "fourth wife" if "two or three" other wives were living and three new ones were married. On the other hand Prof. Sarkar makes an apparently contradictory statement at page 281 of his "*Shivaji*," which is probably a correct representation of the facts of the case. At page 281 Prof. Sarkar states, "On the 8th (June), Shivaji took a fourth wife without any state or ceremony. Shortly before he had married a third." The sarcastic reference of Prof. Sarkar in the foot note at page 281 to the desire of Shivaji to assert his right to hear vedic mantras in sacramental ceremonies really furnishes to us a clue to the mystery of these late marriages. However this would limit the number of Shivaji's marriages in 1674 to two, one after the thread ceremony and the other after the coronation, and not *three* as stated by Prof. Sarkar at page 428. He had lost one of his wives about the month of March in that year. (Narayan Shenvi's letter, Factory Records, Surat, Vol. 88).

In the bakhar of Ramdas Swami, there is a statement that besides three wives Sayibai, Soyerabai and Sagunabai, Shivaji had two concubines. Sabhasad states that besides Sayibai, Shivaji had six other wives; but he does not mention the names. This statement is not corroborated in any of the bakhars. Mr. Rajawade in his "*Sankirna Lekh Sangraha*" printed from the *Granthamala* states on the authority of a paper found at Tanjore that Shivaji had *eight* wives. The paper describes the names and parentage of only six of them, whence it is concluded that the other two were concubines. The date and authority of this document are doubtful.

Mr. Kincaid following the genealogical tree of the Shedgaokar Bhonsles gives the names of seven wives of Shivaji (1) Sayibai, daughter of Vithoji Mohite Newaskar, (2) Putlabai who committed *sati*, (3) Soyerabai of the Shirke family, mother of Rajaram and of a daughter Dipabai, married to a Maratha noble named Visajirao, (4) Sakwarbai, mother of Kamaljabai who became the wife of Janoji Palkar, (5) Lakshmibai, (6) Sagunabai, mother of a daughter named Nanibai, the wife of Ganojiraje Shirke Malekar, and (7) Gunawantabai. Of this list Putlabai,

Lakshmibai and Gunawantibai are described as childless. Besides the daughters, Dipabai, Kamaljabai and Nanibai, Kincaid mentions a daughter of Shivaji by his first wife Sayibai, who was given in marriage to Harji Raje Mahadik of Tarale, governor of Jinji, and he mentions a fifth daughter in a foot note also to Sayibai. This princess was Sakhubai, given in marriage to Mahadji Naik Nimbalkar of Phaltan, from which family came Dipabai the wife of Maloji Bhonsle. As regards this marriage, the Phaltan state records tell an interesting story. Bajaji Nimbalkar had become a Mahomedan, and wanted to come back to Hinduism. Jijabai, the mother of Shivaji, interested herself in the subject and got the priest of Shinganpur to re-admit the Maratha Mahomedan to the fold of his religion and caste, and in order that no doubt might be left on the subject she brought about a marriage alliance between him and Shivaji, whose daughter Sakubai by his first wife Sayibai (who according to most accounts herself came from the Nimbalkar family) was, at Jijabai's instance, given in marriage to the son of Bajaji. This story illustrates the solid work done by Jijabai in the matter of Hindu unity and religion. Shivaji purchased the patelship of a village in Taluka Purandar for 1200 pagodas and conferred it upon his son-in-law.

Mr. Sardesai names three wives and three daughters of Shivaji in the genealogical table at the end of his ***Riyasat*** and in this list Rajkuwarbai is given as the name of the princess who in the genealogy followed by Mr. Kincaid is named Nanibai and is described as the wife of Ganoji Raje Shirke. Nanibai was perhaps the pet name of Rajkuwarbai.

CHAPTER XXXI

SHIVAJI'S FORTUNES AND POSSESSIONS

THE life story of Shivaji has been told in the preceding chapters. It is proposed in the present chapter to make an attempt to estimate the extent of his power, possessions and wealth at the time of his death. Nor should it be quite an uninteresting subject to make such an audit of his wealth and possessicns, seeing that it furnishes an index to the measure of his success in his ceaseless toils of over thirty-six years, in that war of redemption which he had embarked upon against the despotism of the Mahomedan rulers of the country. At the time when the Rajah Shahaji transferred his allegiance from the fallen house of the Naizam Shahi sultans to that of the still prosperous Adil Shahi dynasty and in the service of that government entered upon the sphere of his proconsular authority in the Karnatic, he had left his Maharashtra jahgirs, as we have seen, under the able administration of the loyal Dadaji Kondadev. These jaghir estates comprised the districts of Poona, Supa, Indapur, Baramati and a portion of the Maval country. This was the sole patrimony derived by Shivaji from his illustrious father at the time he embarked upon his political career. Even these districts were held on the sufferance of the Bijapur government and were saddled with feudal burdens. That government was in a position to have cancelled or annexed these jahgirs at any time. To what extent, on entering personally upon the possession of these jahgirs, as a representative of his father,–jahgirs which had originally been conferred as rewards of service and pledges of the gracious favour of the reigning sultans,–Shivaji turned them into the nucleus of an independent kingdom, and what final proportions that kingdom had assumed at the time of his death, this is briefly the survey we enter upon in this chapter. It is necessary to acknowledge the fact that anything like an exact survey is impossible. However the different chronicles about Shivaji furnish us with most valuable material for such a survey, in the shape of the lists and inventories they have compiled of forts and territories, of specie and jewellery, and the family and state fortunes of Shivaji's kingdom. And there is reason to surmise that these inventories had been practically prepared during the life of Shivaji. For young Sambhaji had proved a scapegrace, had already committed treason and joined his father's enemies, and it was feared that sooner or later he would wreck his father's estates. Shivaji had, therefore, these lists compiled, so as to facilitate, when it should be deemed necessary, a partition of all his estates and possessions between Rajaram and Sambhaji, and it appears from some of the chronicles that he had been thinking of such a plan.[1]

Taking the account in Chitnis's bakhar as our guide, we may make fourteen divisions of Shivaji's territorial possessions. Chitnis describes at full length the number and names of the forts comprised in each division. The full lists of these names are reproduced in the original Maratha text by Mr. Keluskar, but in this English version it has seemed advisable to abstain from a dreary catalogue of names, although it has its historical value, and to indicate only the most important positions falling in each territorial group or division. The territorial divisions[2] mentioned in the bakhar above referred to are as follows:—

(1) The Maval territory situated among the Sahyadri mountains or the Western Ghauts. This region comprised the modern talukas of Maval, Saswad, Junnar, and Khed. This territory included, in all, eighteen hill forts. The more famous among them, which have often been referred to in

---

[1] *Vide* Sen's *Shiva Chhatrapati*, extract from *Sabhasad* page 132 and the lists from page 133 to page 149.

[2] Each of these territorial units constituted a prant, (or a subha according to the Mogul terminology,) and was governed by a subhedar, who exercised the jurisdiction of a modern district collector and magistrate. As regards area some were almost as large as a modern district, others only equal in size to a district sub-division, but in a military sense the latter would often constitute a more important charge than a Prant of a relatively larger area.

the foregoing narrative, were :—Rohida, Sinhagad (or Kondana), Kelna, Purandar, Lohagad, Rudramal, Rajgad, Rajmachi, Torna, Visapur, Wasota and Shivneri.

(2) The territory of Satara and Wai. This division comprised eleven forts, of which the following have played an important part in the preceding narrative, viz., Satara, Parali or Sajjangad, Pandavgad, Wandangad and Chandangad,

(3) The territory of Karhad, which comprehended four forts, viz., Vasantgad, Macchindragad, Bhushangad and Kasaba Karhad.

(4) The territory of Panhala, which comprised thirteen forts, conspicuous among which were Panhala, Khelna (Vishalgad), Pavangad, Rangna and Bavda.

(5) The territories of Konkan Bandhari and Naldurg. This extensive division included fifty-eight forts, of which the most noteworthy were the following:—Sindhudurg, Vijayadurg, Jayadurg, Ratnagiri, Suvarnadurg, Khanderi, Underi, Kolaba, Anjanwel, Revdanda, Raigad, Pratapgad, Prabalgad, Mahuli and Lingana. Most of the forts mentioned in the beginning of this list were sea-forts.

(6) The territory of Trimbak, which comprehended twenty-five forts, among which those of Trimbak, Chandwad and Sindhgad may be mentioned.

(7) The territory of Baglan, which comprised seven forts, among which were included Saleri (Salheri), Muleri, and Nahava.

(8) The territory of Vangad etc., which included a great part of the modern district of Dharwar. This division comprised twenty-two forts, including Chitradurg, Kanchangad &c.

(9) The territory of Phonda-Bednore, which comprised twelve forts, the chief of which were Phonda, Kalburga, Mangrol and Krishnagiri.

(10) The territory of Kolhar-Balapore, which comprised twenty-seven forts, among which the following may

be mentioned, viz., Kolhar, Shriwardhangad and Bednore-kot.

(11) The province of Shrirangapattan, which included twenty-two forts.

(12) The territory of the Karnatic and Jagdevgad. It comprised eighteen forts, among which Jagdevgad, Mallikarjungad and Ramgad may be mentioned.

(13) The territory of Vellore, which included the modern district of Arcot. It comprised twenty-five forts, chief among them being Arcot, Trimal, Trivady, Sajara, Gojara &c.

(14) The territory of Chandi (Jinji) which included six forts.

As previously observed, Chitnis gives the whole catalogue of these forts, *seriatim*, classified under the fourteen territorial divisions. Besides these, a long list of other forts can be gleaned from the other chronicles, which Chitnis seems to have overlooked. Of all these forts--and the total for the fourteen divisions in Chitnis's list alone exceeds two hundred and sixty—one hundred and eleven are stated to have been erected by Shivaji himself, by one of his chroniclers, who also gives a full list of such forts; but other authorities concur in restricting the number of such forts to eighty-four.

[1] The contents of Shivaji's treasury at the time of his

[1] Prof. Jadunath Sarkar has published in the Modern Review (January 1910) under the heading "The Legacy of Shivaji", extracts from the Tarikh-i-Shivaji, a Persian manuscript. The extract under reference gives an inventory of the various kinds of property left behind by Shivaji. Prof. Sarkar thinks from the internal evidence that the Persian manuscript is a translation from Marathi sources and was composed about 1780.

Prof. Sarkar divides Shivaji's "Legacy" under the headings, treasure, wardrobe, specie, jewels, grain, rice, dal, armoury, stables and slaves. Under the heading treasury are described quantities of various metals, and specie. The number of hons or pagodas given in this list is about 381 lakhs only. There were besides gold ornaments and blocks of copper, silver, bronze, steel, ironware and lead vessels. Under the second heading are catalogued various kinds of kinkhabs, dupetas, silk shawls etc., also paper, running up to 6,500 quires. Under specie are also included various kinds

death are described by the chronicle writers with over-flowing details. Diverse kinds of gold and silver coins, representing the coinages and devices of distant nations, are mentioned in these lists. Of the gold coin, called gubbar, gumbar or gadar, we find an estimate of one lakh; of gold mohurs, two lakhs; of putlis (worth about five rupees each), three lakhs; of imperial or padshahi pagodas, thirteen lakhs and a half. Then follow different kinds of pagodas viz: Sangiri pagodas, twelve lakhs and three quarters; Achutrai pagodas, two lakhs and a half; Devrai pagodas, three lakhs; Ramchandrarai pagodas one lakh; Gooti pagodas, one lakh; Dharwad pagodas, twelve lakhs; miscellaneous gold coins (consisting of pagodas of twelve other species), three lakhs; Satlam pagodas, one lakh; Ibrahim pagodas, one lakh; Shivrai pagodas, four lakhs; Cauveri pagodas, fifteen lakhs; Pralkhati pagodas, two lakhs; Pamnaik pagodas one lakh; Advani (Adoni) pagodas, three lakhs; Jadmal pagodas, five lakhs; Tadpatri pagodas, one lakh and forty thousand; Tuti (Tuticorin ?) pagodas, one lakh; Vellore pagodas, half a lakh; Sailya Ghat pagodas, two lakhs; pagodas with the pennant device, five lakhs; and gold ingots, equal to twelve and a half candies in weight. Among the silver coins are mentioned rupees, five lakhs; *asarpadi* coins, ten lakhs; the mosque-inscribed silver currency of Dabul, of Cheul, of Busrah, twenty-five, ten, and five lakhs respectively; of silver ingots and plate, ten lakhs of pieces, fifty candies in weight. As regards jewellery and precious stones, it is said to have been of the then value of two crores of pagodas. All kinds of precious stones are mentioned in these lists, viz:—rubies, emeralds, turquoises, sapphires, pearls, corals, topazes, and diamonds. Besides one crore of pagodas' worth of valuable cloth is reported to have been stored in the treasury.

---

of scented oils and perfumes and the quantities vary from one candy to 50,000 candies. Then come jewels, including all kinds of precious stones. Under the heading grain are also included ghee, mica, indigo, sulphur etc. The list of armour is interesting and includes cotton, resin and wax. Under the heading of stables, we have a total of 37,000 horses of all sorts. Slaves are also mentioned.

As to the army, the private paga mustered a cavalry force of eighty thousand, and the shiledar or cavalier horse, twenty-five thousand. The infantry force of Mavalis and Hetkaries included one hundred thousand men. This number does not include the garrison soldiers detailed on duty at the various forts. Detailed lists of cavalry and infantry officers are to be found, which it is not convenient to reproduce *in extenso*. Among the cavalry officers may be mentioned Hambirrao sir-nobut, Anandrao Hapt hazari (*sapt hazari* or commander of seven thousand), Netaji Palker, Manaji (Man Sing) More, Swarupji (Rupaji) Bhonsle, Gondji Jagtap, Khandoji Jagtap, Santaji Jagtap, Dhanaji Jadhav, Netoji Katkar, Kankde, Kathe, Santaji Ghorpade, Telangrao Nimbalkar, Venkaji Jumledar, Gangaji Shirke, Maloji Nimbalkar, Krishnaji Powar, Bhalekar, Udaji Powar, Parsoji Bhonsle, Nemaji Shinde, Krishaji Ghatge, Birje, Tambe, and many distinguished scions of the historic families of the Mohites, the Shirkes, the Bhonsles, the Nimbalkars, the Powars, the Angres, the Pansambals, the Mahadiks, the Thorats and other noble houses. Among the distinguished infantry officers may be mentioned, Yessaji Kunk sir-nobut, Suryaji Malusare, Mal Sawant, Vithoji Lad, Bhikji Dalvi, Trimbakji Prabhu, Kondji Farzand, Tanaji Malusare, Subhanji Naik, Bajirao Pasalkar, Baji Prabhu Deshpande (of the Hardas Maval country), Baji Murar Deshpande (of Mahad), Hiroji Farzand, Krishaji Bhonsle, and many others. This list contains the names of many Prabhu officers. As to the naval squadron of Shivaji, one or two chronicles mention a classified list, from which it would appear there were at least six hundred and forty of such vessels, smaller or larger, as could be fitly used for war. However other chronicles, without going into particulars, state that Shivaji had above a thousand vessels on the sea. Of the largest class, which the chronicles call[1] *gurabas*, there were

[1] These are the *grabs* of the English records.

thirty; next after them of the *galbat*[1] class, or ships of the line, one hundred; of *mahagirees*, or ship-castles, one hundred and fifty; of smaller gurabas, fifty; of transports, sixty, and of smaller craft, of various sizes and denominations,[2] two hundred and fifty. The sea-forts were, as we have seen, an important feature of Shivaji's naval policy, some of which have already been mentioned in the catalogue of the Konkan forts. But they may bear repetition here. The principal of these naval forts were Kolaba, Khanderi, Underi, Anjenwel, Ratnagiri, Padmadurg, Sarjakot, Vijayadurg, Gahandurg, Khakeri, Suvarndurg, Rajkot and Sindhudurg. Shivaji's naval forces generally lay anchored under cover of these fortresses of the sea. But the names only of a few of the naval commanders are mentioned in the bakhars. Among those mentioned are Darya Sarang, Mainaik Bhandari, Ibrahimkhan and Daulatkhan.[3] There is reason to believe, though the names are not extant, that many families of the Koli and Bhandari castes distinguished themselves by their naval service under Shivaji, as in the neighbourhood of these sea-forts, many distinguished families belonging to these two castes are found to have risen into prominence about that time.

Of the Brahman officers who rendered such conspicuous service to Shivaji, a few may here be mentioned, viz: Moro

---

1 Called galwets or gallivats in English records.

2 Such as pal, jug and machavas (i. e. munchwas of the English records).

3 Of these naval commanders some were Hindus and others Mahomedans. Sabhasad describes Daria Sarang as a Mahomedan and Mainaik as a Hindu of the Bhandari caste. Ibrahimkhan and Daulatkhan were evidently Mahomedans. Prof. Sarkar tries to show (*Shivaji* p. 337, foot-note) that the name of the Darya Sarang is a Hindu name, but it might as well be the name of a Konkani Mahomedan as the suffix "*gee*" or "ji" in *Ventgee*, is used both by Hindus, Parsis, and Mahomedans on the Bombay Coast. Further, contemporary European authorities have mutilated Indian names to such an extent, that it is difficult exactly to say what Indian name the name "Ventgee" really stands for. For the bravery of Daulatkhan, see the end of Chapter XXVIII. Darya Sarang is Persian for "*admiral of the ocean*" and *Mainaik* is mixed Arabic and Sanskrit for *captain of the water*. Mainaik is a common name among Kolis and Bhandaris.

Trimal Pingle, Nilo Sondev, Apaji Sondev, Ramchandra Nilkant, Raghunath Narayan Panditrao, Annaji Datto, Balaji Raghunath, Narhar Ballal Sabnis, Ravji Somnath Subhe, Janardhanpant Hanmante, Dattajipant Waknis, Shamji Naik Punde Potdar, Shankraji Nilkant, Raghunath Ballal Korde, Krishna Joshi, Narhar Anandrao, Niraji Ravji, Pralhad Niraji, Dattaji Gopinath Bokil, Timaji Keshav Naik, Krishnajipant Mathure and others of the same family, and a host of others. One of the bakhars gives a list of Prabhu officers in Shivaji's service, mostly civilians. Among the prominent names in the list are Balaji Avji Chitnis, Chimnaji Avji Daftardar, Shamji Avji Karkhannis, Trimbak Vithal Khasnis, Chando Narayan, Ragho Ballal and Nilkant Yessaji Parasnavis.[1]

The lists in the bakhars, whether as regards the statistics of Shivaji's wealth or the names of his gallant officers, civil and military, cannot be regarded as final or exhaustive, nor have we attempted to quote them here *in extenso*, but only as specimens of what is to be found in the Marathi authorities upon this subject. Fuller lists can be found in the Marathi original of this biography, some of them having been patiently reconstructed from a careful study and comparison of the various bakhars. And in concluding this survey it is but fair to observe that the names of many a gallant commander of Shivaji's hill-forts have been lost to posterity.

[1] Of course the names of many Prabhu officers in the cavalry and infantry are included in the preceding lists.

CHAPTER XXXII

CHARACTER

WHILE tracing the record of this eventful career, which we have endeavoured to present, to the best of our ability, by a lucid exposition of the chronicle histories and other material bearing on the subject, the thoughtful reader can ponder in his own mind upon the talents and virtues that claim his tribute of praise, and pronounce an impartial judgment upon those faults and short-comings which hostile critics have sought to discover in the character and career of our hero. We cannot however altogether refuse to take upon ourselves the burden of a comparative estimate and a critical examination of the conduct and character of Shivaji, and to summarize briefly the result of the inquiry. Further, in taking the reader over the mazy episodes of this narrative, the author has had to refrain from criticism and comment, for fear of diverting attention from the story. As a set-off to the restraint observed on those occasions, we deem it both a duty and the exercise of a right,now that we have arrived at the endof the narrative, to make a few general observations on the great character and career revealed in these pages, and to set forth our views on the legacy of thought and action, of wisdom and inspiration, that this noble career has left behind as a common heritage to the people of Maharashtra and perhaps of all India. It is hoped that the estimate now presented to the reader will be accepted in a kindly spirit and any errors that may have inadvertently crept into the account will be generously ignored.

Nil ex omni parte beatum. This ancient earth of ours has yet to produce a perfect man. Perfection cannot be expected of the children of men. No hero, however great or virtuous, can be an exception to this law. From this point of view, our hero may have had his faults and deficiencies, which but proclaim a human origin and human frailty and enlist sympathy and forgiveness. With an expanding circle of duties and responsibilities and a widening intercourse with persons whose interests are in perpetual conflict, conflict of duties must often arise and culminate in actions which at first sight may appear censurable. But until a proper scrutiny of such actions is made by an austere and unbiassed judge, the author of them can never attain his true place in the estimate and opinion of men. Those who have benefited by his actions will continue to praise him at all times, those who have lost by them will never cease to revile his memory. And both these parties in doing as they do seem but to follow the common instincts of human nature. It is only when a neutral and strictly judicial mind comes to examine the two sides of the question and calmly establishes the true character of the person concerned, that the latter obtains his real place in history. Shivaji has not yet had the good fortune to have his actions studied and scrutinized by a rigidly dispassionate but competent historian.[1] The present writer cannot claim such a position. He does not aspire to formulate a final verdict. He frankly professes himself to be a Maharashtrian at core, and he would make no secret that he is too enthusiastic an admirer of Shivaji, to pose as an independent critic. But he feels himself constrained to state here at

1 Mr. C. A. Kincaid in his "History of the Maratha People" Vol. I has vindicated Shivaji from the attacks of his foreign critics and traducers, especially as regards his conduct in the Chandrarao More and Afzulkhan tragedies. He displays a more genuine sympathy for the Marathas and the great Maratha leader, than is done by Prof. Sarkar, who under a guise of analytical criticism traces almost all the actions of Shivaji to the love of plunder and belittles his institutions, though the same analytical examination would go to show that a good many things he has said in the earlier part of his biography are unsaid by him in the last two chapters, especially in the last ten pages. Compare for instance Sarkar's remarks at p. 114 and in the foot-note at pp. 366-67 with the confession at page 493, and the imputations of cowardice at pages 223 and 225 with the remarks at pages 490 and 492. On the whole the impression produced while perusing Sarkar's book is not that he is writing a *Life of Shivaji*, but that he is following the movements of the Mogul armies or interpreting the ill-informed opinions of the European factors at Surat, Rajapur, Bombay or Madras.

some length what the voice of Maharashtra has generally to say about Shivaji, and what answer she has to make, and has been making, to the strictures passed by Mahomedan historians and blindly followed by British imitators.[1]

THE CHARGE OF REBELLION.

The first charge is ingratitude and treason towards the Adil Shahi State of Bijapur. This, according to the hostile critics of Shivaji, places him in the same category as the lawless and rebellious *polygars*, or the refractory barons, of the time. These critics dwell upon Shivaji's ingratitude towards a power that had taken his fugitive father under its protection at a critical juncture in his life, his baseness in abjuring the authority of such a power, his insolent and unprovoked defiance. What then? Was the sense of family obligation to press upon him like a dead weight and crush out of existence all finer sense of manliness and independence? And was it to be imputed to him as a fault if he refused to endure the yoke of a life-long servitude, under the scourge of an alien tyranny, while the rayats were oppressed, while the faith of his fathers was trodden under foot? Was it dignified for one, who was animated by a spirit of true devotion to his country, by a feeling of common interest with the rest of his compatriots, and an enthusiastic fervour for the national religion, to wear the mask of peaceful sloth or dedicate himself to a life of passive and listless pleasure, depending on the capricious bounties of an alien dynasty towards his house? Or was it rather the case, that this time-serving indulgence was a

1 The following remarks of Mr. Kincaid, (History of the Maratha People, Vol. I page 271) bear out our contention :—"Shivaji has by a curious fate suffered more at the hands of historians than any other character in History. They have one and all accepted as final the opinion of Grant Duff, which again was based on that of Khafikhan .....And while judging Shivaji with the utmost harshness, they have been singularly indulgent to his enemies. The thousand basenesses of Aurangzeb, the appalling villainies of the Bijapur and Ahmednagar nobles have been passed over with a tolerant smile. The cruel trick by which Ghorpade betrayed Shahaji has provoked no comment. Shivaji, however, is depicted as the incarnation of successful perfidy, a Cæsar Borgia......etc."

passing phase, an uncertain and slippery advantage, which he might be called upon to relinquish at any moment? And with such feelings dominating his breast, was he still to address himself to the venal arts of a court parasite or glib-tongued loyalist? Or was he not rather more true to the better side of his nature, when, feeling the power within himself and spurred by its compelling force, he devoted himself entirely to the meditation of plans and labours for the emancipation of his countrymen? The history of the world clearly demonstrates that founders of great dynasties are rarely free from the stain of rebellion. But the blot on their escutcheons is more than compensated for by the splendour of their triumphs. The stain is forgotten, the glory only remembered. So ought it to be with Shivaji. That he extricated his country from the mortal grip of an alien despotism and gave his countrymen their first cordial draught of liberty after centuries of misrule, is of itself no small service to the people of India. It is a permanent debt, nor can we ever hope to repay it. That this independence did not endure upto our generation is in no sense a fault of Shivaji. The fault, if any, must be laid, as students of history know, at the doors of those who succeeded him in the sacred duty of conserving the liberty he had won at such a heavy sacrifice. Had Shivaji failed in his heroic enterprise of laying broad and deep the foundations of an indigenous and independent power, towards which the revolt from the Adil Shahi state was to be a stepping-stone, our hostile critics would not have remained satisfied with pouring out the vials of their virtuous rage upon his "rebellion", but would have exhausted upon him every weapon from the armoury of calumnious reproach. But his success having saved him from such an open attack, they still fling against him the reproach of rebellion, content if they can succeed, be it ever so little, in tarnishing his glory. A charge of this kind would appear more graceful and even pardonable from the pen of a Mahomedan historian; but when European historians, who know or ought to know no other allegiance than that which is paid to the ideal of liberty, make themselves parties to the reproduction of the same language of calumny, their conduct cannot but appear ridiculous. It would have been according to the fitness of things for these historians to have given an impartial verdict upon one who so dauntlessly and triumphantly asserted the liberties of his country. But it is difficult to preserve the balance of impartiality in all things and at all times, and it is evident that had we continued to possess that independence for which Shivaji bled and toiled, these historians would have hesitated to pronounce such a sweeping indictment.

THE CHARGE OF TREACHERY.

The second charge brought against Shivaji is his alleged treachery and cruelty. To a superficial observer of Shivaji's record, and in particular to a Mahomedan observer, it would seem that there was much to lend countenance to such a view.[1] But when we survey the vastness of his enterprise and the limited resources at his disposal, we of Maharashtra cannot but vindicate the expediency, the opportuneness and the ripe wisdom of his plans and stratagems. For a mere jahgirdar to take up arms against

[1] The Romans found consolation for the defeats inflicted upon them by Hannibal by charging him with treachery and cruelty. But what modern historian does now seriously believe in the "*Perfidia plus quam Punica*" with which Livy charges him? As to the charge of cruelty, who now thinks it sustainable, having regard to the conditions of ancient warfare? And yet in this case an Aryan nation accused a Shemitic commander of cruelty. In the case of Shivaji historians of a Shemitic bias have flung the charge of cruelty against an Aryan enemy. It needs no answer. It is at least satisfactory to note that not even the worst of his hostile critics have found a weak spot in his character so as to level against him the other accusations which Roman prejudice rightly or wrongly fastened upon Hannibal: "Nihil veri, nihil sancti, nullus deum metus, nullum ius iurandum, nulla religio" (no truth, nothing sacred, no fear of the gods, no regard for oaths, no religious scruples). Verily Shivaji has not fared much better at the hands of his Mahomedan critics than Hannibal did at the hands of his Roman historians. And yet the modern world gladly acknowledges Hannibal's greatness! So must it be with Shivaji.

the triple powers of the Bijapur, the Golconda and the Mogul States was at no stage a light matter, and to the contemporaries of the youthful Shivaji its rashness presented itself in its most disheartening form. The very guardian of Shivaji, Dadoji Kondadev, shuddered to think of the probable consequences of the wild and quixotic adventures of his patron's son, and the reader knows how this anxiety exhausted the strength of this loyal veteran and brought him to death's door. It was, therefore, a foregone conclusion that stratagem and policy were indispensable tools for the pioneer labours of deliverance. Without an appreciable measure of these qualities, and certainly in the total absence of them, Shivaji could never have succeeded in accomplishing even the least of the amazing exploits of his wonderful career. Much less could he have given to his Maharashtra countrymen, if only for a temporary period, the joyful experience of liberty. With the Bijapur government past the zenith of its power, with the Mogul emperor making tremendous strides towards paramountcy over all India and pouring out his mighty armies and unlimited resources to accomplish the destruction of Shivaji, his armoury of stratagem proved equal to every occasion, furnished the means of ready defence, and enabled him by a process of ceaseless corrosion to dissolve and wear out their authority. But this must not delude us into the belief that he knew no arts save those of stratagem or that he practised them against all persons and on all occasions. Those that lent a willing ear or made offer of loyal and manly service for the promotion of his noble enterprise, experienced nothing but frank and honourable treatment at his hands. To meet Afzul or Shaista Khan on a fair field of battle, with the overwhelming hosts that marched under their command, was beyond the scope of any practicable method of defence on the part of a general like Shivaji, operating as he had to do with forces quite out of proportion to those of his antagonists. There were but two alternatives to choose from, either to lead his scanty army to certain death and massacre at the hands of a relentless invader, to relinquish for ever the higher aims and purposes of his life and to court infamy and ridicule in the eyes of all people, or by a bold and skilful use of strategy and guile to cut the ground from under his opponents' feet, entrap their forces and annihilate their power. And if he chose the latter of these alternatives, we at any rate, the people of Maharashtra, cannot afford to be censorious. Treachery of a deeper dye has disgraced the records of other conquerors, treachery the whole purpose of which was the violation of the liberties of innocent nations and the lust for foreign territory. Shivaji's conquests were redeemed from this stain by the nobler purposes by which they were inspired, the sacred cause of the redemption of his people's liberty, their deliverance from a foreign yoke. His stratagems were bound to wear the complexion of treason and treachery in the jaundiced eye of the. Mahomedan sovereignties, who were compelled most relunctantly to acknowledge the sovereign independence of the people of Maharashtra. Had Shivaji stickled for the point of honour, when horror upon horror menaced the tranquillity of his people, the fury of Islam would have ridden triumphant over all, and the name of Maratha would never have been blazoned broad in the world's history. With the invader thundering at the city-gate and breathing revenge and destruction, while meek morality is quivering helplessly amid a scene of blank desolation and dismay, there is no choosing between the furies and engines of war. The political wisdom of the world and the standards of practical morality have recognized the necessity, under such circumstances, of repelling the enemy by every means at one's command. Besides where defeat is sure to carry down into irretrievable disaster and destruction not only one's own self but thousands of dependents and followers, the crisis requires the commander inexorably to put aside the ordinary ethical standards for the time, and ensure the safety of the lives and liberties of his people, even at the sacrifice of the ordinary rules of human conduct. Add to this a state of society in which for centuries together there had been no peace, in which the standards of political morality were not the refined standards of modern times. Consider how Afzul Khan would have gloried, if he had succeeded in his treacherous plots to murder or imprison Shivaji. Consider to what depths of iniquity Shaista Khan would have descended, in order to arrest or otherwise get rid of the elusive Maratha warrior. It will then be seen that the killing of Afzul Khan or the raid upon Shaista Khan, far from redounding to Shivaji's discredit, claim, by the boldness and brilliancy of the plans employed, no small tribute of praise and admiration. It is but natural that those, who smart under a sense of loss by reason of the sensational escapades and stratagems of Shivaji, should, in season and out of season, revile his memory. But there is no excuse for European historians to follow blindly in their lead.[1]

THE CHARGE OF CRUELTY.

Let us now consider the charge of cruelty and vindictiveness. Even a superficial survey of the career of Shivaji

[1] Without prejudice to the defence of Shivaji in his dealings with More and Afzulkhan (vide pp. 141-143 and pp. 152-172) we may say that similar instances of stratagem and treachery are to be found in plentiful abundance in the history of the time on the side of the Moguls and the Deccan sultanates. We may instance the unsuccessful attempt of the Adil Shahi chief, Baji Shamraj, with the aid of the Mores of Javli, to entrap Shivaji on his return from Mahad; the successful trick of Baji Ghorpade against Shahaji; the proposal of the Raja Jaysingh to arrest or murder Shivaji, after his escape from Agra (Vide Sarkar's Shivaji pp. 197-98). The most atrocious instance is Aurangzeb's plot to capture Golconda in 1657 by sending Sultan Mahomed with an army, which was admitted by the unsuspecting Golconda chief as a marriage escort to accompany the Mogul prince to Bengal. Nothing could exceed the meanness of the fraud employed by Aurangzeb on that occasion or the ruthless rapacity of the Mogul army. As to treachery between the British and Shivaji, we have the treacherous aid the Rajapur factors gave to Bijapur when Shivaji was personally besieged at Panhala in 1660, while all the time the factors professed neutrality, and the worse instance of the abuse of the rules of naval warfare by Keigwin and Minchin in the battle round Khanderi island. Mr. Kincaid draws attention to the slaughter of the Macdonalds of Glencoe, in the comparatively refined times of William III.

will suffice to convince us that this charge is absolutely unfounded. It was a settled principle with Shivaji never to cause wanton bloodshed. The prisoners of war taken by Shivaji were never cruelly treated.[1] On the contrary they were often entertained in a manner befitting their rank, furnished with articles of apparel, horses and travelling expenses, and permitted to return home. In fact Shivaji's generosity towards prisoners of war was such as to put to blush the vaunted civilization of modern nations. The Mahomedan rulers of the time used to practise the vilest barbarities upon their victims, forcing them to embrace the faith of Islam, detaining them in prison and even selling them into slavery.[2] No instance of such barbarity can be urged against Shivaji. Towards the foe who surrendered his arms and gave himself up unreservedly to his mercy, Shivaji showed such an absolute courtesy and generosity that the erstwhile foeman blushed at his enmity and gladly took service under such a leader. And it has already been seen in the preceding narrative how such foemen when turned into devoted servants spared neither their fortunes nor their blood in their loyal association with the great cause. It would, therefore, appear that the charge of cruelty cannot be maintained. This unfounded opinion about Shivaji's cruelty might have arisen in consequence of the vengeance wreaked upon Baji Ghorpade, and some are prepared to admit the savageness of the revenge taken upon him. They admit that Baji Ghorpade deserved punishment, but

---

1 *Vide* reference to Grant Duff's remarks in the foot-note to pages 324 and 330 and the testimony of Khafikhan himself in the foot-note to p. 335.

2 Compare the campaigns of the Sidi, the initial campaign of Shaistakhan, and the last campaign of Dilerkhan, 1678 to 80. Dilerkhan's cruelties (*Vide* Sarkar p. 419) caused even the most cruel of the Maratha kings, Prince Sambhaji, to protest against them. How many Mogul campaigns against Shivaji and Bijapur were stained with enslavement of helpless women and children? As against this, what has Khafikhan to say as regards Shivaji's conduct towards women and children? (*Vide* Sarkar's Shivaji pp. 62-63 for a sample of Aurangzeb's orders for a campaign of wholesale cruelty against Shivaji's people.)

they hold it as an unwarrantable cruelty that for one man's guilt, the male adults of his family, his relatives and dependents, should have all been put to the sword. But the heinousness of Baji Ghorpade's guilt must likewise be considered. For the aggrandisement of his family and to win favour in the eyes of his Mahomedan sovereign, he had undertaken and carried out the most nefarious betrayal of a Maratha compatriot, and that too of one who was of the noblest rank among his countrymen. To what dire results the treachery was likely to lead is already known to the reader. As a loyal and affectionate son, Shivaji would have been obliged entirely to give up his plans of liberty and independence. As it was, for nearly four years, till Shahaji was at complete liberty, he had almost to sit down in an attitude of passive silence. When these things are borne in mind, the fearful revenge taken upon Ghorpade, under the overbearing impulse of two dominant passions, an intense fervour of filial affection and a devouring love of independence,[1] may find some mitigation, if not excuse.

THE CHARGE OF FREE-BOOTING.

The third head of accusation against Shivaji is an inordinate greed of money, which it is alleged, led him to a perpetual campaign of plunder and devastation against the peaceful subjects of the Mahomedan powers. And it is further contended that this rapacity of plunder led to manifold disturbances and to insecurity of property. Some Maharashtra writers have themselves admitted that there is a partial truth in this allegation. But a knowledge of the real character of Shivaji's actions will exonerate him from that degree of culpability with which these objectors have been wont to charge him. In the first place we must give him this credit that from first to last in his deep-laid schemes of independence, the free-booting campaigns he pursued were inspired by higher motives than the mere

[1] It is clear from the Shivdigvijay that Shivaji raided Mudhol at his father's express order. *Vide* Shivaji's letter in Kincaid, Appendix p. 178.

accumulation of private wealth. He had to face simultaneously the concerted fronts of three hostile monarchies, and what sacrifices in men and money were involved in the continual and unyielding struggle with their immense armies can be better imagined than described. How but with the hope of pecuniary reward was he to maintain the loyalty and devotion of his soldiers, if he expected them unstintingly to co-operate with him in the realization of his ideals, holding their lives cheap and seeking a deathless martyrdom in the deadly struggle with the powers of Islam? Then again, Shivaji could not but increase the strength and efficiency of his armies to the best of his resources. How was he to meet the vast army charges which the maintenance of such a large force was bound to entail? How was he to maintain at the height of military efficiency those hundreds of forts upon which the security and expansion of his independent power depended? How was he to increase the number of these forts, when his defensive programme made the erection of them in their tens and their hundreds a matter of imperative necessity? How was he to maintain these equipments on the slender revenues of his own sterile dominions? And if that was not possible, what then? Should he not levy contributions on the dominions of his enemies by what in every form and feature must have appeared as plundering campaigns? It was inevitable. The avenues of public credit which are available to modern nations were not open to our leaders in the mediæval times of Indian history. Great wars may now be embarked upon with the help of public credit, depressing the subjects in perpetuity under the yoke of the national debt and the exhausting burden of increasing taxation.[1] The appalling statistics of the national debt among the leading nations of the modern

[1] The reader should clearly understand that this opinion was expressed in Mr. Keluskar's original Marathi edition of 1907. This observation applies to the whole paragraph. The author was scarcely aware when he wrote this in 1907 that Germany was shortly afterwards going to furnish a concrete illustration of the truth of his strictures.

world cannot be contemplated without a gasp and an ominous presentiment that either these nations must be over-whelmed by a general bankruptcy or their helpless multitudes ground down for ages under the crushing mill-stones of a monstrous taxation. And yet can it be maintained for a moment that the giant wars of these nations are all entered upon for the purposes of defending their integrity from aggression or wresting their independence from the thraldrom of a tyrant? What is the cause of these inter-national feuds, but the folly, ingratitude, and perfidy of some tyrant prince or lustful minister, for whose wicked sport or ambition thousands and hundreds of thousands of innocent subjects perish and for whose saturnalian carnivals millions of groaning, tax-ridden bondsmen have to pay the price, from generation to generation? It is but fair to Shivaji to contrast his plundering but regulated methods of replenishing his war treasury in the prosecution of his patriotic war of independence, intended for the benefit of unborn generations of his countrymen, with the unjust and unlimited spoliation of unborn generations, for the purpose of supplying the sinews of unjustifiable wars, which modern finance has made easy to the modern tyrant, for the wanton violation of the liberties of other people. He did not fetter his poor subjects in perpetuity by the imposition of an impossible burden of taxation in order to vindicate their liberty. He chose rather to fulfil the just and unerring law of nemesis, forcing the alien spoliators of his people's fortunes and liberties to pay the price of their spoliation in direct proportion to the cost of redemption, and in that repayment those of his Hindu compatriots had to join as contributories who had risen to the height of their affluence under an alien patronage.

And if these exactions and benevolences were expended upon the sacred cause of independence and became the principal feeders of his war exchequer, we, the people of Maharashtra, again can scarcely call him to a strict account or tax him with immorality. To expatiate on the immorality of procuring money by the tactics of plundering campaigns is, under the circumstances, tantamount to saying in so many categorical terms that he ought not in any case to have devoted himself to the task of redeeming the liberties of his countrymen and conferring on them the blessing of an independent sovereign state. If we consider how heavy must have been the annual expenditure for the maintenance of a hundred thousand cavalry and infantry in a state of effective readiness and to keep all contented, from the meanest foot-soldier to the highest commander, by a system of prompt and punctual cash payments, and how small a proportion of that outlay could at that period have been safely met by taxation from the territories under Shivaji's permanent occupation, we can readily conclude that nothing short of an importunate necessity drove him to this system of predatory war. Add to this the consideration that a storm of invasion had been brewing for a long time and was bound to burst with unmitigated fury when Aurangzeb found himself free to let loose the avalanche of his northern armies upon the fruitful valleys of the south and whelm every landmark in the general deluge. A wise king like Shivaji had to make a decent provision against that upheaval. And if this were called avarice, it would be an abuse of words. In short, who would place Shivaji in the category of those sovereigns that wallowed in sordid avarice like Mahmud of Gazni, with his seventeen invasions of India and his hoarded heaps of countless wealth, and the sorrowful tears he shed at having to part, at the hour of death, with those untold treasures?

THE CAMPAIGN REGULATIONS

Whether these plundering campaigns were carried on in a blind and unregulated style, or were subject to a system of regulated discipline, is a subject that now claims our attention. In a foregoing chapter[1] we have seen the the campaigning regulations of Shivaji. We have noticed the strict regulations for protecting the peasant and

[1] *Vide* Chapter XXIV, pp. 388-391.

cultivator from harm, the permanent injunction against the arrest or abduction or violation of the modesty of women and children, the studied observance of respect for mosques and temples, saints and fakirs, imposed upon the soldiery. No small measure of wholesome restraint was exercised upon the campaigning hosts by the severe regulation that all booty obtained in the course of the campaign had to be accounted for to the state treasury. In consequence, as neither soldier nor officer had an opportunity of appropriating to himself the spoils of the campaign, he had so much the less temptation to lay violent hands on anything and everything that came in his way. It was impossible for them to seek to enrich themselves by robbing the helpless inhabitants of their possessions. The evil hordes that disgraced the Peshwas' campaigns at a later epoch of history, those vampire hosts of Pindaris and plunderers that followed in the wake of the regular army and spread havoc and desolation wherever they went, venturing not seldom to cut off the food and fodder supplies of the regular expeditionary forces themselves, this class of free-booters could never thrive under Shivaji. Moreover, it is pertinent to observe that those chiefs and merchant princes of the enemy country who quietly paid the contributions levied upon them in proportion to their fortunes and made no attempts to evade their burden by hiding their treasures, never came in for any sort of rough treatment at the hands of Shivaji's followers. Then again those burghers, who voluntarily subscribed among themselves the tribute demanded by the invaders and paid it at the city gates were never disturbed by the invading forces, who as a rule withdrew straightway from the walls, the moment their demand was satisfied. Those ruling chiefs and princes who had bound themselves to pay an annual tribute, purchased a permanent immunity for their territories from the hardships attending upon these campaigns. At a later stage of his career, when the Bijapur and the Golconda kingdoms undertook to pay a fixed annual tribute, there was a cessation of these hostilities against their territories. When again these same states broke their treaties and desisted from the payment of the stipulated tributes, these campaigns were renewed, to the great loss of the wealthier part of their population. Nor could it be said that Shivaji's followers carried fire and sword wherever they went. The naked sword, the flaring fire-brand were never used against the houses of the poor. Such wanton cruelty was never practised by his troops. The scouts brought faithful reports as to the possessors of hoarded wealth, and only such men, as a rule, experienced the fury of his soldiers' onslaughts, to escape scatheless in their turn, on surrendering their wealth. Judging by these facts, we must conclude that to denounce Shivaji as a cruel and rapacious marauder is to cast an unmerited slur upon his character.

THE UNDERLYING PURPOSE OF THIS POLICY.

Another circumstance which serves to explain the employment of this policy is its effectiveness for the purpose intended, a fact not often appreciated at its true worth by Shivaji's critics. The continual incursions and exactions of tribute and plunder, with the resulting diminution in the revenues of the Mahomedan powers, sapped their strength by a slow process of attenuation, and compelled them to seek a friendly reconciliation with an enemy possessed of such powers of punishment, if they wished to be left unmolested in their government. The treaties with Bijapur and Golconda, by which these kingdoms agreed to pay fixed tributes, were, as we have seen, the immediate consequences of this policy. In addition to these tributes Shivaji, in consequence of the arrangement made with the Mogul government, exercised the claims of chauth and sirdeshmukhi upon the territories under Bijapur.[1] He intended to make similar levies upon

[1] As Mahomedan historians have made the charge of plundering (European critics following suit), it is pertinent to observe that a Mahomedan emperor not merely sanctioned but encouraged Shivaji's plundering, as long as it was directed against the enemies of the empire. This was

Golconda, but had to postpone his plans for a time on account of the campaign in the Karnatic. Further than that, he was continually endeavouring to get similar claims acknowledged over the Mogul provinces in the Deccan, and had he lived longer, there seems little reason to doubt that he would have succeeded in getting those claims allowed. That this policy of crippling the revenues of the Mahomedan powers by the demands of chauth etc. was sure to lead to their decay and deprive them of their very teeth and claws, while Shivaji's own state waxed proportionately in strength and resources, is so evident, that we must give him the credit of having intended it as a means to a higher end. And the policy was justified by its fruits.

But was it not wanton wickedness, while attempting to cripple the Mahomedan powers, to harass their poor and innocent subjects? The answer to this question is that the subjects of these powers were never indiscriminately harassed. Shivaji's vengeance fell on the rich, a part of whose wealth he sought to transfer to the sacred cause of liberty and independence. It was the wealthy Mahomedans who generally suffered, and the few Hindus who had enriched themselves under their tyranny. They were forcibly required to pay their contributions. No amount of persuasion would have induced the subjects of the Mahomedan powers to part voluntarily with a portion of their superfluous wealth. If then a few Hindus were required to make a sacrifice under compulsion for the permanent benefit of all, this cannot be pronounced wicked. We must always have a regard for the ultimate object of Shivaji, and in the light of it no stain of dishonour can be seen in these actions.

IMPERIAL GREED.

But then it is objected that sordid love of empire was

---

done under the solemn sanction of treaties; witness the treaties with Jay Singh, Jaswant Singh and Muazim. In theory at least it was not plunder, but contributions exacted under the names of chauth and sirdeshmukhi. The Emperor did not like the exactions when the same were levied from his territories.

the motive cause, and that for the excesses of political greed no excuse or extenuation is possible. This is a sweeping charge and calls for a restatement of the true character of the life-work of Shivaji. One original motive for the foundation of an independent power was no doubt to win his personal independence from the Mahomedan monarchies, and it may be freely admitted that when Shivaji started upon his Herculean labours he had this object before him. But to say that this was the sole aim of all his labours and that the higher purpose of accomplishing the emancipation of his Hindu brethren from the long night-mare of the Mahomedan thraldom never came within the range of his thoughts and political vision, is to make too large a demand upon our credulity. The men whose sympathies and services he first enlisted for the realization of an almost chimerical enterprise, would never have permitted themselves to be harnessed to his cause regardless of self or personal fortunes, had he not instilled into their hearts the love of liberty and kindled an enthusiasm for independence. When we contemplate the secret of Shivaji's success in winning over the Brahman envoy of Afzul Khan and the Rajput princes, Jay Singh and Jaswant Singh, we cannot but conclude that in every case it depended on his skill in impressing upon these persons the nobility of his mission to overthrow the power of the Mahomedan monarchs and in stirring up their latent patriotism. These persons were not so utterly lost to a sense of honour, as to have otherwise, however strong the temptation, connived at and shown sympathy with Shivaji's enterprise. Those who accuse Shivaji of an inordinate love of power, must needs be reminded how on three or four different occasions, even at the height of his glory, he was laid hold of by tremendous spiritual transports, that alienated him for the time being from affairs of state and diverted his mind exclusively to meditation on spiritual things. And let them think too of the difficulties of the perplexed ministers, who on the occasions of these spiritual transports found it a very difficult task to bring him round to a just appreciation of his temporal duties. To compare him with Alexander, Tamerlane, Babar, Aurangzeb, and other ambitious conquerors is to misjudge the man. The fields they piled with slaughter, in their career of blind ambition and aggrandizement, at the expense and sacrifice of the liberties and fortunes of independent nations, arouse universal horror and can never obtain our forgiveness. Shivaji's ambition was redeemed from this taint. It was natural to hold that Hindustan was for the Hindus and that the Hindus only had the right to rule in Hindustan. It was natural to consider it a grave sin against nature that the stranger and the alien should enter and dominate over the land and persecute the children of the soil. To expel such unjust and oppressive tyrants from the motherland and vow to make it again the scene of a free and prosperous indigenous sovereignty, was in itself a blessed and righteous undertaking. And what wonder is it, if he, who voluntarily embarked upon this enterprise, has laid all India under a permanent debt of gratitude? Not personal ambition itself can detract from the merit of such an achievement. Apart from the motives with which a person sets out to accomplish an object, the accomplishment itself, if it conduces to the good of society, has an inherent title to obtain our gratitude and admiration. On this hypothesis, granting for the moment, that personal ambition and aggrandizement were the springs of conduct that inspired Shivaji, we cannot see that even such a view of his life's work detracts from the merits of the actual accomplishment. The few foreigners that suffered eclipse from the higher grandeur and glory of his deeds might vent their spleen upon him and fling at him every term of reproach and ridicule. It is all ineffectual bluster. The founders and champions of liberty, in all the world's history, have always received their meed of praise at the hands of impartial and disinterested historians. They have earned the historians' ungrudging applause for building their nation's happiness on the firm basis of liberty. Among such patriots Shivaji has every right to take a prominent place. And he will keep it.

THE CHARGE OF SELFISH AMBITION.

He has been accused of an inordinate thirst for power: he has been charged with self-seeking and self-love. Self-love never made a man think of the weal or woe of another. Self-love consults nothing but self-interest at all times and places. What particular aspect of selfishness is seen in Shivaji, and in what part of his career can it be discovered? Had his end been merely to attain an empire for no higher gratification than the instinct of selfish pomp and pleasure, why should he have carried forward even to the darkening shadows of death the laborious prosecution of an ephemeral enterprise? Why rather should he not have given himself up to the voluptuous enjoyment of the wealth that he had got together by years of toil? With all the means of sensual gratification at his command, why did not the epicurean philosophy of life commend itself to his attention even for a moment?[1] When we survey the daily routine of his life, we are impressed with his austere regard for duty, which scarcely left a moment unclaimed to be turned to the service of pleasure. His duties towards the public, the administration and good government of his state, the defence and expansion of his kingdom engrossed all his physical and intellectual faculties. As can be seen from a close scrutiny of his career, he scarcely ever took a holiday to recoup the continual strain upon his mind and body. Against one who showed this stern resolve to deny himself all rest and relaxation, until he had accomplished the liberation of his country from the tyranny of Islam, this imputation of motives of self-seeking and self-exaltation, appears peculiarly extravagant. His overflowing wealth

[1] Mr. Kincaid speaking of the period when Shivaji made his youthful decision to take upon himself the task of liberating his country, aptly contrasts him with the Trojan Paris on Mount Ida, caring not for the promise of Hera or the smiles of Aphrodite, but without a single backward glance, placing the golden fruit in the hands of Pallas Athene (page 132).

and resources were scarcely employed, if at all, for purposes of personal pomp and splendour. His dress was of a severely simple style, nor had he a weakness for jewellery. That style of magnificence in his state processions and durbars, which was indispensable to maintain his position in the eyes of foreigners and of subjects alike, was all that was observed. Nor can the selfishness of avarice be urged as a charge against one who was most munificent in rewarding merit. The disposition to practise false economy by doling out inadequate remuneration to the officials in the service, without regard to the positions they occupied in the state, never occurred to his mind. There was no failure to please those by whose labours he had purchased his fortunes. But above all the paramount feeling in his breast with regard to his material gains was that they were to be invested for the defence and expansion of an independent power, for the welfare and advantage of his people, and for the vindication, if possible, of the liberties of the land of the Bharatas from the tyranny of Islam. It is no exaggeration to affirm that he was thoroughly imbued with the idea that he held his wealth in trust for his countrymen, to guard and augment it, not to fritter it away in personal enjoyment. When such were the guiding principles of his career, principles held to firmly from first to last, the charge of selfishness must certainly fall to the ground.

Ambition is no ambition unless wedded to selfishness. The ambitious monarch is he who is actuated by an uncontrollable desire to achieve greatness, to extend his sway over multitudes of vassal princes, and to spread the fame of his name to all the quarters of the globe. And at first sight, it would seem excusable to argue that Shivaji became a victim to this infirmity of noble minds. Were it so, however, the moment this absorbing passion was itself absorbed into the wider scheme of the restoration of Hindu autonomy, the passion was transfused into patriotism and ambition purged of its baser dross. However a correct estimate of the sum total of Shivaji's achievements cannot but lead us to the belief that almost from the moment of the inauguration of his noble enterprise, he was animated by a conscious purpose and governed by an irresistible impulse bidding him, as it were, go forth into the world and turn the night into day, till the restoration of liberty and independence should be accomplished. And it would be no exaggeration to affirm that he believed this was the mission of his life and the measure of his success in achieving this object was also the measure of his fulfilment of life's duties. And from that fervent faith sprang those deeds of heroism and valour which the world will never cease to admire.

The charge of ambition is sometimes based upon the fact that at the time Shivaji set out upon his campaign of freedom, he had to overthrow the power of many a Hindu baron who had set up an uncertain independence on his own account. And it is asked, if Shivaji's object was to establish his independence, why should he have drawn the sword against Hindu brother chiefs labouring in the same direction? Does not this circumstance in itself prove his selfish determination to have independence for himself and deny it to others? And do not these instances conspire together to brand the unrighteousness of his ambition? These objections are again based upon a misconception of the real inwardness of Shivaji's labours. If the deliverance of his countrymen from an alien yoke was the true objective of the hero's enterprise, the dismemberment of the country to be delivered into innumerable groups of independent principalities, waging endless wars with one another or leading their brigand forces into the territories of the alien rulers they had seceded from, would have been a fatal caricature of his plans. The tenure of power by such lawless barons is at best of uncertain duration, and the government they have revolted from is sure to find an occasion to overthrow them, one after another, and so to vanquish all. If then Shivaji thought it necessary to win over to his cause the unruly strength of these lawless chiefs and revolted barons, or, failing that, to attack and annihilate their strongholds so as to clear the path for the expansion of his own advancing power, in either case the result was its own justification. The same can be said of Shivaji's attitude towards those towering figures of the Maratha nobility that owed their allegiance to the Adilshahi dynasty. Their opposition had to be disarmed either by the methods of persuasion and peace, or by means of war and devastation. If the labours of Cavour and his compatriots for the restoration of a united and independent Italy from the anarchy and the conflicting claims of the European powers, or if the successful organization of the German empire on the basis of national unity by the Kaisar William I,—if these achievements have elicited the approbation of all right-minded and impartial historians, the labours of Shivaji, upon which such criticisms are made, are certainly entitled to the same respect. It is not at all fair to seek to belittle his work by harping upon his ambition or his selfishness. Without these occasional acts of apparent injustice on his part, the people of Maharashtra could never have drunk deep at the fountain of liberty. For the greater and more lasting happiness of the greater number, if a few had to undergo temporary hardships, such actions cannot be altogether condemned.

THE CHARGE OF COWARDICE.

And when the objector comes to the end of his arguments, he flings the reproach of cowardice against Shivaji. This charge of cowardice is made against him, by a train of syllogisms somewhat as follows:—Had it not been for his cowardice, he would not have resorted to artifice and stratagem. The truly valiant man fights and wins his victories by challenging his foe face to face and never resorts to snares and wiles and hidden ambuscades. Shivaji followed the baser tactics of this sort. *Ergo* he cannot be ranked as a brave warrior. A perusal of the preceding narrative will clearly prove that this sort of reasoning is a ludicrous travesty of the facts. This argument presents in the form of a caricature what is undoubtedly true of Shivaji's generalship, viz. that a great part of his victories he earned by his strategy rather than by his valour. He was always cautious and circumspect in all he did. Rashness and blind daring had no place in his science of war. On every occasion he made a calm calculation of his strength and of that of his enemy. What could be easily accomplished, without shedding the blood of his people, he usually contrived to accomplish by right manœuvring and stratagem. It was his invariable principle to avoid bloodshed as much as possible. And had he not possessed a fertile mind quick to devise and invent what the varying needs of the hour demanded, there would have been no occasion to-day to chronicle the events of his life or to write a history of the Maratha people. Before the masses of his enemies, his scanty troops would certainly have melted away in no time. The labours he had begun would have ended in failure. His very name would have been numbered among the numerous tribes of outlawed rebels and irregular polygars. In short, instead of the unanimous praises, echoed from lip to lip, rendered to him as the founder and architect of Hindu liberty and independence, his name would have passed current as a bye-word for failure and reproach. Need we dwell any longer on the historical purblindness that would confound strategy with cowardice, and discover in it an imaginary cause for censure? The folly itself we can never censure too much.

ANOTHER SCHOOL.

Let us now turn to another school of critics, and this time the critics are themselves Maharashtrians. Some of their pet hypotheses are calculated to lower, in however modest a measure, the greatness of the life-work of Shivaji. We propose, therefore, to review at some length some of the leading theories formulated by this school of historians.

THE BHAGWAT DHARMA AND NATIONAL INDEPENDENCE.

The first of these hypotheses may be restated briefly as follows. The spread of the Bhagwat Dharma (the Bhagwat religion, i. e. religion as expounded in the Bhagwat), in all parts of Maharashtra, obliterating in a great measure the distinction of high and low, tended to a fusion of castes and consequent unity. With a deepening conviction that all mankind are the children of a common father, and that but one road to salvation lay open to all, the feeling was more largely spread among the thinkers of the time, that as in spiritual, so like-wise in temporal matters, it was proper for them to exert their united endeavours for the advancement of any cause that represented the common good of all the people. It is further alleged that the name Bhagwat Dharma came to be changed into Maharashtra Dharma (i. e. the Maharashtra religion) by the saint Ramdas Swami, who constantly inculcated the fostering protection and expansion of the faith upon Shivaji and other leaders of Maharashtra. Therefore, was it, according to this theory, that Shivaji and his followers were able to accomplish the arduous task of resuscitating the liberty and independence of their country.

The first point to be considered is whether in the time of Shivaji or in the period immediately antecedent to his career, the ethical creed of the Bhagwat Dharma had generally spread throughout the length and breadth of Maharashtra. For all over Maharashtra were to be found the pharisaical representatives of the orthodox Sanatan Dharma engaged in a campaign of bitter persecution against the exponents of the Bhagwat faith of Love, as described in the biographies of the poet Mahipati. Then again the devotion of the saints of the Bhagwat school clustered round the shrine of the god of Pandharpur, which they magnified as an earthly Elysium above all holy places, but it can never be said that all Maharashtrians at the time acknowledged such a belief or joined in such an estimate. It will be extremely rash to maintain that the god Vithoba of Pandharpur, who was the object of the single-hearted devotion and allegiance of these Bhagwat saints—saints who co-ordinated a firm belief in the abstract principles of Vedantism with devotion to a concrete image of the Deity—was in an equal degree an object of worship and devotion to all the people of Maharashtra. For contemporaneously with the faith of the Bhagwat saints there flourished other cults in Maharashtra. Secondly, the religion of faith and love associated with the Bhagwat saints was not in all respects antagonistic to the orthodox Sanatan Dharma dogmas. It could not, therefore, be said that the Bhagwat Dharma was in any form revolutionary. What could be truly said about it is that it was widely propagated by the saints of the Maharashtra school beginning with the times of Dnyandev. Nor is it in any sense a historical fact that the labours of these saints extinguished the differences of caste and that such an extinction of caste differences kindled the flame of a strong feeling of Maharashtrian unity. For a hypothesis of this kind there is absolutely no warrant in the actual state of Maharashtra society in those times. If the saints and other votaries of Vithoba, when engaged in the spiritual duties at the holy shrine itself, showed a slight disregard for the strict observance of caste obligations, still who would solemnly affirm that on returning to their homes and villages they persevered in their indifference to caste rules and continued the heterodox usages in their ordinary social life? Like the orthodox people around them, in the matter of food and drink and in the settlement of marriage alliances, they observed the distinctions of high and low, sanctioned by the precepts of orthodox Hinduism. It would, therefore, follow that the liberal principles of the Bhagwat school professed by the saints of Maharashtra had not materially altered the condition of Hindu society at the time. How could it be maintained that if this creed had never come into existence, those that supported Shivaji would never have been inspired to support him? Could it be said that any of his great co-adjutors was a votary of that type who annually made a pilgrimage to the shrine of Pandharpur or otherwise an active supporter of the

Bhagwat creed? No historical evidence to this effect is extant. The Maratha chronicles themselves have nothing to say on this point. As to Shivaji himself and his forefathers, the worship of Shiva and Shiva's consort, Bhavani, under various names, seems to have been hereditary in the family, and on the most critical occasions Shivaji was in the habit of consulting the oracular decrees or utterances of that tutelary goddess. From this it could be seen that his faith was not anchored firmly or exclusively in the Bhagwat creed, but that to his death he was likewise a votary of the goddess Bhavani. In the latter part of his career, indeed, by reason of contact with Ramdas Swami and the effects of his spiritual precepts and society, it may be concluded that some change might have been wrought in his sentiments of devotional allegiance. Even Ramdas himself had specially enjoined upon him to cultivate his usual devotions to Shiva and to make and worship in honour of that god a crore of votive images of sand and so to merit the special grace of that deity. And as a faithful disciple he must be credited to have fulfilled the mandate of his preceptor. From this it must be inferred that Shivaji was originally a staunch follower of the Shaiva creed—the worship of Shiva—and that latterly by communion with Ramdas his allegiance to the god Shiva was divided with other objects of worship. As, however, Shivaji died not long after the spiritual intimacy between the disciple and the preceptor had sprung up, it is very difficult to speculate with certainty as to what would have been its ultimate effects, had it lasted longer. As Shivaji himself was a Shaiva with a pronounced bias for the worship of the goddess Devi (or Bhavani), so were his followers from the Maval country, from the Ghaut uplands, from the Konkan lowlands—whether they were Maratha shiledars, bargirs, or hetkaris—mostly of the Shaiva bias, with their special tutelary deities, the god Khandoba of Jejuri and the goddess Bhavani of Tuljapur. The images of these deities under various names are to be found consecrated in various parts of Maharashtra, and in praying for their propitious grace and favour, the people thought, lay their chief duty in this life, as could be seen from their religious rites and ceremonies and social usages. To take an example, with what eclat and enthusiasm the Marathas observe the feast-day of Dasara is known to all[1] It follows, therefore, that the theory that the people of Maharashtra flocked to Shivaji's standard, on account of the general leaven of liberal ideas caused by the Bhagwat school in the social conscience of Maharashtra, is fundamentally erroneous. Can it even be said that the great leaders of the Brahman and Prabhu castes, who so enthusiastically co-operated with Shivaji in the great cause of freedom, did so or were able to do so, either because they were Vaishnavas and followers of the Bhagwat school or because of any effects the Bhagwat school might have wrought upon their minds?

THE BHAGWAT DHARMA AND ITS NATURAL FRUIT.

We must therefore conclude that the multitudes that thronged to Shivaji's banners and the national work upon which he directed their labours were inspired, not by the teachings or the propagation of the Bhagwat faith, but by the personal magnetism and enterprising spirit of the hero himself. To ascribe even a part of the merit of the great achievement to the Bhagwat faith and its propagators is —and with a heavy heart we have to say it—to misrepresent the actual circumstances of the case. The truth is that the self-denying spirit inculcated by the saints of Maharashtra had for well-nigh three centuries crushed out of existence the spirit of self-assertion. The sages who identified Ram and Rahim, the saints in whom a holy calm and a self-less spirit predominated over all impulses of the human heart, the zealous enthusiasts whose minds were estranged from the glamour of this world and dedicated to the service of the Most High and the quest of salvation,—these were not the men to think of the bubble

---

[1] The Dasara is the auspicious day following upon the Devi Puja festival of nine days and nights (*Navaratra*).

glory of this world, but only of delivering themselves from the world's trammels. To them temporal joys and sorrows were alike; this was the burden of all their exhortation to mankind. Such gentle spirits were not the men to exhort their followers to take up arms against Islam. If we exclude the work of Ramdas Swami, this sort of advice can nowhere be found in the writings of the saints of Maharashtra. To them, that regarded the world as a mere bubble, with all its panorama of earthly things, how could the mundane thought of a political revolt suggest itself? This ascetic and self-denying habit of mind had been so deeply ingrained in our people, that for three centuries together, with the accumulating horrors of the Mahomedan misrule, no doughty Maratha with his valiant arms, nor sagacious Brahman with his ripe statesmanship, came forth for deliverance. What little morsel in the way of emolument or advancement the Mahomedan princes flung to them they were content humbly to accept. All the while the trumpet voice of the Bhagwat faith was ringing in the air, but if they did prick up their ears and listen, it was not to be inspired to start upon an impetuous race for the goal of freedom and independence, but to be the more confirmed in their slavish indolence and self-satisfied vassalage. Nay, when the cry of freedom was taken up in earnest and the standard of independence unfurled by Shivaji, we know how many were the nobles and statesmen, both Maratha and Brahman, who tried to damp his enthusiasm. Can the advocates of this hypothesis point to a single instance of a great warrior or statesman who was inspired to join the standard of Shivaji, under the impulse of the awakened feeling of national unity born of the Bhagwat faith?

Had the impulse of such a national consciousness been in existence from before Shivaji's times, the great leader would have been spared the harsh measures, which at the commencement he had to take against certain contumacious Brahman and Maratha sardars,—measures which in the opinion of rigid moralists cannot square with the abstract standard of moral rectitude. The Brahman statesmen of the order of Moropant Pingle, Abaji Sondev and Dattaji Prabhu, veterans of the calibre of Balaji Avji, Baji Prabhu Deshpande, and Murar Baji; Maratha commanders of the chivalrous gallantry of Tanaji Malusare, Prataprao Guzar, and Hambirrao Mohite,—this great muster-roll of glorious names,—were each and all attracted to Shivaji's standards, spontaneously by the ambition to carve out a fortune and a name for themselves, and gradually, as the lotus blossoms and displays itself in sympathy with the rising orb of the sun, were the more generous passions and enthusiasm of their heart kindled and set aglow by the supreme influence of their leader's noble spirit and character. To trace the causes of the national triumph to the lives and teachings of those saints and ascetics who turned their backs upon all social intercourse is unwittingly to deprive the author and vindicator of our national liberties of a portion of that glory to which he is fully entitled.

SHIVAJI—A DEFENDER OF THE NATIONAL RELIGION.

And here a question may be raised: Was there, or was there not, at the basis of Shivaji's stern resolve to free his country from the oppression of that Mahomedan misrule under which it lay gasping, a faith born of a patriotic enthusiasm for his own and his people's religion? The answer to this question is an emphatic "Yes". From his earliest infancy, the love of the national religion had been implanted in the tender mind of Shivaji: to the hour of his death, the buoyant religious enthusiasm of his early years continued to sway and dominate his mind. Nor would it be too much to affirm that it was precisely owing to this dominant feeling that the anti-Mahomedan sentiments of the starting-point of his career were first excited in his breast. But side by side with the love of religion, arose the love of political independence and it ever grew stronger and stronger, as the years passed on. The kindled flame of the twin-patriotism, love of country and love of the country's gods, inflamed his soul, and with an iron will and quickened enthusiasm he applied himself to the accomplishment of his great exploits. But it will never do to forget that mere religious enthusiasm without the quickened stimulus of national liberty, could not, of itself, have accomplished much: the kindred enthusiasms, the passion for religious freedom and for political freedom, even blended into one, could not have accomplished much, unless they had been accompanied, as they were accompanied in the case of Shivaji, by the important asset of an unrivalled creative spirit and an enterprising and organizing faculty. The effective combination in the same person of these three forces,—enthusiasm, patriotism and a creative faculty,-has given us as the resultant of their joint operation a glorious record which is an inspiration and a legacy to the world. But it cannot be said that Shivaji's enthusiastic love of religion was engendered in him only on account of the propagation of the Bhagwat faith. For the lives of the Bhagwat saints were full of gentleness and love. Theirs was a catholic generosity and toleration. In their hearts was no room for pride or hatred. A religion that consistently identified Ram with Rahim could admit of no parochial or even national patriotism in religion. Nor is there any evidence to show that Shivaji himself was an active propagator of this Vaishnav cult. His faith was deeply rooted in the Sanatan Dharma, with the result that, to the moment of his death, his simple piety and faith in the goddess Bhavani never faltered or forsook him. If he did instill in his followers and supporters a passionate love of religion along with the worship of liberty, it was not by any means with any material aid of the Vaishnav or Bhagwat Dharma. The religious love and pride he inculcated in them was the love of the orthodox or Sanatan Dharma, with its belief in the sanctity of kine and Brahmans, its injunctions for the observance of caste distinctions, its recognition and encouragement of idol worship, and its exhortation urging the value and necessity of all ceremonial usages. And it cannot be disputed that the conduct of Shivaji himself personally and that of most of his followers was in full accord with the precepts of the orthodox religion, inasmuch as in none of the extant bakhars is there the least evidence to the contrary.[1]

It may, of course, be objected that in those districts which were chiefly the scenes of Shivaji's great activities, there was a goodly number of Vaishnav or Bhagwat saints like Tukaram, that the noble events of the peaceful lives of some of them, at any rate, were daily coming before his eyes, and that as to Tukaram himself he was held in the highest esteem and reverence by Shivaji. If such was the case, the objector proceeds, could it be held that the Bhagwat faith of spiritual love wrought no effect upon the mind of Shivaji? The answer to this objection is that the saints including Tukaram were, on account of the stainless purity and sanctity of their lives, objects of reverence and veneration to Shivaji, who lost no opportunity to listen to their eloquent discourses or to enjoy the privilege of social or spiritual intercourse with them. But the idea that these holy men had anything to teach or impress that exceeded the scope, or was in any way incompatible with the teachings of the Sanatan Dharma, or that their manners were in any regard subversive of the accepted traditions of the

1 The first effect of the freedom and revival of religion was in the direction of orthodoxy. This is clearly shown by the opposition of the Shastris to the coronation of Shivaji, their bigoted attitude in calling him a Shudra, and their refusal to allow the Kayastha Prabhus the rites of Kshatriyas until Gaga Bhatt taught them their folly. Prof. Sarkar finds in these caste differences the root cause of the Maratha failure and thinks the seeds of that disunion were noticeable enough already under Shivaji and that the "cohesion of the peoples in the Maratha state was not organic but artificial, accidental and precarious, dependent on the ruler's extraordinary personality," and that it "disappeared when the country ceased to produce supermen." Prof. Sarkar fails to find in Shivaji's rule an organized attempt at communal improvement, the spread of education or the unification of the people. But surely it is too much to expect Shivaji to have set himself up as a social and religious reformer. Is it possible to believe that Babar could have combined in himself the functions of Akbar, Chandragupta of Ashoka, Guru Govind of Guru Nanak, George Washington of Abraham Lincoln, or Cromwell of Calvin?

orthodox faith, never once occurred to his mind; neither did these saints themselves believe there was anything new or startling in the doctrines they propounded.[1] The differentiation of their doctrines from the traditional modes of thought belongs to the modern critic. The charge of a conscious participation in the active process of revolutionizing the traditional modes of religious thought can in no sense be laid at the door of the simple, pious and unassuming generations of those times. Why speak of the past? Even in our own days, though the Vaishnav modes of thought are still current, though in nearly every Maharashtra village, the votaries of the Pandharpur god are yet to be found, though at seasons of the annual pilgrimages hundreds of thousands of pious pilgrims repair to the holy shrine, none ever thinks there is anything particular about it,— none has ever observed that the practice of the pilgrim rites has in the least conduced to liberalize the minds of the devotees or to wean them from the trammels of caste or caste-pride.

---

[1] The late Justice Ranade lent the weight of his great scholarship to the support of the theory that the teachings of the Maharashtra saints and the revolution in religious thought which they brought about by their teachings were a determining factor and a powerful operative cause of the political revolution brought about by Shivaji. The idea underlying this theory is that just as in Europe and particularly in England the reformation in religion was followed by political reform or revolution, a similar event took place in Maharashtra in the time of Shivaji. As regards the theory of a revolutionary change in religion attempted by the Maharashtra saints, it is interesting to notice that Mr. Rajwade (who attributes Shivaji's work to the inspiration of Ramdas) observes that "The kind of religious reform referred to by Mr. Ranade can nowhere be seen in the writings of the saints. These saints did not mean to turn their backs upon gods and temples, and differences in caste, religion and language. Mr. Ranade's dissertation about the saints is without any foundation and does discredit to his historical research. He does not seem to have grasped the true meaning of the phrase "Maharashtra Dharma." He has fathered upon the saints ideas which they never even dreamt of. Mr. Ranade credits them falsely with advocacy of the ideals of abolition of castes, abolition of idol worship, interdining between Brahmans and Mahars etc." Though we do not agree with Mr. Rajwade over the Ramdas question, we agree with him in repudiating this doctrine of a revolution in religious thought brought about by the saints of Maharashtra.

RAMDAS SWAMI NOT AN INSPIRER OF SHIVAJI.

To say, therefore, that on account of the liberal ideas propagated by the Bhagwat School, and on that account only, either Shivaji himself, or the counsellors and warriors who supported him were inspired to undertake the cause of independence, is to say more than can be borne out by the actual circumstances of the times.[1] Further than this, we have to examine the claims made in the latter part of the above hypothesis that the credit of the whole achievement belongs fundamentally to Ramdas Swami. For, says the hypothesis, the Bhagwat Dharma was described by the Swami as the Dharma of Maharashtra and Shivaji was exhorted by him to his dying day to protect and foster it, with the result—impossible otherwise even to dream of—that the great hero applied himself to the great cause of liberty and successfully carried it through. That this claim is impossible to maintain we have conclusively proved towards the end of Chapter XXIX. We cannot retrace the whole ground again. Our modern critics have based this claim upon the current belief that Shivaji entered into bonds of spiritual vassalage to Ramdas Swami so early as the year 1649,—a belief propagated by the fantastic biographical narratives about the Swami and confirmed, on the blind authority of those narratives, by the chronicler Chitnis and the author of the Shivdigvijaya. But the traditional date of the first meeting of Shivaji with Ramdas, and, in consequence, of the solemn enrolment of Shivaji among the circle of the Swami's disciples, has been proved to be false and unfounded, and the most authentic and convincing evidence has now been brought before the

---

[1] From this disquisition it should not be assumed that in our opinion the Bhagwat Dharma is not superior to the Sanatan Dharma. It is beyond doubt that those who follow it and consistently act up to the principles they profess are likely to be a hundred times more liberal in thought and action and feel more keenly the equality of man and man than the followers of the orthodox system. The object of the present disquisition is only to ascertain how far the claim, made by the modern partisans of the Bhagwat School, that the creed in question contributed vitally to the revival of the political independence of Maharashtra is justifiable.

people of Maharashtra, which brings down the date of the first interview with Ramdas Swami, and the consequent discipleship, to twenty-three or twenty-four years later. The whole fabric based upon the assumed traditional date must, therefore, topple down and, great as the other merits of Ramdas Swami may be, not the least particle of Shivaji's glory can be rightfully transferred to his account. Granting, however, that the authentic evidence now forthcoming was not accessible and we had still to go upon the orthodox tradition, even upon this basis it does not appear the right sort of thing to award such a large share of the glory of the great achievement to Ramdas Swami. For it is clear that even prior to the year 1649, at least some five or six years before that date, Shivaji had decided upon his noble project and commenced his pioneer labours. However the eulogistic character of the first epistle of the Swami to Shivaji clearly shows that the latter could not have, as early as 1649 or even for fifteen or twenty years thereafter, merited those praises which are there recited about him. Further, the towns or villages of Wai, Karhad, Satara, Parali etc., which are mentioned in the traditional accounts as the scenes where the first meeting between the preceptor and the disciple and the initiation ceremony took place, were not conquered by Shivaji till the year 1672–73. The Das-Bodh, the *magnum opus* of the Swami, the contents of which have supplied such a strong support to the hypothesis, does not seem to have been analytically examined by its advocates. That with all these difficulties, and improbabilities serious historians should have given the credit of Shivaji's restoration of the religious and political independence of his countrymen to the exhortation or inspiration of Ramdas Swami seems passing strange to us.[1] If, as it has now been proved, the first meeting

[1] The last of these historians are Prof. H. G. Rowlinson in his "Life of Shivaji" and Mr. Kincaid in his "History of the Maratha People" Vol. I. It is strange that these historians accept the date 1649 as the year of Shivaji's meeting with Ramdas. The latter reproduces some of the miracle stories about the saint and follows for all purposes the bakhar

between the *guru* and the disciple took place in 1672, it follows that Shivaji had already come very near his goal, before he was able to avail himself of the Swami's advice. It may, of course, be alleged that supposing Shivaji had not personally met the Swami, he might have heard of him and received instructions from one or the other of the Swami's disciples. But this position again is quite untenable. For the orthodox bakhar of the Swami itself says that Shivaji had heard about him only once or twice and that the little he had heard he had forgotten before the first meeting. Therefore, it follows that the imaginary endeavours for a "political regeneration" ascribed[1] to Ramdas Swami had

or chronicle of Hanmant, called the *Ramdas Charitra*, with all its farrago of truth and fiction. Prof. G. C. Bhate in his Marathi work, "Sajjangad and Samartha Ramdas" has thoroughly exposed the unreliable character of this bakhar. (See especially pages 91 to 105 of this work.) Prof. Sarkar dismisses the whole controversy with the remark that the evidence produced by the Ramdas coterie is neither adequate nor free from suspicion.

1 In the first number of the sixth volume of the Marathi Magazine "*Shri Saraswati Mandir*" (viz. the number for *Chaitra*, *Shaka* 1828) Mr. V. K. Rajwade states as follows :—"In Shaka 1600 (i. e. 1678 A. D.) all over Maharashtra, there were 1200 followers of Ramdas Swami, propounding his ideas and prosecuting the campaign of his work; that when one reflects on the fact that in Shaka 1600, one thousand and two hundred men were actively engaged in the propagation of one creed and the fulfilment of one cause, it can be conceived what an engine for the political re-generation of the country had been created by the Swami; and that the conclusion is irrepressibly forced upon us that in Shaka 1600, the entire Maharashtra was completely permeated with the ideas and the work of the Swami". (page 33, *ibidem*). To what conclusion this statement is intended to lead us, the acute reader can see at a glance. In effect, it means that the whole credit of the political regeneration of the country is to be assigned to Ramdas Swami, that Shivaji was a mere tool and puppet, who did not actually contribute much to the achievement. We are, therefore, called upon to believe that till this engine of the Swami was in motion, all that Shivaji had toiled for upto 1672-73 A. D. was merely labour lost; till then Shivaji's followers had no zeal for liberty, till then Shivaji's labours had not inspired his liegemen to sacrifice their lives for the attainment of that noble object! In short, here we have a curious specimen of a biassed historian drifting away from the truth. Upon the authority of this statement, another admirer of Ramdas Swami has been induced, in an article published in the issue of the Marathi weekly, "Shri Sayaji Vijaya" of the 24th November 1906, under the title "Ramdasi Sampradaya" or the Ramdas School, to indulge in

till this date, viz. 1672, not yet been inaugurated, nor can it be seen, judging from the biographies of Ramdas Swami or the bakhars of Shivaji, how far further they were prosecuted after this date. Of course, one is at liberty to close his eyes to the facts of history, to give a free play to the creations of his fancy, and even to give publicity to his wild speculations. But when the attempt is made to give currency to such fanciful theories under the guise of historical research, we can only deplore the credulity of our people.

THE MAHARASHTRA DHARMA.

A collateral part of this hypothesis is that the Swami gave the designation of the Maharashtra Dharma to the Bhagwat faith, and that the Swami having himself propagated the faith by his teaching and exhortation, the embers of patriotism were re-kindled in all hearts throughout Maharashtra. But in the first place, it is a debatable question, whether the Vaishnav or Bhagwat cult of the votaries of the Pandharpur god was in all respects congruent with the creed of Ramdas Swami, or acceptable to him. An analytical examination of the Das-Bodh reveals the fact that the creed of him who composed that work was in some respects different from the cult of the Vaishnavas. Moreover from this time forth when the cult of Ramdas began to spread in Maharashtra, it was with certain specific

---

further travesty of the subject. It would seem that the frenzied adulation of the Swami's votaries has now reached its boiling point, and the pity of it only is that the distinguishing symptom of the fever should be a desire to distort the truth and to belittle Shivaji. It may be here remarked with reference to the above extract from Mr. Rajwade that the latter proceeds to state that the Ramdas conventicles were to be found throughout Shivaji's kingdom, even at Tanjore. It should, therefore, rather be inferred that the spread of Shivaji's power encouraged the propagation of the Ramdas School. This seems in fact a more credible view to maintain than the opposite view that the Ramdas School propagated the expansion of Shivaji's dominions. Mr. Sardesai in his 'Marathi Riyasat' (1915 edition) page 111, makes the emphatic statement that "it was Shivaji's enterprise that inspired the political thoughts in the Das-Bodh and to say that it was the Das-Bodh that inspired Shivaji's labours for Swarajya is to misrepresent cause and effect."

differences from the Vaishnav cult. The followers of the Ramdas cult, as a rule, were not sworn devotees of the Pandharpur god, and made no annual pilgrimages to that shrine. Nay the story is well known, to those at least who have read the orthodox biographies of Ramdas Swami, of the miracle that took place, when he was once taken under pressure to Pandharpur.[1] It follows, therefore, that the easy creed of the guileless Vaishnav saints of Maharashtra was to some extent different from the school founded by Ramdas, though to all practical purposes based upon the orthodox or Sanatan religion. But surely it also follows that the designation "Maharashtra Dharma" could not have been used by the Swami with special reference to the "Vaishnav" creed as forming a distinct system of religion by itself. It is impossible to understand the words "Maharashtra Dharma" as meaning the "Duty" of "Maharashtra" as if there were some well-defined and exclusive system of Maharashtra Duty. It is strange that our critics should follow a wrong scent, leaving out of sight the plain and straightforward meaning of the expression. The present writer takes the Marathi compound, "Maharashtra Dharma" to mean the Dharma of the Maharashtra people. This compound expression, used by the Swami, first in his eulogistic epistle to Shivaji, and later, in his exhortative epistle to Sambhaji, cannot bear any other meaning. At the time when the first epistle was composed, Shivaji had conquered a great part of Maharashtra and as the result of the overthrow of Mahomedan dominion, the people of those parts, as in many other matters so also in religion, had become independent of Mahomedan interference. It is with reference to this desirable order of things in Maharashtra that the Swami praises Shivaji, in his epistle to him; while in the one addressed to Sambhaji, he exhorts him to foster and promote this liberty of religion. Had Shivaji been a native of the Karnatic, and being so, had he founded an

[1] The miracle referred to here is the story chronicled by Mahipati and others that the God Vithoba transformed himself into the God Ramchandra in order to please Ramdas.

independent kingdom in that province and fostered the liberty of religion among the people of that soil, the Swami would assuredly in that case have testified to the fact that the *Karnatic Dharma* had, in some measure, survived owing to Shivaji, in the same manner as he did actually affirm in the epistle under consideration, that the Maharashtra Dharma had survived in some measure on his account. Moreover, there is the interesting circumstance to be considered, that the compound form "Maharashtra Dharma" does not occur in any other poems of Ramdas Swami. It was, therefore, used by the Swami, only in these contexts, while expressing his appreciation of the work of Shivaji. With such a flimsy basis, to say that the term "Maharashtra Dharma" was purposely brought into vogue by the Swami for the express purpose of stirring the depths of Maharashtra patriotism, seems to us an unwarrantable presumption. As to the epistle to Sambhaji, the words, "Muster together all the Marathas you may, extend the Maharashtra Dharma etc."[1] seem to have been the Swami's first and last address to the young king on the subject. For the Swami died soon after in the same year in which this epistle was addressed to Sambhaji,[2] and there is no record that after his demise his disciples any further prosecuted the enterprise suggested in this epistle. The admirers of the Swami must not forget that mere speculation is out of court in the investigation of such a historical question. To

[1] The words here quoted "Muster together all the Marathas you may, extend the Maharashtra Dharma" do not occur in Ramdas Swami's epistle to Sambhaji, as it has been published in the edition of an old bakhar of Ramdas Swami, printed and published by the Jagadishwar Press. These words do not also occur in the epistle, as it has been published, in the printed and published edition of Mr. Chaubal's Life of Ramdas Swami. It is difficult to imagine why such an important passage should have been omitted or eliminated, unless indeed it was thought to be an interpolation in the authentic text of the poem, subsequently introduced by some over-zealous admirer of Ramdas Swami.

[2] The epistle in question was composed in *Shaka* 1603 (i. e. end of 1681 A. D. or commencement of 1682) in the month of Paush (December–January). Ramdas died in the month of *Magh* (January–February) in the same Shaka.

conclude, the contention that the sentiments of patriotism, love of religion, of independence, of liberty,—the contention that these passionate feelings were, for a long time to come, kept alive in the hearts of the Maharashtra people by the precepts of a recluse like Ramdas Swami, has a smaller share of probability and credibility about it than the claim made for Shivaji, that it was principally on account of his solid achievements and the trails of glory he left behind, that these noble virtues sprouted and thrived in the hearts of the Maharashtra people. On the capture and execution of Sambhaji, when Aurangzeb conquered and almost crushed the fair provinces of Shivaji's kingdom, the indomitable heroes who for nineteen weary years continued the ceaseless war of independence, with such spirit and pertinacity, and who in the end by their forays brought the exhausted invader to his knees,—these dauntless heroes could surely not have owed much guidance or inspiration to the conventicles of the followers of Ramdas Swami, especially when the beacon-light of Shivaji's example burned steadily before their eyes, to direct and inspire: when the warriors and statesmen trained in Shivaji's stern discipline stood amongst them, to counsel and execute. His alone the glory! A heedless spoliation to assign a particle of it to any magic verses of Ramdas Swami!

THE OLD MARATHA ARISTOCRACY.

There is yet another hypothesis on the subject of Shivaji's achievements. It may be stated as follows:—In the various provinces of the Bahamani kingdom, many Brahman civilians and Maratha warriors had risen to eminence with a new sense of power throbbing in their hearts. When these men saw in Shivaji a leader of promise, gifted with the talents and the wisdom for the foundation of an independent state, they gradually came over to his side, with the result, that, by their active co-operation, Shivaji was enabled to lay the foundations of an independent monarchy.

It cannot be said that a close scrutiny of Shivaji's whole career reveals any grounds for such an assumption. Not one among the great circle of his counsellors could have claimed an apprenticeship in the Mahomedan service or boasted of a father or grand-father who had gained his laurels in the Mahomedan monarchies. Not one of his great generals had ever held a substantial jahgir under the Mahomedan sovereigns.[1] There is no authority to assert that Netaji Palkar, Prataprao Guzar, Hambirrao Mohite, Santaji Ghorpade, Khanderao Dabhade, Dhanaji Jadhav, and the other great warriors who surrounded Shivaji had ever held any hereditary jahgir fiefs before rallying to his flag. Most of them must have been petty deshmukhs or mokasdars, many of them must have rallied to Shivaji's flag, when the revenue rights of deshmukhs and mokasdars were gradually abolished in the Swarajya territory, and by dint of their valour and service under the flag, they must have slowly paved their way to rank and honours. The great representatives of the ancient Maratha chivalry of Shivaji's time were the Nimbalkars of Phaltan, the Ghorpades of Mudhol, the Manes of Mhaswad, the Savants of Wadi, the Surves of Shringarpur, the Mores of Javli, the Shirkes and the Dalvis. These remained to the end loyal vassals of Bijapur; these constantly fought for Bijapur against Shivaji, the first three families especially; and none of the rest would ever have cared to join Shivaji, had not the latter forced them at the point of the sword. It is thus not true to say that Shivaji got the cheap assistance and the unbought experience of the great jahgirdars for the prosecution of his plans. The nobles and counsellors who supported his throne had deliberately elected to serve him from the ambition to improve their fortunes. At the time when they rallied round his standard, they were not moved merely by the impulse of patriotism, the altruistic impulse to throw the weight of what little power they possessed on the side of one

[1] Except that in his temporary secession from Shivaji, Netaji Palkar held a mansab of five thousand in the Mogul army, but, as Prof. Sarkar observes, was still supposed to be attached to the army of Shivaji.

who had embarked upon a national cause for the common good of them all. Such an estimate of the movement is not supported by the sources of information that are available to us. These impulses of patriotism were gradually excited in them, the more they came in contact with their great leader. He impressed them with his faith; he inoculated them with his ideas; he charged them with his hopes, his surging passion, his buoyant enthusiasm for liberty and independence. This is, therefore, one of those theories which attempt vainly to diminish the glory of Shivaji's achievements.[1]

"SWARAJYA" NOT CON-TERMINOUS WITH MAHARASHTRA.

And yet another assumption before we have done with this part of the subject. This last hypothesis is that Shivaji's endeavours for freedom and the foundation of a free state were predetermined by the great king to be restricted to Maharashtra. This again is not true. It is clear that Shivaji was inspired with the high desire of emancipating all India from Mahomedan thraldom and had vowed the restoration of liberty of religion for the Hindus and a Hindu paramountcy over all India.[2] Had his ambition been restricted to Maharashtra, it is difficult to see why he should have conducted an eighteen months' campaign into the heart of the Karnatic, and brought those conquests by means of forts and out-posts under a permanent occupation.[3] Again in 1679-80, when he made the important treaty with Masaood Khan, the Prime Minister of Bijapur, why should he have stipulated for a declaration of the independence of his father's jahgir and taken it into his possession? The present author is inclined to believe that the statement of certain bakhar writers that Shivaji had

---

1 Of course, Shivaji had many officers who had gained experience under Shahaji,

2 Mr. Sardesai in his Marathi Riyasat (1915 edition), pp. 381-82, expresses the opinion that Shivaji seems unquestionably to have intended to establish his Swarajya even beyond the confines of Maharashtra.

3 Prof. Sarkar affirms that Shivaji's object was only to get plunder, and the quarrel with Venkoji was a mere excuse for a plundering campaign. Surely this would be a feeble motive for an enterprise of such pith and moment. Nor does the ascription of such a motive accord with Sarkar's estimate at pages 492-93.

determined to carry his victorious arms down to the promontory of Rameshwar and keep the conquests under his permanent occupation has more credibility about it; and it is more than probable that had he been allowed a longer lease of life he would have realized his object. It is clear that an important motive for the prosecution of the Karnatic compaign was to bring about a delimitation of the southern boundaries of the Bijapur state, in the manner that by his earlier campaigns he had delimitated its narrowed frontiers on the west and the north. And in this there was the ulterior design of crippling its power for good and preparing it for a final extinction, when the proper opportunity should present itself. Another object which the campaign was designed to secure was to checkmate the authority of Golconda from the south. Even when Shivaji retired from the Karnatic, the generals left behind in that province were charged with instructions to extend their conquests eastward to the Madras coast and reduce the country under the Maratha flag. Thus he seems to have deliberately chosen a policy of extinguishing both the Deccan sultanates by a process of continued abrasion of their southern as well as their northern frontiers. For the complete domination of the western coast, he had equipped a strong naval force, and he was always casting about for plans to make it stronger and surer from day to day. What but the desire of undisputed domination over the western sea could be the significance of those endless wars with the Sidi, those desperate struggles for the extermination of the Abyssinian power? Shivaji's flags were floating in Guzerat; upto Daman and Surat he had advanced his military stations. Between 1670 to 1680 scarcely a year elapsed without the tramp of Shivaji's light horse being heard in the valleys of Guzerat. The Mogul reigned over those valleys, still intoxicated with a sense of power, and Shivaji knew a single false move on his part would imperil his whole position in that province. With his usual policy of a cautious advance and his consistent refusal to tempt fortune, where he knew the odds were against him, he refrained from attacking the central head-quarters of the Moguls at Aurangabad, though many a time he had led his victorious squadrons, scouring and plundering the country, right upto the gates of that city. But from this it would be wrong to infer that the overthrow of the Moguls was beyond the scope of his ambition. Consider how he conducted himself towards Jay Singh, when the latter came down upon him for the conquest of the Deccan. No stratagem or intrigue was employed against Jay Singh, as against his predecessor, Shaistakhan. The one was conciliated, the other entrapped. The difference between the methods pursued in the two cases is surely an eloquent testimony to the difference in the policy intended. For how did the situation stand? There was Diler Khan battering the walls of Purandar fort. He had battered the fort a long while, without solid success. That one fort had kept a large division of the Mogul army in play, not without inflicting some punishment upon it. There was Jay Singh who had shot his last bolt and had failed to take Sinhagad. Shivaji was not yet driven to desperation. He could still have afforded, had he been so minded, to play fort against fort, army against army. And with all this he personally visits Jay Singh's camp, plays a studiedly humble part with the proud Diler Khan, sues for a treaty, and accedes to the request of Jay Singh to visit Agra. Surely there must have been some policy in all this. And he knew Aurangzeb,–knew him to be a perfidious man, a crafty ruler, a relentless enemy. When with all this knowledge, he deliberately ran the risk of putting himself in the power of such a formidable man, knowing his hostile feelings towards himself, we must needs presume he did so out of some deeper design. To the present writer the whole event appears as a part of a profound and far-reaching policy. This policy was to win over to his cause a powerful Rajput prince like Jay Singh, cultivate friendship with other Rajput nobles and through the intercession of Jay Singh win their sympathy with a view to the further prosecution of his enterprise, to obtain a proper insight into the political situation in the north, and procure the sanction of the Mogul power for a complete subjugation of Bijapur and Golconda. The story of his career reveals to us that more or less successfully he accomplished all his objects. As the Maratha jahgirdars of the Deccan had passed completely under the suzerainty of the Mahomedans and never thought of uniting together for the common object of setting up a free and independent government, so also had the Rajput princes of the north dwindled into feudal vassals under the Mogul throne, looking no farther than to their individual interests.[1] Shivaji doubtless desired to bring before the eyes of these indolent princes the ideal of independence he was endeavouring to realize in the south and to inspire them with a determination to follow in the north the example of his brilliant accomplishments, with his full support and co-operation. In the light of such a purpose we can well understand those last expressions of regret and disappointment, which according to the bakhar writers, as described in chapter XXX, he gave vent to, while the shadows of death were fast closing around him. Nor could it be said that the laudatory description of Shivaji's objects and achievements, which the Raja Shahaji, on returning to the Karnatic from his valiant son, gave to Venkoji by way of exhortation, was all mere rhetoric and hyperbole. Small matters these, but they serve to throw much light on the breadth of his political purposes and outlook. That he did not live long enough to accomplish his ulterior object is no reason for narrowing the bounds of his vision and aspiration.

---

[1] It is interesting to observe that these views of the author are corroborated in almost every particular by Mr. Sardesai in his 'Marathi Riyasat' (1915 edition, pages 382-84). Among the Rajput princes who caught the inspiration of Shivaji's struggle for independence was the Raja Chhatrasal of Bundelkhand who moulded his career upon that of Shivaji. Chhatrasal visited Shivaji's court in the winter of 1670-71 and offered to serve him against the emperor. The Maratha king asked him to start a campaign of independence in his own country. (*Vide Chhatraprakash*, Canto 11, which deals with Chhatrasal's visit to Shivaji, also Prof. Sarkar, *Shivaji*, pp. 236-37).

Thus far we have considered the criticisms made upon Shivaji and his work by critics of two divergent schools: first the alien scholar who would fain discover many a blemish in his character and accomplishment,and secondly the Indian scholar, often betrayed into sweeping generalizations that tend to impair Shivaji's greatness. We have endeavoured at some length to show the falsity or superficiality of the estimates of both these schools of criticism.

TRAITS OF CHARACTER.

It only remains to review, in a final estimate, some of the leading traits of the character of this great leader. Some aspects of that glorious character have already been touched upon in the fore-going part. For a lucid treatment of this part of the subject, we propose to estimate his conduct, from four different points of view, viz: his conduct in politics, his conduct in private life, his family affections, and his religious sensibilities.

CONCILIATION AND MAGNANIMITY.

In politics, it will be difficult to exaggerate the boldness and enterprise, the valour and strategy which he displayed in carrying through the arduous task of opposing three Mahomedan powers and up-building in their place an independent power of his own creation. Illustrations of these high virtues are to be found so abundantly on every page of his glorious record, that we may save ourselves the trouble of dilating separately upon them.[1] But for the successful foundation of an enduring empire, other virtues are needed, besides those mentioned. For one who proposed to himself the accomplishment of an enterprise that bore at

[1] The testimony of Aurangzeb, the inveterate enemy of Shivaji, would suffice to prove his greatness :—

Aurangzeb exclaimed on hearing the news of Shivaji's death :—"He was a great captain, and the only one who has had the magnanimity to raise a new kingdom, while I have been endeavouring to destroy the ancient sovereignties of India; my armies have been employed against him for nineteen years, and nevertheless his state has been always increasing." And this estimate of Shivaji was made by a man who had formerly called him "a mountain rat!"

first view such a visionary and impracticable aspect, the faculty of the highest importance was the art of enlisting popular sympathy and conciliation. This was possessed by Shivaji in a degree scarcely equalled by any leader of men in the world's history. His gentle and persuasive discourse had in the earliest prime of his youth captivated the hearts of the lesser gentry of the Maval country and of other neighbours and secured their cordial participation from the commencement of his whole enterprise. This sort of fascination Shivaji was able to exercise upon all persons who once came in contact with him, instilling in them feelings of love and respect towards himself and rousing them to a sense of appreciation of the great cause he had taken in hand and a patriotic resolve to help it forward, to the best of their endeavour. With this personal magnetism Shivaji never failed to find either loyalty or integrity among friends and supporters. This quality was strengthened by another, which plays no small part in the friendships of political leaders, especially in retaining them. This was liberality. Few rulers could have equalled Shivaji in his open-handed liberality towards his followers. Rewards and presents were scattered with a bountiful profusion according to the respective deserts of officers and men distinguishing themselves. Their stipends were regularly paid. On great occasions in their families they received extraordinary allowances and gifts of his royal bounty. Shivaji was always careful to make adequate provision for the families of those who laid down their lives in his wars. The nearest heir of the deceased,—son or brother,—if found fit, was admitted to the service of the state, according to his position and capacity. This feeling of security about their families and dependents was an added spur to his soldiers to give of their best in the service of their master, even at the sacrifice of their lives.

IMPARTIALITY AND APPRECIATIVENESS.

Another quality that goes a long way in securing the will and enthralling the hearts of the enthusiastic multi-

-tude is the faculty of discerning and appreciating merit. This again was possessed by Shivaji in an eminent degree. With an instinctive precision he assessed the true worth of his servants and officers and entrusted them with duties according to their level. In proportion as their rising valour and virtue displayed themselves, they earned their titles and promotions, without fear of partiality. The reservation of places of high honour or emolument for personal friends or relations was not known in his system. The claims of merit were in all cases duly weighed; there was no fear of unfair supersession. Thus the even chance of promotion was a present stimulus to every loyal heart. Another high principle regulating the relations between this leader and the multitudes he led was his unrivalled capacity of rousing and developing the feelings of probity and loyalty among his followers. When he charged a man with a duty, however arduous or important it might be, he depended upon him to execute it, with a sense of security and confidence. In choosing the man for the duty, he had measured his aptitude and trustworthiness. Upon entrusting the duty to the man there was no ground for distrust or misgiving. Personal envy or malice could harm no loyal servant in the opinion of such a master. Such men had no access to Shivaji's ear. When the public character of an officer of state was such as to give some cause for suspicion, his practice was first to institute a private investigation through the machinery of his secret service, and upon the result of this information to order a public inquiry and a just scrutiny of the evidence produced. This feeling of trust in the honour and integrity of his veterans inspired high and low with a serene confidence that a loyal perseverance in the diligent discharge of their duties was a sufficient guarantee of their continuance in their respective offices. With the growing sense of security, the virtues of loyalty, integrity and devotion took root and blossomed in all their glory.

FRIENDLINESS AND CANDOUR.

His chosen advisers shared his secrets and participated

in all his plans and projects. He courted their criticism of every measure, he appreciated the suggestions they deemed it proper to make. Their opinions were not merely followed but were eagerly sought after. Against his friends and ministers, he practised no mask or disguise. His aims and purposes stood transparent before them. The insolence of power never misled him into any act derogatory to the self-respect of his counsellors. In him his ministerial circle never found a conceited dictator, but a sincere and affectionate friend. Thus was loyalty reconciled with the spirit of self-respect, and the sense of personal prestige thus preserved, flowed back into a general stream of loving pride and loyal reverence for the throne.

PERSONAL INDUSTRY.

The trust and confidence he frankly reposed in his men was never abused. The friendly attitude involved no forfeiture of authority. The cultivation of the spirit of self-respect among his servants and courtiers did not lead him to connive at abuse of power or proved negligence. Retribution in proportion to the fault descended irrevocably upon the offending minister, however high his office. The strictness of his justice made him dreaded as his courtesy made him loved. It ensured a continuity of loyal but efficient service. It rendered effective the control and domination exercised upon such a numerous body of officers and made them amenable to any service that might be demanded of them. His personal example was a source of perennial inspiration to his officers. Inured to habits of industry and patience from his earliest years, he had developed in himself every virtue and faculty, both for the acquisition and the administration of a kingdom.[1] On the field of battle, it never was his wont, as is the case with many princes and generals, to place himself as an idle spectator in a position of security and watch his squadrons

[1] This aspect of the character of the hero-king will remind the reader of the wonderful character-sketch of Hannibal as portrayed by Livy. (Livy XXI, 4).

hurling themselves upon the enemy. Sword in hand he took the first place in the field and put forth before his admiring hosts the most dazzling examples of bravery, of courage, and of art. No commander in all his army could have the vanity to boast of a better display of military qualities. He was not a king who sent forth his armies on distant and perilous campaigns and contented himself with lolling upon his couch in slothful ease enjoying the fruits of his generals' triumphs. Hence no general, flushed with triumphs under his auspices, could create a faction at Shivaji's court and dictate terms to his liege lord and sovereign. Such a thing was impossible with Shivaji. The campaigning season saw him always engaged in active arms in one or the other theatre of his wars. He was never given to idling away a moment of his life. The glory of his greatest generals paled before his, their vaunted valour was dimmed in the splendour of his exploits. The same was true of the character of his leadership in civil affairs. In the administration of forts, in the organization of the land revenue, in the tact and finesse of diplomacy, he was never excelled by any of the distinguished men who served under him. This perfect balance of virtues, this aggregation in the same person of such diverse and opposite elements of strength, this unique versatility of faculty set him far above the most towering personalities of his court. It was this that the sage Ramdas Swami meant to express, when, in his epistle, he addressed Shivaji as "*Sarvadnya*," or lord of all science.

PERSONAL MAGNETISM.

This versatility is, therefore, the secret of that extraordinary personal magnetism he exercised upon his servants. This is the key to that rivalry of good deeds and loyal service he inspired among his people. This is why to the Maratha soldier praise from his lips became the greatest palm of victory and the sacrifice of blood and life too cheap a price for the honour. In presence of that unique personality, they were right willing to be his thralls, for therein, they fancied, lay the consummation of their lives. And as gradually the loftiness of his views and the sacredness of his patriotic purpose dawned upon their vision, a sense of religious piety diffused itself in their conception of loyalty and honour, which held disloyalty a sin, and treason, a pollution. Penetrated with these feelings of loyalty and patriotism, never a shadow of disaffection or treachery crossed their minds.[1] During the captivity at Agra, when for eight months the light of Shivaji's presence was cut off from his Swarajya domains, during the events and vicissitudes of the Karnatic campaign which for eighteen months detained him on a distant soil, no commander or counsellor in the home country ever thought of defection. The full significance of this circumstance can be appreciated by us only if we pause to consider what troublous times those were and how contagious of anarchy. But this mystery is easily resolved when we consider–and only when we consider–the iron grip by which Shivaji held men's hearts and affections, by the splendour of his personality and heart-ravishing virtues.

ORIGINALITY.

Originality, as in every great leader of men, played no unimportant part in moulding his great career. The idea of the foundation of an independent Hindu power, in the times in which it was conceived, required the exercise of a noble faculty of imagination. Under the auspices of the Mahomedan powers such a number of Maratha warriors had risen to high command and become the founders of so many jahgir seigniories, and yet none had ever conceived the thought of an independent Hindu monarchy. Could it be said that the love of country, the boast of national religion, the horror of Islam were in all cases alien to their thoughts and feelings? It is clear that the cause of that sluggish contentment which made them willing to hug the bonds of

[1] The defection of Netaji Palkar described by Khafi Khan was a temporary affair and he again served under Shivaji, and it was because he was such an able servant of Shivaji, that the Moguls at Aurangabad had him arrested, on the flight of Shivaji from Agra. A doubtful case is that of Sambhaji Kavji in the war with Shaista Khan.

their servitude was want of imagination. It was eminently the possession of this faculty that led Shivaji to conceive his proud ideal and devise plan after plan to achieve that noble end. That imagination he had developed from his youthful years. That imagination is the index of his intellectual calibre. His mind was quick to grasp and inquisitive to observe. As there were no limits to his observation, his knowledge of a practical subject was always up-to-date. His own observation and experience of things was being constantly supplemented by the experience and observation of others; and the impressions that checked, confirmed and enriched his original ideas were ineffaceably registered in his mind. Nor was it a mere retentive faculty in which he excelled: his reason was equally acute and penetrating. It was this combination of intellectual faculties that enabled him to direct his knowledge and experience of things upon the successful prosecution of his noble enterprise. It was this that made him a master of resources, an audacious wielder of giant plans and projects. It was the secret of his patience, the basis of his perseverance, the soul of his enterprise. That imagination flowed from a copious stream and failed not of ready response in times of greatest exhaustion. It enlisted for him even as an inexperienced tyro the sympathy and co-operation of men grown hoary with experience and knowledge. They rallied to the cause of the young warrior so wise for his years. They lent themselves whole-heartedly to turn his plans into deeds, his dreams into reality. This profound faculty again and again came to his rescue in every crisis of his career. It was the driving force in all his character, its essence, its vital principle.

LOVE OF INDEPENDENCE.

Another important element of his character was independence of spirit. This has been the characteristic of exalted genius in all ages. Such spirits cannot thrive in an atmosphere of dependence. Their regard for self-respect is so fine and exquisite a quality that it instantly revolts from any cause that would bring it under an eclipse.

Theirs is the philosophy of a crust of bread with liberty. The golden trappings of servility are distasteful to their restive spirits. Shivaji envied not his father, he disdained his liveried pride, his purple servitude. Thus though he knew that in his efforts for independence there was a certain risk of failure, he prosecuted them with the utmost vigour from his constitutional abhorrence of a life of gilded dependence. And this though an elder of the authority and experience of Dàdàji Kondadev was constantly dinning into his ears the advantages of a golden mediocrity and the dangers of his high-soaring pursuits. But he adhered to his purpose. Even when soon afterwards, the life of his father, dearer to him than his own life, stood in danger, by reason of his steadfast adherence to his high resolve, he refused to disavow that purpose, relying on his masterly resourcefulness to deliver himself from his immediate difficulties. The episode of the captivity at Agra is a vivid illustration of this trait in his character. In the presence of the emperor, in full view of the assembled court, in the emperor's own capital, he gave vent to his feelings of injured dignity at the mean treatment accorded to him. It was a quality of a heroical magnitude, for it does honour to every hero, and a total absence of that virtue reduces man to a nonentity. Shivaji guarded against insult, against injury, against insolence. Hence that roll of glorious deeds, elevated above the level of common mediocrity, hence that triumphant illustration of the glory of an exalted spirit translated into the exaltation of an entire nation. Into this focus of a splendid independence, converged together his valour, his chivalry, his enterprise, his equity, his temperance, in short, every single ray of his virtue, both public and private. It is a characteristic of such an exalted virtue to keep up a ceaseless endeavour for the promotion of all those qualities that add to its brilliance and the elimination of those faults and blemishes that however partially eclipse its grandeur. Further than that, such a noble spirit learns, by personal experience, that the true seat of supreme felicity lies in the happiness of the multitude, and the consummation of his brilliant career, in the growing prosperity of the people committed to his charge. It is for the reader to judge how brilliantly the career of Shivaji stands this supreme test of a magnificent character. That magnanimity of spirit gave us for a while the superlative gift of national independence and its exquisite glory, transcending and surviving our fall, still stands before the world to bear eloquent testimony to the national spirit and grandeur of the Maharashtra people.

AS AN ADMINISTRATOR.

As a civil administrator he presents himself as the friend of the people. It is unnecessary to recapitulate in this place the administrative reforms already described in a previous chapter. He was at all times studiously anxious for the happiness and prosperity of the cultivator, the artisan and the tradesman. He laboured hard to deliver them from the harpies of extortion and misrule; he was solicitous to give them the facilities of an easy and efficacious, and at the same time, expeditious system of judicature. To promote the smooth and regular working of the wheels of administration, avoiding every possibility of friction or overlapping jurisdiction, he had devised, as a preventive against every form of anarchy, the system of the *Ashta Pradhan* cabinet, a constitution that had suggested itself to no Indian king before him. The differentiation of the various labours of administration and assignment of each specific head of duty to a separate minister, the joint supervision of the entire cabinet, with his personal vigilance superimposed upon all, seemed to his mind the most absolute guarantee of a just and salutary administration for the equal benefit of all classes of his subjects.[1] With this view he divided

[1] Prof. Rawlinson in his "Life of Shivaji" criticises the council as a bureaucratic system of administration. Supposing it were so, it gave a better guarantee of deliberation in those exciting times and certainly a better and more orderly form of government. But the supervising presence of a responsible king made all the difference. The king bore a large measure of responsibility himself. This prevented the constitution from sinking into a bureaucratic machine, while the existence of the council

his own jurisdiction and allotted shares of co-ordinate authority to his great ministers of state, spreading the fame of their names and their proven merit and chivalry, along with his own, to all the corners of his kingdom. However high-placed an executive officer in his service might be, he never failed to receive condign punishment, upon being convicted of oppressing the people. While the affairs of the administration of each local chief were subject to the supervision of the cabinet minister in charge of the department, his conduct as an administrator was also watched and reported upon by a staff of confidential agents in the secret service of the sovereign. These were always on the move, each in his appointed circle in the Swarajya territory, watching, detecting, reporting the conduct of officials in public life. The government officials thus lived in the constant dread that their sovereign would not fail to have due information and exact the prescribed penalties, should they oppress the people or exceed their authority in any way. This check upon the official reacted to the advantage and security of the multitude. We have moreover seen in chapter XXIV the various regulations of Shivaji's government for the encouragement of agriculture and the protection of the agricultural population.

A BENEVOLENT RULER.

An outstanding feature of Shivaji's administrative system was the equality and impartiality of his government towards all subjects; and it will be no exaggeration to assert that scarcely has any sovereign equalled him in the practice of this virtue. Of course his subjects were divided into castes; but employment in the state service was open to all castes and each according to his competence was eligible for the fulfilment of offices in the state.

prevented the kingship from sinking into an irresponsible despotism. Prof. Sarkar points out that Shivaji's council was in no sense a cabinet and that it lacked the solidarity of the British Cabinet. Naturally so, because there was no parliamentary institution. A "British Cabinet *without* a Parliament" would be a most monstrous form of bureaucracy that could be imagined.

Thus all castes were gratified and contented with his rule. He never showed any undue partiality towards men of his own caste. Even in the case of Mahomedan subjects there was no caste prejudice as regards state service. Those who were loyal amongst them and capable of carrying out their duties, were appointed to positions of trust and honour.[1] It was largely owing to this impartiality as regards caste, that there were no mutinies or treason in his government. To subjects of all castes he was an object of equal veneration.

IN PRIVATE LIFE.

As regards his private life, it must be stated that the chronicle-writers, for the most part occupied with a recital of political changes, have scarcely left any record of Shivaji's private life. In consequence, very little can be said upon this subject. But it may be affirmed that he led a pure life. He was simple in his dress and habits. Free from any vice, he did not even indulge in any sort of levity or jests. His great passion was to listen to the recitals of the poets, the kirtans, and the readings of the puranas. For other forms of entertainment he had neither the inclination nor the leisure. Men of special talents, attainments and learning were handsomely entertained and remunerated. The services of such men were permanently engaged about the court, when their talents were found to be of utility. Shivaji was likewise careful in extending hospitality to friends and relations, nobles and princes, according to the degree of their position and status. The insolence of pomp and power did not estrange him from the duties and relations of private life, nor did the giddiness of success betray him into any form of excess or iniquity.

FAMILY AFFECTIONS.

Turning to Shivaji's family life, we must again complain of the scanty record left by the bakhar-writers. We have seen in many parts of the preceding narrative the proofs and the extent of his filial affections towards both

[1] It will be noticed that Shivaji's admiral in the naval war with the Bombay Government in 1678 was a Mahomedan (Vide Chapter XXVIII).

his parents and his fraternal solicitude, after his father's death, for his only surviving brother. Though the successful architect of his own fortune and the founder of a noble state, neither vanity nor conceit ever betrayed him into any act of disrespect or inattention towards his parents or of insult or violence against his brother. And this at a time when Aurangzeb reigned at Delhi, when the excesses of filial revolt and fratricide had passed into a gospel of political necessity. It is unfortunate that we have no record of Shivaji's relations with his wives. But in the absence of any indication to the contrary, we may positively affirm that he was not uxorious, and never led himself into any improper acts upon their advice.[1] It was his firm belief that women should not interfere in politics. Even his mother was not permitted to do so, much less his wives. From this, however, it cannot be inferred that he had no affection or respect for them. As to his senior queen, Sayibai, the bakhar-writers tell us he loved her to adoration. For womanhood in general he had a chivalrous regard and veneration. Hence the standing regulation of his army not to molest any woman on any account, with the result that violation of female modesty or any outrage against them has never been charged against his soldiers. Shivaji's own example in this matter, from his early youth, was an abiding inspiration to his soldiers. The case of the daughter-in-law of Mullana, the governor of Kalyan, cannot have been forgotten by the reader. If such was his general attitude toward the weaker sex, it may be surmised that he could not have been disrespectful or indifferent to the feelings of his wives. For his sons he had naturally

[1] The picture which Prof. Sarkar (pp. 427-28) draws of intrigues within Shivaji's harem, in the closing years of his life, is drawn largely from imagination and for the rest depends on the partisan vapourings of the Shivadigvijaya. This chronicle displays a pecular bias against Soyarabai and what is stated in it as her wicked plots against Sambhaji, and even against Shivaji, must be taken with caution. All that can be said with certainty is that Shivaji's last days were saddened by Sambhaji's revolt and wayward manners and that Soyarabai tried adroitly to use the prejudice against Sambhaji to advance the prospects of her own son Rajaram.

a strong feeling of affection, and he had taken care to give them a proper education and train them for the duty of governing the state he had created for them. With all this when his elder son began to sow his wild oats and turn to all manner of wickedness, even to the extent of outraging female chastity, he would not permit to his son a license he denied to others and straightway ordered the scape-grace prince to imprisonment. In short, the brief survey we can afford to make of Shivaji's family relations sets him forth before us as a good son, a good husband, a good father, and a good brother.

RELIGIOUS ENTHUSIASM.

With a brief notice of Shivaji's religious attitude, we may conclude this sketch of his character. At different stages of his biography, and especially in chapter XXIX, we have made observations on his religious temperament. Without repeating those observations, we need only state here that the impulses of religious pride and enthusiasm implanted in his tender mind from his earliest years, went on expanding apace as he grew older. How absorbing the religious passion of Shivaji was can be best ascertained from the three or four recorded crises of his religious experience, when he prepared to turn his back upon his labours of independence and dedicate himself for the rest of his life to spiritual pursuits. The reader will doubtless remember the convulsive spasms of spiritual agony which shook his whole being at the shrine of Mallikarjun, on his way to the Karnatic, upon his southern campaign, and how, at the height of that paroxysm, he resolved to lay down his life as an offering to the deity. We have also seen how eager he was to pay proper respect to sages and saints, to supply the needs of the learned and the pious, to spend his treasures upon shrines and temples, upon Brahmans and the expounders of the sacred books. And to his intimate counsellors it was always a standing menace, that this religious enthusiasm might at any time get the better of all his secular aspirations and dominate his mind to such an extent as to withdraw him altogether from temporal cares. But the tradition of the vision seen by Maloji—when the tutelary Bhavani appeared to him in a dream and assured him that it was ordained that an illustrious conqueror would be born of the Bhonsle name, to inaugurate a new era of independence and to deliver the children of the soil from the oppression of Islam,—this tradition was always before his mind and that of his mother, and the feeling gradually arose within him that his people were destined to see the fulfilment of that prophecy in himself, that his genius stood above the ordinary level of human beings, that his life was a mission for the gratification of the intense longings of the Aryan land and its crown of glory was to persevere till death in the vindication of the liberties of the Aryan people from the yoke of Moslem despotism, by the foundation of an independent empire. The conviction that the tutelary Bhavani spurred him on towards this goal incited him at every crisis of his career, to present his fervid vows before her throne. This devotion was rendered from a heart filled with a fiery faith and zeal, with the effect, as it seemed to him, that he was always near her and delivered himself, under her oracular inspiration, of prophecies of deliverance and victory. From this his unsympathetic critics have rushed to the conclusion that this was a piece of hypocrisy and simulation, practised on purpose to gull the multitude and play upon their superstitious credulity, so as to win them over to his side. In short it is alleged that personally Shivaji did not believe in this sort of foolery and used it as a tool to delude the masses. As regards this, we have only to observe that Shivaji did not seek deliberately to practise imposture upon the people. He was himself quite as sincere a believer in the divine communications as any of his people. In his time it was a universal practice throughout Maharashtra to conjure up the spirit of one's tutelary deity and consult the person who was supposed to be the medium of her spiritual presence, for an oracular expression of opinion or advice in any difficulty, and traces of this practice still survive in many parts of the country. It cannot be said that this "spiritual mediumship" is in all cases founded on conscious hypocrisy. The depths of this "psycho-pathia spiritualis" have yet to be sounded. From this point of view it would appear that the exciting cause of these oracles was something deeper than simulation: it was excess of piety, it was credulity, but sincere and earnest. In the throes of a great dilemma which taxed the wits of his counsellors, when the intellect became overcast and saw no way towards safety, the great leader had recourse to prayer, under the stress of his excitement; and in that state of abstraction, thought mingled with devotion, until he seemed to glow under an unearthly influence and finally uttered, in that exalted condition of mind, his trenchant decisions, amidst a world of travail. These utterances were taken down by the attendants, and both the leader himself and his followers regarded them as an oracle of the tutelary goddess. Such was their confidence in what they assumed as her mandate, that they set about the most audacious project or enterprise, without the least misgiving about the ultimate victory. When their operations were, in such cases, repeatedly crowned with success, experience confirmed the pious multitude in the belief that their hero was under the special favour of the goddess Bhaváni, and produced in them the fullest confidence in his victory. In short, it is scarcely just to apply the cold standard of modern rationalism in speaking of an extravagance of religious faith and experience that characterized the social psychology of those times, or to attribute it to conscious hypocrisy or fraud.

We have so far essayed to estimate the character of Shivaji and examine the various criticisms passed upon it. It may be admitted that to some of our readers this estimate may appear biassed, but it seems to us to be our duty to set forth in all sincerity the Maharashtra view of the worth and greatness of the hero of this biography, and we cannot pause to consider, whether or not, this view of our hero's character may square with the arbitrary standards and prejudices of others. It is an undisputed fact that the venerable name of Shivaji is the most beloved name and the most treasured possession in the hearts of all the Maharashtra people, if not of all India. The question by what force of character and endearing virtues he has thus enthroned himself in our hearts has not yet engaged that share of attention which it deserves. In consequence of this neglect, many a prejudice has gathered round his name, and a good deal of ungenerous prudery and divergent criticisms have been paraded against him. If the present work may contribute to however small an extent to clear away these trivialities and superficialities of prejudice, to bring home to people's mind the full image of his real greatness and to perpetuate on a firmer and clearer basis our sentiments of pride and gratitude towards him, that will be taken by us as an ample return for our labour.

And here we pause. The object of this sketch is in the first place to confirm that awakened enthusiasm for the great name of Shivaji, which has taken possession of all Maharashtra and almost the whole of the Indian continent, and secondly to give the reader a more vivid insight into his constructive genius than has hitherto been possible. Such a complete insight is impossible of attainment without concentrating our mind and bringing it into focus upon the whole of that career as a constituted unity. Two centuries and a third have rolled since his demise. During this long period his name has been celebrated by diverse writers, both in prose and verse. No small number of Mahomedan and European historians have written about him, according to their lights. He still lives in his fame. But no systemetic attempt has yet been made to bring his actions and glory into one focus, to examine their synthetical effects, and then to estimate the character of those maculae or dark spots that are said to stain the lustre of his career and to eclipse his glory. This attempt the present author has made according to his lights and ability. It is for the reader, and the Indian reader in particular, to appreciate it.

APPENDIX I

MALOJI AND SHAHAJI

In an article on this subject in the first number of the Quarterly (Marathi) of the Bharat Itihas Sanshodhak Mandali, 1921, Mr. Vasudev Shastri Khare has examined the careers of Maloji and Shahaji and made certain speculations on the part played by Shahaji as the inspirer of Shivaji's programme, which in part corroborate and in part conflict with the views expressed in the text. Mr. Khare supports the claim of the Bhonsles to consider themselves Rajputs and points out that Maloji's father, Babaji made use of the title *Raja* (Rajwade XV, Extract No. 367), before Maloji had earned any honour from the Nizamshahi state. Mr. Khare controverts the view that Maloji began service under Lukhji Jadhav on such a low salary as five pagodas per month, holding that if his fortunes were so depressed as to compel him to serve on such low terms, he could not have married the sister of such a chief as Vangoji Naik Nimbalkar of Phaltan. He believes that Maloji must have taken service with the Nizamshahi state and his corps was then transferred to the Jadhav family, as the latter were the head of the Maratha forces attached to the Nizamshahi state, and he thinks it probable that this connection with the Jadhav family sprang up in the regime of the father of Lukhji Jadhav. He thinks that the person who forced Lukhji Jadhav to give his daughter Jijabai to Maloji's son in marriage was, not so much the reigning sultan, Murteza Nizamshaha II (*alias* Buran Nizamshaha), who was a minor and a puppet, but Malik Ambar, who was already then (A. D. 1604) the mainstay of the Nizamshahi state. He holds that the Maratha Bakhars and other historians are wrong in stating that the marriage of Jijabai with Shahaji took place in the sultan's presence at Daulatabad (*vide* p. 14. *supra*) He maintains that it must have been celebrated at Periuda (Paraude), which was then the Nizamshahi capital, since Malik Ambar who had revived the state after the fall of Ahmednagar and the capture of Bahadur Nizamshaha (the ward of

Chand Bibi) in 1600, installed his puppet prince at Perinda until the foundation of Khadki (the modern Aurangabad) near Daulatabad, in the year 1607, when this new town became the Nizamshahi capital. As to this, it must be said that the Mahomedan chroniclers like Ferishta also give the date 1600 or 1601 for the revival of the Nizamshahi state by the Ahmednagar nobles and state that the capital of the puppet king was Perinda (Parande or Parenda), but it is doubtful whether at so early a period as 1600 or 1601 Malik Ambar had become the *de facto* king of the Nizamshahi state. Such a position he must have attained by the year 1609, when he re-conquered Ahmednagar for the Nizamshahi state. In the *Modern Review*, Vol. XXII No. 129, (p. 247), Prof. Sarkar states that "Buran Nizamshaha (Murteza Nizamshaha II) became a puppet of Malik Ambar about 1609." There were strong factions in the Ahmednagar state, (*Vide* p. 17 *supra*) and Malik Ambar could not have all at once made himself a *de facto* king, but must have risen, slowly, as the power of the other nobles declined. His chief wars with the Moguls were fought in the reign of Jahangir, rather than of Akbar. Malik Ambar died at the ripe old age of eighty in 1626 and he must have been a leading noble of the state in 1600, though he began his career as an Abyssinian slave. There is nothing impossible in the view that the patron of Shahaji at the age of 30 years should have also been a patron of Maloji at a time when Shahaji was 10 years of age, but it is not so easy to believe that he was already then a *de facto* king. Mr. Khare himself states in his article (p. 9), that till Malik Ambar became fifty-four or fifty-five years of age (i. e. till 1600 or 1601 A.D.) he was quite an obscure person.

On the authority of a bakhar in the Tamil language entitled the "*Shiv Bharat*", Mr. Khare thinks that including Shivaji, Jijabai bore six children to Shahaji, of whom the first four died in childhood, (Shedgavkar p. 11), the first to grow into manhood being Sambhaji, the fifth child, born in 1623 (*Vide* p. 51 *supra* and foot-note). Mr.

Khare thinks the date of the birth of Shivaji given in the Jedhe Chronology, viz: March 1630, to be more correct than the date given by most of the bakhars, viz: April 1627. Mr. Khare ridicules the theory that Shahaji married his second wife, Tukabai Mohite, on account of any disfavour with Jijabai and is so far happily in agreement with our view on this subject (*Vide* pp. 55 and 66 *supra*). He holds that this marriage with a daughter of a Bijapur noble, celebrated at Bijapur, in honour of which he received certain grants of land from the Bijapur durbar (Shivadigvijaya p. 53) must have taken place after Shahaji had taken up permanent service under Bijapur, i. e. after 1637. But he makes this marriage an important thread in a speculative web about Shahaji's purposes which he weaves in the rest of his article. He says this marriage was purposely contracted by Shahaji, in order to throw dust into the eyes of the Bijapur authorities, so that while in one direction, Shivaji could go on laying the foundations of an independent power under his own secret guidance and inspiration, he could easily disclaim all responsibility, by saying that he had quarrelled with Shivaji and Jijabai. The theory is too subtle to believe in. It is impossible to believe that even a great master mind like Shahaji should enter upon a simple event in his family life like a second marriage, with such deep-laid political schemes in his head. The rest of the article is taken up with the attempt to show that from beginning to end Shivaji entered upon his task, under his father's inspiration. So far as this theory gives the death-blow to the popular view, sanctified by Grant Duff, that Shahaji was opposed to the plans of Shivaji, it is acceptable to us and has been maintained in these pages. But it is too much for us to view Shivaji's labours as the mechanical execution of ready-made schemes presented by his father. The officers lent by Shahaji were of great service to the youthful hero, the example set by Shahaji was even of still greater service, the many proofs of his father's encouragement and assistance, which he received from time to time, were most valuable in stimulating his enterprise : but it is difficult to believe that the whole plan was laid out by Shahaji already as early as 1637 or 1639, (or even 1643 as sometimes alleged) and entrusted for execution, with an insufficient army and with hopelessly inadequate financial resources, to a promising but after all a raw and inexperienced *boy* like Shivaji. who in the year 1639 was, according to Jedhe, scarcely *nine* years of age,—even if by any gift of observation or prophecy it could be predicted that that boy would turn out a prodigy of genius, and even if that boy were assisted by Shahaji's officials. It seems to us more natural to assume that the ideas of liberty and independence, which were implanted in Shivaji by nature, were fostered by the sympathy of his mother and the example of his father, and with that example before him, he carved out his career and made his preparations from about 1643 to 1648, when the wisdom and the bravery and the perseverance he displayed evoked from the sagacious father cautious acknowledgments of his sympathy, approval and encouragement. (*Vide* foot-note to pp. 94, 95)

As to the reflections of Mr. Khare about the motto of Shivaji's seal and the use of it at a time when Shivaji was barely ten years of age, nothing more need be added to our remarks in the foot-note at pp. 107, 108 *supra*.

APPENDIX II

ANANDRAO BHONSLE AND HAMBIRRAO MOHITE

THE perplexing question as to the identity of Anandrao, one of Shivaji's great generals, has been referred to in the foot-note to pp. 344, 345. Sarkar (*Shivaji*, p. 260 and foot-note) identifies Anandrao, the lieutenant of Prataprao Guzar, with Hambirrao, who succeeded Prataprao to the office of Sir-nobut, when the latter was killed in the battle of Jessary. He says " Anandrao, a lieutenant of Prataprao, rallied the disheartened army of his chief. Shiva (Shivaji) appointed him Commander-in-chief in succession to Prataprao, gave him the title of Hambirrao, and ordered him not to return alive without defeating the enemy." In his foot-note to this passage, Sarkar says, "I here follow the account of Narayan Shenvi (interpreter to the East India Company, Bombay), written at Raigad only a month later, on information supplied by Shivaji's ministers." Sarkar adds that Sabhasad and Chitnis give the new commander-in-chief's name as Hasaji (Hansaji) Mohite. With full knowledge of this, Sarkar identifies Hambirrao with Anandrao. He is quite consistent in this identification throughout his account of the Karnatic compaign, but breaks down all of a sudden when he comes to describe the last operations against Dilerkhan, when the latter was besieging Bijapur. For here he speaks of Hambirrao and Anandrao as different individuals. He describes Anandrao as baing in command of 2,500 men sent to relieve Bijapur (p.417) and again mentions him as being in charge of a cavalry force of 10,000 operating in the south, while Shivaji himself marched with the other half of his army into Khandesh, plundered Jalna and on the return fought with Ranmast-khan, in which battle *Hambirrao was wounded.* This would show clearly that in this context Anandrao is taken as quite a different individual from Hambirrao and to this extent Sarkar is inconsistent with his former account.

Whence came this Anandrao all of a sudden, a general of such acknowledged merit and experience, as to have been put in command of a squadron of 10,000 horse against such a redoubted Mogul general as Dilerkhan, while Shivaji himself, with Hambirrao, was carrying his flying columns into another theatre of war?

The fact is that this Anandrao was not a new general who then blazed into a sudden glory, but is the same Anandrao whom Sarkar had previously mentioned at page 260 of his *Shivaji*, the only mistake being his identification of this general with Hambirrao *Mohite.* This Anandrao was a *Bhonsle.* There are many references to him in Sabhasad and Shedgavkar, as well as in Jedhe. He was probably the same general who figures in most of the bakhar lists as Anandrao *Haft-hazari*, or commander of 7,000, rather an unusual distinction in Shivaji's army, the more common rank under the Sir-nobut, being that of the *Panch-hazari* or commander of 5,000. There must have been a special reason for this unique distinction of *Haft-hazari*, which almost stands on a parity with the Sir-nobutship itself. Verily the status of Anandrao becomes a case of "*A Sir-nobut and no-Sir-nobut*", i. e. a commander who was as good as a Sir-nobut without the title.

The first mention of Anandrao in Sabhasad is at page 63. There this general is named Makaji Anandrao. Everywhere else Sabhasad speaks of him simply as Anandrao. At page 63 Sabhasad says:—"And Makaji Anandrao, the natural son of Maharaja Shahaji, and Venkoji Datto, a Brahman, a great military sardar of renown, who had left the service of the Maharaja (i. e. of Shahaji) and come to the Raje (i. e. Shivaji), these the Raje exalted and invested with the rank of *Panch hazari*. And Prataprao Sir-nobut and Venkoji Datto and Anandrao and other Sardars...... these he (Shivaji) took with him......and marched straight to Surat." It follows then that Anandrao was a natural son of Shahaji and had served under his father, and began service under his brother as a Panch-hazari, at least about 1670, if not earlier. Jedhe seems to hint at his serving, under Prataprao Guzar a year earlier in the Maratha contingent that co-operated with Prince Muazzim at Ahmednagar. He is often mentioned as a brother officer along with the Brahman Venkoji Datto, taking part in the same exploits, both having come over together to Shivaji's court *from the service of Shahaji*. This would mean either that they came in the life-time of Shahaji, i. e. before the end of 1664 or that they came from Tanjore after his death. There is, however, no reason why Sabhasad should not be taken literally when he describes them as "leaving the service of Shahaji", so as to mean that they left him in his life-time. This subject is further discussed at the end of

Appendix IV and we will provisionally hold that Anandrao joined Shivaji before 1664.

Later on Sabhasad mentions him as second in command under Prataprao Guzar, sharing in his exploits, being in fact a sort of "*fidus Achates*" to him. He took part in the battle of Vani-Dindori after the plunder of Surat and is mentioned among the four honoured victors on the field of Salheri. At a later stage Sabhasad describes him as accompanying Shivaji in his retreat from the Karnatic (p. 91) and here Anandrao is clearly indicated to be a different individual from Hambirrao, since the latter was left behind to co-operate with Raghunathpant Hanumante. According to Sabhasad, Anandrao accompanied Shivaji to Kopal and Lakshmeshwar upto Sampgaon (Belgaum district), while Manaji More (one of the great officers who had also accompanied Shivaji) was left behind at Kolhar. The Shedgavkar bakhar corroborates all this, giving additional details. At page 63 (and *Errata* p. 2) he is described as a "*palak lek*" or illegitimate son of Shahaji and as coming over, along with Venkoji Datto, to Shivaji's service as a "Panch-hazari", accompanying him to Surat and serving in the battle of Vani-Dindori. At page 76 he is mentioned under the name "*Anandrao Farzand Bhonsle*" and is described as having been honoured among the greatest victors of the battle of Salheri. At pages 88, 89, he is described as accompanying Shivaji in his retreat from Jinji, when Raghunathpant and Hansaji Mohite (Hambirrao) were left behind. It should be noted that this bakhar always speaks of *Hansaji* Mohite as *Asoji* Mohite. While speaking of some of these events this bakhar mentions Anandrao under the name Anandrao *Farzand Kuwar* (i. e. kumar or prince), so that there is no doubt that the same Anandrao is meant as the one who took part in the battle of Salheri and who is there called Anandrao *Farzand Bhonsle.*

The Jedhe Chronology corroborates this with more details. At p. 188, we are told that on the cessation of peace with the Moguls, Prataprao and Anandrao left the camp of the *Shahazada* (prince Muazzim) at Aurangabad and came away to Raigad. At p. 190 we have an account of the battle of Salheri and we are there told that Prataprao and Anandrao captured Bahlolkhan (i. e. Ikhlaskhan, the son of Bahlolkhan) and Mahakam Singh and Darkoji Bhonsle, together with eleven elephants and 1,700 horses. At p. 191 we are told that Prataprao Guzar and Anandrao fought with and defeated Bahlolkhan (i. e. Abdul Karim) near Bijapur. This was the battle of Umrani. On the same page Jedhe records the battle of Nivte (or Jessary) in which Prataprao fought with Bahlolkhan (Abdul Karim) and was killed. But within one month after that battle, as related by Jedhe, Anandrao defeated Khidarkhan (i. e. Khizarkhan) at Sampgaon. Now this battle Prof. Sarkar has transferred to the credit of Hambirrao consistently with his mistaken identification of Anandrao with that hero. But according to Jedhe (as also Sabhasad and Shedgavkar), the constant companion of Prataprao in almost every engagement was Anandrao, not Hambirrao, and the latter, as seen from other statements of Sabhasad and Shedgavkar was a different individual altogether from Anandrao. According to Jedhe, about two months after the battle of Jessary (or Nivte), Shivaji reviewed his army at Chiplun, where it was cantoned for the rains and then it seems that the title of Sir-nobut was formally conferred upon Hambirrao Mohite. Sabhasad (p. 79) also expressly states that "Shivaji came in person to the army, went with the forces to Chiplun, and remained there. Then after reviewing his army, he looked for a man for the Sir-nobutship and lighted on one Hansaji Mohite and conferred on him the title of Hambirrao and apppointed him Sir-nobut." This is repeated by Shedgavkar, page 79. It is possible that during this interval of two or three months between the battle of Jessary (Nivte) and the appointment of Hambirrrao Mohite, Anandrao, who had all along been second in command under Prataprao Guzar, had to *act* as Sir-nobut, and he perhaps deserved to be promoted to that post, as the man who had always been next under Prataprao and who had rallied the Maratha forces after the death of Prataprao. (The account given in the text that Hansaji Mohite rallied the army of Prataprao Guzar and was immediately appointed Sir-nobut with the title of Hambirrao is based on the version of Chitnis, which requires to be corrected in the light of these facts). But the bar sinister of illegitimacy perhaps stood in the way of his being admitted to the permanent rank of Sir-nobut, which carried a place in the Ashtapradhan Cabinet, and Shivaji with his orthodox notions and having a regard for the feelings of the high minded Maratha nobles in his command, may have deliberately conferred the appointment finally upon Hansaji Mohite. The temporary command of Anandrao might have led to the mistake of Narayan Shenvi, which has misled Prof Sarkar into wrongly identifying Anandrao with Hambirrao Mohite. It is true that on a later occasion another illegitimate son of Shahaji was made viceroy at Jinji, but he was kept practically under the control of Hanumante and had no place in the Ashtapradhan Cabinet. It was perhaps on this occasion that the extraordinary mansab of *Haft-hazari*, or command of seven thousand, was conferred upon Anandrao, so that he had practically the power of a Sir-nobut, though that dignity was not formally conferred upon him.

According to Jedhe, Anandrao accompanied Shivaji on the Karnatic expedition, and was with him on the return march, while Hambirrao was left behind with Hanumante at Jinji. He was present at the capture of Gadag-Lakshmeshwar. He completed the capture of Vellore in conjunction with Hanumante (August 1678). He captured Balapore in April 1679. At this time perhaps a junior officer of the name of Anandrao was rising into prominence, for at this point, the captor of Balapore is described by Jedhe as the "senior Anandrao." No further entries about Anandrao are recorded by Jedhe; but Prof. Sarkar describes his exploits in the final war between Dilerkhan and Bijapur, at a time when Shivaji and Hambirrao began to plunder

Khandesh, in order to divert Dilerkhan from the siege of Bijapur.

It is clear from this sketch that Anandrao was one of the greatest generals of Shivaji, one who next to Shivaji himself had inherited the best of Shahaji's valour. It is a mystery how his exploits came to be buried in oblivion. The reason was probably the same which, as surmised above, had deterred Shivaji from conferring the honour of the Sir-nobut upon him.

[Shivaji's son Rajaram was married to a daughter of Prataprao Guzar and also to a daughter of Hambirrao Mohite (Shivadigvijay, p. 287 and Sardesai's *Riyasat* Genealogy p. 2). Our foot-note to p. 481 should be corrected in this light].

APPENDIX III

THE BATTLE OF KHANDERI

WITH reference to the account of the battle of Khanderi at page 507 and foot-note, it seems to us advisable to quote the original account of Keigwin himself in reporting the battle to the British authorities. An extract from his letter is given below in his own English, without altering his spelling, punctuation marks and capital letters.

Let us prefix to this quotation a brief account of the beginning of the battle. At daybreak on the 18th October 1679, "*Shivaji's Armada*", as Keigwin calls it, bore down on the small English squadron with sails and oars, firing as they came from Cheul. A *grab* (or *guraba*) in charge of a Mr. Gape was the nearest to Shivaji's armada. Mr. Gape was a civilian and the naval or military commander of the vessel, (which was a guraba christened the *Dover*), was Sergeant Maulverer. Next to the *Dover* was the *Revenge*, a British frigate, under the command of Capt. Minchin, a sea-captain in the Company's service and Lt. Keigwin, commandant of the Company's land forces in Bombay. The British force comprised eight vessels in all. Soon after the commencement of the battle, Mr. Gape struck his colours and surrendered to the Marathas. Speaking of this act of Mr. Gape, Keigwin writes in his letter, "What accident befell him (Mr. Gape) I know not, but half a mile before the enemy was up with him, *his ensign and top-sail was struck*". On seeing this act of cowardice, the rest of the English squadron were seized with panic and fled, and the *Revenge* was left alone to face the enemy, one ship against about forty Maratha vessels. The Revenge is usually described to have fought gallantly and to have sunk five of the Maratha vessels and to have pursued the rest to Nagotna. Quite a miraculous feat in the history of naval warfare, which the history of Orme, the Bombay Gazetteer XIII and above all Sarkar's *Shivaji* require us to accept without questioning! But the report of Keigwin himself betrays the cloven hoof. His report of the battle was written on the evening of the day of his triumph, no doubt after he had helped himself to copious libations of "*that accursed Bombay Punch*" compounded of our home-brewed Bombay *bevada*. Here goes Keigwin's account of his own treachery:

"Seeing ourselves alone, Captain Minchin and my selfe encouraged our Souldiers and Seamen admonishing them what disgrace it would be to Christians to be prisoners to heathens, but courageously to defend, and fight the enemy bravely they unanimously said they would live and dye with us, wee promised to show ourselves forward for their example, we hal'd up our sailes the Enemy thinking we were as easily swallow'd as the other, came up our sterne, with 24 Grobs I know not how many Galwets, I ordere'd our men not to fire until the word of Command, Soe when they came within Pistoll Shot, and they finding us mute, thrust themselves forward in their boates to enter, but wee discharged our Sterne Chase with Round Shot and Patridge, and presently our blunderbuses and small shot so smartly ply'd, that checkt their drums and Pipes, and in halfe an hour, wee beat them from their Guns and Musquets and brought them by the Lee."

This passage shows the dodge played by Keigwin and Minchin. Although they did not *"strike their ensign and top-sail"*, as Mr. Gape had done, they, to all intents and purposes, put Daulatkhan and the Marathas under the belief that they were going to surrender, as Mr. Gape had done, and when the Marathas advanced to board their frigate and accept their surrender, they treacherously opened fire. No wonder that the Marathas quailed before this unexpected offensive. Our only regret is that Prof. Sarkar, who has made so liberal a use of the British authorities should have failed to quote just this passage, which is to be found in the India Office Library, *Original Correspondence*, No. 4665. As it is, Prof. Sarkar's reflections at page 358 of his *Shivaji* are absurd.

Capt. Minchin had a few years before fought a duel with a Mr. Hornigold, British factor; and President Aungier had occasion to denounce the event, attributing it to the use of the "accursed Bombay Punch", indulgence in which was too notorious, "to the shame, scandal and ruin of our nation and religion". Both Capt. Minchin and Mr. Hornigold had been fined fifty "zeraphins" each, a "zeraphin" being equal to twenty pence. Keigwin afterwards rebelled but though the governor, John Child, spoke of him as a "notorious, noughty rascal" and wanted to have him hanged, he managed to escape and died in an attack on a town in St. Christopher, in the West Indies.

APPENDIX IV

RAGHUNATH BALLAL KORDE

THERE are two officers of Shivaji, who are constantly confounded with one another. Both are spoken of as Raghunath Ballal or as Ragho Ballal. The surname of one is Korde and that of the other Atre. Even Mr. Kincaid has confounded them. The Bakhars rarely use the surnames and hence the uncertainty. The title *Sabnis* is often found used of each of them. An attempt is here made to separate the exploits of these two men. Both were apparently Brahmans. The name Korde also occurs in the Kayastha Prabhu caste, which has led Mr. B. A. Gupte in Sen's Sabhasad (*p. 69*) to conjecture that Raghunath-*pant* Korde being a Prabhu, the name is a mistake for Raghunath-*rao* Korde. The point is well argued in the '*Vividhdnyan-Vistar*' (Marathi), February 1921, p. 70 This Korde was a brother-in-law of a Brahman officer of Shivaji.

Of these two officers, Korde entered into Shivaji's service earlier and served him longer. Sabhasad says (p. 7) that Raghunath Ballal was one of the officers whom Shahaji sent from Bangalore, along with Shamrao Nilkant (Peshwa), Balkrishnapant (Muzumdar) and Sonopant (Dabir). Raghunathpant came to Poona as Sabnis or paymaster. The name Korde is first mentioned at page 47, where we are told that he was a brother-in-law of Sonajipant Dabir. Korde besides being a Sabnis was constantly employed under Shivaji on the duties of a Dabir, or plenipotentiary. We find him employed in Shivaji's earliest overtures with the Moguls at the time of Shahaji's captivity. (See foot-note to p. 126 and 130). Sabhasad says he was engaged on the mission to Chandrarao More and that he killed him and his brother. We have seen Jedhe has quite a different story to relate (Jedhe p. 180–181) and we have shown (*Vide* pp. 141–142), that Chandrarao More was not murdered, but executed. Korde was probably sent to Javli to bring about a settlement of the dispute. When Sonopant Dabir, who acted as Shivaji's *vakil* to Shaista Khan (Jedhe p. 185), died in 1665 (Jedhe p. 187), the duties of foreign diplomacy fell upon Korde, for he went on an embassy to Aurangzeb at Agra, after the armistice made with Jay Singh (Sabhasad p. 47), although in treating with Jay Singh, the *Panditrao* was employed. Shivaji was accompanied to Agra by Trimbakji Sondev (the son of Sonajipant Dabir, a relation of Korde) and was met there by Korde himself (Sabhasad p. 47, 48). Trimbakji and Korde were practically fulfilling the duties of Dabir and when Shivaji escaped from Agra, both Trimbakji and Korde were seized and imprisoned. (Jedhe p. 188). They had been left behind on diplomatic business at the time of the flight of Shivaji. It is possible that on account of the captivity of these two kinsmen of the late Dabir Sonaji Pant, the vacant office of Dabir was at last conferred upon Somnathpant. The two kinsmen were freed about eight months later, when a new treaty was made with the Moguls (Jedhe p. 188). While recording this event Jedhe speaks of Trimbak Sondev as Trimbak Sondev *Dabir*, but it is not clear whether that title was ever actually conferred upon him. At p. 57, Sabhasad states that Pralhad Niraji was made a Deputy to the Sabnis or Deputy Paymaster of the Forces. Korde perhaps still held the office of Sabnis, though more often employed on other duties. He was again sent on a mission to Muazzim at Aurangabad (Sabhasad p. 60), the result of which was the grant of a Mogul mansab to Sambhaji. Thereafter the office of Sabnis was conferred upon Pralhad Niraji, about 1668. Korde is now neither Sabnis nor Dabir. What was he promoted to? There is reason to believe that he now served on the Konkan coast. In 1669 Shivaji began a desperate war with the Sidi. Korde had already once fought against Sidi Fatteh Khan of Janjira, (*Vide* p. 183 *supra*). The hand of Korde may possibly be seen, though the name does not appear, in that intrigue by which Fatteh Khan, the Sidi Chief, was won over in 1670 to surrender the sea-fort of Janjira. (*Vide* p. 319 *supra*). But the plot was nipped in the bud and the rival chiefs put Fatteh Khan in chains, transferred their allegiance to the Moguls, and saved Janjira (1671). Ten years before the Sidis had lost Danda-Rajpuri to Raghunath Ballal *Atre* (not *Korde*). In 1671 the Sidi chiefs made a determined effort to recover Danda-Rajpuri (*vide* p. 334 supra and Khafi Khan in Elliot VII 290--92). *Korde* was the Maratha governor of Danda-Rajpuri. Korde was taken by surprise during the Holi carnival and was defeated and slain. The garrison were cut to pieces and the women and children sold as slaves. The name Atre given at page 334 is due to an oversight.

Atre, the original conqueror of Danda-Rajpuri, had died long before this event. Both Messrs. Kincaid and Sardesai have frequently confused Atre with Korde. Mr. Kincaid not only speaks of Atre as having been killed by the Sidis at Danda-Rajpuri in 1671, but he mentions Atre as Shivaji's ambassador to Chandrarao More.

Raghunath Ballal Atre was the man who was put in command of the corps of 700 Pathan mercenaries who came to seek service under Shivaji, (*vide* page 147 supra). He distinguished himself by his defence of the fort of Panhala after Shivaji's escape to Vishalgad, in 1660. For this he was highly honoured (pp. 191-192). He was next appointed to lead the Maratha forces against the Sidi of Janjira. The first Peshwa Shamraj Ranzekar had been defeated by the Sidi (p. 148 supra), and though some ground was regained by Moro Trimal Pingle, the Sidi had raised his head again (p. 178 supra). Atre was sent against Janjira with a large army. (*Vide* Sabhasad p. 67 and p. 192 supra). He retrieved the Maratha losses, and captured the harbour-town of Danda-Rajpuri (p. 192 supra). He died soon after this in 1660 and the Abyssinian power began to rise again. (Sabhasad, p. 67). The name Korde occurring in the text at page 196 should be changed into Atre.

Unfounded statements are sometimes made that Korde's prospects in Shivaji's service were cut off on account of his unauthorized murder of Chandrarao More. It is argued that Korde and Sambhaji Kavji murdered Chandrarao by an unauthorized act, that Shivaji was not a party to the murder, and that in consequence Korde was not appointed to any position of trust after that event. But More was *not* murdered and this defence is fantastic. Even Mr. Kincaid has tripped by taking up this line of defence. This defence was urged by Mr. P. B. Joshi in a paper read before a Marathi literary conference and is the subject of a foot-note in Sardesai's Riyasat, p. 238. Nor did Sambhaji Kavji, whose name is also mentioned in that affair, come into disfavour with Shivaji, till his desertion at Shaista Khan's invasion. (See p. 224 and foot-note).

A word may be added about Atre's successor in the Janjira war. This was Venkoji Datto, the companion of Anandrao Farzand Bhonsle. Sabhasad (pp. 67, 68) says that this commander went and utterly devastated the Sidi dominions and annexed their land. In a battle that followed, he killed 300 Abyssinians and captured their horses. This took place in August, 1660.

[A doubt arises here. Did Venkoji Datto and Anandrao, who according to Sabhasad (pp. 63 64) came together to join Shivaji's service, leaving that of Shahaji, actually come in the life-time of Shahaji? That would be before 1664, the date of the first sack of Surat. But Sabhasad mentions them as immediately employed in the second sack of Surat, 1670. But Venkoji Datto was employed under Shivaji already as early as 1660, as we have just seen, i. e. even earlier than the first invasion of Surat. We have a shrewd suspicion that somehow or other the Marathi Bakhars have made a jumble of the two invasions of Surat. They remembered only the particulars of the latter invasion, while their calculation of the amount of booty brought (" five crores of hons " according to Sabhasad) is likely to be more true of the first sack of Surat rather than of the second. The very fact that the bakhars are otherwise silent about the first sack of Surat is suspicious. There is certainly some confusion. The statement that Anandrao and Venkoji Datto left the service of Shahaji and were soon afterwards employed in an invasion upon Surat, joined to the fact that Venkoji Datto had been in Shivaji's service already in 1660, would lead us to infer, that Sabhasad, while giving the particulars of the second invasion of Surat (1670), is thinking confusedly of some matters that belong to the first invasion.]

Amatya—A minister, the head of the finance department.

Amir—A nobleman.

Aryavarta—India, so called because it was first settled in by the Aryas.

Ashta Pradhan—Eight ministers, or the cabinet of eight ministers.

Bakshi—A paymaster of the forces, also commander.

Bairagi—A recluse.

Bargir—A trooper that is mounted and equipped by the state that employs him, opp : to Shiledar.

Bhagwa Zenda—The red-ochre coloured ensign.

Chamar—A fly-whisk ensign of Indian royalty.

Champak tree—A kind of flower tree.

Chitnis—A secretary.

Chouth or Chauth—One quarter of the land revenue of a district.

Chowries—Ornamental hair-tassels.

Dabir—A foreign secretary, or envoy.

Daftar—A record, a register.

Dakshina—A present to Brahmans.

Daroga—A superintending officer, clerks, guards &c.

Dasara—A grand Hindu holiday in the early part of October.

Desai—A hereditary officer, the head of a district. He is the same as *deshmukh.*

Deshmukh—A hereditary officer, the head of a district (paragana). His duties in the district correspond with those of the patil in the village.

Deshpande—A hereditary officer of a mahal. He is under a deshmukh. His office nearly corresponds with that of kulkarni under a patil.

Devi—A goddess, usually the consort of the god Shiva, also called Gauri, *Bhavani* and by other names.

Dewan—A minister.

Dharmashala—A rest-house.

Divali—A great festive Hindu holiday in early November, the Feast of the Lamps.

Durbar—A royal court.

Durva—A kind of grass reckoned holy.

Fakir—A Mahomedan anchorite.

Firman—A mandate, a fiat.

Fouzdar—A garrison commander or police officer.

Gadkari—A garrison man in connection with a fort.

Gandha—A pigment for the forehead or body (of sandal wood, saffron, &c.).

Ghatmatha—A table-land on the Sahyadri mountains, or the Western Ghauts.

Ghorpad—Iguana.

Gosavi—An anchorite.

Guru—A spiritual preceptor.

Guraba—Galley with strong deck, and two or three masts, of 300 tons, a naval ship.

Haft-hazari—(Hapt-hazary) A commander in charge of seven thousand soldiers.

Havaldar—A commander of five decuries ; a chief officer in charge of a fort.

Hazari—A commander of one thousand soldiers.

Inam—A grant in perpetuity without conditions.

Jahgir—An assignment by Government of lands &c.

Jamdar—Office curator, the officer in charge of the treasure and jewels.

Janjira—Maritime fortress.

Jari-patka—A cloth of gold banner.

Jumledar—A commander over two havaldars.

Kabulayats—Agreements.

Kalawant—A singer or musician.

Kamawisdar—A civil commissioner in charge of a town.

Karbhari—An administrator of a jahgir-estate etc.

Karkhana—Ware-house, an arsenal, commissariat etc.

Karkhannis—An officer in charge of departmental stores.

Karkun—A clerk or petty revenue officer.

Khan—Honorary suffix to Mahomedan names.

Kasba—A chief town of a mahal (district).

Khasnis—A special steward.

Killedar—An officer in charge of a fort.

Kirtan—A religious service in honour of a god with music and singing, and moral discourses.

Kos—A measure of distance, equal to about 2½ miles.

Kosha or Mahal—Treasury, mint, stables, parks etc.

Kotwal—A chief officer of police or constabulary of a town.

Kulkarni—An officer of a village under the patil. His business is to keep the accounts of the cultivators with government and all the public records.

Mahar—One of the depressed classes.

Mang—One of the depressed classes.

Mahalkari—A taluka officer.

Masa—A measure equal to the 12th part of a tola.

Mansabdar—An officer holding a rank or command in the cavalry etc.

Mantri—(Waknis) one of the ministers whose duty was to keep the private records and correspondence.

Mirasdar—An hereditary officer usually holding some land in a village; petty landlord.

Mohur—A gold coin worth from Rs 15 to Rs. 20.

Mokasdar—A farmer of the revenue of villages given in inam.

Morchel—A brush of peacock feathers. It is waved over idols, rajas etc.

Mouza—A village.

Mulukhgiri—Active service on hostile soil.

Mutaliq—A deputy.

Muzumdar—Accountant-general.

Nagarkhana—A bandroom.

Naik—Commander or captain or corporal of a company.

Nazar—A state present.

Navratra—The nine nights devoted to the worship of Devi, preceding Dasara.

Omrah—A nobleman.

Pagoda—The same as *Hon* or *Hun*, a gold coin worth about 3 to 4 rupees.

Paga—A body of horse under one commander; the state cavalry.

Padres—Christian missionaries.

Panch-hazari—A commander of five thousand soldiers.

Panchayat—An assembly of arbitrators (usually five).

Pandit—A learned man.

Pant—Honorary suffix to names of Brahmans.

Pant-Sachiv—One of the eight ministers keeper of government records.

Parasnis—Persian translator.

Patwari—An officer of a village, a land steward &c.

Pawada or powada—A ballad.

Peshwa—A prime minister.

Peshkhush—A premium by annual instalments.

Phadnis—An assistant to the Muzumdar.

Pir—A Mahomedan saint at whose shrine vows are made and offerings presented.

Potnis—A cashier.

Polygar—A revolted rayat setting himself up as a chieftain living in woods and fastnesses and employing himself in levying contributions and marauding.

Prabhawal—An ornamental silver plate.

Prant— district.

Puja—Worship of an idol, or priest.

Pujari—A priest.

Quilledar—An officer in charge of a fort.

Rao—Honorary suffix added to proper names among Deccani people.

Ramoshi—A hill tribe.

Rang-Panchami—The fifth day of festivities during the Holi holidays.

Riyasat—A regime.

Sabnis—A paymaster.

Sachiv—A minister, same as Surnis.

Salaam—A salute.

Sanad—A sealed paper of authority or patent.

Sannyasi—An ascetic.

Saranjam—Military grant for the maintenance of an army corps.

Sardar—A nobleman.

Sati—A woman who burns herself with the corpse of her deceased husband.

Senapati—A chief general, same as *Sirnobut*.

Shalas—Karkhanas.

Shaivism—A sect devoted to the worship of the god Shiva.

Shakas—An era which commences from the birth of Shalivahan i. e. about 78 A. D.

Shastras—Hindu scriptures which lay down duties in life.

Shiledar—A horse soldier who provides his own horse.

Shimga—A great Hindu holiday, the same as *Holi*.

Shirastedar—A head clerk.

Sirdeshmukhi—One tenth of the revenue.

Sir-lashkar—Chief commander.

Sir-Naik—Chief commander.

Sir-Nobut—Commander-in-chief.

Subhedar—Military officer over five jumledars; a governor.

Sumant-(Dabir)—A minister of foreign affairs.

Surnis—A record-keeper.

Swarajya—Self-rule.

Tat-sirnobut—Chief Commander of the ramparts.

Toran—A lintel from which leafy branches, garlands of flowers &c. are hung; a festooned arch.

Turufdar-Talukdar—A revenue officer under the mamlatdar.

Vaishnavism—A sect devoted to the worship of the god Vishnu.

Vakil—(Bokil) an agent; an envoy.

Vatan—Grant of land.

Viziership—Premiership.

Waknis—Record-keeper; a home secretary.

Zemindary—The rights of a hereditary officer who collects land dues etc.

Zenana—Harem.

Note:—The terms *Chitnis*, *Phadnis*, *Sabnis*, *Muzumdar* denote major or minor offices, according to the context. When attached to the whole realm or the *Ashta-pradhan* cabinet, the terms denote high ministerial or secretarial posts; when attached to a fort or regiment, they denote minor offices. *Sabnis* may be Paymaster of the Forces (a secretarial post) or paymaster to a regiment or company.

ERRATA.

Page 14 **Doulatabat** should be **Perinda**, or **Parinda.**

Page 45, foot-note, **Jonathan Scott** should be **Scott Waring.**

Page 196 **Korde** should be **Atre.**

Page 237 **is lost** should be **was lost.**

Page 334 **Atre** should be **Korde.**

Page 365 **Next them** should be **next after them.**

Page 387 **Though servants of the state** should be **As servants of the state.**

Page 387 **While they drew** should be **though they drew.**

Page 481 Foot-note (1) should be corrected in the light of the concluding paragraphs in Appendix II.

Page 543, foot-note, **The Ramdas's** conventicles should be the **Ramdas** conventicles.

Page 593 **Dattaji Prabhu, veterans** should be **Dattaji Pant; Prabhu veterans.**

Page 624 **Systemetic** should be **systematic.**

There are some minor typographical errors.

Opinions on the Life of Shivaji Maharaj.

The Bombay Chronicle (Bombay) :—" We warmly recommend this work to our readers. It is a book for all time and deserves to be chewed and digested."

The Maratha (Poona) :—" The work is certainly more substantial and more readable as an historical work than both the monographs of Prof. Rawlinson and the legend-laden history of the Marathas by Mr Kincaid. We welcome the advent of an author possessing such ability and command over the English language as Prof. Takakhav and feel sure that his present book will supply a long-felt want.........English composition is a very useful weapon for practical warfare with English critics and for hacking our way out through the thick lines of prejudices with which Maratha history is surrounded "

The Statesman (Calcutta) :—" There is nothing but well deserved praise for the way in which Prof. Takakhav has acquitted himself of his self-imposed task..........The book is well printed and singularly free (for books in English printed in India) from typographical errors."

The Civil and Military Gazette (Lahore) :—" The lovers of impartial history will be grateful for a book which gives us an account of the leader who did more than any Hindu within historical times to weld the Hindus into a nation ....The views expressed in this chapter (on the character) are very interesting and the author certainly adduces many points in support of his contentions."

The Century Review (Allahabad) :—" It is interesting to find a worthy life of the Great Shivaji, written in the finest style, and containing many illuminating details. The author is to be congratulated on the very comprehensive work he has produced. Shivaji has hitherto been known as a marauder and a wandering brigand. To-day he is differently known and respected. The fact that His Royal Highness the Prince of Wales only recently unveiled the statue of this great Indian must give Shivaji a permanent place among the great rulers of India. He worked to a great and noble end and his life shows him to be an empire-builder of no mean stamp, with a statesmanship possessed by few indeed. The book is worthy of careful perusal, especially by those who wish to learn more of the great leader of India."

The Educational Review (Madras) :—" The book before us makes the laudable attempt of constructing a life of Shivaji with sufficient fullness from internal sources, that is, the native chronicles and *bakhars*, subjecting the information gained from these to adequate criticism in the light of the external sources of information available so far.........The work shows acquaintance with the most recent work done upon various parts of Maratha history and exhibits a ready tendency to criticise every conclusion arrived at from the Maratha sources alone, by Persian sources......... We commend the performance on the whole as a satisfactory effort at a life of the Great Maratha Hero.........We need hardly say more than commend the book to the consideration of all students of history, for careful study and sympathetic criticism......The work is welcome as it is brought out at a time when the memorial to Shivaji received its foundation from the hands of His Royal Highness the Prince of Wales."

The United India and Indian States (Calcutta):—"The biography rightly contradicts the accepted version about the tragedy of Afzal Khan and vindicates Shivaji who met guile with superior guile........It is a welcome addition to the biographies of the famous hero mainly written from an Indian stand-point and we recommend the book to all lovers of Indian history."

The Simla Times—"One of the chief merits of the biography is that Shivaji lives in its pages. He does not appear therein as a mere figure of his times or as a creature of environment, but his personality dominates the entire scene and his character gives colour and animation to his surroundings.........In the pages of this book may be read what Shivaji's dauntless courage, persevering energy and practical wisdom actually accomplished during his life-time."

The Mysore Patriot—"In the present work Shivaji is depicted as the director and entrepreneur of the greatest movement for the assertion of national liberty and independence that India has known in pre-British times. His character, his institutions and the greatness of his work are set forth at length very excellently and elaborately in the succeeding chapters of this valuable publication.........We can say that the present work is an attempt to give a faithful likeness of Shivaji and an estimate of his great work chiefly based upon the indigenous *bakhar* chronicles of the Marathas. The book under review gives a complete account of the career of Shivaji and a critical exposition of attitude towards the hero. We confidently recommend this valuable publication"

The London Times—"It is time to revise the traditional English estimate of Shivaji's work. As Dr. Macnicol says in his 'Foreword', we can no longer regard him as having 'won his supremacy by treachery, assassination and hard fighting'; for, even if we make allowances for the partiality of Marathi historians, upon whom this history admittedly relies, Shivaji stands out as a man of immense determination, of unlimited resourcefulness, of great powers of administration and of high military genius.........When the writer seeks to wipe out every stain from his hero's character, he proves too much; the greatness of Shivaji's achievement is his sufficient epitaph, and, like other great men, he is not without blots upon his escutcheon. For all that, the author has in many respects shown us the founder of the Maratha Empire in a new light, and that, we take it, was his object."

St Xavier's College Magazine (Bombay):—"This story of Shivaji's life is related by Prof. Takakhav with great brilliancy and ability but with a bias for his hero........Prof Takakhav's book is a contribution of permanent value to the study of the real character of Shivaji. It stands midway between Mr. Kincaid's history and Prof. Sarkar's 'Shivaji', which are good examples of two opposite extremes of historical method and research......... Prof. Takakhav's book is for all time."